STUDIES IN ENGLISH LITERATURES

Edited by Koray Melikoğlu

Annie Gagiano

Dealing with Evils

Essays on Writing from Africa

Annie Gagiano

DEALING WITH EVILS

Essays on Writing from Africa

ibidem-Verlag
Stuttgart

Bibliographic information published by the Deutsche Nationalbibliothek
Die Deutsche Nationalbibliothek lists this publication in the Deutsche Nationalbibliografie; detailed bibliographic data are available in the Internet at http://dnb.d-nb.de.

Bibliografische Information der Deutschen Nationalbibliothek
Die Deutsche Nationalbibliothek verzeichnet diese Publikation in der Deutschen Nationalbibliografie; detaillierte bibliografische Daten sind im Internet über http://dnb.d-nb.de abrufbar.

Cover illustration:
Janey Gagiano, 2013.

Second, Revised and Expanded Edition

ISSN: 1614-4651

ISBN-13: 978-3-8382-0687-5

Printed in the United States of America

Contents

Preface to the Second Edition

This collection of essays examines a wide range of African texts from different periods and different parts of a vast continent. These text-centred essays were brought together to give readers a sense of the wide range of African writing – in terms of themes, forms and implied contexts – but also because, despite the need to resist lazy homogenising remarks about Africa, Africans and African writers, there are certain discernible underlying coherences even among works as varied as those analysed in the essays that make up this collection. The novels and other written records of Africa may be said to carry a greater social, historical and even political responsibility than comparable texts in other parts of the world. This is the case because of the continent's late literacy, broadly speaking, as well as the widespread and diverse forms of oppression – ranging from colonial suppression and underdevelopment to postcolonial instances of dictatorial African rule or conditions of violent chaos – and the stifling effect this has on public utterance. The analytical essays contained in this volume are attempts to draw attention to the significance of texts such as those commented on here as contributions to an archive of knowledge of different parts of and historical eras in Africa *and* to showcase the treasury of its literary art, even if the perspective employed is applied to a sample and limited (as it is here) to texts written in English or available in English translation.

The writers' readiness and ability implicitly to analyse and creatively to confront the troubling, dangerous, perplexing or malign aspects of the societies from and of which they write, articulating the complex stresses from different sources to which African individuals have been subjected and the creative and courageous ways in which many among them have responded, are the qualities that inspire the writing of the essays in my collection. The subtlety and literary complexity that I attempt to highlight here are the signs – not of authors taking refuge in art from difficult socio-cultural and political situations, but of writers profoundly concerned with the African sites and times that are closest to them. My commentaries and contextualisations inevitably reflect my own geographical, academic, racial and political realities, biases and choices. There are more texts from the southern than of other parts of Africa discussed here, and not only is there a geographical imbalance, but many, many glaring omissions of other and equally significant African texts and issues. In this regard, no collection this brief could be inclusive. Nevertheless it is my hope that my essays may prompt readings and re-readings not only of the African writings addressed here, but of the many other texts by African authors already available or being and to be published – a rich and valuable resource[1] for Africans but of equal pertinence, in the issues they address and the compelling shapes they give to their thought, to the entire world.

The works discussed here were primarily[2] penned or recorded in English – the colonial language that has been so widely appropriated by African writers and so adroitly used by them to re-map their own life-world in verbally sophisticated gestures registering both independence and connectedness in the ironies of modern African selfhood. "Modernity began in 1492", states Enrique Dussel, "with Europe thinking itself the center of the world and Latin America, Africa, and Asia as the periphery" (132). This arrogant self-elevation will only end, he suggests, "through a process of mutual, creative fecundation" in "corealization with its once negated alterity" (138). I link this with Frantz Fanon's emphasis on the need to "do battle for the creation of a human world – that is, a world of reciprocal recognitions" (155). The great Zimbabwean writer Yvonne Vera insists that Africans "are not isolated things. We exist", she says, "in co-operation with other nations. So we need to put into place methods of communication" (389). But she also expresses her need and desire "[t]o explore, not with romanticism, women's characters. But with accepting the violence that accompanies their existence" while attempting "to underst[and] the intimate complexity of their mental worlds, and their emotions," and to explore "those moments of tragedy without [. . .] withdrawing from them" or "covering up" (385).[3] Issues of subjectivity and the various and contending power forms besetting it; different forms of cultural hybridity, 'authenticity' and abrogation and post- and neocolonial condi-

---

1 See my essay "Book Keeping in Africa" as well as my column "The African Library" published since 1999 in *Litnet*, an electronic journal (http://www.litnet.co.za); a column that by mid-2014 numbers more than a hundred entries in a series of "profiles" (rather than reviews or articles) on texts by African authors from countries all across the continent.

2 The exceptions are the *Dwaalstories* of the elderly Khoikhoi or San Hendrik, recorded in Afrikaans by Marais, Salih's *Season of Migration to the North* – an English translation of the Arabic original – and the translated novel *Little Mother* by Cristina Ali Farah, originally written and published in Italian (for fuller references see chapters 1, 8 and 15).

3 Vera validly here highlights her depiction of women characters in her writing, but I count her profound, incisive and finally empathetic representations, contextualising certain male characters, among her greatest achievements (see Gagiano, "Reading" and "Barbed").

tions as well as gender matters and the plight of many of Africa's children are some of the subjects dealt with in the texts and in my discussions of them.

African English writing does not grow primarily out of the textual world of canonical (or contemporary) English literature, but emerges from the complex translations of local realities into a language now skillfully articulating *African* visions. Yet, by writing in a language of world-wide access, the writers of this continent lay claim to a shareable truth and sphere of experience and exhibit a border-crossing aesthetic power in their texts. Acknowledging, grasping (on the imaginative level) and coping with what are frequently dreadful or emotionally and morally taxing circumstances (as my collection's title phrase, "dealing with evils," indicates), these texts testify to their authors' refusal to allow such conditions – whether psychic or social realities – to overwhelm, cow or silence them and they implicitly insist on our grappling with them to understand situations urgently in need of addressing. Their delineations of African evils and opportunities and of the tangled roots, both African and (originally) foreign, of these conditions, not only demonstrate various ways of contending with difficulties or succumbing to them; of using chances or failing to do so. Their texts are also, themselves, *enactments* of various ways of addressing our difficulties. In a poem by the American poet Wallace Stevens that remarkably employs certain African references, he suggests that narrative artists and poets proceed to "tell the human tale" (456) which transforms disaster by imaginatively narrating it from beyond the event. The same point was made in a wonderfully African way by Chinua Achebe (*Anthills* 124) in insisting on the social supremacy – above either the worker or the warrior – of the teller of tales, narrating the difficult "story of the land," which can vividly record and transmit the heroism even of the defeated.

Bakhtin in his essay "Discourse and the Novel" writes that "[t]he word in language is half someone else's. [. . .] it exists [. . .] in other people's contexts, serving other people's intentions: it is from there that one must take the word, and make it one's own" (293). This remark seems to me extraordinarily useful in highlighting the difficulties *and* the achievements of the modern Europhone African author. In my own analyses of African writing it is my practice to investigate and to articulate primarily the implicitly analytical qualities of the fictional text that percolate through the representational and stylistic aspects of the work, rather than to impose a theoretical perspective upon the writing and subjecting the author's vision to that perspective; I want theory to serve the text and choose those points from theoretical or critical texts that I believe can contribute enlighteningly to its fuller understanding and appreciation. "Theory oppresses,"

Trinh T. Minh-ha reminds us, "when it wills or perpetuates existing power relations, when it presents itself as a means to exert authority – the Voice of Knowledge" (42). Nana Wilson-Tagoe, a critic I respect, writes:

> We need a wider interpretive framework not only for reading contemporary texts of culture against the grain of nationalist theorizations but also for exploring productive tensions between social science discourses on culture and the performative narratives that enact contending and liberating forms of cultural identification. (225)

I link this observation with Maria Pia Lara's remark that the productivity of written work requires two interlinked processes of what she calls "reflexivity": one such process starts "when an author is creating an exploratory moral quest for identity through the written word," and the other (Lara writes) is "related to" such a quest by "readers 'in the act of reading', which is itself a highly reflexive moral search" (16) – *if* it is a serious and attentive reading of a work worthy of being taken seriously, I would add.

It is my hope that this collection will contribute to the understanding that Africa's creative writers are vital to the re-imagining of our rapidly changing continent in its numerous and diverse societies. Tendencies to interpret as "authentic" only those texts that portray pre-colonial, rural or tribal Africa trouble me, as does a tendency to limit understanding of the continent's postcolonial literary production that countenances mainly those works that write back to the period and dominant vision of colonial occupation of African regions. Africa has a postcolonial *present* in which new oppressors exert other forms of exploitation or debasement upon their citizens. In a 2002 address to a gathering of African writers and scholars, Mia Couto reminded us that "the bad are not always outside," and he insisted that "[t]he principal enemies of hope are the fabrication of regimes constructed on the basis of crime, war and misery" (3). The main title of my collection is intended to replicate Couto's view of the fine balance between the castigation of evils and the opening of doors to the future of Africa in the memorable and resonant writings framed in the essays of this compilation.

In his beautifully lucid, Portuguese inflected English, Couto on the same occasion said to his fellow Africans: "[w]e are becoming, more so, alone with our historic responsibility of creating another history," and he concluded: "[w]e have to build our nations in the house where our dream belongs so that our children do not have to import even their dreams" (3). The archive of African creative writing or verbal art, a sample of which I present here, is a great social resource whose importance can hardly be overestimated. African writers who are forced into exile or choose to live abroad continue to write back to the people and places on this continent and are maligned if read as primarily addressing audiences elsewhere; like the authors who remain in Africa, their vision contributes to the needs of their local compatriots. Achebe has referred to the "universal creative rondo" by which "*stories create people create stories*" ("What" 162; emphasis original). Africa's diverse "stories," while especially pertinent to Africans, require of all who hear or read them to reach out imaginatively and to join in the endless undertaking to humanise our world – a world in which ignorance, neglect and prejudice towards Africans come in many guises. What Simon Gikandi calls "the difficult relation between the work of art and the politics of everyday life" (4) is a serious challenge that the texts discussed in the pages that follow invite us to meet.

Works Cited

Achebe, Chinua. *Anthills of the Savannah*. London: Heinemann, 1987.

___. "What Has Literature Got to Do with It?" *Hopes and Impediments: Selected Essays.* By Achebe. New York/ London: Doubleday, 1989. 154-170.

Bakhtin, "Discourse and the Novel." *The Dialogic Imagination: Four Essays.* Ed. M. Holquist. Transl. C. Emerson and M. Holquist. Austin: University of Texas Press, 1981. 269-422.

Couto, Mia. "The Impact of African Writing on World Literature." Unpublished Address to the Indaba Cape Town Seminar. 2002. (Quoted with the author's permission.)

Dussel, Enrique. *The Invention of the Americas: Eclipse of "the Other" and the Myth of Modernity*. 1992. Trans. M. D. Barber. New York: Continuum, 1995.

Fanon, Frantz. *Black Skin, White Masks*. 1952. Trans. L. Markmann. St. Albans, Hertfordshire: Paladin, 1970.

Gagiano, Annie. "The African Library." <http://www.litnet.co.za/african-library>. (Older entries archived at http://www.oulitnet.co.za/africanlib/default.asp.)

___. "Barbed Wire and Dreams in Late Colonial Rhodesia: Yvonne Vera's *Butterfly Burning*." *Emerging Perspectives on Yvonne Vera*. Ed. Helen Cousins and Pauline Dodgson-Katiyo. Trenton, NJ: Africa World Press, 2012. 145-164. Originally publ. under the title "Buried Hurts and Colliding Dreams in Yvonne Vera's *Butterfly Burning*," *Acta Scientiarum Arts & Culture* 31.1 (2009): 41-52.

___. "Book Keeping in Africa." *Mapping Africa in the English-Speaking World: Issues in Language and Literature*. Ed. Kemmonye Collette Monaka, Owen S. Seda, Sibonile Edith Ellece, and John McAlister. Cambridge Scholars Publishing, 2010. 43-68.

___. "Reading *The Stone Virgins* as Vera's Study of the Katabolism of War." *Research in African Literatures* 38.2 (2007): 64-76.

Gikandi, Simon. "Theory, Literature, and Moral Considerations." *Research in African Literatures* 32.4 (2001): 1-18.

Lara, Maria Pia. *Moral Textures: Feminist Narratives in the Public Sphere*. Berkeley, Los Angeles and London: University of California Press, 1998.

Minh-ha, Trinh T. *Woman, Native, Other. Writing Poscoloniality and Feminism*. Bloomington and Indianapolis: Indiana UP, 1989.

Stevens, Wallace. "Puella Parvula." *The Collected Poems of Wallace Stevens*. New York: Random House, 1990. 456.

Vera, Yvonne. "The Place of the Woman is the Place of Imagination": Yvonne Vera interviewed by Ranka Primorac. *Emerging Perspectives on Yvonne Vera*. Ed. Helen Cousins and Pauline Dodgson-Katiyo. Trenton, NJ: Africa World Press. 2012. 375-389.

Wilson-Tagoe, Nana. "Representing Culture and Identity: African Women Writers and National Cultures." *Africa After Gender?* Ed. Catherine M. Cole, Takyiwaa Manuh, and Stephan F. Miescher. Bloomington and Indianapolis: Indiana UP, 2007. 223-238.

Listening for the Mediated Voices of the Southern African Khoisan in Hendrik's *Dwaalstories*: Ironies and Wonders

Assessments of the present state of the Southern African Khoisan people's life and culture fall into three main categories: (1) a belief in the virtual extinction of the people, with the traces (mainly in rock paintings and engravings) seen as faint, vanishing and enigmatic, arousing at best a romantic nostalgia; (2) an insistence on the recognition of the Khoisan cultures and languages that are still viable, despite the inevitable processes of modernisation and social deterioration (for example, the Nama language in South Africa has an estimated 6,000 speakers)[1] along with a sense of the value of the store of knowledge possessed by older members of existing groups; (3) a recognition of the both initiatory and enduring relevance of Khoisan cultural work from earlier times as a resource that is still (despite many filters and inevitable distortions) to some extent "available" in the present.

The larger context to this essay, which cannot be ignored, is the bleak scenario of the precarious survival of some of the Khoisan peoples and their cultures, and of the dwindling expressive and revivalist possibilities for the remaining languages. The clearest evidence of this precariousness is the rapidly dwindling number of *contemporary* speakers of Khoisan languages. Cognisance needs to be taken of the threats to these cultures presented by land confiscations and by forced relocations; by racial contempt and suspicion often shown towards the Khoisan by members of a wide spectrum of other cultures, and by the relentless, inevitable modernisation that is occurring in Botswana, Namibia, South Africa and Angola – the four regions where Khoisan people (or their inheritors) are found in significant numbers.[2]

The debasement and dislocation of one such group has been unforgettably described by the Namibian poet Dorian Haarhoff. In a poem titled "San Song" he

---

1 According to Nigel Crawhall, a linguist at the South African San Institute (SASI), as reported in *The Weekly Mail & Guardian* 12-18 Sept. 1997, 28-29.

2 Recent (available) information gives a figure of just over 105,000 "contemporary Bushmen" in southern African countries, with almost 50,000 in Botswana, almost 40,000 in Namibia, almost 10,000 in Angola, under 5,000 in South Africa, just over 1,500 in Zambia and 1,275 in Zimbabwe (Smith et al. 65). Several articles in South African newspapers have recently highlighted the plight of those San people (or Basarwa) who are being ejected from the Central Kalahari Game Reserve by the Botswana government – see, e.g., the article by Tony Weaver. At the beginning of 2006 this dispute was still continuing.

depicts the gawked-at and debased existence of a Khoisan group formerly employed as trackers by the South African Defence Force, in the following sardonic description: "literary clans of pre and post / Van der Posts, praise / the primitive pre-cursor / grunter-gatherer, pristine man" (Haarhoff 851). Improvements in the conditions of life of these and other remaining Khoisan groups may nevertheless be achieved through the many attempts being made to consolidate their interests and to preserve and revive their cultures. First Nation status is being sought for the Khoisan peoples through representations to the United Nations Organisation.

A useful, brief introduction to the complexities of the study of Khoisan people's lives in the past and present is to be found in a published keynote address[3] by Professor Phillip Tobias, the renowned anatomist-palaeontologist of the University of the Witwatersrand in South Africa – a paper titled "Myths and Misunderstandings about Khoisan Identities and Status" (19-28), in which Tobias states quite firmly (necessarily, in the face of many prejudices, however self-evident a point it may seem) that "the genetic make-up of the Khoisan relates them more closely to the peoples of Africa, than to any other people" (23). Tobias writes that

> The evidence of San-like figures in the thousands of prehistoric rock painting sites scattered in a wide arc from the Drakensberg and the Maluti mountains down to the folded mountain ranges of the Eastern and Western Cape, shows that the San were in earlier times distributed all over southern Africa and, to judge by the paintings, looking very much as they do today. (28)

In an early (1964) study of the ecology of the San people, Tobias saw in the "preNeolithic economy [. . .] of the Bushmen [evidence that] culture predominates over biological considerations in ensuring survival" (qtd. by himself in "Myths" 24) because the "inventive genius and flexibility" of these societies provided the qualities ensuring their survival on this continent – probably over almost 30,000 years.[4] It has been said that "San rock art is a monument to the

---

[3] Given at the "Khoisan Identity and Cultural Heritage" Conference held in Cape Town, July 12-16, 1997.

[4] The earliest South African rock art has been authoritatively dated as approximately 26,000 years old (see Lewis-Williams 11).

breadth, subtlety and interrelatedness of San thought" (Lewis-Williams; qtd. in Tobias 25).[5]

San or Bushman culture is in our time inextricably linked with, though in some ways distinguishable from, Khoikhoi culture – hence the blanket term Khoisan. According to the specialist historian Elphick, Khoikhoi people probably acquired cattle in the area now known as Botswana and spread southwards, displacing (to some extent) but also to a large extent socially interacting with the aboriginal San groups, their Khoikhoi language and social status becoming dominant. Unlike (*broadly* speaking!) the exclusively hunter-gatherer Bushmen, the Khoikhoi kept livestock (sheep and cattle), although they also relied on veld food like the San, often employing and intermarrying with them (Elphick 10-42). Tobias confirms this by referring to "evidence that domestic animals [have] been in South Africa for about 2,000 years" and to "evidence that hunting and herding had co-existed for a long time" in this part of the continent (26).

The historian Noel Mostert has written rather beautifully that "Khoikhoi words crack and softly rustle, and click. The sand and dry heat and empty distance of the semi-arid lands where the Khoikhoi originated are embedded in them." He adds: "But so is softness, greenness. They run together like the very passage of their olden days" (35). Touched as it is by a sort of tender nostalgia, Mostert's description brings one to the point of the extreme scarcity, the scantiness of verbal recordings of Khoisan expressive culture. Because so much of the knowledge, lore, skill and wisdom of these peoples is irretrievable, the little that is available has taken on especial value.

Amongst academics and others interested in these early southern African cultures it is well known that (from about 1860) a German philologist then working in Cape Town, Wilhelm Bleek, and his English sister-in-law Lucy Lloyd, learnt and also devised an orthography for one of the numerous Cape San languages (/Xam), producing some 12,000 pages of transcript from their /Xam informants with accompanying English translations. This is an invaluable archive concerning the beliefs and social practices of a particular San culture, the evidence recorded at the time of (and clearly registering) the colonial disruption in the Cape region, when Khoisan people were subjugated, enslaved and often ruthlessly hunted down (leaving out of consideration the depredations of smallpox and

5 Presumably most readers of an article such as this are aware that, "San" being a pejorative Khoikhoi term for the designated people, there has been a reversion among some scholars to the term "Bushman," even if this name, too, has been resented.

other "imported" diseases). There is a scattering of other verbal records in both English and Afrikaans, but the Bleek-Lloyd collection[6] is likely to remain the chief documentary source for a verbal expression of a particular Khoisan group's vision of life in an earlier southern Africa.

To say this is not to overlook the limitations and probable distortions of even these records, since they were transmitted under the constraints of highly unequal social relations between the recorders and the informants, who patiently dictated their lore to outsiders (Bleek and Lloyd) with a very recent knowledge of the language. The information was translated by the latter into a language (English) perhaps not particularly well fitted for communicating the lineaments of the original culture. A contemporary researcher among the Ju/'hoan (San) people warns against "the ultimate linguistic colonisation, that of a local oral tradition by the literate mind-set" (Biesele, "'Different People'" 7) – a warning one might need to "apply" retrospectively to recognise that even the treasury which the Bleek/Lloyd transcripts and translations represent was established with somewhat unreliable, perhaps distorting instruments.[7]

As an extension of this warning, Biesele records another caution – against what I would call museumisation (which is a form of commodification) of earlier cultures such as those of the Khoisan. She writes in an article: "We try to 'fix' other peoples in categories learnable by rote, and the result is that individuals become invisible. The ways they are transforming themselves [. . .] [t]heir great, current histories of themselves flatten into trite minor fictions" ("'Different People'" 15).

Along the same lines, Helize van Vuuren warns against the "use [of] glib phrases" such as "reconstructing voices from the past," and on the tendency to "romanticis[e] these 'little people' [. . .] as symbolising the original South African presence." She asks: "But are we perhaps merely recolonising exotic material into our defunct white canon with the aim of revitalising it?" (211). There is probably no escape from the accusations of exploitation and contamination attendant upon the contemporary researcher's efforts, for, as Tony Morphet has

6 The collection is housed in the University of Cape Town library; small selections from it have been published (see my bibliography).

7 Compare Mathias Guenther's comment on the Bleek/Lloyd archive: "The social and emotional tensions and strains marking the relationship between the researchers and narrators presumably left their mark on the narratives that were presented" (Guenther 88). See also the article on the photographs of the Bleek informants by Webster.

noted, "there is no independent Bushman archive," we must simply acknowledge "that all forms of collective memory can now only be mediated through the formal archive of established social power" (98). Even a conference such as "Against All Odds"[8] (held to celebrate Africa's indigenous languages and literatures), in being funded, among other instances, by such bodies as the World Bank and the Ford Foundation was to *some* extent an example of this (inevitable?) infiltration of the "original" – by the powerfully modern, probably alien cultures – which is the dark side of globalisation.

Since the subject of my essay is a little group of four Khoisan tales (taking up just over 20 small pages of print) that were told, recorded and published *in Afrikaans*, I shall touch briefly on some aspects of the development and function of this language in South Africa. Languages become powerful usually through the politically dominant position of their speakers, and what could be termed "white" Afrikaans is no exception to this pattern. In an essay titled "Building a Nation from Words: [on] Afrikaans language, literature and ethnic identity [from] 1902-1924," Isabel Hofmeyr refers to the

> diversity of the [Dutch-Afrikaans] dialect [as having] partly to do with the historical trajectory of the lowland Dutch dialect spoken by the seventeenth-century [white] settlers [in South Africa]. In confronting the language of the slaves [that had been brought here] – Malay and Portuguese creole – along with Khoisan speech, this Dutch linguistic cluster had partly creolised. In later years it picked up shards of German, French and Southern Nguni languages and a goodly layer of English after 1806. (96)

Then followed a struggle by white speakers of the language, waged mainly against English colonial denigration, to establish Afrikaans as a language of what the historian-philosopher-anthropologist Ernst Gellner terms "high culture" – which in the South African context meant establishing it as a middle-class, "white" language, distinct from the Afrikaans spoken by those classified "non-white."[9] To this day the term 'Afrikaans' (including of course its associate, 'Af-

8 It was at this important conference (held in Asmara, Eritrea in January 2000, and titled "Against All Odds: African Languages and Literatures into the Twenty-First Century") that an earlier version of this essay was presented as a paper.

9 Hofmeyr in her article makes important points concerning the struggle to achieve the status of an established language for Afrikaans. I cite three quotations from her article (note that there are quotations *within* her quotations):

rikaner') is all too frequently taken as demarcating a "white" racial-linguistic identity.[10] As spoken by whites and eventually established as one of the two "official languages" of the apartheid dispensation, Afrikaans thus became the marker of white domination, whereas, as spoken by other (darker) South Africans, it became the marker of their subjugation. Introducing a 1933 publication, *The Early Cape Hottentots*, the anthropologist Schapera noted:

> In Little Namaqualand descendants of the old Naman are still found in fairly considerable numbers. Here, too, their tribal cohesion and culture have been completely destroyed by contact with the Europeans,

---

a) The columns of Preller's paper *De Volkstem* soon began to carry innumerable articles which began the long task of making Afrikaans respectable. Some of these spoke about 'Taal en Self-Respek' [Language and Self-Respect]. Others attempted to legitimate an Afrikaans language struggle by referring to similar developments in other parts of the world, most notably Flanders but also Quebec, Wales and Ireland. Subsequent articles began to emphasise the links between Dutch and Afrikaans, which made the latter a 'white man's language', and gave it an entree via Dutch into that font of civilisation, the Graeco-Roman tradition. Through these debates carried out in various journals, the people involved refined their objectives. The first was to try and standardise a middle-class variant of Afrikaans. The point was made in many ways, but nowhere more clearly than in the following sentences:

'Language unity is the natural outcome of national unity, the necessary precondition for a national culture. In a situation where there are a variety of dialects, language unity can only be achieved when one of these dialects becomes hegemonic.' (Qtd. in Hofmeyr 105)

(b) See the statement made by one Van Rijn in 1914: 'Afrikaans is no *bastard tongue* [. . .] It is a true *white man's language*, Dutch to the core.' (Emphasis original). Qtd. in Reinecke *et al.*, *A Bibliography*, p. 322. By about 1910 D.F. Malan was linking Afrikaans to Dutch, German and French, 'the natural inheritors of the civilisation and art of the old Greeks and Romans'. Qtd. in Schoonees, *Die Prosa*, p. 13. (Qtd. in Hofmeyr 119 n.)

(c) For attempts to exorcise the 'coloured' nature of Afrikaans, see 'Is Afrikaans Plat?' [Is Afrikaans a common or vulgar language?], *Die Huisgenoot*, August 1919, and then the debate on this article in *ibid.*, November 1919. (Qtd. in Hofmeyr 120).

10 A point made, *inter alia*, in a text proclaimed as the first Afrikaans novel by a "coloured" South African, *Vatmaar* by A. H. M. Scholtz, which claims the language for a mixed-race community in the face of a snobbish tendency (among white speakers of the language) to denigrate their use of the language. Scholtz's text is now available in an English translation (see my bibliography).

> and they have also absorbed a good deal of white blood. A few of the older people still know their own language, but the great majority now speak only Afrikaans, the regular medium of intercourse even amongst themselves. (xiv-xv)[11]

Along with this linguistic domination (and the political domination of which it is the marker) went another sort of domination, which the South African born novelist Bessie Head (in an essay) described in the following terms:

> A sense of history was totally absent in me and it was as if, far back in history, thieves had stolen the land and were so anxious to cover up all traces of the theft that correspondingly, all traces of the true history have been obliterated. We, as black people, could make no appraisal of our own worth; we did not know who and what we were, apart from objects of abuse and exploitation. (66)

Given this truth, all possible forms of re-attribution and recognition, whatever the ironies and complicities involved in such work, do need to be undertaken. Focusing on such a neglected South African cultural resource as the Khoisan *Dwaalstories* can be a small contribution to the reconfiguration of the past and (even, perhaps) the present of South African society.[12] As a mere exercise in romantic nostalgia it would not be worth undertaking, however; the only worthwhile aim would be to recognise in these tales a time-transcending contribution to present-day social realities,[13] which (as I hope to demonstrate) they do certainly offer.

---

11 Compare the following citation from another anthropological study: "Owing to the prominent part Afrikaans, or some form of it, plays in the daily life of the Korana, it became the medium in which most of our conversations were carried on" (Engelbrecht 203).

12 The collection *Dwaalstories*, with the name of Eugène Marais as author, was recently reissued (in Afrikaans) by the publisher Human & Rousseau (Kaapstad/ Pretoria 2007), simultaneously with the first published complete translation into English of this collection (including the introduction by Marais). The English translation: Eugène N. Marais. *The Rain Bull and other Tales from the San*. Translated by Jacques Coetzee. Illustrations by Katrine Harries. Cape Town / Pretoria: Human & Rousseau, 2007. ISBN-13 978-0-7981-4833-7.

13 Compare Biesele's reference to "the hidden teaching capacities and the sense-making functions of folklore and dramatic games" and to "expressive forms [as] articulat[ing] meanings that must be shared in order to perpetuate society as an entity of shared understandings" (*Women Like Meat* 192-193).

These *Dwaalstories* (a title meaning *meandering*, or *wanderers'*, *tales*) are particularly significant in offering a portrayal of a Khoisan society (or societies – the stories seem to depict a degree of cultural variation) as fraught with its (or their) own social tensions. All too common is the tendency amongst present-day commentators to see those societies as pure, utterly harmonious and socially blameless communities – a perspective I find problematic because such romantic idealisation is finally a form either of condescension or of misrepresentation in that it denies full human status (which must include recognition of the harmful capacities of individuals and societies) to the Khoisan. As E. N. Wilmsen puts it, this leads to the position where the Khoisan "can be pan-human only by being pre-human" (19). In a comment I see as paralleling Wilmsen's, Anne Solomon insists that "interpretations of the rock art which prioritise the transcendent at the expense of the mundane must be seen as unacceptable; and an approach which emphasises or proceeds from the religious is as much a 'tranquil' account that conceals historical realities" (56).

But it may not be necessary to dichotomise the religious (both as the transcendent and as the moral dimension) from the historical, in the way that Solomon suggests here. For, in stories like the *Dwaalstories* – simultaneously social documentation and social assessment – these perspectives coexist in mutually enriching ways. In his major essay "A Review of African Oral Traditions and Literature," Harold Scheub says that "myth is a metaphor, and because of that it is a narrative device" (3). This may be taken to mean that in myths which represent "recognisable" social formations and events, the process of recognition or understanding follows the thread or clue that the story-line provides.

Scheub offers ways of considering what he terms "tales that [. . .] have epic dimensions" (14) – a description which I believe fits the *Dwaalstories*, or which I would like to extend to apply to them. To Scheub such tales (with "epic dimensions") transcend the schismatic distinction between what is considered *either* religious *or* historical material, as well as between materials classified *either* oral *or* literary – in an argument I find compelling and liberating. Scheub writes that

> the refocusing of attention from things done to who does them is critical, not only to an understanding of the oral tradition and its permutations, but to a comprehension of its ties with literature.
>
> While Trickster and Hero[ine?] stand alone, each yearns to be an insider. But it is not *being* on the inside that is important, it is *becoming* an insider. *Being* an insider means accepting the society as it is.

> *Becoming* one means altering the society to accommodate what an individual stands for, not the other way round. The shift is revolutionary. (14)

For, in creating such redefinitions, "the hero's vision and his [or her] struggle have to do with the future" (14). In "this breaking of a cyclical pattern," Scheub writes, "the epic character moves away from the tale character towards the historical figure. [. . .] But the break is the thing, for it allows the introduction of realism into the oral narrative" (15).[14] In what follows I shall attempt to indicate that Hendrik's *Dwaalstories* exemplify the kind of tale that Scheub refers to as simultaneously "religious" and "historical," and as transcending the oral-literary divide.

The *Dwaalstories* were four among those (the others now lost) told by a venerable old man of at least a hundred years old, a narrator identified as a Bushman (i.e. San) by the white Afrikaans writer Eugène Marais,[15] who recorded them. Of the teller, we know only his advanced age and his Afrikaans name, Hendrik, as well as the fact that he was an itinerant visitor to the farm in the Waterberg region (in the Northern Province of present-day South Africa) where Marais, himself at this time something of a pariah due to his hopeless morphine addiction, stayed. It is likely that Marais's friend Tindall, son of a Wesleyan missionary who was a pioneering student of Khoisan languages in northern South Africa and Namibia, first interested Marais in these cultures (Rousseau 170). Marais was also interested in the success another early Afrikaans writer,

---

14 Scheub continues the argument to make the point that "History and fiction have come into a tentative union in the epic, making possible the birth of the novel" (15; compare also 46).

15 A political adversary of and (in the local context) "liberal" campaigner against President Paul Kruger of the Transvaal (Boer) Republic before the Anglo-Boer War and a political activist against British domination in South Africa during and after the war; a gifted and pioneering naturalist – one of the very first to study groups of primates in their natural habitat, who also developed important theories concerning termite behaviour; a fiery journalist in his early years, who took a British law degree, acquired a great deal of medical and especially psychological knowledge, read widely in science and philosophy; made jewellery; a very important pioneering creative writer in Afrikaans (whose home language was more English than Afrikaans) and an author of scientific articles and studies; as well as an incurable and almost lifelong morphine addict, who died by suicide – these are some of the many and (in contrast with the Khoisan "Hendrik") well documented roles played by Marais.

Von Wielligh, had achieved in collecting and publishing Khoisan tales in Afrikaans (Rousseau 194). A visit to Marais by a friend, the German artist Erich Mayer, in 1913 resulted in a fine ink portrait of "Ou [=old] Hendrik" (as the storyteller was known). It was perhaps at this time that Marais first heard the *Dwaalstories*.[16] The tales were first (serially and separately) published in 1921, in a popular Afrikaans women's or family magazine, *Die Huisgenoot*.

---

16 A vexed aspect of Marais's position vis-à-vis the Khoisan is the fact that he wrote the following (in an essay, titled "The Yellow Streak in South Africa," which was never published):

> The psychologist finds so many ape-like mental attributes [in the San; Marais is writing as a naturalist who extensively studied primate behaviour and is evidently vaguely echoing the Darwinian ideas of his time] that it is difficult to avoid the conclusion that nothing more than the skeleton of an articulate language separates them from the anthropoids. And to the comparative anatomist the thing seems beyond question. The profound somatic differences between the Bushman and the lowest human race precludes all idea of a common human species [. . .] Everything points to a near ape-ancestry and to an ape-ancestry different from that of the rest of the human race.

To this Marais added:

> And it is a singular thing that this ape-like being [. . .] the first cousin to the chimpanzee, should yet be the only true native South African artist. He was the first and only engraver and painter; the only musician; a poet and storyteller whose genius would compare favourably with that of any human race of a far higher degree of culture. And wherever the yellow streak has polluted the stream of "higher" South African blood it has prepotently carried with it this masterly strain of artistry. The so-called Bushman is our true and only Bohemian. With a broken-backed fiddle, a hoarse concertina and a bottle of virulent brandy he can still at will transform the wilderness into a joyous paradise. And withal, a sense of humour always proof against all miseries and vicissitudes.
>
> (Qtd. in Rousseau 266)

As Tobias comments, "What a strange mixture of pejorative and racist ideas with what high praise for the San artistic accomplishment!" (22).

Elsewhere, Rousseau (his biographer) notes further evidence of Marais's preoccupation with the idea of generic differences between "Bushmen" and other humans: "According to Marais, the tiny bony projections on the human lower jaw were somehow related to the power of speech. In the Bushman, he believed, as in the ape, there were tiny holes instead of knobs, which indicated the Bushman's less advanced stage of development" (Rousseau 389-390).

Marais acknowledges regretfully that he never recorded any of the stories *verbatim*, but testifies that he did write down "a few" immediately after the telling. These details (and what follows) are mentioned in Marais's introduction to the first collected edition of the *Dwaalstories*, published in 1927 with the abovementioned portrait of Old Hendrik (who had died at "over a hundred years old," shortly after this likeness was sketched in 1913) as its frontispiece. In this introduction, Marais refers prominently and knowledgeably to Bleek's transcriptions of a San language (discussed earlier in this article). Marais draws a distinction between San tales which, imperfectly transliterated into Afrikaans, are near-gibberish, and those which have the power to move their listeners imaginatively. Marais seems to assign the stories to a children's audience (and, it would seem, one of white Afrikaans children!), yet his references to Bleek, to the complexities of San storytelling and to European "equivalents," as well as the trouble he took both in recording the tales and in scrupulously acknowledging the authorship of "Old Hendrik," indicate a definite recognition of their value.

The ironies of undervaluation and exploitation are more evident in the later white Afrikaans literary establishment's reception of the tales than in Marais's

---

Shocking and disappointing as these statements seem, coming from the recorder of the *Dwaalstories*, it should perhaps be noted that although his *practice* (both socially and artistically) contradicted these ugly, narrow-visioned prejudices, Marais was perhaps (in these statements) yielding to ideas for which he should not be held the sole scapegoat. Indeed, even the great Senegalese scholar Cheikh Anta Diop could (in a footnote in his *The African Origin of Civilization – Myth or Reality* (1974) refer equally disparagingly to the Khoisan (in order to express contempt towards certain whites): "These Whites are *savages* today, *in the Bushman or Hottentot sense of the word*; they make masks, grimacing and tormented, indicating a cosmic terror equalled only by the Eskimo" (Diop 164; my emphasis).

Very similar sounding to the white Afrikaner Marais's assessment (quoted above) of the San is the comment by the Botswana historian S. M. Molema in his important work *The Bantu Past and Present*: "Amongst the lowest of the world's inhabitants, they [the San] exhibited some traits of the most advanced [. . .] Much lower in the scale of humanity than the Bantu around them, they showed greater advances in some arts – such as painting – than they. In their folklore, too, [. . .] if they did not actually surpass, they were not surpassed by the Bantu" (26).

And for good measure one can add here an 1850 quotation from the famous British missionary David Livingstone's writings: "The Bushmen of the desert are perhaps the most degraded specimens of the human family" (161). See also my own essay, "'By What Authority?' Representations of the Khoisan in South African English Poetry."

dissemination of them. Quite simply attributing the excellence of the stories entirely to Marais himself, the doyen of Afrikaans poets, N. P. Van Wyk Louw, wrote that Marais "here [i.e. in the *Dwaalstories*], in 'visions,' caught occasional glimpses of what Afrikaans [literary] art can be. Purer than he ever managed to convey in [his] poetry" (Louw 136; my translation of the Afrikaans original). One later critic suspects that Louw may have alluded (in choosing the term 'visions') to Marais's well known morphine addiction – a point she then simply extends to the speculation that Hendrik may have told the tales while under the influence of marijuana (Gilfillan 153-156). A contemporary Afrikaans literary critic even told Marais's biographer, Rousseau, that he "could not believe that Marais had himself written the tales" (Rousseau 262) – denying (it seems) *both* Marais *and* Old Hendrik the verbal capacity to have composed these masterpieces! The poem quoted at the end of the present essay was by Marais himself attributed to the character "Joggom Konterdans" who is an artist-figure featuring in the tale told to him by Hendrik. For generations this poem has been taught in South African schools as a composition by Eugène Marais who was (as he himself insists) its *transcriber*. Few pupils were ever taught that the poem had been taken from its context in one of the *Dwaalstories*, let alone that the original visionary or poet was a Khoisan person expressing an imaginative and conceptual understanding particular to his own, now neglected or half-buried South African culture.

Yet it is, of course, impossible to establish what was lost – or gained – by the mode of transcription of these stories. Marais himself ends his introduction to the 1927 edition by regretting that much of value was lost because of the delay between his initial hearing and subsequent recording of the stories. He refers to unusual "Afrikaans-Bushman words and expressions," not all of which he could recall, and adds observations on the inevitable impoverishment (in the transition from oral to literary mode) of the recorded version of the tales because of the absence of appropriate accompanying gestures, natural mimicry and (facial) expressions (Marais 1927: 7; my translations). Marais's awareness of translation as a form of betrayal (*tradurre tradire*, as the Italians say) is therefore fairly sophisticated.

Scheub's may (again) here be a useful perspective: he reminds us that "in ancient Egypt, the craft of the scribe was 'the greatest of all professions'; [. . .] the scribe was the mediator between the oral performer and his audience." Scribes, Scheub tells us, "felt free to rephrase, rearrange and transpose." In this, he sees a metaphor for the transition from the oral to the literary mode, and a model of their possible mutual enrichment – "The two media continued their parallel development; [. . .] there is no unbridgeable gap between them; they constantly nourish each other" (Scheub 16).

Putting the above suggestions to the test brings one to the stories themselves and to the brief illustrations from them that can be contained in an article like this. The thematic outlines of the four *Dwaalstories*, are as follows: in the first one, the exposure of untested fame as undeserved, meeting the braggart's severe punishment for betraying his social responsibility at a time of crisis; in the second, the non-violent overthrow of unearned power; and, in the last two tales, unrecognised (female) excellence winning through. Because of constraints of space, it is only possible to summarise briefly the greater part of the most substantial of the four stories, the one that Marais placed second in the published collection, which bears the title "The Song of the Rain." The story is subtitled "A Coranna Wander-story," a reference which identifies it explicitly with a Khoikhoi group (the Coranna). Although Marais consistently refers to "Bushman stories" and to "Old Hendrik" as a "Bushman," details such as references to the keeping of livestock and to settled dwellings, as well as a reference to Heitsi-Eibib, the great (mythical) hero-ancestor of the Khoikhoi (in this and in one other story) point to their being of Khoikhoi origin – but then, the distinction between San (or Bushman) and Khoikhoi was (and is still) often blurred, both in fact and in description.

"The Song of the Rain" tells of a period of great suffering and near-starvation amongst the members of a smallish community, due to a terrible drought. The emergency resource that should be made available to all members of the community during such a crisis – a fountain or water-hole which never dries – was given into the keeping of the foremost musician and composer of this small social group, with express orders to guard it from common use, *but* to allow access to the water by other members of the community during any critical drought. Yet this man has grown arrogant and selfish and has come to see his caretaker's role as that of an owner with a personal possession, refusing to share the resource.[17] The other (ageing) man who might defeat the usurper in a musical con-

---

[17] Compare the following:

> Moreover, land ownership is loosely defined; the 'owner' or 'master' [. . .] of a territory, or of a permanent water hole that defines it, exercises a form of 'responsible stewardship', [. . .] in the words of Richard Katz, Megan Biesele and Vera St Denis, [he is] 'more an informed person

test is unequal to the task, himself a foolish and vain person. Quietly, secretly, however, an outsider-figure by the name of Krom [or Bent – i.e. crooked, or crippled] Joggom Konterdans – whose full name seems to signify the stigma he bears as a hump-backed person, as well as his innovative, inventive genius in its allusion to the art of dancing "differently"– sets about constructing a new musical instrument according to the ancient lore of his people.

When the instrument is at last complete and the composition is performed, "Counterdance" (as one might render his last name in English) is recognised by the old grandmother and cultural authority of the community (who is named Na-si-Tgam) as their potential saviour. I now cite my own English translation (from the Afrikaans original) of the concluding part of the story (Marais 19-21; my unpublished translation 9-10):

> And she handed him the small mirror which she long ago polished from the black horn of a rhinoceros, as well as the great copper neck-ring of Heitsi-Eibib.
>
> And that morning when the light dawned Counterdance sat at the Steep Stone inside the yard fence of the Berry Trees; this is at the tip of the Skew-water; he had turned his back towards the yard-side. And in front of him he had propped up the rhinoceros horn mirror, so that he could see everything behind him; and his whole body was gleaming with the tail-fat. And around his head dangled three tassels of mongoose skin; and around his neck was the great copper neck-ring of Heitsi-Eibib.
>
> And he composed the Song of the Rain.
>
> And Jacob Tame-One [the tyrant-figure who refuses to share the water: I have freely translated his name from the Afrikaans], when he took the trumpet and opened his mouth wide to blow it, was suddenly dumb-struck. And his little ones rushed from the yard-side shouting: "Our Dad, our Dad, there's someone on the marker stone at the Skew-water who shows only his back. And the people are dancing in their shelters."
>
> And Jacob Tame-One made a grab for his panga, and he shouted for the warriors, but there was no reply. He heard them saying: "Klips! [i.e. "Gosh!"] That is a Master musician, that one."

---

who can care for a water resource so that it can be shared than an exclusive holder of rights to that water.' (Smith et al. 73)

And Tame-One struck the big drum, and he called out: "Today I'll invite *all* the vultures! Today will be the great battle of the Berry Trees!" And he crept up on Counterdance behind the thorn shelter of the Skew-water.

And Counterdance sang the Song of the Rain, and he played his violin [the stringed instrument he had so painstakingly constructed].

And Tame-One saw his own people go to meet him [Counterdance], and they danced and spoke admiringly to Joggom Counterdance. And at the top of the hill he saw the old crone Nasi-Tgam and she spread the black skin cloak out wide, and behind her followed the people from all the other yards, with calabashes and ostrich egg-shells ready for the water, and he felt his heart weakening.

And Bent Joggom Counterdance played the Song of the Rain, and he peeped into the mirror.

And then Jacob Tame-One tossed his panga into the Skew-water, and sat down in the dust, and he called out: "My children, my children, your old father's riding-horse is dead!"

And on that day the old crone Nasi Tgam re-intoned the Law of the Berry Trees, and it was Bent Joggom Counterdance who distributed the water.

The Song of the Rain
(By Bent Joggom Counterdance)

First she peeps slyly over the mountain-top,
And her eyes are shy;
And she laughs softly.
And from far off she beckons with one hand.
Her bracelets shimmer and her necklaces shine,
She calls softly.
She tells the winds of the dance.
And she invites them, for the yard is wide and the wedding grand.
The big game rush up from the plain.

They dam up on the hilltop.
Their nostrils stretch wide,
And they swallow the wind;
And they bend down, to see her faint tracks in the sand.

> The little folk under the earth hear the drag of her feet,
> And they creep closer and sing softly:
> "Our Sister! Our Sister! You've come! You've come!"
> And her necklaces shake,
> Until even the ancient ones on their sleeping mats wake up in the night
> And they talk in the dark;
> And her copper ring catches the last light of the sun.
> On her forehead is the fiery plume of the mountain eagle;
> She steps down from the heights;
> She spreads out the grey kaross with both her arms;
> The wind loses its breath.
> Oh, the dance of our Sister!

Thus ends this tale and my citation of my translation, in which I left the term "kaross" (a skin cloak or blanket) untranslated.

Scheub says that "African oral *and* literary works have had as their central aim the work of transforming the order prevailing in reality" (Scheub 46; emphasis added). He goes on: "the performance is not simply a reflection of that culture; it is the essence of an experience of history and art. The work of art bridges the generations" (Scheub 46).[18] These words seem eminently applicable to "The Song of the Rain," and to the other *Dwaalstories*. As a presentation of the possibility of the transcendence of brute power by creativity, of the idea that creative energy and vision are as socially necessary and fulfilling as rain is to the earth, bringing relief in times of dire need, it is hard not to feel the power and value of this tale – both its enduring relevance and its testimony to the value of

---

18 The puzzled tentativeness of the following comments by Roger Hewitt may be contrasted with Scheub's authoritative remarks (Hewitt is wondering why he – Hewitt – singled out one of two particularly "complex" San tales from the tales and statements, mainly from the Bleek/Lloyd collection, that he studied in his book): "But there is no *a priori* reason why cultural depth and complexity should coincide with aesthetic enjoyment. However, there is no doubt that these versions are singular [. . .] they seem to point to a line of enquiry into the relationship between aesthetic evaluations and the cultural density of narratives [. . .]" (232-233).

Some of Achebe's careful considerations of the relationship between narrative art and social "usefulness," in his essays, indicate that Hewitt's distinction between what is "art" and what is socioculturally useful or enlightening, may be a false one – such as Achebe's blunt statement that "Art is, and was always, in the service of man" (*Morning* 19). See also his essay "What Has Literature Got to Do with It?"

the well-nigh vanished culture from which it emanated. Its intimation of the unsuspected potential carried by a fully attuned artistic vision (characterised by its delicacy, ecological and social sensitivity and by the exhilaration it evokes by means of an imaginative insight shown capable of dethroning the brute orders and demands of the merely mighty) is a notion that the members of the human race keep on forgetting and constantly need to be reminded of.

The ironies of the survival of the *Dwaalstories* in the language of a people in many instances so hostile to the Khoisan themselves are plentiful, but the sense of wonder that these stories generate remains undiminished. Through all their meanderings the tales have retained – as well as proved – the vitality of a culture recognisably wise, playful and celebratory in its pursuit of the joy of survival, though not without social stresses and individuals who exacerbate or cause them. Without inducing mere self-indulgent nostalgia in their readers (since the *Dwaalstories* depict quite tough social struggles, adjustments and tensions), these four stories give enlightening glimpses of a Khoisan culture that is (still) inclusive and self-adjusting, probably at a stage pre-dating major Euro-colonial or rival ethnic incursion. That we can still, today, catch the vivid glimpses of that vanished lifestyle in a language that was and was not its own, is unsettlingly ironic – and yet almost miraculous. I conclude on the expression of a desire by //Kábbo (a name which means "dream"), one of Bleek's San informants, a wish rendered as follows in English: "that I may listening turn backwards (with my ears) to my feet's heels, on which I went; while I feel that a story is the wind" (qtd. in Bleek and Lloyd 303). How astonishingly that image expresses the *Dwaalstories*' elusive, enriching and ever-free qualities.

Works Cited

Achebe, Chinua. *Hopes and Impediments: Selected Essays*. New York: Doubleday, 1989.

___. *Morning Yet on Creation Day*. London: Heinemann, 1975.

___. "What Has Literature Got to Do with It?" *Hopes* 154-170.

Biesele, Megan. "'Different People Just Have Different Minds': A Personal Attempt to Understand Ju/'hoan Storytelling Aesthetics." *Current Writing* 7.2 (1995): 1-17.

___. *Women Like Meat: The folklore and foraging ideology of the Kalahari Ju/'hoan*. Johannesburg: Witwatersrand UP, 1993.

Bleek, Wilhelm and Lloyd, Lucy. *Specimens of Bushman Folklore*. London: George Allen, 1911.

Diop, Cheikh Anta. *The African Origin of Civilization: Myth or Reality*. Trans. Mercer Cook. New York: Lawrence Hill, 1974.

Elphick, Richard. *Khoikhoi and the Founding of White South Africa*. Johannesburg: Ad. Donker, 1985.

Engelbrecht, J. A. *The Korana: An Account of Their Customs and Their History – With Texts*. Cape Town: Maskew Miller, 1936.

Gagiano, Annie. "'By What Authority?' Presentations of the Khoisan in South African English Poetry." *Alternation* 6.1 (1999): 155-173.

Guenther, Mathias. "Attempting to Contextualise /Xam Oral Tradition." *Voices from the Past: /Xam Bushmen and the Bleek and Lloyd Collection*. Ed. Janette Deacon and Thomas A. Dawson. Johannesburg: Witwatersrand UP, 1996. 77–99.

Haarhoff, Dorian. "San Song." *SA in Poësie / SA in Poetry*. Ed. Johan van Wyk, Pieter Conradie and Nik Costandara. Pinetown, South Africa: Owen Burgess, 1988.

Head, Bessie. *A Woman Alone: Autobiographical Writings*. Oxford: Heinemann, 1990.

Hewitt, Roger L. *Structure, Meaning and Ritual in the Narratives of the Southern San*. Hamburg: Helmut Buske Verlag, 1986.

Hofmeyr, Isabel. "Building a Nation from Words: Afrikaans Language, Literature and Ethnic Identity, 1902-1924." *The Politics of Race, Class and Nationalism in Twentieth Century South Africa*. Ed. Shula Marks and Stanley Trapido. London: Longman, 1987. 95-122.

Lewis-Williams, David. *Discovering Southern African Rock Art*. Cape Town: David Philip, 1990.

Livingstone, David. *Missionary Correspondence 1846-1856*. Ed. I. Schapera. Berkeley: University of California Press, 1961.

Louw, N. P. van Wyk. *Vernuwing in die Prosa: 3de Uitgawe 3de Druk*. Pretoria: Academia, 1981.

Marais, Eugène N. *Dwaalstories*. Cape Town: Human and Rousseau, 1959.

Molema, S. M. *The Bantu Past and Present*. Edinburgh: Green, 1920.

Morphet, Tony. Rev. of *Miscast*. *Pretexts: Studies in Writing and Culture* 6.1 (1997): 95-99.

Mostert, Noel. *Frontiers*. London: Jonathan Cape, 1992.

Rousseau, Leon. *The Dark Stream: The Story of Eugène N. Marais*. Johannesburg: Jonathan Ball, 1982.

Schapera, I. Introduction. *The Early Cape Hottentots – Described in the Writings of O. Dapper, 1668, W. ten Rhyne, 1686, and J. G. de Grevenbroek, 1695*. Ed. and trans. I. Schapera and B. Farrington. Cape Town: The Van Riebeeck Society, 1933. i-xv.

Scheub, Harold. "A Review of African Oral Traditions and Literature." *African Studies Review* 28.2-3 (1985): 1-72.

Scholtz, A. H. M. *A Place Called Vatmaar*. Cape Town: Kwela Books, 2000.

Smith, Andy, Candy Malherbe, Mat Guenther, Penny Berens. *The Bushmen of Southern Africa: A Foraging Society in Transition*. Cape Town: David Philip, 2000.

Solomon, Ann. "Representations and the Aesthetic in San Art." *Critical Arts* 9.2 (1995): 49-64.

Tobias, Phillip V. "Myths and Misunderstandings about Khoisan Identities and Status." *The Proceedings of the Khoisan Identity and Cultural Heritage Conference*. Organised by the Institute for Historical Research, University of the Western Cape, held at the South African Museum, Cape Town, 12-16 July 1997. Ed. Andrew Bank. Cape Town: Institute for Historical Research, University of Cape Town, 1998.

Van Vuuren, Helize. "The Tin Shack Bushmen of Kagga Kamma." Rev. of *In the Tradition of the Forefathers. Bushman Traditionality at Kagga Kamma. The Politics and History of a Performative Identity*. By Hylton White. Cape Town: UCT Press, 1995. *Alternation* 2.2 (1995): 207-211.

Weaver, Tony. "Last of the First." *The Big Issue* 41.4 (1995): 20-21.

Webster, Christopher. "The Portrait Cabinet of Dr Bleek: Anthropometric Photographs by Early Cape Photographers." *Critical Arts* 14.1 (2000): 1–15.

Wilmsen, Edwin N. "First People? Images and imaginations in South African Iconography." *Critical Arts* 9.2 (1995): 1-27.

Marecheran Postmodernism: Mocking the Bad Joke of "African Modernity"

> When the other speaks, he or she becomes another subject,which must be consciously registered as a problem by the imperial or metropolitan subject.
>
> – Fredric Jameson, "Modernism and Imperialism"

If I may add one more generalisation to those that have been broadly accepted concerning the European Enlightenment, it would be this: that the pronouncements on colonised peoples and phenotypes made by the most authoritative thinkers of the *Aufklärung* are characterised by an almost uniformly complacent, confident solemnity. Perhaps such authoritative racial arrogance is the inevitable expression of European internal consolidation and external expansionism. To illustrate the point, here are some examples:

> The superabundance of the iron particles, which are present in all human blood, and which are precipitated in the reticular substance through evaporation of the acids of phosphorus (which makes all Negroes stink) cause the blackness that shines through the superficial skin; and the high iron content of the blood seems also necessary in order to forestall a slackening of all parts. The oil of the skin which weakens the nutrient mucus that is requisite for hair growth, has permitted hardly even the production of a woolly covering for the head. Besides all this, damp heat promotes strong growth in animals in general; in short, the Negro is produced, well suited to his climate; that is, strong, fleshy, supple, but in the midst of the bountiful provision of this motherland lazy, soft and dawdling. (Kant 22)

> Africa is in general a closed land, and it maintains this fundamental character. It is characteristic of the blacks that their consciousness has not yet even arrived at the intuition of any objectivity, as for example, of God or the law, in which humanity relates to the world and intuits its essence [. . .] He [the black person] is a human being in the rough. [. . .]
>
> Africa [. . .] does not properly have a history. (Hegel; qtd. in Dussel, *Invention* 22)

> By a dialectic which is appropriate for surpassing itself, in the first place, [European] society is driven to look *beyond* itself to new consumers. Therefore it seeks its means of subsistence among other people which are inferior to it with respect to the resources which it has in excess, such as those of industry. This expansion of relations also makes possible that colonization to which, under systematic or sporadic form, a fully established civil society is impelled. Colonization permits it that one part of its population, located on the new territory, returns to the principle of family property and, at the same time, procures for itself a new possibility and field of labor. (Hegel; qtd. in Dussel, *Invention* 25)

> Against the absolute right of that people who actually are the carriers of the world Spirit, the spirit of other peoples *has no other right* (*rechtlos*). (Hegel; qtd. in Dussel, *Invention* 24)

> I am apt to suspect the negroes, and in general all the other species of men (for there are four or *five* different kinds) to be naturally *inferior* to the whites. There never was a civilized nation of any other complexion than white, nor even any individual eminent either in action or speculation. No ingenious manufacturers amongst them, no arts, no science, On the other hand, the most rude and barbarous of the whites, such as the ancient GERMANS, the present TARTARS have still something eminent about them, in their valour, form of government, or some other particular. Such a uniform and constant difference could not happen, in so many countries and ages, if nature had not made an original distinction betwixt these breeds of men. Not to mention our colonies, there are NEGROE slaves dispersed all over EUROPE of which none ever discovered any symptoms of ingenuity; tho' low people, without education, will startup amongst us, and distinguish themselves in every profession. In JAMAICA indeed they talk of one negroe as a man of parts and learning; but 'tis likely he is admired for *very* slender accomplishments, like a parrot, who speaks a few words plainly. (Hume 252 n.)

The link between this powerful, totalising discourse (illustrated in the above examples) and the need to validate the great surges of colonisation that emanated from Europe has often been pointed out – indeed, a persuasive reading of Enlightenment thought as perhaps primarily if unconsciously a mode of validation of European expansionism has gained considerable currency, as may be illustrated in more contemporary pronouncements such as the following:

> Truth is, in other words, a *social relation* (like *power*, *ownership* or *freedom*): an aspect of a hierarchy built of superiority-inferiority units; more precisely, an aspect of the hegemonic form of domination or of a bid for domination-through-hegemony. Modernity was, from its inception, such a form and such a bid. The part of the world that adopted modern civilization as its structural principle and constitutional value was bent on dominating the rest of the world by dissolving its alterity and assimilating the product of dissolution. The persevering alterity could not but be treated as a temporary nuisance; as an error, sooner or later bound to be supplanted by the war of truth against error on the plane of consciousness. The order bound to be installed and made universal was a *rational* order; the truth bound to be made triumphant was the *universal* (hence apodictic and obligatory) truth. Together, political order and true knowledge blended into a design for *certainty*. The rational-universal world of order and truth would know of no contingency and no ambivalence. The target of certainty and absolute truth was indistinguishable from the crusading spirit and the project of domination. (Bauman 232-33)

> The categorization of the three worlds is, of course, a consequence of Enlightenment philosophy, implicitly grading civilization progress through the standards of northern Europe and America. Modernity in the Third World is necessarily the economic, cultural and political imposition on non-European societies of the European Enlightenment that in this century has been exposed to radical critique. (Lee 40)

> That modernism is itself an ideological expression of capitalism, and in particular, of the latter's reification of daily life, may be granted a local validity [. . .] Viewed in this way, then, modernism can be seen as a late stage in the bourgeois cultural revolution, as a final and extremely specialized phase of the immense process of superstructural transformation whereby the inhabitants of older social formations are culturally and psychologically retrained for life in the market system.
>
> (Jameson, *Political Unconsciousness* 236)

The following quotation in my main text nevertheless illustrates the persistence with which the upsurge of Euro/Western prosperity (which we label "modernity") has continued to mask the extent to which it rested on, took advantage of or simply ignored the "Third World" or colonised countries' misery.[1] The pronouncements following here are by the influential philosopher/anthropologist Ernest Gellner:

> I mean, there are two things to be said in favour of modernity. One, it's inevitable and second, it's good. And it's not good because it's inevitable, but it's good on top of being inevitable. But it is very important that it is inevitable. I mean, mankind first of all has now got hooked on a style of living to which he would like to get accustomed and simply will not, freely, without the most appalling political disasters, accept some kind of reverse policy and a serious romantic rejection of the modern world. You know, that particular programme is just unthinkable, incidentally would involve the elimination of vast numbers of people who simply wouldn't then be able to survive. So it's simply not a remotely realistic alternative. But on top of that, I mean it

---

[1] Dussel writes:

> The ambiguity of the realization of modernity, on the part of the "open society" of *late* capitalism, finds itself limited by what we call the developmentalist fallacy. That is, it would like to extrapolate, to impose the model (and the philosophy that derives from it) of late and central capitalism, in the very same straight line of development without discontinuity, on peripheral capitalism (of Africa, Asia and Latin America; or in other words, to more than 80 per cent of global capitalism, if we take its population numerically), underdeveloped and, as is said in such developmentalist ideology, "delayed." The "delay" of peripheral capitalism is a "before" with respect to the "after" of "late" capitalism. What is not taken into account, in this eurocentric ideology, is that there is no such "before." Since 1492, the periphery is not a "before," but an "underneath": the exploited, the dominated, the origin of stolen wealth, accumulated in the dominating, exploiting "center." We repeat: the developmentalist fallacy thinks that the "slave" is a "free lord" in his youthful stage, and like a child ("crude or barbarian"). It does not understand that the slave is the dialectical "other face" of domination: the as-always, the "other-part" of the exploitative relation. The peripheral world will never be able to be "developed," nor "center," nor "late." Its path is another. Its alternative is different. Liberation Philosophy gives expression to this "dis-tinction."
> (*Underside* 5)

> seems to me positively good that we should have overcome scarcity, that economic and political conflicts in society should have ceased to be a zero sum game, that it would be possible to avoid unnecessary physical suffering. I think on all that we can agree. ("Tough" 36)

In the last section of the Gellner quote, the use of the plural pronoun "we" is particularly striking. To this reader, at least, it seems to signal simultaneously an unconscious exclusiveness and a complacent arrogance or triumphalism that stands in the direct line of inheritance of the Enlightenment philosophers.[2] Given Gellner's considerable standing in Western academia it can be taken as an index of the enduring power of the self-legitimising narrative of modernity as the heir to, or extension of the Enlightenment. In their *Dialectic of Enlightenment* (1979), Adorno and Horkheimer detect a sort of protesting too much element in the apparently celebratory discourse of Enlightenment. They describe it as "mythic fear turned radical" because of its claim to inclusivity: "Nothing at all may remain outside because the mere idea of outsidedness is the very source of fear" (16). They are in tune with the liberation philosopher Enrique Dussel when they declare that what modern men "want to learn from nature is how to use it in order wholly to dominate it and other men. That is the only aim. Ruthlessly, in despite of itself, the Enlightenment has extinguished any trace of its own self-consciousness" (40).

Dussel criticises philosophers like Habermas for describing modernity as a purely European event by arguing that "while modernity is undoubtedly a European occurrence [originating "this history of world domination"], it also originates in a dialectical relation with non-Europe" (*Invention* 9).[3] The nature of that

---

2 In a much earlier publication, Gellner had stated the point even more bluntly: "if a doctrine conflicts with the acceptance of the superiority of scientific-industrial societies over others, then it really is out" ("New Idealism" 405). It is this *rhetoric* of superiority (illustrated clearly also in the above quoted examples) that is so striking and widespread.

In *Culture and Imperialism*, Said in a comment on Conrad's *Heart of Darkness* mentions that "in telling the story of his African journey Marlow repeats and confirms Kurtz's action: restoring Africa to European hegemony by historicizing and narrating its strangeness" (198).

3 Dussel writes: "A European definition of modernity, such as Habermas's, overlooks how *European* modernity constitutes all other cultures as its *periphery*" (*Invention* 32-33). Compare Dussel's reference to "the traditional Eurocentric thesis, flourishing in the United States, modernity's culmination, [which] is that moderni-

relation is, however, of a peculiar kind. According to Dussel, "[t]he *ego cogito* (of Descartes from 1636) was not the original philosophical expression of modernity. Before, the *ego conquiro* ('I conquer,' in first place with Hernán Cortés in 1519 in Mexico) had to undergo the practical experience of Europe's 'centrality,' of its superiority [. . .]" (*Underside* 217).[4]

In conquering the territories and cultures which it invaded, argues Dussel, "Europe never discovered (*des-cubierto*) this Other as Other but covered over (*encubierto*) the Other as part of the Same, i.e. Europe" (*Invention* 12). This point accords with Adorno and Horkheimer's, above. Dussel uses two expressions, "the myth of modernity" (the pattern of thought that declares "the suffering of the conquered and colonised people [. . .] as a necessary sacrifice and the inevitable price of modernisation" [64]), and the "fallacy of development" (the idea of a route or evolution towards modernisation[5] along which the colonised

---

ty expanded to the barbarian cultures of the South undoubtedly in need of modernization" (*Invention* 10).

4 Compare also: "The experience not only of discovery, but especially of the conquest, is *essential* to the constitution of the modern ego, not only as a subjectivity, but as subjectivity that takes itself to be the center or end of history" (Dussel, *Invention* 25).

Dussel also writes the following (in an endnote): "Germán Marquinez Argote defended a thesis, the *Interpretación del 'Cogito' cartesiano como modelo de hermenéutica latinoamericana* (Bogotá: University of Saint Thomas Aquinas, 1980), in which he compares the 'I conquer' with the 'I think.' He provides cogent texts showing the awareness Descartes had that his world had actually discovered a new world" (*Invention* 148).

5 The sociologist Raymond Lee (University of Malaysia) points out some of the attendant ironies in the following two quotations:

> Thus, it is plausible to say that modernisation in the developing world, with its frenetic drive to develop and consume, cannot occur without the political manipulation of ethnic and nationalist sentiments. Different groups of people, separated by space and time but brought together by the fiat of colonialism and independence, must now forge an ideal of national community in order to catch up with the modern standards of the developed world. There is a belief that nation-building in the developing world predicated on Western notions of modern selfhood and self-determinism can result in the creation of national wholes with minimal emphasis on cultural heterogeneity and increased inte-gration of diverse population units. That this notion has universal application is [. . .] nothing but a fallacious assumption accepted by many people in the developing world. (35)

region will have to follow the colonising economy [53, 64]) in order to indicate how Europe/the West justifies and explains the brutalities of conquest to itself.

C. E. Pletch has with subtle sarcasm described the profound, resultant split into the three "worlds" of the "globalised" twentieth century:

> The third world is the world of tradition, culture, religion, irrationality, underdevelopment, overpopulation, political chaos, and so on. The second world is *modern*, technologically sophisticated, rational to a degree, but authoritarian (or totalitarian) and repressive, and ultimately inefficient and impoverished by contamination with ideological preoccupations and burdened with an ideologically motivated socialist elite. The first world is *purely modern*, a haven of science and utilitarian decision making, technological, efficient, democratic, free – in short, a natural society unfettered by religion or ideology. (574; my italics)

A central distinction necessary to this discussion ("modernity" vs "modernism") is usefully delineated in the quotation below. It helps to move the present discussion into the realm of cultural responses to the modernisation process. In a lengthy footnote from his *Modernity and Ambivalence*, Zygmunt Bauman writes:

> The definitional discord is made particularly difficult to disentangle by the fact of historical coexistence of what Matei Calinescu called "two distinct and bitterly conflicting modernities." More sharply than most other authors, Calinescu portrays the "irreversible" split between "modernity as a stage in the history of Western Civilization – a product of scientific and technological progress, of the industrial revolution, of the sweeping economic and social changes brought about by capitalism – and modernity as an aesthetic concept." The latter (better to be called *modernism* to avoid the all too frequent confusion) militated against everything the first stood for: "what defines cultural modernity is its outright rejection of bourgeois modernity, its consuming

---

> Thus, the industrial nationalism of the developing world *makes* both the authoritarian strategy by which industrialisation is introduced as a development package of modernity, and the ethnic or subethnic inequalities that ensue from the asymmetrical distribution of privilege in a socially stratified and culturally diverse system. (36)

> negative passion" (*Faces of Modernity: Avant-Garde, Decadence, Kitsch* (Bloomington: Indiana UP, 1977), pp. 4, 42); this is in blatant opposition to the previous, mostly laudatory and enthusiastic portrayal of the attitude and achievement of modernity [. . .]
>
> I call "modernity" a historical period that began in Western Europe with a series of profound social-structural and intellectual transformations of the seventeenth century and achieved its maturity: (1) as a cultural project – with the growth of Enlightenment; (2) as a socially accomplished form of life – with the growth of industrial (capitalist, and later also communist) society. Hence *modernity*, as I use the term, is in no way identical with *modernism*. The latter is an intellectual (philosophical, literary, artistic) trend that – though traceable back to many individual intellectual events of the previous era – reached its full swing by the beginning of the current century, and which in retrospect can be seen (by analogy with the Enlightenment) as a "project" of *postmodernity* or a prodromal stage of the postmodern condition. In modernism, modernity turned its gaze upon itself and attempted to attain the clear-sightedness and self-awareness which would eventually disclose its impossibility, thus paving the way to the postmodern reassessment. (3-4)

I want to look briefly now at Joseph Conrad's novella *Heart of Darkness* as an archetypal European modernist text – using it as a hinge towards a discussion of the writings of the Zimbabwean author Dambudzo Marechera. In agreement with Bauman (above), I see Conrad's European modernist novel as manifesting the beginnings of an expression of doubt concerning the adequacy or completeness of knowledge of the European expansionist undertaking, along with the dawning but insistent recognition of its doubtful legitimacy.[6] Conrad does, unmistakably, in this text expose *and* subject to a profoundly felt moral indignation both the "fallacy of development" and the "myth of modernity" that Dussel mentions (see above, and compare: "If modernity is about the production of order then ambivalence is *the waste of modernity*" [Bauman 15]). Yet Achebe's well-known critique of the Conradian text as *simultaneously* anti-imperialist and racist is hard to fault (see his essay "An Image of Africa: Racism in Conrad's

6 Lee writes that "[m]odernism in this sense suggests a type of consciousness emerging from the very process of modernization itself to react politically and culturally upon the system that promotes it" (54).

Heart of Darkness"). If one prefers to avoid the tendentious term "racist" – and there is a strong tradition of readings of the Conradian text that include the frame-narrator Marlow in its author's ironic gaze, rather than conceiving of Conrad's purpose simply as using this figure to ventriloquise authorial convictions – a central problem in accounting for the nature and effect of this text remains its depiction of the African area and its inhabitants. A description such as the following in Conrad's short novel –

> The earth seemed unearthly. We are accustomed to look upon the shackled form of the monster, but there – there you could look at a thing *monstrous* and free. It was unearthly, and the men were. No, they were *not inhuman*. Well, you know, that was *the worst* of it – this suspicion of their not being inhuman. It would come slowly to one. They howled and leaped, and spun, and made *horrid* faces [Marlow's description is presumably of an African dance, or ritual]; but what thrilled you was just the thought of their humanity – like yours – the thought of your remote kinship with this *wild* and passionate *uproar*. *Ugly*. Yes, it was *ugly* enough; but if you were man enough you would admit to yourself that there was in you just the faintest trace of a response to the *terrible* frankness of that *noise*, a dim suspicion of there being a meaning in it which you – you so remote from *the night of first ages* – could comprehend. And why not? The mind of man is capable of anything – because everything is in it, *all the past* as well as all the future. (96; my italics)

– *or* Marlow's reference to "the sunlit face of the land" as masking "the lurking death, [. . .] the hidden evil, [. . .] the profound darkness of *its* heart" (92; my italics) ascribes to both the region and its people *simultaneously* a quality of unknowability[7] to or by the European subject, *and* a conviction or certainty of its/their evil. [8]

The currently prevalent reading of *Heart of Darkness* that takes the text as a cunning expression of Conrad's insight (revealed through the figure of Kurtz) that "enlightenment is a form of barbarism, that the West's Other is the West it-

---

7 Notably, 'impenetrable' is one of Marlow's favourite adjectives.

8 The words "horrid," "ugly" and "terrible frankness" in the above quotation presumably indicate the observing Marlow's shuddering, shamefaced sense that the Africans' dance that he witnesses is an unashamed revelation of the basest instincts of humanity.

self" (During 452) is not invalid. It does, however, overlook the extent to which Conrad employs and (I would contend) endorses the ancient and persistent European stereotype of "Africa" as representing, in the present, the past of the "developed" West. The expressions "the night of [the] first ages" and "all the past" confirm this: *even as* Marlow is rebuking a European sense of ethnic difference and superiority, he is thus re-endorsing the notion of "primitive," unrestrained evil passions as an inherently African condition.

One can link this to the following questions: do the very expressions "modernity" and "modernism," as applied to "Western" conditions (whether sociopolitical and economic, or cultural and aesthetic) not claim for *a part of* the world, the command of an *entire* time-frame? Is there not in the "logic" of the very discourse of modernism, a strong trace of the "developmental fallacy" and the "myth of modernity" – to use Dussel's terminology? Are the different parts of the world at different "stages of development" – or should we simply recognise that we are trapped in a power hierarchy of monumental proportions that has (predictably) not budged an inch since the conquests of other territories by Westerners? As I read Marechera (more fully discussed further on) these challenging questions are among those to which his text implicitly subjects European ideas of modernity as well as notions of modernism.

Heart of Darkness is indeed a massively scornful critique of (particularly) the Belgian colonial enterprise, subtly yet recognisably played off by Conrad against the (implicitly validated) "superior" British "civilising mission." It is *also* a text in the tradition of the effacement of Africa (regions and peoples), of the reduction of these "dark" presences to a mere backdrop to the activities (both admirable and culpable) of Europeans (cf. my essay "Blixen, Ngugi" contrasting renditions of Kenya by Ngugi wa Thiong'o and Karen Blixen). Perhaps, despite its author's undoubted concern for the plight of colonised people, Conrad's text is thus another expression of the "mythic fear" (quoted above) to which Adorno and Horkheimer refer. The very title *Heart of Darkness*, even though most intelligent readings apply the expression to Kurtz's own "horror" (first inflicted; later felt), has remained as an expression in the "Western" vocabulary; a dismissive catchphrase[9] for referring to social collapse, power abuse and other disasters

9 Compare: "Up until the 1950s, the education of Africans was predicated on their relocation from the darkness associated with the "tribal" to the sweetness and light of colonial institutions" (Gikandi, "Chinua Achebe" 7).

In another book the same author writes: "if the ideals of modern bourgeois society were framed and justified within the theater of colonialism, colonial society was

manifested in African societies – with little or no recognition of the extent to which these failures are interlinked to continuing (neocolonial) exploitation by European and other Western power centres, both political and economic.

As a critique of modernity and the modernisation process, the modernist novel – as exemplified by *Heart of Darkness* – can thus be described as implicated in or compromised by the system which it criticises (and which produced it). In his extensive comments on Conrad's novella, Andrew Gibson refers to the "totalising discourse" employed by all its European characters, reading this tendency as indicating the "triumph of Western metaphysics as it is ensured by and properly indistinguishable from the triumph of Western power" (60). Although he reads the Marlow figure as "project[ing his] own drive to totalisation" onto Kurtz, Gibson also sees "Marlovian discourse" as "pervade[d by] [. . .] a sense of epistemological dead-end [. . .] [in] the amazed encounter with alterity – an alterity that will subsequently be brusquely subdued." This "baffl[ing]" encounter, writes Gibson, "lies at the very roots of the European experience" (of this period, presumably) (62).

The ideas in the above citations fit in with the distinction drawn by Bauman between modernism and postmodernism (and, for the purposes of this essay, between a modernist text such as Conrad's and the writing of an African (post-) modernist such as Marechera). "Pretences of knowledge," writes Bauman, can be doubted in two ways: *either* one points out that there are events for which the "available knowledge" does not have a convincing or universally accepted narrative (and this, he says, is modernism), *or* one notes that the narrative offered by this knowledge system is not the only, or the best, or the most reliable account possible (and this, according to Bauman, is postmodernism). There is not actually a chronological succession, since both kinds of doubt have manifested themselves "as long as science itself" and between them, as a "co-presence," Bauman suggests, produced "that modern culture which prodded modernity on its road to postmodernity" (238).

Now an African postmodernist[10] would of course notice the partiality (to make that term a pun) of European modernism in ways significantly different

often written as the space deprived of, or undeserving of, such values as individualism and citizenship" (*Maps* 7).

10 Buuck makes the point that "[i]n the contemporary period, Western critiques of the grand metanarratives of history have begun to take hold within the postcolonial world as well as in the metropole [. . .] [but adds that] within the realm of autobiographical fiction, only Breytenbach, Head, and Marechera have seriously focused

from the way a "Western" writer would – and would need to articulate such a "doubt" (to use Bauman's term), or recognition of irony, in a manner sensitive to the realities of power distribution ("cultural" as much as political) of his or her time. In his novel, *Saints and Scholars,* the British Marxist Terry Eagleton writes: "A colonial territory was a land where nothing happened, where you reacted to the narrative of your rulers rather than created one of your own" (104). In a recent essay Rasheed Araeen refers to "art which is produced within the historical space of modernism," making the following points:

> As this space is controlled institutionally, some works are legitimated and are placed within a historical genealogy while others are ignored or suppressed. This historicisation, however, is not based on the nature of the work but on the racial, ethnic or cultural background of the artist; which thus excludes the modernist or avantgardist work of artists from cultures other than of European origin on the basis that modernism is ontologically a European phenomenon. In other words, the eurocentricity of modernism is constructed and maintained largely on racial grounds by which the supremacy of the white subject is maintained. (77)

There is probably a broad truth in this accusation of "Western" myopia, given how ghettoised studies of African writing, even of novels in the Europhone languages, remain. In his introduction to the essay collection *Modernism/Postmodernism*, the editor Peter Brooker observes that

> [a] map which shows the South of England, the Eastern seaboard of North America, and which marks in Paris, Trieste, perhaps Berlin and Vienna but not Moscow, Petrograd or Milan is not an acceptable map of "the" world, but might be the map of a certain cultural mentality,

---

on the self and the construction of identity while also challenging conventional narrative form" (119). His list might be extended with the addition of names such as Henry Lopes, Mia Couto and Yvonne Vera (among African writers).

Klopper states that Marechera raises "the problem [. . .] whether there is a role at all for postmodernist poetry in the postcolonial state" (126). According to Chennells, Marechera was "acutely conscious of the trap within protest literature: an imperial/anti-imperialism exchange, a contestation between a metropolitan authentic and an authentic which reveals itself once imperialism is out of the way both guarantee that the debate is being conducted in the terms imperialism has laid down" (49).

> and is, as it turns out, the "map" of an Anglo-American construction of modernism. The same general point applies to postmodernism. However internally different its main versions, their common geography stretches to the American West, Canada and Australia, and until recently would show little else, even of Europe, beyond Paris and Frankfurt. (4)

A brilliant avantgardist such as Marechera, after (co-)winning the fiction prize of *The Guardian* in Britain in 1979 for his first substantial publication, was allowed subsequently more or less to disappear from public view (see Veit-Wild, *Dambudzo Marechera* 185-378). His problem was certainly in part that of the category-jumper, the "unclassifiable" writer: highly sophisticated in employing postmodernist techniques, yet writing of African experiences and settings and (*tout court*) exemplifying the supposed paradox: an African intellectual utterly proficient in the whole gamut of "Western" cultural and academic discourse.

Marechera during the ten years of his major writing was, one might say, considered both too African for Europe and too European for Africa. His own, oft-quoted comment (in this regard) remains the most eloquent expression of dilemma: "I have been an outsider in my own biography, in my country's history, in the world's terrifying possibilities. It is, therefore, quite natural for me to respond with the pleasure of familiar horror to that section of European literature which reflects this" (Marechera; qtd. in Veit-Wild, *Dambudzo Marechera* 364).

Marechera thought of identity as "an act of faith, impossible to verify" and regretted the "paradox that modernism has been from the start identified with difficulties and, on a continent still barely literate, modernism has, therefore, been condemned as being irrelevant on African soil" (qtd. in Veit-Wild, *Dambudzo Marechera* 370).

Marechera noted approvingly Achebe's use of a Yeats quotation in titling *Things Fall Apart*. In his own case, he had to deal with considerable objection from African critics for being "Euro-modernist" (see Shaw 6-9; Gagiano, *Achebe* 206, 250 n. 25). Even the influential critic Simon Gikandi who has recently stated approvingly that "Marechera's subjects [. . .] took the existence of this African literature [Achebe et al.] for granted [. . .] [as much as] the idea of [. . .] a Pan-African culture" ("Chinua Achebe" 6), had stated over two decades earlier, in his 1979 reader's report for Heinemann (Nairobi), that

> [w]here to place Marechera's novel, is the seminal question in trying to make a decision whether to publish or not [. . .] "Black Sunlight" is

> an absurdist novel – Beckettian in style and approach. It is a novel without any relatives in African creative writing. There is no plot as we know it. The story-line here reminds one of James Joyce [. . .] But this is the kind of writing that has not had any appeal in this part of the world and can easily go unnoticed. (Gikandi; qtd. in Veit-Wild, *Dambudzo Marechera* 214)

Black Sunlight, one of the Marechera texts I mainly deal with in this essay, was in fact initially banned in Zimbabwe for alleged "obscenity" as much as for its "difficulties" (to use Marechera's own term). It is a novel which could be described as using postmodernity as both a political and a philosophical critique of sham modernity[11] and the sham(e) of enforced, late modernisation – as well as being an expression of devastating mockery of, *as well as* the existential angst resulting from being black in the "white" twentieth century (*Black Insider* 73, 87, 105). One commentator has written: "If Marechera looks unAfrican at times it is because any opposition as radical as his is literally unlike anything which has preceded it in Europe or Africa" (Volk 310). The modulations of tone and theme in *Black Sunlight* are brilliantly deployed and it opens, in one of the most unforgettable comic scenes in Anglophone African writing, on a passage overtly and devastatingly parodying *Heart of Darkness* (1–13).[12] The postmodern effect is discernible in the narrator's reference to the scene as a "view" and the initial Conradian echo is clear in the description of this "view" as comprising "gigantic humid trees shutting out the sun" (*Black Sunlight* 1).[13] Equally noticeable is the author's use of *Verfremdungseffekt* in making the entire narrative one that blows in through "the open window [. . .] that fucking window of fiction" (1). In this reference he rings the changes simultaneously on Henry James's "house of fic-

---

11 Although in the essay I deploy an argument that Marechera's is a postmodernism "of a special type," Hassan's well known checklist of salient qualities of postmodernism ("versus" modernism) tallies remarkably well with the features of Marechera's writings (Hassan qtd. in Brooker 11-12). Compare also Riemenschneider (407) and Veit-Wild (*Teachers* 261) on Marecheran postmodernism.

12 For a different perspective on this scene cf. Stein 61.

13 Marechera in an interview stated unequivocally that *Black Sunlight* was set in Zimbabwe (Veit-Wild, *Dambudzo Marechera* 220), but the scenery here is evidently that of Conrad's Congo rather than of Marechera's country of origin. Gikandi writes that "the most prominent insignia of Africanness in modernism is the forest. The African forest would hence appear to negate the ideals of culture and civilization" (*Maps* 169). It is this kind of assumption that Marechera is mocking here by means of his *Heart of Darkness* parody.

tion" image and, I would suggest, on Virginia Woolf's ideal private retreat – the well-known "room of one's own" of the (privileged) female writer.

The audacity, the immensely sophisticated joking going on here also utilises the perspective on an African "chief, black as human beginnings" as he considers the mere thought of "White meat [. . .] White cunts. White arses [. . .]" – sufficient to produce a "gigantic erection" (*Black Sunlight* 1, 2), in comic contrast with (Conrad's) Marlow's fastidious withdrawal from the idea of even remote "kinship" with African frolickings (cf. the passage quoted earlier). An essay of the present length is too short to investigate all the different dimensions merely of the widely allusive, multilayered opening scene of *Black Sunlight*. Simultaneously with its outrageously hilarious effects (such as the reference to the narrator's view, once he has been strung up, head down, in the chief's chicken yard for his disrespectful remarks, of the African scene as a "mirage [. . .] becom[ing] some long ago beastiality [. . .] cleaning its jaws with toothbrushes made of hairy men" (7)[14], Marechera's Rabelaisian or sardonic humour does not sell out to or cater for "Western" racial contempt; it mocks or exposes it. Hence, the anthropologist symbolically named Blanche Goodfather, the narrator's former lover, is described as "roam[ing] the earth [. . .] ferret[ing] out the few bits and pieces of authentic people reducing them to meticulous combinations of the English alphabet" (4; cf. Stein, Chennells). This naïveand clearly reductive kind of (re)search is contrasted with the black narrator's "insecurity, in search of [his] true people"[15] but finding only "'Mere/Cari/Cat/URES'" (10). He knows he is "sometimes all the time [. . .] In the wrong skin. This black skin" (4).

In passages such as the final citation above the reader can discern that, woven into the teasing fun of the opening scene, Marechera twists some profoundly felt, melancholic and eventually tragic recognitions of the exclusionary, contemptuous, dismissive effects of "European" racism towards Africans. Like the naked Blanche Goodfather[16] (in Oxford, or in Africa), it will join in the sexual

---

14 Compare the *Heart of Darkness* echo in another passage: "I willed my heart to stop wheezing horror-horror" (*Black Sunlight* 9).

15 Note nevertheless that in closely proximate sentences, the narrator declares, first, "These are my people. I am their people too" and "Europe was in my head, crammed together with Africa, Asia and America" (*Black Sunlight* 3-4).

16 In another passage, Marechera tellingly contrasts a black and a white body – for instance, he endows his description of the chief's black body with such grotesqueries as the following: "everywhere tufts of hair sprouted out of the sweaty swamp of flesh. The fantastic physiognomy of my great chief suggested sudden and barbaric impulses, crude and insatiable appetites, dark and grim events"; whereas the

"experiments" that explore "the lurid sunken depths [. . .] in *our* bodies" (5; my italics), but it will without warning "eras[e]" the memories of a yearlong relationship, reducing the narrator to a "stain of horror [. . .] an inky blackness" and a "terrified ghostly shape, cringing into the trees" (81). Even an Oxford degree, supposed apex of "European" accomplishment (under Western eyes, no doubt), may have the effect of "making the monkey monkier" (*Black Sunlight* 77), i.e. result in the continuing denigration of the African intellectual as subhuman.

It is in the complexity – as much an emotional as an intellectual, philosophical *range* of awareness – of Marechera's considerations of the dimensions of *existenz* and experience in our time that he in my opinion outpaces what I earlier referred to as the solemnities of the major Enlightenment philosophers, or the modernist author's *angst*. Utterly unfrivolous, even his most blatantly comic writing sounds out profound existential concerns and modulates into issues of tragic import and moral questioning. In *Black Sunlight*, particularly, this author confronts (in postmodern style) the problem that "the development of social and national and international man is one long denial of" what he calls "the very life within us [. . .] The spark that sets creation on fire." And so, "the more we 'progress', the more we think as that progress demands and the less we think and feel as the life within us demands" (*Black Sunlight* 65, 66). Not only is the "spark" to which Marechera's narrator refers our "primitive" or non-modern, elemental energies and impulses, but it also contains what Marechera terms our "humane considerations" (62, 68; cf. 30, 74). His anguished, complex response to "progress" or modernity is, I suggest, the sign of his "postmodernity," read here as an advance in thought on such examples of political and philosophical "modernity" as the passages from Gellner and Conrad quoted earlier in this essay.

Which is not to suggest that Marechera had anything like a comfortable, let alone a complacent, sense of himself or his thought as "superior" – indeed, he was all too aware of many African intellectuals' probable rejection of his writing. He seems (almost uncannily) to have forestalled the banning of *Black Sun-*

---

adventurous British anthropologist (Blanche Goodfather), even though she is an isolated white woman "bathing nude," does so both elegantly and powerfully because she is (even in Africa) swimming "in the tanned and glittering glory of her European tradition" (*Black Sunlight* 6). But the parodic (Conrad-style) description of the chief's body is offset by other, respectful remarks, such as the narrator's comments that the chief "in his heyday, [was] a mighty wrestler, a casanova, a fair and just man" (6).

light itself by writing in this novel of a character very similar to the author having his poems "objected to [for] the 'vulgar words', the unintelligibility"; the African student audience he addresses asserting that "workers did not understand him and his modernistic European manner" (110). Moreover, Marechera faces and acknowledges the pertinence of the accusation of nonparticipation and elitism directed at the artist-writer (in contrast with the political activist) when he puts in the following parenthesis close to the conclusion of *Black Sunlight*: "Steve Biko died while I was blind drunk in London. Soweto burned while I was sunk in deep thought about an editor's rejection slip" (114).

To introduce the discussion of *The Black Insider* as another, though very different kind of postmodernist Marecheran text, a citation in which Marechera uses a critic's points to describe texts resembling his own is a useful one:

> The critic and lecturer Neil McEwan, in his book *Africa and the Novel*, argues that, far from imitating the practice of past generations of European writers, African novelists have extended the possibilities and uses of fiction. He notes that the Soviet critic Mikhail Bakhtin has offered a category of narrative whose unifying factor is a "carnival" attitude to the world. This category includes writers from different backgrounds. They range from Aristophanes, Lucian and Apuleius (the first African novelist, perhaps) to Dostoevsky by way of Rabelais and Dean Swift. I add John Fowles and Günter Grass, and the Nigerian, Wole Soyinka, in *The Interpreters*. *Don Quixote* is quite at home. The world of such novels, says McEwan, is complex, unstable, comic, satirical, fantastic, poetical and committed to the pursuit of truth. The hero can travel anywhere in this world and beyond. Fantasy and symbolism are combined with low-life naturalism. Odd vantage points offer changes of scale. Heaven and hell are close and may be visited. Madness, dreams and day-dreams, abnormal states of mind and all kinds of erratic inclinations are explored. Scandalous and eccentric behaviour disrupts "the seemly course of human affairs" and provides a new view of "the integrity of the world." Society is unpredictable; roles can quickly change. Current affairs are treated with a satirical, journalistic interest. Genres are mixed. Stories, speeches, dramatic sketches, poetry and parody exist side by side. This category of novel is called the menippean. It is no longer necessary to speak of the African novel or the European novel: there is only the menippean novel.
> (qtd. in Veit-Wild, *Dambudzo Marechera* 363-364)

To which Marechera added: "I do not like this century, past or future. I do not like to live under the backside of a medieval god or a nuclear bomb, which amounts to the same thing. I am no mystic, yet no materialist either. I believe in nature but refuse to live with it in the same room" (qtd. in Veit-Wild, *Dambudzo Marechera* 364).

In *The Black Insider* Marechera debates, essentially, issues of African post-modernist identity. The discussions that make up the substance of the novel's "events" are simultaneously philosophical (sometimes to the point of absurdity or pedantry), and of agonising intensity. The setting of the conversations and long monologues being armageddon-like (since both the plague, a bomb, and hordes of warmongers conspire to wipe out all the participants at the end of the text, and these forms of destruction are imminent throughout), this creates the sense of the mocking irrelevance as well as the extreme urgency of the questions that are discussed throughout. Early in the text the narrator refers to his own position: "Cool eyes seethe with reading and gaze out of the window on to a war-paralysed city where multitudes each day succumb to the despair of hunger, disease and homelessness" (*Black Insider* 32).

This is both phantasmagorical and a merely realistic description of conditions in many African countries such as Zimbabwe. In the eyes of the narrator, even the "ability to read and write" allows "endoparasites" such as "culture, tradition, history or civilisation" (33) into our minds. Considering the spread of the "Indo-European group of languages" and their role in "colonisation, trade, conquest," Marechera's narrator laments the global brainwashing process (to extend his image likening language to water) which causes "your thoughts [to] think of themselves in the words you have been taught to read and write" (37).

This text, too, is laced with (albeit corrosive) humour, such as the narrator's remark that he "fear[s] death by drowning in one of T. S. Eliot's poems" (47), cleverly maintaining his central image of flooding to represent mental and cultural colonisation. It is in *The Black Insider* that Marechera deploys the following (now fairly well-known) mocking catalogue of types of African writers, which of course exposes the "Western" classificatory, "anthropologising" and finally reductive approach to the products of this continent:

> "I've never met any black writers. Are you angry and polemic or are you grim and nocturnal or are you realistic and quavering or are you indifferent and European? Those are the categories, I think," she said and neat creases delicately bracketed her wide mouth.
>
> "I write as best I can," I replied, at a loss for words. (49)

One of the small cast of characters (or discussants) in this novel is named Otolith, referred to as a "black Hamlet," who in his "Elizabethan costume [. . .] could fancifully have been the horror which Kurtz saw at the *Heart of Darkness* Brussels suburbia [. . .] the real noble savage" and "a burnt-out case clutching Africanity in one hand and a bottle of whisky in the other" (56). For all its absurdist weirdness, this description is noticeably full of scathing digs indicating how modernisation has harmed gifted Africans (like Marechera) with its false promises of acceptance. Over and over again Marechera returns to the point of the inappropriateness of "development" that is "applied" from outside, to others' benefit, rather than a growth from within. One example is his narrator's reference to "subjects and jobs [. . .] steeped with Graeco-Roman thinking which ha[s] nothing to do with the dusty townships we had come from" (63). To live in the twentieth century, Otolith asserts, is to be "born black in a white environment" (87).

Despite the accusations and lamentations subtly interwoven into this sophisticated text, Marechera here, too, maintains the type of cool "distance" that escapes all three of the limiting categories to which white academics such as Liz (in the passage from p. 49, quoted above) would relegate African writing. And in its evident confidence, sophistication, robustness and wry humour, we see Marechera the consummate postmodernist quietly exposing the inappropriateness of the diagnoses of certain commentators (the voice being that of the character Marechera names, in another clever intertextual reference, the African Schweik):

> Some psychiatrists today diagnose disenchantment with social structures as a disease and proceed to inflict a cure on the patient. Some of our greatest writing [he then adds in the next breath, without pointing the irony by means of a 'yet' or a 'but'] comes from writers in a state of mind of disillusion, disenchantment and dismay. (94)

Even though the alliteration in the last three nouns, above, adds a further self-teasing effect, this text, too, is not finally, primarily comic in its *effect*, although it makes use of that mode. For the narrator, who uses the simple, patriotic expression "my country," reflects also how others, "brilliant students" (like the author himself, a pointed allusion) feel as if "[their] country nourishes [them] solely in order to break their spirit on the anvil of crude racial antagonism," their only other option being "the bitter and inconsolable experience of losing [their] nation" (104). For here Marechera scathingly rejects what "the machine of the nation-state gave the citizen[:] a prefabricated identity and consciousness made up of the rouge and lipstick of the struggle and the revolution" (105). What is conveyed by these seemingly insouciant statements is that African modernity enforces a bitter choice between a crude, fervently nationalistic posturing, or rejection and alienation from one's people – "the sense of having lost our nation was indivisible from the feeling of the nation having lost us" (105).

It is interesting that a writer with such a strong reputation for avantgardism and intertextuality nevertheless insists that, more than by any other author, he was "influenced to a point of desperation by the dogged though brutalised humanity of those among whom [he] grew up" in Vengere township (Marechera qtd. in Veit-Wild, *Dambudzo Marechera* 1). This point should be borne in mind when such a spectacularly postmodern text[17] as Marechera's earliest publication, *The House of Hunger*, is examined. Marechera puts modernist perspectives to local, political use, likening the exclusionary effects of racist colonial social structures to Franz Kafka's *The Castle* (Veit-Wild, *Dambudzo Marechera* 10). In an important interview he said that he had taken the form of this novella from reading the German nineteenth-century novella, especially from Kleist (Veit-Wild, *Dambudzo Marechera* 26). Referring to the text he produced after his own return (from Britain) to what had become Zimbabwe, he found that what he considered his task here, to "write like Franz Kafka or James Joyce or explore the subconscious of our new society" (Marechera qtd. in Veit-Wild, *Dambudzo Marechera* 39) was frowned upon by the new powers-that-be.

Yet he persisted. In *Mindblast*, perhaps his most popular text in Zimbabwe, Marechera paradoxically wanted both to help heal the "fragment[ation]" of Zimbabwean society because of its colonial/racist past and to give expression to the "many voices," even "contradictory" ones, that he heard around him (Veit-Wild, *Dambudzo Marechera* 311). Toni Morrison has written that African-American women "had to deal with 'postmodern' problems in the nineteenth century and earlier [because of] [. . .] certain kinds of dissolution, the loss and the need to reconstruct certain kinds of stability" (qtd. in Brooker 213). Marechera in 1986 said in a public address that his "task as a writer was to take the

[17] Isabel Hofmeyr has said of the "folktale" passage in *The House of Hunger* (79-80) that although "oral narrative [is] a form often assumed to be traditional in theme, *premodern* in literary style, and order-affirming in its ethical orientation[,] the type of narrative we see here is in fact *postmodern*, grotesque, and subversive" (Hofmeyr 88; my italics).

veins of modernism, symbolism, futurism that had developed in poetry and transfer them to the language of prose" (qtd. in Veit-Wild, *Dambudzo Marechera* 367). This was a belief he held, and expressed, with intense passion and a political as much as an aesthetic commitment.

> Write the poem, the song, the anthem, from what within you
> Fused goals with guns and created citizens instead of slaves.
>
> Do not scream quietly

read three memorable lines from one of his poems (*Cemetery* 195). The unique achievements of this author, and the way his large range of writings develops our notions of postmodernism and our understanding of the ironies of African modernity, need far greater recognition than they have so far been accorded. African scholars need to work hard to focus more attention on the intellectual productivity of this continent, whereas many Western scholars need to make more effort not only to make the acquaintance, but to pay sufficient attention to African authors in order to respect and understand their insights and their art. The alternative, Eurocentric, closed circle was succinctly described by Gertrude Stein in a lecture (scathingly?) titled "What Is English Literature":

> If you live a daily life and it is all yours, and you come to own everything outside your daily life besides and it is all yours, you naturally begin to explain. You naturally continue describing your daily life which is all yours, and you naturally begin to explain how you own everything besides. You naturally begin to explain that to yourself and you naturally begin to explain it to those living your daily life who own it with you, everything outside, and you naturally explain in a kind of way to some of those whom you own. (41)

Works Cited

Achebe, Chinua. *Things Fall Apart*. Oxford: Heinemann, 1958.

___. "An Image of Africa: Racism in Conrad's *Heart of Darkness*." *Hopes and Impediments: Selected Essays*. By Achebe. New York: Doubleday, 1988. 1-20.

Adorno, Theodor and Max Horkheimer. *Dialectic of Enlightenment*. London: Verso, 1979.

Araeen, Rasheed. "Sleeping with the Enemy and Re-visiting Postcolonial Theory." *Third Text: Critical Perspectives on Contemporary Art and Culture* 56 (2001): 75-78.

Bauman, Zygmunt. *Modernity and Ambivalence*. Cambridge: Polity, 1991.

Brooker, Peter. "Reconstruction." Introduction. *Modernism/Post-modernism*. Ed. Peter Brooker. London & New York: Longman, 1992.

Buuck, David. "African Doppelgänger: Hybridity and Identity in the Work of Dambudzo Marechera." *Research in African Literatures* 28.2 (1997): 118-131.

Chennells, Anthony, and Flora Veit-Wild. "Unstable Identities, Unstable Narratives in *Black Sunlight*." Chennells and Veit-Wild, *Emerging Perspectives* 43-55.

___, eds. *Emerging Perspectives on Dambudzo Marechera*. Trenton, N.J. & Asmara, Eritrea: Africa World Press, 1999.

Conrad, Joseph. *Youth, Heart of Darkness, The End of the Tether*. London: Dent, 1946.

During, Simon. "Postmodernism or Post-Colonialism Today." *Post-modernism: A Reader*. Ed. T. Docherty. London: Harvester Wheatsheaf, 1993.

Dussel, Enrique. *The Invention of the Americas: Eclipse of "the Other" and the Myth of Liberation*. Trans. Michael D. Barber. New York: Continuum, 1995.

___. *The Underside of Modernity: Apel, Ricoeur, Taylor, and the Philosophy of Liberation*. Trans. and ed. Eduardo Mendieta. New Jersey: Humanities Press International, 1996.

Eagleton, Terry. *Saints and Scholars*. London & New York: Verso, 1987.

Gagiano, Annie. *Achebe, Head, Marechera: On Power and Change in Africa*. Boulder, Co and London: Lynne Rienner, 2000.

___. "Blixen, Ngugi: Recounting Kenya." *Ngugi wa Thiong'o: Texts and Contexts*. Ed. Charles Cantalupo. Trenton, N.J.: Africa World Press, 1995.

Gellner, Ernest. "The New Idealism." *Problems in the Philosophy of Science*. Ed. I. Lakatos and A. Musgrave. Amsterdam: Van Nostrand, 1968.

___. "The Tough and the Tender." *Voices: Modernity and its Discontents*. Ed. Bill Bourne, Udi Eichler and David Herman. Nottingham: Spokesman (in association with Hobo Press), 1987.

Gibson, Andrew. *Postmodernity, Ethics and the Novel: From Leavis to Levinas*. London and New York: Routledge, 1999.

Gikandi, Simon. "Chinua Achebe and the Invention of African Culture." *Research in African Literatures* 32.3 (2001): 3-8.

___. *Maps of Englishness: Writing Identity in the Culture of Colonialism*. New York: Columbia, 1996.

___. "Reader's Report on 'Black Sunlight for Heinemann,' Nairobi." *Ambudzo Marechera: A Source Book on his Life and Work*. Ed. Flora Veit-Wild. London & Munich et al.: Hanz Zell Publishers, 1979.

Hegel, Georg Friedrich Wilhelm. *Enzyklopädie*. Stuttgart: Frommann-Holzboog, 1969.

___. *Lectures on the Philosophy of World History*. Trans. H. B. Nisbet. Cambridge: Cambridge UP, 1975.

Hofmeyr, Isabel. "Not the Magic Talisman: Rethinking Oral Literature in South Africa." *World Literature Today* 70.1 (1996): 88-92.

Hume, David. "Of National Characters." *Essays Moral, Political and Literary*. Ed. T. H. Green and T. H. Grose. Vol. 1. London: Longman, 1979.

Jameson, Fredric. "Modernism and Imperialism." *Nationalism, Colonialism, and Literature*. By Terry Eagleton, Fredric Jameson, and Edward W. Said. Introd. Seamus Deane. Minneapolis: University of Minnesota Press, 1990.

___. *The Political Unconsciousness: Narrative as a Socially Symbolic Act*. London: Methuen, 1981.

Kant, Immanuel. "On the Different Races of Man." 1775. *This Is Race: An Anthology Selected from the International Literature on the Race of Man*. Ed. Earl Count. New York: Henry Schuman, 1975.

Klopper, Dirk. "The Outsider Within: Marginality as Symptom in Marechera's 'Throne of Bayonets.'" Chennells and Veit-Wild, *Emerging Perspectives* 121-135.

Lee, Raymond M. "Modernization, Postmodernism and the Third World." *Current Sociology* 42.2 (1994):1-64.

Marechera, Dambudzo. *The Black Insider*. Comp. and ed. Flora Veit-Wild. Harare: Baobab, 1990.

___. *Black Sunlight*. London: Heinemann, 1980.

___. *Cemetery of Mind: Collected Poetry*. Comp. Veit-Wild, Flora. Harare: Baobab, 1992.

___. *The House of Hunger*. London: Heinemann, 1978.

___. *Mindblast or the Definitive Buddy*. Harare: The College, 1984.

Pletch, C. E. "The Three Worlds, or the Division of Social Scientific Labor, circa 1950-1975." *Comparative Studies in Society and History* 23.4 (1981): 565-590.

Riemenscheider, Dieter. "Short Fiction from Zimbabwe." *Research in African Literatures* 20.3 (1989): 401-411.

Said, Edward. *Culture and Imperialism*. London: Vintage, 1994.

Shaw, Drew. "Transgressing Traditional Narrative Form." Chennells and Veit-Wild, *Emerging Perspectives* 3-21.

Stein, Gertrude. "What Is English Literature?" *Lectures in America*. Boston: Beacon, 1985.

Stein, Mark. "*Black Sunlight*: Exploding Dichotomies: A Language Terrorist At Work." Chennells and Veit-Wild, *Emerging Perspectives* 57-72.

Veit-Wild, Flora. *Dambudzo Marechera: A Source Book on his Life and Work*. London: Hanz Zell, 1992.

___. *Teachers, Preachers, Non-Believers: A Social History of Zimbabwean Literature*. London: Hans Zell & Harare: Baobab Books, 1992.

Volk, Daniela. "In Search of My True People: Universal Humanism in Marechera's Writing." Chennells and Veit-Wild, *Emerging Perspectives* 292-312.

Anomy and Agony in a Nation in Crisis: Soyinka's *Season of Anomy*

Soyinka's many plays, his autobiographies, essays, direct political statements and his first novel, *The Interpreters*, are probably all better known than and, if relative obscurity is an index of absence of admiration, more highly rated than his second novel, *Season of Anomy.*[1] The richness of this 1973 text is nevertheless in one way measurable by the fact that it is one of the few African anglophone novels brought irresistibly to mind when so disparate and wide-ranging a list of topics as bodies, identities, subcultures and repression is mentioned. It is a sustained, complex and intensely dramatic evocation of the ancient and urgent question of how violent political and social repression is to be opposed. Its crowded canvas is crammed with the presence of bodies – whether vulnerably alive or in heaps as corpses – with a range of disparate social and political identities, the presentation of one main subculture (Ayiéró) and the overwhelmingly insistent power of ruthless repression.

A common criticism of Soyinka's work (apart from irritation with his flamboyantly erudite and complex English[2]) castigates what is seen as his "substitution" of "myth" for "historical consciousness."[3] So, for example, Geoffrey Hunt writes:

> In our view the work of Wole Soyinka is one of the highest cultural expressions of this neo-colonial class-ambivalence. It is a modern variant of romanticism. [. . .] for he is undoubtedly a romanticist and in fact displays [. . .] all the general features of the European romanticists [. . . such as] mystical holism [. . . and an] emphasis on imagination and emotion tending to irrationalism. This mystical unity is evoked by means of word-painting. [The work displays . . .] an unlocated dissatisfaction with the present [. . . a] sceptical assessment of science and technology [and . . . e]xtreme individualism [. . .]. (67-68)

---

1 The novel was first published by Rex Collings (London) in 1973. The Nelson paperback edition appeared in 1980 and the Arena edition (to which page references in this paper apply) in 1988.

2 Geoffrey Hunt provides a quotation: "Meanwhile, the masses of working people in Nigeria go on as before, unable even to read the books which Soyinka writes in florid English" (89).

3 With these criticisms may be contrasted the generous praise of Soyinka's work by such writers as Isidore Okpewho and Abiola Irele (Gibbs and Lindfors, 348-350).

Hunt also refers to "[t]his romantic and mystical presentation of the past" in Soyinka's writing, calling the author "a neoromanticist" (83-84). He describes what he calls "[t]he 'return to the source' in Soyinka's universe [as] an escapist response, an attempt to recapture tradition which can only take place in the realm of pure consciousness" (89).

Another critic, George Moore, after quoting Biodun Jeyifo's strictures against "the entirely unrelieved idealist foundation and direction of his arguments" in Soyinka's *Myth, Literature and the African World*, goes on to say: "The same substitution of mythic for historical consciousness has been deplored by other Nigerian radical writers like Femi Osofisan and Kole Omotoso, though all acknowledge Soyinka's talent" (217-218).

In a more recent essay, Brenda Cooper offers similar criticism: "His lifework has been to fashion and re-fashion the myth. [. . .] if not ultimately to succeed in forging social harmony, then at least to offer the hope of individual regeneration through the enactment of ancient ritual. (This is particularly the case in his second novel, *Season of Anomy*, published in 1973.)" (57).

Abdulrazak Gurnah's comments on *Season of Anomy* are comparable to Cooper's (above). Gurnah writes that

> *Season of Anomy* valorises myth over the demands of language and voice. Political dispositions are presented without irony and are often overtaken by a tough-talking 'radical' voice, and the fiction of competing languages and metaphors in which *The Interpreters* [Soyinka's earlier and only other novel] is written deteriorates, at worst, to the cartoon language of student politics. Despite the great power of the set-piece scenes of the killings, *Season of Anomy* is undercut by the very passion which is at the heart of its argument. (79)

These are serious criticisms which could be described as dismissive. Soyinka's own words from an interview given two years after the publication of *Season of Anomy* make clear that, in its author's eyes at least, his is the very opposite both of the glibly immature "radical[ism]" of which Gurnah accuses him and of the myth-preoccupied romanticism mentioned by other critics:

> The realism which pervades some of my work and which has been branded pessimistic is nothing but a very square, sharp look. I have depicted scenes of devastation, I have depicted the depression in the minds even of those who are committed to these [i.e. to "revolution-

> ary"] changes and who are actively engaged in these changes simply because it would be starry-eyed to do otherwise. (Qtd. in Agetua 39)

In the opinion of this essay writer Gurnah's and the other critics' harshness is surprisingly unjust or ill-considered. Their comments seem, moreover, to reiterate what might be referred to as a myth *about* Soyinka's writing which cries out for refutation. *Season of Anomy* (this essay will argue) is not a work in which any mythical consciousness (either the author's or any of the chief protagonists') plays a dominant role. The so frequently noted point that both the names of the central couple – Ofeyi and Iriyise – and the quest of the principal male figure to rescue and retrieve his beloved call the Ancient Greek myth of Orpheus and Eurydice to mind should not lead one to overlook the fact that the novel does not rely on that faint allusion being recognised by the reader. In any case, because there is a vague chance that Iriyise may revive, the thrust of the myth has been altered and adapted.

In view of the novelist D. H. Lawrence's sensible warning, "Never trust the artist. Trust the tale" (Lawrence 297), the defence (or perhaps the introduction) of *Season of Anomy* here will draw on the work itself. It is my purpose to refute the prevalent suggestions that Soyinka in this novel uses myth (even to the relatively minor extent that he does make various mythical allusions) in an escapist or "romantic" fashion to suggest any facile "solution" to social disaster. In fact (my two main points are:) the disaster of horrendous proportions that follows on Ofeyi's plan to instil Ayiéró's communal lifestyle and values throughout the country shows the *anti*-romantic trend of the writing, and (secondly) the novel gives no central role to myth, either African or European in origin. Ayiéró itself was founded when the first members of this community "broke away from [. . .] the earliest working theocracy on the coast" (9), while the ethos they practise is referred to as "a way of life" or "a philosophy" rather than "a religion" (10-11). Of *Season of Anomy* it might, indeed, be said that the novel takes on the most cherished of the myths of political radicalism: (a) that opposition to repression, if principled and sustained, will eventually succeed; (b) that heroic individuals[4]

[4] Is it possible that the "unsympathetic" critics (of *Season of Anomy* and of Soyinka) from whose writings I quote in the essay tend to overlook the ironic distance between the author and the chief protagonist (despite the incidental similarities – such as a tendency towards flamboyant defiance and mockery – in the attitudes of both Ofeyi and Soyinka towards tyrannical authority), perhaps reading the depiction of Ofeyi as a romanticised, self-congratulatory self-portrait by Soyinka? If so,

(say, in the Ché Guevara mould) can make a significant difference on the political scene – refuting both, though with a profound, even tragic awareness of the sadness of this recognition.

The principal subculture featured in this novel is the isolated, neo-pristine rural community of Ayiéró by which Ofeyi, the chief protagonist, is inspired to attempt his scheme of political liberation of his oppressed country. In the words of Pa Ahime of Ayiéró about the Ayiéró "farming and fishing community" (11): "[i]t works, it is upright and balanced because we have made it so" (8). But to Ofeyi, this "pocket Utopia"(26), this "tiny pond" (6) ignores "the hideous hunger of the living world" (25). Despite Pa Ahime's warning to him that "sowing the wind" may mean "reaping the whirlwind" (24), Ofeyi is convinced that "[t]he waters of Ayiéró need to burst their banks" (6). His grand political plan is to use Ayiéró's wholesome identity to inoculate the "old stock" of the decadent and exploitative society – the country at large. The plan is vague but simple: to forge solidarities across ethnic and provincial boundaries in the workplaces across the country where the men of Ayiéró have employment, to re-inspire the demoralised society on whom the power-mongers have a stranglehold of domination and to charge the people's consequent despair with a new hope. An equally simple brutality on the part of the oppressors is more than a match for Ofeyi's idealism, however, as the teaching of one of the four grotesque rulers (at a "champagne dinner" for his three cohorts) makes clear. He (Batoki) is the most brutally direct of the four rulers and it is said of him that "the genius of their language was Batoki himself" (139). These are his words: "'I know my people – they are cowards! [. . .] When you have killed a couple of them and put away some tens behind bars, the rest will [. . .] toe the line. If they don't, add a zero to the numbers. [. . .] If that doesn't break them kill a few thousands and take no more prisoners. [. . .] If that fails I give you permission to call me a bastard.'" (137)

There is nothing akin to student politics nor anything cartoon-like (to use Gurnah's terminology) about the above evocation of brutality to anyone considering Nigeria's recent history (or, say, Rwanda, or Kosovo, or Algeria). Massacre of a local population instigated by and serving the ends of those in political power may be a technique favoured by human grotesques, but to label Soyinka's depiction of such rulers "cartoon-like" is to miss the serious, carefully constructed and warning analysis in his writing, derived from political experience. His

---

they overlook the central fact that Ofeyi's whole scheme is in fact shown to cause much greater disaster to the country than it sets out to alleviate.

prescience as a commentator is shown in the way the following passage from *Season of Anomy* "predicts" the Ogoniland disaster of later years:

> [N]o stream remained unpolluted, no pool existed in which a man could throw a stone without bursting a bloated skin of decay. Not even the wells, for in their mindlessness the hordes of the Cartel [the commercial arm of the military-political association whose members are the four main political goons] had not refrained from soiling the needs of the living for pure sources [. . . In the novel, the corpses of the victims become] the gruesome debris [which is . . .] tipped in reservoirs. (193)

Indeed the passage has the ambience of myth or parable, but Soyinka's writing has the kind of mythical dimension which probes and exposes and is a careful instrument of assessment – it is not a blurring (either a romanticising or a sensationalising) myth which is created here. Soyinka *shows* us here (to use words spoken elsewhere, later) that "tyranny negates the nation" ("BBC interview" qtd. in Quayson 30). Moreover the finely crafted writing in this novel uses the images of sources and of pollution with intelligent care, linking and *placing* them in aid of an unromantic understanding of the fearsomeness of unchecked power.

Filmed or televised images of genocide tend to bypass the sated conscience of a sensation-weary world. Because Soyinka takes such care to give us, in *Season of Anomy*, not just reels of footage of carnage but the caring, hurting, thinking observations of Ofeyi, the man who is partly responsible for much of the bloodshed – since it was his plan which released the terrible vengeance and brutal self-defence of the four tyrants – we are prevented from detaching "the visuals" from the feeling imagination. Hence the generalisation about polluted reservoirs (in the passage quoted above) irresistibly recalls to the reader Ofeyi's terrible discovery, when he goes on a sort of pilgrimage to the dam construction at Shage, that the miasma covering the water surface emanates from hundreds of corpses of slaughtered workers (169-175). In this place a real solidarity had developed between the Ayiéró men and the local co-workers, but not even they could be saved in time. This is because another brutally astute ruler – Zaki Amuri – has turned repression of all citizens into a scapegoating of the more prosperous and the ethnically and religiously distinct citizens – those originally from the Ayiéró region. So the "expatriate" Ayiéró workers are systematically "ethnically cleansed" by the Cross-River Muslim people (their religious affiliation being lightly indicated).[5]

The notion of "anomy" has many dimensions in this novel. It is pinpointed by Ofeyi as the condition of a population blackmailed and seduced by power to serve its ends – though it horrifies him, he understands its irresistible nature. He refers to it as "the insidious process of mass infection" affecting those "exposed daily by proximity, hunger and need, human weakness and deprivation" (92). Anomy is also recognisable in the despair, guilt and horror that threaten to overwhelm Ofeyi when he gets the news of the systematic extermination of the Ayiéró men whom he had enlisted as political activists (90-91; 105). Anomy can also be detected in the *counter*-brutalities of the brutally repressed population against the Cartel's cohorts and servants (reminiscent of South African "necklace" killings), events independent of Ofeyi's idealistic scheme (107-110). The eventually cowed fear and surrender of invaded, militarily controlled cities and regions (129; 133) is another manifestation of the condition of anomy. It is referred to as "the grim temptation [. . .] to succumb to the peace of amnesia" (136), "a dead [. . .] serenity" (133). Even "grief" can become a "cocoon" (310).

Myth is an instrument of interrogation in this novel – not a mindless apolitical escapism. References to genocidal bloodthirstiness as a "plague" or "epidemic" (309), or as "the infection of violence" (303) are not a dismissal of the process as inexplicable, but express the urgent understanding that a healing must be achieved from so vicious, terrifying and *infectious* a condition: "For this was not a mere question of slaughter. A relish had coloured their actions, a deep hunger of perversion both in inventiveness and magnitude, [. . .] a vengeful outrage on the face of humanity" (276) .

Ofeyi *is* shown momentarily but convincingly entertaining the idea that the genocidal impulse is a "metaphysic[al] condition called evil" (276) which may be ethnically and even climactically locatable (276), but these futile wonderings measure the desperation of the need to find "a cause beyond mere differences in culture, beyond material envy" for a fierceness so ghastly that men can slice off the womb of a frail woman in advanced pregnancy – another slash at a "source" (201).

---

5 By the fact that their attacks are on Christian congregations and in the detail of their "white robes." The period preceding and during the Biafran War in Nigeria did have this dimension of a religious war of the "Muslim North" against the (mainly) "Christian East"of Nigeria, the latter area containing Igboland.

The question "How to cope?" (or, better formulated in Ofeyi's words: "how to answer what is happening here" [233]) is also addressed in source imagery. There is Ofeyi's dream of jackal-faced hordes ("the dreams of Anubis, the jackal-headed one" [159]) in which he begins to understand how he, too, might become a "[s]lavering" (176) destroyer if he took on the human packs on their own terms. Besides warning him of the contamination of engaging with evil ("the mob infection" [160]), this is naturally also a subconscious acknowledgement of human kinship – *in inhumanity*, in bestiality – with those whom he usually tends to think of as incomprehensibly vicious.

When the memory of his nightmare vision recurs, his thoughts veer from imagining the killing hordes to envisioning his own possible response to them:

> [. . .] they rushed dragging their young brood with impatience, abandoning them in headlong plunge towards the scent of an inhuman banquet. [. . .] a sensation close to what he had experienced in Iriyise's room came over him, that of being alone in the world. Only this time, he saw where the rest of mankind had rushed, and now his was the only consciousness observing the dark pulsating chasms of tearing, grasping, clawing, gorging humanity. He stood on the humped ridges, the proud-horned bearers of the healing elixir whose bronzed torsos reclined above the laden troughs. And there in his hand, Ahime's scalpel of light. The bulls did not await his command, his barely breathed, 'Plant the horns'. They turned their throats to the sunset and awaited the moment of sympathetic bleeding. With barely a gesture he moved from bull to bull, the fountains leapt up and rushed down the chasms of unbeing, rushed towards the banqueting ravines and inundated them from end to end.
>
> He looked upwards at the shifting cloud-humps in the sky as yet undarkened by a hint of rain and muttered – When again? (176)

Ofeyi is both comparing and contrasting this wish-fulfilment vision with the scene near the opening of the novel which Soyinka describes in loving detail to indicate Ofeyi's reverent response to the dignity, wholesomeness and beauty of the humane, earth-bound Ayiéró lifestyle. It is the ritual funeral feast of the former Ayiéró ruler, during which Pa Ahime presides at the sacrifice of the beasts whose meat will feed the multitudes attending the obsequies. In the passage quoted above, Ofeyi fantasizes about another sacrifice, this time of the killing mobs themselves, as the "final solution" and he places himself (in imagination) above and *outside* "where the rest of humanity had rushed," "clawing" and cannibalistically "gorging" (176). He imagines having the power to "command" (176) floods of sacrificial blood from the very hills in order to drown the killing hordes – like the "healing elixir" the Ayiéró leader had released from fourteen snow-white bulls (14-17); described *there* as the "opening" of "red sluices for the land's replenishment" (17). But in Ayiéró, the ritual shedding of blood was from beasts, to produce sacred food, so Ofeyi's parallel is shown to be questionable, in fact, a distortion. Despite Gurnah's accusation of adolescent escapism *in the writer*, one can see in the later passage (176) that Soyinka is exhibiting a foolish but poignant yearning in Ofeyi for a *deus ex machina* solution to the unbearable. Soyinka shows Ofeyi to be (here and throughout the novel) a fine and sensitive witness, however, his thinking at this point is unmistakably though not unsympathetically ironised *by the writer*. At the end of the passage Ofeyi "look[s] upwards at the shifting cloud-humps [. . .] as yet undarkened by a hint of rain," "mutter[ing] – When again?" (176). These shifting clouds are *not* the solid flanks of cattle, however, and the fact that rain will *not* come from them confirms that "the land's replenishment" (17) is a far-off dream, however poignant the yearning it expresses.

The bleakness of Soyinka's vision of this blood-polluted nation raises an issue which is vividly present throughout this novel: the feasibility, even the *possibility* of resistance within a context of genocidal violence. Besides the (greater) political scheme of opposition to tyranny heretofore discussed, other forms of resistance occur in a range of manifestations which on the one hand underlines the inadequacy of forms of attempted resistance to entrenched and ruthless power, while on the other hand showing that anomy has not yet numbed all sectors of the people. Such resistance includes the curses and prayers *against* the power Cartel and its servants by victims and victim communities (130-133) and is shown in the sly verbal campaigning of Ofeyi's popular songs and slogans – "Root out the climbers and rotten creepers / They don't-sow-nothing but ardent reapers" (60).

We see it also in Iriyise's kicking and screaming as she is kidnapped (153) and in the astonishing, protective courage of the deformed Cross-river man dubbed the "Lion of the Tabernacle" for his role in saving an Ayiéró congregation from slaughter (276-277), as well as in the resolute stand for the necessity of political assassination by the character nicknamed "The Dentist" (Ofeyi's ally and critic). If it comes to a body count or a measure of the relative political strength of the two "sides," however, this is absolutely no contest. The devastation is dire. Power, corruption and savagery are utterly victorious. Soyinka produces no working political solution or plan to save the situation. In fact, resistance has worsened the situation of the victims to formerly unimaginable dimensions. The question to settle, I believe, is whether this is political evasiveness or dishonesty on the writer's part. It is my impression that Soyinka is suggesting that there are – in Africa as elsewhere – humanly engineered patterns of behaviour that cause destruction and dehumanisation on a scope beyond the reach of political explanation or rectification.

To suggest this is not an evasion, political immaturity or moral incapacity. It is a retreat (like the withdrawal to Ayiéró on which the novel concludes) or a withdrawal (to reinvoke Soyinka's important metaphor around which I have organised this essay) to a source. This notion is no mere mystification and has a political dimension, though it is primarily what one might call a "spiritual" or even (in the widest sense of the term) a religious idea. It is the notion found in many myths and probably itself the source of much human mythmaking, storytelling, art and religion. It is the idea that "where there is no vision, the people perish" (Achebe, "Mapping" 25). Our chief illustration of it in the novel is Ofeyi's unblinking but unremittingly compassionate gaze and his refusal to give up the attempt to recover the woman he loves from the clutches of the tyranny. It is that gaze that makes the almost unending sequence of slaughter (shown in the novel) continue to *matter*. It is also found in the expression of Ofeyi's friend Taiila's eyes, the "oceans of sadness" (271) of her pity (despite her youth and her isolating privilege and inexperience), as it is in the still, comatose form of the probably dying and desperately ill Iriyise – Ofeyi's rainbow woman who at the end of the novel releases the hulking prison guard Suberu[6] to a new loyalty. The symbolic force of Iriyise's presence is recognised even by the hard-bitten Dentist as an inspiration and a rallying point for the Ayiéró people and those who are their allies against tyranny. She is the human embodiment of hope against odds, despite defeat, because the apparent futility of rescuing a comatose person nevertheless revives the determination to continue opposing the oppressors, biding the time.

---

6 Suberu's role as prison guard and his name supposedly recall Cerberos, the many-headed dog who guards the entrance to Hades in Ancient Greek mythology. But Suberu is a man, albeit one whose humanity has been all but erased – and we are shown that under Ofeyi's appeals and exhortations this "hidden" humanity begins to recover.

Soyinka's has been one of the early voices castigating the Western and African world's hypocritical, twisted racism in initially failing to acknowledge the awfulness of African incarnations of dictatorship such as Idi Amin's. He has said that "human beings [tend to be] cannibals all over the world" (Duerden 173) and has denounced "the complicity of leaders [referred to as "fellows" of bloodthirsty tyrants like Amin and Bokassa] who turned a blind eye to the inhuman conduct of these despots" ("Twice Bitten" 117). Most recently he has written sarcastically how foolishly the Nigerian political situation (during Abacha's reign) was misrepresented to readers "bemused [. . .] by plaudits for something variously titled 'the democratic process', 'elections', 'a transition programme'. It is not merely the media, but governments and their policy advisers that delude themselves and their constituencies with references to these non-events in accents of solemnity," Soyinka wrote, himself criticising politically "romantic" falsification as pernicious ("Nigeria" 19).

Cancers in bodies (*Anomy* 226) and social plagues can be noted for the damage they wreak. No cure seems near. In showing this, Soyinka is not glib. I see glibness rather in Gurnah's own "tough-talking 'radical' voice," to turn his confidently dismissive comments on *Season of Anomy* (79) against himself. Indeed, it is the purpose of this essay to question the validity of what might be termed Gurnah's (and others') *delegitimisation* of conceptualisations of super-violence[7] such as Soyinka's by terming it 'mythical.'

Against Gurnah's contention that the situations and discussions (what he terms the "[p]olitical disposition") depicted in the novel are "presented without irony" (Gurnah 79), I would suggest that they are (on the contrary) permeated with a deeply ironic consciousness. The novel illustrates that a political vision may take on some mythical dimensions as a way of recognising the existential irony of situations in which human beings are faced with the ungraspably awful and with their own ignorance and helplessness in the face of it.

Soyinka in this novel exhibits a range of responses to and a series of attempts to oppose triumphant brutality, all of which are shown to fail. None of these attempts can succeed in a society where the springs of hope have themselves been poisoned by a kind of "total" violation of humanity – the social (and psychic) condition of anomy. What Gurnah approvingly calls "competing languages and metaphors" (79) *do* collapse in societies where terror reigns. To show that this is so is not to hide from "historical consciousness" (Moore 217) in "mystical holism" or to be "romantic and mystical" (Hunt 67, 83), nor is it to use "cartoon

---

7 I coin this term to indicate any type of "total" social collapse into violence.

language" (Gurnah 79). These critics' descriptions seem markedly inappropriate to the hard look Soyinka takes at people faced with overwhelming destabilisation of social norms. Contending with extreme and harrowing tyranny, Ofeyi perhaps represents the principled "non-violent" response and The Dentist the principled and selective use of retaliatory violence. Their discussion of their partly opposed attitudes and their attempts to resolve the matter "in practice" by visiting the home of one of the tyrants (107-118; 177-191) ends in predictable irresolution. The activist accuses the idealist of being a useless dreamer, whereas the idealist warns the activist of moral contamination. Is it "an escapist response" to show that each attitude ironises the other? Is the withdrawal to a small outpost where social health has been preserved to be labelled mere cowardice or collapse?

Critics like Hunt (67-89), in the passage cited on the first page of this essay, seem to me to be using a strangely twisted pseudo-Marxism to attack thought, writing, even consciousness itself in *accusing* Soyinka of "word-painting" (68). Yet "consciousness" is the inescapable condition of human beings, none of whom lives wholly absorbed in the present, being plagued and stirred (as Ofeyi is – movingly) by both memories and aspirations. Hunt seems to allude clearly to the concluding section of *Season of Anomy* when he writes "The 'return to the source' in Soyinka's universe is an escapist response, an attempt to recapture tradition which can only take place in the realm of pure consciousness" (89).

Of course the bedraggled group, overwhelmingly defeated and 'outclassed' by the Cartel's strategic and power advantages are – in going back to Ayiéró – making a "return to the source." Their doing so would be the kind of falsification of political realities which a critic like Hunt implies *if* Soyinka had presented the retreat naïvely as a solution – even an end! – to the terrible trouble of this period. However, it is an insensitive and seemingly wilful distortion of the tone of this novel's conclusion, if that is the suggestion. Tiny victories and comforts there are, and Ofeyi – or the narrator – notes (in the novel's final sentence) that, "[i]n the forests, life began to stir" (320). Undeniably there is an inkling or a premonition of hope in that detail. But is all history not dependent on the strange truth that human life-forms continue even when all had seemed lost? Perhaps *Season of Anomy* as a whole *is* an "enactment of ancient ritual" (Cooper 57). It seems inappropriate, however, for literary critics to delegitimise any author's (re-)tellings of old human stories when many of these are the myths we live by. As Achebe has written: "*stories create people create stories*" ("What" 162; emphasis original). A more "academic" version of this insight reads as follows:

> As soon as we recognize the value of the subjective in individual testimonies, we challenge the accepted categories of history. We reintroduce the emotionality, the fears and fantasies carried by the metaphors of memory, which historians are so anxious to write out of their formal accounts. And at the same time the individuality of each life story ceases to be an awkward impediment to generalization, and becomes instead a vital document of the construction of consciousness, emphasizing both the variety of experience in any social group, and also how each individual story draws on a common culture: a defiance of the rigid categorization of private and public, just as of memory and reality. (Samuel and Thompson 2)

The large range of communities and subcultures shown in *Season of Anomy* is one of the most remarkable and impressive features of this work. Instead of some homogeneous imagined community Soyinka shows us a diversity of groups and lifestyles distinct and sometimes murderously competitive in their differences – whether ethnic, cultural, moral, religious, economic or class-based. On the other hand the four tyrants, representing different ethnic, social and ideological spheres, have no difficulty in "cooperating" with murderous efficiency. Soyinka's diffident (rather than overweeningly confident) creative comment on writers' sense of nationhood may be appended here: "[Is the] nation [which authors] know [. . .] not simply one of their imagining"? (Qtd. in King and Ogungbesan 174). It can be seen how remarkably and ironically Soyinka here anticipates Benedict Anderson's famous dictum about the nation as an imagined community (Anderson, *Imagined*).

Metaphor (to respond to another of Gurnah's categorisations of Soyinka's novel) is used with particular and shocking irony in this novel – for Ofeyi's hopes of a wholesome growth from Ayiéró into the larger nation are inverted when the poisonous growth of violence and ethnic hatred instead contaminate the people and are entirely predominant. The final words of the novel ("In the forests, life began to stir" [320]) do in my reading primarily indicate an enduring hope. Nevertheless, the metaphors of growth and of seasons by means of which Soyinka organises the "movements" of his narrative (titled in sequence "Seminal," "Buds," "Tentacles," "Harvest," and "Spores") function in a deeply ambiguous fashion to emphasise that *both* poisonous *and* wholesome growth may be ineradicable – the tyrannic impulse as enduring as the courageous, compassionate urge which we see in the novel's 'sympathetic' characters.

Early in his career Soyinka wrote that

> [t]he writer is the visionary of his people, he recognizes past and present not for the purpose of enshrinement but for the logical-creative impulse and statement of the ideal future. He anticipates, he warns. It is not always enough for the writer to be involved in the direct physical struggle of today, he often cannot help but envisage and seek to protect the future which is the declared aim of contemporary struggle. (Soyinka, "Choice" 3)

Season of Anomy uses abundant, *awfully* vivid descriptions as well as myth, language and voice to show competing languages and metaphors, and the great power of Soyinka's descriptions of human devastation is not undercut by, but originates in the passionate anguish of the observing protagonist – the source of which is, unmistakably, the passion in the author himself for that justice without which the sanctity of humanity cannot be recognised or even shown to exist. Nor would these ideas be detachable from Soyinka's discovery during two years of imprisonment (mostly in solitary confinement) that *The Man Die[s]*[8] in him who yields up the stance of opposition to tyranny.

Works Cited

Achebe, Chinua. "'Mapping Out Identity': An Interview with Chinua Achebe." *The Classic* 3.1 (1984): 24-25.

___. "What Has Literature Got to Do with It?" *Hopes and Impediments – Selected Essays*. New York: Doubleday, 1989. 154-170.

Anderson, Benedict. *Imagined Communities: Reflections on the Origins and Spread of Nationalism*. London: Verso, 1983.

Agetua, J. *When the Man Died*. The Midwest Newspapers Corporation, Benin City, 1975.

Cooper, Brenda. "The Two-faced Ogun: Postcolonial Intellectuals and the Positioning of Wole Soyinka." *English in Africa* 22.2 (1995): 44-69.

Duerden, Dennis and Cosmo Pieterse, eds. *African Writers Talking: A Collection of Interviews*. London: Heinemann, 1972.

Gibbs, James, and Bernth Lindfors, eds. *Research on Wole Soyinka*. Trenton, N.J.: Africa World Press, 1993.

Gurnah, Abdulrazak. "The Fiction of Wole Soyinka." *Wole Soyinka: An Appraisal*. Ed. Adewale Maja-Pearse. London: Heinemann, 1994. 61-80.

---

8 Alluding to the "prison memoir" Soyinka wrote, to which he gave the title *The Man Died: Prison Notes*.

Hunt, Geoffrey. "Two African Aesthetics: Soyinka vs Cabral." *Marxism and African Literature*. Ed. George Gugelberger. London: Currey, 1985. 64-93.

Jeyifo, Biodun. Rev. of *Myth, Literature and the African World*, by Wole Soyinka. *Positive Review* 1 (1978): 15.

King, Bruce, and Kolawole Ogungbesan, eds. *A Celebration of Black and African Writing*. Zaria: Ahmadu Bello UP, 1975.

Lawrence, David Herbert. *Selected Literary Criticism*. London: Heinemann, 1967.

Moore, George. *Twelve African Writers*. London: Hutchinson University Library for Africa, 1980.

Quayson, A. "Wole Soyinka and Autobiography as Political Unconscious." *The Journal of Commonwealth Literature* 31.2 (1996): 19-32.

Samuel, R. and P. Thompson, eds. *The Myths We Live By*. London and New York: Routledge, 1990.

Soyinka, Wole. BBC Interview during *Africa 1995*. 1995.

___. "The Choice and Use of Language." *Cultural Events in Africa* 75.3 (1966): 3-5.

___. *The Interpreters*. London: Andrè Deutsch, 1965.

___. "Listening to the Drums of Civil War." *Weekly Mail and Guardian* July 22-28 1994. 37.

___. *The Man Died: Prison Notes*. London: Collings, 1972.

___. "Nigeria's Great Charade." *Weekly Mail and Guardian* July 18-24 1997.

___. *Season of Anomy*. 1973. London: Arena, 1988.

___. "Twice Bitten: The Fate of Africa's Culture Producers." *Publications of the Modern Language Association* 105.1 (1990): 110-120.

Finding Foundations for Change in Bessie Head's *The Cardinals*

> Who is the story-teller? Of whom is the story told? What is there in the darkness to imagine into being? What is there to dream and to relate? What happens when I or anyone exerts the force of language upon the unknown?
>
> – N. Scott Momaday, "The Man Made of Words."

Three factors – that *The Cardinals* (1993) is the only one of Bessie Head's novels set in South Africa (the scene being the Cape Town area during the late 1950s[1]), as well as the recognisable autobiographical elements[2] of this work (her earliest known novel), added to the accident of its very recent "discovery" and belated publication – endow this work with considerable interest for those engaged in South African cultural studies. It would be a mere curiosity if it were not what it is: the unmistakable demonstration of a major literary talent in the making. Yet it is at the same time a bafflingly difficult novel to grasp imaginatively with something of the elusiveness or hiddenness of the chief protagonist's nature colouring the work as a whole. Some of the reasons for this quality are: the scattered, far-flung, erratic writing style and episodic design of the novel, an impression of elusive underground connections and a forward-flowing investigation of matters of profound importance, its off-hand, breezy colloquialism through (or despite) which one senses the lyricism of this writer's craft, and the pulp "romance" frame into which are poured questions and experiences of eroticism, political force, self-validation and personal commitment.[3]

The chief character in the novel, a young woman known as Mouse, is even near the end of the work described as "a shambles of unfocused atoms" by

1 See *The Cardinals*: "Today is Wednesday, September 28th, 1959" (33).

2 See Bessie Head's "Notes from a Quiet Backwater I" for details in which her early circumstances coincide with Mouse's: "No details were ever available about my father [. . .] At birth I had been handed to a Coloured foster mother [who . . .] was paid a pittance [. . .] " (3). Mouse's employment by a newspaper caned *African Beat* evidently recalls Head working in Cape Town for the *Golden City Post*, one of the *Drum* publications. In an anthologised essay Susan Gardner writes that "[t]he circumstances of Bessie Head's biography appear to be so idiosyncratically inauspicious it can seem miraculous that her creativity flowered at all" (227).

3 See Barbara Harlow's *Resistance Literature* for comments on the ways in which resistance narratives challenge literary conventions and generate new literary paradigms (85, 115).

Johnny, the man who loves her (127). From my descriptions above, it may seem that his expression is equally applicable to the novel as a whole, which could thus only be judged a naïve attempt at novel-writing rather than a finished achievement. What I shall be arguing in this paper is that the roughness of this work, its lack of "finish" (in several senses of the word) is a strength worthy of careful reading – this roughness is exactly appropriate to the notion of aspiration (as a lifestyle) that seems to be its hidden theme.

In 1972, in the concluding section of a short piece called "An African Story," Bessie Head wrote:

> South Africa made white people rich and comfortable, but their ownership of the country is ugly and repellent. They talk about South Africa in tourist language all the time: "This grand and sunny land," they say. The cheap, glaring, paltry trash of a people who are living it up for themselves alone dominates everything, infiltrates everywhere. If one is a part of it, through being born there, how does one communicate with the horrible? That is why South Africa has no great writer: no one can create harmony out of cheap discord.
>
> It is impossible to guess how the revolution will come one day in South Africa. But in a world where all ordinary people are insisting on their rights, it is inevitable. It is to be hoped that great leaders will arise there who remember the suffering of racial hatred and out of it formulate a common language of human love for all people.
>
> Possibly, too, Southern Africa might one day become the home of the story-teller and dreamer, who did not hurt others but only introduced new dreams that filled the heart with wonder. (*Woman* 102-103)

Earlier, in 1963 (i.e. probably soon after finishing *The Cardinals*, for which the presumed dates of composition are 1960-1962), in a "Letter from South Africa," she had written: "Maybe I am going to pieces. One of the slobs who are left behind [that is, in South Africa, at a time when so many of her friends had gone into exile] told me rather scornfully the other day that I was not a freedom fighter. I have to admit that it is the truth" (*Woman* 14).

Yet *The Cardinals* is one of those works implicitly illustrating the case for story-tellers and dreamers to be considered freedom fighters rather than romantic escapists. The feature of the novel that indicates this is the perpetual engagement of both Johnny and Mouse, not only with each other, but with the place and circumstances in, by and out of which they live. Encountering each other, they in fact intensify their scrutiny of their land and their articulation of its meaning – parallelling the process by which Head demonstrates to the reader that loving involves politics down to the furthest recesses of the psyche and that (conversely) political force frights the intimate moments of individual encounters. Erecting distinctions between private and public spheres is shown in this novel to be the mark of the hypocrite[4] – nor are such tidy fences respected in this narrative, which moves constantly in and out of descriptions of Johnny and Mouse's feelings for each other and of encounters indicative of the politically constituted society in which they live. In the "sequencing" in chapter 8 (77-85) Head's style itself constantly transgresses these barriers. The narrative moves from the "snugly" ensconced Mouse in her private bedroom to Johnny's entrance and account of the life of his sister, a prostitute at ten to help keep their family, and then to his generalising distinction between "rules" of society and "suffering." This is followed by PK's arrival with the news of a rural township "riot" to which he, James and Johnny travel, Johnny's existential distinction between political commitment and his type of "uncommittedness" (82), and finally his return home and first declaration to Mouse of his love for her, the chapter concluding with the paradoxical juxtaposition of Johnny's insistence on irrevocable "commitment" in love with the declaration that he lives "without a code or a law." The way the novel intertwines "private" and "public" is evident even in such a bald summary.

It is their capacity for passion which – openly in the flamboyant Johnny and in a hidden fashion in Mouse – sets these two off from those around them. In them, passion is "responsibility." The rareness, the felt riskiness of responsibility, is emphasised by a fringe figure in the novel, the unnamed stranger with whom Mouse strikes up a friendship. He says of "[r]esponsibility" that "[m]ost people fear it" and he refers sardonically to "[t]his other man, that everybody hopes will bear the responsibility for them, [who] just isn't there most of the time" (36). The "wild man" Johnny employs the term in his fiercest condemnations – "PK is responsible for this mess" (64) – and in his later injunction to Mouse: "It is a great responsibility to be a writer at this time" (72).

Political force, conversely, is identified as inevitably irresponsible, just as it requires the relinquishing of individual responsibility for its hold on people's lives. For this reason, power in such an autocracy as the South African system

4 See such examples as Mona (102), PK (81) and James (93) and note Johnny's distinction between himself and "James and PK" (87).

must attempt the control of passion. *The Cardinals* is, then, a document demonstrating that "private" passion is one of the strongest and most important forms of opposition to political control. The piece of South African legislation known as the Immorality Act (of 1927, amended in 1957), banning sexual relationships or marriages between members of "different races," is the master narrative against which Head tells the constellation of stories that she calls *The Cardinals*. The sorts of "stories" (as newspaper reports are appropriately referred to in the novel) that make it into daily print are some of these and are set off against many other accounts of life in South Africa at this time – especially as witnessed and told by both Johnny and Mouse.

Head's novel is preceded by her note to readers that "*The Cardinals*, in the astrological sense, are those who serve as the base or foundation for change (page facing p. 1). This piece of authorial information is probably the strongest clue to the direction taken by this unusual novel and to the importance Head attaches to the work. It claims for both Mouse and Johnny the status of initiators or pioneers. It cautions us not to mistake the novel for simple realism, unconscious autobiography, sociological portrayal of earlier apartheid conditions in the Cape, or erotic/neurotic wish fulfilment by its author. Like Head's other novels, then, *The Cardinals* has the dimensions of a parable.

At the core of this story is the fact that Mouse is the product, and Johnny the survivor, of the *same* failed, though initially successful, relationship which transcended class difference as well as the barriers of South African "Immorality" legislation.[5] This fact is also a mystery, since neither of the two has any suspicion of their biological relationship. It is not the law nor the police that ends the spontaneous union between Johnny, then a poor young fisherman, and Ruby, the young woman from a privileged background who is Mouse's mother, but Ruby's momentary snobbery and cowardice and her resulting shame due to this betrayal. She denies knowing Johnny to her "dancing partner," Paddy. Unable to forgive herself for this severance of the spiritual connection between herself and

5 Evidently I disagree on this point with Dorothy Driver, who writes in a review that "Mouse's mother is not white" (16-18). Despite reluctance to participate in pigmentation babble, and despite the narrator's reference to Ruby's "dark brown face," I hold out on this point because it seems to me of thematic significance. I suggest that Head avoids the vulgarities of race classification terminology, but nevertheless builds in numerous other indicators that make it seem extremely unlikely that Ruby's family would not be classified "white" (50-60). The "high society" women with whom Johnny has destructive relationships to "get his own back" on Ruby for abandoning him are undoubtedly "white" women.

Johnny, she commits suicide, whereas their baby (who will be dubbed Mouse) is dumped in a Cape Town slum, described as follows in the novel's opening paragraph: "It was a large area of tin shacks, bounded on the one side by a mile-long graveyard and on the other by the city refuse dump and the sea. A national road separated the slum from the refuse dump" (1).

This wry, blunt style of writing is characteristic of the whole work. It insists on the stark ordinariness of the bleak scene, taken for granted by most of those who drive by on the "national road" – to whom the location of such a slum between dump, graveyard and sea no doubt seems appropriate. The passage is of course imbued with that social vision which the work as a whole conveys. It is the strange placing of the opening word "It" that draws attention to the environment as if it were a character or a force in its own right. Its function is to make us see why the novelist does not bother to show or name politicians or a party in her portrayal of apartheid society. The system has become a place, a non-community of victims, and the words "bounded" and "separated" indicate the compartmentalising thought process referred to above as a false tidiness – for the slum is also chaos, the sign of irresponsibility, a dump for thrown-away people. It is easy enough to sense the resonances and ironies of the word "national" (attached to "road") as a reference to a ruling political party which perverts precisely its *national* duty by creating or allowing such ugliness, "separat[ing]" and scattering people. It is out of this ugly cess, this non-community[6] that Mouse struggles onto the little ledge represented by *African Beat – The Paper of The People*, of whose "emptiness and bold vulgarity" (12) she is all too well aware.

It is in the newspaper office that Mouse encounters the hard-bitten Johnny, for whom her claim to his long-hidden tenderness lies in her writing talent, so badly smothered in the slick newspaper world where Mouse flounders from one unsuitable and cynical assignment to another. The editor PK tells her: "This paper is paying you only to write a dirty story" (18), and later she is "[put] on courts" for "[r]eady-made stories [. . .] immorality cases and [. . .] death sentences [. . .] at least one story brought in every day" (44). Head shows Johnny initially in association with the newspaper's editor, a white liberal of the time, and with the other male journalist, an aspirant novelist with a mean, gossipy soul. Johnny

---

6 Johnny refers – with characteristic intensity – to this particular slum as "an oozing, indiscriminate mixture of muck, incest and hell-fire," as a "swamp" and a "dumping ground." With this should be compared his discerning description of the socaned improvement/alternative of government-built townships as well as his perspective on the "riot" (see 28, 19-20, 80-81).

moves slowly into an open alignment with Mouse. Most of the novel is a record of his arduous wooing of the woman neither knows to be his daughter (a fact they are never likely to discover). If Johnny has, before knowing Mouse, led a dissolute life of brief encounters with a series of white "high society bitches" (46) – half conscious vengeance on Ruby for abandoning him – Mouse's psychological damage has penetrated more deeply, leaving her a lonely woman who freezes out potential relationships by means of a self-protective barrier for her "thin skin" (116). The narrator gives her shrinking from human relationships the dimensions of animal terror: her "fright" is said to be "dumb" and she is referred to as an "unwanted stray" who had to learn that she should "not answer back" those who could at any time "throw [her] out" from any of the ten "homes" in which she was "placed and replaced" (10). "Year by year she had become more and more silent and her inner retreat was [sic] almost to the point where no living being could reach her" (10-11). Johnny's perceptiveness and the correctness of his diagnosis is validated by the author (22, 23, 29) when he warns that "there's bound to be an explosion" (29).

Although neither Mouse nor Johnny is aware that their sexual union (about to occur, one is led to believe, as the novel ends) is in fact incestuous, Head makes clear that these two are in any case taboo-breakers and that this is the source of her interest in them. Miscegenation is their history, Mouse being the child from and Johnny, unknowingly, the father in such a union. The form of passion which the white South African government outlawed as "Immorality" becomes, as Head designs the novel, a theme that haunts Mouse's and Johnny's professional and emotional lives, the epitome of all that restricts the unfolding of the self in such a society as South Africa. Head associates Mouse's self-defensive emotional withdrawal with the term "reserve" and refers as narrator to the "tight shell of reserve and retreat" (107) out of which she needs to be "draw[n]." This coincides with Johnny's insistence that to be a writer Mouse will have "to break off the bolts that are keeping [her] locked up" (75). Evidently, political oppression and social deprivation are by these images incorporated in Mouse's instinctual behaviour: it is a sort of reflection of apartheid. Mouse's emotional stuntedness as much as Johnny's "expense of spirit in a waste of shame"[7] are subtly represented as products, or rather as pathetically inadequate forms, of protest against the mindset that legislates its hatred and fear into the sexual area where the roots of all life lie. The slow deployment of the process by means of which Mouse and Johnny move closer to each other looks, if read one way, very much

[7] Shakespeare's Sonnet 129, lines 1-2.

like a pulp "romance" of the 1950s; read in another way, it is a steely look at one of the few forces strong enough to be resistant to an apartheid society.

The omniscient narrator's voice, often beyond Johnny or Mouse, informing the reader of connections of which the two of them are unaware, also blends easily into the thoughts of both these cardinal characters. The validation of their points of view contrasts with the dry scorn reserved for would-be taboo-breakers – like Mona, a sophisticated dabbler in political causes[8] who is sexually fascinated and harshly rebuffed by Johnny. The cheapness of such frivolous lust in which the transgression of the legal racial barrier serves only as added titillation,[9] is accentuated by the background of politically and personally ruinous love or sexual encounters between white and black people, accounts of which abound in the novel. Head cleverly uses the newspaper office setting to draw in many anecdotes of so-called "Immorality" acts, especially through Mouse's assignment to the court cases where those arrested for this form of social transgression appear. Interestingly, these are mostly not of the "great but doomed love" type. Mouse, with Johnny's encouragement, attempts to understand the selfdestructive urges that bring prosperous white men "of the business-type," as she calls them (110), to have brief encounters with women who are (in Mouse's words) "real tramps in the sense that they have an unwashed look and give off an overpowering odour of urine and woodsmoke" (110). The slum, it seems, despite being dumped far off, will not go away and cannot be forgotten.

Away from the vulgarity required for the newspaper reports by its editor,[10] Mouse writes wonderingly of how "the business-type man"

> stares blankly and mutely, struggling not to look too closely at the doom that awaits him, silent about the cause that led to his downfall. Could it not be that for months he had had no normal sex relations

---

[8] Exposed as such especially by the detail, in a novel so much concerned with the obscenity of "Immorality" legislation, that she would allow her children to attend an "integrated" school "on condition that it's not co-educational" (96)!

[9] The nature of Mona's approaches to Johnny may be judged by one brief quotation: "'We don't have to be conventional in this unconventional atmosphere', she said" (97).

[10] See the middle section of page 18 (especially PK's "This paper is paying you only to write a dirty story"), slyly and tellingly contrasted by Head with PK's preferences for the "human interest side" of a report which endorses the apartheid hegemony.

> with his [sick] wife [. . .] Or, is it not simply that to the sex urge, harsh legislation and repugnant odours are of no account? (110-111)

The comment on these groping thoughts of Mouse's from one of Johnny's former lovers, the "nonchalant" Liz, is a patronising and patently insincere "very interesting" (111). Counter to this is Johnny's expression of his own different way of *seeing* Mouse, "different from the rest" of women he has been involved with because of her "[c]ourage and complete sincerity" (113). What draws Johnny to Mouse is something he inarticulately and yet tellingly describes as "the inside part" – he says that "[s]he's got something inside her that agrees with my system" (65). This, as even the predatory Liz realises, has made Johnny give Mouse "that part of [him other women] could never reach" (112). Mouse has at last agreed to share Johnny's house with him, although she still rebuffs him sexually. Feeling contaminated by Liz's visit, with "waves of anger beating out of him," Johnny "stretch[es] out his arms" and kisses Mouse "with a ferocious despair [so that] a feeling of tenderness over[comes] her alarm and she [winds] her long, thin arms about his neck in an instinctive gesture of comfort. It reache[s] him and ease[s] away his anger" (114).

Notable in this brief episode is the shame and indignation Johnny feels at the "meaningless[ness]" of the type of sexual involvement he formerly pursued with "sophisticated" white women. In addition, there is the maternal role Johnny plays as he attempts to bring a "woman" to birth out of the "child" (131) Mouse who is in her early twenties. The verbs in the above passage the gradual process of entwining growth towards Johnny from Mouse's side – *despite* her weeping because she fears that she "cannot love," "cannot give" (88). Having together survived the onslaught of Liz's visit, Mouse and Johnny return – to the writing up and probing of the society in which they live. Johnny contributes to and pursues Mouse's thoughts about Immorality Act victims, using her reference to the "look of death" (114-115) on the faces of the men on trial. In his view these men are the suicidal registers of the "abyss" on whose edge the society teeters (115). But when he comments on the "insanity" of the whole system being exposed in sexual conduct and its "neurotic," even "crazed" legal repression, he honestly and immediately turns to acknowledge that Liz is "just one out of about a hundred women" with whom he has himself been "messing around" (115) – "mess" being his favourite expression of disgust at an absence of social wholesomeness.

In these seemingly rough-and-ready ways Head indicates some of the linkages between sex and politics, private intimacies and a huge public system. She shows it also by the natural, unpredictable oscillations of conversation in the kitchen scene, which proceeds from Mouse's reference to the way a nasty remark of James's "pierced" *her* "thin skin" (116) to Johnny's expression of his willy-nilly "car[ing . . .] about Africa and its destiny" (117), to his comments on his sense of the writer's vocation which is followed by his observation of Mouse's eyes as "beautiful [. . .] exalted [. . .] two pin-point lights of concentration" (117). Somehow the quiet Mouse, despite her grieving sense of inadequacy, is unmistakably the more eloquent presence of the two – but it is through Johnny's generosity of feeling that the reader is enabled to see this. Both Mouse and Johnny urgently compel each other to change – he is more overtly demanding of her and she is more inwardly compelling towards him.[11]

At this point it is probably appropriate to examine Head's indicators of the nature of Johnny's feelings for Mouse. Some of the passages quoted may show how close Johnny seems to the favourite male lead in many pulp romances, the "masterful,"[12] male "saviour" of the damsel in distress. Johnny does refer at one point to "this dense wall in which [Mouse] has enclosed herself" (65) as if in a faint echo from the fairy tale. No sword hacking through brambles will get to Mouse, though. As Johnny recognises, "I just have to convince her that I can help her with this writing business" (68) and, earlier on, "There's only one hope of reaching that clot of a woman [. . .] Writing" (68). Yet it is evident that Head endorses and values Johnny's feelings for Mouse and I suggest that readers need to take account of this. The author nowhere invalidates the indicators of Johnny's role as, to some extent, that of a saviour of the psychologically damaged Mouse. Implicit authorial endorsement is discernible, for instance, in the choice of image Head applies to Mouse's first participation in creative co-operation

---

11 The metaphor of the human couple as a figure for the ideal of social relationship and "belonging" features strongly in Head's work at this time – compare the following, from one of the slightly later pieces published in the collection of "meditations" and short stories published with *The Cardinals*: "Nothing can be right until a man and a woman make all things meaningful through each other" ("Where" 152).

12 Dorothy Driver, in the review referred to in footnote 9, criticises Johnny's conduct towards Mouse with some asperity. She writes: "But he most certainly does have a code or law regarding women, including Mouse: his behaviour is oppressive and exploitative. 'Battered' [. . .] by these contradictions, Mouse hides [. . .] Writing can barely free her from this state" (18). Evidently my reading differs from Driver's on this point both in how I see Johnny and how I imagine Head to be employing Johnny in this narrative.

with Johnny: when she is "working on the story Johnny had given her" she is "like a child learning to walk" (37).[13]

It is nevertheless interesting to note the extent to which Head twists "true-love knots" into the "iron pokers" of uncomfortable social and political realities in apartheid South Africa. Mouse's distress, for instance, is rooted in the nature of her birth, in her narrow escape from rape by her slum stepfather, in her unwanted and unloved childhood and young womanhood, and in the way she is "taunted" by her colleague James and patronised by the newspaper editor PK (15); ugly male attitudes from which "the battering effect of [Johnny's] personality" (15) at first seems indistinguishable. Her arrival at the newspaper officer, for instance, is described as follows:

> Both men [James and Johnny] battered her with the amused contemptuous looks in their eyes. The short man with the cynical grin [James] said: "Well, look what the cat brought in."
>
> The other man [Johnny] said: "A Mouse." (14)

The echo of the verb "to batter" draws attention to the sense of social, especially sexual onslaught, which causes Mouse's necessary self-hardening and withdrawal, and her initial categorization of Johnny with the other two men.

The fact, made known to the reader but not to the protagonists, that Johnny is Mouse's father, is another feature of the novel that shatters the conventional love story frame. It extends into an extremity, a shock factor, the recognition that "Immorality" legislation (and likewise the larger system from which it emanates) severs the most essential of the human bonds required for psychic survival or wholeness.[14] It is entirely likely that Head is in this respect responding novelistically to her severance from and ignorance of the identity and personali-

---

13 Compare Head's later comment which appears in a letter to Patrick Cullinan, dated 20 February 1965: "You know – that funny book I sent – *The Cardinals* – I started to create a mythical man there and he has since appeared everywhere. I write about him all the time – yet he is not flesh and blood reality. But every time I need to say something about love – he's always there – so conveniently [. . .] He gets better and better with each story [. . .] He is [. . .] 'Africa' and the 'Beautiful Birds Dancing in the Sun-Wind' and 'Earth and Everything' [references to the slightly later pieces printed with *The Cardinals*]" (Cullinan 66-71).

14 Compare Head's alarmed and alarming observation of the "almost complete breakdown of family life" in Botswana (*A Woman Alone* 57).

ty of her own father.[15] Yet her response to this politically created deprivation is not neurotic lamentation but tough, courageous, stocktaking thought – a creative broadening of the base of an individual tragedy. Many South African novelists have tackled the miscegenation theme[16] – Head is perhaps the only first-rate writer who does so "from within," herself the product, like Mouse, of a cross-class, cross-race union. I agree with Margaret Daymond[17] that the incest theme is desensationalised, but I would add that it becomes in Head's hands a metaphor for *recovery*, in the fun range of its meaning, as well as a sign of the difficulty of such healing within the South African "mess." In an important passage, Johnny says of his own childhood: "We just grew up like a lot of animals," and speaks of incest by dichotomising "suffering" from its cause, the "rules of society" (78). This can be linked with his earlier statement that "you cannot feel like the underdog and at the same time feel you belong to a country," enjoining Mouse to "help throw some of those false standards overboard" (72).

The creative surprise in this novel is Head's avoidance of the tragic perspective adopted by other writers which treat of the "Immorality Act," Head – almost coolly – underplays impressions of doomed love drama and wreckage and inevitable defeat. In her account, a tough energy and determination encounter the political, social and psychic barriers – and begin to surmount them. Head's is a liberation fable, a carefully inspirational account, fiercely refusing political fatalism. Perhaps this is the most interesting reason why this work is so queerly breezy and bracing in both its style and theme, for in this way Head, who may be thought to be writing a self-portrait in her depiction of Mouse, is certainly doing so no less in her portrayal of Johnny. An early passage in the novel begins with Mouse in a dreary mood at the newspaper office:

---

15 In the autobiographical "Notes From A Quiet Backwater," Head writes: "I was born on July 6, 1937, in the Pietermaritzburg mental hospital. The reason for my peculiar birthplace was that my mother was white and my father black. No details were ever available about my father beyond the fact that he worked in the family stables and took care of their racehorses" (*A Woman Alone* 3).

16 Some of the obvious examples (in English only) would be Peter Abrahams's *Path of Thunder*; William Plomer's *Turbott Wolfe*; Alan Paton's *Too Late The Phalarope*; Dan Jacobson's *The Evidence of Love*; Lewis Nkosi's *Mating Birds*; Nadine Gordimer's *A Question of Loving*. See also Lewis Nkosi's "Sex and the Law in South Africa" in his *The Transplanted Heart* (22-30).

17 Daymond is the editor of *The Cardinals*, for which she provides an excellent introduction in which the incest issue is widely discussed. See also D. J. Driver's comments on this point (17).

> The day was grey and bleak and rainy. She stood at the office window and felt crushed as she watched the relentless downpour of the late spring rain.
>
> Click, bang, CRASH. And in burst Johnny like the sun. She turned.
>
> "Hello Mouse," he said breezily. "I wrote another short story last night.
>
> Read it and then re-write it the way you think it should be. Make the people real. I want to give that bastard James [The would-be novelist, their colleague] a jolt out of his doltish complacency [. . .]
>
> The kind of writing I'm concentrating on is going to get rid of government and systems for good. Here. Catch!"[18]
>
> She, caught it eagerly. His enthusiasm carried her along with it. (31)

This is actually how and where Mouse begins to function as a writer: through Johnny's *recognition* of her. Of course the elemental associations – "like the sun," "breezily" – endorse the invigorating force of Johnny's personality and especially of his engagement with Mouse, as do the verbs "burst" and "[c]atch." Head does not make Johnny fatherly towards Mouse in any obviously tenderhearted way. Mouse's mother Ruby remarked to a much younger Johnny: "'You are very rough with me [. . .]. Not even my father talks to me the way you do, but I like it. Often those who talk softly and sweetly hide a stabbing cruelty in that softness and sweetness" (53).

Nor is Johnny paternalistic towards Mouse. Head puts in a few light touches to establish this, for instance, by contrasting him with the frivolously condescending editor PK (who is not obviously unkind to Mouse): "I admit she can't write the stuff we want but I'm not going to get her fired [. . .] Ever since she's been around I've been fathering her. It makes me feel great: PK, sex-maniac, plays father to sweet young innocent thing" (27). To offset possible, if unlikely impressions that Johnny's rough and insistent caring for Mouse is a mere seduction game, we have James's words to her, fairly late in the novel: "if you're not physically attractive to Johnny, you're damned attractive to me. I know your

---

18 Compare Head on her novel *Maru* (1971) – it "ought to liberate the oppressed Bushmen here overnight" – where Head's tone is very similar to Johnny's in its exuberant yet urgent attitude towards political oppression (*Gesture* 125).

type. They're real hot mamas in bed [. . .] The trouble with you is that you're morbid. You just need a good rape" (94).

Yet Head leaves readers in no doubt of the intensity of Johnny's desire for Mouse, and of the power of her slowly awakening sexuality. In this respect too the author is interested in an inclusive vitalism, depicting escape from, rather than opposition to, political fences, showing "The Cardinals" reaching after fuller life.[19] Never, though, does the "pretty solid rainbow" (114), as Johnny calls Mouse, leave its footing in the South African soil. Both Johnny and Mouse have come from slums and the "home" to which they go is a "small white-washed house" (136) in District Six. Beyond that we are not told where they may have moved or reached. Head could not have known when she wrote *The Cardinals* that District Six would be razed nor that she herself would gradually and painfully come to reject in *A Question of Power* (1974) – the ideal of sexual partnership as an alternative to or haven from racist oppression.

When Johnny makes Mouse the offer to help her to become "the kind of writer [she] want[s] to be," it is accompanied by his insistence that "Africa may not need us but we need a country like Africa. It's just a part of this joke called Life. We need a country the way we need food and clothes [. . .] [but] you cannot feel like the underdog and at the same time feel you belong to a country" (72).[20]

In Johnny's definition, underdogs are those on whom the conquerors "impose false standards" (72). He knows also that "laws and rules of society are made by men and women who know nothing about suffering" (78).[21] *Suffering*, then, is what Johnny cares about in Mouse – it is the "inside part" (65) of her which he mentions when he struggles to explain what fascinates him about a woman who seems so unlikely to attract him. But he and Mouse want more than victimhood – their attempts are, through their writing, to insert a new dynamism in their society. Mouse is becoming a writer, Johnny is throughout the novel stimulated by her presence to comment copiously on the craft and purpose of creative writing in a stunted society.

---

19 Compare a sentence from "Where is the Hour," in the volume that includes *The Cardinals*, and written a few years after the novel: "We may liberate ourselves from alien oppressors, but when do we come alive to ourselves?" (152).

20 Compare 117. The tightly paradoxical formulation of Johnny's determination (in his own words; emphases added) "to *stand for non*-commitment" is noteworthy, as a clue to his character.

21 See Head's statement in "Africa": "The only reason I always admit pain is that it seems the only constructive emotion" (p. 143).

Helping Mouse to "focus all [the] scattered pieces" (133) of herself (as Johnny hopes to do), he encourages her, as an artistic exercise, to "concentrate [the] [. . .] vastness [. . .] mood [. . .] purpose and the flow and rhythm" (134) of the city in which they live. The *motif* of rejoining what is scattered is central to the novel. There are important passages in which words such as "tapestry" (35); "correlate" (75, 88); "knit unit" (p. 103); "well composed" (135) and "not in bits and pieces" (134) occur. Through Johnny, Head suggests that the act of communion (in love) or of communication (in writing) is the only alternative to "mess" or chaos, which he links paradoxically with rules and laws – and with the mere pretence of defying these. Mouse, the slum girl, becomes by the end of the novel the artist who overlooks and envisions the city's "interweaving patterns," perceiving that "[i]ts purpose is to sustain human life. Its destiny is perpetual expansion" (135). It is when this has been written that Johnny invites Mouse to "go home" with him. The blossoming of Mouse as a writer here is shown by Head to coincide with her casting-off at last of the rigidity with which she has until now repressed her sexual yearnings. Yet "home" is simply "safe": there is no suggestion that this couple will live in a hideaway huddle, "wrapped up in each other." Instead the suggestion is of persistent aspiration for them both: a living un-ease that will continue to engage them not only with each other, but with their society and its hampering of human life.

The Cardinals is not likely to be hailed as a great work – its power and importance are likely to be overlooked by many readers, exactly as Johnny's seriousness of purpose is obscured by his apparent flippancy, and Mouse's purity and strength are concealed by her seeming timidity. What I hope to have conveyed, though, is the salutary toughness of this work – its refusal to concede that, even as crushing a political system as apartheid, can be made the excuse for *not dreaming*. It "refuses" both apathy and melancholy. Much later and much more taxingly, Bessie Head would re-address the *monster despair* in *A Question of Power* (1974). This is her first skirmish with that beast – I think a victorious one.

Works Cited

Cullinan, Patrick. "I Try. In Bits: Letters from Bessie Head 1963-1982." *New Contrast* 21.4 (1993). 66-71.

Daymond, Margaret J. Introduction. *The Cardinals*. By Bessie Head. vii-xviii.

Driver, Dorothy. "Gestures of Expatriation and Belonging." *Southern African Review of Books* 5.5 (1993). 16-18.

Gardner, Susan. "Bessie Head: Production Under Drought Conditions." *Women and Writing in South Africa: A Critical Anthology*. Ed. Cherry Clayton. Johannesburg: Heinemann, 1989. 225-235.

Harlow, Barbara. *Resistance Literature*. New York and London: Methuen, 1987.

Head, Bessie. "Africa." *Cardinals* 141-144.

___. "An African Story." Head, *Woman* 101-103.

___. *The Cardinals: With Meditations and Short Stories*. Ed. and introd. Margaret J. Daymond. Cape Town: David Philip, 1993.

___. *A Gesture of Belonging: Letters from Bessie Head, 1965-1979*. Ed. Randolph Vigne. London: S. A. Writers, 1991.

___. "Letter from South Africa." Head, *Woman* 13-15.

___. "Notes from a Quiet Backwater." Head, *Woman* 77-79.

___. "Where is the Hour of the Beautiful Dancing of Birds in the Sun-wind?" Head, *Cardinals* 150-159.

___. *A Woman Alone: Autobiographical Writings*. London: Heinemann, 1990.

Momaday, N. Scott. "The Man Made of Words." *Literature of the American Indian: Contemporary Views and Perspectives*. Ed. Abraham Chapman. New American Library. New York: Meridian, 1975. 96-108.

Nkosi, Lewis. "Sex and the Law in South Africa." *The Transplanted Heart*. By Nkosi. Benin: Ethiopia, 1975. 22-30.

Blood Gets a Voice: Unity Dow's *The Screaming of the Innocent*

Throughout the world, in the late twentieth century, it seems, the phenomenon of sexual – or, better termed, morbid or transposed sexual predation with children as victims (frequently ending in murder), has been noted (it appears) with increasing anxiety and anger. From regions as different culturally and as far apart geographically as the city of Atlanta in the American South and the city of Edinburgh towards the north of Britain, novelists such as the prominent African-American author Toni Cade Bambara (in *These Bones Are Not My Child*, 1999) and the well known and hugely popular Scottish crime-writer Ian Rankin (in *Dead Souls*, 1997) have addressed this topic. There is hence no intention, in the present discussion of Dow's harrowing text, to suggest that the violation of (especially girl) children's bodies, or the taking of their lives, are practices peculiar to the Batswana culture, or to intimate that (especially male) adults' abuse of children is limited to postcolonial or particular to African societies. Confirming this point is the fact that over a period of nine months the following newspaper accounts[1] appeared in South African newspapers, reporting the following occurrences and analyses:

a) that the *South African Sex Worker Education Advocacy Task Force* has estimated that one of every four sex workers in Cape Town is a child, and that the main reasons for child prostitution are poverty and a rising demand for sex with children; that local girls are commonly kidnapped in broad daylight in public places, gang-raped, forced to take drugs and into prostitution;
b) that highly sophisticated syndicates bring children to South Africa from south-east Asia, eastern Europe and east Africa and less sophisticated syndicates also bring in girls from Southern African countries to serve the local sex trade;
c) that a new *testimonio*-type text titled *Never Been At Home!* by the South African Zazah Khuzwayo, a woman who grew up in rural KwaZulu-Natal, establishes that "submission to the father [in her case an especially brutal

---

1 Sources: a) and b) from the *Cape Times* of 18 Dec. 2003 (confirmed by an account in *Rapport* of 30 May 2004, drawing on a UNICEF report); c) from the *Cape Times* of 8 Apr. 2004; d) from the *Cape Times* of 22 Mar. 2004; e) from *The Sunday Independent* of 4 Apr. 2004; f) and g) and h) from the *Cape Times* of 18 Dec. 2003; i) from the *Cape Times* of 15 June 2004; j) from the *Cape Times* of 5 July 2004.

paterfamilias] is elementary law – at whatever cost to the family," and that the text highlights "the role that custom plays in oppressing women";

d) that Liberian women in March this year felt compelled to march against a spate of ritual killings, especially of children and mainly of girls, explaining that "business people and politicians [. . .] buy charms for power and luck made from [. . . victims'] body parts";

e) that a new Nigerian novel, *Graceland*, tells of a boy's growing up experience that includes his being sodomised by his uncle, masturbated by a policeman during interrogation and getting involved in cocaine trafficking and then in the trade in body parts;

f) that French police at the end of last year conducted their largest series of raids on [evidently *known*, but nevertheless free] paedophile suspects after a nine-year-old girl's disappearance near Paris;

g) that at the same time the British school caretaker Ian Huntley and his female accomplice were on trial for the murder of two pre-teen British schoolgirls *and* (from the same day's paper)

h) that the European Parliament has passed new rules to regulate the illegal trade in human organs (here it *may* indeed be mainly adults who are involved, who sell "voluntarily," but predictably the example cited refers to "Moldova, Europe's poorest country");

i) that jurors in the trial of a Belgian child rapist and murderer who had abducted, abused and killed a series of young girls were considering their verdict;

j) and that the President of Afghanistan had decreed the death penalty for criminals who removed body parts from kidnapped children, while the Interior Minister of that country stated that several hundred children had been abducted in recent years in many cases to remove their body parts for sale overseas, despite the raising of the penalty for kidnapping a child from 15 to 20 years.

If Dow's novel is, then, an exposure of the social structures and practices that allow or even enable the wealthy to prey on the poor, the male on the female and the adult on the child, this pattern of predation is found almost everywhere and (to quote the title of a recent Women and Law in Southern Africa Research Trust publication from Botswana) there is *No Safe Place* for the most vulnerable members of the human race. Clearly, though, the screaming of the innocent emerges most often from among the wretched of the earth – *whether* the abuse comes from afar (e.g. as sex tourism *to* "Third World" countries or as the exportation of "Third World" girls to the sex rings of the wealthier societies), *or* from the more powerful local males; often within the home, the extended family, the community, or members of the upper echelons of the local society. Moreover, this form of predation tends to rely for its continuing functioning on networks, either international or local – networks that cut across borders and classes.

The enduring popularity of crime fiction may well testify to the "fascination of the abomination" (Conrad 50) for large numbers of readers and viewers, a fascination ranging from the genteel shudders engendered by Agatha Christie's British crime novels to the obvious appetite fed by the baroque violence and gore of television "police" series, or the intellectualised, existential depictions of crime and bloodshed in *noir* films. Crime fiction has also become a popular form of writing in southern Africa, as two recent MA studies by Chigidi and Mphahlele attest. One way of establishing Dow's un-frivolous, non-sensationalist authorial morality is through recognition of the close connection between her professional life as a human rights (and women's rights) activist, lawyer and High Court Judge in Botswana (of which she is the only female member); another lies in the consistency with which, in her three novels to date,[2] she assails abusive patriarchal practices in her society – as well as its deeper, ancient patriarchal *structure* – as the "original sin" or bedrock on which this and other forms of contemporary gender crimes rest.

The particular evil on which the focus falls in this, Dow's second novel, is the killing of so-called "hairless lambs" (prepubescent girls) for the purpose of brewing *dipheko* (known as *muti* in South Africa): the word meaning "'traditional strengthening medicines'" (*Screaming* 59). But like many (perhaps most?) crimes, it becomes a palimpsest of different stages and kinds of crime: as one good woman in the novel says, the case depicted here "isn't unique" in that "very few ritual-murder cases are [. . .] solved. Children, especially girls, disappear or die under very mysterious circumstances, and no-one's called to account. And when the villagers demand answers, we, the government, are the very ones who try to shut them up" (146).

Dow allows us to distinguish gradations of evil and involvement in this crime ranging (for example) from the relatively minor to the major: the minor contributors are those – usually intimidated and manipulated policemen or junior officers – who are caught between two kinds of overwhelming and superstitious fear (of the perpetrators' power, and of the victim's need for justice or vengeance)

---

2 These are *Far and Beyon'* (2001); *The Screaming of the Innocent* (2003); *Juggling Truths* (2004).

and who invariably end up assisting the cover-up, whereas the major criminals are the awe-inspiring and terrible "big men" who both crave the perverse sexual thrill of the ritual murder and require the manipulative power they believe it grants them. Dow carefully delineates and distinguishes between these different roles: the victim's mother asks the police officer who is manoeuvred into setting up an attempted cover-up of the murder: "'Why are you running away from the truth? Who are you protecting?'" (68), while a junior officer admits "'I just want to be transferred [. . .] These people [the perpetrators] are powerful: I don't want to end up dead or mad. I can't sleep at night; I can't eat'" (74). When the manipulated officer referred to above protests to his superior, the latter (the station commander) tells him: "'Detective Sergeant Senai, [. . .] listen to me carefully. [. . .] the child was killed by wild animals – *full stop!* If I want you to go and detect anything [. . .] I'll tell you!'"(74-75). At a later point in the novel, a young man makes a spot-on diagnosis of the killers: "'generally the killing's a male thing – men already successful wanting to go even higher: [. . .] an assistant minister wanting to be a full minister; a deputy headmaster wanting to be a headmaster; a businessman planning to expand his business [. . .]'" (168-169).

The victim's mother Molatsi never gets to identify or personally confront the big men, but she addresses the police on two occasions – first when,

> [t]he tired, anguished family [. . .] stood up to leave [the police station, and she . . .] looked back. [. . .] In a soft voice, she'd said, 'Man of government, as you go about your job, just remember: I haven't lost a goat, and my cow hasn't been hit by a car. My daughter was killed – by people who expected you'd do nothing about it.' (65)

And in a later, considerably harder tone when she says: "'She was killed for *muti; dipheko*; *ditlhare*: traditional medicine. [. . .] we all know it [. . .] The question is [. . .] Who are you protecting? You come here [to the village], telling us stories about lions. That's nonsense'" (68). But all that these minor men yearn for is a "transfer" (74) in order to get away from the crime that is haunting their lives, despite their merely peripheral role; they lack the courage or selflessness to resist either superstitious fear or open intimidation – as they would have to if they were to assist the victim's family.

The bereaved mother's cousin says roundly: "'Everybody knows it's big people who commit ritual murders, not small men with little influence'" (68), and the sophisticated lawyer Boitumelo later confirms this: "'ritual murders aren't committed by poor people'" (171). By building these remarks into her text at the level of gossip Dow demonstrates how embedded an evil the practice of ritual (child) murder is, and that in some way the conspiracy of silence allowing it to persist extends *throughout* this society: it remains a reality, she suggests, because it is mythologised (by most), instead of being addressed.

This structure of mythology within which the crime of ritual murder secretly flourishes extends beyond the superstitious awe aroused by the deed itself, Dow demonstrates. This is why the chilling, eery opening chapter shows the main plotter ogling and drooling at the sight of his happily playing future victim (a girl of eleven), yet he is simultaneously described with cutting sarcasm as a pillar of society; there *are* many rumours about the sources of Mister Disanka's success (5), but he remains, incontrovertibly, "*by all accounts*, *a good man*" (1; emphasis added). What is a good man, then? One who is very rich, prominent in local affairs and as prosperous in the choice of a discreet wife as of discreet mistresses, with a mother to help maintain the proper familial-political balance among them all (1-8).

Dow again plays on the word "man" when the chief criminal and his cohort choose a third co-conspirator, by articulating their idea of what "a *real man*" (their expression) is: it is one with "a hard heart, a heart of stone," who is "willing to do" what they call "the ultimate thing": taking part in the killing of "a hairless lamb" (21). A "lamb" that should have been nurtured and grown to maturity, who should have been able to have *heirs*, is to be slaughtered; yet, shockingly, the mutilators/murderers refer to this deed as "harvesting" (5).

In the village there must be a small man, poor enough to be cheaply bribed and intimidated into assisting the big men. Such a villager is found – and so strange are the workings of guilt and fear that for a number of years after *participating* in the murder he plays the role of the victim's mother's chief comforter in the village. He is described by all who know him (and this is, of course, yet another mythological stereotype) as a "dear old man" (54).[3] Dow in her own relentless detective tracking of the deeper sources and conditions permitting the single main crime or event (which is the focus of the simultaneous, but more superficial detective thriller structure of the text), constantly uncovers her society's underlying, malignant patriarchy: early in the novel the sarcastic narrative voice states that, to attain the hugely powerful and responsible position of a chief, "no training [is] required" and "there [is] neither an entry age nor an exit age," so

[3] Cf. the reference to him as a "sweet man" and a "good man" (118) and as "gentle" (177).

that "it [is] conceivable that a mad man could be a chief. And people existed who argued that quite a few mad men had indeed been chiefs" (10).

The "pillars" of this society (Dow [22] again sarcastically, actually uses the cliché) are represented by the four main conspirators to the murder (the fourth being an ambitious deputy minister who later becomes the Minister of Safety and Security – a further instance of Dow's corrosive sarcasm); these four form a male network or structure consisting of some of the most ruthless, corrupt and powerful men in this society.[4] But the novel does not contain only horror, gloom and fury; hence there is what may be termed a counter-network of those (not only, but mainly women) who oppose and resist the evil doings of the former group, although they are more dispersed and not all, not always, and not all *knowingly*, interlinked. The figure around whom most of the text's positive energies coalesce is a young woman, Amantle, who already has a history of standing up to the government's bullying. Significantly, this brave spirit was nurtured by a poor but caring family who chose her, the one most thirsty for knowledge although the youngest, and a girl, from among her many siblings, as the first and only one of their family to be sent to school.[5] This family's cooperation and unselfish sacrifice and fostering attitude also constitute a network (26-27; 34-35) – but an admirable one.

The main or most visible counter-network (to the conspirators') also centres on Amantle – in the novel, two of her female lawyer friends unashamedly identify its unifying ideals as those of "justice and truth" (132, 203). It is unsurprising that Amantle remains the central figure, in fact the true leader of this "movement": her own modest self-assessment is that "amazing things tended to happen to her," but the narrator adds that she never ran away from such strange occurrences "as most people would: she became intrigued and involved" (101). Like most fictional female detectives, Amantle is feisty – she is *not* "obedient" (90)

---

4 See p. 14 ("he could trust the headmaster to look the other way") and p. 20 ("Mr Disanka had long viewed Mr Sebaki as being a potential partner"). The influence of the rapist "witchdoctor" (who "fathered" Neo on Molatsi, her mother) *and* the predatory imaginings of her main murderer, are framed in the same language of entrapment, hunting and prey which echoes eerily in the little girls' two skipping songs quoted on pp. 5 and 7.

5 Dow subtly contrasts this truly *loved* girl-child (Amantle, "the baby of the family" [27]) with the merely spoilt, supposedly favourite girl-child of Disanka the chief criminal – known as "Debaby" from being her "Daddy's baby" (4). Amantle's father is a clearly benign, gentle yet strong parental figure, as generous and progressive (despite the family's poverty) as her mother and siblings are.

or: not burdened with awe of "superiors" or males; "relentlessly articulate" (89) and an excellent "networker" (103) – in other words, someone around whom people rally, since she inspires trust and earns affection. Between Amantle and her friend and lawyer Boitumelo, they win over another brilliant young woman lawyer, Naledi, to their cause, as well as Amantle's fellow voluntary worker, a young man who is her friend, Daniel – another young volunteer worker who helps them, and who has his heart and his head in the right place. But this group of educated, younger people have the advantage of the groundwork laid earlier by the courage and the refusal to be intimidated (by authorities) of the villagers among whom Neo's (the victim's) mother lives.

Another figure who has no actual links of cooperation with Amantle's friends, but who is in many ways a more matronly version of the same spirit, is Mrs Molapo – as Director of the Organisation for National Service (which is here a *social* service), she is fearless in raising challenging questions to (and in questioning the bona fides) of the group of powerful male government officials among whom she is the most junior and only female member. It is Neo's mother's, and Amantle's and Mrs Molapo's still unanswered, and (in this patriarchal context) unanswerable questions that lucidly echo and amplify the screaming of the innocent victim – in contrast with those who can or attempt to silence them. Two other echoes, one muffled, and one articulated just too late, *would have* swollen the outcry against the crime to sufficient strength. The eyewitness (participant's) account of the old man in the village is delivered to Amantle and her friends just (and only) *after* the bloodstained and rediscovered clothes of the victim – containing the only provable evidence of the perpetrators' participation in the murder – have been returned to the police (since the minister, who had actually been involved in the killing, had in a public statement "guaranteed" a "proper" investigation this time). The old man after this confession commits suicide – to silence the screams of his conscience that have made his life a horror ever since he took part in the crime. Another crucial witness, the daughter of the main perpetrator (a young woman who had, as a girl, detected her father's involvement in the crime), continues to prop up the façade of the respected father whom she actually knows to be a child mutilator and murderer, and from whose home she herself has fled. Yet she refuses to cooperate with Amantle's group when they sense that she has important secret knowledge.[6]

6 Interestingly, as a young girl she "plays detective" to uncover her father's and his co-conspirators' crime of ritual murder of a girl; the torch she had lent her father, which has blood on it afterwards, she cleans but keeps as a ghoulish memento of

In conclusion one might contrast two images featured close to the end of the text: that of the "thin waist" of the victim's grieving mother, versus the "large" size of the murderous Minister: the latter "clearly someone who ate well and often" (196, 197),[7] we are told. The crime has been "privately solved" and the criminals "exposed" to an inner group, but the bitter sarcasm of the end – which ensures yet another cover-up – demonstrates that if society is unjustly – one might say criminally – constituted, evil prevails; crime succeeds; innocents' screams are silenced and those who uncover the truth are unable to exact punishment or make a public exposure of the perpetrators' guilt. Yet, Dow's text itself constitutes a political act by amplifying the innocent's screams through its unflinching facing of one of the most awful aspects of her society – and by detecting and exposing those who at this stage are still both escaping justice *and* ruling the roost.

The "naked newborn babe" of pity is aroused in any sensitive reader by the horror of the deed – a pity that is enjoined to transform itself into an avenging angel "striding the blast" – to appropriate the anguished words of Shakespeare's Macbeth (1.7.21-22) – another murderer of innocence. We do need the courage to *use* fury and outrage to tackle the real horrors of our world, transforming sorrow into an indomitable determination to champion and protect the vulnerable and the innocent from the predations of the gruesomely selfish abusers of power. In writing a text like *The Screaming of the Innocent*, Unity Dow has not only described the work of characters who can be described as women warriors, but has herself done what Maria Pia Lara urges feminist reformers to do, by

> entering into the convoluted, interlarded language of public life with illocutionary force, with such creative rhetorical power and non-

---

his crime and her consequent rejection of him – without shining light on the crime by exposing her father. Even though she now hates him, the patriarchal myth of the protective father as mainstay of the family is still too powerful for her. She, too, has been "spoilt" (if in a somewhat different way from her younger sister, "De baby"), and lives in a complicated state of depression, emotional confusion, and guilt.

7 Cf. Disanka's (the main perpetrator's) butchery business and the way his daughter surreally associates the blood of the near-raw liver that he likes to eat, seen dripping down his chin, with the blood and the bits of flesh of the victim-girl which she saw him and his co-conspirators bringing home to share out.

institutionalized resources that one's own and other's identities seem to require a reconstructed narrative of the social, one that is coded in much more democratic, egalitarian and humanitarian terms. (136)

Works Cited

Bambara, Toni Cade. *These Bones Are Not My Child*. First publ. in the U.S.A. by Pantheon (Random House), 1999. New York: Vintage, 2000.

Chigidi W. L. "The emergence and development of the Shona detective story as a fictional genre in Zimbabwean literature." MA thesis University of South Africa, 1997.

Conrad, Joseph. *Heart of Darkness*. *Youth, Heart of Darkness, The End of the Tether*. London: Dent, 1902.

Dow, Unity. *Far and Beyon'*. Melbourne: Spinifex, 2001.

___. *Juggling Truths*. Cape Town: Double Storey (Juta), 2004.

___. *The Screaming of the Innocent*. First publ. in Australia by Spinifex, Victoria, 2001. Cape Town: Double Storey (Juta), 2003.

Lara, Maria Pia. *Moral Textures: Feminist Narratives in the Public Sphere*. Cambridge: Polity Press (in association with Blackwell), 1998.

Mphahlele, L. L. "The Detective Novel In Northern Sotho: A Comparative Study." MA thesis University of South Africa, 1989.

Rankin, Ian. *Dead Souls*. London: St Martin's, 1997.

Shakespeare, William. *Macbeth*. *Complete Works*. Ed. P. Alexander, London and Glasgow: Collins, 1951.

Women and Law in Southern Africa Research Trust (Botswana). *No Safe Place: Incest and Defilement in Botswana*. Gaborone: Lightbooks (a division of Lentswe La Lesedi), 2000.

Two Late Apartheid-Era Novels: Balancing the Books in the South African Present

> Reconstructing the literary history of South Africa is first a matter of circulating between different corpuses, opening up libraries and removing books from their pre-assigned shelves.
>
> – Alain Ricard

Although hopefully not ultimately incompatible, the simultaneous imperatives of both deracialising the present and remembering the racist past of South African society are proving hard to reconcile. The Ricard quotation above (119), although functioning on a rather different scale than this article does, points to a way in which the juxtaposition of alternative accounts of the apartheid era – divided primarily by what race was made to mean during that period – can serve to throw some light on circumstances still (de)pressingly present in their social consequences, yet fast coming to seem encumbering, embarrassing and even uninteresting, especially to many younger South Africans. Two years ago, a colleague teaching at a campus a stone's throw from Sharpeville reported that hardly any of the undergraduate students in her predominantly black class could tell her what had happened there in 1960, or knew the date, while the Robben Island Museum Council chairman, Ahmed Kathrada (himself a prominent veteran of the island prison), was recently reported as having said that "collections like [the Mayibuye Archives on the island] were needed to educate young people who were largely ignorant of the struggle" (5). Many white South African students, again, complain of being burdened with the sins of earlier generations or declare themselves "force-fed" on (and embarrassed, or even bored by!) the topic of apartheid/racism. Even if thought of, more responsibly, as agonisingly shameful, brutal, or appalling, the apartheid past needs to be borne in or brought to mind in ways that will remind or teach South Africans of the different but linked lives lived under apartheid – our brutally divisive but commonly constitutive past – as a tool by means of which to make sense of the present. Works of literature, reflecting as they do social conditions refracted through individual experience, provide one of the most accessible means of educating younger readers concerning the conditions of earlier periods.

A poem from the second (British) colonial era in South Africa (the initial colonisers were the Dutch) can serve to illustrate how profoundly embedded racism has been in the South African social structure since early colonial days. The sardonic speaker in a 1920s ballad-style poem by Thomas Pringle, a Scottish poet, observes how "Dutch *and* British *in a band* / Are come to rifle [rob; plunder] Cafferland" (the term used to refer to AmaXhosa regions at that time). My (added) emphases stress this poet's sense of whites/Europeans colluding against the racially different indigenes. Pretending complicity with the European settlers' plundering frenzy, the speaker in the poem asks sarcastically and rhetorically: "How can Dutch or English care / for Africans with woolly hair?" (Pringle 38). Over a century later, in the short lyric "Under Tracy's Folly, 1930," David Wright's poetic speaker recalls (as a child) visiting the ruins of Anglo-Boer War breastworks that would have been built for either Boers or British "by [the] native hand" of the black indigene over whose appropriated land Europeans and European settlers were warring, while the *further* persistence of racial subjugation is recorded in the last line, a recollection (by the white speaker) from a later time: "*our* Zulu gardener built a wall like that" (Wright 144-145; emphasis added). In a 1990 poem, again, Peter Horn mocks the willed amnesia of many white South Africans concerning apartheid injustice and atrocities: "Somewhere there must have been a past / but we don't seem able to remember it." The poem concludes in a stanza reading: "So far we have not been able / to ascertain what crimes we are supposed / to have committed / if any: there are only vague rumours" (249-250). Instances of "denialism" still persisting in response to the hearings of the Truth and Reconciliation Commission's hearings confirm Horn's sarcastic mockery.

Although white poets like those quoted above bear witness to the injustices and crimes practised in the name of supposedly valid racial distinctions over so many decades of South African history (and reflected in literary texts), there was formerly a *relative* dearth of accessible black voices in the literary writings analysing or depicting racism in South Africa. The reasons for this – such as deliberate silencing, political persecution, inadequate access to education, lack of publication opportunities and of adequate encouragement (from the literary establishment) – are obvious. Texts by black theorists from elsewhere (like Fanon's) used to be banned in South Africa. That ban betrayed the apartheid practitioners' fear of the power of analysis (applied to local racist practices) and of those exhortations to action – particularly, to violent resistance – contained in the Fanonian and other texts (notably in *The Wretched of the Earth* of 1967). Analyses of the virulence and persistence of racism remain pertinent under South African conditions, where widely differing social, political and psychic histories of various peoples need to be respected and/or resuscitated *whilst* appropriate reconciliatory practices, policies and philosophies need to be developed for the good of all.

Comments and pronouncements by non-South African black theorists of race (such as Fanon, Cabral, Du Bois and more recent analysts), although made in different geographical and political contexts, cast useful light on local quandaries and agonies. In the re-issue of *'There Ain't No Black in the Union Jack': The Cultural Policies of Race and Nation*, Paul Gilroy expresses recognition both of the "ideological work" that goes into making "signifiers" of racial categories and of the (resistant) "struggle that determines which definition of 'race' will prevail" (39), while Stuart Hall stresses his own sense of Gramscian theory as "one of the most theoretically fruitful [. . .] sources of new ideas, paradigms and perspectives in the contemporary studies of racially structured social phenomena" ("Gramsci's Relevance" 440). Whilst recognising the importance of all these (and other) theorists' work, the present article holds out for the educative value rendered by the vicarious immediacy of depicted individual experiences of large social patterns (such as apartheid) – *experienced* conditions of which literary texts are perhaps the most complex and vivid renditions. The two novels on which this essay mainly focuses render intelligible the racist social edifice constructed by apartheid's "architects" (H. F. Verwoerd was notoriously known as such an "architect"). At the same time they provide insights that preclude any facile use of shallow multicultural ideas in the South African context. In his most recent text, *After Empire*, Gilroy (recalling Du Bois) warns against "underestimating" the damage done to "notions of human fellowship and solidarity" and emphasises that the "racial order" of the present "cannot be undone by fiat, by charity, or by goodwill" (38). The public debate in South Africa in 2005 oscillates between constant accusations of "playing the race card" (made against public commentators reiterating apartheid's harms and the consequent continuing necessity of restitution imperatives) and as many remarkably premature celebrations of the supposed defeat or disappearance of racism from this society. Both "African humanism" (or *ubuntu*) and "Western humanism" are used as rallying cries that are unmistakably (verbally and conceptually) marked by forms of racial exclusivity and sectarianism in their very terminology – despite the human inclusivity they also strive to imply. As Aldon L. Nielsen has noted, "our language is the body that carries the virus of racism" (12).

While in South Africa the explicit discourse of race will necessarily persist alongside the multiple, newly deligitimised and nowadays more carefully disguised, muted, or "privatised" expressions of racism, the often invidious but historically embedded links between notions of race and of identity – of racial or racist identity; identities that are racially conceived – constitute an inescapable social, political and psychic *problematique*. Enrique Dussel's description of euro-centric racism and its role in colonialist subjugation as "an ideological construct which deforms world history" (10) is accurate and nowhere more apparent than it has been in South Africa. Yet Fanon himself – who uses the term "nationhood" for a decolonised, deracialised, geographically located identity – warned in 1961 of the pendulum swing of racism, writing in "The Pitfalls of National Consciousness" of the aftereffects of subjugation when "the nation is passed over for the race, and the tribe is preferred to the state." This process he labelled "retrogression" (119). In the revised edition of *Between Camps: Nations, Cultures and the Allure of Race*, Paul Gilroy echoes Fanon's point: "the shortcuts into solidarity that race affords," he writes, "look especially attractive in the aftershocks of injustice and victimage" (xi). Even though power has irrevocably changed hands in South Africa, there are worrying signs of racial encampments being re-established or re-entrenched. This is especially (and disquietingly) obvious in certain white Afrikaner circles, persistently ideologising what they claim is "Afrikaner culture" in proclamations containing either subtle undertones or glaringly militant expressions of racism – while old antagonistically mustered racial categories of "coloured" and "African"[1] re-emerge as dangerous tensions even within the Western Cape provincial legislature and the governmental practices of the ruling African National Congress, as they do in disputes about local housing allocation for the poor and formerly dispossessed.

In her 1997 article "Identity in the making," a South African educational authority, Mala Singh, acknowledged that "with all its contradictions, apartheid was a powerful allocator of identity" (120). In other words, the legislation and power practices of the state established or confirmed affiliations that have not disappeared with the cancellation of those laws or the changes in government since 1994. As Singh says: "we will have to engage with the sedimentation of previous dispensations and debates about identity" (121). Balibar posits that

---

1 Black South Africans, members of Bantu cultures, are commonly termed "Africans," whereas "Coloured" (not always capitalised) is a more contentious term, since it was devised in apartheid South Africa as a convenient "catch-all" categorisation of those South Africans who are neither "black" nor white, but the offspring of cross-racial unions, or descendants of the aboriginal Khoisan peoples or of those enslaved Asians that were brought here from India and Malaysia. A majority of "coloured" South Africans lives in the Western Cape region.

"there are no identities, only identifications" (187), however, identifications (whether chosen or imposed) are no less powerful in effect for their being recognised as reifications or strategic alignments. The pulling power – as well as the evanescence – of identifications is noted in an eloquent (cited) passage by J. Souter: "ambiguous and cross-corporal cohabitations," she writes, "they unsettle the I" (qtd. in Hall and du Gay 6). Souter's description gives expression to the inescapable *uncanniness* of identifications – to the way racial identifications, for instance, can be slapped on an individual at any moment as an insult – or as a powerfully persuasive exhortation to solidarity. These functions of racial and racist discourse have by no means disappeared in South Africa – hence, examining some of the ways in which they were used during the late apartheid years (as illustrated in the chosen novels) can prove instructive to those grappling with what Mala Singh describes as "the question of reshaping identity in all its different dimensions [as] inextricably tied to the struggle to realise social and economic justice and equality for all the citizens of the country [South Africa]" (123).

Predictably, South African literary critics have been drawn into the local transformation and identity debates with all their racial over- and undertones. A voice of especial authority is and has been that of the writer and academic Njabulo Ndebele (at present rector of the University of Cape Town):

> Standing between [black and white] is a chasm of engineered ignorance, misunderstanding, division, illusion and hostility. It highlights the national tragedy of people who have lived long together, but could do no better than acknowledge only their differences. They have done so with such passion as would suggest that perhaps they sensed something in common between them, which neither of them was prepared to acknowledge. ("Liberation" 22)

Ndebele made this comment fifteen years ago, but its substance is reiterated by Leon de Kock in his editorial introduction to the recent collection titled *South Africa in the Global Imaginary*: "these objects of culture," he writes of the various cultural-linguistic products of the region, "have seldom been aware of each other, despite their geographic contiguity" (De Kock, introduction 1). De Kock proposes the trope of a "seam" as fitting for what he terms "the crisis of inscription in South African writing following colonisation" – in his view, this image of a seam functions in an appropriately paradoxical fashion to register simultaneously "the effort of suturing the incommensurate" and the existence of the (incommensurate) "gap" that such writing attempts to bridge, or to coexist with (11). If the Ndebele quotation above highlights the "chasm" between race-cultures in South Africa and De Kock advances the "seam" metaphor, Stephen Gray (in an earlier assessment) thought to close the local cultural-racial divide (at least in the realm of thought) – daringly, or by sleight of mind! – by defining the divide *itself* as the central, shared property or what he refers to as the South African literary-cultural "system": "our system," he declared, "is not divided, but it is about division. That is our common heritage, and comparisons may begin with confidence only from that common point" (21). The position most adequate to the urgencies of the South African position, however, is perhaps that which Michael Chapman advanced in an essay concerned with the writing of literary history. Chapman, a highly prolific and influential critic, literary historian and anthologist, emphasises the necessity of "an ethical base" – both authors and critics are regarded by him as participants in "a social activity concerned with justice." His statement of the point that "[literary] exploration proceeds according to a dialectical relation of past significance to present meaning" is especially relevant to the analysis presented in this essay ("Writing" 42).

Other local critical positions range from those focusing comments on what they see as an explicit and fairly simplistic intention in apartheid-era writers wishing to produce texts directly contributing to political liberation (e.g. Carusi 97; Oliphant 234), to those criticising the persistent "realism" of (black) South African writing of that period (e.g. Nkosi "Postmodernism" 77; Parry 104) and others striving for a balanced "examin[ation of] the relation between ethical and aesthetic questions" (Attridge and Jolly 2; compare Attwell 154 and Bethlehem 97). My own approach to the novels I discuss in this piece is to consider them primarily but not exclusively as two examples of originary myths – a perspective that I have also employed, explicitly and implicitly, in two earlier articles on more recent South African texts ("South African Novelists" and "Adapting the National Imaginary"). The present article may also be contrasted with a recent essay in which I have criticised the racial characterisation of (particularly) black South Africans in the apartheid-era and post-apartheid texts of J. M. Coetzee, whose representations of South Africa have been given compelling but disquieting force by his international (and South African) fame as an authoritative painter of local social "realities" ("'Racial' Characterisation").

Achebe reminds us that "*stories create people create stories*" (Achebe 162; emphasis original) – a succinct and vivid articulation of the point that Kath Woodward phrases more ordinarily, as follows: "vital elements in the construction of national identities relate to myths of origins" (155). Achebe's centralisation of the role of novels as modern myths of origin and identity for human groups parallels Benedict Anderson's well-known emphasis on the function of novels in the establishment particularly of Western democracies. Whether such texts can function as powerfully in multilingual postcolonial societies (like South Africa) with low literacy rates (and in view of the preponderance of cheaper, more popular forms of culture) is a moot point. For if "the written text is a social situation [. . .] exist[ing] in the participation of [. . .] writers *and readers,*" as Ashcroft has rightly observed (Ashcroft 59; emphasis added), both critics and commentators need to concern themselves with texts as much as with their accessibility in the public domain. The two novels discussed here may, however, be considered as fairly closely commensurate with the flood of "border" (i.e. border war) stories written in South Africa by white (especially Afrikaans) authors, many of them former young conscripts, and with the less abundant but significant and more recent presence of texts concerned with the armed struggles of the A.N.C./M.K.[2] At the same time it is worth noting that the experiences of white conscripts and of mostly black militants, and the social and political contexts of these undertakings, are still strongly present in public discourse in South Africa, at all social levels.

Both the novels under examination here can hence be approached in the recognition that "narrative identity is" – as Maureen Whitebrook puts it – "simultaneously subjective and intersubjective," involving "answerability and responsibility and the capacity for negotiation" (10). In attempting to entangle rather than merely to juxtapose the two chosen novels with each other, my aim is to respond to both texts not only as vivid documentations of individual lives, particular racial groups' experiences, or of a specific period in South African history, but to pay attention to something that was perhaps insufficiently recognised at the time of their publication (Langa's in the later eighties; Galgut's at the beginning of the nineties) – a reaching out for understanding to what I believe was in the first place a wider *South African* audience (rather than for international fame). Neither author engages in the gestures of international literary "high culture" and both writers rely extensively on readers' local knowledge – however, in making this point I am alluding not so much to details of style as to the tonal qualities of lament that predominate in Galgut's, and of questioning

2 The armed wing of the African National Congress, *Umkhonto we Sizwe*, was known as MK. Examples of texts depicting its activities are Serote's *Scatter the Ashes and Go* and Nkosi's *Underground People* (both 2002).

exhortations that colour Langa's text (respectively). This point links with the idea of the function of novels as foundation myths, because in the local context the bitterness of the experienced situation at the time of the novels' setting had to be acknowledged simultaneously with the urgent imperative to move into a "better time," one that would not come easily or automatically. These texts, I would propose, depict the dreary or anguishing past as bedrock, an undeniable presence as much as an unlikely, unpromising foundation on which the edifice of what came to be rather facilely termed "the new South Africa" had to be erected. In studying texts of this kind – works of considerable but understated literary merit and of great social relevance, but overshadowed at the time of their publication and subsequently by the (ironically!) almost exclusively white-authored, internationally prize-winning texts of authors such as Brink, Gordimer and Coetzee – one is engaging in a type of restitution. For not only is the South African historical, sociopolitical and literary-cultural canvas shown to be larger and more varied (than it would seem by limiting study to the "big names"), but the lived reality of the bad time from which many South Africans have made some advance is reviewed as both a past to and still a presence in wherever "we" (South Africans) are now.

Neither Langa's nor Galgut's text attracted much critical attention at the time of their publication (or subsequently); there is, however, a 1998 essay on gay (male) writing by Michiel Heyns in which Galgut's novel is one of the two foregrounded texts and a 1995 article on Langa's, by Jabulani Mkhize. I engage with these critical writings in what follows on the assumption that reviewing such indicators of the two novels' reception (from my present-day perspective) should also form part of any argument concerning the usefulness of the texts in the recuperative, investigative task/s of assessing cultural and racial identities "available" in South Africa then and now – eleven years into a democratic dispensation.

Mkhize's account, while contextualised by his recognition of the contribution writers felt compelled to make to the liberation struggle against the apartheid state, construes Langa's novelistic aim as that of "winning ideological assent" from his readers (53, point repeated on 54) – only to castigate the author, eventually, for being "at odds with the democratic character that a collective programme of political action is supposed to uphold," because of the text's "central focus [in Mkhize's view] on an individual character" (57). In my own view, most of the faults Mkhize finds with the text stem from his own ascription to it of various rigidly and ideologically defined goals – which, when the novel is found not to fulfil them, are taken as the proof of its (ideological *and* aesthetic) failure. Much of Mkhize's dissatisfaction with Langa's novel is based on the novelist's own declaration in a 1989 newspaper piece that he wanted to "show the human face of the ANC" – in order to counter the South African government's propagandist description of the Movement's fighters as "terrorists" (qtd. in Mkhize 53-54). It is his reading of *this* statement that ties Mkhize's argument about Langa's novel into something of a knot, I believe. This critic's insistence on reading Langa's text as "counter hegemonic" *yet* "ideological" (terms used over and over on p. 54 and elsewhere) overlooks what seems to be the clear meaning of Langa's stated intention – to *de*ideologise the characters, while recognising their contribution to a political and military struggle – or their failures. It would be my contention that this text would have held little interest for present-day readers, except as a documentary example of literary propaganda, if it had striven primarily to fulfill Mkhize's prescriptive insistence on what he calls "the text's ideological function" (60).

I would refute several of Mkhize's charges against aspects of Langa's novel, from the text itself – such as the critic's claim that the young man Mbongeni, who is in fact referred to in Langa's novel as a "monstrosity," a traitor and one of the "serpents" who are "in league with the regime" (*Rainbow* 130; 173; 174), is given "apparently [authorial] sympathetic depiction" (Mkhize 57). Nor is it to my mind valid to say of the text that it has a "central" focus on Khetiwe (a young woman, sister to Mbongeni but politically at odds with him) and that her "heroine's consciousness is inflated" (Mkhize 57; 59) – since Khetiwe, Mbongeni and a third sibling, Thokozani, in fact function (along with their elderly father, the government-deposed village chief Ndungane) as a microcosm of the range of political and personal choices made by black South Africans during the late apartheid years (along with several other foregrounded characters).

Taking issue with Langa's novel (or: with its supposed "ideological" profile), Mkhize contends that the novelist "downplay[s]" the Ndaweni villagers' "communal effort of resistance" (Mkhize 58). But that is not the primary focus of Langa's novel. Through (chief) Ndungane and others' eyes, we are shown (from the very first, to the near-final pages of the novel, as in many passages in between) that Ndaweni village has a proud and consistent history of resistance to many forms of oppression – applied directly by the apartheid government (at various times), or by proxy, by the sub-state organisation and militiamen of Inkatha (referred to in the novel as "the Brotherhood") and the co-opted (KwaZulu) homeland authorities.[3] Langa's novel is in fact unusual in the South African literary context in that, comparably to Lauretta Ngcobo's *And They Didn't Die*, it pays tribute to a *rural* community's resistance to apartheid. But Langa's canvas is a large one, and he depicts a wide spectrum of social settings and political roles – armed peasant resistance (*Rainbow* 1-2; 13; 52; 56-61; 91-92; 123-138; 157-176); political vengeance squads (9); industrial protest action (61-62); militant trade unionism (63-65; 77; 140; 191); student activism according to the principles of the Black Consciousness movement (71-75); ANC recruitment, and MK armed action (85-91; 101-102; 105-106; 108; 113-119; 157-168; 182-185; 187-191) as well as informal engagement with and exhortation of urban (township) blacks (39-40; 144-148; 191). Langa also notes a white (female) journalist's contribution to the struggle (151-155), contrasted with Mbongeni's shamefully selfish pursuit of fame and eventual betrayal of his family and his people. Mbongeni's role as urbanised, luxury-loving (black) traitor is matched by the malicious and effectively destructive political role of the (understandably) martially embittered rural matron, MaCele. In between we are given glimpses of many, many "unorganised" black South Africans struggling to survive – cowed, resentful, apathetic, criminal, or merely head-down practical in their roles and lifestyles. In painting such a broad social and communal canvas, so much of which is not ideologically tinted, Langa's socio-political and psychic portrait is not only more "believable" and reliable than it would have been if it merely fulfilled the "objective ideological function" that Mkhize ascribes to it (60), but indeed an artistic achievement that can educate today's youth, in particular, about the political and personal choices made by the young (and some older) people during this (late apartheid) period. Langa's powerful, vivid depiction of black South Africans at a time of near despair, his delineation of the sacrificial courage of a minority and his recognition of the dreary squalor of townships and neglected, oppressed rural black areas can link this narrative with the achievements and failures of the present dispensation.

---

3 In what is widely thought of as a "balkanisation" strategy, the apartheid government had set up semi-independent "homelands" for various black cultural-ethnic groups, allowing "cooperative" leaders some authority. KwaZulu was one such homeland; in it, those conservative traditionalists who cooperated with the government in opposing resistance to apartheid and affiliation to the A.N.C. were united in an organisation named Inkatha. Intense and often bloody rivalry between members of Inkatha and the A.N.C. persists to this day in the province of KwaZulu-Natal.

Heyns's article (or its section on the Galgut novel) is more circumspect and carefully qualified than Mkhize's trenchant essay; however, in its emphasis on gay experience and political perspectives within the late eighties in South Africa, it too (to my mind) reveals some blind spots and predilections that are somewhat at odds with (in particular) Galgut's depiction of his central character. Patrick, the traumatised young man who is the focaliser of this text (far more than Khetiwe is in Langa's novel), does not in fact reveal a clearcut or unmistakable (gay) gender identity. Whilst Heyns initially notes – concerning Galgut's and another author's texts – "that in their very different ways, they do consider the white gay man as *white man* in a racially divided society, and thus suggest ways of positioning a gay agenda in a context with, as it were, other things on its mind" (Heyns 113), his use of the expression "gay agenda" foregrounds that particular idea as the ideology of the Galgut text (as Mkhize foregrounds a "democratic" political ideology for Langa's novel).

Heyns recognises Patrick's alienation from the "world of male [*macho*] camaraderie" represented by his father, brother and the South African army – in which he serves as conscript, at the time of the Namibian liberation struggle – and he appropriately cites Galgut's statement (in a contemporary newspaper interview) that he "see[s] apartheid in its entirety as a male mythology" (qtd. in Heyns 113). But Heyns's presentation of the novel's single physically homosexual encounter as a definitive reaching towards a gay identity – rather than as primarily a rejection of the *macho* soldiers' world – is questionable. So too is Heyns's assumption that, when Patrick tells his mother that he has been "in love" only "once," but did not know it "at the time" (Galgut, *Beautiful* 109), he must be referring to the fellow soldier, the thoroughly unprepossessing Lappies, with whom he had "fumbling sexual contact" (Heyns 114) on a single occasion. There is the less likely possibility that Patrick is referring to the rather pathetic "girlfriend" with whom he corresponded during his stint in the army ("on the border" – as white South African conscripts used to describe apartheid military duty in "South West Africa" [the later Namibia] and Angola), as well as the more likely reference to the close childhood relationship he had with a "coloured" farmworker's daughter on his maternal grandparents' farm in the Cape Province. Concerning this latter friendship, Patrick says: "I loved her as much as my age [eight to ten; the girl of roughly the same age] would allow" and he adds a poignant detail: "she was my first friend and I've not had another" (Galgut, *Beautiful* 33, 35) – the latter remark significantly including his army time, placing in perspective his "friendship" with Lappies.

Heyns does notice and acknowledge that "amongst the many male possibilities in the novel there are at least two, possibly three, that are potentially liberating" – appropriately listing both the young white South African Andrew Lovell who became a political activist in the Namibian liberation struggle and Godfrey Eichab, a Namibian, a SWAPO[4] organiser, but more contentiously he (Heyns) includes Patrick's fellow conscript Lappies (though qualified as a "more ambiguous [third, liberating] possibility") (Heyns 115) – even though Lappies was merely *as* timid (both sexually and ideologically) as Patrick himself. I do not, therefore, accept Heyns's suggestion, however carefully qualified at this point in his article, that to Patrick the choice of a gay gender identity presents itself as a viable or adequate alternative (to the white male brutalities around him and to his apathetic, despairing sense of alienation) at this or at any other point in the novel. Reviewing his army experience, Patrick calls Lappies "merely a companion"; he says that "he had ceased to be even that" after their awkward sexual contact (Galgut, *Beautiful* 112). Certainly there is much in the delineation of Patrick's character that fits a stereotypical pattern of the formation of male gay identity: as a boy he is recognised as exceptionally sensitive, uninterested in most "masculine" activities, repelled by his father but very close to his unhappily married mother. Yet there are many *more* markers identifying Patrick as a fairly typical white South African boy than as (potentially or actually) gay: his is indeed an identity struggle, but it is not primarily or importantly focused on the gender issues it raises, as I shall demonstrate more fully below. Particularly significant, too, is his eventual, muted, but politically and psychically significant break with his frivolous mother.

Heyns declares (if again in a faintly tentative formulation) that "for Patrick himself, the *primary liberation*, the one that is not mentioned at all or only by implication, would presumably be an acceptance of his sexual identity" (Heyns 116; emphasis added). The last three words make clear that in his view not only is Patrick's "identity" unmistakably gay, but "coming out" as a gay male is considered an adequate, even a salvific "liberation" for the damaged, troubled young man.

The fairly assertive remarks quoted above from Heyns's article are succeeded by several demurrals ("But [. . .] only [. . .] only [. . .] at least [. . .] whereas [. . .] if [. . .] also [. . .] but" and a final "perhaps" [Heyns 116-117]). He concludes

4 SWAPO, the South West African People's Organisation, was the principal liberation organisation fighting for Namibian independence from South African political and military control.

that "Perhaps what Galgut's novel most effectively dramatises is the perplexity of the white male homosexual in South Africa, who cannot allow himself even the luxury of a struggle for his own liberation" (Heyns 117). This sentence, which opens Heyns's final paragraph on this text, nevertheless suggests that he reads Galgut's novel's (and perhaps its author's) major albeit unacknowledgeable preoccupation as the difficulty of acknowledging a gay male identity within a highly *macho* white culture. Although I agree that "perplexity" is an appropriate description of Patrick's frame of mind, I read its main cause differently, as I shall outline below, before returning to Langa's text.

Galgut prefaces his novel with a brief extract from the Sophocles play *Ajax*, an excerpt in which the attitude of being "*careful* / With every moment, every sight" (emphasis added) is contrasted with the unthinking rashness represented by "warrior stars and furious men" (qtd. as motto in *Beautiful* n. pag.). What is at stake in maintaining (with difficulty, in the face of dominant aggressions) one's sense of "care" towards life is worthwhile existence itself, this extract makes clear. The quotation is carefully chosen and well placed. Galgut's central character and focaliser, Patrick, is a young white South African, a former conscript (of the apartheid army) who served in "South West Africa" against Namibian freedom fighters. After the death in action of his only friend there, Lappies, Patrick suffers a severe nervous breakdown and is (honourably) discharged from the army, but still suffers from post-traumatic stress disorder, making him dependent on medication.

It is well known that white South African conscripts as well as Permanent Force soldiers suffered a high rate of war traumatisation. Despite all the years of apartheid indoctrination and the particular justifications of the military incursions into neighbouring states, the general (largely race-based) injustice as well as particular atrocities involved caused many (young) men to break down, as Patrick does. "Border war" experiences resulted in the writing of a great many "border stories"; as mentioned above, most of these were written in Afrikaans.[5] In a late nineties essay, Njabulo Ndebele argued that "English-speaking [white] South Africans have yet to acknowledge their willing compliance, by developing their own particular version of oppression, in the oppression of black people" (Ndebele, "Memory" 27). Galgut's low-key text had by then, I believe, quietly attempted to address exactly that point, although the novelist also subtly

5 Mark Behr's well known *The Smell of Apples*, which touches on an Afrikaans conscript's "border war" experiences, was translated into English by the author from the original Afrikaans.

emphasises that the South African "border wars" of the late eighties are yet another example of whites' colluding against blacks – as Pringle's early poem put it, of "Dutch and British in a band / Are come to rifle Cafferland" (Pringle 38). For although Patrick's father is a wealthy English-speaking businessman, his mother is an anglicised Afrikaner and his formative experiences are presented as ranging between childhood visits to his dour Afrikaner grandparents' farm and, at home, his humiliating failures to join in his *macho* father's and brother's sporting and hunting escapades.

Patrick is a self-conscious, timid and vulnerable child born into a brutalising environment, both domestically and socio-politically. He is not presented as an appealing personality, even though he is certainly pitiable – more "pathetic," though, than dissident in any principled way from the brutal codes of the dominant males he encounters at home and in the army. Patrick's alliances with his mother (at home) and with Lappies (his fellow conscript, in the army) are examples rather of shared weakness than of shared values. From the novel's strange title one senses that something in Patrick has gone awry, has been twisted away from what is wholesome. The obscure symbolism begins to clarify as we are told that Patrick on a return visit to his now widowed grandmother's farm finds the cries of slaughtered pigs "hideous," whereas as a youngster he considered them "beautiful." This strange comment seems to indicate Patrick's – or Galgut's – belief that childhood innocence can matter-of-factly accept deeds of killing for survival purposes, even in play, whereas in his broken young adulthood Patrick associates pig-sticking with the ugliness of the war deaths he has caused and witnessed. Moreover, he seems to associate himself, more in a demeaning than a morally empathetic way, with the creature being so efficiently slaughtered – a weak, ugly victim to be consumed for others' benefit.

Galgut deftly indicates Patrick's implicated position in the rural racial economy represented by his Afrikaner grandmother's farm. His cooptation into (or, as Ndebele puts it in the above quotation: "compliance [. . .] in the oppression of black people" [Ndebele, "Memory" 27]) is shown not only in his *not* refusing to serve in the apartheid army (as the young [white] members of the End Conscription Campaign in South Africa, for instance, did do), but depicted as a tendency stemming from his early childhood. When his affectionate and cheerful (though intermittent) farm relationship with a little "coloured" girl – the one really warm and happy, uncomplicatedly loving alliance of Patrick's life, a pre-puberty friendship – ventures into childish sexual exploration, a Calvinist and apartheid-induced taboo kicks in as a sudden revulsion. To cover up and protect himself from the shared guilt and fear of punishment he experiences, Patrick resorts to brutal and racist bullying of his little friend. He threatens, not only to "get [her] into big trouble," but warns her that he will get his *oupa* (the Afrikaans word for grandfather emphasising the old man's patriarchal status and land ownership) to throw "out" her farm labourer father (i.e., evict their whole family from the farm by firing the girl's father from his job there). The point is added that Patrick "never played with her again" (*Beautiful* 35). The lasting and tragic effect of this rupture is registered when the adult Patrick tells us that "she was my first friend and I've not had another," although he had "loved her as much as [his] age would allow" (35; 33). At a childish level this is a primal apartheid experience, in a society where so many love and sex relationships "across the colour line" ended in the betrayal, intimidation and abandonment of black women by white men.[6] (Many white South Africans of the apartheid period played happily together with blacks as children, especially on farms, only to withdraw or to separate themselves into white enclaves in early adulthood.)

When Patrick's shallow-minded, now divorced mother (with whom he lives after his discharge from the army) takes a Namibian lover ("Professing not to notice he was black, she revered him solely because of it" [47]), it is Patrick who ends up respecting and loving this man, Godfrey Eichab, whereas his mother soon abandons her black lover for a distinctly racist, white Afrikaans farmer from South Africa – seemingly reverting to the social values inculcated by her (fairly standard) rural Afrikaner origins. Godfrey's passion for Patrick's mother is tempered by his recognition of her superficial moral and political feelings; he even slaps her during a quarrel, but is much cast down when she ends the relationship. Godfrey's effect on Patrick's life will be long-lasting, however. Although Patrick focuses more consciously on the assassinated Andrew Lovell[7] as a counter-example to himself and as an inspirational figure, it is through and along with the black Namibian Godfrey, who so generously and compassionately accepts the unhappy, disturbed young man (after all, a recent "enemy soldier"

---

6 Numerous South African novels – from early examples such as Richard Plomer's *Turbott Wolfe* (1925) and Bessie Head's *The Cardinals* (written 1960-1962, though only published in 1993) to very recent ones such as Zakes Mda's *The Madonna of Excelsior* (2002) treat the topic of love/sex between white and black in apartheid South Africa – relationships which were, notoriously, forbidden by law.

7 The figure of Andrew Lovell is probably based on the example of a young white Afrikaans man, Anton Lubowski, who became a leading SWAPO member and was the victim of political assassination in Namibia.

and killer!), that Patrick sees what it might have been like to make common cause *against* apartheid oppression (despite being a white man).

Patrick begins to recognise how selfless, courageous (and dangerous!) dedication to a land and its people (like Godfrey's, and Andrew Lovell's – even though the latter was not only white, but not a Namibian) is achieved and maintained – and how tellingly such commitment and hard-earned "belonging" contrasts with his own profound existential alienation. Although he remains to the end somewhat in limbo (emotionally as much as racially-politically), Patrick demonstrates the beginnings of a chosen disassociation from white racial hegemony. This happens when he is moved to awe by Lovell's political martyrdom; runs away from an ancient German who has returned to "South West Africa" to strengthen the white vote; deliberately shocks a white woman by telling her that his white mother and the black Godfrey are lovers; and when he hands out pamphlets (to whites) advertising a SWAPO rally that will also serve as Andrew Lovell's funeral. At the latter event, the way he has been accepted as co-worker with, almost a younger brother or son to the Namibian Godfrey, makes Patrick see the latter as "father[ly]" and "avuncular" (*Beautiful* 147) – movingly (but probably unconsciously), as a worthy alternative to his rich, insensitive white South African father. Although Patrick's emotional fragility propels him momentarily back into an attack of anxiety, depression and alienation, he has healed and grown sufficiently towards the close of the novel to criticise his mother for ending her relationship with Godfrey, realising that an "enormous" change has occurred in him (158; 159). Even though he is forced to return to apartheid South Africa in the company of his mother and her next (prospective) lover, the crassly *macho* and racist farmer Blaauw, Patrick has acquired sufficient moral and emotional strength to disaffiliate himself from her and her new relationship, announcing quietly that he has decided to go and live on his own (169).

Stuart Hall has made the point that "it is only through the relation to the other, [. . .] to precisely what it lacks, to what has been called its *constitutive outside* that the positive meaning of identity can be constructed" ("Who" 4; emphasis added). I would want to suggest by means of this article that students of South African literature, history and society need to engage in constant and conscious acts of *linking juxtaposition* as they deal with accounts of the apartheid past. Sentimentality and cynicism are opposite but twin dangers in retracting the bloodily and brutally divided routes by which the present political settlement was achieved, and the work of growing into a South African community treasuring cultural and spiritual connections more than divisions has only just begun.

Just as many young whites still need to break out of a racial cocoon (to a large extent maintained by means of economic privilege) in order to free themselves from racial crassness and complacency and to learn compassion and respect for their compatriots, young blacks can benefit by being shown the enormous weight of peer pressure and political indoctrination to which whites were subjected. Without a sense of the grievous harm inflicted by apartheid, whites can have no deep understanding of their society, whereas blanket villainy ascribed to whites, without distinguishing different degrees of compliance with or resistance to apartheid among them bodes ill for their future even in a democratic and therefore (at present) majoritarian black dispensation, while the black youth may also inadvertently trivialise the sufferings of earlier generations.[8] A white poet, Ingrid de Kok, emphasises the acts of "mourning, recovery and remembrance" (61) that are still required, while Njabulo Ndebele looks to the future "convergence" of the "stories of millions of those recently emerged from oppression" with "the story of the agony of the contemporary Afrikaner family" ("Memory" 25). The same critic has warned against the danger of "conviction without knowledge," and has seen a "pamphleteering" of the past (or the future!) in the texts South Africans study as unhealthy (Ndebele, "Against Pamphleteering" 142). One might "apply" these ideas in considering the educative, enlightening use to which texts like the two novels under discussion here may be put in order to create what I would term an *accessible otherness* for (particularly "post-apartheid") South Africans.

If Galgut renders accessible something of the "agony" of young white alienation during the late apartheid era, obscure (because not fully acknowledged) guilt, and a timidity about moving out of old racial zones (attitudes still present among many Afrikaners and English-speaking white South Africans, more than a decade after the supposed end of apartheid), it is in a text like Langa's that one finds a vivid, moving and convincing account of the growth towards an unshakeable (if at the time still unfulfilled) resolve among black South Africans in particular, determined to achieve the dignity of liberation from the humiliation of racial contempt and oppression. But Langa's black communities are not ideo-

---

8 In a recent interview, Nadine Gordimer mentioned how "people" [South Africans] tend to "forget" the past, or find it unimaginable, relating how in her presence the teenage son of the poet Mongane Wally Serote (who was deeply involved in the liberation struggle) asked his father (on the topic of the "pass" black South Africans were obliged by law to carry): "How feeble. Why didn't you just throw it *away*?" (320).

logically "purified"; there are complex tensions and many shades of feeling in his rendition of the lives of rural Ndaweni villagers and of the Durban city dwellers of Umlazi township. Langa's text, like Galgut's, gives prominent recognition to the formative, socialising influences of family life that, even when resisted or "left behind," continue to affect individual identities; this "family focus" (emphasising the role of parents and siblings in socialisation processes) is one of the strongest links between these two texts. In *A Rainbow on the Paper Sky* the benign patriarch Ndungane and his warm, strong wife Nomusa are revered but not feared by their three children, but, as in a majority of black South African families, the racist economy and apartheid pressures separate the family members. Like Galgut's text, Langa's has a youth focus – particularly on the three Ndungane children Mbongeni, Thokozani and Khetiwe (the latter the youngest, and the only daughter). While Ndungane (a chief deposed by the apartheid government for his politically resistant activities) continues to lead his rural community under persistent political pressure and even murderous attack, the three children lead entirely different and almost totally separate lives in the city (Durban). Mbongeni, a musician, becomes spoilt by success and is seduced by luxury, fame, sexual and alcoholic indulgence, eventually openly betraying his family as well as the liberation cause that they espouse. His decadence is briefly contrasted with the feisty courage of a white woman, a journalist with whom he has one of his numerous affairs (*Rainbow* 148-156). Mainly, though, Mbongeni is contrasted with his slightly younger brother Thokozani, his much younger sister Khetiwe, and other young black people.

Langa's novel is an unobtrusive, multilayered *bildungsroman*, especially in its portrayal of Thokozani and Khetiwe, both of whose growth towards a full moral-political awareness is lucidly yet subtly indicated, and illuminated by the narrator's charming humour and ethical seriousness. Thokozani is converted to fervently evangelical Christianity in his early days in the city – convincingly shown to be the emotional and moral shelter he uses to help him, a country boy, in dealing with the harsh pressures of apartheid city life. After an unfair arrest he loses his job, but is gradually politically conscientised through becoming active in a trade union. Refusing to betray colleagues who engineered the death of a brutal (black) bosses' spy at work, Thokozani is tortured and given a lengthy prison sentence – a dreadful and dehumanising experience that he barely survives. What we are shown in several other scenes – first, when he leads stranded black travellers on a night walk after the train they were on crashes in a storm, then when he insists that keeping a promise made to a former fellow-prisoner (since executed) is more urgent than alleviating his own exhaustion or hunger, and when he prevents a township mob from murdering a white man whose car has run over and injured a black schoolgirl – depicts Thokozani's gradual growth in strength as a leader – and the novel ends as he returns to his family subsequent to addressing a political rally after the death of his sister (at the hands of the state security forces) and his father's sentencing to lengthy incarceration on Robben Island. At the end he is the one who has taken up the cudgels of the struggle and who understands it as a humanisation process.

For her part, Khetiwe (who is much younger than her two brothers) leaves her parental home at the age of eight to go live with her father's sister (who runs a township shebeen) and to attend school in Durban. Dissatisfied with her bullying black headmaster's attitude, she finishes her studies privately and becomes a nurse, at this time beginning to mingle with the black student youth in Durban, idealistically imbued with the Black Consciousness ideas of the time. Aware of her political commitment, her first "boyfriend," the political activist and poet Mark Mboghozi, directs her to her hospital colleague, a young black woman doctor (Shelley), for formal recruitment into the (at the time banned) ANC. As balancing counterpart to the politically risk-taking youths, Langa at this point introduces Duma, a young man who grew up with Khetiwe's brothers in Ndaweni village, but who has since become a both menacing and bumbling, politically co-opted police officer.

In the latter part of the novel Langa depicts what in this article might be termed the other side of apartheid war and soldiering (in contrast with Galgut's portrayal of the government forces), focusing especially on the leader, Hugh, of a guerrilla group[9] that infiltrates the forest outside Ndaweni village, where they introduce sophisticated armaments and give military training (and agricultural assistance) to selected villagers. Hugh's (and his colleagues') idealistic and ideological enthusiasm and strict discipline are tempered by encounters with older leaders like (Khetiwe's father) Ndungane, as well as the ancient *inyanga* (herbal healer) Ndimande. The latter asks Hugh challenging questions about the way a post-liberation democratic government would deal with the high levels of criminality in South Africa – questions that remain pertinent today, and which confirm that Langa's vision in this text is more "careful" and much broader than anything a "correctly ideological" tract could convey, and that it has not lost rel-

9 The account in the novel is based on an actual episode during the period of armed resistance to and insurgency against apartheid oppression (a point Mkhize confirms in his article).

evance. In addition, the text convincingly depicts a sudden but deep love developing in the midst of danger, duty and secrecy between Khetiwe, who has returned to the village to run a clinic (with her doctor friend, Shelley), and the young guerrilla leader, Hugh.

The deaths of young people in this text occur because of military activity – Khetiwe's friend, the poet Mark, dies in a bombing raid on a neighbouring country where he was attending a cultural convention, while Khetiwe and Duma are shot when the guerrilla group's presence is betrayed by MaCele, a female villager with a valid but vindictive grudge against her husband (who is part of the armed resistance movement in the village). Ndungane is sent to Robben Island, imprisonment that at his age he will "not survive" (191). The alienated characters in Langa's text that are comparable to Patrick (in Galgut's 1991 novel) are Khetiwe's elder brother Mbongeni and the policeman Duma, who dies when shot by Khetiwe – not, as Mkhize avers in his article, because she is "trying to defend *herself* against the security forces" (59; emphasis added), since she might have escaped, but to warn and to protect Hugh and the other MK guerrillas, who are alerted by the sound of the shots and escape in time (*Rainbow* 191-192). Thokozani at the end of the text realises with great sadness that his musician brother Mbongeni "wasn't going to survive" (192) – whether he means that his irresponsibly decadent lifestyle will destroy him, or that his soul has been contaminated by his cooptation into the apartheid system, or even that he may incur "revolutionary justice," is unclear, but not finally significant. Those of the young people who do "survive" would include Mark (through his poetry and in Shelley's memory); Thokozani in his now established political and familial roles; the young MK commander Hugh (even though he has lost his beloved Khetiwe); Shelley and above all, Khetiwe. Even though her dead body is dangled by helicopter above the village as a brutal, terrorising warning against political resistance, the local people who loved her see in this that "their shrines had stretched to embrace the skies" (191). She becomes the new "rainbow" reassuring them of hope beyond the inundating deluge of apartheid – a suggestion confirmed by the depiction of her little niece, also named Khetiwe, Thokozani's daughter – at the very end of the text (192).

There are many other significant points of "comparable contrast" by means of which contemporary readers of these texts can trace the contours of apartheid's divisive socialisations and the way these resulted in black and white South Africans *seeing* their country differently and from opposed perspectives – such as the depictions of townships in the two novels (e.g. *Rainbow* 13; 17; 37 and

Beautiful 42; 54-55; 57-59) and also of landscape, or even ways of "relating to" the land – for example in Godfrey's "electrifying" touch of the desert sand in Namibia, and Patrick's and his mother's hill walk (*Beautiful* 86; 108-109), comparable with Khetiwe's and Hugh's intense and appreciative awareness of the forest and the river at Ndaweni in northern Kwazulu-Natal (*Rainbow* 113-114; 122-123). The links between and differences in racial visions, psychic and social identifications and political orientation in a comparison between the particular characters shown in the two novels (and the explicitly described or implied attitudes towards one another of various South African groups) have been touched on in the course of the preceding analysis. A central and saddening aspect of both texts is the contemporary reader's sense of the curtailed or thwarted dreams of most young South Africans who were subjected to the harshness and the hardening demands of the conditions of the time – whether they were black or white. Yet, and partly because of the martyr-heroes Khetiwe Ndungane (in Langa's novel) and Andrew Lovell (in Galgut's), there is also a sense of muted hope in both these texts, perhaps intensified by readers' hindsight from the perspective of the freer present. As the poet Mongane Serote wrote in his 1994 publication *Come and Hope with Me*, "we do not want any civil war," and "the seed of this hope is buried deep" (18; 19). In the eighties, the same poet (in his poem called "The Breezing Dawn of the New Day") had insisted both that "we keep the record" which is "the story of our country," and that "our national life / [. . .] must grow now" (140).

Maria Pia Lara, a Mexican philosopher, writes in a feminist context but in terms applicable to the racist fissures and tensions of South African society in the past and present, that "differences are an important part of what should be regarded as worthy" and that "solidarity enters here because it is through others that one can define one's own identities" (157).[10] Racism's virulence relies on an insistence that others' identities are reprehensible – hence racists desire to "write off" and to "wipe out" both those others whom they cannot bear to recognise, and their histories. This article concludes, hence, with the summarising suggestion that in the difficult task South Africans face, of accommodating one another not only politically, but socially and personally, texts like those discussed here are valuable aids. Simplistic demonisation of whites and contemptuous dismissal of blacks are attitudes implicitly rejected in both these texts –

---

10 Compare Fanon: "Many members of the mass of colonialists reveal themselves to be much, much nearer to the national struggle than certain sons of the nation" (116).

Galgut's novel "correcting" the first and Langa's the second named of these simplifications. A favourite line from a white poet's acknowledgement of complex engagement with and alternative to the many layers of white South African racism comes to mind: "put on the skin and look out" (Wilhelm 208). Novels like the two discussed in tandem in this paper make possible vivid glimpses into "our own otherness" to "emerging" South Africans in particular, whatever the racial or cultural perspective they read from, and enable non-South African readers to form a more complex and balanced impression of the country's tragic past. While Mongane (Wally) Serote's novel *To Every Birth Its Blood* (1981) may stand as the most magisterial, complex and searingly poetic rendering of South Africa under apartheid, more low-key versions of that system's effects have validity and both documentary and psychological value to work enlighteningly under the present "same-yet-different" conditions in this society.

To observe that literary studies involve and affect our perceptions of society, past and present, is not to reduce the study of literary texts to propaganda, but to recognise that accounts of familial, social, psychological and political life do not exist in airless aesthetic compartments. The two novels discussed here have power and relevance and spring from deep feelings of compassion and outrage – they are complex, demanding works of verbal art. Achebe says that "art is [. . .] an alternative in the imagination to the reality all around us" (qtd. in Jeyifo 11), while Peter Hallward observes that "what goes by the name of artistic or creative writing" continues to "open a fragile space of relational detachment and imaginative engagement" (334). Such a space allows us vicariously to participate in, and assess, ways and kinds of life different from our own, enlarging the imaginative space within which we exist. This article has attempted to indicate how, by means of juxtaposing particular writings, the compartments of present-day South Africa, and the various, often rigid compartmentalisations of race, may have alternatives played off "beside" them to give greater balance to our historical and social vision.

Works Cited

Adam, Ian, and Helen Tiffin, eds. *Past the Last Post: Theorizing Post-Colonialism and Post-Modernism*. New York: Harvester Wheatsheaf, 1991.

Achebe, Chinua. *Hopes and Impediments: Collected Essays*. New York: Doubleday, 1989.

___. "What Has Literature Got to Do With It?" *Hopes and Impediments*. By Achebe. 154-170.

Anderson, Benedict. *Imagined Communities: Reflections on the Origins and Spread of Nationalism*. London: Verso, 1983.

Ashcroft, Bill. *Post-Colonial Transformation*. London and New York: Routledge, 2001.

Attridge, Derek and Rosemary Jolly, eds. *Writing South Africa: Literature, Apartheid and Democracy, 1970-1995*. Cambridge: Cambridge UP, 1998.

Atwell, David. "The Experimental Turn in Black South African Writing." De Kock, Bethlehem, and Laden 154-179.

Balibar, Etienne. "Culture and Identity (Working Notes)." Rajchman 27-32.

Behr, Mark. *The Smell of Apples*. London: Abacus, 1996.

Bethlehem, Louise. "A Primary Need as Strong as Hunger: The Rhetoric of Urgency in South African Literary Culture under Apartheid." De Kock, Bethlehem, and Laden 94-116.

Boehmer, Elleke, Laura Chrisman, and Kenneth Parker, eds. *Altered State? Writing and South Africa.* Sydney and Mandelstrup: Dangaroo, 1994.

Carusi, Annamaria. "Post, Post and Post: Or Where is South African Literature in All This?" Adam and Tiffin 95-103.

Chapman, Michael. "Writing Literary History in Southern Africa." Smit, Van Wyk, and Wade 40-50

___, ed. *The New Century of South African Poetry*. Johannesburg: Ad. Donker / Jonathan Ball, 2002.

___, ed. *The Paperbook of South African English Poetry*. Johannesburg: Ad. Donker, 1986.

De Kok, Ingrid. "Cracked heirlooms: Memory on Exhibition." Nuttall and Coetzee 57-71.

___, Leon. Introduction. De Kock, Bethlehem, and Laden 1-13.

___, Louise Bethlehem, and Sonja Laden, eds. 2004. *South Africa in the Global Imaginary*. Pretoria: University of South Africa Press and Leijden: Koninklijke Bril, 1986.

Distiller, Natasha, and Melissa Steyn, eds. *Under Construction: 'Race' and Identity in South Africa Today*. Sandton: Heinemann, 2004.

Dussel, Enrique. *The Invention of the Americas: Eclipse of "the Other" and the Myth of Modernity*. New York: Continuum, 1995.

Fanon, Frantz. "The Pitfalls of National Consciousness." *The Wretched of the Earth*. Trans. Constance Farrington. Harmondsworth: Penguin, 1967. 119-165.

Gagiano, Annie. "South African Novelists and the Grand Narrative of Apartheid." *Journal of Language and Politics* 5.1 (2005): 97-109.

___. "Adapting the National Imaginary: Shifting Identities in Three Post-1994 South African Novels." *Journal of Southern African Studies* 30.4 (2004): 811-824.

___. "'Racial' Characterisation in the Apartheid-Period and Post-Apartheid Writings of J. M. Coetzee." Distiller and Steyn 38-49.

___. "Two Bad-Time Stories and a Song of Hope." *Literator* 23.3 (2004): 161-177.

Galgut, Damon. *The Beautiful Screaming of Pigs*. Reading: Abacus, 1991.

___. "An Extended Cry against Male Mythology." Interview with Jane Rosenthal. *Weekly Mail* 14-20 Aug. 1992: 34.

Gilroy, Paul. *After Empire: Melancholia or Convivial Culture*. Abington: Routledge, 2004.

___. *Between Camps: Nations, Cultures and the Allure of Race*. London: Routledge, 2000.

___. *'There Ain't No Black in the Union Jack': The Cultural Politics of Race and Nation*. Chicago: University of Chicago Press, 1991.

Gordimer, Nadine. Interview with Hermione Lee. Nasta 315-326.

Gray, Stephen. "Some Problems of Writing Historiography in Southern Africa." *Literator* 10.2 (1989): 16-24.

Hall, Stuart. "Who Needs Identity?" Introduction. Hall and Du Gay 1-17.

Hall, Stuart, and Paul Du Gay, eds. *Questions of Cultural Identity*. London: Sage, 1996.

Hall, Stuart. "Gramsci's Relevance for the Study of Race and Ethnicity." Morley and Chen 411-440.

Hallward, Peter. *Absolutely Postcolonial: Writing between the Singular and the Specific*. Manchester and New York: Manchester UP, 2001.

Head, Bessie. *The Cardinals, with Meditations and Short Stories*. Ed. M. J. Daymond. Cape Town: David Phillip, 1993.

Heyns, Michiel. "A Man's World: South African Gay Writing and the State of Emergency." Attridge and Jolly 108-122.

Horn, Peter. "Good Morning South Africa." Chapman 249-250.

Jeyifo, Biodun. "Literature and Conscientization: An Interview with Chinua Achebe." Jeyifo 3-19.

Jeyifo, Biodun, ed. *Contemporary Nigerian Literature: A Retrospective and Prospective Exploration*. Lagos: Nigeria Magazine, 1985.

Kathrada, Ahmed. "Journalist Boosts Mayibuye Struggle Archives." Comment *Cape Times* 26 May 2005: 5.

Langa, Mandla. "People Who Love, Live, Sing and Die." *New Nation* 29 Sept. – 5 Oct. 1989: 11.

___. *A Rainbow on the Paper Sky*. London: Kliptown, 1989.

Lara, Maria Pia. *Moral Textures: Feminist Narratives in the Public Sphere*. Cambridge: Polity, 1998.

Mda, Zakes. *The Madonna of Excelsior*. Oxford: Oxford UP, 2002.

Mkhize, Jabulani. "The Human Face of the Movement: Mandla Langa's *A Rainbow on the Paper Sky*." *Research in African Literatures* 26.1 (1995): 53-60.

Morley, Dave, and Kuan-Hsing Chen, eds. *Stuart Hall: Critical Dialogues in Cultural Studies*. London: Routledge, 1996.

Nasta, Susheila, ed. *Writing Across Worlds: Contemporary Writers Talk*. London/New York: Routledge, 2004.

Ndebele, Njabulo S. "Against Pamphleteering the Future." Ndebele, *Rediscovery* 133-144.

___. "Liberation and the Crisis of Culture." *Southern African Review of Books*, Feb. – May 1990: 22 – 23.

___. "Memory, Metaphor and the Triumph of Narrative." Nuttall and Coetzee19-28.

___. *Rediscovery of the Ordinary: Essays on South African Literature and Culture*. Johannesburg: COSAW, 1991.

Ngcobo, Lauretta. *And They Didn't Die*. Pietermaritzburg: Natal UP, 1999.

Nielsen, Aldon L. *Writing Between the Lines: Race and Intertextuality*. Athens and London: University of Georgia Press, 1994.

Nkosi, Lewis. *Underground People*. Cape Town: Kwela Books, 2002.

___. "Postmodernism and Black Writing in South Africa." Atwell and Jolly 75-90.

Nuttall, Sarah, and Carli Coetzee, eds. *Negotiating the Past: The Making of Memory in South Africa*. Cape Town: Oxford UP, 1998.

Oliphant, Andries W. "Past and Present: Literature and Freedom in South Africa." Oliphant, Delius and Meltzer, 2004: 233-239.

Oliphant, Andries W., Peter Delius, and Lalou Meltzer, eds. *Democracy X: Marking the Present, Re-Presenting the Past*. Pretoria: Unisa, 2004.

Parry, Benita. "Some Provisional Speculations on the Critique of 'Resistance Literature.'" Boehmer, Chrisman, and Parker, 1994. 11-24.

Plomer, Richard. *Turbott Wolfe*. London: Hogarth, 1925.

Pringle, Thomas. "The Honey-Bird and the Woodpecker." Chapman, *Paperbook* 37-39.

Rajchman, John, ed. *The Identity in Question*. New York: Routledge, 1995.

Ricard, Alain. *The Languages and Literatures of Africa: The Sands of Babel*. Trans. Naomi Morgan. Oxford: James Currey, 2004.

Serote, Mongane Wally. "The Breezing Dawn of the New Day." *Selected Poems*. Ed. M. V. Mzamane. Johannesburg: Ad. Donker, 1982. 138-141.

___. *Come and Hope with Me*. Cape Town and Johannesburg: David Philip, 1994.

___. *Scatter the Ashes and Go*. Braamfontein: Raven, 2002.

___. *To Every Birth its Blood*. Johannesburg: Ravan, 1981.

Singh, Mala. "Identity in the Making." *South African Journal of Philosophy* 16.3 (1997): 120-123.

Smit, Johannes A., Johan van Wyk, and Jean-Phillipe Wade, eds. *Rethinking South African Literary History*. Durban: Y Press, 1996.

Whitebrook, Maureen. *Identity, Narrative and Politics*. London and New York: Routledge, 2001.

Wilhelm, Peter. "With my Father in the Bar at Naboomspruit." Chapman, *Paperbook* 208-209.

Woodward, Kath. *Understanding Identity*. London: Arnold, 2002.

Wright, David. "Under Tracy's Folly, 1930." Chapman, *Paperbook* 144-145.

Mongane Serote's *To Every Birth Its Blood*: Painting the True Colours of Apartheid

Over the years to come as the system slowly withers away, reassessments of the literary representations of apartheid are bound to occur. This essay contends that Mongane Serote's *To Every Birth its Blood*[1] is the most profound and adequate literary examination of this phenomenon yet written in English, despite the (at present) far greater fame – measured in sales and in international as well as local awards and also in the amount of critical attention (so far) attracted – of especially Brink's, Breytenbach's, Gordimer's and Coetzee's renditions of the subject. The undeniable stature of the aforementioned writers has been built up over many years, whereas Serote's work has remained in relative critical obscurity. Literary criticism relating to *To Every Birth* published hitherto includes essays by Barboure; Ndebele; Sole; Trump; Visser; Gagiano; Watts and Wilkinson.

Sole's second essay on *To Every Birth* ("This Time") is particularly sharp in its criticisms of Serote's novel, at times verging on condescension and sarcasm; e.g.:

> Agreement on the need to destroy apartheid and on the central operative role of the Movement becomes, unwaveringly, agreement as to the means involved under the auspices of the Movement. Such a conception is circular and self-justifying. Here, most tellingly, the problems caused by the ambiguous presence of the movement (simultaneously organisation and mass of people) can be seen. (72)

> We are left, finally, with a 'poetic' sense of politics which falls short of being able to deal with the struggles and contradictions likely to occur in a post-apartheid South Africa. (73)

> Interpersonal and psychological processes are transplanted wholesale into the realm of political relationships, and psychic repression and disjuncture are merely seen as an index of the socio-political [. . .] The idea of harmony being the socio-political state following on the defeat of colonialism is again common to much African fiction immediately before and after formal independence [. . .]; a conceptualisa-

---

1 In this essay the page references are to the Johannesburg: Ravan Press, 1981 edition of this work. The Heinemann edition appeared in 1983.

> tion compellingly inadequate in the face of subsequent political and economic events on the continent. (74)
>
> [T]here is evidence in the text of remaining contradictions, repressed yet still lingering beyond the author's explanatory powers. (76)

There is a large measure of agreement between the criticisms of Serote's novel by Sole, Visser and Trump.

The apartheid subject is a huge one. The great bulk of South African literature could be said to have been influenced by either the hatching or the full-fledged presence of this enormous political force. Early intimations of apartheid are discernible in the very beginnings of South African literature, e.g. in Sol Plaatje's novel *Mhudi* (1930). Sepamla's *A Ride on the Whirlwind* (1981) and *Third Generation* (1986); Tlali's *Amandla* (1981); Mzamane's *The Children of Soweto* (1982) and Langa's *A Rainbow on the Paper Sky* (1989) are novels comparable in subject and to some extent in setting with *To Every Birth*. Among the novels of J. M. Coetzee, *Age of Iron* (1990) is most overtly concerned with apartheid. An essay like this cannot undertake the taxonomy of the anti-apartheid novel and makes no more than cursory references to a handful of the other writers on the subject. "The literature on apartheid is so extensive today," Neville Alexander has remarked, "that no single person could study all of it in the span of a lifetime" (9).[2]

This chapter can be (re-)introduced by a quotation from the preface by A. Adu Boahen[3] to his work, *African Perspectives on Colonialism*:

> First, although there is no theme in African history on which more has been written than that of the rise and fall of colonialism in Africa, most of these authors have looked at the subject primarily from an Euro-centric point of view. Their principal pre-occupations, in spite of the recent noise that has been made about African resistance, have been the origins, structure, operation, and impact of colonialism. The crucial questions of how *Africans* perceived colonialism, what initiatives and responses they displayed in the face of this colonial chal-

[2] For wide-ranging works on apartheid approached from historical or cultural perspectives, see the works by (or edited by) La Guma; Lapping; Lonsdale; Marks and Trapido; Motsoko; Plaatje; Posel (as well as Serote's *On the Horizon*).

[3] Boahen is the editor of the UNESCO *General History of Africa*, vol. 8.

> lenge, and above all how they reacted after the forcible imposition of colonialism have not been systematically dealt with.

Merely mischievous as it would be to label South Africa's famous anti-apartheid white writers "Euro-centric," there is a sense in which the Boahen quotation parallels the pattern of "fame distribution" roughly sketched in the opening paragraph of this chapter. What Boahen says here is irresistibly reminiscent of two quotations by Chinua Achebe. The first was written some time ago: "The story we had to tell could not be told for us by anyone else no matter how gifted or well-intentioned" (*Morning* 70).[4] More recently, Achebe has written that "stories are not innocent; [. . .] they can be used to put you in the wrong crowd, in the party of the man who has come to dispossess you" ("African" 7).

Literature is a mode of knowing and undoubtedly those who best know the oppression of apartheid are those within the bruised heart of the country, whether they live in "townships" or in rural slums. Such writers as Gordimer and Coetzee clearly acknowledge their more peripheral relationship to the subject in gestures of authorial tact – the muteness of Friday in *Foe* and the uncomprehended and yet "understood" tirade by July in *July's People* being but two examples which illustrate these authors' refusal to speak on behalf of black South Africans. Yet the centrality of such voices from within as Bessie Head's, Eskia Mphahlele's, Mazisi Kunene's, Miriam Tlali's, Sipho Sepamla's and Mongane Serote's still needs to be critically reclaimed. The South African past itself is likely to undergo a considerable process – and effort – of cultural decolonisation and redefinition in the years to come.

I

> Every writer seeks reconciliation, in the inner recesses of his soul, between private life and social action.
>
> – Mbulelo Vizikhungo Mzamane

South African writers have been particularly conscious of a need or a duty to make "a gesture of belonging" in their work.[5] The overwhelming presence on the local scene of the apartheid system has by some been considered detrimental

---

4 Compare Serote in a U.S.A. interview: "We learned that it is only black people in South Africa who understand what has happened to them, and who know what they want." (cited Chapman, *Soweto Poetry*, p. 112).

5 These are the words which end Bessie Head's novel, *A Question of Power* (206).

to the creation of worthy writing, due to the inevitable temptation to address apartheid's definition of blacks as contemptible and of whites as worthy by straightforwardly inverting it, in a natural attempt to redress the social imbalances in the idealising sphere of culture. Consequently Mphahlele could say: "I'm sick of protest creative writing and our South African situation has become a terrible cliché as literary material" (*Down Second Avenue* 199). The anthropologist Hannah Arendt famously referred to "the banality of evil." One might say, then, that one aspect of a South African writer's dilemma in confronting the workings of apartheid is to show this *banal* quality, but to do so in ways that creatively transcend the immediate impulse towards mere condemnation – in other words, to retain an exploratory approach to the subject. Njabulo Ndebele's well-known essays on this point, chiefly his essays "Turkish Tales" and "The Rediscovery of the Ordinary," are cogently argued and have been deservedly influential. He makes one explicit reference to Serote's novel, judging that although the novel "attempts to deal with the ordinary concerns of people [. . .] within the broad political situation in the country," in the end "the spectacle takes over and the novel throws away the vitality of the tension generated by the dialectic between the personal and the public" ("Rediscovery" 55). It will be evident that the present essay, while to some extent employing the criteria used by Ndebele, argues for greater recognition of the success of Serote's novel in meeting those same standards.

The quotation from Mzamane which heads this section alerts one to the tension between the sensitive individual's instinct to guard the privacy of the very experiences which are the source of verbal art and (as counter-pull) the writer's felt need to bring to public expression those forms of experience which are hardest to acknowledge – for instance such feelings as shame, impotent hatred, despair and bewilderment – the dragon's teeth of apartheid – all this in a context where there are demands on writers for uncritical or obvious commitment to "prevalidated" social or political action. Bluntly, how does a writer avoid pamphleteering and yet make his or her work contribute to a social need as urgent as that experienced by apartheid's victims?

The argument of this essay is that Serote succesfully addresses this dilemma in different ways which demonstrate the subtlety and power of his art. These methods or negotiations of his will be addressed in turn.

In the first place, he immerses us throughout in the deep meanderings of his characters' moods. By using this term I do not mean feelings only, or any superficial "moodiness," but those profound and involuntary assessments of the condition of the self (the "state" of the "soul") as it is affected by surrounding realities. Social scientists of many kinds such as historians, sociologists and political scientists have attempted to delineate apartheid. Nadine Gordimer earned the Nobel prize for literature and J. M. Coetzee almost equal fame to a large extent *because* they are taken to be subtle analysts, evaluators and chroniclers (and resisters) of apartheid – which they undoubtedly are. What sets Serote's novel off from these other writers', though, is his ability to depict convincingly the "inner recesses" (Mzamane, "Writer" 3) of individuals who are at the centre of victimhood within the system, whereas Gordimer's and Coetzee's "black" characters (inevitably) remain peripheral and type-cast.[6] In other words Serote's characters are, without being in the least banal or unbelievable heroes, "ordinary," but depicted with extra-ordinary sensitivity. The depiction of their "private life" (Mzamane) is hence a "social action" on the part of the author.[7] It is his contribution to an understanding of the way this public (political) system penetrates into the supposedly inaccessible "recesses" of the self. Serote shows us how apartheid *humiliates* its victims with its tentacular, overshadowing hold on their lives. Almost every sentence in this novel carries the imprint of apartheid – whether in references to social realities, physical details or inner feelings. Tsi (the main character) says at one point: "Everything we could claim immediately left bloodstains on our fingers [. . .] Nothing was happening. Everything: a tumour! That was when I realised that South Africa was my home" (70-71).

Such passages as those occurring on pages 28-32; 51-63 or 316-320 both *represent* and implicitly *analyse* apartheid and illustrate the power and importance of this text.

We are moreover shown this process of psychic invasion without the writer compromising his or our sense of the victim's full human stature. That is why the modulations of Serote's portrayal of especially such characters as Tsi, Yao and John are so interesting. These figures are the loners, the losers, the escapists (generally and comparatively speaking) among the novel's large cast of characters. Their deep melancholy is explored for our understanding of the demoralis-

---

6 On this point compare such analyses of Gordimer's work as Kathrin Wagner's *Rereading Nadine Gordimer* (especially 115-165) – a subtle and balanced (re-) evaluation of this writer's work, as well as the essays by Paul Rich; Michael Marais and Lewis Nkosi on Gordimer's and Coetzee's work.

7 Compare Serote's blunt statement in his "Words for a Cause: A Writer's Role in Change": "In South Africa, writing portrays the state of the people. I portray apartheid" (Serote: *On the Horizon*, 13).

ing effect of the apartheid system. Their private feelings are the register of the awful power and range of the public, social phenomenon which apartheid is more generally taken to be, thus showing its encroachment on the psyche itself. Barboure comments astutely on Serote's exploration of this issue in *To Every Birth*:

> Imperialism is not only [. . .] exploitation [. . .] but the uprooting of languages and customs [. . .] [i]t [. . .]can be tracked to the most intimate roots of speech and signification. [. . .] culture is so vitally bound up with one's common identity that there is no need to argue for its relation to political struggle. (215)

Readers are necessarily warned against the naïvety of assuming simple correspondence between authors and the (chief) protagonists of their novels, whilst at the same time one must recognise the undeniability of the link between what a writer has lived and what s/he records in (his or her) writing. It is difficult not to sense a *degree* of "authorial agreement" between, say, Maureen Smales of *July's People* and Nadine Gordimer and between Mrs Curren of *Age of Iron* and J. M. Coetzee. Both these novels are rightly said to be acts of exposure of the limitations of "white" liberalism within the South African contexts. Nevertheless Gordimer's final freeze-shot of the sprinting Maureen and Coetzee's melancholic image of an old and dying but bitterly honest Elizabeth Curren – caught as she feels between hateful Nat politicians or police and the mere harshness of the iron-hard black youths she encounters – indicate that both authors "centre" these women (in their novels) against a "background" (or "black ground") in such a way as to valorise the women, however ironically qualified the valorisation may be.

However great the exposure of the limitations of "liberalism" in *July's People*, the authorial empathy with Maureen is evident in the way she is contrasted both with the limitations and inadaptability of her husband and with the generally rather petty concerns attributed to her (former) servant (July), for whom the author establishes no solid sense of dignity or intelligence – both men and their possible future(s) are forgotten as the novel ends on what seems a vaguely intended "heroic" gesture of Maureen's (her much-disputed sprint towards an arriving helicopter). Indeed Gordimer may be accused of "sexing the revolution," if Maureen's sprint prefigures the way Hillela (in *A Sport of Nature*) beds and marries black men. Of *Age of Iron*, Marais says that it "is haunted by a sense of its own social insignificance" (22), as if Coetzee in this novel were confronting his own authorial marginalisation in a society or generation – and a situation – which (in Mrs Curren's simplistic dichotomy) "do[es] not believe in words [and] think[s] only blows are real, blows and bullets" (*Age of Iron* 133).

Yet there is a discernible awkwardness in the ambiguous endorsements of both authors' female protagonists, due to their manifest(ed) failures – amongst which the chief failure must be their inability to achieve social integration. If (or even though) it is apartheid that is the chief cause of their separateness (Mrs Curren's from her daughter, from repulsive whites, from repelling blacks – and Maureen's from July and his "people" as well as from her husband and children and from the "revolutionary destiny" (Clingman 203) of acceptance or death that may await her "beyond" the ending of that novel) both protagonists are nevertheless so isolated as to be lacking in that type of social significance which we call representativeness.[8] They are like the eggs on the edge of a clutch; unlikely to hatch; hard to read as directors to a future (either personal or political). Nor does Gordimer or Coetzee in these two novels convey to the reader any strong sense of a meaningful future (for white and/or black South Africans) "despite" or "beyond" the two fading protagonists: the authorial vision, too, seems cowed and curtailed.

Having recorded these (evidently disputable) readings I want to return to Serote's foregrounding of Tsi Molope and the further presence in his novel of the characters Yao and John. Compared with the obvious political activists in the novel – such as Oupa, Onalenna, Tuki, Mandla – these other three (Tsi, Yao, John) might be referred to as "inactivists." It is nevertheless noticeable that when Serote locates the act of his own writing of the novel *To Every Birth Its Blood* by adding the place names and dates "New York – Gaborone – Kanye 1975-1980" on its last page (368), this directly parallels the movements (and the initial absence) of Yao during the crucial period of South Africa's political life which the novel depicts – known usually as "'76" and referred to in the novel as the "days of Power and the time of the school children" (171 and elsewhere). Yao's letter to John in response to the news of the death by police fire of

---

[8] Both portrayals are also somewhat lacking in "practical" credibility on several points. Wagner and Margaret Lenta have made such comments on Gordimer's portrayal of Maureen; as far as Mrs Curren's depiction by Coetzee is concerned, her *complete* isolation from friends, (ex-)colleagues or relations of her own race, class or age (in a Cape Town suburb!) is not credible, nor is the township debate scene (in the midst of shootings and a panic-stricken, angry and running crowd) at all convincingly imagined.

Nolizwe (John's beloved) is particularly interesting in this regard (174-175). In other words, if one is to make the same kind of link between author and character as in the interpretation of Gordimer's and Coetzee's novels above, Yao is an obvious candidate to be identified as an "author figure": "difficult," deeply concerned and yet excluded by his absence (see the letter, 174-175); all this is experienced by him as a profoundly disturbing dilemma. Another and probably more noticeable "author-figure" in the work is, naturally, Tsi Molope, whose thought is the chief filtering consciousness of this novel – obviously so throughout all the first part (1-163) and also when he is brought back by the author to conclude the novel as reevaluator of its events (324-326; 343-358; 367-368). Tsi, too, can be parallelled with Serote – in the account of his parentage (*To Every Birth* 28-30), because of his gangster boyhood and early adult life in Alexandra and his year's schooling in Lesotho, in his (young man's) indulgence in alcohol and in his eventual escape to Botswana. As the chief *witness* in the novel he "enacts" what the novel as a whole does: describing what apartheid feels like to its main victims:

> Does it not feel like mud, mud we have to wade through, mud we have to sink into? What are we going to do? [. . .] Everything had become so futile. There was nothing I envied or liked about my father or mother. They seemed trapped in a painful terrible knowledge. I feared for the children [. . .] What is going to happen? Torn Streets. Smell. Dongas. Dirty water in street [. . .] Township. Alex. What is this mess? Our home. Our country. Our world. (53-54)

This, then, is another way in which "private feelings" modulate into the "social action" of writing in such a novel as *To Every Birth its Blood*.

Several interviews with Serote have been published. Especially illuminating are some of his comments in the interview with Wilkinson which was published in *Index on Censorship* in 1988. In this he indicates that his first impulse to write came to him because "most of the things that you read don't have anything to do with the life that you lead. At this stage I really felt that I could write about my life as I know it." He says here that "[b]eing black means at one level being threatened all the time," but that "one begins to understand [. . .] why it is necessary to be hopeful about life [. . .]" Referring to "the Black Consciousness era" in his life, he judges that they "didn't take the history of struggle into consideration [. . .] we had to search for a history of struggle." Serote does not shirk the painful realisation towards which the novel moves: "That it ha[d] become necessary not only to die for freedom but also to kill for freedom – very unfortunate discoveries [at which people only] [. . .] arrive [. . .] [when things are at their] worst [when perpetual] oppress[ion is the only alternative]" (104-106).

Later in the interview Serote says that he aspires to the creation of a proper point of reference "for [his] people [, having] [. . .] experienced this very deep wealth which the world has forgotten [. . .] [of which it needs to be] remind[ed]." Commenting reticently on his own nine months in solitary confinement and on the police torture to which he was subjected, Serote mentions the experience of "very severe pain which changes your life completely" (104-06).

I suggest that despite evident self-reflexive/reflective ironies, Serote's "relationship" with his character is less uncomfortably ambivalent than Gordimer's and Coetzee's with theirs in the two novels mentioned above. Such a purely intuitive comment rests on aspects of the novel that make Tsi seem a (self-?)forgiven figure who has taken up the spear dropped by his heroic and tragic nephew Oupa through telling Oupa's story – a sort of Horatio to Oupa's Hamlet.[9] Tsi comes to the reader as someone irreparably *damaged* by apartheid. His dislocated wanderings constitute the novel's main metaphor for what this system does to black South Africans: making them psychically homeless in the land of their birth. Homelessness is the central metaphor of this novel (Gagiano 84-91). Tsi represents his dislocated, disillusioned, harmed society. Serote's subtle and delicately networked deployment of this image of homelessness must rank as one of the great achievements of South African writing. It may be surmised that an uprooted and exiled Serote re-roots or re-orientates himself by means of this profound study of the psychic cost of apartheid and that the author's "private feelings," too, are transformed into a significant act of social solidarity. Here Achebe's *Anthills* passage might again be invoked, in which the point is made that "Recalling – is – Greatest" – because in the storyteller's "new-found utterance our struggle will stand reincarnated before us" (124-25). A somewhat more melancholic vision of the contribution of the (exiled) writer can be found in the concluding stanza of Arthur Nortje's moving poem, "Native's Letter" (from his collection *Dead Roots*):

> Darksome, whoever dies
> in the malaise of my dear land

[9] At the end of Shakespeare's play Horatio is enjoined by Hamlet to "tell [his] story" as an act of love, much as Tsi has been telling his nephew Oupa's "story" (see 324-26; 351-52). Compare Achebe's "only the story can continue beyond the war and the warrior" (*Anthills* 124).

remember me at swim,
the moving waters spilling through my eyes:
and let no amnesia
attack at fire hour:
for some of us must storm the castles
some define the happening.

Before leaving this part of the discussion the figure of John is also worth discussing. John "literally" mediates between the melancholic drifter Tsi and the group of committed activists shown in the novel, since he "begins" part II of the novel when Tsi is temporarily left behind. He "feels" to the reader at first indistinguishable from Tsi – as if he is "another" Tsi. In the same way that Tsi is a bystander compared to his brother (significantly named) Fix who is imprisoned on Robben Island and compared to his activist nephew Oupa, John stood by helplessly and even hid behind a pillar when his beloved Nolizwe (whose name links her with the idea of the nation) was gunned down by the police (164-66; 169). It is said of him that "John stood strictly on the periphery of things" (171) and this apparent passivity is shown to exasperate his more obviously "committed" friends, who suspect him of "self-pity" (177). But they are wrong. Although John had an earlier history of "political failure" (when detained, he had given "names and addresses" to the police under threat [167]), his condition after witnessing Nolizwe's death is not what it seems (that of a "broken" or demoralised person), but the entirely different condition of "a deadly man," because it is his understanding that his and Nolizwe's "love [. . .] would otherwise rot and be vulgar" (168). (In the final conversation in the novel between Yao and Tsi [356-358] the topic is similarly the revolutionary power of love.) John's life of suspended animation hence becomes one of full activism as he joins the Movement (252-254) and participates in one of the chief acts of anti-apartheid vengeance shown in the novel (305-306). This is another example of Serote's way of both achieving (as a writer) and showing (as a witness) the link between the "inner recesses" of experience on the one and "social action" on the other hand, to which the Mzamane quotation refers.

II

this dichotomy between the political and the aesthetic

– John Povey

This section of the discussion addresses the issue articulated in the Povey quotation above by means of demonstration rather than by means of argument. The reader's attention is directed to a long extract from *To Every Birth*, namely the section that describes Oupa's dying moments in police custody and then transfers to a discussion between another young revolutionary (Themba) and an old soldier of the struggle (Mmaphefo) in the rural setting of Walmanstadt on pages 312-315. To save space this rather long passage is not quoted in full. It begins on page 312 at line 27 (i.e. towards the bottom of the page) and starts with the words "Oupa began to weep," continuing until page 315, line 20 (mid-way down the page), ending on the words "towards the door which led outside."[10]

In the opening words of the selected passage Oupa's "weep[ing]" (312) is a response instead of a reply, since it enacts a refusal to answer the question by his (police) interrogators and torturers who are demanding that he provide them with information (which of course would involve a betrayal of his comrades to the system). His weeping is, indeed, simultaneously the sign that he is counting the cost (his own life) of such a refusal to "cooperate." The (misnamed) "security" policemen pressurise and taunt him by saying that his own "family is talking" and that he (Oupa) is "going to tell [. . .] all of it" (312). The words of the interrogators ironically and tragically invert Dikeledi's bemused and slightly condescending words when she is surprised to discover that the younger Oupa belongs to the Movement: "Oupa, I have heard that so many times" and "You are so funny, talking like that" (251). What might earlier have seemed like (Oupa's) slogans and clichés are now being heroically – and terribly – confirmed. He evidently does *not* tell on his comrades and such silence "speaks volumes. (Serote conveys Oupa's resistance through silence implicitly, by certain deliberate "gaps" and "slips" in the text.) We are told that Oupa's head is "hooded." This near-suffocation treatment to which Oupa is subjected is known to have been one of the favourite methods of the South African "security" system to elicit information from "suspects." The suffocation is given symbolic overtones

10 These page and line references are to the Ravan edition of *To Every Birth*. For the Heinemann (AWS) edition, the page and line references are 175 (line 29) to 177 (line 9).

in a paragraph preceding the cited passage: "His scream was *choked* by the wet canvas. [. . .] He tried as hard as he could to scream. Nothing happened. *Nobody heard him scream*" (312; emphases added). One could compare with this Serote's accusation that "the world has forgotten" in his *Index on Censorship* interview with Jane Wilkinson (106), and with Yao's words that "when we love we cannot forget" (*To Every Birth* 357). The nightmarishly recurrent method of state torture (of which Serote had personal experience during his own period in police detention – see the Wilkinson interviews) is indicated by the vivid detail of a repeated word: "covered [. . .] *again*. His cock shot out *again*" (312; emphases added). Serote's ability to write political analysis (of the persistence and power of the apartheid system and the terrible endurance required of those who resist it) at the same time as he is (as an artist) clearly and memorably "painting" this episode, illustrates his ability to surmount the dilemma posed in the Povey quotation at the head of this section. The writing in such a passage is simultaneously profoundly cherishing, deeply indignant *and* intensely political. It could be said to achieve a tragic grandeur, quiet and understated as it remains.

Let us now focus on the report of Oupa having an erection at this of all moments, a detail some readers might imagine "unlikely" or "vulgar." It is of course the involuntary spasm of a body *in extremis*. This occurs long after Oupa was "badly smashed" (307) at an earlier stage of his capture. In the meantime he has also been forced to take his clothes off: "Strip, you dog!" (310), increasing the vulnerability and exposure of the body. The outrage done to his flesh is also written in this humiliatingly "ill-timed" erection, shocking evidence of both the exposure of the self and the invasion of the body by so brutal a system. It is to be compared to Tsi's farting and peeing (despite the desperation of his attempts to "contain himself") when he is assaulted by the police (89), and to the degradation he experiences there. One might describe Oupa's erection as a "screaming" of the body itself in a situation where (immediately prior to the analysed passage) "[h]is scream was choked by the wet canvas [. . .] He tried as hard as he could to scream. Nothing happened. Nobody heard his scream" (312). But the novelist is making *us* hear the scream in a passage that is agonising to read. Oupa's erection has the pathos of life-affirmation and -yearning by a doomed person, and the "standing" penis is a sign prefiguring Oupa's final gesture when he hauls himself erect to say his dignified words of belonging and of validation: "'Yes, I am a member of the Movement,' he said" (313). Those, I feel, are the central words of homecoming in this novel. The gesture of his rising to say them in his agony makes them, not a confession, but a proclamation. He literally and nobly "rises above" his torturers' degradation of his body.

Then Serote (at first sight abruptly) transfers the narrative to the rural setting of Walmanstadt where the landscape itself is "read" by Themba (whose name, of course, means 'hope'). Meticulous consideration by the reader reveals how carefully the subtle linkages between the two juxtaposed passages are established, in order that the Walmanstadt passage serves as a sign of the continuation and growth of the struggle in which Oupa has now become a casualty – even an "ancestor" as his name (despite his youth) indicates [since "Oupa" means 'grandfather']. Themba's first thought about the Walmanstadt landscape is that "[t]he silence here is stubborn" (313), which of course recalls Oupa's refusal to "assist the police in their enquiries." The words "silence" and "stubborn" also echo from a *much* earlier passage: "But the silence was stubborn [. . .] The silence here is graceful" (11), where the almost identical expression indicates (as it does here) the "resistance by endurance" motif, which could more simply be called *fidelity*: the people's belief in their right to their own land.[11] On page 11, the expression occurs in the setting of Alexandra's graveyard, paradoxically more "alive" than the oppressed township itself because it enshrines the dead and revitalises thoughts of resistance in those who meet there ("Old Man Zola" and Tsi) – as described in another remarkable passage (10-19).

In the Walmanstadt passage, the "setting" itself as well as the cattle and sheep owned by the inhabitants are "protect[ed], like a womb, like a mother" (313) by "[t]he silence" – and it is a silence that is living, since it "spreads" (313). A city boy, the young revolutionary "Themba fe[els] naked" here in this quiet backwater – but in hopeful contrast with Oupa's nakedness, Themba's is that of enlightenment, of someone "suddenly" seeing a larger picture, seeing that the [whole] land and all of those who are more land-bound than himself (such as the peasant farmers of Walmanstadt or the mineworkers he next thinks of) *are* "involved" (in the full sense of the term) in the political struggle in which he has been playing (he now realises) a relatively small part. This dawning realisation is akin to Serote's allusion (in the Wilkinson interviews) to his and others' *later* awareness that Black Consciousness adherents were too unaware of and cut off from their

---

11 Compare "The movement is an idea in the mind of a people; a resolve that it will never accept the process of defeat [. . .] the real issue [is] that the people want and need their land" (327). Contrast the many references in the novel to the dreary feeling of "defeat" (e.g. 17, 59, 60, 78 [79: "we have been beaten into submission"], 82 and 326).

people's past. Hence the dawn image ("day") and the imaginative, embracing re-interpretation of the word "underground" (313). The simple, beautiful "conclusion" ("The meaning of underground, Themba told himself, was hard work" [314]) shows Themba the revolutionary achieving an insight which perhaps echoes but also exceeds Marxism in its physical and spiritual immediacy – the knowledge that a country is "earned" by those who work its soil: "Their eyes were shining. [. . .] The people here carried with them the smell of water and the smell of the soil. They seemed to come from underground" (314).

In another "abrupt" shift, the old soldier of the struggle Mmaphefo (who plays the part of "mother" – or "grandmother" to most of the young revolutionaries) discusses the habits of snakes with Themba, who is unused to these creatures. Subtle details of the imagery indicate that the snake itself symbolises "[t]he Movement": the expression "in motion" (314) being the first clue. A moving snake is said to look "like flowing water" (which recalls the dam image associated with the Movement on page 272 and perhaps the epigraph topping page 65), while the word "glows" in the penultimate line on page 314 echoes from the third line on the same page. "If you cannot touch it, how can you fight it?" (314) indicates not only the slipperiness of snakes, but the inviolate, unconquerable nature of the people's aspirations and dreams of reclaiming their land, while the "ability to strike at lightning speed" (315) reminds the reader of the acts of revolutionary vengeance depicted in the novel. This should be linked with Mmaphefo's laconic observation that "[s]nakes don't go out looking for people to bite" (314) – i.e. the violence of the struggle is (implicitly) defended as a provoked violence. (Compare Themba's slight querying of this notion on page 315, lines 13-16.)

The selected passage ends with the elderly woman's "struggl[e]" to come "upright" (315) from her formerly sitting posture – reminiscent of Oupa's final act of resistance after torture. Again there is the suggestion (here slightly and benignly comical and indulgent, as the old woman overcomes the physical decrepitude to which she constantly refuses to submit) of indomitable courage and of "stubborn" (313; 11) resistance, a mode of being that is natural, heroic and also "graceful" (11) – despite immediate physical appearances. To this may be compared the depiction of Old Man Zola (12-19) and the old woman (Ma-Maria) to whom Dikeledi speaks after the bombing (279-84). At Mmaphefo's place, too, there is a suggestion of homecoming through struggle; we are told that "[t]he distances between the house [i.e. the "four thatched rondavels"] gave Themba the feeling of bountiful space" (315).

Serote's images for the Movement are all organic. Its existence is perhaps first hinted at in the epigraph which tops page 65 (a river/journey); it is then described on pages 272 ("like the wind"); 318 ("The Movement [. . .] is as old as [. . .] the first San [. . .] who was killed by a bullet [. . .] as young [as the revolutionary schoolchildren of '76 and later] [. . .] is the eyes which see how [. . .] white [and] dry [poverty is]); 326 ("like an old tree [. . .] [it] spreads and spreads its roots"); 327 ("an idea in the mind of a people"); 359 ("like the sea [. . .] deep [. . .] vast [. . .] reflective [. . .] calm [. . .] rough and tough [. . .] it moves and moves") and even (I suggest) on pages 331-32 (where it is linked with the movements of the freed cattle which startle Tuki). Despite the heavy weather which some commentators have made of Serote's employment of this image, it is evidently a poetic and profoundly-felt symbol and cannot fairly be criticised for not indicating a political programme, since it is itself the ideal which inspires political activity. It is, in the fullest sense of the word, an *existential* aspiration and reality.

In this section of the essay the aim has been to illustrate that the political force and forthrightness of Serote's writing combines wonderfully with its aesthetic delicacy and vividness. The passage chosen for analysis is by no means exceptional; there is an artistic and political integrity[12] at work throughout the novel. Despite its well-known function as an affectionate "nickname" for the A.N.C., Serote's use of the term "[t]he Movement"[13] is not to be interpreted as a narrowly party political expression – this comment being validated by his deliberate widening of its meaning to include all those who toil and hope under oppression (as in the middle section of the passage analysed above).

---

12 Two points are to be linked with the term 'integrity':
(a) the (inter-)connectedness of the whole novel, to the mind of this (essay-)writer the crucial point overlooked in Visser's article on *To Every Birth*;
(b) the accusations that have more recently been levelled at Serote concerning his party political and organisational activities, whether taken as valid or denied, should not (again, in the eyes of the present essay-writer) be allowed to overshadow analyses of his work, "belonging" (as it does), once published and studied, no longer to the writer but to the culture at large.

13 Which may also function as an unconscious echo of the "Black Consciousness *Movement*" (emphasis added).

III

the story of the land

– Chinua Achebe

In another part of the brief quotation from Achebe's *Anthills of the Savannah* from which the epigraph to this section of my essay is taken, the author speaks of the god Agwu (elsewhere identified by Achebe as "the capricious god of diviners and artists" [105]) as "the god of healers": "Agwu is the right hand a man extends to his fellows [. . .] *to serve the compound*" (125; emphasis added). What is implied here by Achebe's reference is the social function of art: the larger spiritual forces working though the individual artist in the interests of whole communities. "Political" as such art is likely to be for a society in the throes of oppression or during a process of agonising adaptation, it could not serve its purpose by being political in a narrowly partisan way. Something broader and more visionary must inform the writing.[14] This idea is well captured in Achebe's brief expression, which is quoted at the head of this final section of the discussion.

The issue of (relative?) non-partisanship in so evidently politically "committed" a novel as *To Every Birth its Blood* needs to be further argued, which shall be briefly done. For a novel to qualify as "the story of the land," it needs to exhibit also such features as inclusivity and representativeness – the vision it communicates must be a communal one (*pace* Achebe, above). This assessment of Serote's novel finds that it amply satisfies those criteria.

(i) Non-partisanship

Clearly this novel is unfriendly towards the political position held by the "architects" and upholders of the apartheid system. South Africa has not produced much creative writing that unashamedly upholds the doctrine of racial stratification; being "anti-apartheid" as a novelist is almost a given of this occupation (notwithstanding that the political power of apartheid has been ruthlessly inventive, shrewd, alert – in short, as Foucault would say, "productive"[15] in multi-

14 Compare Es'kia Mphahlele's monograph *Poetry and Humanism* and Mazisi Kunene's introduction to his poetry collection *The Ancestors and the Sacred Mountain.*

15 "We must cease once and for all to describe the effects of power in negative terms [i.e. by saying]: it "excludes," it "represses," it "censors," it "abstracts," it

ple other ways). The notion of non-partisanship used here is hence an adapted one; *To Every Birth* does show the two "sides" involved in the liberation struggle in the stark harshness of their encounter. Amongst the "white" characters the tough, vicious policemen, the racist lift operator, the "dominee" farmer, the "liberal" white sympathisers and their limitations (referring here to David and Sue; Anne and Dr. McLean) are all clearly and vividly delineated and individualised where the observing perspective warrants it (Oupa's torturers, for instance, would not be "identified" and could not be named by him). Amongst the "black" South Africans shown in the novel a wide spectrum of attitudes is shown, ranging from the pathetic Morolong to the heroic Oupa, whose youthful political idealism is so terribly validated in his death – Tsi occupying a type of "middle" position. The analysis (74-79) of the role of the "bantustan chief" (76), Lerato, and of the "BSO" (77) – Black Students' Organisation – is notable, as is the description of the political role and development of the Ramono family (e.g. 218-21; 228-39), Ramono being a Mandela-type figure. Despite the wide range of people he depicts, Serote manages to endow all characters with a solid humanness – even a betrayer like Mpando, the assassinated police officer, is depicted with at least a touch of poignancy (260-61), indicating the intelligent broadness of Serote's vision.

(ii) Inclusivity

The range and sweep of to *Every Birth* is large. A loose count of characters comes to something in the forties! All of these are individualised as if "known" by the author or observer; even the "bit parts" (like the racist lift operator Mr Koek) are vividly realised. Serote shows us households and families; communal occasions (like the funeral of the freedom fighter Willy); street scenes and rural settings; events and meditations; journeys and indoor moments. Nor is the effect ever that of a mere mosaic or catalogue, despite the sudden transferences that "re-place" the reader from time to time. Different sections of the novel are successfully held or linked together by the narrative and (mostly) chronological flow of the writing, by the gravity of its mood and by the sense of a huge process of *national* adaptation and painful growth which it depicts.

(iii) Representativeness

That the damage inflicted by apartheid is not limited to the "black" citizens of South Africa is a very old point indeed. The examination of the various ways in

---

"masks," it "conceals." In fact, power produces; it produces reality, it produces domains of objects and rituals of truth" (*Discipline and Punish* 194).

which this system skewed "white" lives may be described as the strongest thrust of Gordimer's writing, for instance. It is nevertheless to be acknowledged that Serote is foremost among those novelists in English who could most successfully depict the circumstances of the people whose lives have been most crucially affected by this policy. To say this is not to dismiss or undervalue the significant novels of Sol. Plaatje, Peter Abrahams, Alex la Guma, Richard Rive, Es'kia Mphahlele, Lewis Nkosi, Miriam Tlali, Sipho Sepamla, Mbulelo Mzamane or Mandla Langa (Bessie Head's being a "special case") – and then there are the short story writers and poets. Yet Serote has an unmatchable ability to convey the localised, *directed* nature of his vision by welding poetic density and subtlety with documentary vividness.

An important point here is the nature of the experiences depicted in the novel, bearing Ndebele's strictures against novelistic sensationalism[16] in mind. It is striking how much "space" and "time" in this novel are devoted to showing the domestic circumstances of people's lives, and the brilliance and sensitivity with which Serote paints the often uneasy, painful and subtle oscillations of personal and intimate relationships is noteworthy. A very small proportion of the novel, in the end, is devoted to direct political action: its concentration is on the inward "digestion" of events and political circumstances.

Although most of what Serote shows us in this novel occurs in Alexandra or "greater Johannesburg," pains are taken to make evident that (in Serote's eyes) this place is a microcosm of the larger reaches of the land that lie beyond it – partly because its occupants have links over the length and breadth of the country. Serote has said that "Alexandra was for me a definition of the way blacks lived in our country as a whole" (Seroke 30). To this one may compare these words said of Ramono: "every day now seemed to draw him away from his house, as he began to know and understand *his country*" (*To Every Birth* 221; emphasis added).

---

16 As articulated especially in his two essays "Turkish Tales" and "The Rediscovery of the Ordinary," Ndebele was perhaps to some extent anticipated in these essays (11-36 and 37-57) by one of Lewis Nkosi's ("Fiction by Black South Africans"), published in the collection *Home and Exile and Other Selections* (1983), with these generalising comments occasioned by a short story of Bloke Modisane's: "the excitement is external [. . .] and does not come from the inner tension of creative talent confronting inert matter [. . .] we can detect [no] underlying moral imagination at work" (132).

(iv) Communality

Serote's interest in the communal aspect of his society is revealed by the immense interest shown in the course of this novel in (especially) the family networks and other linkages that bind people together (and which, of course, are also frequently shown to break down).

The main thrust of Achebe's expression "the story of the land," however, is towards the communal purpose or function of an artist's creation – as Achebe puts it elsewhere, "art [. . .] in the service of life" (*Morning* 19).[17] This quality is demonstrably present in *To Every Birth* – especially in the deeply compassionate, empathetic quality of the writing which creates Serote's characters. D. H. Lawrence claimed that "[i]f the novelist *honours* the relationship[s depicted in a novel], it will be a great novel" (111). Similarly, one might say that Serote "respects" the people he shows us and hence the actual and larger community from which they emanate. Such respect is validated by also "containing" necessary criticism; it is an *understanding* and not a blanket, or token, forgiveness of the failures and weaknesses of apartheid's victims. In this respect, the depiction of Tsi Molope and the novelist's placing of him (rather than some more heroic figure) at the centre of the book can be certified as a fine artistic and political choice.

Lastly, it is the spirituality, the visionary and "forward-looking" quality of this novel that confirms its communal function. This quality permeates the whole work, but becomes most evident towards its end – for instance in the harrowing and poignant, drunken conversation (353-58; especially 357-58) between the "exiled" Tsi (his status is ambiguous and he has a sense of guilt about his family [346-49]) and Yao, in which Yao tells Tsi that "'[t]he question is whether we are still able to love, you know [. . .] you see, when we love we cannot forget, and this means that we know a lot about hatred. [. . .] we loved Oupa – shit, now we know too much.'" (357)

Other examples from this section of the book which indicate Serote's sense of communalism are the reassuring force of the oracular reference to "[t]he movement" at the start of chapter 15 (359); Tsi's feeling that "[t]he first leg of the journey is now well and truly in progress" (367); that "we can wait and they cannot" (367); and of course the famous image of the woman in the throes of birth on the last page of the novel: "Her vagina, open like the lip of the earth, the lip of the sky when the sun pours out, was red with blood" (368).

---

17 The full quotation reads: "Art for art's sake is just another piece of deodorized dog-shit. Art is, and always has been, in the service of life" (*Morning* 19).

The "promising" images of suffering here associated with dawn and the imminence of birth are offset by the presence of a groaning and "shattered" (365) man and by a last reminder that Tsi abandoned his family and country so that he still has to "get back" (368) – a term implying not only return, but the regaining of the country.[18] The *complex* poetic and moral texturing of Serote's writing which controls the whole length of the novel is thus maintained to its end; its broadness and visionary generosity make no facile posturings of easy victory. The ruthlessness, determination and power (or, indeed, the efficiency and "intelligence") of the apartheid state are clearly recognised. Compare Tsi's sardonic comment: "I still give Verwoerd a pat on the shoulder for this lovely package that he gave the Bantus, I do" (74). The author's political sanity is hence confirmed. Both celebration and lamentation are blended into the writing; it remembers from within.

To Every Birth thus has both a documentary and a commemorative quality. Walter Rodney said that "[t]o be colonized is to be removed from history." But "[f]or record, for history, for memory" (357), we have this and other books; arks from the ugly past of apartheid, in "our battle to reclaim a home for ourselves" (79) – a central quotation from Serote's novel.

A good man in another context has written: "Whether perpetrators and supporters or victims, that past will never be put behind us until we share some common understanding of the injustices of apartheid. For this we need to listen to each other's stories [. . .]"[19]

According to Chinweizu et al., African literature does present "a community discussing its experiences with itself" (241). In *To Every Birth Its Blood*, not only the tragedy and degradation, but also the grandeur of the South African land and people are shown. In the words of Tsi's grandmother:

> 'Child you must know, in the darkness of your past, where you come from, and in the faint future where you are going, that you were issued by loins which bathed in the fire that made the lightning, that dared

18 Compare Fanon's words: "The immobility to which the native is condemned can only be called in question if the native decides to put an end to the history of colonization – the history of pillage – and to bring into existence the history of the nation – the history of decolonization" (40). This comment is more or less echoed by Said: "To become aware of one's self as belonging to a subject people is the founding insight of anti-imperialist nationalism" (214).

19 Victor Honey, past facilitator and chairperson of the Stellenbosch Negotiating Forum, in a community newspaper (*Eikestadnuus* 17 Feb. 1995: 11).

> the clouds to join and curl into the blood of man, that you were like the plants, so merged with the soil, and water, and wind, and the sun and the moon, that your past is so scattered, nothing could hold it, that you have a future to build.' (88)

Her words speak to us all.

Works Cited

Achebe, Chinua. *Anthills of the Savannah*. London: Heinemann, 1987. 124-125.

___. *Morning Yet on Creation Day: Essays*. London: Heinemann, 1975.

___. "African Literature as Restoration of Celebration." *Kunapipi* 12.2 (1990): 1-10.

Alexander, Neville. *Southern African Review of Books* Nov./Dec. 1994: 9.

Barboure, Doriane. "Mongane Serote: Humanist and Revolutionary." *Momentum: On Recent South African Writing*. Ed. M. J. Daymond, J. U. Jacobs, and M. Lenta. Pietermaritzburg: University of Natal Press: 1984. 171-187.

Boahen, A. Adu. *African Perspectives on Colonialism*. Baltimore: Johns Hopkins UP, 1987.

___, ed. *UNESCO General History of Africa*. Vol. 7. London: Heinemann, 1985.

Chapman, Michael, ed. *Soweto Poetry*. Johannesburg: McGraw-Hill, 1982.

Chinweizu, O. Jemie and I. Madubuike. *Toward the Decolonization of African Literature*. Vol. 1: African Fiction and Poetry and Their Critics. Enugu: Fourth Dimension, 1980.

Clingman, Stephen. *The Novels of Nadine Gordimer: History from the Inside*. Johannesburg: Ravan, 1986.

Coetzee, J. M. *Age of Iron*. Harmondsworth: Penguin, 1990.

Eagleton, Terry. *Literary Theory: An Introduction*. Oxford: Blackwell, 1983.

Fanon, Frantz. *The Wretched of the Earth*. Trans. Constance Farrington. Harmondsworth: Penguin, 1967.

Foucault, Michel. *Discipline and Punish: The Birth of the Prison*. Trans. Alan Sheridan. New York: Pantheon, 1977.

Gagiano, Annie H. "Serote's Novel and Visser's Criticism." *English Academy Review* 6 (Dec. 1989): 84-91.

Glegg, Jane. Review of *To Every Birth its Blood* by Mongane Wally Serote. *Staffrider* 5.1 (1982): 34-35.

Gordimer, Nadine. *July's People*. London: Jonathan Cape, 1981.

___. *A Sport of Nature*. Cape Town: David Philip, 1987.

Head, Bessie. *A Question of Power*. London: Heinemann, 1974.

Kunene, Mazisi. *The Ancestors and the Sacred Mountain: Poems*. London: Heinemann, 1982.

La Guma, Alex, ed. *Apartheid: A Collection of Writings on South African Racism by South Africans*. New York: International Publishers, 1971.

Lapping, Brian. *Apartheid: A History*. London: Grafton, 1986.

Lawrence, D. H. *Selected Literary Criticism*. Ed. A. Beal. London: Heinemann, 1967.

Lenta, Margaret. "Fictions of the Future." *English Academy Review* 5 (1988): 133-145.

Lonsdale, John. *South Africa in Question?* Cambridge: Heinemann, 1988.

Marais, Michael. "'Who Clipped the Hollyhocks?': J. M. Coetzee's *Age of Iron* and the Politics of Representation." *English in Africa* 20.2 (Oct. 1993): 1-24.

Marks, Shula, and Stanley Trapido, eds. *The Politics of Race, Class and Nationalism in Twentieth Century South Africa*. London: Longman, 1987.

Motsoko, Pheko. *Apartheid: The Story of a Dispossessed People*. London: Marram, 1984.

Mphahlele, Es'kia. *Down Second Avenue*. Garden City, New York: Doubleday, 1971.

___. *Poetry and Humanism: Oral Beginnings*. Johannesburg: Witwatersrand UP., 1986.

Mzamane, Mbulelo. *The Children of Soweto*. Johannesburg: Ravan, 1982.

___. "A Writer in a Fragmented Society." Address to the *New Nation* Writers' Conference. Johannesburg: Dec. 1991. 3.

Ndebele, Njabulo. "Turkish Tales and Some Thoughts on South African Fiction." *Rediscovery of the Ordinary: Essays on South African Literature and Culture*. By Ndebele. Johannesburg: COSAW, 1991. 11-36.

___. "The Rediscovery of the Ordinary: Some New Writings in South Africa." *Rediscovery of the Ordinary: Essays on South African Literature and Culture*. By Ndebele. Johannesburg: COSAW, 1991. 37-57.

Nkosi, Lewis. "Fiction by Black South Africans." *Home and Exile and Other Selections*. London/New York: Longman, 1965, rpt. 1983. 131-138.

Nortje, Arthur. *Dead Roots*. London: Heinemann, 1973.

Patel, Essop. "Mongane Wally Serote: Poet of Revolution." *Third World Quarterly* 12.1 (Jan. 1990): 187-193.

Plaatje, Sol.T. *Native Life in South Africa before and since the European War and the Boer Rebellion*. Kimberley: Tsala ea Batho, 19[13?].

Posel, Deborah. *The Making of Apartheid 1948-1961: Conflict and Compromise*. Oxford: Clarendon, 1991.

Povey, John F. "English-Language Fiction from South Africa." *A History of Twentieth-Century African Literatures*. Ed. Oyekan Owomoyela. Lincoln and London: University of Nebraska Press, 1993. 103.

Rich, Paul. "Apartheid and the Decline of Civilization Idea: An Essay on Nadine Gordimer's *July's People* and J. M. Coetzee's *Waiting for the Barbarians*." *Research in African Literatures*, 15 (1984): 365-393.

Said, Edward W. *Culture and Imperialism*. New York: Knopf, 1993.

Seroke, Jaki. "Poet in Exile" Interview. *Staffrider* 4.1 (1988): 30-32.

Serote, Mongane Wally. *Behold Mama, Flowers*. Poetry. Johannesburg: Ad. Donker, 1978.

___. *Come and Hope with Me*. Poetry. Cape Town: David Philip, 1994.

___. *To Every Birth Its Blood*. Novel. Johannesburg: Ravan, 1981.

___. *The Night Keeps Winking*. Poetry. Gaberone: Medu Arts Esemble, 1982.

___. *No Baby Must Weep*. Poetry. Johannesburg: Ad. Donker, 1975.

___. "Now We Enter History." *Culture in Another South Africa*. Ed. Willem Campschreur and Joost Divendal. London: Zed, 1989.

___. *On The Horizon*. Essays. Fordsburg: COSAW, 1990.

___. *Selected Poems*. Poetry. Ed. M. V. Mzamane. Johannesburg: Ad. Donker, 1982.

___. *Third World Express*. Poetry. Cape Town: David Philip, 1992.

___. *A Tough Tale*. Poetry. London: Kliptown, 1987.

___. *Tsetlo*. Poetry. Johannesburg: Ad. Donker, 1974.

___. *Yakhal'inkomo*. Poetry. Johannesburg: Ad. Donker, 1972.

Sole, Kelwyn. "'The Days of Power:' Depictions of Politics and Community in Four Recent South African Novels." *Research in African Literatures*, 19.1 (Spring 1988): 65-88.

___. "'This Time Set Again': "The Temporal and Political Conceptions of Serote's *To Every Birth Its Blood*." *English in Africa* 18-1 (May 1991): 51-80.

Trump, Martin. "Serote's *To Every Birth Its Blood* and Debates within Southern Africa's Literature of Liberation." *Staffrider* 9.2 (1990): 37-49.

Visser, Nick. "Fictional Projects and the Irruptions of History: Mongane Serote's *To Every Birth Its Blood*." *English Academy Review* 4 (1987): 67-76.

Wagner, Kathrin. *Rereading Nadine Gordimer: Text and Subtext in the Novels*. Johannesburg: Markew Miller Longman and Wits UP, 1994.

Wilkinson, Jane. Interview with Mongane Wally Serote. *Index on Censorship* 5 (1988): 104-106.

___. "Mongane Wally Serote". Interview. *Talking with African Writers: Interviews with African Poets, Playwrights, and Novelists*. London: Heinemann, 1992. 175-182.

___. "Serote's Cities: (De-)Constructing South African Urban Space." *Altered State? Writing and South Africa*. Ed. Elleke Boehmer, Laura Chrisman, and Kenneth Parker. Sydney: Dangaroo 1994. 91-99.

Watts, Jane. *Black Writers from South Africa: Towards a Discourse of Liberation*. London: Macmillan, 1989. 211-250.

Shakespeare, (Fanon,) Salih: Can the Black Man Love the White Woman? Can the White Woman Love the Black Man?

> [. . .] an old black ram
> Is tupping your white ewe.
>
> – Shakespeare, *Othello* 1.1.87-88

> Differences of race are irreducible and between two beings who love each other they cannot fail to produce exceptional and instructive reactions. In the first superficial ebullition of love, indeed, nothing notable may be manifested, but in a fairly short time the two lovers, innately hostile, in trying to approach each other strike against an invisible partition which separates them. Their sensibilities are divergent; everything in each shocks the other; even their anatomical conformation, even the language of their gestures, all is foreign.
>
> – Abel Hermant (late nineteenth-century "physiologist")

Shakespeare's interest in black (usually North African) subjectivity is initially manifested in the early play *Titus Andronicus* (presumed date of composition 1594), and he shows from the first a recognition of racial identity as a power factor. Aaron, the black slave and outsider, as servant-slave supposed a mere incidental appendage of a defeated enemy queen, manipulates and wreaks vengeance upon the paleskinned Roman Andronici and all but succeeds (this by means of his continuing sexual relationship with the Gothic queen Tamora, who has in the meantime married the Roman emperor) in implanting his own child on the Roman throne, as heir to the empire – but the baby's dark skin puts paid to his plan. In his unmasking of power built on violence,[1] Shakespeare in this deeply sardonic play repeatedly ironises notions of barbarity.[2] Conventionally and complacently applied to Aaron as the notion is (compare 5.3.4: "This barbarous Moor"), the vengeful power structures of Roman "civilisation" are in this play

---

1 Shakespeare in this play depicts Roman "civilisation" as a structure of violence (established and maintained by its exercise). The play opens with two brothers demanding violence from their followers to validate their rival claims to the imperial throne (e.g. 1.1.1-17) and ends with the vicious, vengeful torture of Aaron (5.3.178-82) and Tamora (5.3.194-97).

2 Compare my article "'Barbarism.'"

exhibited as no less "barbarous" (1.1.131), "unnatural and unkind" (5.3.47) than the cultures of those beyond the Roman pale.

Tamora the "milk-white" (5.1.31) Goth is romantically and sensually disposed towards the "lovely Aaron" (2.3.10-29), her "sweet Moor" (2.3.51). Aaron's attitude towards Tamora is entirely pragmatic. He treats her brusquely, insisting on his own political purpose of "Vengeance" (2.3.38) in contrast with Tamora's amorousness (2.3.30) – giving her just enough assurance of devotion (as "empress" of his "soul" [2.3.40]) not to offend her. Privately, he speaks bluntly of her as an instrument by means of which he can piggyback into the very centre of power (2.1.1-25). Now a merely nominal slave, Aaron also boasts of the (now) empress Tamora as "fettered" to *him* "in amorous chains" (2.1.15). In other words, he has emotionally and erotically enslaved her, and her devotion to him is a tool with which he can wreak havoc in Rome. The ultimate victim of the vengeance is the young Roman woman Lavinia: raped, tongueless, with her hands severed; "righteously" executed by her father as soon as she has assisted at *his* murderous revenge banquet. Aaron prefigures Iago in his destructive scheming, but for one main difference: whereas Iago is icily uncaring, Aaron's love for his new-born child is expressed in the words full of tenderness and pride in which he addresses it[3] – whereas Tamora has sent Aaron the baby with the order to "christen it with [his] dagger's point" (4.2.70) (since to her the black baby is a mere danger, and a political embarrassment).

Titus Andronicus is a highly intelligent, sardonic study of politics, presented in the mode of melodrama. Shakespeare's further examination of the "darker" outsider and his futile and thwarted vengeance against a " white" social power bloc in *The Merchant of Venice* (1598) is a considerably more nuanced work. In it, anti-Semitic prejudice against Shylock is subtly linked with Portia's disdain towards the "complexion" of the Prince from Morocco (2.1.1 and 2.6.79), and the callous earlier reference to the Venetian clown Lancelot's seduction of a young servant – his "getting up of the Negro's belly"[4] (3.5.36-37).

---

3 "Sweet blowze, you are a beauteous blossom, sure" (4.2.72, and following). The terms of Aaron's first greeting to his child are in their tone reminiscent of a well-known passage in *The Winter's Tale* (2.2.62-66) in which Paulina describes the new-born Perdita. See also 3.3.45 in this play, where the soft-hearted courtier Antigonus addresses the baby princess Perdita as "Blossom" (like Aaron his own baby in *Titus Andronicus*).

4 In the next sentence Lancelot is told: "The Moor is with child by you" (3.5.37), and in this juxtaposition the interchangeable use of the terms "Moor" and "Negro" is noticeable. Both the rebuke and the bantering disavowal which follow (3.5.35-

In the figure of Desdemona Shakespeare may seem to have incorporated elements of Lavinia (from *Titus Andronicus*), innocent white female victim[5] of a black man's wrath. Both women "represent" a power structure without being personally powerful. But the great, late tragedy is incomparably subtler and more wrenching in its effect because in both Othello (initially) and in Desdemona there is a deep, naïve innocence which leads them to imagine each other, and their union, as existing beyond the reach of the envious, racist social pressures of their context, as if such a relationship could retain an inviolate purity. Desdemona is, of course, described as "the more angel" (5.2.131) because she retains her faith in Othello beyond his vicious, misplaced suspicion and even his murder of herself. Such an "overcompensating" love is itself not unimplicated in the structures of the racial and continental demarcations of the time, however. Desdemona, whose sense of human practicalities is generally superior to Othello's[6] (a pattern characterising the gender roles in most heterosexual love relationships depicted by Shakespeare), dismisses (by implication) Othello's appearance, the markers of his race and nation, by saying that when she fell in love

---

45) make clear that the seduction and the resulting pregnancy and child are being dismissed as unimportant, because of the woman's race and class position. On Elizabethan use of racial terms such as 'Moor,' see the fascinating essay by Daniel J. Vitkus, as well as the essay by Boose. See also my own essay on *The Merchant of Venice*.

5 Lavinia is a much less appealing or sweetnatured figure than Desdemona, and Shakespeare invests little moral energy in delineating her beyond indicating her sharp tongue and her snobbery as well as the racial colouring of her (and her husband's) vision (2.3.66-79), however unjust and horrifying her eventual fate is.

6 The textual detail often taken to illustrate the point most vividly occurs in the depiction of their first reunion in Cyprus:

Oth. O my fair warrior!
Des. My dear Othello!
Oth. [. . .] O my soul's joy
[. . .] If it were now to die,
'Twere now to be most happy, for I fear
My soul hath her content so absolute,
That not another comfort, like to this,
Succeeds in unknown fate.
Des. The heavens forbid
But that our loves and comforts should increase
Even as our days do grow. (2.1.182-199)

Compare the essays by Grennan and by Neely.

with him, "I saw Othello's visage in his mind" (1.3.252). Her creed of moral tolerance may contrast with Othello's absolute idealism – she knows "men are not gods" and that honeymoons don't last (3.4.146-148) – but whereas Emilia is immediately alert to the threat, Desdemona declares Othello "made of no such baseness / as jealous creatures are," thinking that "the sun where he was born / drew all such humours from him" (3.4.23-27). Hence her attitude essentialises Othello, albeit idealistically. He may have the "honours" and the "valiant parts" (1.3.253) which made her prefer him to "the wealthy curled darlings of [her own] nation" (1.2.68), but had she considered the social insecurities of the Venetians' lone black general, she might have been more circumspect in her pleas (to him) for Cassio's reinstatement. Having seen Othello initially as a tower of strength, Desdemona fails to imagine his weakness and vulnerability. The narrator of Salih's novel exclaims at one point: "How strange! How ironic! Just because a man has been created on the Equator some mad people regard him as a slave, others as a god" (Salih 108).[7]

Iago, the villain of the tragedy, evil as his machinations are, is probably not primarily a racist.[8] He recognises that, had he been let alone, Othello would have made "a most dear husband" (2.1.286) to Desdemona. What Iago does know, though, are the paired fears in a racist society – notions of "the black peril" on the "white" side, and on the other hand, anxieties about social contempt from and exploitation by whites, felt by those who are "black." Iago knows, fiendishly, how to arouse and manipulate and unleash these terrible and mutually de-

---

7 Fanon writes: "To us, the man who adores the Negro is as 'sick' as the man who abominates him" (*Black* 8). Compare the words of academic "Englishman" in Salih's novel, who says of "the English Left" that their favouring of Mustafa Sa'eed was mere tokenism, and adds that "the same exaggerated emotional energy bears either to the extreme right or to the extreme left" (Salih 58-59).

The point has more recently been reiterated by Ben Okri in his piece on *Othello*: "Those who hate black people and those who romanticise them mean the same thing [. . .]" (564).

8 Compare two quotes from the essay by Little: "throughout, [Othello's] blackness continues to elude" (311); and "It is Iago who most adroitly pushes Othello towards the (re)discovery of his black origins" (316). See also the essay by Adelman. When he is first shown "working on" Roderigo, Iago declares: "these Moors are changeable in their wills," but he follows this (almost within a breath) with the comment on Desdemona that "she must have change, she must" (1.3.347-353) – suggesting an equally promiscuous appetite in "Moors" and a "Venetian," most probably without himself believing this of either Desdemona or Othello.

structive furies. Thus he changes the vivid image of a faithful Desdemona in Othello's mind for its hovering, initially unacknowledged counterpart: Desdemona the scheming cuckolder. She *becomes* the "super-subtle Venetian" (1.3.357) in Othello's mind, a type of her nation, no longer herself, the "pity[ing]" woman who fell in love with him out of her individual tenderness and courage (of which her father had been unaware – 1.3.94-98).

As Iago intensifies his insecurities to a pitch of hysteria, Othello in fact himself becomes more cunning and manipulative, more like Iago, more "Venetian." He tells Desdemona an elaborate lie that fetishises the handkerchief he had earlier given her as a love-token. We learn by the end of the play, after Desdemona's murder, that (in Othello's own words) this handkerchief was merely "an antique token my father gave my mother" (5.2.217-18), a simple pledge or family heirloom. But when Iago has poisoned his mind against Desdemona and Othello has already irrevocably betrayed his wife by turning and cleaving to Iago[9] (instead of to Desdemona) as his anchor and guide in Venetian society, Othello tells another story[10] about the handkerchief:

> Oth. That handkerchief
> Did an Egyptian to my mother give,
> She was a charmer, and could almost read
> The thoughts of people; she told her, while she kept it
> 'Twould make her amiable, and subdue my father
> Entirely to her love: but if she lost it,
> Or made a gift of it, my father's eye
> Should hold her loathly, and his spirits should hunt
> After new fancies: she dying, gave it me,
> And bid me, when my fate would have me wive,

---

9 It is by now a critical commonplace that in the scene (3.3.335-486) where Iago eventually kneels beside Othello and pledges him his support in "avenging" the supposed cuckoldry (by Desdemona and Cassio) to which Othello believes himself subject, their act resembles parodically a wedding scene of a conventional bride and groom and, thus (psychically) Othello and Iago's "cuckoldry" of Desdemona. The monstrous conception of suspicion in Othello's mind will issue in the murdered bodies on the marital bed, all three people betrayed by Iago (see, e.g., essays by Parker and by Gross.)

10 The essay by Gross also focuses on this passage, making several points similar to my own, but with a different "slant"; see also the comments (on this point) by Lemuel A. Johnson (170-173).

To give it her; I did so, and take heed on't,
Make it a darling, like your precious eye,
To lose, or give't away, were such perdition
As nothing else could match.
Des. Is't possible?
Oth. 'Tis true, there's magic in the web of it;
A sibyl, that had number'd in the world
The sun to make two hundred compasses,
In her prophetic fury sew'd the work;
The worms were hallow'd that did breed the silk,
And it was dyed in mummy, which the skilful
Conserve of maidens' hearts.
Des.I' faith, is't true? (3.4.53-73)

What is noticeable from the first three lines here is that Othello in his exoticising description of the napkin is culturally alienating Desdemona; he is excluding her from "his" world, as he feels (through Iago's persuasion) excluded from Venetian society and its supposed easy promiscuities. The same Othello who soothingly, half mockingly assured Desdemona's father Brabantio that the "only [. . .] witchcraft" (1.3.169) he had used to "charm" Desdemona[11] was to tell her the story of his life, now threatens her with the inevitable (or even already irrevocable!) loss of his love for her, and with the damnation to which he will attempt to send her as he later strangles her. He does this because *his* "soul" has been caught by the "perdition," the whirling "chaos" (3.3.91-93) which his own betrayal of loving trust has brought about.[12] It is noticeable that marital love is im-

11 Compare Fanon: "Why not, for instance, conclude that the father revolts because in his opinion the Negro will introduce his daughter into a sexual universe for which the father does not have the key, the weapons, or the attributes?" (*Black* 117 – written with no reference to Brabantio or the play *Othello*). Iago's innuendo, "lascivious Moor," certainly expresses this phobia (1.1.126).

12 Shakespeare heightens the poignancy of the betrayal by showing us that Othello half anticipates, perhaps even half *wills* that dreadful loss: "Excellent wretch, perdition catch my soul, / But I do love thee, and when I love thee not / Chaos is come again" (3.3.91-93), he had said earlier, just before Iago's first innuendo struck him. Was he giving Iago an opening here? Why does he, to *this* man, expose both his love and his dependency? Is he already beginning to turn (on) to Iago the trust that should be put in Desdemona, because of the intensity of his sexual-cultural insecurities in Venice? The point is, of course, to recognise Othello's

agined in this speech as a species of conquest or male defeat ("subdued"), precariously held against loathing; that Othello's tone is coercive and threatening and warns of the "perdition" (a significantly recurrent term in Othello's discourse, from 3.3.91) which (since the handkerchief *is* already lost) is now imminent. Love is debased and reified ("Make *it* a darling like your precious eye"; emphasis added – punning on "I"?) into a piece of embroidered cloth, something like a passport, without which Desdemona will no longer be "amiable" (i.e. loveable). For the bond of admiration, desire, trust and loyalty that existed between them, Othello has substituted the *ersatz* "magic in the web" of the handkerchief, a kind of invented and exclusive Africanism.

The handkerchief is associated with death, not life – the deathlike, infertile, eerie and supposedly absolute purity of "conserve[d] maidens' hearts," with references to "worms" and to "mummy" that obscurely bring notions of putrefecation to mind and that point forward to the pure *but dead* Desdemona of the play's end. This fetishisation of chastity will eventuate in Othello's swinging back to the counter-absolutism, once he has been reassured of Desdemona's sexual faithfulness, of describing the murdered woman as a "pearl [. . .] / richer than all his tribe" (5.2.348)[13] – never bringing the Venetian woman home, or achieving the "increase" of "loves and comforts [. . .] as [their] days [might

---

insecurity (*and* Desdemona's social security and confidence) as markers of their respective social positions, rather than as "personal," or moral weakness (or strength), respectively. See Mahoney, "The Social Construction of Whiteness." Felperin writes: "As the living symbol of high Venetian culture, Desdemona is not simply a wife to Othello but the legitimating agent of his acculturation" (78).

13 That a pearl (besides its preciousness) is usually of a pale, whitish hue, and that the reference by a black man to "his tribe" calls (so-called) black people to mind, can be no accident. Compare the words of Louis T. Achille: "In so far as truly interracial marriage is concerned, one can legitimately wonder to what extent it may not represent for the coloured spouse a kind of subjective consecration to wiping out in himself and in his own mind the colour prejudice from which he has suffered for so long. It would be interesting to investigate this in a given number of cases and perhaps to seek in this clouded motivation the underlying reason for certain inter-racial marriages entered into outside the normal conditions of a happy household" (qtd. in Fanon, *Black* 51).

Othello's resemblance to the "abandonment-neurotic" described by Fanon (*Black* 54-58) has been noted by some critics. In himself he combines, however, this condition with that of the *alienated* black person who finds himself within a "white" structure (on which the rest of Fanon's text concentrates). See (e.g.) the essay by Burton.

have] grow[n]" (2.1.194-195) which Desdemona had hoped for. She, ironically, prophetically assumes the role of her mother's "maid call'd Barbary" (4.3.26). Although the name of this woman, whose beloved "prov'd mad" and forsook her (4.3.27-28), may be no more than a version of the English name Barbara, in the context of this play's geographical and ideological scheme of reference (such as Othello's disapproving silencing of the "barbarous brawl" offending "Christian shame" and carrying, as he puts it, threatening overtones of the faithful "turn'd Turks" [2.3.161-163], along with the constant refrain of references to Othello as the "Moor"),[14] it is difficult to overlook the suggestion of the pampered Venetian lady Desdemona having now assumed the position of the seduced and abandoned black servant girl. The way the sad song of a woman's abandonment in love recalls the African queen Dido's fruitless attempt to waft her beloved Roman Aeneas (an Asian becoming an European) back to her, by using a wand of willow, has also been noticed.[15]

Othello's fractured subjectivity provides the cracks through which Iago's poison can enter his mind, corroding two marriages and crushing five lives, letting in (as Ben Okri says) "the terrors that are at the heart of the play" (562): that the real peril, the real time bombs in our societies are not signposted by skin colour, but are the grudge-bearing "insiders" who are not superficially distinguishable; those who are believed to be "honest" like Iago. But Okri is also critical of the Othello Shakespeare conceived, calling him "the white man's myth of the black man," called "noble" by the whites who use him – "a negative myth [or warning] for black people in the West" (564).[16] It is no wonder that the man Othello,

---

14 An important and highly enlightening article concerning the racial and religious tensions of the historical period before and during the period of the writing of *Othello* is the essay by Vitkus (see footnote 4); see also the essay by Smith.

15 See *The Merchant of Venice*: "In such a night / Stood Dido with a willow in her hand / Upon the wild sea banks, and waft her love / To come again to Carthage" (5.1.9-12). See also Parker's essay (95-98 especially) and Hall's book.

16 The words quoted in the following passage might have been written to describe the position of the Moorish Othello, in his role as Venetian general: "serv[ing] his adopted country in the land of his ancestors [. . .] ma[d]e him wonder whether he was not being betrayed by everything about him, for the white race would not accept him as one of its own and the black virtually repudiated him" (qtd. in Fanon, *Black* 49). Jyotsna Singh's excellent essay on *Othello* and *Season* is well worth reading on the ambiguities of Othello's position, as is Barbara Harlow's. Edward Washington holds that "Othello has not forgotten that he is black, [but . . .] seeks [.

whose transition from Venetian military employment to civilian life began with the self-exoticising stories of "anthropophagi" and other tall tales of deformed and subhuman Africans[17] should end by slaughtering himself *as* a "circumcised dog"; "a malignant and a turban'd Turk" (5.2.353-357) – self-sentenced in terms of a racist stereotype and notably, not because he betrayed the individual, faithful Desdemona in an act of *personal* failure and venom, but as one who "traduc'd the [Venetian] *state*" and (it seems) all European Christendom. Lemuel A. Johnson (a Sierra Leonean, now U.S.-based, theorist) refers to him as "this very estrangeable man" (123). Othello, in other words, allows himself to fulfil the alienating prophecy that white racism makes about "even the best" of blacks. In doing so he destroys the best of the whites and the best in himself, the human "kindness"[18] that always needs acknowledgement for life to prosper. Othello's

---

. .] personal success through the politic 'humanization' of his blackness in Venice" (173).

17 Compare the following, from Lemuel A. Johnson's text (110-111):

> De Certeau's terms of reference thus allow for a response to *Othello* that would focus on the ways in which the Moor of Venice encourages surplus identities of himself; in which he is complicit as a witness against himself. That being the case, whether by cold calculation or in grandiloquent self-advertisement, there is telling irony in the fact that Othello does bear witness against himself with that "traveller's history" of his life, in a Venice that was already predisposed to a certain understanding of his racial and sexual type. For he does embroider and carry on so: about Cannibals and Anthropophagi; about rocks whose heads touch heaven; and about men whose heads grow beneath their shoulders. The awkwardness of Othello's place in the scheme of things and his "'dilated' traveller's tale," Patricia Parker observes, thus re-opened "to Venetian (and English) eyes exotic worlds beyond the direct reach of vision."

18 See 4.2.161-165: "Unkindness may do much; / And his unkindness may defeat my life, / But never taint my love," in which the poignancy of Desdemona's words relies on one's recognition of the pun on "unkindness," which means (simultaneously) (1) lack of compassion, kindness, or gentleness; (2) alienness (being of a different "kind"); (3) unnaturalness or inhumanity (behaving unlike "human kind" should or does). Her declared refusal to allow her love for Othello to become "taint[ed]," even in the face of the "evidence" (his harshly unloving attitude towards, even detestation and hatred towards herself) of course contrasts with the extent to which Othello has allowed the tainting of his conception of Desdemona to occur. But both Othello and Desdemona are unrealistic; both their eyes are clouded by the cultural-racial tensions of the context. Desdemona's dying words, it

type of "black soul" is (as Fanon says, and as Shakespeare[19] may have sensed) "a white man's artefact" (*Black* 2). It takes more than a single Desdemona to undo such damage. In *Black Skin, White Masks* Fanon says, with reference to what one might term the struggle for the achievement of full subjectivity, that

> human reality in-itself-for-itself can be achieved only through conflict and through the risk that conflict implies. This risk means [. . .] the transformation of subjective certainty of my own worth into a universally valid objective truth.
>
> [. . .] I do battle for the creation of a human world – that is, of a world of *reciprocal recognitions*. (155; emphasis added)[20]

– a quotation clearly useful to the understanding of the predicament of the protagonists of both main texts here discussed.

My subtitle for this essay, I discover in retrospect, may actually be an unconscious echo and adaptation of a Fanonian question: "can the white man behave healthily towards the black man and can the black man behave healthily towards

---

is worth noting, are: "Commend me to my *kind* lord" (5.2.126, emphasis added) – a significant recurrence of a key term.

19 V. M. Vaughan says of *Othello*: "I think this play is racist, and I think it is not" (70). It would be some years later than *Othello* (dated at c. 1604) and then in his depiction of the superb Cleopatra, that Shakespeare would (*Antony and Cleopatra* being dated approximately 1608) portray an African woman so confident of her own worth and selfhood that she could emotionally overcome and lovingly forgive (unlike Othello!) the temporary betrayal of her European lover Mark Antony (see 2.5 and 3.3 in this play). Caliban, son of the shadowy but definitely North African Sycorax in *The Tempest* (1611), is probably Shakespeare's last powerful portrayal of an African; a subject who (as we know) has achieved immense resonance in the area of postcolonial studies as a "representative" character functioning to expose and challenge colonial racism (see e.g. the "Brief Conclusions" chapter of my *Achebe, Head, Marechera: On Power and Change in Africa* (275-278). Notably, the journey that leads into the tempest of the play's title was occasioned by the marriage of the Italian princess Claribel to a North African – the King of Tunis (2.1.75-76; 5.1.212 in *The Tempest*).

20 On the final page of *Black Skin, White Masks* Fanon confirms these ideas (in another typically male-inflected passage) about the need to "achieve" subjectivity, as follows: "The Negro is not. Any more than the white man. Both must turn their back on the inhuman voices which were those of their respective ancestors in order that authentic communication be possible. Before it can adopt a positive voice, freedom requires an effort at disalienation" (Fanon, *Black* 165).

the white man?" (*Black* 120) – a question to which the preceding reference to "reciprocal recognitions" is the ideal answer; the eventuality aspired to. But Fanon also indicates uncompromisingly how great a distance has to be travelled before such recognitions can become possible – without his (at this point) bringing in the gender issue, which I highlight. Fanon also indicates the possibility of false routes towards disalienation or full subjecthood which may be followed by the alienated or disintegrated black (male) subject, in a passage that seems to anticipate (or at least describe) the conduct of Salih's major character (Mustafa Sa'eed) in *Season of Migration to the North*: "[T]he Negro who wants to go to bed with a white woman. In the latter there is clearly a wish to be white. A lust for revenge, in any case. [. . .] White civilisation and European culture have forced an existential deviation on the Negro" (*Masks* 12).[21]

The legend that builds up around Mustafa Sa'eed emphasises that he was "the first Sudanese to marry an Englishwoman" (in fact, "a European of any kind") (55); "one of the darlings of the English left" (58); a "conqueror" (60) who is said to have boasted laughingly: "'I'll liberate Africa with my penis'" (120). In this complex, enigmatic novel, Tayeb Salih (the Sudanese author) builds up a dense palimpsest of often conflicting, contradictory impressions of Mustafa Sa'eed. He does this partly by means of the device of filtering our knowledge of this main character through the impressions of him garnered by the unnamed narrator – *like* Mustafa Sa'eed, a Sudanese who returns after prolonged study in Britain.[22] This narrator is a much more hesitant personality than Mustafa Sa'eed – he is in many respects more successfully reintegrated into his original village context, yet also envious of the man who so impresses everyone and who seems to be of more useful service to the village than himself – in his returnee's role as

---

[21] On the interpretation of some critics that Mustafa Sa'eed's bedding of British women is a (politically effective) campaign of anti-colonial liberation, the following Fanonian comment is also relevant: "Racialism and hatred and resentment – 'a legitimate desire for revenge' – cannot sustain a war of liberation" (*Wretched* 111). See also Matar's essay on *Season*.

[22] For interesting comments on the function of the narrator and on his and/or Mustafa Sa'eed's relative importance, see the essays by Amyuni; Ihsan Abbas; Abu-Haydar; Khairallah and Matar, a.w.a. the essay by Davidson (not in the *Casebook* on *Season*). Salih himself has stated that in this novel he deliberately created a "conflicting world" with "two voices" (with reference to Mustafa Sa'eed's and the narrator's) to force the reader to make up his/her own mind, since the usual assumption of identity between author and the first person voice is here not sustainable (qtd. in Amyuni 16).

a civil service bureaucrat. But the narrator gradually develops a burning hatred of the mysterious Mustafa Sa'eed (134; 166).

The extent to which this Sudanese novel (originally written in Arabic; published in Beirut in 1967 and in 1969 in its first English translation) signifies upon[23] Shakespeare's *Othello* is made explicit at several points in the text, for example when Mustafa Sa'eed answers the question as to what his race is by saying "'I'm like Othello – Arab-African'" (38). In order to seduce the questioner, a white woman (one of his many sexual conquests, all heartlessly undertaken), Mustafa Sa'eed tells her (the description is his own) "fabricated stories about deserts of golden sands and jungles where non-existent animals called out to one another"; he also arouses in her a sardonically noted "Christian sympathy" (38). These details distinctly call Desdemona's initial attraction to Othello to mind.

But that the African novel rings many changes on the European play is equally recognisable. It does so in some respects, I believe, by treating the *Othello* situation as a myth that requires re-examination – a study that can lay bare some of the deep wounds and wrongs of the skewed relations between the "races" *and* the "sexes." The Sudanese novel traces the intimate and intricate connections between the international phenomenon of colonialism (on the one hand) and what is here treated as local, "traditional" destructive patriarchy (on the other). It is a brilliant study of the intertwinement of racism and sexism.

The narrator's unmistakable initial fascination with Mustafa Sa'eed exposes, as this reading of the novel will argue, the misleading glamour that this strange man exudes (his good looks are frequently noted). That the glamour is false is indicated both in the way the Englishwomen (of various ages and classes) whom he seduces with no intention of marriage relate to him, (i.e.) in terms of a "racist romanticism" (or "romantic racism") of the kind Edward Said has more recently

---

23 Henry Louis Gates Jr, in his *The Signifying Monkey*, identifies "signifying" as a practice of satirical or ironic or mocking response (or implied comment), an echoing or mimicry of a powerful original which is challenged by being re-enacted with a difference. Barbara Harlow in her essay on *Othello* and *Season* makes the point that Salih's text can be seen as "participat[ing]" in the Arabic literary tradition (called *mu'āradah*) of "retaliatory" writing (75). Jyotsna Singh sees Salih's novel as exemplifying the "counterdisciplinary" and "revisionist" strategies of non-European writers in the sixties (299). (Singh also refers to Fanon's ideas in her essay, though not as extensively as I do.) Makdisi describes *Season* as "a radical intervention in the field of postcolonial Arab discourse" (805).

exposed in *Orientalism* (1979),[24] and (secondly) in the utterly cynical "conquest" mentality of the African seducer. In Mustafa Sa'eed, I suggest, Salih has combined features of Shakespeare's Othello with those of his villain, Iago. Like Iago he is a demonically effective scene-setter,[25] seducer and destroyer (three white women who associate with him commit suicide; the fourth is murdered by him). Being an invader and (supposedly) a "conqueror" (60), he has (however) taken on the same hue of those on whom he is supposedly avenging himself[26] – as Othello (in my reading of Shakespeare's play) to some extent becomes a Iago even as he "turn[s] Turk" (2.3.161) in his murder of Desdemona.

I want to draw attention to a small but (I believe) crucial detail in Salih's text.[27] During his trial for the murder of his English wife (Jean Morris) Mustafa Sa'eed thinks to himself, whilst his defence lawyer refers to him as a "noble"[28] person "whose mind was able to absorb Western civilisation but it broke his heart," that the exculpatory argument is simply "untrue," for (as he puts it here), "*I am no Othello. I am a lie*" (33; emphasis added). These latter words indicate that Mustafa Sa'eed holds on to the image of the Moor (Othello) as (unlike himself) an uncomplicated, dedicated lover; a "true" African as much as a "true" lover, diabolically misled and manipulated by the fiendish European, Iago. As the narrator's understanding of Mustafa Sa'eed's ambiguity slowly grows into an eventual detestation of the man, this process is marked (I suggest) by a slight

24 See (e.g.) "'How marvellous your black colour is! [. . .] the colour of magic and mystery and obscenities'" (139); or: "she cried out ecstatically: 'The Nile'" (39); or: "'you are beautiful beyond description'" (143).

25 See the description of his rooms, both in London (e.g. 30-31) and in the Sudan (the narrator calls this room a "museum," judging that Mustafa Sa'eed "want[ed] to be discovered, like some object of value" and castigates his "limit[less] [. . .] egoism and [. . .] conceit" [154]). See also Geesey's intelligent discussion of "hybridity" notions in the novel.

26 See Mustafa Sa'eed's declaration: "I, over and above everything else, am a colonizer" (94).

27 A. A. Abbas is the only other commentator on Salih's novel whom I have found drawing attention to the variation between the two statements, but he reads its significance somewhat differently (see p. 34 in his *Casebook* essay). Harlow's comments distinguish politically between Othello and Mustafa Sa'eed, emphasising the ironies and injustices of the south/north encounter and reading Salih's Mustafa Sa'eed as a sort of sardonic corrective of the "western sentimentalism" of Shakespeare's text.

28 Othello is, of course, referred to as "noble" (in the eponymous play) almost as often as Iago is called "honest."

and probably unconscious change in his recall of the words quoted and italicised above. The narrator remembers Mustafa Sa'eed, at this later stage, as having stated "*I am no Othello. Othello was a lie*" (95). This apparently slight error in his recall occurs significantly as he listens, "as though it came to me from afar," to the "sobbing of Hosna Bint Mahmoud, the Sudanese woman whom Mustafa Sa'eed had married (and apparently widowed by his suicide) after his return to Sudan. Othello is here identified as a liar by the narrator, I believe, to indicate his slowly growing awareness (perhaps brought about because he is falling in love[29] with Hosna) that Othello (like Mustafa Sa'eed) in fact betrayed *both* his race *and* his wife – as/and in Mustafa Sa'eed's case, his race and *both* his wives.

Mustafa Sa'eed's relationship with Jean Morris is distinctly perverse. Because she sets herself up as the one "unconquerable" woman in the London circles where he operates, Mustafa Sa'eed becomes besotted with, enslaved and degraded by her; she tempts and taunts him into the act of murder (by a sexualised, ritualised knife stabbing) which simultaneously takes her life and destroys his "occupation"[30] in Britain. He thinks of that murderous moment, however, as the "completion" of his whole life (68):[31]

> 'I have bedded [he says melodramatically of his relationship with Jean Morris] the goddess of Death and gazed upon Hell from the aperture of her eyes – it's a feeling no man can imagine. The taste of that night stays on in my mouth, preventing me from savouring anything else.' (153)

---

29 See 104; 112; 132-133; 141.

30 Cf. *Othello* 3.3.363: "Othello's occupation's gone" (words said when he first believes Desdemona to have cuckolded him and recalled when he has been brought to his senses after murdering her – before he *resumes* the "military" role in killing himself in punishment for the murder).

31 Compare 155-165, e.g. "For me this moment of ecstasy is worth the whole of life," comparable to Othello's words on being reunited with Desdemona in Cyprus (see footnote 6). Desdemona, like Hosna, has a more "domestic" sense of love and fulfilment (see, again, footnote 6) – when asked by the narrator whether she had loved Mustafa Sa'eed, Hosna answers: "'He was the father of my children'" (90). The perversity of Mustafa Sa'eed's feeling for *his* (white) wife is both like and unlike Othello's for Desdemona. Discovering the probable evidence of this first wife Jean's infidelity (another man's handkerchief!) in their bedroom, Mustafa Sa'eed seems both anguished and titillated (162). See especially Mustafa Sa'eed's description of the moment of the murder as simultaneously satanic and an "ultimate reality," or fulfilment (165).

Looking at the painting Mustafa Sa'eed made of Jean Morris and placed as a shrine-like centrepiece in his secret room, the narrator can now ask demythologising questions about her: "Was this, then, the phoenix that had ravished the ghoul? [. . .] [That] had made [Mustafa Sa'eed] swallow such degradations?" (155).

Aside from these speculations, the narrator's dominant feelings at this point, he says, are those of "bitterness and hatred, for after all those victims [Mustafa Sa'eed] crowned his life with yet another one, Hosna Bint Mahmoud, the only woman I have ever loved" (141). That the narrator is himself married to another woman[32] of course implicates him, too, in the idea of betrayal. The main point I intend (and which I believe the author wishes to convey), however, is that the destructive relationship between the black man Mustafa Sa'eed and his white European wife Jean has everything to do with the later, horrifying death of his second (African) wife, Hosna. In my interpretation the "symbolic logic" connecting the two wives' shocking deaths (for both of whom the narrator blames Mustafa Sa'eed, in the passage just quoted, even though the latter perpetrated only the murder of Jean Morris) indicates a profound and dangerous failure and inability to love in Mustafa Sa'eed as a man of fractured subjectivity.[33]

Mustafa Sa'eed appears in the narrator's eyes to have achieved an enviably successful and complete reimmersion in Sudanese village life after his return, his own situation appearing more problematic in this respect. Only gradually and

---

32 She *may* be a "white" woman: the narrator makes no reply when the elderly Bint Majzoub teases him by saying, "'We were afraid [. . .] you'd bring back with you an uncircumcised infidel for a wife'" (4); he also never names or describes this wife beyond mentioning that the villagers pay no attention to her (when he and she return there to visit), but lavish all their attention on their daughter (63).

33 In a cynical response to one of his white victims' emphasis on humanity's need of "courage and optimism" (revealingly *linked* with the narrator's Sudanese grandfather), Mustafa Sa'eed declares: "'I for one shall continue to express myself in this *twisted* manner'" (41; emphasis added). On one of the papers the narrator finds in Mustafa Sa'eed's secret room is the written declaration that he and Jean Morris had loved each other in a "twisted" manner (151). Fanon states, in a passage that "comments" on the diseased nature of Mustafa Sa'eed's notion of love, that the "person I love will strengthen me by endorsing my assumption of my manhood" and that "authentic love will remain unattainable before one has purged oneself of that feeling of inferiority or that Adlerian exaltation, that overcompensation, which seem to be the indices of the black *Weltanschauung*" (*Black* 31). Salih himself reportedly declared: "'I read Frantz Fanon after I finished writing *Season* and I discovered that I was in total agreement with him'" (qtd. in Abbas 30 n.).

almost obscurely does the author make clear to the reader that Mustafa Sa'eed is in fact a classic case of (in Fanonian terms) the Manichean, divided, colonised subject.[34] In England he sets up a seducer's lair crammed with a hotchpotch of African exotica (incense, etc.). Back in Sudan and to all intents and purposes now a village farmer, father of two schoolgoing sons, he maintains a large secret room to which neither his wife nor anyone else is allowed access during his lifetime – it is a replica of an educated British gentleman's drawing room,[35] crammed only with English books. Fanon says that "the colonial world is a world cut in two" (*Wretched* 29); here we have a man who, because he is so severed, cannot be "true"; unintegrated, he lacks integrity, and is incapable of faithfulness – much like Othello.

Mustafa Sa'eed may or may not[36] have drowned (as the narrator apparently believes) on the night of his disappearance (when the Nile had flooded) and may or may not have intended suicide; what his final letter (which he prepares for and leaves to the narrator) makes clear is that he deliberately planned, prepared for and intended leaving his wife and his sons.[37] It is therefore a distinct possi-

34 Fanon famously introduced the idea that "[t]he colonial world is a Manichean world" (*Wretched* 31), a notion adopted by later theorists such as Homi Bhabha and Abdul JanMohamed. Earlier, Fanon had written that "[i]n the case of the African especially, white society has smashed his old world without giving him a new one" (*Black* 131), calling the idea of a fractured subjectivity to mind.

35 The room has a "glistening" dining-table; a "silver candelabrum"; a "ceiling of oak" (138) a.w.a. "Persian rugs" and a "real English fireplace" (136). Of the conference hall in Khartoum we are told that it cost "more than a million pounds," with its "corridors of white marble brought from Italy"; its "chandeliers the size of a [. . .] camel"; its "smooth and shiny" platform (119). Mustafa Sa'eed's room is evidently similar to the opulent hall, scandalously and hugely expensively constructed of European materials, at which Africa's despicably neo-colonial rulers gather – men scathingly described by the narrator as "smooth of face, lupine of mouth, their hands gleaming with rings of precious stones, [. . .] and with shoes that reflect the light from chandeliers and squeak as they tread on marble" (Salih 118-119). Salih's character represents the *continental* (neo-colonial) schizophrenia.

36 His body is never found *and* the reader is repeatedly told what a strong swimmer he was.

37 In the letter he writes (of his sons, aged seven and nine): "How I *would have* liked to stay on with them, watching them grow up [. . .] I do not know which of the two courses would be the more selfish, to stay on or to depart. In any event I have no choice [. . .] That *distant call* still rings in my ears. I *thought that* my life and mar-

bility that his "drowning" may have been staged to cover up his abandonment of his Sudanese wife and sons in order to respond to the (to him) irresistible and persistent seductive pull of the West and of European women (and an opulent, urban lifestyle). His Sudanese wife Hosna tells the narrator that she sensed that Mustafa Sa'eed was "hiding something"; that he "spen[t] a lot of time *at night* in that room" (91; emphasis added), from which he excluded her. She also witnessed his "European talk" *in his sleep*, when he would repeat "Jeena Jeeny" (91) – evidently, the name of the Englishwoman Jean Morris, whom he had married and murdered. He leaves the narrator to witness Hosna's anguished "lamentation of a woman for a husband she did not know" (92), and makes *him* responsible for his (Mustafa Sa'eed's) sons' welfare.

Brought up by a widowed mother, with little communication or show of love between himself and her, Mustafa Sa'eed had as a young boy chosen an English, colonial education, becoming or discovering (in the process) a "mind [. . .] like a sharp knife, cutting with cold effectiveness" (22). This knife image[38] is recalled when he finally "overcomes," "satisfies" and "impresses" the taunting Jean Morris – by stabbing her to death, at the moment both confess "love" for each other![39] Though Mustafa Sa'eed may have hoped that the narrator would be able

riage here would silence it. [. . .] But mysterious things in my soul and in my blood impel me towards *faraway parts* [. . .]" (66-67; emphases added). The narrator describes this notion as the "pursuit of a foreign mirage" (93). Compare 29; 33; 93 and 157, on which Jean Morris is described as a "mirage." The image emphasises insubstantiality, a belief in an illusion, and a desire for a world "other" than the dry North African context.

38 Early during the first marriage, in emotional and sexual bafflement, Mustafa Sa'eed "stood over [Jean Morris] with a knife in [his] hand" (158); on the night of the murder, he says, "I put the blade-edge between her breasts [. . .] I pressed down the dagger with my chest until it had all disappeared between her breasts" (164). Fondly recalled as it is, the obscenity of this eroticised act is emphasised by its mimicry of sexual intercourse or rape. The entire relationship with Jean Morris is described in terms of images of warfare, mostly phallic ones (see e.g. 34; see also the images of conquest, mountain scaling and the driving in of tent pegs or flagpoles which Mustafa Sa'eed applies to his other sexual liaisons, e.g. 41). He refers several times to himself and his history as resembling the inevitable course of an "arrow" (e.g. 27) – an image which of course also indicates his eschewal of personal responsibility and his adoption of a *conquistador*'s role.

39 Mustafa Sa'eed's own analysis of the quality of the feeling between himself and Jean Morris is found on a scrap of paper in his room: "It was not hatred. It was a love unable to express itself. I loved her in a twisted manner. She too" (151).

to protect her, his abandonment of Hosna leaves her vulnerably exposed in a patriarchal village where even the most enlightened of the younger village men declares to the narrator that "'Women belong to men'" (99), and that Hosna's forced remarriage to a seventy-year old village roué is unavoidable. As she had earlier threatened (96), when this old man attempts violently to rape Hosna after their marriage, she stabs him and kills herself (124-129).

The murder and suicide weapon in this case is not literally, but symbolically, the same blade that had killed Jean Morris, and here, too, it is symbolically wielded by Mustafa Sa'eed, whose inability to achieve an integral subjectivity had left him at the mercy of the predatory[40] Jean Morris, so irredeemably enslaved to her memory that he has left his betrayed and socially vulnerable Sudanese wife and sons. Hosna, in her turn fascinated by Mustafa Sa'eed and made fascinating and "foreign" (89) by her marriage to "the stranger" Mustafa Sa'eed (129), becomes the prey of village patriarchy, in "need" (as men like her father and her second husband, and even most village women, see it) of being "subdued."[41] The bloodiness and awfulness of the deaths of Mustafa Sa'eed's two wives and of Hosna's second husband are understood by the narrator as being linked: in seeing the dead Hosna as the last of Mustafa Sa'eed's "victims" (141), and in judging the two deaths as equally "obscene," in fact even as "merged," by associating an image in his mind of Hosna as sexually overcome and violated by "the aged Wad Rayyes," and another of the "two white, wide-open thighs" (87) of Jean Morris which enticed Mustafa Sa'eed to murder (the second image having been indelibly implanted in the narrator's mind by Mustafa Sa'eed's narration of his life story). The narrator thus indicates a surrealist, subconscious

40 Compare: "Having been a hunter, I had become the quarry. I was in torment" (159). Jean Morris gives no evidence of what I have termed "romantic racism" in her attitude towards Mustafa Sa'eed (like his other white victims), in fact, Fanon's words in the following passage are (rather) applicable to her: "Western bourgeois racial prejudice as regards the nigger and the Arab is a racism of contempt; it is a racism which minimises what it hates" (*Wretched* 131). Her attitude indicates a decadent, self-destructive and irresponsibly frivolous motivation, sado-masochistic enjoyment of her perpetual humiliation of the helplessly besotted Mustafa Sa'eed.

41 When the narrator suggests, mildly, to Hosna's elderly (at that stage still only) aspirant second husband that she might be allowed to "do as she pleases," he "burst[s] out into a crazy fit of rage" and declares that she will have to marry him, since women in the village are in the charge of their menfolk (97, 98); her father "swore at her and beat her," saying a daughter who "wouldn't listen to him" would make him a "laughing-stock" in the village (122). See also 124-129.

recognition of racial and sexual victimisation as associated[42] diseases contaminating (bedevilling!) the social life of human beings.

Both these texts study the bedevilment of sexual, familial and social life by the racist and sexist parodies of human beings which fear or its twisted twin, the will to dominate, creates in our minds[43] about one another (or ourselves), most devastatingly about those with whom we have intimate dealings. If racism finds a kind of apotheosis in situations of sexual insecurity, sexism is (it seems) exacerbated to extremity by "racial" anxiety or hatred.[44] Power postures are assumed and individuals reduced to incidental, generic attributes in destructive and deadly ways – not only on battlefields, but in bedrooms. Talking about these issues is extremely difficult and always (as we say) "touchy"; both Shakespeare and Salih have made important contributions to what Fanon calls "the world-wide struggle of mankind for his freedom" (117), especially by their incorporation of the female dimension of that struggle (which Fanon underplays). In these two thoughtful, haunting texts, neither writer underemphasises the anguishing uncer-

---

42 Salih very carefully structures the build-up of this association: first, the narrator expresses "the same feeling of embarrassment" at "overhear[ing] the love play [a questionable term, as p. 128 makes clear!] of old Wad Rayyes with his [other] wife," and at having been made to imagine Mustafa Sa'eed's image of Jean Morris as "two thighs, opened wide and white" (48); he *later* "imagine[s] Hosna Bint Mahmoud, Mustafa Sa'eed's widow, as being the same woman in both instances: two white, wide-open thighs in London, and a woman groaning [. . .] under the weight of the aged Wad Rayyes," saying that "*[i]f that other thing was evil, this was evil too*" (86-87; emphasis added); then as he later journeys through the desert (at the time when Hosna is actually being forced into marriage with Wad Rayyes, but before he hears of the murder and suicide) he imagines "The weeping of a woman under a man at dawn and two wide-open white thighs. They are now like the dry bones of camels scattered in the desert" (111); *lastly* there is the (already quoted) passage where the narrator describes Hosna as "yet another" victim of Mustafa Sa'eed's, declaring that Hosna had both murdered Wad Rayyes and killed herself "because of Mustafa Sa'eed" (141; 142).

43 Fanon warns his readers: "The important theoretical problem is that it is necessary at all times and in all places to make explicit, to demystify, and to harry the insult to mankind that exists *in oneself*" (*Wretched* 246; emphasis added).

44 Hernton speaks of "*The racism of sex*" (11) a.w.a. "the sexualisation of racism" (18).

tainties which can produce brutalities, or the extreme intricacy and difficulty of much human intercourse.[45]

Ways of coping may be, like the final act of Salih's narrator, to shout for help (169) or – in the image of Salih's title – to recognise that life is akin to a migration process (168); neither conquest nor enslavement, but an onward circling through the different dimensions of the world, *among* others. I would link this idea with the words of Pieterse and Parekh, that "decolonisation [. . .] requires not [. . .] restoration of a[n] [. . .] alleged pure precolonial heritage, but an imaginative creation of a [. . .] new way of life" (3), to which one might add that it should partake of the dangers, and of the advantages, of our global north *and* south, of our bi-gendered subjectivities, and of our multifarious human race. That Salih learnt from Shakespeare, whereas Shakespeare is extended by Salih, portrays the onward spiralling of this ultimately communal enterprise.

Works Cited

Adelman, Janet. "Iago's Alter Ego: Race as Projection in *Othello*." *Shakespeare Quarterly* 48.2 (1997): 125-144.

Amyuni, Mona Takieddine. Introduction. *Season of Migration to the North: A Casebook*. Ed. by Takieddine Amyuni. Beirut: American University of Beirut, 1985. 11-25.

Abbas, A. Abdullah. "The Father of Lies: The Role of Mustafa Sa'eed as Second Self in *Season of Migration to the North*." Amyuni 27-38.

Abbas, Ihsan. "Sense of Proportion in *Season of Migration to the North*." Amyuni 39-44.

Abu-Haydar, Jareer. "A Novel Difficult to Categorize." Amyuni 45-53.

Bhabha, Homi K. *The Location of Culture*. London: Routledge, 1994.

Boose, Linda E. "'The Getting Of A Lawful Race': Racial Discourse in Early Modern England and the Unrepresentable Black Woman." Hendricks and Parker 35-54, 305-309.

[45] The fragility of human subjectivity is especially memorably expressed by Shakespeare, who refers to the "fear of trust" silencing "the perfect ceremony of love's rite" (Sonnet 23, lines 5-6 in the *Complete Works*). The two main texts here both express the horror and mourning of failed sex and race relationships – yet neither of these works stifles the profound human yearning for their wholesome adjustment.

Burton, Jonathan. "'A most wily bird': Leo Africanus, *Othello* and the Trafficking in Difference." *Post-Colonial Shakespeares*. Ed. Ania Loomba and Martin Orkin. London/New York: Routledge, 1998. 43-63.

Davidson, John E. "In Search of a Middle Point: The Origins of Oppression in Tayeb Salih's *Season of Migration to the North*." *Research in African Literatures* 20.3 (1989): 385-400.

Delgado, R., and J. Stefancic, eds. *Critical White Studies: Looking Behind the Mirror*. Philadelphia: Temple UP, 1997.

Fanon, Frantz. *Black Skin, White Masks*. Trans. L. Markmann. St Albans, Herts: Paladin, 1970.

___. *The Wretched of the Earth*. Trans. Constance Farrington. Harmondsworth: Penguin, 1967.

Felperin, Howard. *Shakespearean Representations*. Princeton: Princeton UP, 1977.

Gagiano, Annie. "Relationships in *The Merchant of Venice*." *Theoria* 71 (1988): 61-77.

___. "'Barbarism' and 'Civilisation' in Shakespeare's *Titus Andronicus* and in Marechera's *Black Sunlight*." *Literary Griot* 10.1 (1999): 13-27.

___. *Achebe, Head, Marechera: On Power and Change in Africa*. Boulder, CO/London: Lynne Rienner, 2000.

Gates, Henry Louis, Jr. *The Signifying Monkey: A Theory of African American Literary Criticism*. New York: Oxford UP, 1989.

Geesey, Patricia. "Cultural Hybridity and Contamination in Tayeb Salih's *Mawsim al-hijra ila al-Shamal* (*Season of Migration to the North*)." *Research in African Literatures* 28.3 (1997): 128-140.

Grennan, Eamon. "The Women's Voices in *Othello*: Speech, Song, Silence." *Shakespeare Quarterly* 38.3 (1987): 275-292.

Gross, Kenneth. "Slander and Skepticism in *Othello*." *ELH* 56.4 (1989): 819-852.

Hall, Kim F. *Things of Darkness: Economies of Race and Gender in Early Modern England*. Ithaca/London: Cornell UP, 1995.

Harlow, Barbara. "Sentimental Orientalism: *Season of Migration to the North* and *Othello*." Amyuni 75-79.

Hendricks, Margo, and Patricia Parker, eds. *Women, "Race" and Writing in the Early Modern Period*. London/New York: Routledge, 1994.

Hernton, Calvin C. *Sex and Racism*. London: André Deutsch, 1969.

JanMohamed, Abdul R. *Manichean Aesthetics: The Politics of Literature in Colonial Africa*. Amherst: University of Massachusetts Press, 1988.

Johnson, Lemuel A. *Shakespeare in Africa (And Other Venues): Import and the Appropriation of Culture*. Trenton, NJ: Africa World Press, 1998.

Khairallah, As'ad. "The Travelling Theater or the Art of Entertaining a Doomed Caravan with Amusing Stories." Amyuni 95-111.

Little, Arthur, Jr. "'An essence that's not seen': The Primal Scene of Racism in *Othello*." *Shakespeare Quarterly* 44.3 (1993): 304-324.

Mahoney, Martha R. "The Social Construction of Whiteness." *Critical White Studies: Looking Behind the Mirror*. Ed. R. Delgado and J. Stefancic. Philadelphia: Temple UP, 1997. 330-333.

Makdisi, Saree S. "The Empire Renarrated: *Season of Migration to the North* and the Reinvention of the Present." *Critical Inquiry* 18.4 (1992): 804-820.

Matar, Nabil. "Tayeb Salih's *Season of Migration to the North*: Circles of Deceit." Amyuni 113-122.

Neely, Carol Thomas. "Women and Men in *Othello*: "What should such a fool / Do with so good a woman?"" *Shakespeare Studies* 10 (1978): 133-158.

Okri, Ben. "Meditations on *Othello*." *West Africa* (23 and 30 March 1987): 562-564, 618-619.

Parker, Patricia. "Fantasies of 'Race' and 'Gender': Africa, *Othello* and Bringing to Light." Hendricks and Parker 84-100.

Pieterse, Jan Nederveen, and Bhikhu Parekh. "Shifting Imaginaries: Decolonization, Internal Decolonization, Postcoloniality." *The Decolonization of the Imagination: Culture, Knowledge and Power*. Ed. J. N. Pieterse and B. Parekh. London: Zed, 1995. 1-19.

Said, Edward. *Orientalism*. New York: Random House, 1979.

Salih, Tayeb. *Season of Migration to the North*. Trans. Denys Johnson-Davies. Boulder, CO and London: Lynne Rienner, 1997. Originally publ. in Arabic as *Mawsim al-Hijra ila'l-Shamāl* (Beirut: Dār al-'Awda, 1967).

Shakespeare, William. *Complete Works*. Ed. Stanley Wells and Gary Taylor. Oxford: Oxford UP, 1988. *Antony and Cleopatra* (1001-1035); *The Merchant of Venice* (425-451); *Sonnets* (749-770); *The Tempest* (1167-1189); *Titus Andronicus* (125-152); *The Winter's Tale* (1101-1130).

___. *Othello*. The Arden Shakespeare. Ed. M. R. Ridley. London: Methuen, 1959.

Singh, Jyotsna. "Othello's Identity, Postcolonial Theory, and Contemporary African Rewritings of *Othello*." Hendricks and Parker 287-368.

Smith, Ian. "Barbarian Errors: Performing Race in Early Modern England." *Shakespeare Quarterly* 49.2 (1998): 168-186.

Vaughan, Patricia Mason. *Othello: A contextual history*. Cambridge: Cambridge UP, 1994.

Vitkus, Daniel J. "Turning Turk in *Othello*: The Conversion and Damnation of the Moor." *Shakespeare Quarterly* 48.2 (1997): 145-176.

Washington, Edward. "'At the door of truth': The Hollowness of Signs in *Othello." Othello: New Essays by Black Writers*. Ed. Mythili Kaul. Washington, DC: Howard UP, 1997. 167-187.

A. C. Jordan's *Tales From Southern Africa*

A. C. Jordan's 1940 novel *Ingqumbo Yeminyanya* (translated into English in 1980 as *The Wrath of the Ancestors*) has a place of honour in Xhosa literature. Not at all as well known is his 1973 collection, *Tales from Southern Africa*, which he wrote in English. In the collection of essays which appeared in the same year, *Towards an African Literature*, Jordan himself wrote that "the English-speaking world knows far less about [the tales about men and women]" than about "myths and animal stories" from Africa (*Towards* 4) and he suggested that "the cultural world is looking for just these and other traditional artistic possessions, of which South Africa itself has not become aware" (14). In 1990 Noverino Canonici wrote that "the folktale tradition [. . .] permeat[es] not only literary forms, but all forms of life" (128), though simultaneously acknowledging many signs of the decline of this cultural resource (134-36; 140-41). If it is true that "cultural identities are formed and informed by a nation's literature" (Toni Morrison 39), the various strands of South African literature may be thought of as dangerously or unhealthily detached from the awareness of those who are non-literate (known to be a large a majority of South Africans). Renewed interest in and use of our folktale resources may be one way of bridging this gap. For, as Isidore Okpewho insists, "the mythopoeic fancy [. . .] concerns itself with the entire spectrum of the social universe" and he recognises its engagement with what he calls "*actualities*" as well as "*mysteries*" (*Myth* 114).[1] In the following brief discussion of Jordan's *Tales* I shall demonstrate how wide ranging and socially pertinent the themes of these stories are.

Without presuming to know the principle(s) in terms of which Jordan selected the thirteen tales included in the collection, this reading finds in his re-telling[2] of

---

1 In "*We Spend Our Lives as a Tale that is Told*," Isabel Hofmeyr concludes: "oral literature quite literally forces scholars to lift their eyes from the page. [. . .] one not only has to confront context as a very material reality, one also confronts anew the complex links that unite producer, text, audience and the world" (181).

2 Scheub in his introduction (Jordan, *Tales*) comments that "the narratives [. . .] have not been retold by A. C. Jordan so much as recast by him" (10). "He used techniques of the short story to bring life to the skeletal outlines" (13) to compensate for the devices (gesture; tone; audience participation; etc.) at the disposal of the oral performer of the *ntsomi* (11-12). In his work *Myth in Africa* (1983), Isidore Okpewho suggests that "the more 'poetic' a tale is, the stronger is its content of intellectual play and thus its availability for exploring larger cultural or existential (as against experimental) issues" (69).

these traditional stories a discernible focus on processes of social adjustment, especially in the overcoming of social crises. They do not merely enshrine reaffirmations of "custom," but portray challenges to, enlargements and adaptations of "custom" itself.[3] It is also evident that this author's interest lies more in the discovery or employment of "internal" mechanisms of adjustment to pressures or threats to the societies which he shows us, than in celebrations of military or muscular force. Confirmation of this tendency is the preponderance of female protagonists in these *Tales*, whether in heroic or in socially transgressive roles (and frequently transgression itself precipitates heroism). The argument of this essay is that Jordan's *Tales from Southern Africa* can be fruitfully read as a composite portrait of societies capable of achieving vital adjustments in response to a variety of challenges.

A good place to begin this brief introduction to Jordan's *Tales* (most of which seem to have been told to him by women: by "the widow, Nofali"; by his great-aunt and by an unnamed "woman from Qumbu" (Z. Pallo Jordan xxii-xxiii) is with the last one in the collection: a hilarious "Parliament of Fowls"[4] story in which all the birds of the world come together in seemingly orderly fashion to choose a leader according to the (apparently) perfectly sensible and appropriate criterion of which of them can stay in the air the longest. The story, in Jordan's handling of it, becomes a brilliantly satirical anecdote, exposing the extent to which a combination of power-hunger, pomposity and chicanery can turn a neatly hierarchical and bureaucratically organised situation into a nightmare of competing political groupings and legalistically irreconcilable contestations: Grass Warbler hitches an undetected ride on the majestic Eagle's back and flutters and flips about in the air triumphantly *after* Eagle's return to the earth, with consequent argument, counter-argument, outrage and scapegoating in a display of ambitious power competition. Although this story is formally one of those ani-

3 In a section of his "general" introduction to Jordan's *Tales* (1-13), Scheub writes that the

> broad theme [of the Xhosa *ntsomi* tradition] centers about the need for an ordered society, a stable and harmonious community [. . .] There is a thematic movement from an impure society through purification and into a healthy social order. This odyssey is often expressed by means of a dramatic enactment of the male and female initiation rites, and usually finds its metaphorical perfection in symbols of nature (9-10).

4 I am alluding to the fourteenth-century English poem by Geoffrey Chaucer, which (many scholars suspect) may contain disguised allusions to contemporary politics, although the ostensible subject is courtly love.

mal fables along the pattern of "Why such-and-such a creature behaves in such-and-such a fashion" (like the two previous *Tales* in the collection: "Why the Cock Crows at Dawn," [260-262], and "Why the Hippo Has a Stumpy Tail," [263-265]), Jordan's "Choosing a King" (266-277) – in its comparative length and in the delightful, biting vividness of its portrayal of individual bird "characters" in recognisable political roles – is evidently a cautionary tale as enjoyable as it is potentially educational. Is it incidental that this *one* story has no female characters?

The tale which Jordan placed first in the collection (18-31) is called "The Turban" – which refers to a woman's headscarf or *doek*. It is a moving, delicately-told story of marital love gone wrong, faintly like Shakespeare's *Othello*, but unlike that play in the degree of emphasis Jordan places on the larger familial and social context of the tragedy. The story features a younger wife, devotedly loved despite her childlessness. The husband has children by his elder wife and so intense is his passion for the younger woman that he resists pressure even from her own family that he take another wife to "compensate" for her barrenness. When both wives gather honey on an expedition, the prudent older woman saves some for her children and her husband. Expecting that his childless wife will have saved even more of the delicacy for him, the husband is so appalled to find that she failed to keep him any that he gives her a blow which, to his horror, kills her. Any remaining sympathy for this man (compromised by his petulance, impetuosity or harshness) is seriously undermined when he proceeds literally to cover up his deed by stealthily burying the dead woman and her belongings before setting out towards her people where both are expected at a wedding festival. As Scheub writes, "It is his ability to continue with life, almost as if in a stupor, as if nothing had happened, that invests the story with much of its horror, and which simultaneously, strongly underscores the love that he had for his wife" (general introduction 16)

A favourite with her people, he is nevertheless summoned from dancing and ritually, wordlessly executed by them when an eery little bird, a "form" of the dead wife's turban, reveals his guilt to them. But the story is put in a realm beyond affirmation of custom[5] when it ends with the dead man's arm rising to press the woman's turban to his heart. Fascinatingly, the story indicates the unusual intensity of this passion as recognised by this society: as *both* destructive

[5] Here I disagree strongly with Scheub, who concludes that "the narrative thus becomes an affirmation of tradition over boundless emotion" (general introduction 17).

(and punished when it goes awry) *and yet* finally, poignantly beyond the reach of the customary, outliving even its own protagonists. The tale is a fascinating introduction to a group of stories of the type usually taken to have the principal purpose of unambiguously affirming social cohesion and time-tried habits.

A tale that in Jordan's telling foregrounds domesticity by showing its disruption and eventual restitution is called "Demane and Demazane" (34-54) after the boy-and-girl twins who are its chief protagonists. The first part of the story is the well-known "amasi bird" episode in which the bird who undoes the field-clearing labours of the parents is captured by the father and ransoms itself in captivity by yielding amasi to his family in a time of general drought. Under peer pressure the twin children break the father's rule of secrecy and the bird escapes. Terrified of paternal punishment, the twins flee into the bush, find shelter and set up their own version of domestic cosiness in the "Rock-of-two-holes," only to encounter a cannibal (or *Zim*) – from whom they escape when a mother-bird, reassuring them that they are loved and longed for at home, flies them home to a reception on their mother's best kaross. One might see this story as portraying a restoration to civil ordinariness and social and familial harmony. Yet it is noticeable that adventurousness is portrayed as admirable; although it cannot last (the amasi bird is lost; the children return home from their camp), it is shown to have been enriching. Like others in the collection, this story foregrounds unusual and transgressive conduct without merely warning of the inevitability of disaster.

A story with a similar pattern of a family break-up and eventual reconstitution is called "Nomabhadi and the Mbulu-Makhasana" (155-177).[6] The first part of the girl Nomabhadi's life takes place in a village where drought and consequent starvation have killed all the children except herself and her two brothers. Jealous of the younger brother's bigger portions, the elder kills him and is himself put to death when his sister reveals the fact. The eeriness and stress of the situation is indicated also in the surrealist detail that *everyone* here has earlier stopped speaking; the sense of doom is intensified when the news of the sibling murder leads the other adults to kill one another – as if that murder has severed some final sustaining ideal. Social breakdown culminates in yet is offset by the parents' decision to send Nomabhadi off to her prosperous uncle while they set fire to themselves and their homestead. Nomabhadi, the sole survivor of the doomed community, fails to obey her mother's final injunction to look neither back nor to left or right. Because of this failure her life is invaded and her role at

6 Compare the *ntsomi* Scheub prints in his book (*Ntsomi* 547-551).

her uncle's homestead usurped by the nearly-human but repulsive Mbulu-Makhasana (perhaps a "recurrence" of the elder brother's jealous greed?). The infiltration of the family by this new form of anti-social greed is abruptly stopped when its uncontainable intensity is exposed in a public ritual or test: the Mbulu-Makhasana's hidden and bound-up tail bursts out and yanks her into a trough of milk. But not even then is the envy of this sub-human creature finally defeated, for a pumpkin plant grows nightmarishly out of the Mbulu-Makhasana's grave and the fruit attacks Nomabhadi while she is being prepared for womanhood. Once again Jordan's telling of the story emphasises not only a need for perpetual vigilance, but for courage, meticulous care and social cooperation. The tale of "Sonyangaza and the Ogres" (193-216) similarly portrays the necessity of a rescue – and here, too, its success is not the sole achievement of the dashing hunter-hero, but comes about partly due to the resolution, spirit and intelligence of both his abducted twin sister and her little half-caste daughter, with the reunion of the three as a family group rounding off and crowning the story (215-216), after the defeat of the ogres.

The tale called "Siganda and Sigandana" (219-237) is a well known story of sibling rivalry that turns murderous. Nevertheless, Jordan's telling intensifies the poignancy in especially two aspects: by portraying the brothers as unusually close and loyal in their tenderly mutual affection and by the strongly empathetic portrayal of the way the beautiful white cow arouses the more cowardly elder brother's envious desire and greed. It is unmistakably a novelist's talent which juxtaposes (the younger) Sigandana's spontaneous and joyous hymn to the loveliness of the white cow (227; given in both Xhosa and English versions) with the guilt-ridden, nervy, fevered musings of the elder brother about this cow (230; after he has abandoned his sibling to probable death in order to steal it). The "happy ending" is deeply shadowed by the earlier brotherly betrayal and the grief (and dismay) it causes both father and brother. What happens is at the end contained by the wider community, from which Siganda expels himself by fleeing from impending retribution.

A more troubling and eerie story of social transgression and exclusion is the one called "The Woman and the Mighty Bird" (241-248): a tale with distinct emphasis on a male power structure in the society depicted here and with little by way of individualising characterisation. The story is starkly told: there is, we are informed, a powerful taboo against going into "the depths of the forest": "[t]he depths were greatly feared by the whole community, and though no one ever gave the reason why, the women were constantly warned by the men never to go anywhere near the tall trees" (241). The woman of the title is, we are told, "beautiful" and "young" (241) and the only wife among the women who, when during a long spell of cold sufficient wood is harder to find, decides to risk going into "the depths," where she finds many bundles of ready-cut wood, guarded by a fearsome and huge bird – "the mighty bird / Of manifold windpipe and manifold dewlap" (243), as he announces himself in a song. He allows her to take a bundle of wood on condition of her promise never to say to "those of Ndela" (245), i.e. her husband's family, that she has seen him – the bird being described in emphatically male terms: "a big tall man"; "a great bull"; "a giant bull" (242). She does this three times; her husband grows predictably suspicious and when he threatens to kill her unless she tells the truth, she admits to having seen the giant bird – who then surges up to the house, causing the husband to faint in a fright, and swallowing the woman before "reced[ing] to the depths of the forest" (248). If the function of this story is merely to endorse a patriarchal social and familial structure, as Scheub suggests in his introduction to it (238-240), there are nevertheless oddities and ambiguities in the temporary duration of a secret pact between the woman and the giant bird and in the initial benefit this brings. The woman is, as has been said, hardly individualised, though the pattern of her conduct seems to indicate that she represents marital (indeed, "female") untrustworthiness and its rightful punishment. *Yet* the bird does not seem to have any sense of alliance with the human male, the woman's taboo-upholding, disciplinarian husband. Perhaps the story can be read as obliquely recognising the unacknowledged or unacknowledgable danger of female adultery in a society that caters for male polygamy (even though *this* husband has only one wife). This story is mysterious in Jordan's handling of it and, if the woman comes across as sly and manipulative, the husband is evidently harsh and unheroic: amongst all the tales this is also the one in which there is least evidence of social mediation.

The story called "The King of the Waters" (179-191) forms an interesting counterpart to the "Mighty Bird" story; Jordan first introduces the ostensible, male hero, the "renowned hunter" (179) prince Tfulako, who is denied a desperately needed drink by the waters of a spring. "The King of the Waters" relents when Tfulako promises him "the most beautiful of [his] sisters to be [his] wife" (181). This peremptory though life-saving decision is reported when he gets home, "[b]ut everybody, including the beautiful princess, felt that this was the only offer Tfulako could have made in the circumstances. So they awaited the coming of the King of the Waters" (182), though no-one knows in what shape he will appear. Nkyanyamba, the "King of the Waters" (182), eventually appears from a cyclone in the form of an inordinately big snake. He takes up his place as a "burden round [the] body" of the princess, "rest[ing] his head on her breasts and gaz[ing] hungrily into her eyes" (182) – an evidently phallic and erotic, but threatening and alien presence. This young woman (to whom the whole focus of the tale now shifts) also betakes herself to "her mother's people, far over the mountains."[7] As she travels, carrying the python, she expresses her revulsion and distress in song, to which the snake replies, also in song, proclaiming his worthiness; as Jordan puts it, they journey "singing pride at each other" (183). On arrival the princess pretends sexual and social capitulation; on the pretext of needing time to beautify herself, she confers with her maternal uncle and his wife to make a plan to save herself. Jordan vividly conveys the shuddering stress of the situation for this young woman, who yet manages to steel herself to execute the family plot. She goes back to the snake so well oiled that, when invited to embrace her, the creature slips down repeatedly and is stunned – she can then go out and lock the door before the hut is burnt down with the python in it. She is nevertheless not declared free and ready to return home until she can handle the skull of the snake with casual fearlessness, deciding to take it back as a washing vessel for her brother: a ritual indicative of her promotion in status attained by her courage and endurance in overcoming lingering fears. A slightly ironic touch at the end is Tfulako's belligerent posture and fierce decision to "save" the sister who has already extricated herself from the coils of "The King of the Waters": the closing song echoes that of Tfulako and his hunters at the beginning (181), but changes it to proclaim the defeat of the snake, largely his sister's victory,[8] which is sung of as a communal achievement (191).

Scheub tends to see all the tales as validations of custom; my reading discerns both validation and interrogation of (some) customary practices in Jordan's telling of the stories. The tale called "Sikhamba-nge-Nyanga" ("She-who-walks-by-moonlight"; 252-259) shows how custom can function to validate the abuse or neglect of exceptionally valuable individuals – a wife is neglected for supposed barrenness, but is capable of giving birth to a daughter of surpassing beauty; Sikhamba-nge-Nyanga should not be subjected to the customarily honoured but naggingly selfish demands of a withered old woman, due to which the whole

---

7 Like Nomabhadi in the tale called "Nomabhadi and the Mbulu-Makhasana" (*Tales* 155-177).

8 Despite the "feminisation" of the focus of the tale after its opening, it is interesting that "the princess" is never named, remaining "Tfulako's sister" (190) to the end.

community (including her own small baby) temporarily loses her. This, too, then, is a story of restitution after loss and exclusion and it shows the need to be flexible, also about "time-honoured" customs; here, too, a young girl (the *mpelesi*; 256) is the unobtrusively daring saviour-figure of the tale.

The two stories which by their unusually lengthy and detailed unfolding achieve the central position in this collection are placed back to back. They are called "The Maidens of Bhakubha" (57-98) and "The Story of Nomxakazo" (108-152) and in both the female protagonists are the main focus of attention and reattest profoundly communal values after social breakdown.

In the land of Bhakubha the princess, the youngest member of a large group of (about two hundred) maidens, is so charming and so much a favourite that she is affectionately nicknamed *Nomtha-we-Langa* (i.e. "Mother-of-the-Sunbeam"). The girls spend their days together and delight especially in swimming in the pools of the river which separates their kingdom from the neighbouring one. They make teasing but courteous acquaintance with the young men of that kingdom, whose prince Sidlokolo picks the young princess as the loveliest among her peers during a playful yet ceremonious encounter. At her first menstruation the lively young princess is, however, obliged to "undergo custom" (60) during a period of social isolation. Mischievously, she plays truant in order to join her friends on one of their picnic outings and she chooses the unknown and feared "Lulange pool" (61) for them to swim in. Just as they intend leaving this pool to return home, they discover that a slimy monster has stretched out on their clothes so that they are obliged to beg him to allow them to retrieve their clothing. This creature, too, is explicitly male and described as gazing lewdly at each maiden as she makes her request. Princess Nomtha-we-Langa alone, the last of the maidens, pridefully refuses until she eventually "screwed her face and so shaped it that it looked as ugly as the monster's" (65), mocking and defying him – to which he retaliates by biting her in the thigh. This transforms *her* into a monstrous version of herself while the "Slimy One" (65) itself disappears. If the wilfulness and disobedience of the Princess have "be-monstered" her, the effects also reach far beyond herself: the story fascinates because it moves beyond the obviousness of retribution to the difficulties of restitution.

Besides indicating the protective effects of sexual schooling which members of this culture are required to undergo, Jordan's telling of the story exhibits the far-reaching social consequences of this crisis and the hugely widespread and socially cooperative effort required to solve it. The story portrays *two* societies remarkable for the degree to which their members generously accept responsibility both for themselves and for others (see especially Jordan's depiction of the deliberations of the Bhakubha court on pp. 70-74). The author heightens one's sense of civilization as the product of human dealings and renewed compacts, compensating for human weaknesses and failings. The social sophistication exhibited here is demonstrated in the way culprits are not simply expelled or ostracised; a *type* of containment is still operative. Jordan is evidently fascinated by and interests the reader in the courtesies of the many human interchanges he depicts. The maidens of Bhakubha are indeed sent into exile, but are given respectable shelter by Prince Sidlokolo of the neighbouring kingdom, while he himself sets out to fight the monster and to find the princess who has herself been sent away to an outpost – it seems, partly to punish and partly to protect her from ridicule – by her own father. In Jordan's vivid formulation, "Sidlokolo and the youths of his age group [. . .] resolved to get themselves fully involved in this matter" (74). The situation is nevertheless subtly entangled and difficult. No monster rises from the pool to the prince's repeated challenges as if to emphasise the a-typical nature of the threat confronted in this story – almost as if to show up the shallower imagining of the typical "rescuing prince" tale where the monster is defeated in battle or through guile. Before setting out to find Nomtha-we-Langa, Sidlokolo is warned by one of the grandmother guardians of the princess that "a rare kind, a deeper kind of bravery" is required by this situation: "the bravery to bear agony" (78). He must promise *not* to try to see her in her altered state. When he and his braves eventually locate her, he is thus overcome with melancholy. For her part, the princess has to endure the bleakness of her isolation as well as her sadness with dignity: "She never sees anyone. [. . .] The door opens ever so little and a hand and arm, all covered with gloves made of buckskin, stretches out to receive the food. [. . .] She walks to and fro, to and fro, to and fro. [. . .] Thinking about home, thinking about the other girls" (82). She has been ostracised, but her deed caused the expulsion of many other women.

Watching from afar the outpost where the princess is kept, the prince and his companions see a strange, towering wall of white (surplus milk that has welled up out of an earth pit) and "just as the first sunbeam of the morning struck it" (92) Nomtha-we-Langa plunges into it and with great joy recovers her own shape. Predictably, she and the prince marry soon after the other maidens are returned home (many of them also marrying young men of the adjoining kingdom). But far more than a superficial happy-ever-after fairy-tale, Jordan has drawn the lines of a social growth process possible only in a healthy and flexibly complex society. Although the miracle of her healing may be regarded as a lucky accident, there is a sense in which it is the culmination of the many caring, tactful and committed efforts made by those in the story who love Nomtha-we-Langa, the restoration of the princess rising – like the milk wall – from their courage and determination to contribute mutually towards the healing of the disrupted community. Something of the complexity of the achievement is recognised in the charming speech of the chief counsellor at the prince's court: "All your fathers, grandfathers, and great-grandfathers at this meeting," he tells the prince, "envy you this great deed" (96), although he killed neither monster nor enemies.

Scheub's introductory commentary (99-107) on the last story dealt with in this essay, "The Story of Nomxakazo"[9] (108-152) is interesting and useful. This is also a tale of a maiden and of her maturing as it affects the fate of a whole nation, but this young woman, whose very name brutally recalls the slaying of men in the battle which took place on the day of her birth (109), is distinctly less pleasant and more obviously spoilt than the princess in the preceding story. Intoxicated by his victory on his daughter's birth-day (in a battle which establishes him as the indisputably most powerful ruler of the region through the defeat of his closest rival), her father the king rashly vows to mark her maturity by bringing her enough cattle to "darken the sun" (110). His is indeed a distinctly warlike, rapacious society – a point subtly criticised by the tone and terminology of Jordan's opening descriptions (e.g. 108-109).

When Nomxakazo duly comes of age, successive offerings of cattle are all met by her smile of contempt (112), necessitating greater and greater devastation of surrounding communities to raid enough cattle. Eventually the scouring warriors encounter an extremely strange, huge creature, *Maphundu* (or "You-of-the-Nodules"), who is strikingly described as a huge tract of the earth itself (113). Showing no respect for "great creating nature,"[10] they raid his abundant herds of cattle. At last Nomxakazo is satisfied: the feasting which follows leaves "thousands of carcasses rotting on the plains" (113). The excess continues until the time for her "coming-out" feast occurs – but then Maphundu arrives to take Nomxakazo away in exchange for his raided cattle. Her father's military might cannot save her. Maphundu first humbles and disciplines her in his own peremptory ways and then deposits her in a cave far from her native land. She is, she

9 A Zulu version of this tale (with an English translation) is recorded in the Callaway collection (181-217).

10 Shakespeare, *The Winter's Tale*, 4.3.88.

discovers, in the country of one-legged cannibals called the Dlungu-ndlebe.[11] Her beauty saves her from being eaten by them and yet again she becomes a king's pampered darling until she is so repulsively fat that they decide to eat her instead. But she prays for rain, and three times the fire is put out, the third time killing the old cannibal king. Now the Dlungu-ndlebe fear her and let her go. "In hunger and hardship she makes her way home, begging for food [. . .] among people whose youthful men have been slaughtered [. . .] homes destroyed [. . .] cattle [. . .] looted, by her father's warriors, to satisfy her father's vanity and hers" (130). Words which by their bleakness and doom-like rhythm hammer home the cost of Nomxakazo and her father's ugly self-indulgence.

She eventually reaches her now wretched home, to be told by her mother that "death ha[s] entered this land" (133). So appalled is she now that she asks: "Who am I that anybody should pity me?" (135) – and that moment of deep self-abnegation begins her recovery and that of her people. If we think of truth and reconciliation in a shattered land, this tale portrays the slow, humbling process needed to soften the previously mighty before repentance can begin.

In the meantime the son of the rival king whom her father defeated decides that, although he wants this most beautiful young woman for himself, he will deliberately humiliate her father by not going through the obligatory marital formalities – also an arrogant illustration of excessive privilege. Nomxakazo is magically enticed and then kidnapped - but she asserts herself and redefines the situation by *consenting* to go to the prince. The abduction becomes a state visit; she so impresses her would-be captors that one old counsellor of the prince's is moved to declare: "She has the heart of a human, she has a liver, she is alive in the head [. . .] she [. . .] means to go back to her people still a maiden – She has [. . .] left us only the straight road to go by – the road of custom" (148).

Not surprisingly, her return home becomes the occasion for a formal proposal of marriage with much bride-tribute in cattle – now her own people foresee that once married she will be "a mother to all homeless wanderers" (152). Her role has inverted: from the destructive daugther she has changed to the saving parent and leader.

Unlike the typical fairy-tale with its focus on personal or perhaps also familial happiness, the author stresses the social, "national" dimensions of the story. Jor-

[11] Scheub points out the irony that these creatures were formerly exiled by Nomxakazo's people because their cannibalism was considered disgusting and sub-human (100); these same proud people have now become more degraded than the cannibals!

dan's telling embellishes and vitalises a story in which devastation among nations and the internal rot of greed are overcome in a process of social restructuring;[12] by the end of the story, representatives of both societies participate together in the re-achieved courtesies of "feasting and rejoicing," their "mingl[ing]" now that of "friendly" people (152). The "Callaway version" or recording of the story (Callaway 181-217) is noticeably briefer in its depiction of what in Jordan's version becomes the reconstitution of social relations – depicted in full and subtle detail. Earlier, the prince had told Nomxakazo: "We thank you for making humans of us" (149). She has also redeemed and rehumanised her own broken people.

Jordan's *Tales* have no ring of nostalgia. If they commemorate and celebrate a proud and complex African civilization to dispel the blind condescension of European racists, they do also point forward to what a combination of peoples in this land must rediscover and regain in their own rites of passage towards mutual recognition. These *Tales from Southern Africa* exhibit the hard-won achievements of communities beset by threats from outside as well as from within, constantly driven to redefine *humanness*. I conclude by citing Toni Morrison:

> The imagination that produces work which bears and invites rereadings, which motions to future readings as well as contemporary ones, implies a shareable world and an endlessly flexible language. [. . .] Living in a nation of people who *decided* that their world view would combine agendas for individual freedom *and* mechanisms for devastating racial oppression presents a singular landscape for a writer. [. . .] How stunning is the achievement of those who have searched for and mined a shareable language for the words to say it. (xii-xiii; emphases added)

---

12 Scheub sees it as follows: "Her odyssey leads her to a respect for custom which has but one purpose: human relations based on respect and made beautiful through love" (*Tales* 107). In his foreword, Z. Pallo Jordan characterises the aim of the traditional ruler as "the reconciliation of parties rather than the interpretation of points of law" (x). He also suggests that A. C. Jordan (his father) "sought to transform the tale into a great collective symbol around which the African people could be mobilized for social and political change" (xxii). It seems particularly inappropriate of the folklorist Richard M. Dorson to single out A. C. Jordan as one of those who "lose sight of the contemporaneity of folklore" (30)!

Works Cited

Callaway, Henry. *Nursery Tales, Traditions, and Histories of the Zulus*. Springvale, Natal: Blair, 1868.

Canonici, Noverino 1990. "The Folktale Tradition Yesterday and Today." *Oral Studies in Southern Africa*. Ed. H. C. Groenewald. Pretoria: Human Sciences Research Council. 128-153.

Chaane, Thokozile. "Orality and Narratives: The Art of Story Telling." Johannesburg: *New Nation* Writers' Conference paper, 1991. 1-3.

Dorson, Richard M. "Africa and the Folklorist." *African Folklore*. Ed. by Dorson. Bloomington, Ind.: Indiana UP, 1972. 3-67.

Hofmeyr, Isabel. *"We Spend Our Years as a Tale that is Told": Oral Historical Narrative in a South African Chiefdom*. Johannesburg: Witwatersrand UP, 1993.

Jordan, Archibald C. *Ingqumbo Yeminyanya*. South Africa: Lovedale, 1940.

___, Archibald C. *Tales from Southern Africa*. Trans. and retold by A. C. Jordan. Berkeley: University of California Press, 1973.

___, Archibald C. *Towards an African Literature: The Emergence of Literary Form in Xhosa*. Berkeley: University of California Press, 1973.

___, Archibald C. *The Wrath of the Ancestors: A Novel*. Trans. from the original Xhosa by the author and Priscilla P. Jordan. South Africa: Lovedale, 1980.

___, Z. Pallo. Foreword. A. C. Jordan, *Tales* i-xxiii.

Morrison, Toni. *Playing in the Dark: Whiteness and the Literary Imagination* Cambridge, Mass.: Harvard UP, 1992.

Okpewho, Isidore. *Myth in Africa: A Study of Its Aesthetic and Cultural Relevance*. Cambridge: UP, 1983.

___. *African Oral Literature: Backgrounds, Character, and Continuity*. Bloomington : Indiana UP, 1992.

Scheub, Harold Ernest. *The Ntsomi: A Xhosa Performing Art*. Ann Arbor: University of Wisconsin microfilm-xerograph, 1969.

___. General introduction. A. C. Jordan, *Tales* 1-13.

Memory, Power and Bessie Head: *A Question of Power*

"Memory says: Want to do right? Don't count on me."
– Adrienne Rich: "Eastern War Time" (1991)

Born in 1937 in the Pietermaritzburg mental asylum where her white mother had been institutionalised,[1] Bessie Head was rejected by almost all of her mother's family, classified "coloured" when her appearance indicated that her father had been (an unknown) black, and became initially a teacher, then a journalist. She left South Africa for Botswana in mid-1964 on a so-called exit permit, having been denied a passport because of her fairly peripheral involvement with the PAC (the Pan Africanist Congress led by Robert Sobukwe). By 1973, when *A Question of Power* first appeared, she had published two earlier novels, also set in Botswana. She was, however, not given citizenship of her new country until February 1979, seven years before her death at the age of 48. In 1982 she wrote the following in an account of her life and writing that she composed for publication in *Drum* magazine, stating points evidently pertinent to the consideration of *A Question of Power* offered in this essay (the quotation vividly illustrates her vision of the inextricable entanglement of personal, political and historical matters in the context of a perpetually dangerous, risky world):

> I feel that people, insofar as they are able, need to have a sense of alertness about destiny, a sort of alertness about their spiritual history.
>
> [. . .] each individual, no matter what their present origin or background may be, is really the total embodiment of human history, with a vast accumulation of knowledge and experience stored in the subconscious mind. [. . .]
>
> The African experience of slavery, colonialism and exploitation arouses feelings of intense anguish and there was a fear in me that monsters would merely change roles, that black faces would simply

---

1 Head's biographer Eilersen has established that Head's mother was not institutionalised *because* she had had a child by a black man, although the evidence of the child's racially "mixed" parentage did lead to her existence being ignored by all her "white" relatives with the exception (initially) of her maternal grandmother, and to her being given up for adoption into a "coloured" family (Eilersen 3-10). See also the article by Birch. Head's father's identity remains unknown.

> replace white faces of cruelty, hate and greed and that the people would bleed forever.
>
> [. . .] in an internal and private way, I perceived the ease with which one could become evil and I associated evil in my mind with the acquisition of power. (*Woman* 77)

The full span of human history is here conceived of as constituting the huge "memory" in which all people participate and for which responsibility must be borne. In Head's thought, minds are so open – both inclusive, and invadable – that Elizabeth's "memories," for instance, range freely over Ancient Egypt (Osiris-Isis); Ancient Greece (Medusa); Ancient Rome (Caligula); Ancient India (Buddha) and refer to the South African political past (1910: the Act of Union) and many other historical incidents and periods. Jacqueline Rose writes: "It is not clear whether we are dealing with an outside-in or with an inside-out situation – the writing doesn't let you decide. Projection is one way, ghosts another, of reading what is taking place" (113).

As an opening perspective on the study of the function and possible contexts of memory in *A Question of Power*,[2] I want to suggest a link between quotations from two pieces by the author. The first (from 1979) reads: "literature is very functional in Southern Africa and bound inextricably to human suffering" (Head, *Woman* 67).[3] The second (written in 1981) states: "Southern Africa isn't like the rest of Africa and is never going to be. Here, we are going to have to make an extreme effort to find a deep faith to help us to live together" (*Woman* 31).[4] Linking the two excerpts involves the recognition that the "extreme effort" to which Head refers in the second of the cited quotations can be thought of as an *ongoing* or continuing suffering incurred in the arduous process of somehow accommodating the supposedly past, yet insistently "self-presenting" suffering, which persists by means of ineradicable memories. In South Africa, where the difficult arts of restitution are all too easily overwhelmed by glib and premature claims of achieved recovery or reconciliation,[5] there is need to call Head's wit-

---

2 I omit discussion of numerous other issues in order to keep the line of argument as clear as possible. In the discussion of *A Question of Power* in my book (Gagiano 152-159) I concentrate on issues of power and transformation.

3 From the essay "Social and Political Pressures that Shape Writing in South Africa" (*Woman* 65-72), first published in 1979.

4 From "For Serowe a Village in Africa" (*Woman* 29-31), extracted from *Serowe: Village of the Rain Wind* (1981).

5 Mamphela Ramphele mentions

nessing to mind. "I fear the countries that have suffered after independence and are going to suffer, have been the ones where people lived in fear," she wrote to Vigne in 1978 (*Gesture* 219).[6] Head deromanticises the "victorious victim" image. Her novel works hard against the self-soothing and socially comforting belief that those who endure and *survive* the "terror of power" (*Woman* 77) are by definition strengthened, ennobled, or triumphant.

I am here of course alluding to the notion of healing-through-telling that was so discernible in the workings (even in the very title) of the South African Truth and Reconciliation Commission. In one of the best accounts of that process, Antjie Krog's *Country of my Skull*, one can, however, see many instances of unsatisfied victims, unassuaged feelings of loss or outrage, or even of recurrent abjection. An example of the latter kind of effect can be seen, for instance, when a former torture victim, at the time of the hearing a prominent member of parliament, is re-humiliated at the TRC event (Krog 73; 76). Many male victims of gross human rights violations, in particular, experience literal or symbolic emasculation or impotence. The so-called "Shepherd's Tale" of the aged Mr Lekotse leads to the following conclusion: "His worth as a father, a brother, a son has been negated [. . .] He'd be happy, he says, if someone would kill him immediately" (Krog 220). The report of the testimony of Mr MP Mhlongo ends: "I'm getting these children, and I suspect I am not the father of the children" (Krog 139). Among the women, even the chairperson of the Gender Commission, Thenjiwe Mthintso, testifies: "Even now [. . .] I feel exposed and distraught" (Krog 179), whilst the relative of a "necklacing" victim, Nozibele Madubedube, tells the TRC: "I saw two of those who grabbed me and my sister in the hall [. .

> a few impediments to the building of a moral culture in South Africa. The first obstacle is that the ghosts from the past refuse to lie down. [. . .] We can talk about the Rainbow Nation as loudly as we like, but we need to confront the implications and the consequences of the fact that a large group of South Africans were made to feel subhuman. Voting in 1994 and again in 1999 did not remove those scars of humiliation, particularly as the majority of people continue to live in squalor, are unemployed and without hope. This inferiority complex is a reality of most people's lives. Until and unless we confront it we will not succeed. In the same vein, the superiority complex amongst white people needs to be confronted (173-174).

6 Compare Elizabeth's warning, in *A Question of Power*, concerning postcolonial politicians' "jump[ing] on the bandwagon of past suffering" (133 and ff.; see 133-135).

.] and they are still [. . .] *nothing* [. . .] only [. . .] now I am also nothing. My life keeps slipping through my fingers" (Krog 136). Particularly memorable, and heartbreaking, is the testimony of Mrs Elsie Gishi: "I have holes [caused by bullets – but evoking the idea of "gaps" in the mind], I can't sleep well. Sometimes when I try to sleep, it feels like something is evaporating from my head. [. . .] My son Bonisile [. . .] was never well again" (Krog 79-80). Her words are strangely reminiscent of Elizabeth's experiences as described in Head's novel.

Despite Head's well-known declaration (in an interview concerning *A Question of Power*) that "Elizabeth and I are one" (Head, *Between the Lines* 25),[7] there are at least two major and especially significant differences between Bessie Head (author and person) and the protagonist of her third "Botswana novel." Firstly, Elizabeth – even though her son knows that she "like[s] to write," as he says when he offers her the gift of a pen (178) – is *not* presented to the reader as a writer, but as a former schoolteacher who became a vegetable gardener and who *may become* a writer, since, by the end of the novel, she begins to devise an account of the period of her "breakdown" (or her "work-out," as Head called it in the Marquard interview [53]). Secondly, although Bessie Head in the course of her correspondence with Randolph Vigne (now published as *A Gesture of Belonging*) relates numerous actual instances[8] where she felt herself or her son to be the object of racial abuse, or of a more generalised racial/racist disapproval (in Botswana), she does not *in the novel* include a single instance where Elizabeth is, by any actual person, so treated or described (in her new country). The omission is remarkable, given the woeful litany, exemplified over many years, in Head's letters concerning her experiences in Botswana.

A list of some of these rejections as she experienced them would include the following examples: (a)"they don't want me here" (*Gesture* 9; written 27 Oct.

---

[7] Compare Kristeva:

> [. . .] a portion of autobiography in a narrative ensures its moorings in reality; but another portion, one of transformation or distortion, that is, the share of fiction, collects the intensity of the subjective bonds that fasten the narrator to others and to himself or herself. And that fictional portion, in contrast with the autobiographical one, acts as a filter that produces a certain discretion, a certain modesty, while changing real-life characters into prototypes. (78-79)

[8] See for example pp. 66-67; 178 and 216 from the Vigne letter collection (Head, *Gesture*), in addition to the examples that are quoted in the main body of this essay. Compare, from *A Question of Power*, the reference to "the Coloured dog, Elizabeth" (129).

1965); (b) "especially the disregard and degradation of women. It's terrible" (18; December 1965); (c) "my own condition which is one of unbelievable isolation" (27; early 1966); (d) "I feel so ill and frightened, Randolph, because the things essential to my survival – like generosity and a rich flow of ideas – I can't seem to find" (31; March 1966); and (e) "but it's been Batswana people I've been fighting with, so God help me, and that does not endear me to anyone, especially as I'm some kind of half-caste. You've no idea how frightened I really am because I thought Africa was my home and now I don't know what to do" (37; August 1966); and the following:

> [(f)] No sooner did he go to school this year than the children at school told him [her son Harold, then first going to school] he is a coloured. Apparently being a Motswana is a very exclusive thing. He kept on complaining about this and I used to break out into a sweat not knowing what to say because I started it in the first place. I don't think he understands words like human being and mankind. Eventually he got assaulted by children twice his age apparently on the grounds that he's an usurper into the race of Motswana, or some filthy specimen. I withdrew him from school because he can't handle such a situation. Neither can I. (64; Oct. 1968)

(g): "People are deadly faithful to their own, not to you, the outsiders. One of the most painful moments of my life came when a Batswana woman said to me, with actual hatred: 'What do you want running after the Batswanas?'" (68; November 1968); (h) "I can't change myself from being a bushman, half-breed or [. . .] into anything to please anybody. I look like a Bushman, who is a despised tribe here. [. . .] There is no-one who is going to un-bushman me" (71; January 1969); (i) "I walked into a shop and asked for half a pound of cheese. The crazy Motswana behind the counter said to me: 'Look here, if you don't treat us with respect, we can't serve you.' What has that got to do with asking for half a pound of cheese in a normal voice?" (83; February 1969); she also averred that (j) "here I am Bessie Head, the Bushman dog [. . .]" (85-86; May 1969) and reported [9] that (k):

[9] The cause of the unpleasantness was said (by Head) to involve the allegation of a secret affair between herself and a member of the Batswana nobility, as well as the scandalously rumoured murder of a (resulting) baby by her, she supposedly having drowned it in a pit toilet – an idea Head found especially horrific and distressing (*Gesture* 87-88).

> a lot of influential people don't like me and how dare I set foot back here. What really made me mad was that they created for me a reputation so horrible [. . .] The thing is they really believed it, those things they confronted me with. Eventually I cornered three of the buggers in a room and started screaming "You bloody bastards" (88; again May 1969)

(l) "There was a woman in my dreams torturing me. She was a black woman, as though I had no right to live on this earth in my own complexion. There was a mocking smile on her face as though nothing I could do would ever make up for the crime of my complexion [. . .]" (108; written January 1970); (m) "Everything went wrong from the time Howard was assaulted. I never seemed to recover and the nightmare was so persistent and inward-turning in my own mind that nothing seems to wash away the horror of this racial business" (112; Feb. 1970);

> [(n)] To tell the truth a racial feeling never entered my mind, except towards what I called "the enemy" [presumably, racist whites] and even there he was too far removed from me to give me nightmares. It is different if a racial feeling is created by people and I mean African, who are also human to you. (121; May 1970)

Head even asked herself (o): "Why did I give my most beautiful lines and experience to a Motswana [in *Maru*] when they all [i.e. local people; Batswana] spat at me for being Coloured?" (124; written June 1970).

Yet, in the novel, *Elizabeth* is the person who yells racial abuse at the innocuous Motswana shop clerk in the event of her first major "public" breakdown (*Question* 49-51). Rooney notes that "on this map South Africa is here too" – in the sense of its influence being felt even in the supposedly "safe space" of Botswana, where acceptance and a sense of social solidarity had been expected (199). In the novel, Elizabeth reverts defensively to mimicry of the very racism that so terrifies her: a complex and shameful memory-effect, it might be called.

In 1979 Head wrote: "That rejection of my application for citizenship was one of the gestures of evil that was done to me. [. . .] They still think they can treat me as the coloured dog" (qtd. in Eilersen 226).[10] This and the other quotations

[10] Head's 1977 application for Botswana citizenship was rejected (no reasons being provided); something that happened repeatedly. She wrote to Vigne at the time: "So, there's not much to go home to" (*Gesture* 216).

illustrate the range and duration of the hurt Head suffered in Botswana and contrasts with the way in which she did write of – and record – these experiences in *A Question of Power*. Despite the avowedly "autobiographical" or "verbatim" nature of the novel (her own words; qtd. in MacKenzie 24), Head's deliberate "omissions" from and adaptations of the "raw material" of her Botswana experiences – as told to correspondents like Vigne – show her to be the shaping, selective *novelist*. Head was using her imaginative powers first to "read" and analyse the experiences she had undergone and then – in her "blabbermouth" role[11] as witness for the exposure of evil – to communicate her understanding of the origins of abusive power use in the unusual novel that she composes. The argument here is not that Head the novelist in writing *A Question of Power* is applying "self-censorship" (so blatantly is the very obverse – exposure of numerous shameful aspects of selfhood – the case here), *or* that she is perhaps afraid to criticise the "new" society. Instead, the creative, self-critical and socially conscious transference or transformation of her material – *in order* to produce a more searching and psycho-philosophically challenging document than "raw" reportage – becomes discernible. "Autobiography" is here therefore both an act of memory and of construction, as well as a deed of social enlightenment, in which what has been learnt can be told and taught to others. The idea of transferable knowledge is suggested by Elizabeth when she queries Tom's acceptance of the "Black Power" idea by saying that she does so "because of what I'm *learning internally*" (*Question* 133; emphasis added). This point can be compared to Boyce Davies's comment on "this process of ordering a life, giving meaning to it, and *rewriting the self*" (287-288; emphasis added). Trinh Minh-ha says of exiled autobiographers that "they do not so much remember for themselves as they remember *in order to tell*" (10, emphasis added).

All readers of the novel are familiar with Elizabeth's words, "The evils overwhelming her were beginning to sound like South Africa from which she had fled" (57), and since to read this novel is to battle with the terrifying complexities of evil felt in the psyche with which it confronts us, almost all readers register this statement as an important clue to its meaning – only to find how little it

---

11 Compare *Gesture* where she refers again to herself as "blabbermouth" (116) and this quotation from the novel: "That was the crux of it, once she knew and was certain of the truth, she would disclose it, no matter if it was the most horrific truth mankind had ever heard" (*Question* 200). This idea may be theoretically expressed as the "political question of [. . .] gaining access to positions of enunciation" (Innes and Rooney 207).

actually explains. For to be persecuted by means of imagined racial rejection (by a black woman), to be sexually humiliated [in the imagination] by a triumphant African male and to have the mind constantly invaded by obscene visions in various forms bears no obvious resemblance to Elizabeth's South African experiences, although these visions are felt by her to be simultaneously grossly evil and deliberately visited upon her alone. Moreover, the reference to South Africa has a "counterpart statement" elsewhere in the novel: "Elizabeth felt that some of the answers lay in her experiences in Botswana" (19). *Both* Botswana *and* South Africa have therefore contributed to Elizabeth's torture; moving to Botswana from South Africa has not effected an escape from power subjection. "Apartheid abjection" persists.

Yet Head wrote, three years after the publication of *A Question of Power*, that she was

> sick to death of all that has been written about [the novel] by white reviewers [. . .], whether racialist or liberal, [for in their eyes] a black man is not a whole man, with whole, horrific, satanic passions [, but] a wee, sleekit, timorous beastie they mowed down with maxim guns a hundred years ago. A black man could not possibly be the characters in my books, so hugely vile, so hugely demonish. (Qtd. in Eilersen 222)

"They [i.e. such reviewers] had to re-set the work in South Africa because this sort of thing [. . .] could not apply to Botswana," she wrote sarcastically to Vigne in 1974 concerning reviewers' responses to *A Question of Power* (*Gesture* 187). She profoundly resented reductive readings of her work that would push it into the mould of the standard protest novel depicting a black victim of white oppression – ironically only another failure to respect the African victim *or* to acknowledge the existence of *African* incarnations of evil and oppression.

This point has its equivalent in the novel, when the narrator, who is a remembering, interpreting commentator, remarks: "Too often the feelings of a victim are not taken into account [. . .] a process of degradation, scorn and wild, blind cruelty *had its equivalent* of wild, savage [desire for] vengeance in her" (98; emphasis added).

What is it that arouses such "vengeance" in Elizabeth that it maddens her? This is not abjection, but its flipside: so desperate is the victim of humiliation to escape its agonies that she allows the furies of a vengeance-lust to boil up in her soul, *hence re-enacting her torturers' roles*. The shock of experiencing her awful past, in which she was racially, morally and sexually humiliated, is *resurfacing* "mirror-fashion" in Botswana, in Elizabeth's mind. This type of haunting is, then, a memory-form. In South Africa, racism caused Elizabeth "permanent nervous tension" (19) in a "torture"[12] that went "on and on and on" (19); secondly, she was told with shocking suddenness at the vulnerable early adolescent stage of thirteen (in the indelible, "cruel" comments of the missionary school headmistress) that she did not have a "home," was "racially contaminated" as well as prone to genetic mental instability and morally tainted because her mother had had sex with "the stable boy, who was a native" (16); thirdly she had been subjected to the subsequent sexual humiliation inflicted by a husband both voraciously and indiscriminately promiscuous (18-19).

Head gives us no recognisable sign, in the novel (beyond the spite shown towards Elizabeth by the Motabeng headmaster, depicted later), of anything done to Elizabeth *by Batswana people* to explain why "her life began to pitch over from an even keel" (21) in the country where she had sought refuge. Yet in the persecutory hallucinations to which she is subjected, her torturers have Batswana incarnations and their "blackness" is emphasised (37; 57; 128). In fact, both "Sello" and "Dan" are said to have actual counterparts in Motabeng village. Though clearly the mix of Elizabeth's South African memories supplies the witch's broth from which the demons who torture her emanate,[13] their having black African embodiments signifies that Elizabeth has discovered that there is, for her, no escaping from the forces of humiliation. As Head wrote to Vigne from Botswana: "Something really went wrong for me to be openly insulted and spat at [. . .]" (Head, *Gesture* 121).

I suggest that the novel rewrites the *social* prevalence of racism that Head wrote about in her letters as a *psychic* persistence. This re-setting occurs because

---

12 In 1963 Head had written concerning what it felt like for a "black" person like herself to live in South Africa: "Every white face that you see passing you by churns you up till you could just cry to be delivered from this unceasing torment of hate, hate, hate" (*Woman* 14). It is to be noted that the reference to the "torment" caused by "hate" may refer either to the suffering caused by being hated, or to a responsive, but anguishing hatred of the persecutor – the latter perspective being emphasised throughout *A Question of Power*.

13 The narrator informs us that "they *played on* her experiences in *South Africa* [where] [. . .] she had been rigidly classified Coloured" (44; emphasis added). Adetokunbo Pearse writes that "Dan's' strategy is to destroy any sense of love or respect Elizabeth may have for herself, and thereby destroy her love and respect for others" (89).

there is no society entirely free of hierarchies, and because the memory of degradation embeds itself in the recesses of the psyche, from which it inevitably resurfaces. Head wrote to Vigne concerning this period in her life: "I was recreating inwardly a past where I continually brought *myself* to death through sheer aggression of personality" (*Gesture* 154; emphasis added) and in the novel we are told that "South Africans usually suffered from some form of mental aberration" (58). Elizabeth learns that she "recognises" the discriminatory workings of power because she understands through her very hatred the gloating delight, the profoundly pleasurable sense of empowerment which victimisation of others produces. The description she sent to her friend Vigne indicates Head's understanding of the slippage from power into evil:[14]

> Hell is like this. I have power and exquisite sensations. I'll give you a little to eat you dog. I'll put my mouth on the spring of your life and suck it dry because I'm really the most important person around here. Now dog, get down to the level I dictate to you. You are inferior. You are filth. I hate you, but ah, I need a dog to lap up a little bit of the exquisite sensations I dish out now and then. I only need dogs around here and you are my chief dog. Crawl, bitch! (*Gesture* 162)

This is clearly reminiscent of Elizabeth's tortures in *A Question of Power* (e.g. the gloatings of "Medusa" and "Dan" in passages on pp. 44; 13; 191; and elsewhere), in which she herself enacts both the victim's *and* the perpetrator's roles in her mind.

Elizabeth's isolation in Motabeng is described as her circumscription by "a barrier of solitude" (11): she is cut off racially, culturally and linguistically from those among whom she now lives. This "empty stage" provides the opportunity allowing her damaged psyche to re-enact the racial, moral and sexual persecution she underwent in South Africa, but now with the torturers in Batswana guises – which is to say, those harmful categorisations are (re-)asserting themselves, with even greater force, as products of her inner self: memories are masked as actual recurrences or reincarnations. The trapped energy of unassuaged resentment and hatred has not died down, but has been resuscitated and

[14] Head's notion of evil is somewhat inexplicit and more like a "working definition": she refers to "the misery and suffering [evil] inflicts on human life"; and to evil as "inflicting harm on others" (*Woman* 63), as well as saying "I associated evil in my mind with the acquisition of power" (77; cited earlier). Her *images* of evil are of extremely selfish, greedy, cruel and obscene acts.

intensified. In Elizabeth's identification of "the feeling behind it – a deep, cringing shame" (117) lies an important clue to what is happening in her mind. Since she naturally hates her persecutors with a profound fury and indignation – the "wild, savage vengeance" (98) earlier referred to – the anger seems a reassurance of how ineradicably *different* the victim of cruel power is from its perpetrator. But the figures in Elizabeth's psycho-drama (who are, of course, the inadequate, weak, but "good" "Sello" who is nevertheless himself the former power figure "Caligula"; the pitiless "Medusa"; and the grotesque "Dan"), *if* these three are not "real people," they are nevertheless not strangers either. They are (it seems) "possible selves."

A number of quotations strewn throughout the narrative hint at this point – such as: "[t]he roots of evil, as a creative, propelling force, had become as close as her own breathing" (85-86) and: "Medusa [. . .] is really the direct and tangible form of [one's] own evils [. . .] power lusts [. . .] greeds [. . .] self-importance" (40), as well as Elizabeth's acknowledgement that she is "living with a strange 'other self' [. . .] [who] has a terrible Medusa hidden away in *his* subconscious" (58; emphasis added) – a mental region which is thus *Elizabeth's* deeper subconscious and deeper self. If, "*wherever* relentless cruelty and hatred erupted, it was like the dark geyser of Medusa's soul erupting" (92; emphasis added), then Elizabeth has herself become the conduit of evil power. The eruption image portrays power as a force slumbering in all human souls.[15] It links with a whole chain of other references to Elizabeth's wrathful vengefulness (at her victimisation) as a "lava" slumbering within her: "One would go stark, raving mad if a deep and endless endurance of human suffering, such as one could encounter in Southern Africa, were really brought to the surface. *Subterraneously* it was a *powerful* willing of the total extinction of the white man [. . .] [a] terrible hatred" (83; emphases added).

We are told that the "disregarded" feeling, a "ferocity" at centuries of victimhood, "rumbled beneath her consciousness like molten lava" (98) and later that "Dan [one of her imagined torturers] [. . .] saw the hidden molten lava within –

---

15 Compare a remarkable passage from Fanon: "The important theoretical problem is that it is necessary at all times and in all places to make explicit, to demystify, and to harry *the insult to mankind that exists in oneself*" (246; emphasis added).

In her wide-ranging, subtle essay on *A Question of Power*, Rose posits that the "universality" Head establishes and achieves in this novel is "the universality of madness" (11-15), but the view I put forward is that Head's is the more disquieting, indelible discovery of the "universality" of the capacity to inflict hurt – to use power evilly – *even* in victims.

'Now, I know what to do with that', he said, triumphantly" (136). Then we learn that Elizabeth "began to believe her own nightmare. It was a combination of Dan and the hidden, molten lava" (140). All these images of a volcanic power smouldering within Elizabeth culminate in the final, great crisis during which she assaults the inanely "Christian" Mrs Jones, when "the propaganda records, the repetitive images of evil, [. . .] shattered her sanity [. . .] The day she broke down she simply howled, and *like a volcano the evil erupted in a wild flow of molten lava*" (171; emphases added).

The notion of memory is used in a strange, much enlarged way in this text. It might be associated with the notion of contamination or complicity. Having been subjected to power as its victim, and having consequently *apparently* escaped from its clutches, only to find that it is living (on) within her own mind, Elizabeth has been forced through experiencing this lingering after-effect of power to acknowledge that it cannot be safely parcelled away in the South African past, labelled "apartheid." The voices of "the soul of the black man," of "the poor" themselves instruct Elizabeth that the "roots" and "creators" of "evil" are "nothing like the white fools shoving us around," but lie in the *ubiquitous* "arrogance of the soul, [. . .] its overwhelming lust for dominance and prestige" (134-135). This is not a comforting, but a "tortur[ing]" (135) thought to Elizabeth. Unlike Conrad's *Heart of Darkness*, in which the weak white soul succumbs, when exposed to the opportunities for evil which "Africa" offers, to an indeterminate[16] "horror! The horror!" (Conrad 149), Head (through Elizabeth) in her novel acknowledges evil personally *and* denies it a racial tag.[17] Through the text Head insists on the taking of responsibility by each individual for all the power forms of society – *even when* one is their victim. This startling, frightening discovery of a dreadful duty which Elizabeth so arduously attains ("the possibilities of massive suffering were being worked out in her" [39]) establishes that her awful experiences are nevertheless a learning process[18] – the difficulty, disturbing effects and immense poignancy of the novel reflect the terrible warning

16 An illuminating comment occurs, when the narrator refers unenthusiastically to "the lofty statements of mankind's great teachers" as "*indistinct* statements about evil" (12; emphasis added).

17 In a letter to Vigne in 1967 Head wrote: "There are really wicked people on this earth. BUT THEY ARE NOT IN CAMPS" (*Gesture* 54; capitals in the original).

18 "There was no beauty or tenderness in her learning" (70) is a statement preceding the list of "fundamental questions" to which Elizabeth is subjected. Compare her reference to "learning, internally" (133), and her later reference to herself as having been "born for this experience" (192).

which is its "lesson": that "[e]vil is a complexity so monumental that everything becomes a tangle of lies" (12).

Once heard, the "roar" (36; 159) of power[19] echoes on and on in the soul. *A Question of Power* offers no glib, enduring or certain reassurance of recovery from the damaging effects of harmful power; its truth is not reconciliatory, but demanding and warning. What Elizabeth's German friend tells her (after relating the incident in which an Afrikaner humiliates an African tea-server), concerning the Jews and the Nazi period (as a supposed historical parallel to South Africa), that "once the liberation came and the war was over" their belief that they were "inferior" and their "cring[ing]" over it "*disappeared overnight*" (46-47; emphasis added), is surely meant to be recognised in the context of this novel as an invalid and foolishly sentimental claim. This false reassurance of the possibility of an "erasure" of the harm caused by power abuse, parallels the other hopeful beliefs which Elizabeth learns to discard – such as belief in a powerful, justice-dealing and rescuing God (200; 86) and the dream of a romantic male soul-mate who will be simultaneously protective, powerful and faithful. The latter (naïve) ideal or yearning constructs the charade that "Dan" upholds for so long.

One description of Elizabeth's actual experience explicitly brings in the "memory" notion:

> So many people ran away from South Africa to *forget it* or to throw it off. It *seemed impossible* then, the *recurring*, monotonous song in her head: 'Dog, filth, the Africans will eat you to death'. [. . .] It broke her instantly. [. . .] There was nothing she could think of to counter it: *I'm not like that. I've never been a racialist.* Of course I admit I'm Coloured. [. . .] Maybe people who are Coloureds are quite nice too, just like Africans [. . .] (47; emphases added)

The pathos of this passage, its *harrowing* effect, comes from one's sense of the extent to which it is saturated with the experience of the recurrence of victimisation and manifests the continuing cringe of the beaten victim.

In the piece published in 1982 in *Drum* magazine, Head (looking back on her own past) wrote:

---

19 Most terrifyingly illustrated when Dan "open[s Elizabeth's] skull [. . .] and talk[s] right into the exposed area" with his "unintelligible [. . .] 'Rrrrrrrrraaaaaaaaa'" (177). It is a gesture enacting *violation* of the individual by power abuse, as well as the invasion of the mind by maleficent power.

> This terror of power and an examination of its stark horrors created a long period of anguish in my life and forced out of me some strange novels that I had not anticipated writing.
>
> It was almost as though the books wrote themselves, propelled into existence by the need to create a reverence for human life in an environment and historical circumstances that seem to me a howling inferno. (*Woman* 77)

This "aftermath" piece both testifies to the way power "terror[ises]" and subjugates its victim in "anguish," and *simultaneously* records how it can impel the victim to "create" that which was formerly unimaginable – because the "need" of "reverence" is intensified in the "inferno." Thus unendurable memory becomes a source of creative energy; it makes possible the recognition of the huge effort of the imagination required to establish a liveable world, *against* the perpetual, insistent thrust of power lust – both outside of, and within people.

In 1972 Head wrote:

> It is impossible to guess how the revolution will come one day in South Africa. But in a world where all ordinary people are insisting on their rights, it is inevitable. It is to be hoped that great leaders will arise there who *remember* the suffering of racial hatred and *out of it* formulate a common language of human love for all people. (*Woman* 103; emphases added)

As in *A Question of Power*, an unsentimental "language of love" would (as Head imagines) be forged *from memories* of the harm caused by racist abuse.

Reminding us that "the novel in Africa has been dominated by historical and hence nationalist themes," Elleke Boehmer asks the question "how are [African] women to find a voice? How are they to interrupt the duologue of colonial master and national father?" – a question which she answers by pointing to such women "giving voice: [. . .] speaking for themselves, telling their own histories" (244). Like the writers Tsitsi Dangarembga and Yvonne Vera after her, Bessie Head had the courage to give voice to the "underground" of nationalism and decolonisation and to the psychic hardships of being female, without any family connections, darker than white and a person of "mixed race" within these (sociopolitically) rigidly hierarchising contexts. Head's insistence on uncomfortable realities, it needs to be recognised, grew out of agonising, shameful memories –

and to overcome that agony and its awful, attendant shame[20] required great effort and daring.

Victim, "blabbermouth" (40), "warrior" (103), Bessie Head produced in this text an enduring testimony to the ineradicable awfulness of violation and abjection and to its horrifying aftermath. Nothing as facile as a "talking cure" is offered in her vision of the contorted memory that succeeds trauma. A huge, slow and arduous effort is required to outmanoeuvre the temptations and seductions that power offers even to its victims. It seems that for Elizabeth it is possible to opt out of hierarchies and power struggles only by embracing the humanly ordinary.[21] Elizabeth bases this insight on *another* memory, one she brought with her from the "slums and hovels" of South Africa (26), a recollection to which she comes back in the end (206). For, in Head's view, "[t]here [is] no direct push against those rigid, false systems of class and caste" (206). All power forms are shown to be forms of "aparting";[22] their only true opposite being presented as acceptance of our own and others' "ordinar[iness]"[23] – the interlinking force which creates community and "belonging" (206). *A Question of Power* ends, all readers remember, with Elizabeth "placing one soft hand over her land," moving from memory into a future with that "gesture of belonging" (206).

The word 'belonging' is crucial. It indicates an achieved dedication that avoids both the arrogance of possessiveness and the humiliation of homelessness. It also points the way out of the memory trap in which victims are caught, for to belong is to be future-directed, like the enduring "land" itself, the soil on

---

20 Compare Elizabeth's reference to "this record inside her head" and (again) to the "feeling behind it [. . . :] a cringing, deep shame" (Head, *Question* 117).

21 A theorist like Nancy Holmstrom emphasises the extent to which both racial and gender "identities" are markers of power subjugation. "Racism, in short, has created the group that needs to struggle against it," she writes (97), and "(hetero)sexism creates the group that needs to struggle against it" (98).

22 Tucker notes that "Absolute power [. . .] relies on the victimisation of *an Other*" (175; emphasis added).

Evasdaughter's reading of Head's text mentions as two of the novelist's main discoveries the recognition that "power over *others* has no good form" (197-199, 205-206) and refers to the "interpretation of *paranoia* as a reaction to power" (77; 81; emphases added).

23 Head emphasises the term "ordinary" by using it over and over as the expression of a major discovery: see 196-206; 31; 39; 63; 79 – and compare: "I am just anyone" (*Question*11).

which Elizabeth lives among plants, creatures and other "ordinary" people (206). Is this attained relief to be imagined as a condition immune from reversion into agonising memories? Such a question remains unanswerable. For Head herself, the plaguing psychic disturbances of the violated would certainly recur, contributing to her increasing addiction to alcohol and her premature death. Perhaps her anguish intensified, as it shortened, the life of this profound spiritual guide, who saw her account of remembered suffering and her vision of its arduous transcendence as a testament to posterity.[24]

Works Cited

Birch, Kenneth. S. "The Birch Family: An Introduction to the White Antecedents of the Late Bessie Amelia Head." *English in Africa* 22.1 (1995): 1-18.

Boehmer, Elleke. "Motherlands, Mothers and Nationalist Sons: Representations of Nationalism and Women in African Literature." *From Commonwealth to Postcolonial*. Ed. Anna Rutherford. Sydney: Dangaroo, 1992. 229-245.

Boyce Davies, Carol "Private Selves and Public Spaces: Autobiography and the African Woman Writer." *College Language Association Journal* 24.3 (1991): 267-289.

Conrad, Joseph. *Youth, Heart of Darkness and The End of the Tether*. London: Dent, 1902.

Eilersen, Gillian Stead. *Bessie Head: Thunder Behind Her Ears. Her Life and Writing*. London: James Currey, 1995.

Evasdaughter, Elizabeth N. "Bessie Head's *A Question of Power* Read as a Mariner's Guide to Paranoia." *Research in African Literatures* 20.1 (1989): 72-83.

Fanon, Frantz. *The Wretched of the Earth*. Trans. Constance Farrington. Harmondsworth: Penguin, 1967.

24 She once wrote about experiencing "a wild terror that I had stumbled upon a world of evil that [. . .] would live forever. [. . .] I felt that I would go through this experience again were I re-born [. . .] if I recorded the evil [. . .] I would read *A Question of Power* and it would save me from such suffering" (qtd. in Sarvan 15). But Head also registered her sense of the public response to the text more despondently as follows (in 1976): "Since the material used is authentic, [. . .] It caused people to pause and consider; [. . .] But generally, at a more sophisticated level, it was branded the work of a deranged mind – [. . .] as such it had its place but was not worthy of regard" (qtd. in Nichols 18).

Gagiano, Annie. *Achebe, Head, Marechera: On Power and Change in Africa.* Boulder, CO & London: Lynne Rienner, 2000.

Head, Bessie. *A Question of Power*. London: Heinemann, 1974.

___. *A Woman Alone: Autobiographical Writings*. Ed. Craig MacKenzie. Oxford: Heinemann, 1990.

___. MacKenzie and Clayton. Interview with Michelle Adler et al. 5-29.

___. *A Gesture of Belonging: Letters from Bessie Head, 1965-1979*. Ed. Randolph Vigne. London: SA Writers, 1991.

___. *Serowe: Village of the Rain Wind.* London: Heinemann, 1981.

Holmstrom, Nancy. "Race, Gender, and Human Nature." *Race/Sex: Their Sameness, Difference, and Interplay*. Ed. Naomi Zack. New York: Routledge, 1997. 95-107.

Nichols, Lee. "In Memoriam: Bessie Head." *ALA Bulletin* 12.3 (1986): 16-18.

Innes, Lynn, and Caroline Rooney. "African Writing and Gender." *Writing and Africa*. Ed. Mpalive-Hangson Msiska and Paul Hyland. New York: Addison Wesley Longman, 1997. 193-215.

James, Wilmot, and Linda van de Vijver, eds. *After the TRC: Reflections on Truth and Reconciliation in South Africa*. Cape Town: David Philip, 2000 and Athens: Ohio UP, 2001.

Kristeva, Julia. *Nations Without Nationalism*. Trans. Leon S. Roudiez. New York: Columbia UP, 1993.

Krog, Antjie. *Country of my Skull*. Johannesburg: Random House, 1998.

MacKenzie, Craig, and Cherry Clayton, eds. *Between the Lines: Interviews with Bessie Head, Sheila Roberts, Ellen Kuzwayo, Miriam Tlali*. Grahamstown: NELM, 1989.

Marquard, J. "Bessie Head: Exile and Community in Southern Africa." Interview. *London Magazine* 18.9-10 (1978-1979): 48-61.

Minh-ha, Trinh T. "Other Than Myself/My Other Self." *Travellers' Tales: Narratives of Home and Displacement*. Ed. George Robertson et al. London/New York: Routledge, 1994. 9-26.

Pearse, Adekunlo. "Apartheid and Madness: Bessie Head's *A Question of Power*." *Kunapipi* 5.2 (1983): 81-93.

Ramphele, Mamphela. "Law, Corruption and Morality." *After the TRC: Reflections on Truth and Reconciliation in South Africa*. Ed. Wilmot James and Linda van de Vijver. Cape Town: David Philip, 2000.

Rooney, Caroline. "'Dangerous Knowledge' and the Poetics of Survival: A Reading of *Our Sister Killjoy* and *A Question of Power*." *Motherlands: Black

Women's Writing from Africa, the Caribbean and South Asia. Ed. Susheila Nasta. London: Women's Press, 1991. 99-126.

Rose, Jacqueline. *States of Fantasy*. Oxford: Clarendon, 1996.

Sarvan, Charles. "Bessie Head: Two Letters." *Wasafiri* 12 (1990): 11-15.

Tucker, Margaret E. "A 'Nice-time Girl' Strikes Back: An Essay on Bessie Head's *A Question of Power*." *Research in African Literatures* 19.2 (1988): 170-181.

Patterns of Leadership in Bessie Head's *Maru* and *A Bewitched Crossroad: An African Saga*

> Southern Africa isn't like the rest of Africa and is never going to be. Here we are going to have to make an extreme effort to find a deep faith to help us to live together.
>
> For largeness of heart is what we need for a civilisation and big, big eyes, wide enough to drink in all the knowledge of the heavens and earth.
>
> A sense of history was totally absent in me and it was as if, far back in history, thieves had stolen the land and were so anxious to cover up all traces of the theft that correspondingly, all traces of the true history have been obliterated. We, as black people, could make no appraisal of our own worth; we did not know who or what we were, apart from objects of abuse and exploitation
>
> – Bessie Head, *A Woman Alone* (31; 50; 66)

Although Head thought of herself primarily as a writer plumbing the depths of evil (Head, *Woman* 63), I would propose her as one of the few authors to consider goodness as something simultaneously mysterious, complex and worth investigating (89): evil in *Maru* and *Bewitched Crossroad* is comparatively banal (à la Hannah Arendt's *Eichmann in Jerusalem*) and uninteresting.[1] Perhaps, though, *A Question of Power* is the missing middle term in this study, it being the work in which Head does investigate the nature of evil (in the form closest to her experience of it – injustice and prejudice, the denial of human status to another)[2] and also the personal, psychic form of leadership-through-suffering.[3]

---

1 Compare Head's 1977 judgement: "because that's what evil is: *Rubbish*" (*Woman* 59).

2 "It was as though, in an internal and private way, I perceived the ease with which one could become evil and I associated evil in my mind with the acquisition of power" (*Woman* 77).

3 There is a trace of this notion in a 1975 comment on Khama III: "The act of suffering persecution for a belief eventually made Khama the victor in the struggle and the leading social reformer of the country. [. . .] he was a compassionate man by inclination" (*Woman* 56).

Generally, the trend of this essay accords with Head's 1978 self-description: "I have always reserved a special category for myself, as a writer – that of a pioneer blazing a new trail into the future" (*Woman* 64).

Out of the confusion which injustice causes, Head emerges with a triumphantly serene and sure recognition of leadership: the transformative energy, courage and vision needed to tackle the tangled stagnation of society as it is. From early on (compare *The Cardinals*) Head seemed to respond to the ugly "mess"[4] of racism and sexism not with despair, but with determination to envision an alternative – the "new world" of *Maru* (68).[5] With time and in her last self-published work, *A Bewitched Crossroad*, she set out to prove that it could be done because it had been done by people like Khama the Great in Botswana, given some luck and some backing. "[C]onfusion" (*Woman* ix)[6] has been said to characterise Head's own life, emphasising its ravagement by brutal neglect and racial ostracism. The deep clarity of her vision of leadership is, then, its most arresting and inspiring quality. I shall characterise *Maru* as a work of vision and *Crossroad* as a work of perception.[7]

I hypothesise that Head's interest in issues of leadership is the natural consequence of her perception of the embedded and dominant qualities of some of the worst features of human society, such as racial prejudice (in *Maru*) and irresponsible land greed (in *Crossroad*) and that this prompts her recognition that

---

Primarily, though, I would draw attention at this point to Head's idea that the sufferer can "bear witness" to the benefit of others – compare her key expression "blabbermouth" (*Question* 40; cf. 200). In accordance with Head's thought in *A Question of Power* that sufferers are explorers or scouts into the future of human development is a poem of Robert Frost's, "A Witness Tree" (Frost 195).

4 See *Maru* 68. In *The Cardinals* the word "mess" occurs more than ten times to describe injustice and incoherence in society.

5 This expression is used insistently in *Maru* to emphasise the need and to "extend an invitation" to transform society (7; 50; 68-70; 128). Head herself in 1975 declared her work directed at the creation of "new worlds" (*Woman* 28). The expression features also in *Crossroad* (75;132).

6 Cf. *Crossroad* (15), where the term "confusion" is used to describe the effect of a Matabele attack, but also applies to the "indiscriminate" killing ("anyone in sight") and to the bestialisation of these human warriors ("roaring like lions").

7 Cf. "It was like *finding* black power and black personality in a simple and natural way" (*Woman* 72; emphasis added).

unless a lead be taken towards the establishment of a better social arrangement, stagnation and profiteering will forever imprison humanity.[8]

In the novel *Maru* (1971) Head sets out to imagine how such leadership might come about. It is the dynamic and complex, *interpersonal*[9] nature of leadership as she conceives it that sets her thought apart from conventional (and, to her, suspect) notions of the "great man" who single-handedly (56)[10] or as the commander of many leads "his people." This common notion of leadership is from early in the novel *Maru* identified as misleading: "There was always the public. A man with a public eye tried to please them" (9).[11] In the novel bearing his name, we first meet Maru, "a born leader of men" (5), working in the fields along with his three associates, but his innovative, strategising mind is made immediately evident: he rejects and redirects ancient African habits of cultivation (6) as firmly as he has rejected conventional kingship to establish "a vision of a new world" (7). The form of kingship he has preferred is both private (a severance from the public life of the exercise of power), exemplified in the small home surrounded by yellow daisies, and "a beginning" (7): this latter term I interpret as signifying that *the kingship of choosing* "the kind of wife everybody would loathe from the bottom of their hearts" (6) is *a socially initiating act*: it is not presented as romantic escapism or abdication. His people may attempt to suppress the socially re-evaluating force of the deed (6-7; 36; 50), but the Masarwa feel its liberating implications and are empowered to challenge those

---

8 In *Maru* (68-70), the writer shows us Maru's dawning recognition of the harm done by racism and of its dangerous, doomed nature.

9 See the section "A reverence for people" at the end of *A Woman Alone* (99-100). Two of her own comments on *Maru* in her letters to Vigne confirm this concept of interpersonality: The novel "glories *friendship* between a man and a man and friendship between a woman and a woman" (*Gesture* 136) and "If there were no love making in the world, racialism and prejudice would never die" (72). Cf. Townsend, "Beyond Racism" 28.

10 Compare Head's own mimicking of critical (mis-?)readings of and complaints against *Maru* (novel as well as character): "No, no, no [. . .] Why do you have to have the god-man the world is waiting for. We don't want this sort of thing anymore" (*Between the Lines* 19).

11 Cf. also the comment on Moleka (*Maru* 9), as well as passages that touch on the issue (68-69, 50, 36).

who would continue to devalue them (126-127).[12] The nature of the revolution is as simple as it is far-reaching: "they were as human as everyone else" (126-127).

Although the novel by its title and other foregrounding mechanisms (such as the prevalence given to his perspectives and his controlling and planning activities) seems to give Maru pre-eminence, there are more interesting ideas that course through this work.[13] Personally and deeply fulfilling as the marriage of Margaret and Maru is shown to be (6-10), it is its consequences, psychological, social and political by nature, that constitute its wider importance. Hence the abrupt shift from the conclusion of the Maru and Margaret history, with which the novel opens, to its real beginnings or roots – the persecution of Margaret Cadmore (Jnr) and the Masarwa people. The love and recognition shown towards Margaret in Maru's tender greeting, "My sweetheart" (10), hinge the story back into Margaret's early days, "with the tin cans rattling: 'Bushman! Low breed! Bastard!'" (11), the actions and expressions in denial of her humanity. Head looks at the interface between prejudice (a social phenomenon) and "oppress[ion]" (11) (a political strategy). As in *The Cardinals*, her telling of a peculiar love story is a tool for the analysis of human communities. These are of two main types: power alliances, or love choices; the former thrives on the habits of prejudice (in terms of rank, or gender, or race – and so on), whereas the latter is characterised by the transgression of boundaries.[14] In *Maru*, we are told of the unholy trinity Seth, Pete and Morafi that "birds of a feather flock together" (42). Theirs is the untroubled affinity of evil, whereas Maru's is the type of mind said to be capable of "embrac[ing] the impossible," disregarding "barriers" (110).[15] In other words, habitual alliances are contrasted with new combinations, which

[12] It is notable that Head uses exactly the same imagery (of the small, stinking room) to apply to her own condition, in a passage written in 1968 (*Woman* 48), as she does to describe the liberation of the Masarwa at the end of *Maru* (126-127). One might add that continuing discrimination against the Masarwa people in Botswana (as reported in the "Open Africa" supplement to the *Weekly Mail and Guardian* of April 1995 and June 1996) is both an irony and a demonstration of the lasting urgency of the novel's issues.

[13] Coundouriotis in her essay well analyses Margaret (Junior)'s seminal role.

[14] In a 1979 note on *Rain Clouds* Head herself explicitly draws such a distinction between two types of society (*Woman* 73).

[15] Notably this directly parallels and echoes an earlier description: Ostracism "had created in her an attraction for the unpredictable, for the types of personality most people could not abide or get along with, and for all forms of vigour and growth outside the normal patterns" (94).

require imagination and courage to initiate.[16] Habitual alliances will have their figureheads who imagine themselves leaders (like the three goons mentioned above), but such "leaders" are mere conformists to the bad old habits of deference (towards the significantly named Totems and their hereditary privileges) and ritualised contempt towards the supposedly subhuman Masarwa. Such pseudo-leaders are, in fact, mere followers, paradoxically dictated to by the lowest common prejudices – they are enslaved or manipulated by those supposed to be following them, a point Maru is shown to grasp (67).[17] People like Seth, Pete and Morafi adhere to what might be called the sandwich structure notion of society, a rigid hierarchy of which they are, because of their relatively privileged position, the unthinking adherents.

I want to come back to the important issue of the interpersonal nature of leadership as depicted by Head. By the time Margaret Cadmore Jnr arrives in Dilepe village and Moleka first and then Maru recognise that this startling woman has the power to change their lives, a great deal else has had to happen to make her effect on them a possibility. I suggest firstly that Head shows us that Dikeledi, Moleka and Maru are already in conventional leadership *positions* in Dilepe, but indicates that each of them has the possibility to change and become leaders in her special sense: as those who can initiate improving changes in a seemingly intractable social structure. Hence, Dikeledi is characterised as "a drastic revolutionary" (25), because she quietly freed Masarwa slaves to become her salaried employees (25), a clear precursor of her brother's more radical social transgression to come. For all his *Don Juan* ways and harsh arrogance (29; 35; 57) towards ordinary people[18] that so upsets Margaret when he drives her: "He'd

---

16 Margaret's ability to enjoy and honour the two goats (themselves adventurous transgressors beyond the usual barriers between animal and human life, and as *images* echoing certain patterns in Margaret's life) fits in here (95-98). It is noticeable how Head transfers and applies the term 'creative' to a socio-political context in Maru's thinking, in this both broadening the concept and aligning him with Margaret's visionary, artistic abilities. She indicates a similar link between the "artistic' and the "political" in the work of the South African resistance leader Robert Sobukwe, whom she held in the highest esteem: "The papers that were issued in a steady stream were the work of a creative artist and not that of a hardened self-seeking politician" (*Tales* 138). These writings are said to be "new and unexpected."

17 Head gives us a clear sense of the prevalence of the figurehead-leader notion by showing that even the otherwise admirably enlightened Dikeledi adheres to it (66).

18 Contrast the comment on Maru at the bottom of p. 110.

grown up making goats and people jump. It was nothing" (28).[19] Moleka's restlessness is indicative of his hidden yearning and capacity for a more disciplined and responsible lifestyle appropriate to the "real husband" (125)[20] and effective administrator (70) he will become after Margaret and Maru's departure: his devotion (33) and submission to his strange and only friend Maru (before the explosion of love rivalry between them) also testifies to such a capacity in him.[21] For his part, Maru's aloofness from the world of petty intrigues and power display (36) makes clear, long before Margaret's arrival, that he senses himself destined for a less predictable role than that of traditional paramount chief or king.[22] He discovers the "gods who spoke to him in his heart" (73) before Margaret's appearance in his life and it is thus that he does not "fall for" her on sight, or on hearing (as Moleka does), but chooses her before meeting her as the one person who would compensate for and complement the "lonel[iness]" (56) within him. We have also been told about him, before his encounter with Margaret, that "[h]is manner towards everyone was of courteous informal respect. [. . .] He set the tone, seemingly, for a new world" (50).

By describing Head's unusual notions of leadership as foregrounding the interpersonal rather than individual nature of this force I do not mean to suggest that she shows us (in *Maru*) people consciously co-operating or "networking" in the corporatist sense of the term. Instead, she depicts a frequently accidental coincidence of energies and opportunities. Although Maru is the most 'aware' member of the web of activities that culminate in a crucial social and political redistribution of possibilities in his society, Head seems to indicate that beyond human agency there are fates or growth forces at work, or at least, waiting possibilities that require recognition to become available to human beings. Maru, hence, is enjoined to obey the gods in his heart (57; 73): they are neither his puppets nor the validations of any selfish strivings (58). Yet such urgings as are

---

19 Head's careful novelistic organisation is evident in her inclusion of a comment (28) on the gentle Dikeledi's careful driving (and talking); if driving represents leadership and power, Dikeledi is clearly "necessary" as an alleviating influence on and partner to Moleka.

20 The lovely and necessary interplay between Moleka's and Dikeledi's personalities and roles (both within their marriage and in their society) is shown in a lyrical passage on p. 83.

21 On p. 82 Head points forward to the eventual transformation of the arrogant, selfish Moleka into a humble and generous leader of the type she respects.

22 A similar point is made about Maru: "nothing was personal to him" (73).

experienced by Maru through these "gods" and by Margaret[23] through the power which compels her paintings (100-101) are in this novel the primary "leaders." On p. 69 in *Maru* the main character's consciousness registers a social and political effect of the presence of these "gods": "[t]hat they were opening doors on all sides, for every living thing on earth." They could be said to be energies inspiring or empowering the liberatory thrust forward of all life.[24]

That these energies are not only impersonal but (rather) interpersonal is confirmed by the co-incidence of Margaret's major painting (of Dilepe village, first truly "seen" by Margaret after her crucial encounter with Moleka [31]) reaching and comforting Moleka after her departure (116) and by the fact that Dikeledi can "match" Moleka's yearnings despite the fact that the initial "unlocking" of his heart happened through his falling in love with Margaret (83). The central statement of the leadership notion as an unconsciously co-operative phenomenon occurs on p. 116: "In this strange tangle of secret events, secretly they all assisted each other."[25]

Outside Dilepe village, in the history of Margaret's birth and upbringing, lies another strong thread that is a component of the creative "[en]tangle[ment]" (116) mentioned above. The passionate, frustrated, common-sense nature (16) of Margaret Cadmore Snr is an important catalysing agent to bring about the eventual blossoming of the yellow daisies (or marguerites). The passionate fierceness of her recognition that the dead, dirty Masarwa woman [Margaret Jr's actual mother, who dies in giving birth to her] "looks like a Goddess" (15) and that the little girl she brings up as an "experiment" (15; 16) cannot be taken from Africa because she owes a debt and must contribute to the improvement of the lot of those Masarwa people (17; 20-21) from whom she (the younger Margaret) has been more-or-less isolated (19) by her relative privilege, gives the older Margaret a pivotal role in this tale.[26] She may be deliberately desentimentalised by the author (12-13; 87; 88), but her bestowal of her own name on her adoptive daughter-servant-experiment does make her a type of ancestor, initiator and

23 Compare Head's own words in which she pays tribute to Margaret's visionary powers and strength of character: "This is the great love story. She *imagines*." "She holds herself together through creativity" (*Between* 18 and 20).

24 Cf. the wonderful "seeding" passage in *When Rain Clouds Gather* (78).

25 Cf. the central paragraph on pp. 73, 104-105; 108 (where we are told that Maru "*through* [Margaret,] sought to gain an understanding of the eventual liberation of an oppressed people" [my emphasis]) and p. 112.

26 Note how the core image of the opening of a door is associated with Margaret Snr (16). Cf. passages where the "influence" of the older woman is described (20; 94).

leader (perhaps precursor) who will see and paint the power and beauty of "ordinary, common" people (107). *Through* his later commitment to the younger Margaret, Maru in turn is sensitised to the Masarwa condition and to the hidden possibilities of all unimportant, ordinary people:

> The women carried water buckets up and down the hill but the eye was thrown, almost by force, towards the powerful curve of a leg muscle, resilience in the back and neck, and the animated expressions and gestures of the water-carriers as they stopped to gossip. They carried a message to [Maru's] own heart: Look! Don't you see! We are the people who have the strength to build a new world! And his heart agreed. Dikeledi, with her delicate expressions and coddled life, was given the same treatment, until she too belonged amidst the vigour of the goats and the water carriers [. . .] a third Dikeledi was emerging who sat alone and aloof and stared with deep, penetrating eyes on the value of her own kingdom. It was as though, once she knew everything and had uncovered her own worth, she would awaken and share her gifts with those who needed them. The portraits and sketches traced this unfolding of the soul. (107-108)

It is through this unique form of energy, which might be termed vision or leadership, echoed in the above passage in the verbs 'uncover,' 'awaken' and 'share' (108), that Head demonstrates how a daughter of an enslaved people, given the gift of education, can unfold her creativity and be connected with hereditary status to become a third, new thing – a transformative, liberating influence (107-108).

In the historical novel *A Bewitched Crossroad: An African Saga* (1984), which took Head ten years to write (Eilersen 260) and which was the last work she published, she returns to the issue of leadership form a different perspective and in a different mode. The scrupulosity of her research and the balanced, carefully considered nature of her judgements are everywhere in evidence in this to date somewhat neglected work (both among students of her work and historians), which is in fact a cunning and beautiful achievement. It is the book which most fully and fittingly answers her own yearning "as an African for a sense of historical continuity, a sense of roots" (*Woman* 86). The strategies of leadership are as central to this book as they are in *Maru*; the strategies of authorial construction operate here under the constraints of brute facts,[27] but testify to the grace and adaptability of Head's talent. In this second part of my paper I wish to examine Head's history of the preservation and emergence of the Botswana state as a type of testing ground or re-examination of ideas concerning leadership as she had earlier embodied them in *Maru*.

The central concept in *Crossroad* is "nation-building" (23), which is mentioned in Head's prefacing "Author's Note," whereas the idea of visionary leadership is discernible in Head's choice of the Marquez citation (8) as introductory epigraph to this work. One of the most fascinating aspects of Head's book is the entirely oblique, even distant presentation of the central leader during the period and in the area depicted: Khama the Great (i.e. Khama III) of Botswana. Although Head referred to the work as her "Khama novel" (e.g. Eilersen 26 and 191) and had long wanted to write such a book even before she began what proved to be the slow and arduous process of its construction, her very fascination with the man proved an obstruction (Eilersen 261).

I would postulate that Head had sensed that a study of Khama's "austere" personality (Head; qtd. in Eilersen 191) would not be sufficient *in itself* to account for the process of social change she was describing and that she was perhaps driven back to a recognition of the context of leadership – the myriad of ordinary people and other influences within which leadership must function – and to the corresponding realisation of the co-operative, (and what I have termed) *interpersonal* nature of leadership impulses – her struggle in writing this work was, she said, "to pull together the whole southern African experience at that time" (Eilersen 260).[28] In this novel, too, the active hostilities of particular individuals and the threats of real events present historical complications – authorially or conceptually tricky terrain to negotiate if she were to maintain the thread of a tale of social development or nation-building. Although the largely singular and dominant role of Khama III is thus recognised in the narrative (we may think of Maruapula's frequent, sarcastically resentful references to him as the "Great Man" (e.g. 68-70), Head's titling of her work emphasises the large de-

27 She wrote elsewhere: "Khama [. . .] fascinates me. But unfortunately the work is slow and heavy and the research, forbidding" (*Gesture* 188). That the work presented a conceptual problem is indicated in her acknowledgement that she had "never [before] bothered to examine what it means to have a fluid, unbending personality [like Khama's] within a power structure, to use power for one's own ends and others" (*Gesture* 171).

28 Some other explanations are given (by both Head herself and Eilersen) in Eilersen's biography (261; 262).

gree of luck involved in the (if I may so term it) unappetising[29] nature of the Botswana region – as far as the great powers and the ambitious men of the time were concerned. Yet we are left in no doubt about the rapacities surging all around the Bamangwato region and are shown that sometimes such volatilities and greed manifest themselves even inside this "hallowed" ground (196).[30]

It is due to the ambience of these vicious energies that the proverbially cool calm and collected leadership style of Khama (Head refers to his "serene, steady personality" and his "quiet, decisive voice" [50; 55]) is a shining exception and a tower of strength to his people.[31] Yet the aloof manner of the man is no sign of his detachment: indeed it is his alertness and his continuous, far-seeing concern for the welfare of his people that are so striking. This man moves (as does the whole work) between the "bushes" and the "stars" mentioned in the quotation leading chapter I (9): he is as deeply involved in the practicalities of water supply (161-163) and weapon acquisition and political or military organisation (49; 53) as he is in the ideological transformation of society (ending human sacrifice; discouraging alcoholism; abolishing the bride price practice; declaring his country a Christian commonwealth).[32] It is his marvellous skills of negotiation – *engaging* those who are amenable to reason or working through them to hold off others or forces who do not seem so appeasable[33] – that Head foregrounds in her writing. She shows him using as wedges the vague promises of protection to secure the independence and recognition of his people.[34] What this emphasises is

---

29 Cf. *Between*: "There was a period of British colonialism. But they so loathed the country because it looked like a desolation to them" (10).

30 Head wrote elsewhere: "The history of Southern Africa fascinates me, not necessarily the miserable history of the Great Trek, the land-grabbing, cattle-grabbing wars and the diamond and gold rushes, but themes that are linked to the eternal stream of mankind's history" (*Woman* 78).

31 Not that Head is unaware of African precursors of his humane style of leadership - she describes the last good Mambo or king of Mwene-Mutapa and his (sub-)chief Mengwe as well as the founder of the Sotho kingdom, Moshoeshoe, as sharing the qualities of enlightenment shown by Khama III.

32 "My people, Jesus, that King of Kings, rules here [. . .]" (40); "Khama became an obsessed reformer" (54), "an enlightened leader of his people [. . .] and a great Christian" (56).

33 E.g. "I wish to avoid all contact with the Boer government except through the government of Her Majesty, the Queen" (123).

34 The greatest example of this strategy is the brilliant combination of appeal, exhortation and careful logic in the letter given to the Warren expedition, an episode ful-

that here, yet again, the leadership notion is virtually devoid of power display, love of privilege or harsh imposition. Despite the strictures of a critic such as Maruapula, he too is shown as somewhat bemused by the skill with which Khama introduces reforms (68-70) so that they are mostly assented to: even "cornerstones" (169) of the Tswana lifestyle are removed and exchanged without major disruption – because these changes have demonstrable benefits and help to disentangle some of the complications caused by rigid observation of custom. Khama's purpose being broadly humane and enlightening, the austerities of his reign are found endurable. It is shown that no challenge to his rule has much appeal:[35] he inspires and impresses (cf. Head *Woman* 56).

Especially fascinating in Head's investigation of the enigma of a leader who can remove many of the organising principles of a society and introduce different ones with hardly discernible disruption (164) is the role in this process of public deliberations and the dispersal and "digestion" of innovations and crucial decisions as aimed towards the future. In one of her letters (to Vigne) she explains her admiration for him as for "a man who goes against the grain" (180). Yet as she shows it, innovation does not take place by authoritarian decree of socio-economic programme. It is distinctly a process of dissemination from Khama through the Kgotla or central parliamentary gathering of male leaders to flow onwards throughout the many wards and households there represented. It is, truly, a democratic structure, flexible and sensitive, ensuring that the seemingly aloof but guiding role of this leader always connects (him) with the people whose welfare is his concern.[36]

> [. . .] all Khama's reforms were to observe this base – a harmonious blending of traditional custom and Christian worship. Large social courtesies surrounded each ritual and ceremony practised by his people.
>
> All the traditional courtesies were retained while the bloody or brutal aspects demanding sacrifice of human life were omitted. (55)

ly described and citing in full this remarkable document (114-121, the letter appearing on pp. 117-119).

35 I refer to challenges such as Sechele's "stirrings" (124); Khamane's bid for power (89) and Kobe's defiance (137-139).

36 Cf. "two of the greatest black leaders the continent may ever know – Khama, The Great, and his son, Tshekedi Khama – men distinguished for their personal integrity and the power with which they articulated the hopes of their people" (*Woman* 70).

Concerning the adoption of Protectorate status, Head shows us how "the chief spoke [. . .] at the same time subtly leading them on and persuading them to accept the negotiations he had made with a foreign government" (116). As the old chief Sebina sagely observes, "[o]ur ideas of leadership must change to suit the times" (120).

But *Crossroad* is not only a "Khama novel" and this (yet again) ensures that the reader is led to recognise the multiplicity of leadership in a healthy society. Head's brilliant strategy of incorporating the Sebina clan history in this work gives us – in the figure of the benign old man Sebina[37] – an image of another leader who, although he subordinates himself willingly to Khama's innovative rule, can measure that man's decrees and practices against a wide and varied experience. He represents an ancient, pre-Christian African tolerance.[38] It is due to the background experiences of the demeaning, almost bestialising practices to which the Matabele subjected his people (15-17; 61; 63; 91) that Sebina can celebrate the apology accompanying the news that six of his people were accidentally killed by Khama's people as the sign that at last they will find a new haven by joining and swelling Bamangwato society (60-63).

In the discussions between the sweet-tempered Sebina and the somewhat unwilling Khama subject Maruapula (67-71; 98-100; 120-121; 137; 171-173) Head creatively inserts the pro's and cons of both the leader's manner and his measures for our consideration. In illustrating the excitement of "the new learning" (78; 79; 80 and elsewhere), she never forgets to offset it against the maintenance of ancient courtesies which demonstrate the essentially humane nature of this society in both its pre-modern and its modernising phases – the communal, structured (66) character of a type of human society from which it is possible for a leader of Khama's fibre to emerge and by which he can be accepted (116). That there are harsh, repressive forces at work within this (as in any other) community, is recognised – for instance, in Maruapula's refusal to allow any member of his family to acquire "the new learning" (71) and in the way this traumatises his son (133-135). Yet in the cheerful, brilliant scholar Mazebe,

---

37 "He [Sebina] had always been a leader of his people [. . .] He came from a rich tradition where the people were governed with affection and justice and where the rules and courtesies of life were always known [. . .] skilled in sorting out disputes and the management of their affairs" (74). In the figure of Mazebe (75) Head introduces a future (educated) generation of leadership.

38 This is a quality which the Christian reformer Khama has not lost, but combines wisely with the new piety: "and from Khama a broad outline and definition of traditional African government and courtesies" (116).

Sebina's grandson, we have another generous leader who shares what he learns with all and sundry (80-83; 133-135).

Head's examination of modernisation strategies, especially literacy, takes a not uncritical look at its principal instrument, the Christian missionary. I would say that both MacKenzie and Hepburn are shown as important and highly useful co-leaders to Khama in his project of the protection and upliftment of his people. She says of MacKenzie that he became "the first person to write of African customs with subtlety and depth" (48) – hence himself a visionary (cf. 104-121; 157), whereas Hepburn is accorded the following praise: "[n]ever had a king had a secretary of state like Hepburn where qualities of integrity and service were paramount" (178). Yet they have their weaknesses and blind spots (73) and the roles of both are beset by the irony that, if these two missionaries are on the whole capable of honouring the human worth and achievements of their host society, they are unfortunately also somewhat exceptional in that respect. Those missionaries in Africa (Head's example here being John Moffat [146-150; 155-156]) who exploit the trust placed in them are evidently misleaders and exploiters of an especially shocking kind in Head's eyes.

In *Crossroad* a great deal of attention is paid to figures I would term anti-leaders,[39] to express something of the scorn in which they are held by the author, though her recording of their influence in the human affairs of the time is careful and correct. An inhumane ethos of one kind or another, insofar as it is shown by Head to govern or inspire a whole movement of people, may also be termed an anti-leader. It is Head's choice to represent the movements north and towards the interior by both the Matabele forces and the Afrikaner Boer encroachments (87-89) as being "led" in this way, rather than by dominant individual figures. In the assumption of dominance; in the terrible, indiscriminate killing cries of the Matabele ("Gwaza! Gwaza! Gwaza!" [15; cf. 19; 91; 156]) and the inhumanely arrogant and dreadful – but politically useful – definition of African indigenes as "schepsels" or creatures (rather than people whose humanity must be recognised [31]) by the Afrikaner Trekkers and their successors, these two powers are shown to be akin. They are alike also in achieving the reverse of nation-building: both are destabilising, disruptive forces which stand directly opposed

---

39 One might term the large disruptive movements of the time (the *difecane*; colonialism as illustrated in the Berlin Conference and in Rhodes's depredations; Afrikaner expansionism) as anti-nation building forces. The last Mambo Tumbale's disastrous, insanely selfish type of rule (13-15) makes him perhaps Head's first example of what I term an anti-leader.

to the "[o]utstanding leaders [who] emerge[d] during this time with the ability to unite many diverse people under them" (23), i.e. the nation-builders. Of the two disorderly forces, the evil of European racism – imposed by military might as much as by political ideology – is measured exactly in its being found to be the worse and more devastating of the two[40] (to the bewildered ears of old Sebina, who had thought nothing could be more fearful than a Matabele onslaught [92; 94]). The Matabele forces sweep through, they kill and plunder and burn, but move on to a settlement where they in their turn become a society beset and eventually devastated by European encroachment, whereas the Boer threat never lets up and perpetually harasses the Southern African indigenes.[41]

Perhaps Head is somewhat tolerant in her depiction of the influence of British imperialism in this region at this time[42], but she is too sophisticated an historian and analyst of power not to show the ironies of "accidental" alliances between British influence and African interests in this area at this time (103), while recognising the broadly humanitarian thrust of abolition of slavery and recognition of local, African rights by British leadership (33). She is moreover a deft analyst of the whole range of representatives of the empire, ranging from such an heroic and principled champion of African rights as the missionary MacKenzie, Khama's early ally and mentor, to the ruffians and scoundrels who scramble for African riches in the basest of ways (160-161). She writes:

> Of all the foreign invaders, to only Britain had been extended an essentially African courtesy, that of seeking the protection of a greater power, with an implicit trust in the humanity and justice of that greater

---

40 Compare *A Gesture of Belonging* (219; e.g. "The Boer heritage is far worse [. . .] ominous") and three passages from *A Woman Alone*: "another power of stunted spiritual and intellectual growth [. . .] this gross, brute spirit" (82); "But a meeting of strange cultures in Southern Africa did not inspire wonder and communication between black and white. It produced a desolate history of moans, lamentations and wars" (85) and Head's linking of racial discrimination with the idea of primitivity: "Primitive man [. . .] was a provincial who raised the barriers high [. . .] That primitive way of life [. . .] underlines the social order of South Africa" (97).

41 It needs to be added that Head's documentation (hence vision) is not racially biased – she is not blind to ugly forms of African power abuse, treachery or land greed (e.g. 100).

42 See 31; 108 – but she dryly records the astounding passing (in 1890, in the British Parliament) of the "Foreign Jurisdiction Act, which gave itself the right to proclaim British sovereignty over any part of the world without previous treaty or agreement with the indigenous people" (176)!

power. The British government accepted this as an innovation they had acquired as part of their empire building. (108)

In the deepest hole of her "anti-leader" hell Head puts the man Cecil John Rhodes (151; 182-183), the imperialist extraordinaire of whom she says so devastatingly that "[a]ll his utterances were ugly" (156) – and shows us how valid and even restrained this judgement is by quoting his sayings, such as "[i]f you want the black man's land, take it" (184) and his grotesque boast: "I have taken everything from them but the air" (193; cf. 152; 184 again; 189). His grinning, florid figure appears the more shocking in the context of this book,[43] where we see so varied an array of those African leaders whose delicate courtesy and innate dignity are conveyed by *their* sayings, in which recognition of others and concern for the quality of human(e) society are so evident, such as the famous words of Moshoeshoe after capturing the cannibal who had eaten his own father: "Men cannot eat stones. Let it all be forgotten" (27; cf. 16; 28; 54; 61).

In Head's first full paragraph describing Cecil John Rhodes she implicitly contrasts his self-aggrandising bent with the *nation*-building intentions of true leaders: "He was building up a political base for himself in the Cape that represented the unity of English and Boer interests and, unlike MacKenzie, wished the imperial factor eliminated, *lest* expansion into the interior of African become identified with 'a sympathy for the natives'" (110; emphasis added).

His instinctive alliance with racist Boer expansionism (110; 149) is another illustration of the "birds of a feather" pattern remarked on in *Maru* (42) and reported earlier in this paper.[44]

That this book ends with the beginning of the failure of Rhodes's selfish ambitions (referring to the notorious Jameson raid) and with the transition of the reader's attention to the "slender thread of survival" (195) of the Bechuanaland Protectorate until the achievement of independence as Botswana in 1966, testifies finally (in Head's own concluding comments [196]) to the quiet power and inspiring beauty of a form of African leadership inviolate in its integrity – at home in and deserving of what she terms "a hallowed land" (196).[45]

---

43 See 109-110. It is more ironic that it is Rhodes of all people who replaces MacKenzie.

44 Rhodes's rapacity is also said to be the counterpart of the viciousness of the Matabele killing machine (156).

45 Note how the terms of this final reference to the *land* echo the earlier description of the *leader*: "The image of Khama now fell upon the land of northern Bechuana-

Like Maru with his interests in preserving the moisture of the clods on the field (6) and like Margaret with her paintings of village women carrying water, Khama is shown by Head to have a communicable vision of "a new world" (131).[46] He alone among African leaders achieves "a voice in Britain" (196) and he does, truly, represent his and his people's portion of African soil (117 - cf. Head *Woman* 87; 70). Indeed, Head tells us that during his lifetime the Bamangwato "became known as *batho baga Khama*, Khama's people" (54; cf. 123) and there can be no more fitting expression on which to conclude an examination of Head's study of leadership in these two works, as it perfectly confirms the ancient African wisdom in the saying that "[t]he king is king by grace of the people" (54; 121): a leader is or should be the visible face and head of a body of people without whom the leader is unimportant; a leader is not a dominator.

It has been said that Head in *Crossroad* (and perhaps similarly in *Maru*) almost excludes or even subordinates women.[47] Of course it is true that no woman is shown in either of these books in an obvious position of leadership. Yet one might be reminded that the Masarwa woman Margaret looks down on the Motswana king Maru as "from a great height" (64) at the moment of their meeting when he is masquerading in the role of petty and prejudiced dictator (59-60; 63-64; 65). Bearing in mind Head's own living experiences it seems absurdly inappropriate to suspect the woman who had written *A Question of Power* of being dazzled by male power or the power of maleness and hence of denigrating

land like a magic bewitchment" (57). Cf. *A Woman Alone*: "like a protective mantle over the land" (94).

46 This expression occurs in *Crossroad* not only on p. 131, but also on p. 75, evidently recalling its prominent use in *Maru* (7; 50; 68-70; 125; cf. *A Woman Alone* 28).

47 See Newell's somewhat disdainful reference to Head "betray[ing] the masculinist bias of her utopian conception." Newell also refers to other critics' (e.g. Nixon's; Chetin's) comment on "Head's mytholigisation of an all-male cast of historical heroes (and villains)" (Newell 77). Newell's somewhat ambivalent (but mainly critical) comment on this issue can be concisely represented by her question "Has Head usurped male historians' roles only in order to narrate His-Story?" (80-81).

With the above criticism, contrast Matsikidze (108) and Ola (72-73) a.w.a. Coundouriotis's comment (this time on *Maru*) that in it, a "feminine story, a romance, acquires deep political meaning as its resolution puts into motion a profound realignment of social structures" (24).

Finally, Head's own words: "You see, simply, leadership and power have so often been in the hands of men" (*Between* 16 - from a 1983 interview). See also her comments quoted in Eilersen (191), and her aspirational claim to the role of "mankind's storyteller" (*Between* 12).

women's contribution to social growth.[48] Though very few women fall within the ambit of her historical survey of the bewitched crossroad of Botswana, their pervasive presence it felt; theirs are the hidden energies without which no advances can be achieved or solidified (83; 141; 165-173; cf. *Woman* 86), even though, as Head showed in *The Collector of Treasures*, they often pay the worst of the price. Head of all people must be exonerated from petty gender-counting criticism. The broadly inclusive vision of this woman writer, woman warrior focuses through the tragic and bloody slush which makes up so much of human affairs on "[t]hat which is double-edged, that which is made of fire, that which is eternally alive" (*Woman* 44; 49), to cite the Biblical quotation she loved. We may apply to this writer Bessie Head, I think, the words she quotes concerning a pharaoh of Ancient Africa, which indicate the generous dimensions of true leadership: she "was most beautiful in [her] greatness, because of the length of [her] roots, for [her] roots bathed in great waters" (*Woman* 50; cf. 103).

Works Cited

Abrahams, Cecil, ed. *The Tragic Life: Bessie Head and Literature in Southern Africa*. Trenton, N.J.: Africa World Press, 1990.

Birch, Kenneth S. "The Birch Family: An Introduction to the White Antecedents of the Late Bessie Amelia Head." *English in Africa* 22.1 (1995): 1-18.

Bryce, Jane. "Writing as Power in the Narratives of African Women." *Kunapipi* 16.4 (1994): 618-625.

Bryce-Okunlola, Jane. "Motherhood as a Metaphor for Creativity in Three African Women's Novels: Flora Nwapa, Rebeca Njau and Bessie Head." Nasta 200-218.

Coetzee, Paulette, and MacKenzie, Craig. "Bessie Head: Rediscovered Early Poems." *English in Africa* 23.1 (1996): 29-46.

Coundouriotis, Eleni. "Authority and Invention in the Fiction of Bessie Head." *Research in African Literature* 27.2 (1996): 16-32.

Cullinan, Patrick. "On the Edge of Everything." *Southern African Review of Books* 41 (1996): 4-5.

Eilersen, Gillian Stead. *Bessie Head: Thunder behind her Ears. Her Life and Writing*. Portsmouth: Heinemann, 1996.

---

[48] This point is to be linked with Head's understanding of the role (contribution; influence) of her own writing in the life and issues of her own and later times: "You should link in with thousands of people – you should be a link in a chain" (*Between* 27).

Frost, Robert. *Robert Frost: Selected Poems*. Ed. Ian Hamilton. Harmondsworth: Penguin, 1973

Gagiano, Annie. 1994. "Finding Foundations for Change in Bessie Head's *The Cardinals*." Paper delivered at the AUETSA Conference hosted by The University of Transkei, July, 1994.

___. 1995. "Bessie Head's Questioning of Power." Paper delivered at the Conference "Women, the Arts and South Africa" hosted by the Gender Studies Programme of the University of Natal (Pietermaritzburg), January, 1995.

Head, Bessie. Interview with Michelle Adler et al. MacKenzie and Clayton. 5-29.

___. *A Bewitched Crossroad: An African Saga*. Cape Town: Ad. Donker, 1984.

___. *The Cardinals: With Meditations and Short Stories*. Ed. Margaret J. Daymond. Cape Town: David Philip, 1993.

___. *The Collector of Treasures/Short Stories*. London: Heinemann, 1977.

___. *A Gesture of Belonging: Letters from Bessie Head, 1965-1979*. Ed. Randolph Vigne. London: S. A. Writers, 1991.

___. *Maru*. London: Heinemann, 1971.

___. *A Question of Power*. London: Heinemann, 1974.

___. *Serowe, the Village of the Rain Wind*. London: Heinemann, 1981.

___. *Tales of Tenderness and Power*. Cape Town: Ad. Donker Ltd.

___. *When Rain Clouds Gather*. London: Heinemann, 1969.

___. 1990. *A Woman Alone: Autobiographical Writings*. London: Heinemann, 1989.

Innes, C. Lynn. "Reversal and Return in Fiction by Bessie Head and Ama Ata Aidoo." Mihailovich-Dickman 69-75.

Johnson, Joyce. "Structures of Meaning in the Novels of Bessie Head." *Kunapipi* 8.1 (1986): 56-69.

Kibera, Valerie. 1991. "Adopted Motherlands: The Novels of Marjorie Macgoye and Bessie Head." Nasta 310-329.

MacKenzie, Craig, and Cherry Clayton, eds. *Between the Lines: Interviews with Bessie Head, Sheila Roberts, Ellen Kuzwayo and Miriam Tlali*. Grahamstown: NELM, 1989.

Mihailovich-Dickman, Vera, ed. *"Return" in Post-Colonial Writing: A Cultural Labyrinth*. Amsterdam: Rodopi, 1994.

Nasta, Susheila. *Motherlands: Black Women's Writing from Africa, the Caribbean and South Asia*. London: Women's Press, 1991.

Newell, Stephany. "Conflict and Transformation in Bessie Head's *A Question of Power, Serowe: Village of the Rain Wind* and *A Bewitched Crossroad*." *Journal of Commonwealth Literature* 30.2 (1995): 65-83.

Nnaemeka, Obioma. "From Orality to Writing: African Women Writers and the Re(Inscription) of Womanhood." *Research in African Literatures* 25.4 (1994): 137-157.

Ola, Virginia U. *The Life and Works of Bessie Head*. Lewiston: Mellen, 1994.

Ogu, Memoye. 1995. "Bessie Head and the Pragmatic Spirit in *Maru* and *The Collector of Treasures*." Paper delivered at the AUETSA Conference hosted by the University of Natal, Pietermaritzburg, July, 1995.

Pearse, Adekunlo. "Apartheid and Madness: Bessie Head's *A Question of Power*." *Kunapipi* 5.2 (1983): 81-92.

Rasebotsa, Nobantu. "Wild Cannon." *Southern African Review of Books* 41 (1996): 3-4.

Sebina, Peter Mazebe. "Makalaka." *African Studies* 6 (1947): 82-96.

Townsend, R. "Beyond Racism: Bessie Head's Vision of a New World." *Unisa English Studies* 32.1 (1994): 27-31.

Townsend, Rosemary. "Life Stories: Fiction and Autobiography in Bessie Head." *An Introduction to the African Prose Narrative*. Ed. Lokangake Losambe. Pretoria: Kagiso Tertiary, 1996.

"Barbarism" and "Civilisation" in Shakespeare's *Titus Andronicus* and in Marechera's *Black Sunlight*

> It is right for Greeks to rule barbarians, mother, but not for barbarians to rule Greeks. For the one is slave, the other free.
>
> – Euripides, *Iphigenia at Aulis* (86)[1]

> Europe [. . .] hath [. . .] all manner of learning, whereas other countries are all of them, overspread with Barbarisme.
>
> – Mercator, *Atlas* (1: 42)

An emphasis on the grotesque and the poignant; the mocking, hyperbolic undermining of cultural stereotypes and of notions of civilisation; an irreverence of attitude; evocations of the intolerable injustice and cruelty of the world; mockery of the state; flamboyance of style and the subversion of stereotypes are qualities which Shakespeare's play and Marechera's novel have in common. In this somewhat experimental piece of "relational reading" I not only wish to examine how the notions of barbarism and of civilisation function (somewhat similarly) within texts so widely separated in time, but am attempting also to make a case for strategic redirection of Shakespearean studies so as to lead on to and link up with newer realities – such as contemporary Africa and its literatures. "The whole debate about what it means to be 'civilised,'" writes Patrick Chabal, "goes on endlessly and evolves according to the circumstances in which we find ourselves. It is tied to the question of identity, an important issue of debate today" (32).

As the pre-eminent metropolitan writer, Shakespeare's texts are continually updated by readings and rediscoveries that the issues of our time can be figured from his works. Aaron, Shylock, Othello and Caliban are figures in the plays whose presence has been highlighted at the time of a global shift towards postcolonial studies.[2] Such figures help to defamiliarise the apolitically "safe" area

---

1 Iphigeneia is herself, of course, a daughter sacrificed to empire by her father.

2 O. Mannoni's *Prospero and Caliban: The Psychology of Colonization* (1964) is one somewhat controversial example. More strictly literary studies include Eldred Jones, *Othello's Countrymen: The African in English Renaissance Drama* (1989) and Kim F. Hall, *Things of Darkness: Economies of Race and Gender in Early Modern England* (1995).

of literary studies – although discussions even of colonisation and its consequences sometimes end with "Shakespeare" still as the only, or main "authority,"[3] overshadowing "local" realities and texts. By welding the Shakespearean to the Marecheran text I aim to illustrate that the partnering of these two authors' recognitions of barbarism and civilisation as *both* perpetually included in the category "humanity" can work to re-alert one to the encapsulating force of established structures and dichotomies – to see both racial and literary classifications as social and mental traps. Destabilising the ruts of the lazy imagination was one of Marechera's chief aims. "Reaching" a text like his *Black Sunlight* "through" Shakespeare's play can re-enlighten *Titus Andronicus* as well as help us to discover the rich darkness of *Black Sunlight*.

Titus Andronicus is in my reading a staging of empire and its ironies. It uses a type of presentation which Marechera's irreverence towards all power forms (in *Black Sunlight*) helps one to recognise. The devouring nature of empire is the chief focus of Shakespeare's "lamentable Roman tragedy" (as the title page terms it). The Roman general and paterfamilias Titus Andronicus is an almost "colourless" personality: a nearly entirely conventional exemplar of "pietas" and patriotism, hence the perfect butt of the black joke at the heart of the form of power expansionism which is empire, even though he seems the complete "insider." Hence Titus, at the beginning of the play, unquestioningly endorses the complacent and *validating* claim of (his) empire, that it represents civilisation. Shakespeare illustrates that, as a nation's power expands and swallows other cultures, it *requires* the myth of "civilisation" to endorse its subjugating role.[4] Titus initially acts almost entirely and unquestioningly in terms of rules and precedents; by contrast Aaron, despite the negative markers of slavery and blackness which identify him as barbarian outsider, easily inserts himself as unsuspected puppet-master into so rigidly structured a society. The conventionality

---

3 South African authors who have analysed the "ameliorative" or "empire-building," "colonising" use of Shakespeare are Martin Orkin (*Shakespeare Against Apartheid*, 1987) and David Johnson (*Shakespeare and South Africa*, 1996).

4 Jan P. Nederveen Pieterse speaks of the "stages of empire" which follow "conquest": "consolidation, exploitation, formalisation and expansion" (192). Robert Young has a useful short history of the development of the notion of "civilisation" in Europe (32-37). He cites J. S. Mill's remark that "farther advanced in the road to perfection; happier, [. . .] is one sense of the word civilization. But in another sense it stands for that kind of improvement only, which distinguishes a wealthy and powerful nation from savages or barbarians" ("Civilisation"; qtd. in Young 35).

of Titus's position, the predictability of his decisions, is underlined by 1.1.67-68, which describes him as "the good Andronicus, / Patron of virtue, Rome's best champion."

Returning to "victorious" Rome (1.1.73 – the very expression made possible through his own military exertions, but transferred to the empire), Titus shows no outraged recognition at the fact that he has meekly "fed" twenty-one (out of twenty-five) of his sons to the insatiable consumer, the monster imperialism. There is a faint nudge from the playwright in 1.1.89 – which reads "Titus, unkind and careless of thine own" – but the apparent self-reproach is immediately cancelled by what follows, in which the dead sons are soothingly consigned to a "[s]weet cell of virtue and nobility." After slaughtering the eldest son of the captive Gothic queen Tamora in a ritual to "appease the shades" of his own dead children (dismissing her moving, motherly plea for her son's life to be spared), Titus is instantly ready to kill *yet another* of his few remaining sons – for resisting subjugation to the demands of the new emperor and for opposing his (Titus's) endorsement of this power-greedy incumbent ruler. The new emperor is Saturninus, whose name may also be associated with the idea of a devouring god/father. Titus's tenderness and magnification are reserved for – of all things – the family tomb[5] and (it seems) for his *dead* sons (1.1.28). It is entirely of a piece with his rigidly hierarchical perception of things that he foolishly endorses the candidature of (predictably) the previous emperor's eldest son and refuses to accept the offer of emperorship to himself. He lauds Saturninus – an unknown, ambitious and wilful young man – as "king and commander of our commonweal, / The wide world's emperor [. . .] Rome's imperious lord" (1.1.251-254), and will pay an extreme price for this blindness.

The nation which has been defeated under Titus's military leadership is identified as "the barbarous Goths" (1.1.28). The irony of this claim is underlined by what follows – the Goths will eventually become the allies by whose aid "Roman civilisation" is saved. The first (attempted) rape of Lavinia is about to occur – *within* empire's maw (compare Ray). Titus's daughter Lavinia is the betrothed of Bassianus, brother and rival of the newly installed emperor, Saturninus. In yet another unthinking genuflection to empire, Titus, who "gave" Saturninus the emperorship, now grants him Lavinia as his wife. Titus's sons thwart such a violation of civic values and move to protect their sister, respecting her prior betrothal (to Bassianus). Whereupon Titus himself slays son number twenty-two for resisting his fatherly will and the new emperor's desire – so entirely subju-

5 "O sacred receptacle of my joys, / Sweet cell of virtue and nobility" (1.1.95-96).

gated is the old general at this stage to the idea of the priority of empire. It is with difficulty that Titus is prevailed upon at least to allow this young man burial in the family tomb, pressurised by the somewhat belated words of his own brother: "Thou art a Roman, be not barbarous" (1.1.383). The grotesque comedy of these early scenes in Shakespeare's only "self-constructed" Rome[6] vividly show up the absurd pretensions to "style" of an up-and-coming power: a sort of political equivalent of the *nouveau-riche*.

The great set piece depicting the point from which the play's later horrors stem is, of course, the scene where Titus – almost primly – defies the anguished begging of Tamora that he spare the life of her eldest son. This plea by the Gothic Queen turns absolutely on the recognition of her and his – and their sons' – common humanity and the values which both their cultures supposedly endorse, erasing differences claimed in words such as "barbarous" and "civilised":

> Victorious Titus, rue the tears I shed,
> A mother's tears in passion for her son!
> And if thy sons were ever dear to thee,
> O, think my son to be as dear to me.
> Sufficeth not that we are brought to Rome
> To beautify thy triumphs and return
> Captive to thee and to thy Roman yoke?
> But must my sons be slaughtered in the street
> For valiant doings in their country's cause?
> O, if to fight for king and commonweal
> Were piety in thine, it is in these. (1.1.108-118)

For one moment the possibility of being "merciful" (1.1.121) flickers into what will become the barbarically tit-for-tat world of this play, but Titus's impervious, imperious rigidity is proof against it. Shakespeare subsequently gives Tamora's other sons, the terrible Chiron and Demetrius, a small discussion of Titus's refusal, in which they link this "barbarous" decision of "ambitious Rome" (to sacrifice their brother) to the contemporary negative stereotype of the

---

6 Unlike all his other "Roman" plays, *Titus Andronicus* has no known source (e.g. in North's translation of the Plutarch *Lives*). However, according to Naomi Conn Liebler a work by Herodian presents "Rome dominated from within by "barbarians" (274).

notoriously inhumane Scythians,[7] much as the playwright was later to give Lear a reference to "the barbarous Scythian / Or he that makes his generation messes" (*King Lear* 1.2.116-118) in a similarly ironic context – when Lear is himself treating his daughter Cordelia in a harshly inhumane way. Only much further into *Titus Andronicus*, when events like his own ostracism from power, the execution of two sons on trumped-up murder charges and the banishment of the last son (for resisting such imperial injustice) have occurred, is Titus at last ready to recognise that his formerly revered empire Rome "is but a wilderness of tigers," that "[t]igers must prey" (3.1.54-56) and that his family provides that food – even *before* he learns of his daughter's rape and dismemberment.

At this point I insert Marechera's reference (in a 1980 essay) to the Rhodesian "record of humiliation and atrocities," which those in the position of domination (colonial or "imperial" whites) "mystif[ied] and transform[ed] [. . .] into the more acceptable dimensions of "responsibility," "civilisation," "frontier-building and the keeping up of standards" – attitudes which Marechera links with "a visceral unwillingness to define the individual by reference to that individual's self" (Veit-Wild 232). The fit is near-perfect. The Shakespearean mirror reflects Marechera's black sunlight.

In *Titus Andronicus*, Titus's daughter Lavinia (who might have married the emperor) is supplanted by the Gothic queen Tamora whom Saturninus weds in a spleen. The Gothic woman is hence declared "*incorporate* in Rome" (1.1.467; emphasis added), even though "[a]ccompanied [. . .] with a barbarous Moor" (2.2.78) – and despite being exposed as "barbarous Tamora" (2.2.118) by Lavinia (the play's notorious rape and dismemberment victim). Tamora is now civilisation's "insider." Yet from act 2, scene 1[8] on, Shakespeare begins clearly to foreground the black man Aaron and it is he, rather than Tamora, who becomes the orchestrator of the web of vengeance in which the Andronici are entangled. His "personal" motives – as distinct from his furthering of Tamora's cause (of vengeance against Titus for killing her son) – are never definitely established. The text hints only, broadly but vaguely, that there is in him a burning resentment against his "slavish" (1.1.517) position, alleviated though it is by his "fetter[ing of his lover, Queen Tamora] in amorous chains" (1.1.514). It seems to be news to an amorously-inclined Tamora when Aaron tells her, "Vengeance is in

[7] 1.1.134-135: "Was never Scythia half so barbarous!"/ "Oppose not Scythia to ambitious Rome." The Scythians lived north and east of the Black Sea at the time of Homer and after.

[8] Or 1.1.500, according to the alternative line readings of the Arden edition.

my heart, death in my hand, / Blood and revenge are hammering in my head" (2.2.37-38). What this suggests is that the terrible penalties he exacts against the Andronici are his own obverted crusade – for he speaks neither as her instrument nor (even) ally here. When, by the end of the play, Aaron's *general* destructiveness (indiscriminately aimed at all those favoured by society) is proclaimed, we may recognise in Aaron both the double and the anti-type of Titus. In "racial" or class terms they seem glaring opposites, because Aaron is the knowing outsider at war with all society and has none of the (in this case) naïve expectations of "justice" (4.3. 51-52) for which Titus continues to yearn until his opportunity for taking culinary vengeance arises – but at that point Titus's grotesque method links him with Aaron. The notorious feast (when Titus takes his gruesome revenge by feeding Tamora her own sons' flesh, blood and brains in a pie at a banquet) merely confirms the self-consuming nature of imperial power. The detailed recipe twice outlined by Titus (5.2.182-200) returns us to the political and arbitrary distinction between a victorious culture as "civilised" and a subordinated culture as "barbaric." However intense his sufferings and sorrow up to this point, and however affecting the mute figure of Lavinia, Titus's vengeance outdoes Aaron's and nauseates as much as it provokes a sort of helpless, wild hilarity. Titus seems to see his "execution" of Lavinia as no more than a kind of moral tidying up, but here yet another of his children is sacrificed to, and by, her father (see Green).

It is a remarkable fact that the execrated Aaron who is made to end his days (half-)consumed, alive, by the earth in which he is buried "breast-deep" and left to "famish" and "cry for food" (5.3.178-179), while anyone who "pities" him will die for "the offence" (5.3.191 – another demonstration of Rome's "victorious" civilization in public destruction of a defeated enemy), is yet the only one of the play's parents who through a combination of determination and guile manages to *preserve* the life of his child (whatever its future role will be). Neatly and triumphantly, the Gothic/Roman empress (Tamora) is re-designated a "ravenous tiger" (5.3.194) at the end of the play, as the Romans recover a "purged" Rome with the aid of the Goths – *all* Roman in the gloamin' now! Yet Shakespeare carefully – much earlier – inserts the detail that the child of Aaron and Tamora might *not* have been black (4.2.154-156) and that the Moor might thus not only have infiltrated the imperial bed, but could also have left his son on the Roman throne. It is a kind of genetic "bad luck" (however predictable) that keeps Aaron's child off the imperial throne, no inherent "deficiencies."[9]

In a play as sardonic and generally brutal as this, the lines in which the villain Aaron addresses his child stand out for their remarkable tenderness, celebratory tone and intimate loyalty – such as "Sweet blowze, you are a beauteous blossom, sure" (4.2.74). In the same scene where he ringingly declares (of his child), "[t]his before all the world will I keep safe" (4.2.112), Aaron re-orders the human colour-coding of their situation in scornful reference to Tamora's lightskinned sons as hypocritical and untrustworthy: "white-limed walls" and "ale-house painted signs" (4.2.100). To note these points is not to forget that the play appears to cast Titus as hero-victim-vindicated (it is, after all, "his" tragedy by the author's naming of the work) or to ignore that Aaron is most blatantly the play's major villain, but to recognise how slyly and sardonically the Elizabethan playwright *nevertheless* undermines the very (complacent and "racial") distinctions which he seemingly endorses, complicating our reading of Aaron's nature by emphasising his paternal fortitude and protectiveness.

That *Titus Andronicus* deals with the condition of empire can be pinpointed most simply in the recurrent expression '"victorious" Rome' (1.1.73) with which Titus salutes his country after his return from war, as it confirms the Roman conquest of a neighbouring nation. Jan Nederveen Pieterse refers to racism as "the psychology of imperialism [. . .] because racism supplies the element that makes for the righteousness of empire" (235). Necessarily the subjugated nations (whether Goths or Africans) must be distinguished culturally from the victors and predictably the schema adopted declares them inferior *in civilisation*, hence barbarous.[10] Here I link back to an African setting where similar codings of nationality played themselves out. In an interview given not long before his early death Marechera used the image of Kafka's *Castle* to describe childhood in a colonised culture and added: "It was so easy to make us kids feel [. . .] that we were a product of an inferior race [. . .]" (Veit-Wild 10).

---

9 See the reference by Green to the child, the "still-railing Aaron" and the cast-out body of Tamora as "signify[ing] what his patriarchy cannot digest" (326).

10 Originally meaning simply 'non-Greek' (see the Euripides quotation at the head of this article), the term became associated with the Berbers (North Africans). George Puttenham in *The Arte of English Poesie* refers to "the rude and barking language of the Africans now called Barbarians" (258). Iago refers sneeringly to Othello as "an erring Barbarian" (*Othello* 1.3.343).

Marechera's personal history, the transition of a Shona township youth from desperate poverty to university in Rhodesia and then to Oxford University, one of the icons of the British empire and civilisation, is openly alluded to in *Black Sunlight*, especially in the hilarious and brilliant opening section of the novel (1-14, especially 4 and 9). Shakespeare's play fades out on Aaron chest deep in the earth, shouting maledictions at the society which has both expelled and engulfed him, whereas we first encounter Marechera's nameless black narrator (one of the few racially marked characters in the book), where he has been strung upside down by his African chief; "swinging" through the "chickenshit" (3) of history, head down (one of many crucifiction images in the novel). The cultural and political paradoxes of an intellectual *been-to*'s existence are urbanely, mockingly outlined in the wit and fun of this passage, which in its intellectual poise and cheeriness balances the deeply melancholic, baffled closing pages of the novel. The opening section is, "chronologically," a type of alternative ending in this intricately designed work, with what follows from the top of the fourteenth page as the beginnings of a biography. In these opening pages of Marechera's novel (1-14) it is especially the Conradian "primitive," "ugly" Africa (as depicted in *Heart of Darkness*)[11] in terms of which the reader is teased – by means of improbably exaggerated images: with "gigantic humid trees shutting out the sun," with the "chief, as black as human beginnings," whose "fantastic physiognomy [. . .] suggested sudden and barbaric impulses, crude and insatiable appetites, dark and grim events," with a reference to "Sadza [= mealie-meal porridge], that supposed cornerstone of [the narrator's] authentic [African] image"; even including the hilariously lurid detail of "some long ago beastiality [. . .] cleaning its teeth with toothbrushes made of hairy men"(!); the fleeing narrator "will[ing his] heart of darkness to stop wheezing horror-horror" until he is returned to "the so-called real world" by means of coffee, cigarettes and whiskey! He knows that, like Conrad's Kurtz, his "voice [is] the biggest thing about" him. He also knows that he is as unappreciated in Africa, even as a mere "court jester" (2; 9), as in Europe, alluding to his (and others') "thin" – i.e. sensitive, easily permeable – "black skin" (in contrast with any Conradian *heart* of darkness, and also contrasting with the glamorous "white skin" of his erstwhile lover at Oxford University, Blanche). Encountering Africans, he reminds himself: "[t]hese are my people. I am their people too" (3). Yet with "Europe in [his] head, crammed together with Africa" *and* other continents, he remains "[i]n search of [his] true people," perpetually "[i]n the wrong skin – [t]his black skin" (3-4), someone

11 See also Chinua Achebe's indignant and impassioned essay on *Heart of Darkness*.

who has "come into the wrong world" (14). His dislocated existence is not unlike Aaron's at the Roman court, but the exploration of that condition (as haunted, and haunting) is far more disturbing and sadder in Marechera's text than in Shakespeare's.

Of the three principal relationships depicted in *Black Sunlight*, the one which lingers long after its break-up and seems most deeply embedded in the narrator's mind is his connection with the Oxford-trained anthropologist whom Marechera pointedly names Blanche Goodfather – and describes as "[t]his intrepid seeker after the ideal human society" (4). It is said of her that "[s]he was a moth fiercely attracted to [. . .] the savage, the earthy, the primitive" (4) – perhaps like Tamora in *Titus Andronicus*? She is remembered in a key passage "before the electric fire wearing nothing but her scholar's gown" (5) – which presumably serves to emphasise that she embodies the "Western" education system to which Marechera was (*despite* the ironies of his position) so deeply attached. In addition to the vividness of this memory of the narrator's on a personal level, it is probably also more generally indicative of the seductiveness of "Western" learning and privilege. Although the narrator imagines re-encountering his Oxford lover (before he actually does so) in Africa with the ironic greeting "Blanche Goodfather I presume" – thinking of Stanley and Mutesa (9), later the memories of the previous collapse of their love affair (in England) hint at the narrator's humiliating sense of "racial reduction" during that break-up. He recalls (in jagged, surrealist images) being ousted from the mansions of "his" Goodfather: "drove me out [. . .] far down at the end of the street [. . .] fighting back the rising breakdown" (75). His first, burning memory which resurfaces when he is given a drugged drink at the anarchist hideaway Devil's End (the outpourings which follow making up the entire concluding half of the work) refers to "[l]anguage" itself – particularly English – as something "[k]notted tightly around [his] eyes like a bandage made of headaches. In a broken glued-together mirror [he sees himself – in "European" fashion] knotting [his] tie [while] English images come out of the barn with a thousand Zulus at [his] heels" (73-74).[12]

[12] In 1983 Marechera wrote:

> The English language was automatically connected with the plush and seeming splendour of the white side of town. [. . .] I was therefore a keen accomplice and student in my own mental colonisation. [. . .] This perhaps is the undergrowth of my experimental use of English [. . .] For a black writer the language is very racist; you have to have [. . .] hair-raising panga duels with [it] before you can make it do all that you want it to do. (Qtd. in Veit-Wild 4)

Despite his “miles of books” and the “Graeco-Roman stains” on his lips, the narrator senses that it was “the desert” (an image I read as representing his Africanness) that drove [him] out” of Blanche’s home and heart (87; 75).

There *is* a thin and deeply buried narrative thread in *Black Sunlight* and discernible hints that the novel is indeed set in Zimbabwe (with memories of England interspersed) are confirmed by the author (Veit-Wild, 220). In contrast with Aaron’s very apparent “outsider” status in *Titus Andronicus* (*by means of which* he manages the inside/demolition job on the Roman state in that play), Marechera’s protagonist is “The Black *Insider*” (Veit-Wild 217; emphasis added)[13] to exploit one of Marechera’s other titles. There are painful hints that a *black* insider in England, for all his brilliance and erudition, remains something like a tame monkey (tolerated for a while as a curiosity and pet), since the narrator’s rejection by Blanche is followed by humiliating reminders of his African (translate: inferior; “uncivilised”) identity such as: “‘You may be a writer but you are still as coal black as I am’” and: “Making the monkey monkier [. . .] to make him no more than a black insider [. . .] Leaving only the paranoid image of the desert [. . .] [T]he doors [. . .] locked in his teeth” (76, 77). He is turned into a “terrified ghostly shape, cringing into the trees” (81) – something no longer human in status, not even real.

The narrator returns to his country and marries the blind Marie whom he has known since childhood. His tenderness towards her is coloured with sadness, as though she represents his own, “wounded” country. Later he has an exhilarating affair with the urban guerrilla Susan, a woman of incandescent vitality who is in revolt against all systems (especially lyrical are pp. 36-37 and 47 – see also 45-51). But he notes a deterioration in his country since before his departure: “[. . .] I returned from Oxford to find the culture and the society of my country broken down, replaced by manufactured images, fiction and fantasy. I could hear Blanche saying: ‘The breakdown of cultures makes the provision of entertainment (even war) a necessity’” (110).

Before this, the narrator mentions that Blanche, when their affair began to go wrong in England, “had begun to talk as though she needed to observe herself clinically from afar whenever I was in her vicinity” (110) – a punning “translation” of the term “detachment” with its hints of fastidious disdain, cultural separation and frigidity. Contrastingly, the narrator throughout uses vitally natural,

---

13 This was the title of the first version of *Black Sunlight*. Marechera also wrote another novel titled *The Black Insider*.

even primitive images in his appreciative and rather beautiful descriptions of sexual encounters (4-5; 36-37; 47; 46; 51).

The "hallucinatory" section of the novel (roughly its second half) is actually its most searing. It is an intellectually or rather imaginatively rigorous indictment of the failure of "modern civilisation" (not/no longer geographically or racially specified). It is not failure to *accommodate* the human person, but failure to *free* what Marechera sees as the flaming singularity of each personality which he identifies as the huge flaw in the design of society. The violence of the anarchic guerrillas – the narrator's friends – reaches towards no end and no "building," but towards an explosion of all encapsulations, including that which is considered and termed "civilisation." The anarchists' "freedom" is *also* ironised, though:[14] "How did one escape? In a rain of bullets? Or seeing red everywhere until the straitjacket came?" (21).

There is a sardonic reference to these anarchists as "[t]errorising the neighbourhood with quotes from Fanon's psychiatric notebooks" (113). What Marechera does is to take the "decolonisation" notion implicit in the Fanonian reference further, to confront (and to confront us with) the need, if the life-spark is not to die out, for continuous liberation from all the enclosing systems[15] which people allow to entrap them. We might then say that Marechera redefines "postcolonialism" as a perpetually aspired to, existential condition.[16] That is why the question of violence (as it is raised in the conversation with Susan, and in the surreal "self-interview," and in the last part of the novel) is so urgent and its definition(s) so wide and searching (see 43-51; 64-72; 56-117).

The victim or "runner" image[17] emphasises that *all* cultures, systems or civilisations persecute and hunt down the signs of human aspirations to freedom. Marechera's images for civilisation or society hence resemble Shakespeare's "wilderness of tigers" (4.1.54): "this created tiger [. . .] these grand designs";

---

14 Compare Marechera's statement that "[i]ntellectual anarchism is full of contradictions in the sense that it can never achieve its goals. If it achieves any goal at all, then it is no longer anarchism" (Veit-Wild 31).

15 Referred to by Marie as "dead things" (22).

16 Compare Marechera's self-description: "I think I am the doppelgänger whom, until I appeared, African literature had not yet met. And in this sense I would question anyone calling me an African writer [. . .] the direct international experience of every single living entity is, for me, the inspiration to write" (Veit-Wild 221). See also David Buuck's essay on Marechera's "life-work" (120).

17 "There is always somebody on the run. From [. . .] judges [. . .] Special Branch [. . .] from the ugly face of tradition" (8-9).

"society [. . .] the lioness"; "What has not been done in the name of some straitjacket?" the narrator asks (50; 69; 88). The "straitjacket" reference ironises the claim to sanity from those who impose social control, implying a "sanitising," "civilising" intention to be achieved by means of the imprisonment of freedom-seeking aspirations. This again may remind one of the "earthing" of Aaron at the end of the play in which Shakespeare confronts triumphant Rome with the gleeful Moor who is actually a product of its own success: chickens come home to roost; colonies are not the defeated inferiors of empires, but their own hatchings (products). Neither Shakespeare's nor Marechera's text shows civilisation "arising" from barbarism, but instead both depict forms of "civilisation" barbarising people through oppression. In Marechera's novel a condition where "[o]ne *thinks* before living" is in itself reviled as decadent (65; emphasis added). In the last part of the play, oscillating references (on the one hand) to Aaron and to Tamora's sons as "barbarous, beastly villains" (5.1.97), to Aaron as "barbarous Moor," "ravenous tiger," "inhuman dog, unhallowed slave" (5.3.4; 5; 14) and as an "irreligious" and "misbelieving Moor" (5.3.120 and 142) contrast (on the other hand) with the words of Titus's son Lucius, victorious (with the aid of the Goths!) and now "Rome's gracious governor," who thanks the "gentle" Romans" before giving his first official command: "Set [Aaron] breast-deep in earth and famish him" (5.3.145; 146; 178). The pattern of irony (from the play's "victorious" opening) repeats itself.

In contrast with the impression of consistent, sardonic detachment in the portrayals which Shakespeare's *Titus Andronicus* (an "early" play) contains, Marechera's novel (his most mature work) is dense, complex and considerably more nuanced than the play, with passages of great tenderness and moving sadness – like that in which the narrator is described "[d]iscovering how infinitely a human condition despair" is (107). There is, for instance, recognition of the "almost domestic" quality of the association and cohabitation of the group of people alternatively described as anarchists or as "the restless walking wounded" (107). What are referred to as "the interior happenings of the house" are yet "indissolubly connected to what was happening out there," not only politically (in their society) but literally "universally" – in "galaxies beyond galaxies" (108). Human relatedness (especially relationships between the narrator and Blanche, Marie and Susan) is very movingly and vividly described by a novelist of great power and skill, as are the restless, questing, and anguished thoughts of the narrator. Mockingly, but poignantly, the narrator's alter ego "proves" his existence by quoting Shylock, "If you prick me, I hurt" (68), but he also acknowledges the (barbarised) insensitivity of the cultural *arriviste* in himself: "Steve Biko died while I was blind drunk in London. Soweto burned while I was deep in thought about an editor's rejection slip" (114). Throughout Marechera's novel, human vulnerability is contrasted with ruthless social efficiency. It is a book of very large reach: clearly a document in civilisation as much as a documentation of violence, to adapt Walter Benjamin's famous words. [18] In *Black Sunlight* Marechera brings all people startlingly and slyly together in two simultaneously sardonic and tragic sentences: "But then everybody must have roots. [. . .] Disease, war, persecution, rapine, these are *our* ancestors, you know" (71; emphasis added). Barbarians are never merely (or "safely"!) "out there."

Works Cited

Achebe, Chinua. "An Image of Africa: Racism in Conrad's *Heart of Darkness*." *Hopes and Impediments: Selected Essays*. New York: Doubleday, 1989. 1-18.

Benjamin, Walter. *Illuminations*. Trans. Harry Zohn. London: Fontana, 1973.

Buuck, David. "African Doppelgänger: Hybridity and Identity in the work of Dambudzo Marechera." *Research in African Literatures* 28.2 (1997): 18-31.

Chabal, Patrick. "The African Crisis: Context and Interpretation." *Postcolonial Identities in Africa*. Ed. Richard Werbner and Terence Ranger. London: Zed, 1996. 29-54.

Conn Liebler, Naomi. "Getting It All Right: Titus Andronicus and Roman History." *Shakespeare Quarterley* 45.3 (1994): 263-278.

Conrad, Joseph. *Youth, Heart of Darkness and the End of the Tether*. London: Dent, 1902, rpt. 1961.

Euripides. *Iphigeneia at Aulis*. Trans. W. S. Merwin and G. E. Dimock. New York: Oxford UP, 1978.

Green, Douglas E. "Interpreting 'her martyr'd signs': Gender and Tragedy in *Titus Andronicus*." *Shakespeare Quarterly* 40.3 (1989): 322-323.

Hall, Kim F. *Things of Darkness: Economies of Race and Gender in Early Modern England*. Ithaca, New York: Cornell UP, 1995.

Johnson, David. *Shakespeare and South Africa*. Oxford: Clarendon, 1996.

Jones, Eldred. *Othello's Countrymen: The African in English Renaissance Drama*. London: Oxford UP, 1989.

---

[18] "There is no document of civilization which is not at the same time a document of barbarism" (Benjamin 248).

Mannoni, O. *Prospero and Caliban: The Psychology of Colonization*. New York: Praeger, 1964.

Marechera, Dambudzo. *The Black Insider*. Harare: Baobab, 1990.

___. *Black Sunlight*, London: Heinemann, 1980.

Mercator, Hondius Janssonius. *Atlas or a Geographicke Description of the World*. 1636. Facsimile edition in two volumes. Introd. R. A. Skelton. Amsterdam: 1968.

Nederveen Pieterse, Jan P. *Empire and Emancipation: Power and Liberation on a World Scale*. London: Pluto, 1989.

Orkin, Martin. *Shakespeare Against Apartheid*. Johannesburg: Ad. Donker, 1987.

Puttenham, George. *The Arte of English Poesie*. Ed. Edward Arber. London: Alex Murray and Son, 1869.

Ray, Sid. "'Rape, I fear, was root of thy annoy': The Politics of Consent in *Titus Andronicus*." *Shakespeare Quarterly* 49.1 (1998): 31-34.

Shakespeare, William. *Titus Andronicus*. Ed. Jonathan Bate. The Arden Shakespeare. London: Routledge, 1995.

Veit-Wild, Flora, ed. *Dambudzo Marechera: A Source Book on his Life and Work*. Harare: University of Zimbabwe Publications, 1993.

Young, Robert. *Colonial Desire: Hybridity in Theory, Culture and Race*. London/New York: Routledge, 1995.

Farah's *Sweet and Sour Milk*: The Noise in the Dictator's Ear

> There is nothing more difficult to take in hand, more perilous to conduct, or more uncertain in its success than to take the lead in the introduction of a new order of things.
>
> – Machiavelli, *The Prince*

However much the situation in and around Somalia has changed – politically, socially, militarily – since the time Farah presented us with his vision of a nineteen-seventies Somalia in *Sweet and Sour Milk* (1979), that vision, of ways to defend or achieve integrity under oppression, and of the importance of doing so, has not lost its relevance. Nor will it, as long as there are oppressive situations (and societies) to contend with. The force of Farah's writing has intertwined roots in two sources. The first is a passionate detestation of tyranny and a conviction that Africans should not allow themselves to be the instruments of their local tyrants and exploiters – it is a belief inherent to his writing; that resistance (as a refusal of victimhood or cooptation) is possible as well as morally necessary. The second equally strong root is his artist's impulse to craft telling and indelible portraits of Africans in complex settings that exhibit how the realities of a globally influenced Africa produce (in any one location) fascinatingly differentiated individual and social responses, ranging from the corrupt to the heroic. Farah's concentration does not fall principally on corrupt use of power, although its profile is highly visible in his texts as the backdrop against or the context within which his main actors function. Instead, he focuses more distinctly on those who contend with power – often and necessarily in secret and sometimes quite privately, in domestic environments – in contrast with those who comply with it.

As the title of this chapter indicates, the focus falls particularly on issues of voice and articulation in this study of *Sweet and Sour Milk*. Two short quotations that succinctly and lucidly suit the perspective adopted here occur in David V. J. Bell's 1975 text *Power, Influence, and Authority: An Essay in Political Linguistics*. The first citation quite simply states: "politics is talk" (10) and the second emphasises that both political power and actions are "built of and around words" (12). Both these remarks can be taken as largely valid as long as one emphasises that speech and writing that influence and reflect political realities are never either disembodied or decontextualised, and that politics lives in everyday speech and private reflection as it does in *speeches* emanating from public platforms (or: disseminated in public documents), in proclamations and laws and in debates and discussions. Derek Wright, a leading Farah critic, states that "[i]n this work, Farah pursues the implications for texts – for his own text – in a mode of reality built on oral discourse and asks what happens to language when nothing is happening – in the sense of being written – in it" ("Zero" 33). The statement alludes both to the fact that the Somali population is at the time that is portrayed in *Sweet and Sour Milk* a largely illiterate people and to the political fact Farah portrays – that the Barre regime of the time relies extensively on an *oral* network of spies in contrast with the central concern for documentation of the state's abuses and terrorist tactics and publishing of these facts by the members of the resistance group.

Late in the novel, Loyaan learns from his murdered twin brother Soyaan's friend and trusted ally Ibrahim (Il Siciliano) that the two of them had worked on a Memorandum titled "Dionysius's Ear" (135) in reference to the Syracusan tyrant's practice of constructing a prison in the shape of an enormous ear, the function of which was to magnify the secret whisperings of his prisoners to one another, to his hearing. They used this allusion to point the parallel with the employment by "the General" (the Siad Barre figure – the Somali head of state who grabbed power in a coup, whose name is never mentioned in the novel) of an enormous network of poor, illiterate "street people": "men and women from an oral tradition" who "daily, report what they hear as they hear it, word by word" (136). Ibrahim names this an "ear-service of tyranny" and contrasts it with the fact that while people can be incarcerated on the evidence of these oral reports, "there are no written warrants" and "two thirds of the prisoners have no files" – hence the life-saving importance of their group's efforts to compile (as in the Appendix to the Memorandum) "a list of detainees who have been forgotten," many of them "illegally detained because of [. . .] mistaken identity" (136). If there is no record of arrest and no trial, a person could be "erased" or obliterated as easily as their written name can be, is the chilling realisation that comes to mind. It is the way power operates at this time in Somalia, in acts of "erasure" of individuals or of the truth of their affiliations, that creates the pervasive, menacing atmosphere of eeriness and uncertainty with which Loyaan has to contend, psychologically as much as politically.[1]

Not only in the streets but in people's own homes are there "listeners" ready to betray others to persecution for "disloyalty," since "[n]othing escapes the

1 Fiona Moolla has characterised *Sweet and Sour Milk* as "structur[ing] a modernist take on the detective novel" (118).

close scrutiny of the security system whose planted *ears* have sprouted in every home" (139; emphasis original). The sinister prevalent atmosphere has made people "inarticulate with fear"; if saying anything slightly "risky" carries so harsh a cost, people "prefer not to speak" (139). It is the un*spoken* dread in which Somalis at this time are forced to live that make Soyaan and Ibrahim decide to form the "Group of Ten" (beginning with eight other friends whom they trust as sharing their principles) who see it as their task to "collect information for a common pool." Their aim is to counter the fear holding people's minds captive and stilling their tongues with "the *written* word, more powerful than the gun" as they believe that this publicising of the regime's brutalities "will frighten" the unjust rulers in their turn (139; emphasis added). Written words and meticulously researched and provable, recorded findings of oppressions and atrocities can "speak up" and "speak out" when the cowed populace cannot. Such writing can also, of course, escape the containment of Somalia itself to make audible the cries of a suffering people.[2]

The citation featured as epigraph to this essay (qtd. in *Sweet* 21) is taken from *The Prince* (1532), the Renaissance political treatise by Niccoló Machiavelli – translated from the Italian original. In Farah's novel the cited lines constitute the first of two underlined sentences from this text, the last book Soyaan had been reading just before his untimely and shocking death. The point made in Machiavelli's remark should, this essay argues, be taken as having overarching significance: its function is to emphasise the magnitude of the risky task taken on by Soyaan and his few allies and the courage and despair resisting determination which is their ethos. Underlined by Soyaan's suspicious death just after the reading of the Machiavelli passage, the citation is one of the guiding messages Soyaan leaves his brother as a political legacy. The grim political and social realism of the pronouncement indicates how absent romantic "struggle idealisation" is from Farah's vision in this, possibly the novel in his growing oeuvre that is most strongly grounded in lived experience within Somalia itself.[3] It is in terms of this point that I strongly dissent from Derek Wright's suggestion that in this novel, Farah responds to the "mode of reality that built on oral discourse" in

---

2 The text also contrasts the erection of monuments of various kinds proclaiming the General's might and the triumph of his Soviet-backed "revolutionary" regime (cf. 73, 11, 130, 132) with the Memorandums and other written records of the regime's doings by Soyaan and his associates, which tell a different story.

3 *Sweet and Sour Milk* was (according to Farah's own testimony, a novel first conceived in Somalia, even though eventually written mainly in Europe (see e.g. Alden and Tremaine 33-35).

Somalia by "retreat[ing] deeper and virtually disappear[ing] into [the text's] 'writtenness'" ("Zero" 33).

Wright also gets it wrong, I believe, when he characterises *Sweet and Sour Milk* as "an obscure and evasive text" ("Zero" 33), for what Farah does is to *articulate*, as vividly and compellingly as he can, the politics of obfuscation on which the Barre power structure (in his reading of it) depends. The murder of Loyaan is a *secret* crime and it is with impressive lucidity (to point the paradox) that Farah depicts the baffling and terrifying context in which Loyaan has to try and decipher this mysterious and terrible event. In the course of his last conversation with Loyaan, Soyaan (his voice interrupted by the hiccups that are the symptoms of his failing breath) mentions the primary political need (in Somalia at this time) for the "demystifica-*hic*-tion of in-*hic*-formation" and of "politics" (20). Later in the novel, on his way to his brief imprisonment by the regime (symbolically and for practical "security" reasons blindfolded), Loyaan thinks to himself about how "[t]he politics of mystification rendered rumours credible" and "kept everyone at bay," since "[p]eople were kept in their separate compartments of ignorance about what happened to other people." Cunningly, "[n]o information was released until a rumour had [first] been published." If his informants report to the General that a particular act of his was met with criticism, "one heard an unconfirmed report" about consequent arrests, but "[t]he papers didn't carry the news, the radio neither" (196). It is because of the covering obscurity in which the regime hides its misdeeds that getting facts about it recorded and published, i.e. written down, is so important. One example that can be referred to occurs in the dispute between Keynaan (the twins' father) and Loyaan about Soyaan's political loyalties, when Loyaan is able to tell Keynaan: "I have documents. I have his writings" and surmises that this is the reason the regime "wanted him [Soyaan] removed, taken out of circulation like a banned book" (94).

The character on whom the focus of the novel (and of this essay) falls is Loyaan, the twin who survives his murdered brother. Loyaan's development into a politically committed and *audible* participant – one who carefully negotiates his way through the moral and political murk characterising (in Farah's portrayal) Somali society under Siyad Barre's dictatorship during the period of Soviet affiliation (roughly, 1970-1975) remains relevant to later times and comparable settings. During 1973 Farah had been on a tour that took him to "the Soviet Union, Hungary, Greece (of the Colonels) and Sadat's Egypt", returning with the idea that "dictatorial regimes, wherever they were, invested power more in their own variety of truths, each of which had a fictive truth to support its validity" – a legitimating claim Farah also dubs "the 'groomed' truth" ("Why" 1596-1597).[4] Many commentaries have addressed this first text in Farah's first trilogy and its "companion" novels – *Sweet and Sour Milk* (1979), *Sardines* (1982) and *Close, Sesame* (1983) titled *Variations on an African Dictatorship* by the author – but much remains to be said about this dense and portentous work.

Farah's re-imagining and re-presentation of the psychological, social, political and historical conditions of the time are accessible to careful reading of the complex balancing of textual details, the hard-hitting insights and profound art of his evocation. The meticulous skill and flair of the writing indicate how seriously he took his responsibility in portraying so dire a situation – a role for which he had initially felt himself under-equipped,[5] despite intense pressure from both pro- and anti-Barre factions among his Somali acquaintances. These competing demands for his affiliation evidently added to the tension in the air; Farah reports that "[a]s the cliché has it, you were for or against the regime of Mohamed Siyad Barre, the self-declared Messiah of the Somali nation" ("Why" 1595). *Sweet and Sour Milk* is deeply imbued with Farah's personal experiences while still living in Somalia. The origin of its vision and passion is traceable to the awakening of his political consciousness after his return to his motherland at a "tumultuous" time after his tertiary studies in India. He wrote of this period (in phrases closely recalling the evocations in the novel) that he remembers it as "noisy' with "badly-sung choruses praising the Generalissimo" – the use of the Italian term for Barre highlighting Farah's contempt for the neocolonial regime of the man in charge of Somalia (since the coup d'état of October 1969). The anxiety which permeated people's daily lives, caused by the terror tactics of the new regime, is vividly evoked by Farah:

> Mornings were vibrant with surprises and shocking news: you heard that so-and-so was arrested on suspicion of anti-revolutionary sentiments; nights were frightening since the sinister National Security Service made dawn arrests without warrants. People sought one another's company and comfort, and in order not to be arrested they formed large gatherings during the brightest hours of the day, singing

4 Compare Loyaan being told that it was after Soyaan's first visit to the Soviet Union that he came back inspired to conduct "research into something of national use" (*Sweet* 122) – the core idea of the "group."

5 See "I feel inadequate and haven't the experience nor the talent" and "I felt more inadequate than ever" ("Why" 1596-1597), as Farah reported in his own words.

> sycophantic songs of the Generalissimo, certain of only one thing: that the NSS would not sweep them away into detention centres but would wait until one was alone, or in bed at home, wait, at any rate, until nightfall. [Those in opposition told] horror stories, after-midnight tales of detention, torture and terror. ("Why" 1595)

In an unforgettable image, Farah recalls observing how "fear began spreading on [people's] faces, as though it were melting butter."[6] Even so, he felt impelled to put his writing to use in an appropriate response to the moral and political exigencies of the time: in his own words: "I gave serious consideration how best to rise to the summons" ("Why" 1596).

Farah was himself not exempt from the terrifying pressures evoked above; he mentions that "the then Minister of Higher Education and Culture"[7] (later to be detained!) and the then "President of the National University" were extremely "frightening in their insistence that it was for my own good that I write something favourable about the revolution" ("Why" 1595). His play *A Dagger in Vacuum* was forbidden performance by the censors on the grounds of its being "scandalously un-revolutionary," whereas the visiting Marxist scholar Walter Rodney "attacked *From a Crooked Rib* [1970, Farah's first published novel] savagely for being a [. . .] bourgeois kind of novel" (qtd. in Alden and Tremaine 33), as a result of which Farah was called in by the authorities for questioning. During the pre-publication process, Farah wrote to his British publishers concerning both *A Naked Needle* and *Sweet and Sour Milk*, indicating his anxiety that the texts, if deemed "undesirable," might endanger his family (qtd. in Alden and Tremaine 34, 199). The worry about the possible fallout from the powers in charge was confirmed when his brother Muxammad (highly placed in the Somali government at this time) intercepted Farah's return from Europe with a phone call that warned him for his own safety never to set foot in Somalia again, but to "[f]orget" it (qtd. in Alden and Tremaine 34-35). Muxammad himself would later lose his post "as a result of the publication of *Close, Sesame*" (Alden and Tremaine 34). But Farah wrote, as he would later say, because he had become

---

6 In an interview, Farah gave a precise date for "*the turning-point in* [*his*] *perception of the regime*," saying that "[i]t began, perhaps, in late 1971, when for the first time in the Somali people's history, people were executed for their political ideals" ("Combining" 183; italicised words as in the original).

7 One can link this reference to authorial experience of state intimidation to Loyaan's confrontation with the Minister to the Presidency and Soyaan's earlier angry meeting with the head of state (*Sweet* 173-184, 226).

convinced of the need to present his own writing and his version of Somalia to the world as "an alternative to the propaganda Siyad Barre's oligarchy released to the world's press as the unchallengeable truth" ("Why" 1597).

In his later life, Farah would contrast his own role as a writer critical about the Somali regime from the safety of exile with those who (like Muxammad) had remained in the country, asking himself: "would I be just as brave if I were in Mogadiscio at this very moment?" and replying: "I am not so certain" (Farah, "Fear" 9). This painfully honest remark needs balancing with the recognition of how influential his texts have nevertheless been in contributing to the exposure of the crimes of the regime against its citizens – nevertheless it is a post hoc indication of the implicit respect with which the author regards the oppositional activists he portrays in the novel, whom he later referred to as "those who do not compromise" (Farah, "Arts and Africa"; qtd. in Wright, "Parents" 96). The analysis presented in this essay contests the validity of a fairly prevalent reading that is coloured by what may be described as a type of political and at times even moral condescension (among the text's critics) towards the clandestine indigenous resistance "Group of Ten" and their activities as portrayed by Farah.[8] At times, comments by even such sophisticated critics as Felix Mnthali come across as if they are rebuking "real people" for not being sufficiently "politically realistic" – as in his repeated reference to the lack (in the activities of the resistance group) of a "recruitment drive" ("Autocracy" 183, 194), while the Farah critic Derek Wright states (in my estimation, inaccurately) that the dissident group "looks to Western liberal humanism for its inspiration" and "has little of its own to put in the place of the coherent tribal heritage which the Soviet-backed ideologues are careful to keep intact and appropriate for their own uses" ("Parents" 96).[9] I argue contra Mnthali that Farah makes quite clear that there is

8 Cf. John C. Hawley, who refers to the members of the younger generation Farah portrays in the trilogy as "sadly lacking in a moral center or clear sense of what might be called ultimate reality and meaning" (77), while Wright states that "Somalia's political uncentredness is matched by the decentred lives of its intellecuals" ("Zero" 36) and he refers to a "motif of uncentredness [as] part of a broader national and continental malaise" ("Mapping" 108). John Masterson (2013) describes their "energies" as "ultimately misplaced" and refers strangely to the "*arguably* ethical imperatives bubbling beneath the surface of *Sweet and Sour Milk*" (29, 36; emphasis added).

9 Cf. Barbara Turfan's (again, in the view of this essay writer, inaccurate) reference to "the wholesale adoption of foreign ideologies" *by the dissidents* (276) – forgetting, it seems, that it is Barre's adoption of Russian ideology and Soviet-style KGB terrorist tactics against which they protest and struggle at terrible risk to

no practical possibility of embarking on more widespread "recruitment" given the two factors of a fanatically repressive (and efficient) regime and a cowed, socially conservative population; his comment therefore is itself highly "unrealistic" in terms of the conditions portrayed (recalling the Machiavelli citation) and insufficiently perceptive of the group members' own awareness of the absence in Somalia of "a tradition of protest movements, trade unions or organised groups of any kind" in contrast with (e.g.) "Egypt, Ethiopia, or Sudan" – countries in which there is a "tradition" of "student movements which can help form or unform governments or shape public opinion" (*Sweet* 139). The moral fury with which Soyaan responds to the execution of ten sheiks (and one woman) by the regime and Loyaan to the murder of his brother and the subsequent distortion of all that he had stood for by the regime and with the cooperation of Keynaan, their father, are the kinds of experiences portrayed as inspiring the two brothers' resistance to the brutal rule of the General (*Sweet* 226, 182), rather than any adherence to "Western liberal humanism" as Wright contends. Wright's approving reference to a "coherent tribal heritage" in the above citation is also greatly at odds with Farah's well known and consistent critique – as powerfully conveyed in *Sweet and Sour Milk* as in most of his other writings – of what he would never term "coherent" or describe as a "heritage," but evokes as the awful, rigidly repressive patriarchy of both state and society in Somalia at this time.[10]

If one studies Farah's portrayal of Loyaan's growth in moral stature as he sets out on and proceeds (against pressure) with his dangerous quest to establish the facts and to understand the circumstances that led to his brother Soyaan's death, it becomes clear that to some extent we are dealing here with heroism in resistance (Soyaan's) and its succession within oppression (Loyaan accepting the political "inheritance" of his brother). Soyaan and his closest allies had knowingly taken an enormous (and in his case, fatal) risk in not only organising, but also expressing and recording, in a few key documents, their opposition to the regime. The impulse to record such dangerous ideas is shown to spring from the

themselves, whereas Turfan describes them as ignorant and uncaring about their compatriots (278).

10 Many (perhaps most) studies of *Sweet and Sour Milk* concentrate on the intersecting patriarchal tyrannies in the homes and the state of Somalia that Farah brilliantly analyses (cf. the Wilhelm Reich citation, 97). Dubravka Juraga's fine essay opens by stating that "[o]ne of the main projects of Nuruddin Farah's fiction is to expose the complicity between the traditional patriarchal family and oppressive political conditions in his native Somalia" (205).

combined intentions of firstly saying the unsaid, the (at a time of tyranny) almost unsayable even if most obvious truth: that the regime is corrupt and tyrannical; secondly, bringing in the virtually unanswerable "second voice" which challenges the monologue which a dictator's voice and pronouncements always are. Thirdly, and as indicated by the term 'Memorandum' which is applied to the subversive document that Soyaan and Ibrahim "Il Siciliano" compose, they choose to commemorate and to remind Somalis of a suppressed truth and of the need to resist oppression; fourthly it is, of course, with the intention of "spreading the word," of disseminating[11] political and social ideas, that these thoughts are recorded. Finally, if we link all this to the idea of passing on a difficult inheritance to his surviving brother Loyaan, Soyaan's writings – some coherent; some confiscated and/or inaccessible; others mysteriously coded or mere scraps – represent Soyaan's "last will and testament": an inheritance to be arduously accessed and "earned" by Loyaan. It had been Soyaan's will and hope to "[inform] the masses of what really was happening" (19) in simple and accessible terms and to demystify the "wicked alphabet of mysteries" in order to explain to people what significance "pregnant letters" like KGB or CIA actually carry; to expose the supposedly "socialist" regime as "fascist" (20). In the context of Machiavelli's warning words and of revelations of the cowed or co-opted state of Somali society and the brutality of the state, this hope must seem an idealist's dream, but his words prove that Soyaan understood that they were only at the very beginning of what would be a very long haul. It also indicates that his hopes include the ideal of working with the broad mass of people and excludes any mere ambitious lust for power.

From his own position of exile from Somalia at that time (not, of course, over yet), Farah is in this novel, especially in his depiction of the characters of the twins Soyaan and Loyaan, imagining the far more risky role of the "*insider*-resister" compared to the relative safety and lesser sacrifice of an escapee; a survivor (like himself). Two lines from a poem by Arthur Nortje, an exiled South African, may serve to establish the distinction between the activist (on the one hand) and the artist (on the other hand) which can be noted here: "for some of us must storm the castles, / some define in happening" (361). In being the record of a sustained and complex effort of imagination and conscience, Farah's text (his

---

11 See the first six-line paragraph on p. 20, in which Soyaan (inter alia) says, even though his voice is already interrupted by hiccups to indicate both his dire physical condition and his indomitable nature: "Tell the *hic* masses in the simplest *hic* of terms what is happening. Demystify *hic* politics" (20).

novel) parallels some of Soyaan's texts' hoped for effects, outlined above – but the novelist is on record as being very aware that, to say from *outside* Somalia that Barre is a corrupt tyrant is easier and safer than to do so inside the country. Even though Farah's statement that his own writing is meant to be an alternative to Barre's "badly written play" (which is Somalia) is well known,[12] opposition and resistance from outside and performed in writing (in English) plays out differently and to a different audience than do political action and writing *within* Somalia. What Farah commemorates and what he implicitly exhorts his readers to uphold, in this novel, is at once more efficiently disseminated outside and less accessible to those inside Somalia, given the author's distance from the country.[13] Most importantly, therefore, *Sweet and Sour Milk* – however much of an artifice; a fiction it is – wants to extend the reach of the "inheritance of heroism" to wherever its seed may fall, in *and* beyond the Somalia of this time. Hence, however intensely Somali-centred Farah's thinking shows itself to be, the novel has, in the end, a much wider reach and relevance; not instead of, but in addition to its commentary on the author's motherland – to which his ideas have of course nevertheless also filtered through, and where they have an especial pertinence.

The propagation of a misleading, fascist notion of heroism is the very idea that Barre's advisors and propagandists are shown to use with Machiavellian cunning as they usurp the memory of Soyaan's life for their own purposes, garlanding the man they had murdered with the title "Hero of the Revolution." In a linguistic pattern characteristic of oppressive systems, single words contain, conceal *and* betray elaborate but powerful hoaxes. For Soyaan's was indeed an heroic life – yet coupling the title of "hero" with a reference to the bogus "Revolution" of the Soviet-dominated period in Somalia undermines everything he considered worth standing for. This cunning stroke on the part of the regime – coopting its most brilliant critic and most effective opponent, Soyaan, is (as Farah shows) reliant on the corruptibility of the most authoritative member of

12 It occurs in his 1998 essay "Why I Write," where Farah stated: "Somalia was a badly written play, I had thought, and Siyad Barre was its author" (10). Compare Loyaan's comment on the fake "Mulki"; presented to him in prison: "All this is like a badly written farce" (*Sweet* 199).

13 When the Somali language gained an orthography, Farah wrote a novel that was (initially) serialised in a Somali newspaper, but publication was stopped when the text "ran afoul of the censors" (Alden and Tremaine 33).

Soyaan's family; within the Somali patriarchy[14] this is his father Keynaan, who is quite shamefully ready to lie about Soyaan's dying moments and to betray the truth of this murdered son's heroically resistant life to re-ingratiate himself with the regime, in order to be accorded unearned and bogus public stature and to reap the monetary benefits that will further his plans of acquiring a third wife. This development occurs because Keynaan (the father) is not only prepared, but all too happy to bear false witness by claiming – as reported in the only newspaper – that Soyaan of all people died with a sycophantic political cliché on his lips: "Labour is honour and there is no General but our General" (99). This supposedly parroted slogan contrasts glaringly with what the son had told the father at their last encounter before the poison administered to Soyaan's system killed him, when Keynaan had been *told* by Soyaan in his suffering, ailing state:

> I am no bearer of anybody's banner. But I feel humiliated, I feel abused, daily, minutely. A friend of mine is in [jail] for anti-Soviet activities. But where are we? What era is this? Is this Africa or is this Stalin's Russia? I am disgusted. As soon as I feel better, I promise you ... (15-16)[15]

Soyaan's voice is cut off by one of the hiccups (brought on by the poison) that will soon kill him – hence, Keynaan's misrepresentation of Soyaan's dying moments is evoked by Farah as a silencing, begun by the regime's agents and perpetuated by Keynaan, in direct contradiction of his son's will; obliterating Soyaan's denunciatory voice by means of a shameful echo of the dictator's empty rhetoric.

It is Loyaan who remembers, honours and is faithful to his brother's unfulfilled intention to "demystify" and "uncover" the evil secrets of the regime (20) – and who is faithful to Soyaan not only because of their shared political convictions, but because of his love and respect for the brother who died while saying his own [Loyaan's] name three times (21). Loyaan understands the unspoken re-

---

14 See p. 95, where Keynaan makes the following pronouncement after Loyaan criticises him for his misrepresentation of the significance and circumstances of Soyaan's death: "I am the father. It is my prerogative to give life and death as I find fit. I've chosen to breathe life into Soyaan. And remember one thing, Loyaan: if I decide this minute to cut you in two, I can. The law of the land invests in men of my age the power. I am the Grand Patriarch."

15 See the top half of p. 198, where Loyaan daringly articulates the same sarcastic political criticism as Soyaan's (quoted above) in his "conversation" with the regime's chief torturer, even though he had not heard Soyaan's earlier words.

quest (and bequest) in that death-bed naming. "In the choir of the nation's sad song: Loyaan's loud lament" (56), reads part of a sentence in an early passage, suggesting Loyaan's inherently, audibly discordant response to the chorus of assent demanded by the regime even before the murder of his brother. In contrast with the self-contradictory and falsifying description of Soyaan in the Minister to the Presidency's pompous and self-serving claim: "I knew him to be a man of great integrity and revolutionary fervour" (177), Loyaan demonstrates his respect for Soyaan by pursuing the cause they both supported – that of articulately opposing the cruel and dishonest regime. Keynaan, their father, lies about Soyaan to please the regime, profoundly shaming and embarrassing Loyaan and alienating Soyaan's true friends and comrades. Even the twins' mother Qumman is seduced by the fabricated account of her son's death because of the reward this reaps. When she tells Loyaan: "[t]he government of this country [. . .] has offered your brother the honour due him"; he reminds her that "[t]he regime, if we come to that, bestows only *dis*honour on one, never honour" (79). Loyaan rebukes and insults his father for accepting a reward to misrepresent the circumstances and significance of his son's death, saying: "Pension, what pension? A mean sum to unlock your rheumatised tongue and make up your rusty jaws function so you can praise [the General]" (88).

Over and over, in this text (as in the above citation), Farah draws attention to the central political significance and the differently contextualised meanings of either speaking or keeping silent – of words as acts and badges of allegiance. Among the general population Loyaan early on notes the widespread, cowed failure to protest, reading it as "the triumph of fear over anger" (39); much later in the text, the point recurs when Ibrahim notes the effects of the hordes of illiterate spies or *listeners* (my own word) employed by the state security system: "So people, inarticulate with fear, prefer not to speak" (139), he tells Loyaan. And later on Loyaan notes that it has become normal not to ask questions or to hold the state officials to account when a loved one disappears: "Nobody ever *asked for the right* to see a husband, a son or a brother" (158; emphasis added). This helps us see the importance and the courage of his own refusal to accept his twin's death by keeping silent. Even when his mother and sister exhort him to lie low, to comply with the compliant who merely "Move. Sweep" and "Don't talk" under the eyes of the revolutionary guards, he cannot so humiliate himself or desecrate his brother's memory (190-192); he gets himself "noticed" and taken into custody for interrogation. In Somalia at this time, if individuals do not raise a stink, official modes of silencing will erase or rewrite the life of a true hero as that of a bogus revolutionary, for: "the paper's [don't] carry the news, the radio neither" (196).

A type of speech (or sound) is nevertheless enforced and squeezed out of the broad body of the people. In order "to eke out an indecent living" or "to stay on" in Somalia, Loyaan notes, "you break and praise [the General]" (74). And again: "immediately their number exceeded five [the limit for legal gatherings, people] found it expedient to sing the General's praises" (89). Farah hints that the General enforces a regime of blasphemy: people go to the Revolutionary Centres, "not to mosques any more" (89), while the praises "there is no general but our General" constitute profane mimicry of the Muslim creed. One brilliant description refers to people "beating the drum and *singing the sycophancies* of the revolution's successes" (187; emphasis added). Some (like Mulki) are forced (or: reportedly forced – since even this may be a deliberately planted, false rumour) to speak and reveal anti-regime plans under torture (see 158).[16] Ahmed-Wellie justifies his own apparent cooperation with the regime by telling Loyaan: "Against the ethics of political violence, the weak have no means of survival other than to collaborate, up to a point, with the powerful. It is while collaborating that strategies can be studied" (159). But it might be the self-justificatory accent in the last sentence that helps Loyaan finally to conclude that Ahmed-Wellie is an "*informant*" (224; emphasis original) to the regime; yet another one who now sings for his supper.

Loyaan, who had never had his brother's focused and efficient manner, being a more passionate and less organised personality, develops a strong sense of purpose in the wake of his brother's strange and premature death. He develops a verbal dexterity under the pressure of his own suspicion and anger, claiming with a disquieting air of knowledge that his brother died of "complications" (35; 46 and elsewhere) – the deliberate obscurity of the term's application being one way of disallowing whitewashing explanations of Soyaan's death as natural or as an event in which the state was not secretly involved. Initially only *inside* his head, he develops a personal "voice," a voice he describes as "giving [him] guidance" (81), and as speaking both "through him" and "to him" (89). It is this voice which, when his feelings are in danger of overwhelming him, "remind[s]" him of his "moral, intellectual and ethical duties" (150).

16 Ahmed-Wellie tells Loyaan that Mulki (who had been Soyaan's secretary and is Ibrahim il Siciliano's sister) "broke under torture," that she "mentioned names" and might have revealed the whereabouts or divulged the contents of one of the secret and "dangerous" Memorandums she typed for Soyaan (158).

That this "inner" will become an "outer" voice is first announced when Loyaan steels himself for his showdown with the sinister Minister to the Presidency in the words: "Tomorrow [. . .] my dialogue with naked power begins tomorrow" (161). It is his greatest achievement and the sign of his growing moral stature (nearly matching his brother's, even though belatedly) that Loyaan has forced the regime's monological power into such a "dialogue" when, in the long, fierce verbal battle with the Minister, in his state office, this lone young man manages to interrogate and intimidate so very powerful a minister and to force crucial revelations out of him.[17] What he does here is to wrest Soyaan's memory (even if only temporarily and not in public, but within the inner sanctum of power) from the regime's grip (170-184). In doing this he is (perhaps unconsciously but unerringly following his dead brother's example) doing what his brother did before him – for Soyaan had, on the day the General had ordered the death by firing squad of the "ten sheiks and [a] woman [who had resisted his reign]" (45), dared to have "the worst of confrontations with the General" himself (226). Soyaan thus had first bravely mocked ("mimicked"), irritated and defiantly stood up to power as Loyaan does with the Minister. Both brothers are prepared to take the consequences of such politically risky behaviour.[18] Neither brother is prepared to be cajoled or bribed into silence.

In the lengthy scene (173-184) of Loyaan's confrontation with the Minister, many references to various kinds of speech and silence occur as markers of the to-and-fro power shifts between the verbal combatants. Not only are the words spoken or withheld markers of greater or lesser power, but they note the difference between Loyaan's moral force and the Minister's political might. As Loyaan enters the Minister's luxuriously furnished office, the latter greets him with the de rigueur exclamation "*Jaalle*!" (172; emphasis original), the Somali translation of the Marxist term "comrade" – a bogus claim to equality of stature that also implies that they are allies in the fake Somali Revolution that has "mar-

---

17 Whereas Wright refers dismissively to this scene as constituting Loyaan's "futile interrogative assault on the minister" and claims that "his lone quest for the truth peters out inconclusively" ("Parents" 95), a more recent critic, R. John Williams, devotes considerable space to a meticulous analysis of this crucial event (169-170).

18 Margaritta testifies that Soyaan had said "he wanted to be found home if *they* came for him" (227; original italicised), knowing that retribution against anyone openly challenging the regime was inevitable. Following his brief detention and interrogation, having been informed of his "posting" to Belgrade (which may be deportation or end in another murder), Loyaan too determines to "prepare for their coming" and states that he "would be ready for it" (208).

ried" Marxist ideology with local traditional patriarchy and pays lip service to Islamic morality. Having got nowhere with his fishing questions (at Soyaan's funeral) to Loyaan about his brother's Memorandum,[19] the Minister had asked Loyaan to "come and see [him]," claiming (with clear ulterior motives): "[*w*]*e* have a number of things to *talk* about" (49), as if they are old comrades in need of "catching up." The "conversation" starts awkwardly, mainly because Loyaan refuses to say anything spontaneous, deliberately creating tension. To steel himself, in his mind, Loyaan instructs himself to "[*w*]*hisper the unspoken secrets of the nation's heart which beats with fright*" (173; emphasis original), indicating that he is here in the role of the spokesman for the oppressed; the one who might make the dictatorial state hear that which it has outlawed or that to which it refuses to hearken. But he is also, as he has guessed, in the presence of the very man responsible for orchestrating Soyaan's murder, and so his role here has both national and personal dimensions. The confidence that strengthens him arises also from Loyaan's conviction that "[t]he tongue of guilt, like a bell's, would eventually sound a confession" (174).

Suavely, the Minister (who clearly carries the counter-conviction that Loyaan will be the one from whom a "confession" can be extricated either by charm or by intimidation) invites him to "speak [his] thoughts," but exactly as at the funeral, Loyaan deliberately and provocatively pretends not to understand, resolving that he will *not* "say anything" and that this will force the Minister to "speak" (175). It is a remarkably vividly imagined scene of *eloquent* but predominantly unspoken enmity, where lines are drawn between the regime's bully (with the full weight of state power behind him) and the supposed underling; Loyaan with consummate skill playing the role of a subaltern who cannot speak (much) managing to *articulate* through his very silences that he will not speak and will not be cowed into doing so, or will alternatively speak and say what the Minister and the regime do not wish to hear. Additionally, Loyaan's conduct "loudly" proclaims his contempt for his brother's murderer, for the chief strategist of a corrupt and evil regime and for that illegitimate regime itself. He is fully aware that his integrity is at stake and that his "word" is his "power" and that his endorsement of the state's conduct is what is being sought from him. Needled by his tight-lipped stance, the Minister nudges Loyaan: "You haven't answered me", and when he remains uncooperative, the Minister resorts to claim-

---

19 "[D]own at the Presidency we wondered if Soyaan showed you or talked to you about a Memorandum he had been working on" (48). (Soyaan had for years been the Economic Adviser to the Presidency.)

ing that it had been Loyaan who had "asked" to "talk to" him rather than vice versa (which the reader knows to be the case) (175).

As soon as Loyaan (deliberately) broaches a politically awkward topic and refers to a person associated with the "Group of Ten," the Minister summons a secretary to "register what [they] say"; it seems (as Loyaan mockingly observes) that the Minister failed to prepare adequately for their meeting by installing a recording device. And since Loyaan demands that the woman be sent away again to prevent this supposedly "private conversation" (as Loyaan absurdly describes it) turning into an official interrogation, the Minister, however furious at Loyaan's intransigence, is forced to dismiss her as required (176). Loyaan holds the cards (of desperately needed information) for the time being. Having calmed his own "agitated tongue" for a moment, Loyaan proceeds to invert the meeting into an interrogation of and not by the Minister – reminding the man of his "telling" him at the burial site that Soyaan's last words were his (Loyaan's) name, three times repeated. The Minister admits this, whereupon Loyaan in words imbued with indignation and outrage relates how, since those dying words were accurately relayed, the Minister and the regime had made Keynaan (their father) "speak a falsehood," even "swear" to its truth and then disseminated this falsehood by publishing the fake dying words proclaiming Soyaan's supposed adherence to the regime in banner-high words in the only national daily. Blandly, the Minister attempts to validate the falsehood, but "Loyaan's waiting silence worsened things all the more" (177). Loyaan draws inspiration from his memory of the probing, truth-demanding gaze of Beydan, Keynaan's second wife, imitating her "super-powered stare" to "[m]ake him speak" and "listen" (178). This flash of recall of the upheld dignity of one of those bearing the brunt of familial and state patriarchal oppression is highly significant and aligns Loyaan again with the most downtrodden of the regime's victims.

Evidently flustered, the Minister dismisses Soyaan's known politically oppositional stance as a "rumour" circulated by "jealous" friends; interrupted by Loyaan's mockery of his unconvincing babble or "talk," the Minister defends the profile drawn as derived from "the horse's mouth," the dead man's (and Loyaan's) father. With harsh insistence, Loyaan derides this "made-up story" and daringly confronts the Minister with the recorded fact that "Soyaan's writings prove that he considered the general a usurper, a tribalist, a fascist of the first grade" (178). When the Minister asks about these documents, Loyaan mocks the fact that he has made him expose his real purpose and in fury and frustration at having been outmanoeuvred, the Minister throws his "pen across the room in rage" (179) – a brilliant use of detail to convey the impotence of fascist power in the face of a principled refusal to cooperate or be cowed. The Ministerial pen is *not* mightier than the "sword" of Loyaan's righteous words and silences; it is unable to write, while the regime fears and seeks to obliterate the Memorandum written by Soyaan's pen, backed by his brother's testimony.

After further verbal sparring, Loyaan homes in on the Minister's probable role in orchestrating Soyaan's murder, demanding to know who the Russian doctor was who (in all likelihood, on the Minister's orders) injected Soyaan with the poison that killed him. It is a clear give-away of his guilt when the Minister's "voice trembled as he spoke in haste to cover the tremor," pretending ignorance. He even turns his back on Loyaan as he states: "I don't know what you are talking about" when so evidently, he does (182). Having created a hero in Soyaan, revelation that he died by poisoning would be a serious blow to the legend the regime seeks to establish. The Minister "suggest[s]" that Loyaan leave, but does so "tremblingly" (184). Loyaan has through his dexterous use of both words and silence achieved a moral victory. Politically, it is a Pyrrhic victory, however, since he has now fully exposed himself as a dangerous enemy to the regime. Farah shows that it could not have been achieved otherwise, and that Loyaan took on the role he did for his murdered brother's sake and in obedience to the promptings of his conscience. Retribution will follow, but he has saved his soul and clearly articulated his "*J'accuse!*" to the murderer.

Apart from this key passage with its recurrent references to speech and silence, symbolically resonant descriptions of the acts and ideas of speaking, writing, singing or chanting as well as writing, or of the inability to perform these actions, feature intermittently throughout the novel. Many, many Somalis are at this time in the position of the wife of one of those arrested in the dawn raids, in response to whose anxious enquiries "no one will tell her anything" (38). Similarly, "[w]hen a person met violent death at the hands of the Security Service [. . .] his family could not ask even to be shown the body" (44). The majority, fearing a like fate, are forced to "clown" by "clap[ping]" and "sing[ing the General's absurdly] astral titles" (39).[20] The Minister's (initially) seemingly odd concern (at Soyaan's funeral) with the nature of Soyaan's "last words" (47) is politically predatory, since the fabrication (a proclamation by Soyaan of loyalty to the So-

---

[20] Cf. "chant the chorus" (57) and Soyaan's sarcastic reference (in a letter to Loyaan) to the fact that any Somali citizen "is expected to buy uncritically [. . .] the General's wise sayings. To stay on, you break and praise. You do this in order to eke out an indecent living for the weaker members of the family [. . .]. If you don't do this, you end up in prison" (74).

mali "revolution" and its leader) they want to put out in the only daily as the words on Soyaan's lips as he died is a propaganda coup. The most revealingly brutal expression of the regime's anxiety about words and reports is in the law or proclamation found recorded on a scrap of paper found in one of Soyaan's pockets:

> *Any person who spreads or takes out of the Somali Democratic Republic printed, reading, spoken, or broadcast matter, or persons in the SDR who display, distribute or disseminate information aimed at damaging the sovereignty of the revolution of the Somali nation will be liable to death.* (52; emphasis original)

Clearly this is aimed at anyone who dares to expose the bogus claims implicit in the words "Democratic," "revolution" or "nation" in the officialese of the regime. And it is in direct defiance of it, and in terms of a righteous, spoken "rage" that Soyaan resolved to "[employ] all the talents at his disposal to describe the chaos" *in writing*, and to do so as accurately and incontrovertibly as possible. The alternative is the conduct of those who also hate the repression but only "talked and talked" since "[t]hat was all they could do" (53). Clearly, Farah's text/s, as much as Soyaan's documents and documentation, are in no way (to repeat Wright's expression) a "retreat [. .] into [. . .] 'writtenness'" ("Zero" 33), but an *advance* into record keeping, incontrovertible evidence and damning illumination of Somalia's murky corners.

All along the streets in Somalia, "monumental placards bearing the General's portrait" are to be seen, "boasting in statistical quotations the progress and success of the revolution." When, on a few occasions, small signs of resistance appear, as when a "costly portrait" of the General has its "eyes [. . .] pierced" and "anti-Soviet slogans [. . .] scribbled on it," retribution is swift and brutal: "This village was purged" the next day; three hundred boys and girls [. . .] taken for interrogation" and "about fifteen" of them "held in custody;" remaining incarcerated: "Untried. Tortured nightly" (111). Unlike the flowing words of the propaganda machine, the General "stammers when talking of social justice" (130); the tremor in his voice (as in the Minister's) giving away the falsity of his claims. For his part, Loyaan is intermittently prompted and inspired by "the voice from within, Soyaan speaking through and to" him (132). It is to shut him up that Loyaan is given the bogus appointment to the diplomatic post in Belgrade that had been intended (without his having been informed of it) for Soyaan. Loyaan asks sarcastically about the "posting" when told of it by the officer: "Bribed with a post, silenced, got rid of?," for he realises that this will in fact be a "deport[ation]" (199).

When arrested, Loyaan is physically silenced: "his mouth filled with a cottony gag" (195). Yet he refuses to be intimidated into keeping mute, even by the regime's top torturer – when this man threatens Loyaan, saying "Don't provoke me," Loyaan replies, calmly and provocatively: "I have, officer" (201). And he insists again that Soyaan did not pass away while singing the General's praises, but died "shouting [his own, Loyaan's] name" (201). Similarly Loyaan refuses to utter the retraction of his accusation that the regime had had Soyaan murdered which the interrogator, the third-highest member of the security, demands of him. Farah indicates a parallel between Loyaan and the goat sacrificed after being tortured at his brother's final funeral service, but the goat is no silent, compliant victim – it bleats, it broadcasts its protests against captivity, torture and death, and manages to sound a warning – as Loyaan, too, does (205; 207-209).

Two other uncowed voices, both those of women, are featured in the novel. Especially important is the voice of the put-upon, maritally abused and neglected as well as unjustly suspected Beydan; the woman married (in a grotesquely insensitive gesture of "compensation" by the regime) to Keynaan, the twins' father: a disgraced policeman who had tortured her first husband to death. "Beydan *had something to say*," Loyaan notes (151; emphasis added). She refers to the Minister to the Presidency with clear contempt as "the one who's made all these declarations," obviously aware of the fabricated, manipulative contents of these official statements, and she is not in the least grateful for this man's attempts to clear her of the blame of having supposedly poisoned Soyaan, whom she had dearly loved (151) and who had stood by her in opposition to both his father Keynaan's abuses of his unjust patriarchal powers and privileges and his own mother Qumman's jealousy of Beydan. She resents the Minister's pompous and discourteously unannounced claim on her hospitality and food, and dares to make this quite clear, telling this powerful politician about women's position under the regime: "When we are widowed, we cry softly lest you or the General hear, lest the Security men return to take away those you haven't already imprisoned. Go and discuss your politics away from here" (152). For openly saying this to the Minister in the presence of her husband Keynaan, Beydan is furiously beaten by her husband despite her advanced pregnancy; Keynaan is incensed at her for embarrassing him by uttering such clearly defiant words. The beating is one of the many instances whereby Farah demonstrates that state and the paterfamilias cooperate to effect the silencing of women and of children – for Beydan had noted and tells Loyaan about the meaningful look the Minister had given Keynaan before he left; clearly an unspoken order to beat the outspoken wife severely for voicing her disrespect of the government official.

The setting of this scene may be domestic, but Farah evidently meant his readers to recognise the serious political significance – indeed the heroism – of Beydan's statement. As has been noted, the memory of Beydan's "super-powered," truth demanding "stare" later becomes an inspiration to Loyaan in his important confrontation with the same Minister when he resolves to "[m]ake him speak. And listen" (178). Ladan (Loyaan's sister) treats the Minister (as in all likelihood the person who engineered Soyaan's murder) with similar disdain, *also* defying the sycophantic patriarch Keynaan's ire (203). On a later occasion Ladan for a second time stares her contempt at the Minister, for Farah knows and shows that looks can speak volumes. It is Ladan who cautions her brother Loyaan to "rebel" "without parting with [his] composure" (193) and it is she who will fiercely and safely guard the dangerous inheritance of the murdered Soyaan's writings from the regime's prying eyes and listening ears when Loyaan is deported.

No such small group can "win" against entrenched tyranny. Yet their voices carry, and the noise they make to disturb the lulling chorus of the sycophants sound an alternative to the helpless wails of the regime's victims which will serve to remind power disquietingly of its own impermanence; exposing the hollow ring of its authoritarian voice. This message is passed on – as happens historically and as is achieved to the benefit of and in warning to other climes and times in a novel of such power and beauty, despite the eeriness and horror it depicts so uncompromisingly. As Farah stated in his famous "Why I Write" essay, "truth is the breath in the air, the breath that someone somewhere in the world will inhale, and then speak, in the end, I say" (12-13). Within the Somalia portrayed in this text, the "message" of resistance remains in the safe keeping of Ladan, the twins' loving and brave sister. Early on, when thinking about the dangerous things spoken by the fatally ill Soyaan and while sitting "silently" by her sleeping brother, "she [had] told herself" that, "[c]ome what might [. . .] she would contain the secret" of "what [he] had spoken in his sleep" (16). Mulki, Ibrahim's sister, is known by her brother to be equally brave and protective. Even if tortured, he says, "she won't speak" – but he knows that her silence and strength in endurance are unlikely to "stop them from coming" for him, too (142), as they do. At the end of the narrative, the newborn son of Beydan (who has died in childbirth) and Keynaan is addressed by the name of "Soyaan" by his half-sister Ladan, who is rocking and comforting him. "Soyaan. Keep quiet, Soyaan" (237), she tells the baby (in the last lines of the text). But it is a naming that "speaks volumes" – the "knock on the outside door" (237 – the final words of the text) announces that the regime's lackeys have arrived to deport Loyaan; the new generation (Marco, Soyaan's son, and little Soyaan) will have to assume the burden of resistance to prevent the continuing "crush[ing of] the anima of man."[21]

In *Sardines*, the last novel of Farah's first trilogy, there is a passage cited from a letter that reads:

> So Soyaan is dead? And nobody knows what has become of Loyaan? Someone saw him briefly in Rome in the back seat of an embassy car. He looked ill, this person said, and his cheeks were puffed up. The others [other members of the "Group of Ten"] are in prison; so is Siciliano; Koschin [who is being kept in an asylum] is broken and foams at the mouth, you say, unable to hold his saliva. (22-23)

The terrible news conveyed in this document conveys the triumph of the ruthless regime over the ideals of the resistant group and its dreadful human cost. It is not the only index by which to measure what the passage tells us, nevertheless. Abdourahman Waberi sums up the core idea of Farah's later novel *Maps*[22] (1986) in the short statement "Truth is body" ("Organic" 775) and in this later novel we find the phrase "[t]he body speaks" (*Maps* 55). Whether we think of a dead body (such as Soyaan's) or of the hurt bodies of the group members, muted, malfunctioning and distorted by torture (as evoked above), bodies utter wide ranging truths. These truths record not only the cruelty of corrupt regimes, but also the nobility of those who risk all to keep alive their insistence on the value and dignity of remaining by choice outside of and apart from power's seduction, seeking fulfilment elsewhere by refusing to stop speaking out and writing about its sins.

Early in the novel Margaritta (Soyaan's lover and the mother of his son Marco), in a scene on a beach near Mogadiscio, "wrote [Soyaan's] name on the sand. The sea washed away her writing" (12). In order to ensure that the courageous histories of resistance to tyranny are not erased, texts like *Sweet and Sour Milk* need to be written, read and returned to. They do the important work of

---

21 As Medina reportedly has termed it (73).

22 This novel is dedicated by Farah "To Muxammad my eldest brother and trusted counsellor" (n.pag.).

complicating and complementing simplistic accounts of African dictatorships and power abuse, for (as Farah has stated): "[a] writer lives in a capsule of visions, ideals – and in the mansions and hallways of his conscience." And necessarily and as a duty, the writer, particularly the African author, "acts like one in whom is invested a people's history" ("Creative" 29).

Works Cited

Alden, Patricia, and Louis Tremaine. *Nuruddin Farah*. New York: Twayne, 1999.

Bell, David V. J. *Power, Influence, and Authority: An Essay in Political Linguistics*. New York: Oxford UP, 1975.

Farah, Nuruddin. *Close, Sesame*. London: Allison & Busby, 1983; St Paul, MN: Graywolf, 1992.

___. "A Combining of Gifts." Interview with Maya Jaggi. *Third World Quarterly* 11.3 (1989): 171-187.

___. "The Creative Writer and the Politician." *The Classic* 3.1 (1984): 27-30.

___. *A Dagger in Vacuum*. Unpublished play.

___. "Fear is a Goat." *Guardian* [Lagos] 1 June 1990: 9.

___. *From a Crooked Rib*. London: Heinemann, 1970.

___. *Maps*. London: Picador, 1986; New York: Pantheon, 1986.

___. *A Naked Needle*. London: Heinemann, 1976.

___. *Sardines*. London: Allison & Busby, 1981; London: Heinemann, 1982; St Paul, MN: Graywolf, 1992.

___. *Sweet and Sour Milk*. 1979. London, Ibadan, Nairobi: Heinemann, 1980.

___. "Why I Write." *Third World Quarterly* 11.4 (1988): 171-187.

Hawley, John C. "Nuruddin Farah: Tribalism, Orality and Postcolonial Ultimate Reality and Meaning in Contemporary Somalia." *Emerging Perspectives on Nuruddin Farah*. Ed. Derek Wright. Trenton, NJ and Asmara, Eritrea: Africa World Press, Inc., 2002. 67-94.

Juraga, Dubravka. "Nuruddin Farah's *Variations on the Theme of an African Dictatorship*: Patriarchy, Gender, and Political Oppression in Somalia." *Critique* 38.3 (1997): 205-220.

Machiavelli, Niccoló. *The Prince*. London: Penguin Books, 2003.

Masterson, John. *The Disorder of Things: A Foucauldian Approach to the Work of Nuruddin Farah*. Johannesburg: Wits UP, 2013.

Mnthali, Felix. "Autocracy and the Limits of Identity: A Reading of the Novels of Nuruddin Farah." *Emerging Perspectives on Nuruddin Farah*. Ed.

Derek Wright. Trenton, NJ and Asmara, Eritrea: Africa World Press, Inc.: 2002. 175-196.

Moolla, F. Fiona. *Reading Nuruddin Farah: The Individual, the Novel and the Idea of Home*. London: James Currey, 2014.

Nortje, Arthur. "Native's Letter." *Anatomy of Dark: Collected Poems of Arthur Nortje*. Ed. Dirk Klopper. Pretoria: University of South Africa, 2000. 360-361.

Turfan, Barbara. "Opposing Dictatorship: Nuruddin Farah's *Variations on the Theme of an African Dictatorship.*" *Emerging Perspectives on Nuruddin Farah.* Ed. Derek Wright. Trenton, NJ and Asmara, Eritrea: Africa World Press, Inc.: 2002. 265-281.

Waberi, Abdurahman. "Organic Metaphor in Two Novels by Nuruddin Farah." *World Literature Today* 72.4 (1998): 775-781.

Williams, R. John. "'Doing History': Nuruddin Farah's *Sweet and Sour Milk*, Subaltern Studies, and the Postcolonial Trajectory of Silence." *Research in African Literatures* 37.4 (2006): 161-176.

Wright, Derek. "Mapping Farah's Fiction: The Postmodern Landscapes." *Emerging Perspectives on Nuruddin Farah.* Ed. Derek Wright. Trenton, NJ and Asmara, Eritrea: Africa World Press, Inc.: 2002. 95-129.

___. "Parents and Power in Nuruddin Farah's *Dictatorship* Trilogy." *Kunapipi* 11.2 (1989): 94-106.

___. "Zero Zones: Nuruddin Farah's Fiction." *ARIEL: A Review of International English Literature* 21.2 (1990): 22-42.

Performances, Ethics and Aesthetics of Wealth in African Literary Depiction

This chapter is devoted to an atypical topic in African literary scholarship; a topic that is nevertheless of great significance in postcolonial African societies, and one to which the three texts selected for discussion – Waguih Ghali's *Beer in the Snooker Club* (1964), Meja Mwangi's *Striving for the Wind* (1990) and Chimamanda Ngozi Adichie's *Purple Hibiscus* (2004) – contribute important insights and evaluative perspectives. While each of the texts manifests serious engagement with the economic dimensions of local societies in ways that are challenging, instructive and complex, these texts could not be said to be primarily intended as economic or class analyses, for in their evocations of the characters, relationships and contexts they portray, the writers allow readers to recognize the interrelated effects of a range of factors, forces and conditions as the social field within which wealth and the wealthy play noticeable parts. The three texts convey no overt ideological perspectives, say, of a Marxist, liberal or capitalist kind. Nor does any of the three present us with reductive interpretations ascribing social inequality, maldistribution of wealth or injustice primarily to the colonial past, even as each of them acknowledges and traces the neo-colonial aspects to the conduct of the "representatives" of wealth (in their texts) and in the role of wealth in the portrayed societies. Reference to "representatives" of wealth indicates the characters in each text who are disproportionally endowed with wealth and the privileges and opportunities it affords them – along with certain handicaps – in comparison with and in relation to other characters, but also within the broad social sphere. The major interest of each author could be said to be in the quality of life that is available to characters in the contexts they display and in the factors contributing to that quality. This intangible, statistically unmeasurable quality is (in all three novels) nevertheless the unstated "measure" used by the authors; a standard of evaluation that overrides the amount of wealth a character commands (or not) or the social status they occupy. The three texts could be seen as implicitly distinguishing between wealth and worth, or between the quantifiability of wealth and the "obviousness" or display of its power and glamour versus quality of life as an immanence, a dimension of being as distinct from power and ostentation as worth is from wealth.

What the novelists do particularly interestingly, using literary art's resources of *telling* detail and of affect and resonance, is to "personalise" wealth in the figures they choose to portray and to show how wealth and the wealthy are socially embedded – especially in vividly detailed portrayals of familial settings. In all three cases evocations of familial settings explore how wealth and the power with which it endows the "representative" character (in none of the three texts the main character) impinges upon characters who are their family members. In all three novels, the main character falls in the latter category, so that in each case we get observations directly or indirectly from someone who is "close to" wealth and its "representative," rather than personally rich. The three very different historical, geographical and demographic settings are necessarily also, both in detailed portrayal and casual allusions to broader contexts, shown to influence the kinds of manifestations of wealth the authors explore, and by means of these differences the three novels both extend and diversify the exploration attempted in this essay.

In the main body of this essay, the performance, ethics and aesthetics of wealth as explored in each of the chosen novels are discussed in turn and in the (chronological) order of the three texts' publication dates. This order coincides with the sequence of the historical periods that are portrayed in the three novels. Coincidences of representational perspective and evaluation among the chosen texts have been broadly outlined above. Nevertheless, in order to avoid creating the impression that they are "studies" of the same social issue or problem, rather than works brought together and juxtaposed in the interests of the essay writer's exploration that here juxtaposes texts that could not be described as related in any readily evident way, the fuller and more detailed analysis of the performance, ethics and aesthetics of wealth in each text is presented more-or-less separately. Occasional enlightening or interesting parallels are pointed out, but each text is foregrounded in turn. This structural choice for the essay follows from the desire to avoid flattening three such vividly distinct and distinguished works into mere variations on a theme. Recognizing the three novels' individual strengths and a refusal to subjugate creative writing, which has its own intrinsic modes of conveying social analyses and psychological insights, determined the chosen format for this chapter. The usefulness of such an approach must be validated in the succeeding sections of this essay, but underlying it is the assumption that it is preferable as far as possible to allow the chosen texts to "speak" or "to be heard" in terms of what insights they yield concerning the chosen topic in not giving primacy to the specifically comparable aspects of these three works. In the final part of the essay, the different strands of analysis will be briefly brought together to see what conclusions can be drawn.

Waguih Ghali's *Beer in the Snooker Club* (1964)

> [. . .] an acre of land in our country is a lot of money. (11)

Ghali's novel is set primarily in Egypt and it is a text as passionately concerned with the fate of this nation as the narrator Ramos (usually referred to as Ram) is – despite the flippancy of his manner. Parts of the narrative are also set in London; the British "Left" of the time (including the communist party) being an important political reference point for Ram and his best friend Font, who are taken to the UK by their older friend Edna, an Egyptian Jewess from a still hugely wealthy family – despite their possessions and businesses having been nationalised or otherwise appropriated by the Nasser government. The time frame is roughly the fifties, starting from the 1952 Egyptian revolution which toppled King Farouk and soon brought Gamal Abdel Nasser to power. The narrator refers to the continuing British military presence, the fallout from the Suez crisis that was precipitated by Nasser's annexation of the Canal and the 1956 British invasion which followed. However, as Nadia Gindy observes, although Ghali's novel is "concerned with change and revolution [it] suggests that nothing really changes" (425). This remark links with the dismay expressed by Ram when, upon his return to Egypt from London (deported for assaulting a policeman during a demonstration against the British Suez invasion), he discovers the extent to which the revolution that both he and Font had so enthusiastically supported before they left, has since been travestied and betrayed. This is how Ram puts it in explaining his disillusionment to Didi, the young woman whom he agrees to marry, towards the end of the novel:

> Anyway, when I came back I saw that life here is exactly as it used to be. [. . .] I mean how can I go and work in a boiling village when *he* [alluding to Nasser, the post-revolutionary head of state] is travelling about in Farouk's yacht which costs a million just for upkeep? And all this nationalization business just makes me laugh, although I don't tell Font that. The money goes to that useless army. Even the Asswan dam; by the time it's completed we'll have increased by ten million. (202; emphasis original)

What galls Ram has everything to do with the issue of wealth and resource redistribution which the revolution was intended to achieve, or at least to foster. Instead, he sees that the "revolutionary" ruler has appropriated the hugely expensive luxury item (and its display) from the feudal monarchy; that the proceeds from the nationalisation of property are not used to alleviate the indigent and improve conditions for the struggling peasants, but are fed into maintaining a pathetically ineffectual army, the officers of which have merely joined the parasitical class of the wealthy who frequent the exclusive pleasures of the Gezira Sporting Club ("where middle-aged people play croquet" like their former British overlords [126]) and other haunts of the rich. As a taxi driver tells Ram: "Before the revolution you could only pick up a fare in the posh districts, now the army people also ride in taxis" from "all over Cairo" (143). Indeed, the formerly disdained occupation of being in the army is (in Ram's rich extended family) now fully acceptable, while the maintenance of the army can itself be seen as a type of display or token performance of national wealth, testifying to the ruler's vanity instead of serving the valid purpose of effectively defending the nation and the resources with which the country is endowed.[1]

Ram's moral, political and social position is complicated, complex and fraught with contradictions. As Susie Thomas puts it, he is "an anti-colonialist who [is] also an Anglophile"; a man sympathetic to communist practices who has consciously "aristocratic tastes" and "a member of the elite" who is simultaneously "an outsider" ("Waguih Ghali"). It is his outsider's station as a penniless, educated and sophisticated member of a rich Cairene Coptic family that places Ram in the position to satirise, tease and mock his rich family members, whom he thoroughly despises for their hypocrisy, moral stupidity and political ignorance, as well as their heartless exploitation of the *fellaheen* – the poor peasants whose labour is one of the main sources of the family's income. Ram is especially scathing towards the unofficial head of their family, the wealthy aunt on whose financial charity he and his mother depend. Ram's mother is a widow whose husband (before his early demise) lost most of their money in unfortunate investments. Although she has refused to fund Ram's tertiary education and has also forced Ram's mother to give up her car, the rich aunt pays for their flat in a respectable neighbourhood. They took in Font, Ram's orphaned friend, as a child and the boys (later young men) share resources and ideals. The novel opens in the opulent home of Ram's richest aunt (one of several, all very wealthy), where he has gone ostensibly to ask for money to allow him to continue his interrupted education in the UK. The political background (we soon learn) is Nasser's land reform policies which are supposed to effect a redistribution of land by restricting ownership to a maximum of two hundred acres. Ram is well

---

1 Ram tells Didi Nackla that "a third of our [i.e. Egypt's national] income [is] being pumped into an army to fight a miserable two million Jews who were massacred something terrible in the last war" (202).

aware that his request for funding will be refused, and in fact uses the opportunity to expose his aunt's hypocrisy and to needle her. The aunt (in addition to several blocks of flats in Cairo) owns ten thousand acres of land, which she is now by law obliged to reduce to the requisite two hundred, and is shown sitting at her desk with her secretary in attendance, signing away (ostensibly as "free gifts") the excess acres. What Ram reveals is that she is secretly (though cheaply) selling the land and pretending to the government to be a major philanthropist. To underscore the quality of life of his family members Ghali introduces as a visitor – a cousin of Ram's. This woman has bought herself a new Cadillac for six thousand pounds (12, 194), absurdly claiming to have been obliged to do so to save on petrol costs; together the two (nastily excluding Ram, who mocks them with pretended commiseration) present themselves as troubled by the rise in the bread price – something that makes no iota of difference to the still undiminished luxury of their lifestyle, but which will cause near starvation among the genuinely poor masses (13). When Ram tells the visitor (tongue-in-cheek) that he has a new plan for exploiting their *fellaheen*, she recoils, telling him that he "mustn't joke about such things" (13). In his compromised though disdainful attitude towards people like this visitor (also a family member), sarcastic mockery is shown to be one of the few forms of protest available to Ram.

Iman Mersal, a contemporary Egyptian novelist based in Canada, in an essay recalls a remark of George Orwell's that described "every joke [as] a tiny revolution" (source not referenced, 670). In her descriptions of a more recent attempted Egyptian revolution, like Ram, she draws a line of permitted humour that excludes "the images of young men and women who died for such dreams" (673).[2] Like Mersal, Deborah Starr endorses Ghali's suggestion that "jokes" are an inherent part of Egyptian culture, indeed have a political function,[3] since they "[unmask] the underhanded dealings of the wealthy classes who cry poverty" and also "expose power relations" (277). Describing himself in the wry phrase "insincere, but honest" (189), Ram contrasts his ironic take on his own position as a *de facto* parasite on his rich relatives who yet maintains the political stand of an enemy to their overarching exploitative and socially parasitical position in

2 Compare Caroline Rooney's "Egyptian Literary Culture and Egyptian Modernity: Introduction." Like Mersal, Rooney cites Ghali's text in the context of comments on "Tahrir Square 2011" ("Introduction" 375).

3 See the collection *Cheeky Fictions: Laughter and the Postcolonial* (2005), edited by Reichl and Stein, for various essays on this topic (including my own, on other texts than the three discussed here).

Egyptian society with its millions of needy people whose indigence they despise. While in London and after Font and Edna (their Jewish communist benefactor and mentor, the woman whom Ram deeply loves) had left to try and contribute to the resistance against the 1956 British occupation of Suez, Ram had briefly joined the communist party in an attempt to find a political home. But he could not remain a party member, for Ram is a person fundamentally different in temperament to Edna who, despite being the only daughter and heir of enormously wealthy parents (dispossessed in Egypt and since living in South Africa), attempts to live like "the people" in a tiny flat, travelling third-class. Font, too, attempts to become a market trader, but he is "rescued" by Ram. Edna in particular as well as Font, are politically sincere and solemn, hence their attempts to confirm their egalitarian convictions in their lifestyle. To Ram, however, it seems like posturing to do this. To him, "[r]iding the tram is Egyptian" (190). Ram comes to realise that, although a privileged member of society (even if lacking any personal wealth), he is better able to connect socially with ordinary Egyptians of all classes and ethnicities than his two dear friends, whom he profoundly respects though bemused by their attempts to "perform" poverty. The openness, candour, warmth and deep humanity of Ram's personality are especially poignantly illustrated in the way he allows a little street urchin to wash a car he borrowed from one of his rich friends; in the way he *notices* the little boy ("He was thrilled – his bare feet contracted with shyness" [32]) and in the way he praises the work done by the boy as "beautiful" (40).

Ram (as narrator) informs the reader that "in spite of all the books we [i.e. Font and he] had read demonstrating the slyness and cruelty of England's foreign policy, it took the Suez war to make us believe it" (58).[4] Though taunted as "Nasser's disciple" (and a "revolutionary") by his rich aunt (47), Ram nevertheless deeply resents the Nasser government. His opposition is not only based on his perception of their mismanagement of the economy, their corruption and inefficiency, but on their cruel persecution (in "concentration camps" where "hundreds of decent young people are dying and being imprisoned" [205]) of specific minorities, particularly Jewish Egyptians, communists and opposition activists. Ram is well aware that the brunt of this onslaught by the state is borne by poorer Egyptians.[5] He has his first major fight with the charming and educated Didi-

[4] Compare Ram's devastating analysis of the greed, hypocrisy and ruthlessness of the British colonial mentality (76).

[5] Compare the following, from the Algerian novelist Merzak Allouache's *Bab el-Oued* (1995): "And naturally, Bab el-Oued [a poor inner-city area] paid the highest

Nackla, a young newspaper reporter – a former lover of his whom Ram is set to marry after breaking up with Edna – on this topic. Didi is the daughter of one of Cairo's wealthiest men, but unaffected and intelligent; a supporter of Nasser's reign despite the likely reduction in her family's wealth resulting from his policies. What Ram points out to her, shouting in fury, is that the Nasser government commits atrocities against its opponents, concerning which Ram has been gathering photographic evidence riskily sent to the newspapers, who fail to print anything. In a mood of anguished anger, Ram reminds Didi of the report that "twelve men committed suicide this week in concentration camps" (205). The prison doctor refused to sign their death certificates, clearly because these were political murders. Ram singles out one particularly poignant case among the twelve victims:

> One of them I had known at the university. A quiet, peaceful boy from Upper Egypt, son of a fellah. He used to live on seven pounds a month he earned working as a cinema usher in the evenings. A scholarly Marxist who had refused to fight against Israel unless Nasser met Ben Gurion for an attempt at a peaceful solution. He went away quietly, his neighbours had told me, and was never heard of again until I saw that picture. (206)[6]

The vicious persecution and state crimes of the Egyptian government are shown to be linked to its especial detestation of opponents who advocate a real redistribution of wealth. But in describing the murdered man (above), Ram pays especial tribute to his integrity, courage and commitment; a quality of life unattainable by those who cruelly wield their wealth and power, or who remain smugly ensconced in lives of luxury and cannot be roused to any exertion to alleviate the suffering of the downtrodden. Achebe compares such a state of being to a build-up of "a layer of adipose tissue over our sensitivity" ("Truth" 149).

Ram's period of risky though secret political activism (gathering the photographs) comes as a surprise to Edna and worries Didi, while Ram never (in order to protect his dangerously naïve and idealistic friend) informs Font of these ven-

---

toll in terms of the children and young people mown down by bullets or savagely tortured during the repression" (*Bab* 75).

6 Earlier, Ram had noted (concerning his exceedingly silly and brash – but very rich – cousin Mounir, that "[h]e was all set to be given high office" whereas "all the other students dying at Suez were from poor families and Mounir and Co. were going to lord it over the survivors" (49).

tures. Generally, though, Ram is not primarily a political person, nor is his focus economistic. As he explains to Edna during their final meeting:

> happiness, to me, is the freedom of two people who love each other to share their lives in circumstances permitting this love to live. When I hear of downtrodden people, of concentration camps, of wars of hunger, of imprisonment, I always think of two people separated in these circumstances. I know that people can't continue to love if they have to share a room with their children, or are diseased or are dirty or are hungry. (183)[7]

Ram's social vision is deeply humane and he earns the reader's respect for his wryly self-critical attitude and his refusal to kowtow to the wealthy relatives on whom he is financially dependent. The complex conscientiousness of this unusual young man shows up in profound contrast to his rich aunt's ugly and fundamentally falsifying, self-justifying resentment even against Nasser's half-baked attempt to achieve greater social equality in Egypt. Ghali depicts a conversation in which the family's *fellaheen* are referred to as an undifferentiated and contemptible mass – "they" – while Ram's aunt and her brother (who lives in the rural area administering the family properties) address the topic of how to get more money from these poor peasants (168-169). In response to his aunt's last, petulantly squealing remark ("That's what we've come to. We starve while the fellaheen owe us money" [169]), Ram quietly punctures the lie she is telling by asking: "Who's starving?" (169) – a question so devastatingly effective in showing her up that she immediately bullies Ram's mother to remove him from her sight lest she have a nervous breakdown!

This aunt's complacency and insensitivity (coupled with the stupidity that results from a refusal to *question* social injustice and maldistribution) have been transmitted to the next generation in the form of her son Mounir. Mounir has spent a few years "studying" in the USA and comes back strengthened in all his brutally simple capitalist beliefs. Ram's aunt (Mounir's mother) attempts to engineer a marriage between her son and the equally wealthy Didi Nackla. It is at least partly to save Didi from this fate (to which her father has agreed) that Ram offers to marry Didi – of whom he is fond and who is in love with him.

Edna (who is some years older than they) had first become aware of Ram and Font when they were eleven-year-old boys. She describes the two of them (at cousin Mounir's birthday party) stuffing their pockets with "enormous amounts

---

[7] Compare a later part of this conversation (185-186).

of cakes and crackers" (109) in order to give these to the gardener's boy (110). This small scene – a cameo of sharing and social redistribution, the bulging pockets of the well-off boys emptied for the benefit of the no doubt skinny gardener's son – is like a tiny, spontaneous and secret "revolution" (in the appropriate childhood currency of party goodies), even if it will have no lasting consequences. Throughout the text, Ram's actions serve this kind of purpose and are somehow heartening and endearing, as well as an exposure of the (by contrast) dully conventional lives of the rich, preoccupied as they are shown to be with trivialities – such as hugely expensive imported clothing, dropping "chic" French phrases into their inane conversations, and being served by hordes of servants. Near the end of the text, Ram consolidates the picture he has drawn of his wealthiest aunt by subtly indicating her obesity. He refers to her "filling a large sofa" (215) and as "wobbl[ing] up to [him]" (216). She attempts to bribe Ram to leave Egypt (and, by implication, give up Didi Nackla for her son Mounir to marry) by offering the money to study and live comfortably in the UK for some years – the money she had formerly refused to provide. But Ram is immune to her bribery – if partly (as he honestly acknowledges) because marriage to Didi will make him financially independent.

Beer in the Snooker Club has made something of a come-back in the contemporary Egyptian context of another struggling, attempted revolution. Ghali's social vision and perspicacity are remarkably demonstrated on this novel which – like a more recent Egyptian novel, Al Aswany's *The Yacoubian Building* (2006) – lays bare the state's wastage of its human resources; particularly in the failure to employ young, talented and skilled citizens and in the thwarting of human aspiration in the most idealistic members of society. Ram's political growth brings him to a recognition of shared humanity, shared plights and similar aspirations. "Gradually," he says, "we [he and Font] began to see ourselves as members of humanity in general and not just as Egyptians" (53). Ram raises a question that resonates into the second decade of the twenty-first century (and beyond?) as he lies with a sleeping Edna one morning, listening to "the call to the faithful." He does so, all the same, with a sense of deep connectedness to his compatriots; as someone who is *not* (as his wealthy relatives and others of their class are) "a stranger to his land" (53). Ram asks: "who is going to climb the stairs and give us a call if a revolution – a real one – takes place?" He answers himself with the "sad thought," that there will be "no one" to do so (121). It is clear that Ghali would rejoice if Ram were to be proved wrong, but such an outcome is yet to be attained.

Meja Mwangi's *Striving for the Wind* (1990)

> 'Money speaks,' said Baba Pesa. 'And it calls me Daddy!' (114)

Striving for the Wind opens by describing this text's "representative" of wealth, whose very name indicates his riches. The description in the opening scene of the setting of this novel sketches how disproportionately much he owns in comparison with his neighbours (the Barus and others):

> From Kambi village a dust road wound its way up the hill past numerously wretchedly poor *shambas* and, after crossing the old Ngobit River, cut through the scrub then whipped back before straightening out past the Baru place to peter out eventually among the barns and the broken down farm machinery in the Pesa compound. This two-track road [. . .] was known as *Njiaya Pesa*, the way of money.
>
> Baba Pesa, the father of money, was the largest, richest man on this hill and the next and the next. He owned three hundred acres of land, hills and valleys, forests and plains, trees and rocks and more cattle and goats and chickens and tractors and things than his ten-acre neighbours had even dreamt about.
>
> He lived in a six-bedroomed wooden house [. . .] surrounded by acres of orchards, barns, cattle sheds and chicken runs [. . .]. (1)

Not only in terms of ownership and home location, but also in terms of bulk and girth, does Baba Pesa tower over those among whom he lives or whom he employs, such as his meagrely fed and paid goatherd, Mutiso:

> From close up Baba Pesa was even more formidable, a five foot seven giant weighing two hundred and fifty pounds to Mutiso's hundred and thirty. In fact Baba Pesa was the biggest man on this hill and the next and the next. Apart from the village chief and Mavuno the seasonal harvest doctor, no one came anywhere near his bulk. He was known to have demolished a bar counter with one angry fist and his voice, at best that of an angry bull, was never known to laugh in genuine mirth. (2)

Discernible in the above quotation are the bullying inclinations of this unattractive man, whose money makes him the most powerful person in his rural (village and farming) context, wielding more authority than the Chief himself and brutally contemptuous of those to whom he refers as "small people of no consequence" (56).

Baba Pesa's homestead used to be the central part of the even larger estate of an old "Boer" (i.e. a white Afrikaner settler in Kenya) who fled the country when *uhuru* came. From Boeserk (the colonist) Baba Pesa has "inherited" more than a fine house, a large Mercedes, many acres of fertile farmland and many implements. Boeserk left Kenya in fear of "revenge for the many and cruel injustices he had inflicted on his African slave labour" (30) on which his wealth was built. While Baba Pesa is not shown inflicting physical hurt on his employees, he is the sort of man who enjoys, even seems to have a need to inflict humiliation on those (i.e. everyone in the village except for the tiny elite[8]) who are much poorer than he is. It is especially in his regular visits to one of the three village bars that that he exhibits this tendency by buying up the entire stock of beer – so depriving the poorer patrons, and ordering their ejection; stating as his reason for this act their indigence, measured in the fewness (a donkey or two; a few goats) of their possessions. Given that Mwangi dedicates this novel "to all those who plough [like Pesa's poor neighbour Baba Baru does] with oxen and count their wealth in goats" (n.pag.), it is clear on whose side the author is. In his bar clearing antics Baba Pesa finds his locally available method of compulsive wealth *display* – a dimension of behaviour that the "representatives" of wealth in all three novels have in common.

Mwangi, by embedding his wealthy character in a network of social and familial relations, shows up his oafishness and prevailing anti-social conduct by contrasting him with other locals. An especially vivid scene, in this regard, occurs when Baba Pesa rushes from the bar, drunk and foul-tempered and full of frustrated fury because the Chief has explained to him that, however poor, Baba Baru cannot in law be forced to sell his ten-acre plot to Baba Pesa. Pesa detests the fact that this poor neighbour's small parcel of land cuts into the three hundred acres he owns. Baba Pesa bursts rudely onto a convivial scene: Baru is entertaining visitors – a group of "old men in tyre sandals and dusty, torn greatcoats" who sit in a circle with their host, "drinking honey beer under the shade of the lone pepper tree in the yard," "each friend getting his share, a horn at a time, as was the traditional sign of togetherness in the old days" (38). Baba Baru has no reason to respect, let alone like, his bad-tempered and ill-mannered

---

8 The narrator refers contemptuously to this little group as Baba Pesa's "local mafia" (64).

neighbour. Nevertheless he offers him the traditional courtesies – a seat on a log, a drink of honey beer from "the horn of friendship" and some freshly roasted meat from a calabash dish. Each courteous offer is rebuffed in turn by the uncouth intruder: "I don't sit on tree stumps", "I don't drink cow's urine" and "'I don't eat from pumpkins,' declare[s] the lord of the land" (40-41), claiming to represent "civilized" modernity.[9] Because money – in large amounts – and what it can buy are the things that principally matter to Pesa, he finds Baba Baru's consistent refusal of his offer to buy his ten-acre plot for "thirty thousand shillings," coupled with the humiliating offer of employment and accommodation (on his land and on his terms) for Baru, his wife and his son, incomprehensible and actually perverse. Pesa has no understanding of Baru's innate dignity; he is equally unconscious of (and uncaring about) the absence (or rather, the opposite) of dignity characterising his own conduct.

In contrast with the communality, conviviality and shared courtesies of Baru's gathering, the narrative elsewhere depicts the unpleasantness, dullness and cowed atmosphere that settles over the bar after Baba Pesas's entry and bullying intervention: "With the little people gone there was no more life left in Tajiri Bar. Baba Pesa bought the beer and the local Mafia drank it, and since they dared not argue with anything he said, conversation came to a dead end. [. . .] so they gave up. Soon after, the party broke up [. . .]" (115). So arrogant and unimaginative is Pesa that even after sex with his under-age "mistress" he can only "tell her how rich he [is] and how much richer he would get" and "of one day owning all of the Laikipia Plains" (132) – a megalomaniac dream. All he can think to do on a Sunday after squirming under the implicit criticism in the Biblical message that a camel will more easily enter the kingdom of heaven than a rich man will – having dutifully accompanied Mama Pesa to church – is to rush around the countryside in order to "show off" his huge, shiny "God-given" car (139). When Baba Pesa for once holds a party, it is with the purpose of raising funds (as if he needs it) in order to send his elder son Juda to the United States for further education; but what is gathered comprises only a few meagre coins, such is the "sheer magnitude of the [vast majority of the] guests' poverty" (92).

Twice in the narrative – indicating how seriously he takes the matter as a case typical of postcolonial African societies, and to what extent the aesthetically unappealing portrayal of Baba Pesa is an outward sign of the fundamentally unethical foundations of his wealth – Mwangi provides the reader with lengthy

---

9 "Don't you know that the age of the pumpkin is past?" is how Baba Pesa puts it to Baba Baru (41).

passages of socio-economic and micro-political analysis. The racketeering, greed, connivance and betrayal of the trust and aspirational hopes of poorer compatriots revealed in this brief historical outline provide an ugly example of the selfish African opportunism on which neo-colonial systems of exploitation rely and are based. Although Baba Pesa did not act alone and could not have succeeded without the "assistance" of like-minded men, the text's focus on this single man's economic advancement gives the account especial impact. Boeserk's settler estate was sold after his departure, as the narrator informs us, to a large group of "smallholders [. . .] displaced by the [. . .] *Mau Mau* war" – the Swahili words referring to the liberation war as led by the Kenya Land and Freedom Army. But, says the narrator, after the apparently successful transference of land to the needy, "what followed was classic" (15). The inexperienced, indigent smallholders, needing money to "develop" their shambas and to educate their children, find themselves "at the mercy of their wealthier brothers." Selling "bit by bit", they end up "landless in Kambi village as struggling businessmen, labourers and village beggars", with Baba Pesa "naturally" the one who "benefited the most from the misfortunes of his neighbours" (15).[10]

Pesa's talent for exploitation – "his shrewdness [. . .] was ruthless and legendary" (15) – had manifested first during the colonial era, when he began by putting away "small savings as a [British] DC's clerk," then increased these by selling eggs in the "sprawling army barracks" of the occupying army as well as smuggling whiskey and selling it profitably in the "African locations" where it was highly desired but "strictly prohibited" (15) by the colonial regime. By these means, Pesa became the one man with the financial capacity to buy what was by far the most valuable piece of available land, on which stand Boeserk's "six-bedroom wooden house, the orchards, the barns [. . .] tractors, trucks and a multitude of farmyard tools" (15).

> By using his little money and his big brain [. . .] he had whittled away at his neighbours, buying a little at a time. He made them offers they couldn't refuse when they couldn't refuse them, forcing some into such indebtedness that they were glad to exchange their land for their freedom; he found others alternative land so they could sell to him and

---

10 In Ngugi wa Thiong'o's *A Grain of Wheat*, the author ascribes this kind of post-decolonisation cheating and greed to the political class, exemplified by the MP who cheats Gikonyo and his group, who exemplify "the peasants who fought the British yet who now see all that they fought for being put to one side" in Ngugi's brief, bitter foreword to the novel (n.pag.).

> move out, and even convinced some they were better businessmen than they were farmers, thus tricking them into urbanisation, until, finally, he had a whole hillside to himself and only Baba Barus's ten aces remained to complete the planned Pesa empire. (15-16)

The second long passage goes into greater detail as to how the poor members of the land buying co-operative were swindled out of their rightful shares:

> When the land-buying company had finally paid off the estate of Boeserk and after the officials that included Baba Pesa had tired of exploiting the members; after they had cornered all the best parts of the land, all the fertile parcels with river and road frontages, all the glades and cattle enclosures; after they had sold off all the livestock and farm machinery to themselves at throwaway prices, indeed when only the good government stood between them and complete alienation of the land from its rightful owners, the barefoot members who had worked so hard to raise the millions with which they had purchased the land and entrusted them with this money in the old misguided belief that a black man did not cheat his brother out of his heritage. When all had been sewn up, the committee of rich and fat old men called in the surveyors to parcel out the land – what was left of it – that is to say the rocky hills and barren *murram* plains where nothing would ever grow, and dish it out to the poor unsuspecting members.
>
> The surveyors, the corrupt crocodile brothers of the committee members and collaborators in the plot to exploit the rest, were the first inhabitants of Kambi Village. [. . .] Later when Baba Pesa and his like had bought off their neighbours and created destitutes in a land that had never before known of such a thing, shanties and ramshackle dwellings had mushroomed around the old camp. Then, naturally, like flies to dung, had come the merchants and the traders, followed by the missionaries and the administrators. Thus had Kambi grown to what it was today – the social, economic and political centre of this hill and the next and the next. (30-31)

This succinct and cutting analysis of postcolonial peasant impoverishment and of rural ghettoisation is imbued by the narrator with strong but implicit moral condemnation at the ruthlessness, brutality and slyness of the process that yields wealth (and power) for the few who drive it. In the detailed information and explanation that it provides, and in the affective power of the bluntness and scorn of the narrator's tone – as well as indignant pity on behalf of the impoverished Kenyans cheated by their own compatriots out of the briefly regained heritage of native soil (of which the colonists had previously deprived them) – a passage of this kind contributes meaningfully to the understanding of corrupt post-colonial wealth creation.[11] The mocking final sentence in the citation above that pretends sarcastically to celebrate the status and significance of this decrepit village, creates (along with the foregoing description) an example of the forgotten, neglected and dying rural ghettoes of the African postcolony, in which the "rich and fat old men" (30), like Baba Pesa, always still flourish.

The morally grotesque quality of Baba Pesa's nature is confirmed in his (and his younger son's) treatment of the Baru family, especially the Baru women. Pesa (afterwards likened to a "hyena" by his victim [68]) attempts in a casual attack to rape Mama Baru, who had accepted a lift from him on her weary way home from the village (67-71). Elijah Pesa similarly tries to rape the teenage Baru daughter Wangari (87-88), while Baba Pesa seduces the naïve schoolgirl (Wangari) with gifts, later rapes her and then makes her his lover, promising her a palatial home and marriage. When she later tells him that she is pregnant, he throws her out of his car (108-110). He also, after killing Baba Baru's only ox in a collision brought on by his reckless driving and his vehicle's poor brakes, makes no apology, merely threatening to sue the heartbroken Baru to the hilt for the damage to his car (149, 158). Although he is in the last part of the text shown in a somewhat softer light, Pesa's assistance to the Barus in ploughing their land with his car is given partly or largely for selfish reasons, as he admits (172) to Juda.

In balance it needs to be pointed out that Mwangi is so fine a novelist[12] that he manages, in his depiction of Baba Pesa, not to present us with a mere brittle car-

---

11 The perspective Mwangi provides in this passage resembles Fanon's in the famous fourth chapter, "The Pitfalls of National Consciousness," in *The Wretched of the Earth*, as well as recalling Achebe's well known image (in *A Man of the People*) of the post-colonial elite taking over the "house" of power and privilege from the colonists, while requiring everyone else to remain outside in the "rain" (*A Man* 37).

12 The text has not attracted as much critical attention as it merits – Johansson's and Kehinde's being the two most substantial analyses. Johansson cites from p. 49 in Currie and Ray's research article concerning what they too term the "corrupt co-operatives and landbuying companies" in which families invested their savings,

icature of monstrous proportions. Pesa is, rather, portrayed as a rather awful man but one who, for all his morally repulsive qualities, is a believable human being who is occasionally (as in his near heroic drive through a dreadful storm and over a flooded bridge to get Wangari, in the throes of a birth crisis, to hospital) capable of more admirable behaviour. His oafishness is also curtailed and offset by those among whom he lives – primarily his humane and long-suffering spouse, Mama Pesa, who manages subtly to alleviate her husband's brutishness by many acts of neighbourly kindness, but also by Juda, his educated, drunken, charmingly eccentric elder son, who has his own firm plans for maintaining the soil and for uplifting the local community (22, 53, 142). When Wangari Baru's pregnancy is revealed and Baba Pesa angrily rejects her, Juda steps in with an offer of marriage to the distressed girl and ends up falling in love with her. Sadly, Wangari dies in childbirth – as the nurse reports to the two devastated families: "It was too difficult for her [. . .] She was too young" (195). The shocking death of so young a person underlines the predatory nature of Baba Pesa and the way he abuses his wealth: the loss of this innocent young life is Mwangi's clearest example of how brutally the rich exact the cost of wealth – from the poor. The twin babies who survive Wangari will nevertheless inextricably connect the indigent Barus with the wealthy Pesas – however unequal these neighbours' present share of the land.

Lastly it must be noted that the ancient goatherd Mutiso, the poorest person in the neighbourhood, is its unofficial leader; respected by all and consulted in all their troubles even if he has, often, nothing but his gentle compassion to offer them (100, 111). It is he rather than the inarticulate Chief or the blustering Baba Pesa who embodies the "untranslateable" Swahili proverb "*kuria uru kwa mu-Afrika gutigiria mundu arie wega!*" (n.pag.) which according to a Swahili speaker's attempted translation means: "The fact that the African does not eat well cannot stop him or her from speaking well!" – thus showing worth where there is a clear absence of wealth.

Chimamanda Ngozi Adichie's *Purple Hibiscus* (2004)

> Papa always sat in the front pew for Mass [. . .] Papa said modesty was very important. (4-5)

"in the hope of getting small land parcels" (qtd. in Johansson, *Shadow* 113), confirming Mwangi's analysis.

Purple Hibiscus, Chimamanda Adichie's first novel, has attracted considerable critical attention and is easily the best known and most widely read and taught text among the three discussed in this essay. Excellent as many of the published analyses are,[13] none of them foregrounds the aesthetics, ethics and performance of wealth in this text – quite validly so, as these elements are, perhaps, more subtly present in the novel than its other aspects (such as its gender dynamics and the issue of voice and silencing and of family politics and cultural-religious tensions). The obvious "representative" of wealth in this novel is Eugene Achike, a major industrialist (he owns a number of factories as well as a newspaper and has two palatial homes) and a fanatic Catholic. Eugene's only daughter Kambili is the focaliser in this text, in which Adichie consistently uses the technique of allowing her reader to see "beyond" what Kambili is able to see (or to acknowledge) about her father. One example of this is Eugene's clearly unhealthily overweight physical condition, which Kambili mentions but on which she does not comment, critically or otherwise – as when, following her father up the stairs, she mentions that "in his red silk pajamas, his buttocks quivered and shook like akamu [. . .], jellylike" (41). She also sees that his cheeks are "rubbery" (42), further mentioning "the mound of flesh that was his stomach" (101), his "heavy breathing" (15) and his "soft chest" (34). Despite his physical condition, Eugene is probably only in his forties, a huge man who towers over those around him (like Baba Pesa does in Mwangi's novel) and when he casually slaps his teenage son Jaja or Kambili in the face, across the dining table (for some trivial infraction of his rules of conduct), the sound resembles that of "a heavy book falling" (69).

In the cumulative effect of all these details, along with the information about Eugene that builds up in the course of the narrative, the reader gathers that this rich man (whose skin also frequently breaks out in suppurating rashes) is a pathologically driven person and a disciplinarian tyrant whose absurdly, impossibly rigid standards of supposedly "Christian" and "civilized" (13) conduct act like traps to allow him to let off steam in psychopathic acts of violent cruelty towards his wife and two surviving children. For, in his embrace and pursuit of capital (which he accumulates much faster than he gives it away – a position of social and financial success which he himself seems to believe springs from his fanatic adherence to his rule-bound, extremist form of Catholicism (47, 196) –

[13] E.g. in articles by Mabura (2008), Tunca ("Ambiguous," "Ideology"), Stobie (2010), Udumukwu (2011) as well as in Brenda Cooper's chapter (2008) from which I cite below.

Eugene is finally an enemy of life. This is shockingly illustrated in the fact that his most violent assaults on his timid wife Beatrice tend to coincide with her infrequent pregnancies, resulting always in foetal death and in deep woe for his family members.[14] A more minor instance of this pattern occurs when Kambili, suffering from severe menstrual cramps, is urged to eat a small bowl of cornflakes so that she can take Panadol. When Eugene, whose huge stomach betrays his own overindulgence in rich food, discovers to his fury that Kambili (supported by her mother and brother) has "broken the Eucharist fast" (101), he takes off his "heavy belt" (102) and whips all three of them.

Yet Kambili holds this violent, ultimately weak, man in awe. Her complicated feelings for her father result perhaps from her sensing in him, despite what has become twisted in Eugene, a deep yearning for love, but also in evidence is her admiration for his wealth and social stature in the midst of so much squalor and need.[15] One sees this attitude, for example, in Kambili's description of their family's second (village) home and in her evocation of the following small scene:

> Our house still took my breath away, the four-storey white majesty of it, with the spurting fountain in front. [. . .] Three little boys rushed into the compound to greet Papa. They had been chasing our [three] cars down the dirt road.
>
> "*Omelora*! Good afun, sah!" they chorused. They wore only shorts, and each one's belly button was the size of a small balloon.
>
> "*Kedu nu*? Papa gave them each ten naira from a wad of notes he pulled out of his hold-all. "greet your parents, make sure you show them this money." (55)

---

14 When Kambili notes that her mother's previous miscarriage (also due to an assault by Eugene) was "almost six years ago" and adds: "I could not even think of her and Papa together on the bed they shared" (21), this signifies more than the normal shyness of a child about her parents having sex. I would argue that it hints that, on the infrequent occasions that he has intercourse with his wife, the subsequent "proof" of this in a pregnancy fills Eugene with guilty shame, resulting in his infliction of violent "punishment" on his wife, probably obscurely blaming her for his "weakness" (see 28-36).

15 Frequently noted by Kambili – e.g. "the half-naked people near the rubbish dumps" (43); "girls much younger" than she, with "moth-eaten blouses", selling food by the roadside (45), or "the unkempt women in Ogbete market" with their "hole-riddled slips" showing under their unravelling wrappers (295).

Elsewhere Kambili refers to the "stretches of gleaming marble floor" (14) and the shiny glass tables in their city home. Adichie hints that the fifteen-year-old Kambili is "dazzled" by her father's wealth and importance; even her much more sophisticated, frequently cynical cousin Amaka refers without a trace of irony to "Uncle Eugene" as a "Big Man" (93).

Eugene is only superficially unlike the swaggering Baba Pesa (so fond of proclaiming his wealth to all and sundry) in his behaviour; and also resembles Ram's awful aunt who manifests her wealth in the grandness of her home and her horde of servants and acolytes. Instead of bragging, Eugene "allows" others to praise him. Breathtakingly, the white priest in the church Kambili's family attends "*usually* referred to the pope, Papa, and Jesus – *in that order*" (4; emphases added). In the village scene cited above, Eugene insists that the little boys inform their parents of his gifts to these obviously underfed children, in conformation of his title *Omelora* – meaning "The One Who Does for the Community" (56). His acts of charity are almost invariably of this ostentatious kind, for example in endowing their church (5, 28)[16] as well as in making large donations to his children's expensive (Catholic) schools. An act like Eugene's *flinging* "some crisp naira notes [from his car] at a beggar sprawled by the roadside" contrasts and is juxtaposed with Kambili's desire (unfulfillable in her familial context) to go in person to the aid of a poor market woman who is being whipped by a soldier in an "urban clearance drive" (44). Adichie underlines the inadequacy of Eugene's charity by subtly reminding readers who know their Bible of the Parable of the Good Samaritan whose acts much more closely resemble what Kambili wants to do here than what her father has done.

Eugene's material success seems in some way (and definitely, in his own mind) due to his embrace of Western values and is coupled with his conviction of his own righteousness, which in turn derives from his fanatical adherence to the extremist and rigidly formalistic form of Catholicism which he was taught by the priests as a boy working for them (as household servant) to give him access to education. He couples this with a contempt for all things Igbo, particular-

---

16 A quality of ostentation, suitably subdued to the environment, is evident in the "steps that *glowed* like *polished* ice blocks" on "one of the *best* altars" in the region and in "the *iridescent* saints on the *floor-to-ceiling* stained glass windows" (28; emphases added), as well as the "*huge* candles and the *ornate* marble altar" (240; emphases added), all in their local church and all paid for by Eugene – who is regularly praised for these gifts, from the pulpit. Compare the mesmerising, fascinating "gleam" (10 and ff.) of wealth and material prosperity that is satirised in Ayi Kwei Armah's *The Beautyful Ones Are Not Yet Born* (1968).

ly the indigenous faith practices and beliefs. Eugene's preference for using English, his opulent homes and his dress style reflect, as Ram's wealthy family's (in *Beer in the Snooker Club*) do, a determination to prove his superiority to and severance from what is African and indigenous – even if this includes his own father, whom he has denied. Eugene allows his children (and even this only under pressure from his village community) a single, fifteen-minute annual visit to their paternal grandfather, provided they neither eat nor drink at the dignified old man's meagre shelter. Papa-Nnukwu's "skinny" body (153) and his bare yard confirm his lament that even though his son "owns that house that can fit in every man in Abba" (their village), he all too often has "nothing to put on [his] plate". He blames himself: "I should not have let him follow those missionaries" (83). But although she is unable to articulate, even to herself, that Papa-Nnukwu is a deeply worthy and devout person, Kambili evidently becomes profoundly aware that he is nothing like the despicable pagan Eugene makes him out to be. In fact, one sees how quickly she comes to love him. Similarly, the worn furnishings and smallness of her widowed aunt Ifeoma's campus flat which at first dismay Kambili, soon come to signify the affection, laughter and lively debates of this family – so unlike the cold luxuries and repression of her own.

In her otherwise perceptive analysis of Purple *Hibiscus*, Brenda Cooper finds it an uncomfortably contradictory and problematic aspect of the text, even a sign of a "suppressed nationalism" (128) and a "false binary" (129), that Adichie – in her (i.e. Cooper's) eyes – "partially forgives Papa [i.e. Eugene] his [domestic] crimes [in] portraying him as a brave fighter for democracy" (129). In my view, Cooper fails to see how very carefully Adichie both parallels Eugene's violent abuse of familial authority with instances of state backed violence and corruption, and how she subtly undermines Eugene's national and international image as an heroic defender of democratic values in the context of state tyranny (the Abacha regime appears to be the one alluded to).

The first example indicating that Adichie sees direct parallels between domestic and state forms of violent tyranny, indeed terrorism, occurs quite early in the text; when we are given the clear proof that Eugene viciously abuses his wife, followed by a brief allusion to a public hanging of three drug smugglers. Both cases are instances of "punishment," but with various serious questions undermining the validity of the procedure. Beatrice, Eugene's wife and Jaja and Kambili's mother, is a slightly built woman. Troubled by nausea one (Sunday) morning because of her pregnancy, Beatrice had initially demurred at joining Eugene in his customary post-Mass visit to the white priest, but complied when her husband responded with barely disguised outrage. Once home, Eugene proceeds with violent blows to "discipline" his wife for her attempt to remain outside while he paid the weekly visit. Clearly such violent castigation is not unusual; Kambili comments (listening to but attempting deliberately to both minimise and "explain away" the thudding blows audible from behind their closed bedroom door to her in her own room): "Sometimes it was over before I even got to twenty" (33). Beaten into an unconscious state, Beatrice is afterwards carried out by Eugene, "slung over his shoulder like the jute sacks of rice his factory workers bought in bulk" and Jaja, expressing no outrage, remarks that "'There's blood on the floor.' [. . .] the trickle of blood, which trailed away [. . .] all the way downstairs" (33). The reader is certainly intended to be horrified by this and by the predictable loss of Beatrice's unborn baby because of her injuries, which the blood trickle signals. This wealthy and powerful man's habitual abuse of those dependent upon him, and their instilled fearful inability to challenge him, are as evident as the extreme injustice and the pathological quality of his spousal "castigation."

In the next paragraph, on the same page, Jaja and Kambili (having been told that their mother will not be returning from hospital that evening) discuss "*[i]nstead* [. . .] the three men who were publicly executed two days before, for drug trafficking" (33; emphasis added). Not only does Adichie highlight the strangeness (under the circumstances) of this "alternative" topic (considering their mother's plight and the familial tyranny within which they are trapped), which indicates these teenage children's inability to confront their father and to "take care of the baby [. . .] protect him" (23) – as Jaja had intended (in view of their mother's previous loss of a pregnancy in the same way) – but it is suggested that either the children themselves, perhaps with their secret "language of the eyes" (305), or the author, notice a parallel as well as a contrast here. More glaring is the contrast between convicted criminals being punished by law and the innocent victims (Beatrice and the baby she was carrying) so grievously assaulted by Eugene that the unborn child dies. But there is also a parallel between an abusive husband out of some obscure and twisted sense of guilt violently hitting his wife and their baby, and an abusive government spectacularly staging its punishment of criminals as a way of demonstrating its power and of deflecting attention from its own, much larger guilt and its failure in the duty of protection of the poorer and weaker by the wealthier and stronger.

The later passage concerns Eugene's role as the owner of a newspaper – such ownership being more obviously linked with his wealth and his power to influence public opinion from "behind the scenes" in the dangerous space that is Nigeria at this time. Eugene had been given a major and internationally significant human rights award – a fact which he "allowed" his fearlessly outspoken editor, Ade Coker, to report in the paper – for "his" outspokenness in criticising the state's human rights abuses. The editor, who is the truly heroic writer-activist, refers to Eugene in the newspaper as "*the bravest man I know*" (42; emphasis original), but as Jaja assures the children's Aunty Ifeoma (Eugene's feisty sister): "they won't touch Papa [. . .]. They know he has many foreign connections" (202). Eugene's wealth and the influence it accords him thus save him from persecution. Not so Ade Coker, as his worried wife knows. She comes to see Eugene because of her anxiety about Ade's arrest for his risk-taking challenges to and exposures of corruption in the state. The rich man's bland reassurance to his employee's wife: "Yewande don't talk that way. Ade will be fine, *I promise you*. Ade will be fine" (38; emphasis added) are exposed only a few lines further when Kambili states that "soldiers had arrested Ade Coker as he drove out of the editorial offices of the *Standard*" (38). He is seriously tortured while incarcerated, and although Eugene on this occasion manages to get him released, the editor's next exposé will cost him his life when a letter bomb is sent to his home.

Kambili reveals the background: "I knew his arrest was because of the big cover story in the last *Standard*, a story about how the Head of State and his wife had paid people to transport heroin abroad, a story that questioned the recent execution of three men and who the real drug barons were" (38). The ability of Big Men to buy those who will be the scapegoats or receive the retaliation to what is done on their behalf and for their profit (since Eugene's Amnesty World award is certainly profitable to him, as is the organised, state-protected crime of drug smuggling to the Head of State) is shown here. Eugene's ability to shield behind others to boast on his behalf (as is done both in his Church and in his newspaper and by the hordes of sycophants with whom he surrounds himself, all unaware of his grotesque domestic misconduct), is an irony and a scandal Adichie certainly intends us to notice – as an effect clearly undercutting and invalidating the apparent suggestion that Eugene is an heroic champion of democracy. His sense of responsibility in not having stopped Ade Coker from taking the further and fatally risky step of exposing the state orchestrated assassination of Nwankiti Ogechi, a major "pro-democracy activist" and a threat to the oppressive state because the "rallies" he held could fill a stadium (199), drenches Eugene in guilt – appropriately so. Unfortunately this tension in him finds outlet in further extreme violence against his children, Kambili bearing the brunt of it this time.

People who do not understand how cushioned Eugene is by his enormous wealth and his international profile, had been worried about *his* safety and cautioned him to "be careful" and to avoid going to "public places," reminding him of "the bomb blast at the airport when a civil rights lawyer was travelling" and of other state assassinations (201). But all Eugene is subjected to is a visit from "soldiers" bringing "a truckful of dollars" in an attempt to bribe him to silence Ade Coker – a bribe that a man as wealthy as Eugene can easily refuse. The only other slap on the wrist he gets is that one of his numerous factories – in which sweet biscuits and drinks are made, his fortune resting on selling such consumer goods to the Nigerian populace – is shut down. By contrast, when Eugene's underpaid, often unpaid, widowed sister Ifeoma is told to "Be careful, be very careful" (231) by the commander of "the special security unit in port Harcourt" and her home is searched by these brutal men "for documents designed to sabotage the peace of the university" (230), such a warning is full of real menace. It is soon fulfilled when Aunty Ifeoma is given "notice of termination [. . .]. For what they call illegal activity" (a trumped-up charge) and given a month's notice to clear out her shabby (but love and life-filled) apartment. She is forced (borrowing heavily from Eugene) to leave Nigeria for the USA with her three children, there holding down two jobs to make ends meet. But in the course of Kambili's narrative, we are shown that Ifeoma in her financially straitened circumstances is a woman who stands tall and who stands up to Eugene. Ifeoma's outspoken criticism of government corruption, her strong feminism and her resistance to authoritarian university mismanagement are not protected by wealth – or by her wealthy brother.

I conclude my analysis of the performance, ethics and aesthetics of wealth in *Purple Hibiscus* by drawing attention to the fact that Adichie like the other two novelists uses the image of body size to draw a contrast between the "representative" of wealth in her text, the overweight Eugene, and others who are spare of body and who are not only physically but spiritually healthy in contrast with Kambili's father – a man unlikely to have lived much longer than the curtailment of his life when his wife decides to kill him by poisoning. The poison is supplied by Sisi, the family housekeeper and one of the abused Beatrice's few confidantes.[17] A death that comes from imbibing administered poison is symbol-

[17] Despite her many years of working as their housekeeper and cook, Eugene only ever refers to Sisi as "that girl" (12, 98, 258), never personally addressing her – a

ically appropriate for Eugene and can be contrasted with the peaceful and dignified death of the father he had rejected merely because he refused to cast off his Igbo practices and convert to Catholicism. Beatrice is saved from jail when Jaja claims to have been the poisoner, but although the family is left still enormously wealthy after half of Eugene's fortune goes to the church, it is evident that all three of them are scarred for life. This is Adichie's example of what I term "the cost of wealth" – the familial or social pattern that the extreme wealth of some is "cannibalistically" exacted from other and weaker persons. Eugene's financial compensation to Ade Coker's young family cannot make up for their loss of a loving husband and father; he cannot buy absolution for his own responsibility in this talented and courageous man's death. Nor can the luxury of their lifestyle ever be enough to balance the vicious cruelties Eugene inflicts on his family, or the resultant "shame and [complicated] grief" (305) of his surviving family members.

Conclusion

These literary evocations of the performance, ethics and aesthetics of wealth in three African contexts are significant contributions to the understanding of economic, social and political currents and of the influence of a multitude of factors informing the power relations in these societies. What I hope to have indicated in the course of this essay are the simultaneous achievements in these impressive novels of literary *art* and of implicit but probing social analysis. Especially important to note, I believe, is the point that authors like Ghali, Mwangi and Adichie have in these three texts succeeded in indigenising African power analysis by locating the primary responsibility for the maldistribution and misuse of wealth in local figures. Furthermore, analyses of African societies tend to foreground poverty, but as these novels remind us, this sadly prevalent condition is perpetually intertwined with local – and not only, or primarily, international – forms of wealth and the power that wealth allows to its possessors.

In the performances or staging of their wealth, Ram's aunt, Baba Pesa and Eugene Achike are three figures who either openly or secretly relish what they assume is the "superiority" confirmed by their wealth – when in fact, as Ghali, Mwangi and Adichie show in these texts, what their wealth allows them is a type of masquerade. Eugene's royal seeming silk pajamas, Ram's aunt's glittering "thirty seater" dinner table and Baba Pesa's roaring Mercedes are badges of

manifestation of social disdain for "inferiors" that again makes him comparable to Baba Pesa (and Ram's aunt) for all his suavity.

privilege, but cannot cover up the ugly dimensions – bodily as much as spiritual – that their lives assume. They show the typical facets of conspicuous wealth consumption – in the commodity forms of clothes, cutlery and cars – that mark performances of wealth across the world, but that are especially glaringly at odds with the lives of most people around them in Africa. Despite their far flung locations, Eugene's protruding stomach, Baba Pesa's bulky body and Ram's aunt's obesity prove the "relatedness" of the three figures not only in their body shape but in the predatory roles they play in their respective societies. They show all three authors concurring in registering the "embodiment" of wealth in these representative figures, and its "cannibalistic," consuming nature.[18]

As was mentioned in the discussions of Mwangi's and Adichie's novels, the matter of the cost of wealth needs to be taken into consideration. Not only in the cases of extreme abuse such as Baba Pesa's rape of Wangari and Eugene's assaults on his family members, but in the contempt that all three "representatives" of wealth exude towards those poorer than or employed by them, these figures of wealth do harm that far outweighs the good that they also (to a greater or much lesser extent) do in their families and communities. Their abuse is also of themselves in eschewing the sources of deeper satisfaction to be achieved in love, labour and self-improvement, and this is externalised in their unappealingly bulky and unhealthy appearance. In this way, the aesthetics and the ethics of wealth are shown to be deeply intertwined.

In no way does this essay attempt to deny that more wealth is desperately needed all over the African continent, and better distribution of it. Africa remains a looted continent, from which the valuable "raw materials" – even intellectual goods – are taken and converted into wealth in and for other societies. But unless the African middlemen (and women) – land owners, business people, heirs of empire or government leaders – begin to show greater responsibility for the welfare of all their people (and welfare always requires a modicum of wealth to allow access to society's benefits), our continent will not prosper and the majority of lives are likely to remain "poor, nasty, brutish and short" – to appropriate the well- known, notorious description of Thomas Hobbes (*Leviathan* XIII 9).

---

18 In *The Bottom Billion: Why the Poorest Countries Are Failing and What Can Be Done about It*, Paul Collier speaks of "*the survival of the fattest*" (42, emphasis original). Compare also J.-P. Bayart's work, *The State in Africa: The Politics of the Belly* and Chinua Achebe's use of the metaphor of eating in *A Man of the People* (1966), which I analyse in *Achebe, Head, Marechera* (92-100).

There are enlightening coincidences in the vision of the role and effect of wealth in the three novels, some of which have been touched on. Several other aspects had to be left unexplored, such as the gender and generational aspects of the situations evoked. Wealth possession is not invariably male, as Ghali's text reminds us, and Africa has its share of matriarchs – benign as well as malign – as well as its better known abundance of patriarchs. Still, the majority of the wealthy on the continent are of course Big Men – in both senses of the expression – like Baba Pesa and Eugene Achike. Wealth misuse also tends to have clear gender dimensions, with women as its victims, co-consumers or as opportunists pursuing the wealthy males. Generationally, complacent wealth possession may simply be transmitted to the next generation (as in Mounir, the indulged and vapid son of Ram's richest aunt) or may be challenged by younger family members like Ram with his satirically mocking, barbed comments on his wealthy relatives, Kambili's troubled attempts to fend off while secretly admitting her father's cruelty and weakness to herself, or Juda's laughter at and contempt for Baba Pesa's greedy aspirations and his swaggering lifestyle. It is made clear that Ram, Juda and Kambili are strongly aware of social injustices and imbalances and that they all three have profoundly humane social instincts, in which there is at least the possibility of hope for improvement of the harsh wealth imbalances on the continent in some pockets of this vast and troubled region of the world.

In all three narratives, the authors' moral-political analytical perspectives are powerfully communicated because the texts use the affective resources of literary art to give resonance to their work. The unattractiveness of the selfish and parasitical kinds and uses of wealth in the three novels concerned functions as an ethical placing in the sense that the wealthy person is given a human "ranking": but this aesthetic portrayal process also ironises the wealth – it is made to seem less overpowering, more socially interconnected and accessible by means of the narrators' specific perspectives on the wealthy Africans they depict so memorably. There is some human poignance, some vulnerability evident in each of them. Thus does the complicating, inclusive compassion of the novelists allow us to feel not only for the victims of their abuses, but to see anew the truth of the proverb that human lives are intertwined and that the abusers of privilege always also harm and deprive themselves.

Works Cited

Achebe, Chinua. *A Man of the People*. Oxford: Heinemann, 1966.

___. "The Truth of Fiction." *Hopes and Impediments: Selected Essays*. By Achebe. New York: Doubleday, 1989. 138-153.

Adichie, Chimamanda Ngozi. *Purple Hibiscus*. 2004. London: Harper Perennial, 2005.

Al Aswany, Alaa. *The Yacoubian Building*. 2002. Trans. H. T. Davies. Cairo: American University in Cairo Press, 2004.

Allouache, Merzak. *Bab el-Oued*. 1995. Trans. A.M. Brewer. Boulder, CO: Lynne Rienner, 1998.

Armah, Ayi Kwei. *The Beautyful Ones Are Not Yet Born*. London: Heinemann, 1968.

Bayart, Jean-Francois. *The State in Africa: The Politics of the Belly*. London: Longman, 1993.

Collier, Paul. *The Bottom Billion: Why the Poorest Countries Are Failing and What Can Be Done about It*. Oxford: Oxford UP, 2007.

Cooper, Brenda. "Breaking Gods and Petals of Purple: Chimamanda Ngozi-Adichie's *Purple Hibiscus*." *A New Generation of African Writers: Migration, Material Culture and Language*. By Cooper. Woodbridge: James Currey, 2008. 110-132.

Currie, Kate, and Larry Ray. "The Pambana of August 1: Kenya's Abortive Coup." *Political Quarterly* 57.1 (1986): 47-59.

Fanon, Frantz. "The Pitfalls of National Consciousness." *The Wretched of the Earth*. By Fanon. 1961. Trans. Constance Farrington. Harmondsworth: Penguin, 1990. 119-165.

Gagiano, Annie. *Achebe, Head, Marechera: On Power and Change in Africa*. Boulder, CO and London: Lynne Rienner, 2000.

___. "Using a Comic Vision to Contend with Tragedy: Three Unusual African English Novels." *Cheeky Fictions: Laughter and the Postcolonial*. Ed. Reichl, Susanne, and Mark Stein. Amsterdam / NewYork: Rodopi, 2005. 257-270.

Ghali, Waguih. *Beer in the Snooker Club*. 1964. New York: New Amsterdam, 1989.

Gindy, Nadia. "'The gift of our birth': An image of Egypt in the Work of Waguih Ghali." *Images of Egypt in Twentieth-Century Literature*. Ed. H. Gindy. Cairo: Cairo University, English Department: 1991. 423-433.

Hobbes, Thomas. *Leviathan or The Matter, Forme and Power of a Common Wealth Ecclesiastical and Civill.* 1651. Ed. Ian Shapiro. Hartford: Yale UP, 2010.

Johansson, Lars. *In the Shadow of Neocolonialism: Meja Mwangi's Novels 1973-1990*. Umea: Umea UP, 1992.

Kehinde, Ayo. "Epidemic of Postcolonial Woes: Meja Mwangi's *Striving for the Wind* and the Trouble with Africa." *Ufahamu: A Journal of African Studies* 30.2-3 (2004): 61-83.

Mabura, Lily G. N. "Breaking Gods: A Gothic Reading of Chimamanda Ngozi-Adichie's *Purple Hibiscus* and *Half of a Yellow Sun*." *Research in African Literatures* 39.1 (2008): 203-222.

Mersal, Iman. "Revolutionary Humour." *Globalizations* 8.5 (2011): 669-674.

Mwangi, Meja. *Striving for the Wind*. Oxford: Heinemann, 1990.

Reichl, Susanne, and Mark Stein , eds. *Cheeky Fictions: Laughter and the Postcolonial*. Amsterdam / New York: Rodopi, 2005.

Rooney, Caroline. "Egyptian Literary Culture and Egyptian Modernity: Introduction." *Journal of Postcolonial Writing* 47.4 (2011): 369-376.

Starr, Deborah A. "Drinking, Gambling, and Making Merry: Waguih Ghali's Search for Cosmopolitan Agency." *Middle Eastern Literatures* 9.3 (2006): 271-285.

Stobie, Cheryl. "Dethroning the Infallible Father: Religion, Patriarchy and Politics in Chimamanda Ngozi Adichie's *Purple Hibiscus*." *Literature and Theology* 24.4 (2010): 421-435.

Thomas, Susie. "Waguih Ghali: 'Beer in the Snooker Club' – 1964." *London Fictions*. 25 April 2014 <http://www.londonfictions.com/waguih-ghali-beer-in-the-snooker-club.html>.

Tunca, Daria. "An Ambiguous 'Freedom Song': Mind-Style in Chimamanda Ngozi Adichie's *Purple Hibiscus*." *Postcolonial Text* 5.1 (2009): 1-18.

___. "Ideology in Chimamanda Ngozi Adichie's *Purple Hibiscus* (2003)." *English Text Construction* 2.1 (2009): 121-131.

Udumukwu, Onyemaechi. "Adichie's *Purple Hibiscus* and the Issues of Ideology in the Constitution of the Nigerian Novel." *Tydskrif vir Letterkunde* 48.1 (2011): 184-204.

wa Thiong'o, Ngugi. *A Grain of Wheat*. London: Heinemann, 1967.

Three Takes on Somali Womanhood in the Eddies of the Contemporary Black Atlantic Context

> we walk in the rubble
> of the African dream
>
> brushing shipwreck from
> our hair & dresses.
>
> This is the country
> of the gone-away [. . .][1]
>
> – Aracelis Girmay

This essay as its point of departure addresses a geographical aspect or implication of the Black Atlantic concept[2] that plays out as part of the decentring or erasure of Africa – the point that, because the Atlantic abuts only on the western side of the continent, the northward dispersal of Africans and the diaspora, exile or migrations of Africans from the East, North and North-East (as well as the South of the continent)[3] are eventualities that would almost inevitably be occluded, ignored or side-lined by a concern with cross-Atlantic movements by and contacts among Africans. If one applies the Bakhtinian notion of the chronotope to Gilroy's influential text, its concentration on the initial dispersing and propelling factors – slavery and colonialism as initiating the forced migrations of those eras whose aftermath in modernity and by means of hybridity he studies – can also be seen as limited and partial in view of the later emigration patterns, exiles and dispersals *and their causes*, focus on which would serve to centralise

1 From the poem "Elegy in Gold" in this poet's second collection, *Kingdom Animalia*. Aracelis Girmay is not Somali, but of Eritrean and Puerto Rican descent.

2 Paul Gilroy in his 1993 text *The Black Atlantic: Modernity and Double Consciousness* employed this term in order to refer to the cross-Atlantic dispersal of Africans to Europe and the Americas mainly because of slavery and to point to the cultures Africans created or contributed to by adapting to life in those continents.

3 The recent rise of Indian Ocean Studies and the broader concept of Oceanic Studies can be seen as responses to an Atlantic focus. See also the earlier article by Ntongela Masilela in the 1996 special issue of *RAL* (ed. Simon Gikandi) articulating assessments of Gilroy's 1993 text, e.g.: "it is a profoundly flawed book because of its exclusionary epistemic cultural politics" and: "[. . .] Gilroy excludes Africa and Latin America" (Masimela 88), as well as Gikandi's introduction to this issue ("Africa" 1-5).

Africa, or at least give greater prominence to what has happened and is happening on this continent and in individual African countries.[4]

It is against this background that it seemed a worthwhile undertaking to bring the so-called[5] "collapsed state" of Somalia and recent fictional explorations of the condition of this African nation to bear on the topic of of the Black Atlantic – the expression being used in this context to refer to a larger oceanic sphere whose "eddies" are here taken to include the Mediterranean and the crossings by Africans of more recent times, and from the northeast rather than the west of the continent. Clearly, it is only Nuruddin Farah's *Knots* (2007) that – because its main protagonist grows up in Somalia, emigrates to Canada and returns to Somalia to recover from an agonising loss and recover her family's property – centrally involves Black Atlantic crossings, though the text is set in a more recent and tighter time-frame than Gilroy's assessed historical-cultural transitions. Safi Abda's *Offspring of Paradise* (2003) is the text among the three addressed here that most closely involves the post-Barre collapse of Somalia – from dictatorship into warlord dominated, bloody mayhem[6] – as first-hand experience, portraying also the subsequent, fanatic neo-missionary menace faced by some Somali refugees in an unnamed (European or North American) country. *Little Mother* (2011, the English translation of the original Italian text, *Madre Piccola*, 2007) by Cristina Ali Farah does have one of its three narrators (the only male one) moving from Somalia to Italy to the U.S., but its two more strongly foregrounded female narrators cross the Mediterranean from Somalia to Italy, all three leaving at different times, although the state of the country likewise propels their exits from Somalia. As may be evident from the foregoing, it is not

---

4 See texts such as the collections of essays edited by Goebel and Schabio and by Oboe and Scacchi – especially the introduction to the latter text and the chapter by Lombardi-Diop – as well as articles by Gabaccia (1, 17, 18), O'Reilly (77, 78), and Owomuela (239) for various examples of attempts to address perceived insufficiencies of the original conceptualisation.

5 Rosa E. Brooks is one voice that has drawn attention to the inappropriateness of the term to certain postcolonial circumstances, writing that implicit in the expression is the notion that at independence the conditions of statehood existed; i.e. can a "state" that had not [yet] become one be said to have "failed"?

6 The words of the 17th-century British philosopher John Locke ring bitterly true for recent Somali history: "I confess [. . .] men should fly from *oppression*, but *disorder* will give them but an incommodious sanctuary. 'Tis not without reason that *tyranny* and *anarchy* are judged the smartest scourges can fall upon mankind [...]" (119; emphasis original).

Africa as an entity but one specific country and its people's particular misfortunes and experiences of disaster causing dislocation that form the focus of the texts and of this paper. The texts and the article are furthermore Afro-centric, but in different ways than the term usually implies: in Nuruddin Farah's *Knots* the possibility eventually begins to emerge of a future in Africa, in Somalia, but in the other two novels Somalia is primarily a haunting memory, although Somali connectedness and a Somali-centric subjectivity – primarily as a religious and linguistic identity or commitment in *Offspring of Paradise* and mainly through familial and social networking in *Little Mother* – can be seen as a largely successful retention of an Afro-Somali sense of nationhood. Versions of Africanness in a Somali form can be said to be central to all three texts; this persistence (despite relocation) of an originary identity is remarkable in view of the settled and comparatively secure life that is available to all the protagonists in "Western" (geographically northern) societies. The "Somaliness" of the various characters is shown to be and to remain their primary and ineradicable identity (Abda's text being intensely critical of the northern "host society," the other two considerably less so).

The selected fictional works "connect" importantly in other dimensions of their Somali Afrocentricity also, within what might be called a late (and enlarged) Black Atlantic space and time-frame.[7] Particularly significant is the three novels' coinciding perspectives on the unbalanced gendering in standard Somali socialisation and the way this plays out in the Somali civil war and the consequent diaspora. All three texts are discernibly gynocentric in their narratives and all explicitly (through their female protagonists) condemn what are perceived here as the dominant types of Somali manhood and the phallocratic nature of the society – a swaggering, ruthless and competitive "macho" culture ascribed by the characters to a majority of Somali men – and hold these responsible for the bloody anarchy and violation of humane social values that brought about the destruction of the country as a "liveable location" for the majority of its former citizens.[8]Although Afro-Somali-centric, the three texts are hence intensely critical of what are seen as central or dominant aspects of this particular African culture. Despite the protagonists' real and enduring Afrocentricity, their depictions of their own culture are in no way sentimental or merely nostalgic. Though many

7 Oboe and Scacchi draw attention to "a brand new route that connects the Black Atlantic and the 'Black' Mediterranean" (6).

8 The introduction to *Little Mother* contains the information that "there are currently more Somalis living abroad than in Somalia itself" (xvii).

of the characters' memories of Somalia are tender and fond, they name and shame (as well as face up to) what they diagnose as the faults of Somali society, and deplore the shocking or disgusting aspects of its history and its present condition. In view of this, it remains important to recognise that all three novels function simultaneously as acts of resistance against the superficial and reductive demonisation of Somalis and Somalia in the global media. The texts do this by way of discussions of the prevalent media stereotypes of their society and people, which the novelists counter through their characters both by depicting a number of admirable, gentle and socially responsible men and (especially) in their representation of courageous and thoughtful Somali women. The novels also counter the popular clichés about Somalia by characters recalling the intellectual sophistication, depth of culture and complex, diverse urban social life (in Mogadiscio in particular) available in Somalia before the disintegration of the state. Examples of violence-crazed, violated or starving individuals and scenes of buildings reduced to rubbish and rubble are present in these works of fiction in order to acknowledge the hugeness of Somali loss, rather than being presented as evidence of their compatriots' allegedly inherently savage tendencies and wolfish natures. Thus these texts lament and commemorate even as they denounce different aspects of their cultural inheritance, finely balancing their portrayals among yesterdays and todays, with faint intimations of tomorrows[9] in complex, responsible, and moving assessments of the state of their nation.

In this article I consider the question how the three chosen texts indicate possible reconfigurations and adaptations of the Black Atlantic conception (or at least, how they can function to measure the advantages of updating its discourse), especially but not only in their centralisation of (Somali) African subjectivity and Somalia's significance as a distinct portion of the African continent. The matters to be examined by means of the three texts are inter alia the following: reimaginings of the topics of Somali nationhood or nationness (as against hybridity); cultural confidence and the role of religious orientation or inculcated values; gender issues as well as power shifts and class change brought about by relocation; cultural recuperation and social (re)connection; evocations of African modernities or contemporaneity and a focus on the present; and returning to or remaining in the homeland and attendant crises as against the affective costs and challenges of the diaspora (as exile). The thickness or density of

[9] Alluding to Nuruddin Farah's text recording interviews with and reflections on Somalis in exile, which he titled *Yesterday, Tomorrow: Voices from the Somali Diaspora*.

evocation in all three novels and the vividness and affective power (including the sense of authenticity, hence validity) which the texts achieve,[10] make them rich sources for exploring these compelling topics (listed above). Metatextually, the article seeks to trace and test how creative fiction functions as an important educational tool or as a source and repository of social knowledge[11] in a world where power imbalances are reflected in the blind spots and clichés of uneven knowledge and severe imbalances in understanding – with the seriously harmful consequences (in misrepresentation, injustice and xenophobia) that result from this.

Knots is Nuruddin Farah's tenth novel and like all his fictional texts set largely in the country of his birth, although Farah (who has in recent years been able to return on visits) has been living in exile ever since the publication of his second novel *A Naked Needle* (1976) made him *persona non grata* to the dangerous Barre dictatorship of the time. Cambara, the main protagonist of *Knots*, is not as compelling a figure as (for example) Medina in *Sardines* (1981)[12] – another strong female figure given a central role by Farah, who is often identified as a male feminist writer – and her engagement with her local compatriots is more in the nature of exploratory rediscovery and reconnection after her return to her native land from Canada, where her Somali husband's affair with his employer (and failure to mind their only child) led to the nine-year-old boy's death by drowning. Cambara's return to Somalia after living in Canada since her teens is propelled by her compulsion to put distance between herself and her now detested husband, and by her attempt to try and recover from her loss and to mourn it. She gives herself the assignment to try and recover her family's property, a large house set in extensive grounds, known to have been illegally seized and

10 In her *Moral Textures: Feminist Narratives in the Public Sphere*(1998), Maria Pia Lara writes of "new historical accounts [. . .] that reveal the bias and distortion of earlier narrations, and where the polluted representations of marginalized, excluded and repressed groups can be challenged and set right" (171) in the struggle "for a group to gain esteem and recognition" (136). Her examples are mainly literary.

11 Stephen Chan berates theorists of war and social upheaval, saying "*How did the 'victim' understand it?* That is a question we do not ask" (101; original italicised), whereas Christine Sylvester (a political scientist specialising in International Relations and Development Studies) tells us to "remember the ghosts about," to consider analysing wars "based on how they are experienced," and testifies that "a well-crafted fictional account of war can impact on [her] research sensibilities like nothing else" ("Pathways" 125, 124, 128).

12 See my article "Farah's *Sardines*: Women in a Context of Despotism".

since occupied by one of the minor warlords who (by means of the gangs or militias of armed teenage thugs which they employ) hold the formerly gracious city of Mogadiscio in their thrall. This bare-bones introduction immediately indicates two possible answers to the badgering question put to Cambara on her arrival by her repulsive cousin Zaak – "Who do you blame?" (1) – by which he seems to refer to the collapse of much that is considered normal social life in the war-raddled city, but which slyly also nudges her bitterness about her son's death, about which he clearly knows a lot. We learn later that Cambara's estranged husband actually had the audacity to call Zaak and tell him his "side of the story." The ambience of male Somali misbehaviour in the examples of the husband, the cousin and the warlord indicates that even a strong woman like Cambara will have her work of recovery (in both senses) cut out for her, given the brutality evident in these men with whom she has had to and will have to engage. Farah at a much later point in the text inserts the misandrist generalisation with which a new and extremely helpful friend to Cambara, another strong and enterprising woman, responds after hearing her guest's narrative. Kiin (the friend) speaks of "the terrible things men have always done to women and gotten away with." She tells Cambara how "saddened" she was to hear of her "tragic loss", and how "it breaks [her] heart now to remember how [her husband] Wardi neglected [his and Cambara's] son." She concludes: "Men are a dead loss to us and they father wars, our miseries" (194). While Farah depicts several very good Somali men whose exemplary conduct and sense of responsibility through care-taking contradict the anti-male sexism of which one might deem Kiin guilty, it is noteworthy that Farah often identifies Somali patriarchy and its phallocratic practices as profoundly intertwined with the forces that have all but destroyed Somalia and pushed over half its people out of their country of birth.[13] What is extremely interesting about Farah's reading of gender into politics is how he sees *male* domestic and "personal" conduct interlinked with (male) public and political actions.

---

13 In Farah's *Sweet and Sour Milk* (1979) the following Wilhelm Reich quotation features centrally: "In the figure of the father the authoritarian state has its representative in every family, so that the family becomes its most important instrument of power" (97), while in *Sardines* the writer matches the head of state (the Barre figure always referred to as "the General") with the sinister matriarch Idil, hell-bent on infibulating Medina's daughter Ubax and a strong upholder of patriarchal values – like Medina's own mother.

In Nuruddin Farah's on-going interrogation of Somali nationhood, there is an evident recognition of the strength and validity of Somali nationhood, but an equally powerful and insistent demand for a reinvention of this culturally cohesive force and of the need for this to begin by male members of the community pulling their weight in correcting ugly gender imbalances and injustices. The novel outlines examples of how this might be done in – for example – the conduct of the gentle medical doctor Bile (once he has recovered from the deep pit of depression in which Cambara found him); the dutiful and down-to-earth Dajaal (an upright former army officer); Odeywaa (the shopkeeper who assists local Somalis in receiving remittances sent by relatives abroad, who is married to a leader of the Women for Peace network in Somalia) and the taxi driver who contemptuously refers to the warlords as "men in drag, every one of them" (134). It is, however, especially through a network of Somali women (to whom the aforementioned men are allies and whom they assist) that Cambara is empowered to stage a play in the war-torn, divided city in her now recovered ancestral home, an abode which is guarded by Dajaal and refurnished with the help of Bile's very dear Irish friend Seamus (who has settled in Somalia). In the play, Cambara gives leading roles to a boy who had survived by becoming feral when his visiting Somali father was killed by a taxi-driver in a set-up; to a youngster who was a member of the youth militia employed by her cousin; to the "rediscovered" mother now reunited with the boy who had run wild and also to Bile – with whom she has fallen in love and who returns Cambara's love. The achievement of all this is crowned by the arrival from Canada of Cambara's mother and her dearest friend, Arda. In some ways an undeniably "romantic" vision of what could be done in the devastated city, often referred to in the novel as perhaps the most dangerous place on earth, Farah's novel nevertheless finely balances hope (given sufficient effort and cooperation – especially among men and women) for Somalia and its people with castigation and the question of "blame" with which the text opens.[14] In contrast with Gilroy's conception of Black Atlantic space being primarily created through forcible "export" of African culture to the "New World," adapted and transformed by centuries of settlement to become the vibrant hybrid forms of culture and lifestyle that fascinate him, Farah's concentration is in no way on the North American (Canadian)

[14] I concur with John Masterson's remark that Farah's "commitment to defamiliarising the hegemonic notion that Somalia has always been, and thus will always be, an incubator of disorder is as resolute in *Knots* as at any other point in his career" (268).

space of settlement – even if comfortable and accommodating as both Cambara and her parents had largely found it. Nor is there much question of hybridity, since their family had been a distinctly "modern"[15] and largely secular small community before moving to Canada. Cambara and her family as well as those local Somalis with whom she connects on returning to Mogadiscio cannot (in the words of Gilroy) be said to transcend "the structures of the nation state[16] and the constraints of ethnicity and national particularity" (19), because they are quite comfortable within that "particularity" and are not shown to experience it as constraining.

What might be termed a reproachful but unbreakable sense of nationhood is immediately evident in the dedication to Safi Abdi's *Offspring of Paradise*. It reads: "To the wronged souls of our land" (iii). In Abdi's novel the emphasis on their Muslim affiliation and moral values among the Somali refugees on whom her text focuses helps one to grasp another dimension of the Black Atlantic's complexity that Gilroy – whose mostly African American subjects shared or came to share Christian affiliation with their new compatriots – does not explore: their maintenance of a different theology is a safeguard against aggressive Christian proselytising to which Abdi's characters are subjected and is a strong centripetal force in their lives. Abdi's central character, the teenage Hana (a little girl of six when the disaster of violent mayhem strikes the nation and their family, pulverising Hana's beloved father before her eyes in an explosion; shooting down her paternal uncle who is attempting to drive them to safety and causing the still-birth of a baby brother amidst the gang-rape that drives her mother temporarily insane and out into the desert night), understandably develops a fiercely denunciatory attitude to the males of her nation, stating categorically that "Somali men as a whole have let the Somali woman down" (237). Though the imam in the Somali refugee community where she lives first with her grandmother and then with a neighbouring woman (her guardian after her grandmother's death, in

15 Cambara's mother does make the concession of pretending to have had her daughter infibulated – a form of pretence that succeeds in saving Cambara from mockery and taunts from other girls in an environment where this ritual cutting is seen as culturally essential (this is while they are all still living in Mogadiscio).

16 Compare Laura Chrisman's suggestion that "the category of the nation supplies the only effective means for interpreting the category of black – or any – transnationality" and that "African nationalism and black transnationalism [be considered] as symbiotic political impulses" (41). One must concede, however, that in Gilroy's initiating text the identification of particular African countries of origin of the subjects he discussed was not possible or relevant to his focus.

the absence of her mother who is still missing) does attempt to placate her, Hana remains scornful:

> And now after so many years of blaming others, putting the blame squarely on the mindless of our nation, the regime of Siyad Barre, the young delinquents, the generals, the thieves and the power hungry, the upright men of Somalia, the men with the clean record, are suddenly so remorseful? (235)

Her scepticism is justified, though her sense of terrible failures of responsibility and deep betrayal is something she imposes also on her female guardian, who (under quite extreme pressure, as her family was fleeing the mayhem in Somalia under the protection of her then half-crazed, clan-besotted elder brother) half-inadvertently abandoned her dearest friend – a member of the clan associated with the toppled dictator now labelled *faqash* (meaning 'rubbish') and considered fair game to rapists and murderers. Hana, after her rescue from the clutches from the crazed would-be "converter" Helen, still maintains: "My people let me down. And it's them that I should blame, not Helen. By the time I came to the gates of this nation, I was a reject, and Helen found a reject. So, what's the big deal?" (342).

Amidst such bitterness, it is noticeable that Hana earlier spoke to Helen, who could not comprehend why Hana would not repudiate her people and the Muslim faith, by saying (in explanation of Somalis' persistent solidarity amidst the temptations available in the new environment, should they religiously and culturally re-align themselves):

> I don't think you'll ever get to know us Somalis, Helen. [. . .] Some of us may seem to you as cutthroats, but at the end of the day, we're family, and especially here in *the wall* [the nickname of the refugee facility where Hana lives for many years; emphasis original]. You could say what we've got here's nothing more than a sibling rivalry gone awry, if you will. [To this she adds:] My grandmother's words, not mine [. . .] I personally can't understand it, but that's how my grandmother saw things: 'It's a mad house out there, and until Somalis get the message bell clear that what they have done to themselves is not only un-islamic but also plain idiotic, they'll never amount to anything.' These are also my grandmother's words. (143)

In the opening words of Cristina Ali Farah's *Little Mother*, spoken by Domenica Axad the Somali-Italian protagonist (one of three narrators), the emphasis falls again on a sense of indissoluble Somaliness: "the knots, clear and tight, that, though far from each other, do not unravel" (1). Though technically a hybrid subject, as her "double" name confirms, this young woman uses the words of a modern Somali poet[17] (*Soomaali baan ahay* – meaning 'I am Somali') to claim a birthright in this nation and refers to her (presumably Somali) "half that is whole" (1). Domenica Axad's memories of the warmth and closeness of the extended family in the compound where she spent the first nine years of her life, living almost like a twin sister with her beloved, slightly older cousin Barni (who lost both her parents) are interwoven with details indicative of the violence and danger besetting them from outside the compound's walls – violence that would (during the Barre years) cause Barni's father's death by firing squad (for political resistance) and the subsequent despair and death of her mother, as well as the imprisonment and prolonged absences of Domenica Axad's father (in hiding from the Barre regime). When Domenica Axad at age 18 attempts to return to Somalia (from where her mother had taken her to return to Italy) and reunite with her father, Somalia has collapsed into bloody chaos and she is immediately taken back to Europe by a male cousin, considering herself now a member of the Somali diaspora, but for many years remains a lost soul, muted and a prey to self-mutilation because of her sense of loss of her father (who disappeared in the violence), of her national-cultural identity and even her sense of selfhood.

Like her cousin, Barni (the second female protagonist-narrator in Cristina Farah's text) also testifies to her affiliative[18] Somaliness – stating: "I hold my country close to my heart" (17), even if (as she says to the Italian journalist who is interviewing her about the Somali community in Rome) "my home is here" (16). Two of the narratives told by Barni demonstrate the paradoxical nature of Somali solidarity in exile. The first concerns her almost helplessly going to the aid of an unknown Somali man, injured in a fire and arrested on suspicion of terrorism – an act of charity and Somali fellow-feeling through which Barni ends up being reunited with her beloved cousin Domenica Axad, guided by the Somali social and familial network in Rome. The second concerns Barni's initially

---

[17] Identified in a footnote (which also dates the poem as a 1977 composition) as "Cabdulaqaadir Xirsi Siyaad, also known as 'Yamyam'" (1).

[18] I allude to Edward Said's distinction between what might be termed the "blood relation" or "passport identity" (the "filiative") and the chosen, elective, "affiliative" identity (*World* 22-24).

hostile and suspicious response to a woman she recognises as Somali, wearing earrings she instinctively identifies as probably those looted from her by reckless young thugs when the mayhem erupted back in Somalia and suggesting to her that the stranger is connected by clan to those youngsters and is therefore an "enemy" to her (Barni). The earrings turn out to have come to Ardo (the other woman) by chance, in Italy, and Barni and Ardo grow to be dear friends to each other – Barni at last admitting to herself that she had allowed her mind to be poisoned by the divisive clan loyalties that played a part in the dissolution of Somalia. She analyses the pull of clan hatred as a (false) duty and that is perpetuated by the fear of exiled Somalis of becoming disconnected from their people – "just a loose thread, with nothing to hold onto, no safety net" (152). Again, Somali unity is seen as strong and enduring, but beset by terrible internal fissures and enmities.

As in the other texts, Somali men's faults are highlighted and seen as exacerbated by exile, to which they are seen to acclimatise with much more difficulty than Somali women (29-30).[19] Barni states that "Islam is [now] taking on the fathers' [shirked] responsibilities" to their wives and children, for the exiled fathers "have washed their hands of them." Hence Barni insists that the now single Somali mothers do "what they can," disgustedly asking: "what kind of an example is a man who cannot even run his own life?" (228). However, Cristina Farah juxtaposes this anti-male diatribe with Barni's own description of how she and Domenica Axad met their old family friend, the saintly and fatherly Gaandi (so nicknamed for his Indian dress style and profound social commitment), in the Netherlands. He had come to Europe temporarily "to raise funds [as] he had chosen to [remain] in [ravaged] Somalia where his [medical; healing] skills were needed" (228). Gaandi is clearly an exemplary, ideal male Somali, selflessly dedicated to assisting his people's recovery. In Italy, the cousins' only surviving paternal uncle Foodcadde – the extended family's provider, in the past, in Somalia; in contrast with his two politically activist brothers, Barni and Domenica Axad's fathers, both now dead – remains a solid rock and takes on the role of their paterfamilias even for family members still living in Somalia, who phone him for advice. The cousins go and visit him in the distant Italian town where he lives, to allow this benign man to meet Domenica Axad's little son, the family's newest member. Domenica Axad yields to Barni's insistence that she also re-

---

19 See commentary on Nuruddin Farah's similarly reproving sense of Somali men's failure and weakness exacerbated by exile in his *Yesterday, Tomorrow* in a section of my "Surveying the Contours" (259-262).

connect with her Italian mother, from whom she had become estranged. Her dual (rather than hybrid) cultural heritage will be transmitted to her little son, to whom she will speak in Italian, but to whom she and Barni (with whom they now live) will at a later age also teach the Somali language. Domenica Axad also has the little boy circumcised – despite the disapproval of the Italian doctors – to "mark his [Somali] belonging on his body" (223).[20] The two women have nevertheless fully *settled* in Italy; as Barni insists, those who come to dwell in a country need to show appreciation for the generosity with which they are received and to interact with their new compatriots; it is not good to be "irrevocably separated from [one's] context" (225). In this text we hence see "Somaliness" remaining largely intact yet relocated transnationally. Domestically and socially, Somali speech predominates, but most women are shown to interact easily in Italian in professional and public spaces.

While I have delineated concerns with gender articulated in the three novels, above, I wish to engage further with this topic to see what these texts contribute to advancing insight about intertwinements of gender, nationality, race and class in the various settings which they portray, and how this can develop conceptualisation of the contemporary "Black Atlantic." Donna Gabaccia, a professor of history, comments that "Atlanticists [. . .] share with globalists the huge challenge of gendering their analyses of change and continuity" and need to explore interactions of class and racialisation, referring to "the badly needed gender analysis of transnational phenomena" (18). Editors Annalisa Oboe and Anna Scacchi, in their Introduction to *Recharting the Black Atlantic*, criticise Gilroy for "fail[ing] to take into proper consideration important identity markers such as class and gender," referring to Gilroy's "panorama of case studies focusing predominantly on middle-class male intellectuals born in the U.S." (4). In choosing the three novels for discussion in this article, their foregrounding of the experiences, insights and perceptions of African women was the most important consideration. Together, the many women's voices in the texts constitute a "Parliament of Women," or perhaps a special forum for the Somali perspective in an investigation of the ways in which the dispersal of African people impinges on women's lives. An important cautionary perspective on the gathering of "evidence" in contemporary engagements with issues of refugeeism and social collapse in the wake of war articulated by Didier Fassin, a former vice-president of *Médecins sans frontières*, may be taken into account at this point:

---

20 The boy's Somali father Taageere remains in the U.S., where he and Domenica Axad married, because of visa problems; he may or may not join them later.

> However, from the perspective of a politics of life and an ontology of inequality, the issue is not that the historical context and geopolitical dimensions of conflicts, the strategic games and contradictory interests, are erased by the representation of war situations given by those whose only interest is in the "insulted and humiliated," to use Brauman's formula. It is rather that if one believes that what distinguishes humans from other living beings is language and meaning and that what makes human life unique is therefore that it can be recounted, as Hannah Arendt asserts, then humanitarian testimony establishes two forms of humanity and two sorts of life in the public space: there are those who can tell stories and those whose stories can be told only by others. With this new dividing line, life is no longer, as it was before, biological (the life that is risked or sacrificed); it is henceforth biographical (the life that is lived but that others narrate). More tenuous and less visible, it is nevertheless essential to what constitutes beings insofar as they are human. At the very time when humanitarian action is shifting from bare life to qualified life, from physical survival to social existence, a new inequality is insinuating itself into humanitarian politics of life. (518)

Vaguely recalling Spivak's notorious unspeaking or gagged subaltern, Fassin's point is nevertheless a different one and I want to use it here to delineate a different consideration, also by "combining" it with certain observations articulated by Christine Sylvester in her essay "Development Studies and Postcolonial Studies." In the abstract for her article, Sylvester (who is herself a specialist in Development Studies) observes that "*development studies does not tend to listen to subalterns and postcolonial studies does not tend to concern itself with whether the subaltern is eating*"; she adds to this her opinion that: "*of the two fields, postcolonial studies has the greatest potential to be a new and different location of human development thinking if it can overcome a tendency to lock into intellectual rather than practical projects of postcolonialism*" (703; emphasis original). It is possible, I suggest, to use Sylvester's urging of postcolonial scholars to return focus to the "gathering [of] narratives of experience through literature" rather than endlessly "theorising postcoloniality" ("Development" 713) as a way of validating the many voices of the imagined characters (particularly the women's) in the chosen texts. Seen in this light, the privileged authors are not narrating *instead of*, but using the powerful energies of empathy generated by ineluctable awareness of the urgent plight of their people to constitute narratives that will draw attention to "real" people and to whether they eat. To come back to Maria Pia Lara, the role of narratives articulating the voices of overlooked people (often women, frequently African) in the public sphere is that, in being as vivid, irresistibly affective and articulate as our available works of creative writing can be, they contrast with the all too often "ignorable" qualities of primarily informative and statistical writing and the melodramatic nature of all too many media representations to reach minds and hearts. Novels of the kind examined here do important work in enlarging the public sphere of recognition.[21] As John Marx puts it, creative fiction "imagines a redistribution of the authority to describe atrocities" (599).

The latter remark is useful as a key to what Nuruddin Farah is doing by means of the imposing, invented female Somali figure of Cambara (in the novel *Knots*, which is throughout dominated in both plot and perspective by the actions, thoughts and feelings of this character) whom I read as the writer's emissary, created in order to start the process of re-imagining Somalia, or at least to present an hypothesis about how the recuperation process could be approached – with networking and art-work playing central parts, along with a firm repression of violence. Since Farah has throughout his extensive oeuvre indicated his diagnosis of the ills of his nation as rooted in the false and ultimately destructive belief in a proper social order being a phallocratic one, it is important and "necessary" that the leaders that in his text point the way to processes of national recovery should be female. It is necessary also to note that the initial impression of Cambara as a sort of "superhero" of near comic-book dimensions (or, say, resembling Lara Croft) is soon qualified when the novelist indicates that, stimulating as her presence is to further change and in helping to bring about healing and begin re-normalisation ("humanisation") of the deeply damaged society, she enters a field where much has been initiated long before she came back – alliances forged, co-operatives formed and healing work undertaken. Cambara is able to "plug into" and move into and along with these flows of social energy that have begun to refertilise the barren wasteland caused by the warlords and their

21 Lara writes of "[women's] narratives that offer a wider conception of 'agents' as moral subjects" (93); of "recognition" that must be achieved by "resignifying the spaces of appearance" (143) and of "[r]ecognition" as "a performative process of acquiring identity" by "us[ing the] institutionalized channels of communicating with others" in order to "[redefine] the limits on traditional views" (157). This, she suggests, can be achieved or effectively contributed to by novels and autobiographies.

henchmen along with the passivity and cowering fear they inculcated among the majority of Somalis. Significantly, the major network assisting her is that of the local "Women for Peace" organisation. In Nuruddin Farah's previous novel, *Links* (2003) he outlined how Bile (with his Irish friend Seamus assisting him) had set up and run The Refuge – a centre for healing, housing and feeding – in the immediate aftermath of the civil war that succeeded the fall of Barre. Although he is ill with appalling depression when she first encounters him, Bile recovers with Cambara's help and in return helps her to improve her play script and to direct rehearsals, as well as acting as onstage narrator in the play whose performance serves to re-unite and re-energise many of the unpaid "social workers" of this society – the great majority of whom are women. In Farah's novel *Maps* (1986) the term "misgendering" (161) occurs; a word indicative of how a macho culture and the undervaluing of its female citizens can skew an entire society and, if brought to a peak of domination, bring about its downfall. If (as Farah established in the course of his numerous interviews with exiled Somalis in *Yesterday, Tomorrow*) Somali women generally cope much better with the upheavals of exile than their male compatriots, it is clear that weakness, cruelty as well as a sort of masculine parasitism were both promoted and hidden by "masculine" posturing and swagger in the pre-war society. Cambara's husband's ruthless exploitation of her initial devotion, her cousin's meanness and resentment towards her, his vicious abuse of his wife and daughters and degenerate, passive lifestyle (to which he reverts upon his return to Mogadiscio) – as well as the relentless, violent warlords and criminalised (thieving, murderous and mayhem creating) youths whom they pay with *qaat* (a stimulant), ill-gotten gains and weaponry – are all of them the ugly fruits of this system; not only male favouring and denigratory towards women, but inducing mere reckless violence as properly "masculine" conduct. Heroism has a different make-up, Farah shows.

Perhaps the most poignant moment in *Knots* occurs when Cambara – wealthy and healthy, protected invisibly by a host of friends and well-wishers – hears the story of the woman Jiijo: bedraggled, exhausted and heavily pregnant with the child of the warlord who "saved" her by taking her as "his" woman after months of nightly rapes by whoever among his henchmen wanted to have sex. The warlord is described by Jiijo as having shown "kindness" to her even though he beat her up the night before her conversation with Cambara, since he did rescue her from the far worse fate of a "comfort woman" holed up in a tiny, dark room for the pleasure of his horde of hooligans, and is not often violent towards her. Jiijo's sad narrative, full of tragic eventualities ever since the end of her childhood as the favoured daughter of a city tailor, is described as "a tale, her own and the nation's"; a point confirmed when Cambara is startled to hear this woman of little education ask: "What help is there for our nation?" (180, 179). Cambara notices Jiijo's "strong sense of personhood" despite her tribulations, and this may be taken as the author's tribute to the downtrodden women of this nation who even in their wretchedness have a sufficiently strong social awareness to sense that their plight exemplifies their nation's sickness and to feel concern for the larger society and the many other tragic tales that make up the national narrative. Jiijo's integrity contrasts with some of the other "veterans" of the civil war whom Cambara has encountered, who "tell the tales of their woes as though they were medals they wear to a gathering of fellow sufferers" and seem to "revel in excluding those, like her, who have not endured the physical and mental pain of the strife" (298). Cambara believes that part of her Somali husband's cruelty towards herself when "dejected" by his memories of the war could be a weak man's scapegoating of an available woman – as if to regain a sense of power and to exact emotional vengeance for his past humiliations (unfairly, on someone not responsible for them). Like her vile cousin beating up his wife and daughters in Canada and (after time in jail there) scuttling back to Somalia to sink into a lazy life dominated by his *quaat* habit, this is another example of Black Atlantic dispersal "exporting" Somali gender injustice to North America – rather than creatively combining with local cultures there. What these examples illustrate is that transplanting of traditional socio-cultural practices may as easily preserve bad habits as stimulate cultural growth.

In *Offspring of Paradise*, Safi Abda depicts some of the most devastating effects of an "exported," profoundly damaging Afro-Somali memory affecting self-image. In Somalia, the despotic rule of Barre and his nepotistic practices produced the label or curse of the word *faqash* (a Somali term meaning 'rubbish') which was applied to the dictator's clan after the toppling of his rule and in the resulting mayhem. This denunciation quickly began to be applied to everyone and anyone who could be associated with his clan even if they had opposed his rule; it began to function, as in other historical contexts (Rwanda; Bosnia; Nazi Germany come to mind) as the validation for genocidal murder and rape sprees by violent and terrified men to prove that they were on the right side. Abdi's seemingly artlessly narrated novel is brilliantly contrived to show the spread of the use of this term as the mayhem expands and the social insanity of the civil war intensifies – the term tolls through the text with its ominous freight of disgust, outlaw status and "exterminability" (3, 16, 17, 19, 20, 21, 24,

28, 29, 30, 31, 36, 47). It is used by a former close friend and neighbour to steal Hana's uncle's escape vehicle; by Mulki's brother to eject her dearest friend into the wilderness (where she disappears – probably kidnapped, gang raped and murdered); eventually, "everyone had become a *faqash*" in "the hell fire that they all called home" (36). In this cauldron, "the killing and maiming of all forms of life became the norm, and the dishonouring of women an honourable feat" (17).

When Hana and her *Ayeyo* (grandmother) are given asylum in an unnamed northern country after two years on the run as fugitives, the television in their small flat abounds with "[w]retched images of Somali women and children" (11), and the child obscurely associates all the women with her lost mother, saying "I know her, [. . .] [s]he has no one to run to" and "[h]er baby will die." *Ayeyo* simply says: "[s]he is us, Hana" (11). By the time Hana is fifteen and the disturbed local woman Helen begins her campaign to convert this Muslim girl to Christianity, she is extremely vulnerable to the anti-Somali and anti-Muslim propaganda of this "dear friend" (who has carefully won her trust by moving into the yawning emotional gap left by *Ayeyo*'s death). Hana's first encounter with contempt as her "inherited" lot occurs at school, where a classmate calls her "dark skull" (275). When Helen more-or-less kidnaps the child to the distant country estate of the director of their group (who call themselves "*the carriers of the cross*"), she begins her process of "softening Hana up" with the aim of getting her to reject her Muslim faith by showing TV clips of the theft of food convoys to aid the starving in Somalia; raided and confiscated by "some crazy clansmen down in Hamar" (Hamar, sometimes spelt Xamar, is Somalis' more usual name for Mogadiscio) (270). Hana tries to resist by reminding Helen that "Christian" Serbs also indulged in mass rape and murder of Muslim Bosnians – i.e. not only Muslim people are villainous. But Helen cannot help being shamed and distressed by these reminders of what her people did ("Hana's head is itching again" [272]) as Helen piles on the televised images of skeletal, starving children and humanitarian aid provided by Westerners. On these reminders of "the African drama" in Hana's country of origin Helen builds the claim: "We feed you. We clothe you and you owe us your life" (270). Though Hana with some feistiness insists on her own inherent worth ("*I am a person*," she says [274; emphasis original]), Helen's tactless reference to Hana's "soul" as having "dropped" into her sphere evidently triggers the obscure and probably repressed memory of the *faqash* label, so that Hana "translates" Helen's words, saying to herself: "*Yes, that's what I'm to Helen, some droppings from Africa! To be molded* [. . .] *into any form the finders wished*" (269; emphasis original). Much later, when Hana has been rescued from Helen and her evident intent to murder Hana, should the girl continue to resist Christian conversion, Hana is still plagued by "a deep feeling of abandonment – a sunken feeling she'd carried for so long" (343); a sense that "[her] people let [her] down." This is why she says: "By the time I came to the gates of this nation, I was a reject, and Helen found a reject" and later, again: "to her, I was nothing but some droppings from heaven" (342, 348). The title of Abdi's text, *Offspring of Paradise*, is probably intended as the Islamic words of comfort Hana needs to remember – and will, eventually, the text suggests.

While her *Ayeyo* was still alive, Hana had made a project of recording everything she remembered about their life in Somalia, and everything her grandmother would tell her. *Ayeyo* muses: "*It's her heritage, a fallen nation's legacy to her own; let the poor citizen record*" (83; emphasis original). Her choice of the term 'citizen' is revealing; it functions as an implicit recognition of status that overrides gender and age prejudice and bestows the right to know and evaluate (and if appropriate, to indict) her nation. Later on, as the terrible memories of Hana's father's assassination, the shooting of her uncle, (obscurely) the violent attack that led to her mother fleeing into the wilderness and the two years (in Somalia) of the homeless wanderings of grandmother and granddaughter unspool, *Ayeyo* says: "*There is no escape for Hana, but to wrap herself up in the* shroud *of her heritage; the only shroud handed down to her by her nation*" (88; emphasis original). The notion of an African cultural inheritance is real here, as *Ayeyo*'s words indicate that Hana's national origins are indelible, yet it is also, clearly, a terrible heritage with which she is burdened and with which she will have to learn to cope – as she does, eventually, the text suggests. While this awful "shroud" cannot be discarded, it is also a form of "cultural clothing" in a foreign land. Hana's grandmother's caring love, her responsible, supportive role throughout Hana's childhood and early adolescence, her deep dignity and piety, are, after all, also an inheritance that has been brought from their African land of origin to sustain them both in the new country. And even though it takes a long time for her to learn to understand and appreciate it, Hana eventually comes to see that Mulki was rightly given the role of her guardian after *Ayeyo*'s death. Alongside the many admirable women[22] portrayed by Safdi – and in equal con-

---

22 There are other examples, such as Amina, the woman who saves the (then) crazed Asha (Hana's mother) from the roadside, nurses her wounds and takes her to live with in her family home, where Asha slowly recovers her sanity and from where

trast with the trigger-happy thugs who overran Somalia after the tyrant Barre's fall – are the fine men such as Hana's father and uncle; Mulki's father, and Abdirahman, who is the imam of their refugee community.

The two leading women protagonists in Cristina Ali Farah's *Little Mother* are also depicted as being in a mutually care-taking relationship – in Italy, as they were as children in Somalia. Farah's title is the rendition (in the Italian language when she wrote the text, as in the English translation) of a Somali term for one's maternal aunt, and it indicates how the strong and lovely tradition of familial cherishing is maintained in the new country, across the "Black" Mediterranean. Barni – even though she early on lost first her father (shot by a firing squad) and then her mother (who could be said to have died of despair, in a household fire not long after) and even though she is not much older than Domenica Axad – had always been the main person assisting her cousin and helping her over her adjustment problems whenever she came back from visits to Italy (her mother's country) and temporarily forgot how to speak Somali. In contrast with the long-lasting refugee status of Hana and her *Ayeyo* (who are very poor after they lost everything in the upheaval of the civil war), Barni and her cousin are fairly well off in Italy after an initial period – of traumatised apathy in Domenica Axad's and of quite lowly jobs as a carer for the elderly in Barni's case. They both become successful professionals; Domenica Axad as documentary filmmaker and editor and Barni as a midwife employed at a leading hospital. In this they contrast with Cristina Farah's third narrator, Taageere, who moves from one low-paying job to another and has lost the social status he had in Somalia. In the adult lives of both women, their Somali connectedness (as outlined in previous sections of this article) remains central. Barni especially, by hosting get-togethers for her friends and cooking them dinners, keeps the networks of "Somaliness" going in Italy, whereas Domenica Axad joins a former (male) acquaintance in a major project of documenting exiled Somalis' lives on film. Like them, Farah's third protagonist Taageere, whose second wife Domenica Axad becomes after they met at a few Somali gatherings in the US, is concerned with "maintaining Somaliness" in the States. Unlike the women, who are happy to adopt a freer lifestyle (of dressing much more "daringly" and less conventional-

---

she is later taken to be reunited with Hana in the northern country. With the Somali women's conduct may be contrasted the condescending, would-be charitable, but (culturally and historically) dangerously ignorant group of women of northern origin who aim to "help" the Somali and other refugee women at the "tea parties" they hold for them out of idle "do-goodery."

ly; smoking and having the occasional glass of wine) in the West, Taageere is shocked to see young Somali girls walking about fairly scantily (in his view, scandalously) dressed. His sexism is cunningly exposed by the author (who does also indicate his more endearing qualities of enthusiasm, loyalty to friends and caring attitude to children and the elderly) during his garrulous and quite one-way "conversation" with his ex-wife, who lives in Italy with their nine-year-old son – whom he has never either seen or paid support for. Shukri (the ex-wife) is told that the boy is his (the biological father's) "possession" (65) and will remain such, and that she is thought a prostitute (a *sharmuuto* [63]) because she lives with a European, even though the latter converted to Islam and they got married by Muslim rites. This is another illustration of differences in the "trends" of male and female Somali behaviour in the new country (as Nuruddin Farah, too, indicated), i.e. that the men tend to be more rigid and unadaptive and expect to be able to cling to entrenched, culturally validated patriarchal privileges and abuses and are generally less successful émigrés.

However, it is to Taageere that Cristina Farah gives the role of commemorating Mogadiscio[23] in some moving passages; he, too, uses the image of a shroud to indicate how "personally" the loss of homeland is registered by Somalis, opening chapter 5 of *Little Mother* with the words "Xamar, shrouded in silence" (120) – Xamar (or Hamar) being Somalis' alternative, "intimate" name for Mogadiscio. He felt that shrouding silence first when the city was under siege by the marauders who murdered, stole and invaded homes, but the image applies also as he looks back at the now destroyed community that was there –"*Xamar waa lagu xumeeyay*. Xamar, they have ruined you," he says, and "*Xamar waa lagu xumeeyay*. Xamar, they have defiled you"[24] – the words slightly differently translated in the text in the second instance. Taageere recalls Mogadiscio as a city "where everyone lived in peace and harmony, in safety and in freedom"; as a "[m]agnificent city on the African coast," but where, "because of the blood and strife these same brothers are fighting among themselves" (127) – a situation he, too, had to flee into the wretchedness of exile and social drifting.

---

23 Unlike in Nuruddin Farah's novel, the translation of the city's name in *Little Mother* is spelt Mogadishu (see glossary, 345); this text also spells the "nickname" of the city differently to the way Abdi does: Abdi's characters call the city Hamar; in Cristina Ali Farah's novel this is spelt Xamar. (The Somali language only acquired its own orthography in the 70s.)

24 Compare Ardo's words to Barni: "The worst thing about this war is the hate it has created between us. [. . .] Mogadishu was a great city, [. . .] [e]veryone lived there" (*Little Mother* 146).

Because the novel focuses on a return from Canada to Somalia of a protagonist who was absent from her country of origin during the outbreak and main part of the civil war there, Nuruddin Farah's *Knots* does not have as much to say as the other two novels about the horrors of that time or about the pain of exile. Elsewhere, Farah (who was himself living elsewhere for that period) does write movingly about the experience of exile from Somalia, which for Somalis means not only being distanced from what was their country, but being deprived of any country they can call their own. Among the many gradations of the African diaspora this must count as one of the most anguishing positions. Farah asks: "what becomes of a person – indeed what becomes of a people – when the country as hypothesis ceases to function. How [. . .] full of inexpressible agony is the instant when it dawns on one that one's country does not exist any more, either as an idea or as a physical reality!" (*Yesterday* 49).

Because of the time gap between (forced) departure from Africa and the formation of the hybrid cultural forms he describes as flourishing in the West, Gilroy's text does not touch on two effects of more recent displacement from the continent (and from Somalia in particular) that Cristina Farah's and Safi Abdi's novels strongly foreground – viz. the horror of the social disintegration of the African society on its home soil, and the profound yearning, nostalgic longing for and deep sense of loss of what had been a sheltering, complex modern African culture that is felt in the new (Western) context. One sees it in the quotes asserting Somali pride in its own distinct social ethos that Domenica Axad intersperses in her opening chapter (*Little Mother* 1-11) and in the enquiries about loved places in pre-war Mogadiscio which a Somali woman returning there from abroad puts to Asha (Hana's mother) at Dubai airport, where their paths cross as Asha is waiting for the flight that will take her away to a reunion with Hana after the years of separation. "'Soon, you'll find a foothold in the ruins'" (*Offspring* 336), Asha reassures her chance companion. She is kindly softening the shock this woman is likely to experience when she sees the now "derelict" buildings and "the broken neighbourhood where women worked like horses. And men grazed like cows [presumably, chewing *qaat*] – that's when they weren't chasing each other down the street with their machine guns, or whatever other ammunition under their disposal" (330). Hana's *Ayeyo* recalls (in their flat in "the wall," long after they have joined the refugee community) that moment when she saw her eldest son (Hana's father), just returned from worshipping at the mosque, "shatter[ing] like a crystal glass" as the assassin's bomb hit him, and Hana, thinking of the same moment, "sees" first herself (a little girl in "a flowered dress with puffy sleeves") then "smells" "the stench of fire and smoke, and then, [hears] the deafening cry of [her mother,] a pregnant woman splashed with [her husband's] blood and rubble" (*Offspring* 84). To balance these terrible remembered moments, Safi Abdi depicts Mulki (who lives in the neighbouring flat) lovingly mending her traditional Somali garments; cooking the dishes of her national culinary tradition and listening to "the richness of her mother tongue" (108) in the recordings of Somali poetry and music.

> She shed tears of joy for having been part of an era of songs and good humor, of Thursday trysts on the beaches, and of Friday lunches taken under the cool shade. Oh, how sorry she felt for Hana and her generation for having known so little, if anything, with which to water down the complete disorder of the [present] day! (*Offspring* 109)

In *Little Mother*, Barni is shown to be haunted by images of poor Somali refugees drowning in shipwrecks[25] as they try to escape from their devastated country (like her aunt Xaliima, who raised Barni after her own mother's death, who is drowned along with several nephews and nieces and hundreds of other fleeing Somalis):

> Boats have been coming and unloading illegal immigrants along Italian coastlines for a long time now [she tells the journalist who is interviewing her]. The tides go in and out and the beaches keep filling up with garbage [using that symbolically loaded word much as Hana did in Abdi's text]: tomato cans, shards of green glass, small tubes of medicine, clumps of tar, and plastic bags, more and yet more plastic bags. And, carried by the sea, lifeless bodies, wearing tattered clothes, their purplish skin blotched with white salt. (14)

The final, harrowing detail (above) carries considerable symbolic freight, and the passage as a whole is one of a deep mourning, not only for the dead (known and unknown), but for the entire, rubbished society.[26] Barni does not seem an

---

25 Lombardi-Diop discusses how, in recent Somali texts written in Italian, the Atlantic slave trade is a ghostly echo (see her chapter in Oboe and Scacchi [162-180]).

26 Compare (in Abdi's text) the use of the term *faqash* (discussed earlier) – both Abdi and Cristina Farah conveying the horror of people reduced to mere rubbish – not only dehumanised, but redefined as discardable, even as pollutants needing to be cleansed from society. Compare the postcolonial Zimbabwean government's term "Operation Gukurahundi" (meaning: 'clear out the rubbish') for the brutal

especially devout Muslim and lives a fairly secular life, but when she tries to help the traumatised, unknown Somali burn victim, struck temporarily mute (who was brought to the hospital where she works), she soothes him by telling him a long tale of the Prophet's mildness and forgiving nature – in implicit contrast with the multiple acts of male vengeance and counter-vengeance that brought Somalia to ruin. As it turns out, the patient (arrested on "terrorism" charges) is himself a protective and tender-hearted man who had attempted to rescue Taageere's sister and her baby from a car wreck that had caught fire in which he thought them trapped. Mostly happy in Rome, Barni goes to the Termini station from time to time because so many Somalis gather there, for that is where she can (in her own resonant words) "plunge her arm again into the burning pools, the pools of memory and separation" (26). Barni is strongly aware of how much harder exile is on Somali men than on women; the men seem "lost" (30) in the new countries. Taageere, for his part, refers to the emotional effect of exclusion from the home country as "a deep and shabby sadness" (57).[27] Elsewhere he speaks of the "immense" and "terrible sadness, depression" (71) that was experienced by a Somali woman of his acquaintance, isolated in icy Finland with many children and a feckless husband. What he felt as exile, Taageere says, was not "rage but disgust" (84) – a self-disgust into which he was sunk for a long time before his budding relationship and marriage with Domenica Axad rescued him from this apathy. She for her part describes "the insanity of feeling lost" (87); of feeling "disgusted with [her]self" and "empty to the very core"(88) after her abortive attempt to revisit Somalia. She realises that she was in fact "sick from too much loneliness" (96). Taageere elsewhere applies a term from an anecdote to the "uprooted" condition: it is like being "expropriated" (170). He even says that "people who are in exile for a long time end up going mad" (178). But Taageere also illustrates the moral pitfalls that male Somalis seem especially prone to – not providing for his (separated) first wife and their son; engaging in foolish money-making schemes and getting arrested – teetering on the edge of serious drug dealing and attendant violence. Domenica Axad, who had abortively attempted to return to Somalia and reunite with her father just as the violent chaos erupted, completely associates herself with the diaspora. She

---

post-election campaign in the Matabeleland region, which took on genocidal proportions. The term "ethnic cleansing," which we use far too glibly, certainly carries the same overtones.

27 One recalls the opening words of Edward Said's essay "Reflections on Exile": "Exile is strangely compelling to think about but terrible to experience" (172).

says that she "internalized its makeup, the absence of a vision, its lack of goals" and its emotional condition of "bewilderment" (217).

Perhaps – as Amina (her rescuer) had said to Asha (Hana's mother) – it will be the "women of this land [who] must overcome, someday, if it be by the grace of Allah" – words that Asha quotes back to Amina at their sad parting (*Little Mother* 329). In *Offspring of Paradise*, we learn that her *Ayeyo* had reassured Hana over and over: "He will look after you Who created you from nothing" (91). In the same text the words of the Prophet of Islam are quoted (as epigraph to one of the chapters): "*That person is not of us who inviteth others to aid him in oppression; and he is not of us who fighteth for his tribe in injustice; and he is not of us who dieth in assisting his tribe in tyranny*" (qtd. in *Little Mother* 51; emphasis original). To indicate something of the complexity and deep historical roots of the Somali crisis, Hana's *Ayeyo* tells her, as a point which "we are all now [only] beginning to understand," that "the malfunction of [Somali] society did not come by chance," but that "there's a whole history behind that demise," with the hope that one day far into the future, Hana might be able to understand and even forgive her people's faults. *Ayeyo* may be alluding to the historical fissures of the Somali people into different colonial enclaves after defeat and invasion by Europeans. The quoted words are her verbal legacy to Hana; words on a tape that gets played to Hana (on *Ayeyo*'s instructions) after her death. She also tells Hana there: "Hana, Allah does not change the condition of people until they change that which is in themselves" (113).

The three texts discussed in this article have, I believe, much to contribute to various necessary and perhaps overdue extensions and adaptations of the "Black Atlantic" concept as we at the present juncture attempt to return Africa and the African continent and countries to a more central position from the half-forgotten rim (periphery, in both space and time) to which Gilroy's important initiating theorisation of the results of large-scale human dispersal from Africa inadvertently seemed to assign it. They are rich texts that stimulate questioning thought and deepen understanding in the ways I have attempted to illustrate and many more. Christine Sylvester wrote in a 1999 article:

> There are plenty of critiques and dreams of development circulating ambivalently in the villages and urban areas of specific Third World locales. The challenge is to reach into those spaces, pull out and analyse the stuff of everyday postcolonial deprivation and desire. And with that knowledge should come plenty of forgiveness – and perhaps some hope too. ("Development" 703)

As the above explorations of their novels show, this is what the three Somali novelists do in and with their texts. It is not helpful to anyone to write off *any* people as "beyond redemption" or any society as irretrievably shattered. Nuruddin Farah, Safi Abdi and Cristina Ali Farah all teach us, great novelists that they are, that the recovery of Somalia is the business of Somalis in the first place, but that this society in its history and in its present, deserves our considered empathy and respect. Vile deeds there have been, but moral anger and denunciation are the right of "the wronged souls of [the] land" (Abdi's dedication), not of self-righteous outsiders. And with the deep and enduring Somali connectedness that all three of these novelists recognise and depict, there is indeed a possibility of "forgiveness" and of "hope." The novelists take up the same sort of duty as that with which *Ayeyo* charged Hana on her death-bed: "Write, for none else will record [the Somali woman's] misery" (95); they also record and archive the larger nation's faults and sorrows and their aspiration for the nation and the land to recover from devastation.

Works Cited

Abdi, Safi.*Offspring of Paradise*. Miami: 1stBooks Library, 2003.

Bakhtin, Mikhail M. "Forms of Time and of the Chronotope in the Novel." *The Dialogic Imagination: Four Essays.* Trans. C. Emerson and M. Holquist. Austin: University of Texas Press, 1981. 84-258.

Brooks, Rosa Ehrenreich. "Failed States, or the State as Failure?" *University of Chicago Law Review* 72.4 (Fall 2005): 1159-1196.

Chan, Stephen. "On the Uselessness of New Wars Theory: Lessons from African Conflicts." *Experiencing War*. Ed. Christine Sylvester. London and New York: Routledge, 2011. 94-102.

Chrisman, Laura. "Black Modernity, Nationalism, and Transnationalism: The Challenge of Black South African Poetry." *Beyond the Black Atlantic: Relocating Modernization and Technology*. Ed. Walter Goebel and Saskia Schabio. London and New York: Routledge, 2006. 29-46.

Farah, Cristina Ali. *Little Mother*. 2007. Trans. Giovanna Bellesia-Contuzzi and Victoria Offredo Poletto. Bloomington and Indiana: Indiana UP, 2011.

Farah, Nuruddin. *A Naked Needle*. London: Heinemann, 1976.

___. *Knots*. New York: Riverhead Books (Penguin), 2007.

___. *Links*. Cape Town: Kwela Books, 2003.

___. *Maps*. New York: Pantheon/Picador, 1986.

___. *Sardines*. London: Heinemann, 1981.

___. *Sweet and Sour Milk*. London: Heinemann, 1979.

___. *Yesterday, Tomorrow: Voices from the Somali Diaspora*. London and New York: Cassell, 2000.

Fassin, Didier. "Humanitarianism as a Politics of Life." *Public Culture* 19.3 (2007): 499-520.

Gabbacia, Donna. "A Long Atlantic in a Wider World." *Atlantic Studies* 1.1 (2004): 1-27.

Gagiano, Annie. "Farah's *Sardines*: Women in a Context of Despotism." *Africa Today* 57.3 (Spring 2011): 259-282.

___. "Surveying the Contours of 'a country in exile': Nuruddin Farah's Somalia." *African Identities* 4.2 (2006): 251-268.

Gilroy, Paul. *The Black Atlantic: Modernity and Double Consciousness*. Cambridge, Mass.: Harvard UP, 1993.

Gikandi, Simon. "Africa, Diaspora, and the Discourse of Modernity." Introduction. *Research in African Literatures* 27.4 (Winter 1996): 1-5.

Girmay, Aracelis. "Elegy in Gold." *Kingdom Animalia*. By Girmay. New York: BOA Editions, 2011. 75.

Goebel, Walter, and Saskia Scabio, eds. *Beyond the Black Atlantic: Relocating Modernity and Technology*. London and New York: Routledge, 2006.

Lara, Maria Pia. *Moral Textures: Feminist Narratives in the Public Sphere*. Berkeley, Los Angeles and London: University of California Press, 1998.

Locke, John. *Two Tracts on Government*. Ed. Philip Abrams. Cambridge: Cambridge UP, 1967.

Lombardi-Diop, Cristina. "Ghosts of Memories, Spirits of Ancestors: Slavery, the Mediterranean, and the Atlantic." *Recharting the Black Atlantic: Modern Cultures, Local Communities, Global Connections*. Ed. Annalisa Oboe and Anna Scacchi. New York and London: 2008. 162-180.

Masilela, Ntongela. "The 'Black Atlantic' and African Modernity in South Africa. *Research in African Literatures* 27.4 (Winter 1996): 88-95.

Masterson, John. *The Disorder of Things: A Foucauldian Approach to the Work of Nuruddin Farah*. Johannesburg: Wits UP, 2013.

Marx, John. "Failed-State Fiction." *Contemporary Literature* 49.4 (2008): 597-633.

Oboe, Annalisa, and Anna Scacchi. "Black Bodies, Practices and Discourses around the Atlantic." Introduction. *Recharting the Black Atlantic: Modern Cultures, Local Communities, Global Connections*. Ed. Oboe and Scacchi. London and New York: Routledge, 2008.1-8.

O'Reilly, William. "Genealogies of Atlantic History." *Atlantic Studies* 1.1 (2004): 66-84.

Owomoyela, Oyekan. "Lost in Transit: Africa in the Trench of the Black Atlantic." *Recharting the Black Atlantic*. Ed. Annalisa Oboe and Anna Scacchi. London and New York: Routledge, 2008. 238-257.

Said, Edward. "Reflections on Exile." *Reflections on Exile and Other Essays*. Cambridge, Mass.; Harvard UP, 2000. 72-183.

___. *The World, the Text and the Critic*. Cambridge, Mass.: Harvard UP, 1983.

Spivak, Gayatri Chakravorty. "Can the Subaltern Speak?" *Marxism and the Interpretation of Culture*. Ed. C. Nelson and L. Grossberg. London: Macmillan, 1988. 271-313.

Sylvester, Christine. "Development Studies and Postcolonial Studies: Disparate tales of the 'Third World.'" *Third World Quarterly* 20.4 (1999): 703-721.

___."Pathways to Experiencing War." *Experiencing War*. Ed. Sylvester. London and New York: Routledge, 2011. 118-130.

Achebe's Children: Resonance, Poignance and Grandeur

Although primarily composed as a contribution to the celebration of the fiftieth anniversary of its publication, this essay is also an academic reconsideration of what *Things Fall Apart* communicates to us as Africans throughout the continent (and also beyond it) in a later time. Hence its title, Achebe's children, does double duty.

In numerous recent novels, African authors depict the fate of the continent's children. In reconsidering *Things Fall Apart*, it became apparent that here, too, as in so many spheres, Achebe has been a pioneer of African letters. But in tracing how carefully, how profoundly attentively Achebe depicts the children who feature in this novel, it seemed that some of the implications of his doing so have been underemphasised or simply unnoticed. From this perspective, Achebe's first novel can been seen as a non-apocalyptic, non-nostalgic text, allowing the recognition that in it, as much as in his more obviously "contemporary" novels, Achebe is addressing the present as well as the future and a primarily African audience.

There is a great deal of "benign mischief" (*Anthills* 125; italics removed) in Achebe's writing and in his "implied relationship" with readers and critics. The traces of his occasional teasing are the confirmation of the multidimensionality and confidence of his art. For as Bakhtin says: "Everything that is truly great must include an element of laughter. Otherwise it becomes threatening, terrible, or pompous; in any case, it is limited" (135). Achebe's own writing provides a motto for this essay. It reads: "they sought in their work to capture the past as well as invent a future." This does not come from one of Achebe's essays on the nature of Igbo art, but is a comment on the urban signwriters who decorate public transport buses in the imagined city of Bassa (which closely resembles Lagos) depicted in *Anthills of the Savannah* (201). In this his latest novel, a text insistently critical of class divisions, Achebe's guiding signals would indicate that with this description of popular, contemporary urban art the author is unobtrusively saying something important about his own art, too – an art whose analysis has sometimes overemphasised Achebe's concern with the past,[1] partly of course because of the overwhelming impact of his first novel and its compelling

---

[1] In an interview with Lindfors, Achebe states the following: "while the African intellectual was busy displaying the past culture of Africa, the troubled peoples of Africa were already creating new revolutionary cultures which took into account their present conditions" (5).

portrayal of the Igbo past. The awareness of the significance of contemporary popular art expressed in the quotation just cited may also recall Achebe's own modest insistence elsewhere (in a 1984 interview): "I don't think any nation is saved by reading one book," and of his recognition of the need for "a long period of exploration and debate" ("Mapping" 25) during which new social forms can gestate and solidify.

Perspectives from three writers originating from geographically very diverse spaces create a frame for the detailed discussion of those aspects of *Things Fall Apart* which are explored in this paper. The first is the critic Olakunle George, a graduate of Ibadan University who is at present Associate Professor of English and Africana Studies at Brown University in the U.S.A. Several of the points raised in his *Relocating Agency: Modernity and African Letters* (2003) illuminate my own critical route. He cautions that, in aligning African letters with "tradition" as against "modernity," we may place our continent's people in the position of an "Other" eternally panting behind the so-called "advanced West" to "catch up" – and that even notions of postcoloniality may trap us into this space (74). He enjoins us instead to "put 'Africa' at the center of an adventure of human minds; [. . .] as the occasion and subject (rather than incidental backcloth or object) of human minds contemplating human affairs" (101). In his recognition that our "creative writers" have "all along been theorists of agency" (104), George signals towards the reading of *Things Fall Apart* that sees the novel representing and reporting on an ongoing African saga in which European colonialism was indisputably a destructive intervention *and* a stimulus to change, but ultimately merely an interruption. George's comments link back to Achebe's own reminder of the need for taking a "long enough view" (interview with Serumaga 17)[2] when assessing the cost of ruin. I address *Things Fall Apart* as a text in which its successors – the four subsequent novels that move towards the present and gesture towards the future – are already embryonically present. George instructs us to "listen closely to storytellers who happen to be African, telling stories designed to get a handle on our shared insecurities *in modernity*" (188; em-

2 Achebe makes the point that, "if you take a long enough view" of cultural or national devastation, you are able to recognise that "society is, in fact, adjusting [be]cause life must go on, no matter what we say" (interview with Serumaga 17). In an earlier commentary on Achebe's vision in *Things Fall Apart*, I drew attention to the author's significant identification of *Things Fall Apart* as a "sceptical" work (*Morning* 4; qtd. in Gagiano, *Achebe* 59), an adjective that should assist recognition that Achebe in his first novel does not simply valorise the Igbo past; that its "sceptic[ism]" extends, so to speak, backwards as well as forwards.

phasis added). Through listening closely to what is said about and by its children, *Things Fall Apart* too can be heard to articulate concerns with contemporary and even future African modernities.

The second critical voice invoked here is that of Mudrooroo, the great Australian writer. Mudrooroo has written:

> A state [i.e. condition; a state of mind], either mental or mythical, lies underneath the ordinary day-to-day consciousness of the Aboriginal character, which sometimes erupts to give certain passages a surreal quality. This again contradicts a first facile reading which sees these texts as simply realist, naturalist, or social realist. This recognition of an atemporal state in itself leads to mixed genre. (*Writing* 172)

Reminiscent of the recognition that anthropologising readings of Achebe's texts have often been reductive, Mudrooroo's word "atemporal" insists that representations of aboriginality are not locked into one set past. Elsewhere, Mudrooroo writes that "history is the past reconstructed for an ever-increasing series of presents" (*Us* 177). It has been said of Mudrooroo that he succeeds not only in creating "a polyphonic dialogue of voices in one time, but a polyphonic cross section of times and spaces" that is "pan-Indigenous" (Archer-Lean 222). Recurrent, persistent engagements with the profundities of Achebe's first novel are sufficient proof that the same quality of polyphonic, pan-Indigenous vision ascribed to Mudrooroo is discernible in this text.

The expression "polyphonic dialogue" in the previous citation recalls the ideas of Mikhail Bakhtin, the influential Russian theorist of the novel who is the third commentator here brought to bear on *Things Fall Apart*. Bakhtin (who died in 1975) makes no reference to African authors and probably never read Achebe. He first developed his theories about what he came to call the "dialogic imagination" in writing about Dostoevsky, and later about Rabelais. Nevertheless, other Achebe critics (such as Kwadwo Osei-Nyame) have also brought this Russian modernist into their analyses of *Things Fall Apart*. The text invoked here is a collection of Bakhtin's meditations titled *Speech Genres and Other Late Essays*, published in English translation in 2004.

In one of these essays, Bakhtin writes that "trying to understand and explain a work solely in terms of the conditions of its epoch alone [. . .] will never enable us to penetrate into its semantic depths," since "works break through the boundaries of their own time, they live in centuries, that is, great time [. . .]". In the same essay Bakhtin writes that literary works "frequently [gain] in significance" and "are enriched with new meanings" as time passes; in the case of great works not merely because new perspectives are provided by new circumstances, but "because of that which actually has been *and continues to be found*" (4; emphasis added) in such texts themselves. Bakhtin actually recommends a readerly position of "outsideness" (7) in the study of a text depicting a culture (like that examined in *Things Fall Apart*). One could extend the notion to a writer depicting such a culture, for (writes Bakhtin): "we raise new questions for a foreign culture" and even: "without *one's own* questions one cannot creatively understand anything other or foreign" (7; emphasis original). The term "foreign" must here be taken to apply also to anyone writing about a text concerned with an earlier period, even the past of one's own culture. Hence Bakhtin's idea can be adapted to suggest that to reconsider and re-interpret a text originating from or depicting another time is not only valid and possibly helpful to the greater understanding of that text itself and of its time, but will be a likely contribution to our understanding of our own time and circumstances. Rereading the great work after the lapse of years (if it is great) will throw its light on the reader's present and future, enlarging and enriching his and her understanding. In Bakhtin's words, "there is neither a first nor a last word and there are no limits to the dialogic context" (170). In these late writings, Bakhtin begins to extend the notion of dialogism to the effective interactions between the text and its innumerable, ever-changing reading contexts that manifest themselves as time goes by. This links with Achebe's own insistence that "art is, and was always, in the service of man" (*Morning* 19); we do not experience *Things Fall Apart* as a text limited either to the time of its setting or that of its publication.

But neither Achebe nor Bakhtin is suggesting that art serves humankind or any particular society merely by soothing or reassuring those who encounter it. Bakhtin elsewhere in the collection cited here also states: "This meaning (in the unfinalized context) cannot be peaceful and cozy (one cannot curl up comfortably and die within it)" (160)![3] If one combines Achebe's comment about art being in the service of man with another of his (from a 1984 interview) in which he said: "And ultimately, I think what literature is about is that there shall not be misrule" ("Mapping" 25), it becomes possible to see that Achebe has no intention of being a comforting artist – neither for African, nor for colonising nations.

---

3 Compare a sentence not often noticed in Fanon's *The Wretched of the Earth*: "The important theoretical problem is that it is necessary at all times and in all places to make explicit, to demystify, and to harry the insult to mankind *that exists in oneself*" (246; emphasis added).

At the same time, his characterisation of "the novelist as teacher" has been distorted by those critics who lose sight of Achebe's own very circumspect and sparing use of the terms "art," "literature" and "novelist". Subtlety and obliqueness, a complex interplay of ideas and often taxing emotional paradoxes (for readers of as much as persons depicted in his novels) characterise his writing – as many *other* critics have indeed demonstrated.

In approaching Achebe's depiction of children in *Things Fall Apart* it is necessary to start briefly with Okonkwo. Four brief sentences will do:

> Okonkwo ruled his household with a heavy hand. His wives, especially the youngest, lived in perpetual fear of his fiery temper, and so did his little children. Perhaps down in his heart Okonkwo was not a cruel man. But his whole life was dominated by fear, the fear of failure and of weakness. (9)

As a very important diagnostician of society, Achebe has often provided more explicit analyses of social issues in his essays and interviews than in the complex, layered ironies of his novels. For readers and critics, such "non-literary" comments can provide (on occasion) a type of toolkit to facilitate articulation and recognition of particular aspects of his creative writing. In commenting on the Okonkwo passage above, remarks made by Achebe in the course of an interview prove enlightening. Here, Achebe says that "literature must try and reach back beyond the modern nation state to the *original politics* that existed" ("Mapping" 26; emphasis added). Achebe's use of the term "rule" in the expression "Okonkwo *ruled* his household with a heavy hand" (9; emphasis added), indicates that the novel engages not only with the clan politics of Umuofia, but with the very origins of politics: in the family itself. And if Umuofia practises an acephalous, androcentric, democratic republicanism, Okonkwo's household is unmistakably dictatorially managed, with techniques of intimidation and punitive practices deeply embedded in its fabric. This family is a small society in which there is also, of course, a great deal of love and profound, spontaneous loyalty; duties *and* enjoyment, but although it is right to recognise that the irony with which Okonkwo is depicted equally embodies a profound authorial compassion, the narrative is clear-eyed about the age-old, dangerous combination of power and insecurity at the depths of his personhood.

Achebe says: "the shaping of consciousness comes from knowing absolutely who you are" and indicates that, as much as it is necessary to retrieve African pride and self-confidence from earlier colonial humiliation, the "negative factors" of postcolonial states (which he here lists as "tribalism [, . . .] corruption, misrule and inefficiencies of all kinds"), are also "the things that the writer helps the society to see clearly and to try to overcome" ("Mapping" 24-25). He adds that "in the discussion and the dialogue" of such points, "something will be distilled which [the writers'] children or their children will immediately recognise: this is what our forefathers fought for" (24). Achebe, who sometimes has had the label of nativism, of an African primordialism, pinned onto him, says in this interview that "identity is not something which hangs like a millstone around your neck. It is something you can hold dialogue with" (24). A further statement previously cited, "And ultimately, I think what literature is about is that there shall not be misrule" (25), is worth calling to mind here, since it insists on the function of literature as future-directed social critique of the present (note the tense of "shall"), rather than a resuscitation of the past.[4]

It would not be just to characterise Okonkwo's familial role simplistically as "misrule" *per se*, but in his finely nuanced portrayal of Umuofia and of Okonkwo's conduct within it, Achebe over and over draws attention to particular instances of familial misrule – some blatant, and others more deeply embedded. If the welfare of the people is the major responsibility of the state, the care of children is the chief task of the parent within the familial *polis*. Although they implicitly rely on him as protector and provider (along with their mothers), the fact that Okonkwo's "little children" live "in perpetual fear of his heavy hand" (9) is surely meant to be recalled when Akunna, "one of the great men in the village" (128), corrects the missionary Mr Brown's misunderstanding of Igbo theology by saying: "In my religion Chukwu is a loving father and need not be feared by those who do His will" (130). The element of immature self-indulgence with which Okonkwo wields his overlordship within his family is an unfortunately vivid reminder of the spectacularisation of political power to which commentators on African societies and their rulers' conduct (such as Achille Mbembe and Mahmood Mamdani) have drawn attention. Kwadwo Osei-Nyami refers to Okonkwo's "outrageous assertiveness" (151). The point here is not to "bemonster" Okonkwo, whose portrayal in this text is one of the peaks of the complex balancing of impressions Achebe achieves here, but to draw attention to the author's analysis of domestic politics as viscerally related to the larger political arena of his own *and later* times. This is a way in which Achebe's injunction to

4 Compare the well-known opening sentence of Achebe's political booklet or statement *The Trouble with Nigeria*: "The trouble with Nigeria is simply and squarely a failure of leadership" (1).

"reach back beyond the modern state to the original politics that existed" (24) can be applied in the rereading of *Things Fall Apart*.

The first part of the following discussion of the three most fully delineated children in *Things Fall Apart* concerns Okonkwo's daughter Ezinma, a happy child who has her mother Ekwefi's devoted love and care and who has a relationship of trust and considerable mutual respect with Okonkwo. As a treasured child, Ezinma grows up confident and secure. Although initially plagued by illness and feared to be *ogbanje*,[5] she becomes a physically strong as well as an intelligent and lively person; interested, articulate and competent. Other women besides her mother are shown to take affectionate interest in her. Ato Quayson in a 1994 article refers to her as "a toughminded and questioning personality" (130). Her precocity is shown in the novel when she (a ten-year-old) tests the claim that "grown up" people are impervious to the heat of cooking utensils, contesting this myth of adult superiority by means of an example from her own observation: "But Nwoye's mother dropped her pot of hot soup the other day and it broke on the floor" (29). Unlike Okonkwo, Ezinma is thus shown capable of analysing and questioning clan lore; she is alert and independent-minded, but not in an aggressive or unpleasant way. Quayson observes that "she joins the ranks of other male characters who *pose* questions of varying interest in the narrative" (130; emphasis original). The subtle allusion to the title of Achebe's text in Ezinma's reference (above) to the dropping and shattering of a pot also needs to be noticed – implicitly it suggests that those who are older and who have authority by tradition may also fail, and that Ezinma has noticed this. Her anecdote about Nwoye's mother inadvertently breaking her pot of hot soup is carefully juxtaposed with the example of Obiageli (Ezinma's half-sister of roughly the same age as herself) breaking her water pot. In Achebe's amusing description, she had been "making *inyanga* with her pot. She had balanced it on her head, folded her arms in front of her and began to sway her waist like a grown-up young lady" (31). Both youthful irresponsibility and a lapse in adult attentiveness can have shattering results, it is suggested.

The conversation among Okonkwo and the girls is a charmingly domestic scene (and it is clearly not an unusual one), in which Okonkwo does feature as a benign and loving father. He sits contentedly eating, in the company of his two little daughters, from the dishes his first and second wives have sent him for

---

5 This term is used in the Igbo culture to refer to a child believed to be fated to die when quite young and then be reborn, repeatedly, causing its parents much suffering unless the condition is "cured" by the traditional doctor.

supper. More than that, when Ezinma seemingly attempts to get Okonkwo to scold Obiageli for having broken her pot, he replies calmly, refusing to rise to her bait, by expressing neither anger nor condemnation, and he even supports the slightly younger Obiageli's way of fending off a possible rebuke. The broken pot is not allowed to make things fall apart, metaphorically speaking, and here Okonkwo upholds the peaceful, companionable and pleasantly conversational familial atmosphere.

Ezinma's sense of protectedness within both family and clan springs from several sources: her mother's devotion and friendship, the approval of her personality that her father from time to time reveals, the care taken by both parents over her initially precarious health and the interest shown in her by Chielo, whose night-time circuitous expedition with Ezinma into the shrine of Agbala is clearly a tribute to the special strength of this girl's character, and possibly an attempt by Chielo to associate her with the protection of a powerful god, even though both her parents respond with such apprehension when she (Chielo) takes Ezinma away from home late at night. The folktale told elsewhere in the text (100-101), which distinguishes between alternative maternal responses (loud in the case of the hen mother, but silent in the case of the mother duck, when the predatory kite snatches a chick) proves that both Ekwefi and Okonkwo are parents of the duck type with reference to Ezinma – in their profound and courageous love for this child, who is safely "returned" to them (101).

Ezinma takes with aplomb to the public attention from many clan members during the hunt for and discovery of her *iyi-uwa*[6] as the cured sufferer, but when Okonkwo is racked by profound but unspeakable grief about the death of Ikemefuna and his own participation in the killing of the boy it is she who, speaking like a parent or a medical authority to a patient, instructs him: "You have not eaten for two days. [. . .] So you must finish this" (i.e. the food she has brought to him) (45). Okonkwo not only loves but admires Ezinma. Yet (in terms of what has been described as his gender neurosis or "imbalance")[7] he cannot express this admiration in terms of her femaleness. Having lost his "preferred son" Ikemefuna, Okonkwo *at this point* (the narrative reiterating the remark three times in as many pages [45-47]) starts expressing the utterly futile wish: "If Ezinma had been a boy I would have been happier. She has the right spirit" (47)

6 The *iyi-uwa* is, in the traditional Igbo belief system, the hidden object that needs to be found by the community healer to "save" the *ogbanje* (the child fated to a cycle of deaths and rebirths) and to "cure" this condition.

7 See, for example, Traoré (69).

– though not, evidently, in the right body. The "yam tendril" (37) Ikemefuna having been severed, not even Ezinma can serve as one of the (now missing) "young suckers that will grow when the old banana tree dies" (47). Ezinma, though deeply loved by her father, is considered constitutionally inadequate and ideologically unsuitable (in Okonkwo's own eyes) to succeed him as a leader in the clan – nor, of course, does the clan culture make provision for female leadership roles except in specific and strictly circumscribed positions (such as Chielo's priestess role).

It must be added that it is her mother Ekwefi rather than her father who provides Ezinma with companionship, training in domestic skills and a social, cultural and political education. Almost all commentators on *Things Fall Apart* have noted the centrality in the novel of the tale of Tortoise and the birds' visit to the feast in the sky, but it is after all only Ezinma among the novel's characters who is privileged to hear it. The tale is a highly sophisticated recognition of the need to analyse the motives of those who speak with a "sweet tongue" – such as Tortoise's in the story which Ekwefi tells, or that of the messenger sent by the District Commissioner inviting the Umuofian leaders to a consultation in his headquarters (69; 138). Whether it is Tortoise's bogus yet effectively persuasive invocation of "custom" (see 69, where the term occurs three times, and 70, where it occurs twice) to stop the birds from questioning his tall tale, or the Umuofians respecting the protocols of intercultural dialogue with the British, greater verbal astuteness might have protected the group vulnerable to predation. Both the District Commissioner and the Tortoise are "great orators" (69) on the dangerous, other side; a phenomenon Ezinma is warned against, as she is against those who glibly claim to represent "all of [us]" (70).

Even when Ezinma is a young adult of marriageable age, Okonkwo "never stopped regretting that [she] was a girl" (124, top and bottom); his compensation is that she agrees not to choose a husband in his (Okonkwo's) mother's clan, but an Umuofian. Notably, he takes satisfaction in the thought that "his future sons-in-law would be men of authority in the clan" (125) rather than considering whether they would be ideal husbands for his daughters. Nevertheless, Quayson is technically wrong when he states that "Ezinma vanishes from the story after the return from exile, and is never referred to again," finding this "problematic" and invoking Hélène Cixous (131). In fact, the narrator informs us that, well after the family's return, Ezinma "had broken her [customary] twenty-eight day visit to the family of her future husband, and returned home when she heard that her father had been imprisoned, and was going to be hanged" (141). She goes immediately to Obierika's house "to ask what the men of Umuofia were going to do about it (141). Such an act shows her assuming an activist and even approaching a leadership role. She is doing as much as she dares and can achieve within the masculinist structure of the clan to help her father. Quayson writes: "There seems to be an unconscious recognition of the potential inherent in Ezinma [. . .] for subverting the patriarchal discourse of the text" (131). I do not, however, see the *text's* discourse as "patriarchal," nor do I think the recognition in it of Ezinma's potential for leadership at all "unconscious" on the *author's* part, however rigidly masculinist Okonkwo's thinking may be. Indeed, Achebe's "art [. . .] in the service of man" is by no means to be taken as an androcentric expression: his art serves human life broadly in its implicit critique of the personal conduct and social conditions he portrays. Achebean compassion is never merely ameliorative.

Our last glimpse of Ezinma in the novel recapitulates her role as a woman whose "parenting" role as it might be termed is respected by Okonkwo (and implicitly, by Achebe); her action here combines compassion and authority. Upon Okonkwo's return from imprisonment with the humiliating marks of the whiplash on his back, Ezinma immediately takes him food that she herself prepares for him. Although Obierika, too, is urging him to eat, Okonkwo who (in his deep anger and resentment) has no appetite, eats "only [. . .] to please [Ezinma]" (142). We do not know how Ezinma's action of defying pre-marital protocol in her premature return to be with her father will affect her future marriage, nor to what extent her father's death in disgrace (despite his warrior heroism and former status) will affect her standing in the clan – or, indeed, how it will affect Okonkwo's other children (except for Nwoye, whose response is described in *No Longer At Ease* 125). Perhaps their father's death by suicide "within" the clan was marginally better for his children than his probable execution by the British would have been, as it was evidently preferable to himself.

If the story of Ezinma's childhood in Okonkwo's household is compared with Nwoye's, this youngster's eventual "disloyalty" to his father is as explicable as Ezinma's enduring, daughterly loyalty to Okonkwo. We first hear of Nwoye and particularly about Okonkwo's attitude towards this eldest of his children towards the end of the second chapter of *Things Fall Apart*. The boy and his relationship with his father are evoked as follows:

> Okonkwo's first son, Nwoye, was then twelve years old but was already causing his father great anxiety for his incipient laziness. At any rate, that was how it looked to his father, and he sought to correct him

> by constant nagging and beating. And so Nwoye was developing into a sad-faced youth. (10)

Achebe's unmistakable indicators of paternal "misrule" are the adjective "incipient" (instead of *evident*) in the reference to Nwoye's clearly only putative "incipient laziness" and the subsequent qualification that the supposed laziness of the boy "looked" like a disinclination to be productive "to his father" – rather than being discernible to an impartial observer. Just at the most vulnerable stage, when a boy begins to wonder what kind of man he might grow up to be, Okonkwo pre-judges the child, not only in evincing harmful "anxiety" (instead of encouraging confidence) concerning Nwoye's potential and his future male adulthood, but in the harsh, even cruel "nagging and beating" to which he subjects him. That this is a completely counter-productive parental strategy is made clear in the ironically contradictory expression "*developing* into a *sad-faced* youth" (emphases added) – leaving Nwoye prematurely melancholic, deprived of the hope and joy that characterise healthy juvenility. Achebe's compassion towards Nwoye at the malforming effect that Okonkwo's child-rearing practice has on the boy reverberates throughout the description. Parents have a crucial role in supporting or, otherwise, undermining a child's self-respect; Okonkwo's expectation of being honoured after his death and of the perpetuation of their culture through an eldest son who is so poorly cultivated by himself as the boy's father is shown up as an absurdity. The political parallel that comes to mind is the practice of selfish power monopoly that does not prepare the ground for its own transmission of power and governing skills to future rulers, in its obsessive concern with the perpetuation of its own particular power incarnation.

Images of yam cultivation feature strongly in descriptions of Okonkwo's relationships with his eldest boy and his foster-son, since "yam stood for manliness" (24). Because he wants his eldest son to be a "great" man and farmer, Okonkwo's resolve to "stamp out the disquieting signs of laziness which he [thinks] he already [sees] in [Nwoye]" (24) is noted here again, prominently, repeating an earlier point in the text (10) and anticipating later comments on his supposed lack of keenness (47). The father's intolerant, lurking anger and tendency to violently disciplinarian (instead of carefully nurturing) paternal conduct is highlighted in his grotesque and terrorising vow: "I will not have a son who cannot hold up his head in the gathering of the clan. I would sooner strangle him with my own hands" (24). While we as readers might dismiss this as mere bluster, it is not likely to be as easily shrugged off by a twelve-year-old boy. Two paragraphs on, Achebe shows up the destructively inappropriate nature of Okonkwo's child educational strategies by quietly shifting into a description of how "the young tendrils" of the yam plants "were protected from earth-heat with rings of sisal leaves" (24), implicit indicators of the vulnerability of young life-forms, whether human or botanical, and of the need to show care and offer protection. Growing up under the strain of Okonkwo's sternness and mistrust in him, it is no wonder that, to Nwoye, Ikemefuna's story of a land where the mere "ant holds his court in splendour and the sands dance for ever" (25) holds a magical appeal in its representation of non-authoritarian joyousness.

It is Ikemefuna's brotherly encouragement that soon enables Nwoye to practise the posture of the required male swagger, "grumbl[ing] aloud about women and their troubles" (37) while obligingly fulfilling household tasks for these women-folk. Because of this change in Nwoye's behaviour, evinced in his doing such jobs as much as in his increased social confidence, Okonkwo now believes it is time to initiate the two elder boys in his household into the next stage – socialising them into his adult male world where prowess is measured by participation in violence and bloodshed. Okonkwo considers anecdotes of war to be "stories of the land" (37)[8] – the persistent but limited masculinist view of history as the sphere of male power display. Poignantly, Nwoye pretends (in order to please his father) that he no longer cares for "women's stories." He does not have the confidence to recognise that he finds boastful accounts of physical prowess much less interesting than the subtle folktales his mother has been telling him. In one example of Nwoye's mother's type of story, Okonkwo's legendary achievement of throwing the cat is symbolically inverted. This is the tale of the bird *eneke-nti-oba*: who wrestles all the world, overconfident of his strength (like Okonkwo), only to be eventually overthrown – by the cat (38)! The other story of his mother's which Nwoye recalls emphasises (like the Tortoise tale Ekwefi elsewhere tells Ezinma) the importance of verbal skills and negotiation in a situation where one's strength is outmatched; where all one can use are the various, appropriate verbal skills of assuagement, intercession and intelligent diplomacy in negotiating with power (38).

---

8 Compare the recurrence of this same expression in the Abazonian elder's cautionary statement that "When we are young and without experience we all imagine that *the story of the land* is easy, that every one of us can get up and tell it. But that is not so" (*Anthills* 124-125; emphasis added). This speaker is a true leader – with quiet eloquence and without arrogance, he attempts humbly to intercede with power on behalf of his people. That he (an elderly man) is jailed for his pains reflects the merely bullying misuse of power.

It is probable that when Okonkwo does "beat [Nwoye] heavily" (41) for bursting into tears when the youngster (now fifteen) overhears his father telling Ikemefuna that he is to be returned to his own clan, this violent response is intended, *not* primarily to hurt his son, but to disguise and hide his own sorrow at the impending killing. Yet the father clearly refuses to accord the boy's grief any validity. Nwoye's sorrow increases to dread when his mother drops her pestle and sighs upon being told of Ikemefuna's supposed return to his own family: Nwoye's profound sense of loss at the departure of Ikemefuna can (in the clan) be accommodated only as "effeminate," as he sits all of that fateful day in his mother's hut with brimming eyes, surrounded by the "deathly silence" of Okonkwo's compound. The ominous atmosphere becomes a certainty of even more dreadful loss when Nwoye discerns in the returning Okonkwo's manner or his facial expression that Ikemefuna has not just been taken away, but killed. He senses his father's participation in the deed, but he also senses the broader cultural validation of the killing of his foster brother in the way he links it instinctively with the required death (by exposure) of all newborn twins. It is at *this* point that Achebe inserts three clear allusions to his text's title, indicating that this first "fall[ing] apart" *within Nwoye* [9] cannot be connected with the arrival of the colonists, nor that of Christianity. What it seems to signify is Nwoye's first, but quite profound emotional severance from his father and from the Umuofian religio-ethical system. In both he seems to sense a deep failure of protective parenting, particularly of fatherhood. And making this moment of break-up Nwoye's more than Okonkwo's gives the boy a far more central place in the emotional logic of the narrative and its metaphoric patterning of cultural adaptation than has usually been recognised in the prioritisation of the father's fate in most accounts of the text. Like Achebe, we need to pay attention to the central importance of familial conditions within the social and political context – a most important resonance of this profound work of literature.

---

[9] That this is an *inward*, i.e. a deep, but not outwardly discernible severance, is emphasised in Achebe's careful formulation, three times repeated: "As soon as his father walked in that night, Nwoye knew that Ikemefuna had been killed, and something seemed to *give way within him*, like the snapping of a tightened bow" (43; emphasis added in this and the following two quotations); as he here recalls the day he first noticed the abandoned twin babies' wailing, Nwoye remembers how he "had felt for the first time a *snapping inside him* like the one he now felt" (43); we are told: "Then something had given way *inside him*. It descended on him again, this feeling" (44).

When Okonkwo returns to society after his grief over Ikemefuna has been overcome or repressed, his sense of loss re-emerges in the twisted form of dismissing Nwoye as an inadequate and unmanly son. This occurs in a conversation with his friend Obierika, with whom he shares a more intimate friendship than with anyone else in his life (47). Okonkwo's contemptuous attitude towards his eldest son[10] is entangled (as Obierika knows) with the man's unassuaged resentment against his own father. No wonder that when (much later in the narrative) the missionaries introduce their God as showing a "tender shepherd's care" (105) towards His children, combined with their emphasis on brotherhood in Christ, this evocation of compassionate fatherliness proves irresistible to Nwoye. The reference to the "happy kingdom" (104) of eternal heaven must indeed recall the "land" of Ikemefuna's favourite story to him, while the missionaries' denunciation of the killing of "innocent children" (105) strikes a powerful chord in Nwoye's soul with reference to the treatment of twin births in the clan. Most especially, we are told, the missionaries' "story of brothers who lived in darkness and in fear" (105; 106) reminds him of those evenings when he and Ikemefuna heard Okonkwo relishingly telling his tales of war and bloodshed – heroic tales forever poisoned (in Nwoye's memory) by his father's subsequent participation in the slaying of his beloved foster brother.

Upon discovering Nwoye's visits to the Christians, Okonkwo blocks the boy's return home. The nature of the bond between them, here as always, is represented by Okonkwo's "*choking* grip" (109; emphasis added) on his son – as an image, this underlines the non-fostering nature of his fatherhood and its stifling effect on Nwoye's personality. Predictably, when ordered not to beat Nwoye, Okonkwo "*left* hold" of his son, after having struck him several "savage blows" with a "heavy stick" (109; emphasis added). This is another of the images of irrecoverable severance or fallings apart (in the title image) in this text. It also shows the limited (primarily authoritarian), containing and constraining relationship Okonkwo has with Nwoye. It contrasts clearly with the natural bond of affectionate, mutual respect and trust we see in the relationship between Okonkwo

[10] The proverb that Okonkwo uses to "prove" Nwoye's inadequate masculinity (in his view), viz. "a chick that will grow into a cock can be spotted the very day it hatches" (47), is often cited with clear approval by commentators on the novel. I believe such approval (based on the assumption that, because Achebe inserts a proverb in Okonkwo's speech, he necessarily approves of the use to which it is being put) to be misplaced, since (as used here by Okonkwo) the proverb illustrates the father's prejudiced and disdainful attitude towards his own son, and its injustice.

and Ezinma. Although the missionary influence does play a part at this stage, it is again Nwoye whose dislodgement from family and hence from his father's culture takes centre stage. Okonkwo cannot emotionally or intellectually deal with or speak to the son from whom he had always/already alienated himself; he can only, violently, oust him from the family. Okonkwo's failure in fatherhood, in the case of Nwoye, is underlined by its contrast with his maternal uncle Uchendu's authoritative, protective and fatherly order when he hears Okonkwo beating Nwoye: "Leave that *boy* at once" (109; emphasis added). By using the word 'boy,' Uchendu insists that Okonkwo's violent beating of the youngster is abusive and unjustified. Families, like cultures, are held together by such nurturing conduct rather than by hierarchical authoritarianism and violence.

We are reading superficially if we fail to discern that Okonkwo does nevertheless feel great grief at the loss of Nwoye, even though he hides these feelings from himself under thoughts of this son's supposedly "despicable [. . .] behaviour"; "crime" and "degenerate and effeminate nature" (110). He dissociates himself from his son to the point of toying with the idea that someone other than himself fathered Nwoye. Seething with self-righteous indignation at this perceived, irrevocable betrayal by his son, Okonkwo is unable to recognise that he himself has all along been betraying Nwoye and has failed in his paternal responsibility to love and cherish this child. In cursing and excommunicating a son for accepting a different set of beliefs to their own, fathers like Okonkwo destroy the opportunity for negotiating cultural adaptation and cross-generational continuity. To say this is not to forget the sense of tragic loss with which Achebe endows the split between Okonkwo and Nwoye, nor his exposure of the ugly glibness with which Mr Kiaga triumphantly declares Nwoye one of those who are "*blessed*" for "forsak[ing] his father and his mother for [God's] sake" (110; emphasis added). Nevertheless it needs to be pointed out that in *Things Fall Apart*, the narrative gives at least as much emotional weight to Okonkwo's responsibility failures and abuses of power concerning Nwoye as it does to the numerous illustrations of colonial abuses of power against him and his people. They are different but potent fissiparous forces outside *and* inside the clan. Obierika's lament over the clan's "sons [who] have joined the ranks of the stranger [. . .] joined his religion" and "help to uphold his government" must be weighed against the fact that these same sons "have been given power" (126) by the colonists. To seek advancement in a new or different dispensation than the paternally endorsed structures of one's upbringing may be a betrayal, may indeed be a despicable yielding to seduction, but it may also be the expression of a natural and normal desire to grow and flourish as one can only do where one is trusted and thought useful. In contemporary terminology, Achebe exposes Okonkwo's persistent "disempowerment" of Nwoye; in "roar[ing]" at Nwoye (109), his anger resembles the clucking of mother hen who yet accepts the kite's snatching of her chick. How ironic and poignant that the Christian name Nwoye takes is Isaac (131); Okonkwo being both like and unlike the biblical figure of Abraham in irrevocably sacrificing *both* of his eldest "sons" (Ikemefuna and Nwoye) in the name of his cultural belief system.[11]

Turning to Ikemefuna, the third of Achebe's children to be discussed here, it is notable that it is the "resonance" of this particular youngster's portrayal that has been most noticed by scholars. Considering how soon he is removed from Umuofia – the community on whose subsequent experiences Achebe expends many, many more pages – the few passages in which he features have been almost universally recognised for their emotional and symbolic potency. Ikemefuna is endowed with perhaps the most beautiful personality the author ever created. If the poignance of Nwoye's painful boyhood and the strength and vitality of Ezinma's girlhood are conveyed by the novel, it is especially Ikemefuna whose presence combines resonance, poignance and a strange grandeur and on whose person some of Achebe's most central ideas rest in this first novel, with echoes in some of his later texts.

The first sentence that names Ikemefuna also tells us that *his* "sad story is still told in Umuofia *unto this day*" (9; emphasis added), which is Achebe's way of signposting the resonance and importance of this young "lad" (as he usually, and affectionately, terms him).[12] Achebe gives Ikemefuna's "story" an enduring life

---

11 In the biblical account Abraham is prepared to sacrifice his son Isaac to prove the strength of his faith in his God, but the deity sends an angel to intervene at the last minute, allowing him to cut the throat of a conveniently nearby ram instead, and the boy's life is saved. Achebe employs Biblical allusions with great care; see e.g. my analysis of the ironic use of such allusions in *No Longer at Ease* ("Symbolic" 231, note 8). Nevertheless I agree with Emeka Nwabueze that the "killing of Ikemefuna is, as Opata suggests, 'an unconscionable act' and not necessarily an offence" (79). "In Igbo culture, Okonkwo should be seen as a victim of capricious fates, a fact" that only "Opata has considered" (169).

12 As we read this comment on Ikemefuna's "story" (9), we ourselves are at that moment "reviving" it and ensuring that it will never be forgotten. Compared to the rich irony of the District Commissioner's condescending comment on Okonkwo's "story" (149) deserving a mere paragraph (in contrast with Achebe's whole novel by means of which he creates and disseminates Okonkwo's story), we see that

both "inside" and in the imagined "outside" of his fiction. Considering that we only witness Ikemefuna's life between the ages of fifteen and eighteen and that he is (in view both of his youth and his status as an outsider and a restitution token in Umuofia) neither a warrior nor a leader nor an orator nor an artist, but only a "boy," Achebe overrides all the clanly standards in successfully allocating to Ikemefuna the emotional prominence and symbolic stature that he has. It is if anything one of the most powerful proofs that Achebe's and Okonkwo's systems of value are not identical, however deeply compassionate the understanding with which Okonkwo, even in his participation in the death of Ikemefuna, is portrayed by the writer. Although Ikemefuna is, like the *osu* in the clan, "set apart" (113) and "*belong[s]* to the clan as a whole" (emphasis added) – rather than being a normal member of a family – he not only "live[s] in Okonkwo's household" (9), but quickly becomes a central presence in it and he is, I think, a central, iconic presence in Achebe's entire oeuvre.

The second instalment of the story of Ikemefuna (in *Things Fall Apart*) follows closely on the narrator's analysis of the deepest source of Okonkwo's insecurity, which is identified as "fear of himself" (10); Okonkwo is (to cite a useful distinction from *Anthills of the Savannah* 46) a "would be strong" rather than a rare, "truly strong" person. In contrast with Okonkwo's deeply hidden "fear of himself," the teenage boy Ikemefuna is made "terribly afraid" when he is plucked from his family for no reason that he has any inkling of and taken "a long, long way from home, through lonely forest paths" (11), all the way to Umuofia, among total strangers. By juxtaposing the descriptions of two kinds of fear on two adjoining pages, Achebe begins to set up a contrast between Okonkwo the lord of the clan and its sacrificial victim-to-be, Ikemefuna.

Whereas Okonkwo "was *ruled by*" his passionate determination to hate both "gentleness" and "idleness," both of which "his father Unoka had loved" (10; emphasis added), Ikemefuna manages to "*overcome* his great fear and sadness" (20; emphasis added). The choice of power terms in both quoted phrases is significant; here already Achebe is contrasting the "truly strong" but gentle Ikemefuna with the "would be strong" Okonkwo. The most noticeable thing about Ikemefuna is his range of knowledge; in Nwoye's eyes, "he seemed to know everything" – but it is knowledge which he shares generously and which balances hunting skills with artistic inclinations, unlike Okonkwo's lopsided overemphasis on violence, power and prestige. Even Okonkwo is not immune to the

---

Ikemefuna, too, is endowed with far-reaching symbolic status by his author and creator.

youngster's sweet, strong presence and he treats him "like a son" with unmistakable signs of trust and confidence in him (20; 21).

Achebe's subtle insistence on stories as repositories and resources of necessary wisdom – social, political and psychological – is a recurrent feature of the *Things Fall Apart* text. In some of his most important essays (such as "Language and the Destiny of Man" and "What has Literature got to do with it?"), Achebe foregrounds the socially educational force of myths and folk tales. Clearly he does not share Okonkwo's dismissal of "women's stories" as trivial and "silly" (54). So, in noting that "Ikemefuna had an endless stock of folk tales" (25), as the enthralled Nwoye observes, Achebe is registering both Nwoye's at this stage unassuaged intellectual thirst and Ikemefuna's ability to be "the tale-teller as teacher." Unlike Okonkwo's (in Nwoye's ears, probably frightening and depressing) "masculine stories of violence and bloodshed" (37), with their all too obviously indoctrinating intention, Ikemefuna's stories are enchanting, inspiring and liberating. In the favourite tale, "the ant holds his court in splendour and the sands dance forever" (25), combining pleasure, art and political order in a magical way within the loving framework of the boys' friendship.

In his essay titled "The Truth of Fiction," first delivered as an address at Obafemi Awolowo University, Achebe identifies as "malignant" or "virulent fictions" the following notions:

> Belief in superior and inferior races, belief that some people who live across our frontiers or speak a different language [. . .] are the cause of all the trouble in the world, or that our own particular group or class or caste has a right to certain things which are denied to others; the belief that men are superior to women, and so on [. . .]. (147)

Though it may be anachronistic to expect an Umuofian elder to realise this, these "malignant" fictions are of course among Okonkwo's most treasured beliefs, but their narrow parochialism all betray the same brittle insecurity, the inability to engage in mental play hence (in Achebe's words): "such fictions assert themselves as facts" ("Truth" 148) – whether for Okonkwo, or for South Africans practising apartheid or (more recently) attacking and murdering fellow Africans as foreigners disparagingly called *makwerekwere*.[13] If our concern with the future of our ever expanding and ever more intertwined world is real, we had

[13] This South African coinage is said to indicate that those so named are deemed "queer, strange people" (a phonetic Nguni adaptation of the adjective 'queer' as meaning 'odd,' without here carrying a gender burden).

better tell ourselves and our children more so-called "women's stories" and stories like Ikemefuna's and fewer so-called "masculine stories of violence and bloodshed" (25). Our own and our children's futures depend on our doing so, and on our rapidly and fundamentally redefining ideals of masculinity – as Ikemefuna does for Nwoye, and as Achebe does by his portrayal of Ikemefuna. That it is possible to be both manly and sensitive is a truth in constant need of demonstration.

When Okonkwo hears "the beat of the drums" announcing the Yam Festival wrestling contest, we are told that it "filled him with fire" and that he "trembled with the desire to conquer and subdue [. . .] like the desire for woman" (30). Okonkwo's type of "pacification" (150) in war, wrestling and sex is juxtaposed by Achebe (on facing pages in the novel) and contrasted with the *peace*-making strength of Ikemefuna. When Nwoye's two younger brothers want to create trouble for their naughty sister Obiageli who has irresponsibly caused her water-pot to fall and shatter, because she was more intent on showing off than in working, Ikemefuna prevents the shattering of the familial peace by silencing them with a single stern look. His maturity and authority and his balancing role in his adoptive family enable him to act in an admirably paternal manner. Not battlefield exploits, but being an encouraging, strong and stabilising centre to the family is Ikemefuna's type of "heroism." Civilisations are often initiated by conquest, but to be maintained they require a balancing fairness towards and the greatest achievable equity among members, for a repressive state is in a perpetual undeclared state of civil war. Like a repressive family, it "cannot hold" (to use another phrase from the Yeats poem that yielded Achebe's title). All along, familial and political parallels co-construct the dense fabric of Achebe's text.

The most poignant and resonant passage concerning Ikemefuna and the one in which his irreplaceable value is most clearly signposted, occurs at the start of chapter seven. The passage is well known:

> For three years Ikemefuna lived in Okonkwo's household and the elders of Umuofia seemed to have forgotten about him. He grew rapidly like a yam tendril in the rainy season, and was full of the sap of life. He had become wholly absorbed into his new family. He was like an elder brother to Nwoye, and from the very first seemed to have kindled a new fire in the younger boy. (37)

Ikemefuna's wholesomeness and the enlivening, even healing effect he has on the whole family are vividly captured in this description. Especially important is the life-quickening effect he has on Nwoye, making the melancholic boy feel loved and valued, in contrast with the inhibiting, even deadening effect his father's contempt and disapproval have on him. The "yam tendril" image suggests that Ikemefuna could have been a growth point for the whole culture, while the word "tendril" in particular stresses the need to nurture what is most valuable *and* vulnerable in any culture – indeed, to "cultivate" it. However validly and inevitably the Oracle may decree the killing within local Umuofian cultural norms, the wrongness of putting such a boy to death comes across particularly on a rereading of the text, when one knows how soon "after" the above passage Ikemefuna is to be cut down. He is excised from the clan as if he represents an alien, noxious growth that is dangerously rooting itself in home ground, while every detail in the narrative evocation of Ikemefuna's being and presence asserts the opposite. Achebe's fine writing holds both perspectives in balance: the grievous fault and failure encapsulated in the killing *and* the knowledge that the act was ordained within the parameters of the culture. The tragic disruption, the brutal shattering that is caused in Okonkwo's family by the Oracle's decree to put Ikemefuna to death is the more deeply felt because it is prepared for by a scene of pleasant and familial communion among Okonkwo, Nwoye and Ikemefuna. In this passage the larger sociopolitical parallel is symbolised by the fact that the three males are shown repairing and strengthening "the red outer walls of the compound." The bonds linking them together as a micro-society have their physical equivalent: "Okonkwo passed the rope, or *tie-tie*, to the boys, and they passed it round the wooden stays and then back to him; and in this way the cover was strengthened on the wall" (39). In a situation that will end in a grievous shattering, this moment of bonding is delicately highlighted. Their peaceful industry is interrupted, for: "quite suddenly a shadow fell on the world" (39). Even though this "shadow" turns out to be the welcome cloud of locusts and is "a tremendous sight, full of power and beauty" (39), it does presage Ikemefuna's demise, in which "a terrible beauty is born" (to cite Yeats's poem "Easter 1916").

Achebe never forgot Ikemefuna. Even as he made him unforgettable to us as readers, he revives his image in later texts. In *No Longer at Ease* Obi refers to "the sad story of Ikemefuna"; how "inseparable" his father and Ikemefuna had been and how his grandfather Okonkwo had "loved the boy" Ikemefuna despite participating in his killing (125). Nwoye, now an elderly Christian (a retired catechist), tells his son Obi how *his* father, Okonkwo, had cursed him for having joined the Christians. However, Achebe twists the tale; even though Nwoye (who has become Isaac) never forgave Okonkwo for the death of Ikemefuna, Nwoye in his late adulthood, as the elderly Isaac, re-enacts the threat of a father's curse and of familial excommunication of an eldest son when he declares Obi's intended marriage to an *osu* unacceptable and "forbidden" – taboo. Obi in his turn breaks off his relationship, so that Clara must seek an abortion. Even though Obi does not wield a machete or surgical knife and is not present at the operation which removes the foetus, the uncanny echo of child-murder is nevertheless there in Obi's own words concerning the death of Ikemefuna: "it was a great wrong that a man should raise his hands against a child that called him father" (126). The "shadow" of Ikemefuna's death and of accepting cruel acts of excision as valid because they uphold clan taboos extends even into the modern Nigeria of *No Longer at Ease*, despite its official creed of social unity across classes and cultures.

It does not seem to me to be an accident that Achebe, in the essay "The Truth of Fiction," chose as his example of a scientific text that he considers to be as significant to society, in its way, as novels and folktales are in theirs, a book by a medical specialist titled *Why Our Children Die* (qtd. in "Truth" 142). Achebe's concern with the young and the vulnerable, and his urgent awareness that, if we do not begin to care better for *all* our children, we are doomed, is enduring and morally complex. As background it may be noted that out of the nearly ten million children worldwide who die annually before the age of five, fifty percent were or are African. The horror statistics of child rape and child murder in South Africa are well known and show no signs of abating, while nearly forty percent of child deaths on our continent occur in West Africa. These are U.N. statistics. Africa faces a crisis of parenting and child care, broadly seen, in our societies' failures to provide properly for our children. While many of the determining factors resulting in these terrible facts are beyond our control, some can be addressed. Achebe indicates that failures of care by familial authorities may lead to our accepting deficiencies in or abuses of state power and authority, as much as we may in conforming to larger cultural or power norms end up betraying our own children. The Somali novelist Nuruddin Farah in his novel *Sardines* prominently places a dictum by the Austrian-American psychiatrist (and psychoanalyst) Wilhelm Reich: "In the figure of the father the authoritarian state has its representative in every family, so that the family becomes its most important instrument of power" (qtd. in *Sardines*, 97). Reading Achebe helps one to see the validity of this statement and also enables one to balance it with the recognition of the vitally creative effects on society at large of lovingly nurturing families and parents; of intelligent, nurturing and *gently* strong authority figures.[14]

Another symbolic "inheritor" of Ikemefuna in Achebe's writing is Ikem in *Anthills of the Savannah* – his bearing an abbreviated version of the same name as Ikemefuna's is surely no accident. But, like Ikemefuna, Ikem too is cut down in his prime by the power-mongers of his society. It is Ikem who warns against "silt[ing] up the canals of birth in the season of renewal" (31). Achebe also built in a vision of an alternative family at the end of *Anthills of the Savannah*, in the scene where Ikem and Elewa's baby is christened "AMAECHINA: *May-the-path-never-close*" (222; original capitals and italics). After the christening, Elewa's uncle arrives, too late for this task (for which he was engaged by Elewa's mother), asking: "Who gave her the name?" He is answered: "All of us" (225). Here Tortoise's bogus claim to represent "*All of you*" (70; emphasis original) in *Things Fall Apart* is inverted and corrected. Elewa's uncle accepts the quiet sociocultural revolution that has occurred in Beatrice's flat and under her "leadership" (229). He prays: "May this child be the daughter of all of us" and "May these young people when they make the plans for their world not forget her. And all other children" (228). One could see this old man's prayer as expressing major part of the Achebean legacy, the great work begun in *Things Fall Apart* fifty years ago, and still to be fulfilled. Some of the ways in which it might be fulfilled are registered in the lengthy and moving christening scene that ends *Anthills on the Savannah*, where so many of the details point to the social as well as familial duty to provide for our children, so that our future and their present might be better than contemporary conditions.

Works Cited

Achebe, Chinua. *Anthills of the Savannah*. London: Heinemann, 1987.

___. Interview with Bernth Lindfors. *Palaver: Interviews with Five African Writers in Texas: Chinua Achebe, John Pepper Clark, Dennis Brutus,*

---

[14] Compare a lively and interesting (quite recent and evidently popular, though probably controversial) Nigerian text on the political effects of the "generation gap" in terms of a split between parental and filial moral values, the novel *Our Children Are Coming!* by Chukwuemeka Ike. It is, notably, dedicated to both "Chinua and Christie Achebe" and another couple (frontispiece). First published in 1990, it was reprinted in 1991, 1996, 2001, 2004 and 2006, indicating the social relevance of the topic to Nigerian families.

Ezekiel Mphahlele and Kofi Awoonor. Austin: African and African-American Research Institute, University of Texas at Austin, 1972. 5-12.

___. Interview with Robert Serumaga. *African Writers Talking: A Collection of Interviews*. Ed. Dennis Duerden and Cosmo Pieterse. London: Heinemann, 1972. 11-17.

___. "Language and the Destiny of Man." *Hopes and Impediments: Selected Essays*. By Achebe. New York: Doubleday, 1989.126-137.

___. "Mapping out Identity." Interview with Chinweizu. *Classic* 3.1 (1984): 24-25.

___. *Morning yet on Creation Day*: *Essays*. London: Heinemann, 1975.

___. *No Longer at Ease*. London: Heinemann, 1987.

___. *Things Fall Apart*. Oxford: Heinemann, 1986.

___. *The Trouble with Nigeria*. London: Heinemann, 1983.

___. "The Truth of Fiction." *Hopes and Impediments: Selected Essays*. By Achebe. New York: Doubleday, 1989. 138-153.

___. "What Has Literature Got to Do with It?" *Hopes and Impediments: Selected Essays*. By Achebe. New York: Doubleday, 1989. 154-170.

Archer-Lean, Clare. "Place, Space and Tradition in the Writings of Mudrooroo." *Mongrel Signatures: Reflections on the Work of Mudrooroo*. Ed. Annalisa Oboe. Amsterdam: Rodopi, 2003. 203-223.

Bahktin, Mikhail M. *Speech Genres and Other Late Essays*. Trans. Vern W. McGee. Ed. Caryl Emerson and Michael Holquist. Austin: University of Texas Press, 2004.

Duerden, Dennis, and Cosmo Pieterse, eds. *African Writers Talking: A Collection of Interviews*. London: Heinemann, 1972.

Fanon, Frantz. *The Wretched of the Earth*. Trans. Constance Farrington. Harmondsworth: Penguin, 1967.

Farah, Nuruddin. *Sardines*. London: Heinemann, 1987.

Gagiano, Annie. *Achebe, Head, Marechera: On Power and Change in Africa*. Boulder, CO & London: Lynne Rienner, 2000.

___. "The Symbolic Dimensions of Achebe's *No Longer at Ease*." *Multiculturalism and Hybridity in African Literature*. Ed. Hal Wylie and Bernth Lindfors. Trenton, NJ: Africa World Press, 2000. 221-233.

George, Olakunle. *Relocating Agency: Modernity and African Letters*. Albany: State University of New York Press, 2003.

Ike, Chukwuemeka. *Our Children Are Coming!* Ibadan: Spectrum Books Limited, 1990.

Lindfors, Bernth *et al.*, eds. *Palaver: Interviews with Five African Writers in Texas: Chinua Achebe, John Pepper Clark, Dennis Brutus, Ezekiel Mphahlele and Kofi Awoonor*. Austin: African and African-American Research Institute, University of Texas at Austin, 1972.

Mamdani, Mahmood. *Citizen and Subject: Contemporary Africa and the Legacy of Late Colonialism*. Princeton, N.J.: Princeton UP, 1996.

Mbembe, Achille. *On the Postcolony*. Berkeley: University of California Press, 2001.

Mudrooroo. *Us Mob. History, Culture, Struggle: An Introduction to Indigenous Australia*. Sydney: Angus & Robertson, 1995.

___. *Writing from the Fringe: A Study of Modern Aboriginal Literature*. Melbourne: Highland House, 1990.

Nwabueze, Emeka. "Theoretical Construction and Constructive Theorizing on the Execution of Ikemefuna in Achebe's *Things Fall Apart*: A Study in Critical Dualism." *Research in African Literatures* 31.2 (2000): 163-173.

Opata, Damian U. "Eternal Sacred Order versus Conventional Wisdom: A Consideration of Moral Culpability in the Killing of Ikemefuna in *Things Fall Apart*." *Research in African Literatures* 18.1 (Spring 1987): 71–79.

Osei-Nyame, Kwadwo. "Chinua Achebe Writing Culture: Representations of Gender and Tradition in *Things Fall Apart*." *Research in African Literatures* 30.2 (1999):148-164.

Quayson, Ato. "Realism, Criticism, and the Disguises of Both: A Reading of Chinua Achebe's *Things Fall Apart* with an Evaluation of the Criticism Relating to it." *Research in African Literatures* 25.4 (1994):117-136.

Traoré, Ousseynou B. "A Metrical Approach to *Things Fall Apart*: A Poetics of Epic and Mythic Paradigms." *Approaches to Teaching Achebe's* Things Fall Apart. Ed. Bernth Lindfors. New York: The Modern Language Association of America, 1991. 69-73.

Yeats, William Butler. *The Collected Poems of W.B. Yeats*. London: Macmillan, 1933. "Easter 1916." 202-205.

___. "The Second Coming." *The Collected Poems of W.B. Yeats*. London: Macmillan, 1933. 210-211.

Acknowledgements

1. "Listening for the Mediated Voices of the Southern African Khoisan in Hendrik's *Dwaalstories*: Ironies and Wonders." Paper delivered at the Against All Odds: African Languages and Literatures into the Twenty-First Century" conference, Asmara, Eritrea, Jan. 2000, under the title "Listening for the Mediated Voices of the Southern African Khoisan: Ironies and Wonders."
2. "Marecheran Postmodernism: Mocking the Bad Joke of "African Modernity." *Journal of Literary Studies* 18.1/2 (2002): 61-84.
3. "Anomy and Agony in a Nation in Crisis: Soyinka's *Season of Anomy*." *English in Africa*. 26.2 (1999): 125-139.
4. "Finding Foundations for Change in Bessie Head's *The Cardinals*." *Journal of Commonwealth Literature* 31.2 (1996): 47-60.
5. "Blood Gets a Voice: Unity Dow's *The Screaming of the Innocent*." Paper delivered at the Annual Conference of the Association for the Study of the New Literatures in English (ASNEL), Johann Wolfgang Goethe University, Frankfurt/Main, 19-23 May, 2004.
6. "Two Late Apartheid-Era Novels: Balancing the Books in the South African Present." Not published before.
7. "Mongane Serote's *To Every Birth Its Blood*: Painting the True Colours of Apartheid." *An Introduction to the African Prose Narrative*. Ed. Lokangake Losambe. Pretoria: Kagiso Tertiary, 1996. 122-130.
8. "Shakespeare, (Fanon,) Salih: Can the Black Man Love the White Woman? Can the White Woman Love the Black Man?" Paper delivered at the International Comparative Literature Association (ICLA) conference. University of South Africa, Pretoria. Aug. 2000.
9. "A. C. Jordan's *Tales From Southern Africa*." *Alternation* 4.2 (1997): 68-80.
10. "Memory, Power and Bessie Head: *A Question of Power*." *World Literature Written in English* 38.1 (1999): 42-57.
11. "Patterns of Leadership in Bessie Head's *Maru* and *A Bewitched Crossroad: An African Saga*." *Atlantic Review* 1.1 (2000): 172-190. Rpt. in *Commonwealth Fiction: Twenty-First Century Readings*. Ed. Rajeshwar Mittapalli and Alessandro Monti. New Delhi: Atlantic, 2002.
12. "'Barbarism' and 'Civilisation' in Shakespeare's *Titus Andronicus* and in Marechera's *Black Sunlight*." *Literary Griot: International Journal of Black Expressive Culture Studies* 10.1 (Spring 1998): 1-15.

13. "Farah's *Sweet and Sour Milk*: The Noise in the Dictator's Ear." Paper presented at the one-day Mellon Colloquium on "Literature and Politics in the Horn of Africa." University of Cape Town [UCT], Cape Town, South Africa. Oct. 2007.
14. "Performances, Ethics and Aesthetics of Wealth in African Literary Depiction." Paper delivered at the EACLALS [European Association for Commonwealth Languages and Literatures Association] conference on "Uncommon Wealths: Riches and Realities." University of Innsbruck, Innsbruck, Vienna, April 2014 under the title, "Colonial Comprador Wealth, Peasant Wealth and Business Wealth in Waguih Ghali's Egypt, Meja Mwangi's Kenya and Chimamanda Ngozi Adichie's Nigeria."
15. "Three Takes on Somali Womanhood in the Eddies of the Contemporary Black Atlantic Context." Not previously presented as a paper or published.
16. "Achebe's Children: Resonance, Poignance and Grandeur." *Blazing the Path: Fifty Years of* Things Fall Apart. Ed. Chima Anyadike and Kehinde A. Ayoola. Ibadan: HEBN Publishers Plc, 2012. 28-59.

STUDIES IN ENGLISH LITERATURES

Edited by Koray Melikoğlu

ISSN 1614-4651

1 *Özden Sözalan*
The Staged Encounter
Contemporary Feminism and Women's Drama
2nd, revised edition
ISBN 978-3-89821-367-6

2 *Paul Fox (ed.)*
Decadences
Morality and Aesthetics in British Literature
2nd, revised and expanded edition
ISBN 978-3-89821-0623-3

3 *Daniel M. Shea*
James Joyce and the Mythology of Modernism
ISBN 978-3-89821-574-1

4 *Paul Fox and Koray Melikoğlu (eds.)*
Formal Investigations
Aesthetic Style in Late-Victorian and Edwardian Detective Fiction
2nd, revised and expanded edition
ISBN 978-3-8382-0593-9

5 *David Ellis*
Writing Home
Black Writing in Britain Since the War
ISBN 978-3-89821-591-6

6 *Wei H. Kao*
The Formation of an Irish Literary Canon in the Mid-Twentieth Century
ISBN 978-3-89821-545-9

7 *Bianca Del Villano*
Ghostly Alterities
Spectrality and Contemporary Literatures in English
2nd, revised editon
ISBN 978-3-89821-714-9

8 *Melanie Ann Hanson*
Decapitation and Disgorgement
The Female Body's Text in Early Modern English Drama and Poetry
ISBN 978-3-89821-605-5

9 *Shafquat Towheed (ed.)*
New Readings in the Literature of British India, c.1780-1947
ISBN 978-3-89821-673-9

10 *Paola Baseotto*
"Disdeining life, desiring leaue to die"
Spenser and the Psychology of Despair
ISBN 978-3-89821-567-1

11 *Annie Gagiano*
Dealing with Evils
Essays on Writing from Africa
2nd, revised and expanded edition
ISBN 978-3-8382-0687-5

12 *Thomas F. Halloran*
James Joyce: Developing Irish Identity
A Study of the Development of Postcolonial Irish Identity in the Novels of James Joyce
ISBN 978-3-89821-571-8

13 *Pablo Armellino*
Ob-scene Spaces in Australian Narrative
An Account of the Socio-topographic Construction of Space in Australian Literature
ISBN 978-3-89821-873-3

14 *Lance Weldy*
Seeking a Felicitous Space on the Frontier
The Progression of the Modern American Woman in O. E. Rölvaag, Laura Ingalls Wilder, and Willa Cather
ISBN 978-3-89821-535-0

15 *Rana Tekcan*
The Biographer and the Subject
A Study on Biographical Distance
ISBN 978-3-89821-995-2

16 *Paola Brusasco*
Writing Within/Without/About Sri Lanka
Discourses of Cartography, History and Translation in Selected Works by Michael Ondaatje and Carl Muller
ISBN 978-3-8382-0075-0

17 *Zeynep Z. Atayurt*
Excess and Embodiment in Contemporary Women's Writing
ISBN 978-3-89821-978-5

18 *Gianluca Delfino*
Time, History, and Philosophy in the Works of Wilson Harris
ISBN 978-3-8382-0265-5

ibidem-Verlag / *ibidem* Press
Melchiorstr. 15
70439 Stuttgart
Germany

ibidem@ibidem.eu
www.ibidem-verlag.com
www.ibidem.eu

HOW TO TRULY LOVE

ANCIENT WISDOM FOR MODERN READERS

■ ■ ■ ■

For a full list of titles in the series, go to https://press.princeton.edu/series/ancient-wisdom-for-modern-readers.

How to Truly Love: An Ancient Guide to a Life of Kindness by Buddhaghosa

How to Speak Freely: An Ancient Guide for Modern Freethinkers and Dissenters by Plato

How to Face the End of the World: An Ancient Guide for Apocalyptic Times by Hesiod, Plato, and Other Doomsayers

How to Be Stoic: An Ancient Guide to Keeping Calm by Marcus Aurelius

How to Live: An Ancient Guide to a Happy Life by Seneca

How to Travel: An Ancient Guide for the Modern Tourist by Herodotus and Fellow Travelers

How to Listen: An Ancient Guide to Learning from Others by Plutarch

How to Compete: An Ancient Guide to the Virtues of Sports by Lucian

How to Find Happiness: An Ancient Guide to the Good Life by Marcus Tullius Cicero

How to Be Grateful: An Aztec Guide to the Art of Gratitude by Pablo of Texcoco

How to Cope: An Ancient Guide to Enduring Hardship by Boethius

How to Feel: An Ancient Guide to Minding Our Emotions by the Buddha

HOW TO TRULY LOVE

■ ■ ■ ■ ■

An Ancient Guide to a Life of Kindness

Buddhaghosa

Selected, translated, and introduced
by Maria Heim

PRINCETON UNIVERSITY PRESS
PRINCETON AND OXFORD

Published by Princeton University Press
41 William Street, Princeton, New Jersey 08540
99 Banbury Road, Oxford OX2 6JX

press.princeton.edu

GPSR Authorized Representative:
Easy Access System Europe - Mustamäe tee 50, 10621
Tallinn, Estonia, gpsr.requests@easproject.com

ISBN 9780691292816
ISBN (epub) 9780691294827
ISBN (PDF) 9780691292823

Library of Congress Control Number: 2026939310

British Library Cataloging-in-Publication Data is available

Editorial: Rob Tempio and Chloe Coy
Production Editorial: Mark Bellis
Text and Jacket Design: Heather Hansen
Production: Erin Suydam
Publicity: William Pagdatoon and Charlotte Coyne
Copyeditor: Jennifer Harris

Jacket Credit: Adapted from Wishva Dilshan, *Mihintale Buddha Prethima*, 2016, CC BY-SA 4.0, via Wikimedia Commons.

This book has been composed in Stempel Garamond

Printed in the United States of America

1 3 5 7 9 10 8 6 4 2

For Emily

The moment we choose to love we begin
to move towards freedom,
to act in ways that liberate ourselves
and others.
—bell hooks

CONTENTS

INTRODUCTION

We live in angry times. Many people find moral value and righteous energy in anger. We deploy it in our struggles for justice, wielding the old slogan, "If you aren't angry, you're not paying attention." We find much in our lives that is frankly infuriating, or at least irksome. And everywhere we turn, we find anger stoked, even celebrated. Even many who find the high temperature of anger in our own lives and the broader culture regrettable assume with a shrug that anger, while unfortunate, is an inevitable feature of human life about which little can be done.[1]

Buddhist thought challenges these ideas and norms by noting the elements of hatred in anger and urging that both emotions be set aside. For Buddhists, anger is painful and destructive not only for those it targets but for the angry person as well. When we are consumed with anger, we see the world aslant; even when we are angry because of genuine harm done to us or those we love, we are filled with a violent and toxic energy that keeps us from taking in the whole picture. Nurturing our resentments, we look for further justifications as we attempt to shore up a damaged ego. Even if we don't act on our anger in retaliation—and if we do, we only fuel an escalating cycle of enmity and reprisal—we still fester and seethe. Or we might try to bury the anger but find that it still gnaws at us under the surface, poisoning our good will and peace of mind in ways we may not even fully realize.

Like many religious thinkers and philosophers across human history, the Buddha taught that we are better off without such anger and toxic emotions. And like other thinkers, he taught that love is the antidote. Love helps us to see more clearly and to connect with the world, rather than throw up barriers against it. And love and kindness always feel much better than hate.

Buddhists also see that love is a kind of freedom. Love, and related experiences like compassion and sympathy, not only benefit others—they also free our own minds from the constrictions and distortions of anger, hatred, envy, discontent, cruelty, and indifference that otherwise enslave us and make us miserable. Love, sympathy, and compassion can cast off these painful shackles and replace them with the freedom to flourish in solidarity with others.

The question then becomes *how*. How exactly does one turn hate and anger into love? *Especially* in the case of trying to love one's enemies and all the angry haters out there. How does one foster the compassion for them that rids us of cruelty and indifference? How does one actually feel happiness instead of discontent or envy from the success of others? How can we truly love others?

The Buddhist techniques in this book are practical strategies for learning how to do just this.

Lovingkindness, Compassion, Sympathetic Joy, and Equanimity

The earliest Buddhist teachings speak of four "sublime attitudes"—lovingkindness, compassion, sympathetic joy, and equanimity.[2] We might find it helpful to see them as four varieties of altruistic love. In Buddhist terms, they are four kinds of "attention" to others, where we come to see them more clearly and without the blinders and blinkers of our negative emotions. These forms of attention—which include active modes of feeling and emotion—require disciplined work and activity to bring them into being.

Lovingkindness is friendliness toward others, attending to them and wishing them well-being and happiness. *Compassion* is being shaken by others' distress and wishing to remove it. *Sympathetic joy* is feeling delight and happiness, rather than envy, at the success and good fortune of others. And the fourth sublime attitude—one to be built only after developing the other three—is *equanimity*, a kind of impartial, nonreactive, and balanced attention to others, come what may.

These four are the same kinds of attention and feeling a mother has toward her four sons: she feels *lovingkindness* toward the little one, wanting him to flourish; she feels *compassion* toward the sick child, wanting him to get well; she feels *sympathetic joy* toward the youth, rejoicing in his beauty and success; and she feels *equanimity* toward her grown-up son as he manages his own affairs (though she has, of course, never stopped loving him). The challenge is to take these very natural dispositions that we already feel toward our loved ones and extend them further and further out toward mere acquaintances, and then even hostile people, extending them eventually in every direction universally. The more we can do so, the more both we and those we encounter in the world are flooded with these happy and peaceful experiences.

Because they can always be extended in scope to more and more beings, and can always increase in depth and habit toward any one being, the sublime attitudes are also called the "immeasurables." They are the constant work of removing anger, hate, envy, and cruelty. Cultivating them should probably never be regarded as entirely finished.

When we learn how to flood others with these beautiful emotions, we achieve freedom from their opposites, and the world becomes a brighter place. To the extent that we can extend these dispositions in every direction without limit or boundary, we experience the world as more spacious, and we inhabit it with greater freedom.

The *Path of Purification*

The text translated here is one chapter of a meditation manual composed by the great fifth-century scholar and commentator Buddhaghosa. Buddhaghosa lived in India nearly a millennium after the Buddha and helped compose commentaries that systematized and elucidated what the Buddha taught. Buddhaghosa traveled to Sri Lanka, where he was entrusted with the ancient commentaries on the sacred texts of the Theravada tradition (one of the earliest Buddhist schools), a large body of scripture that we now call the Pali Canon in reference to the language in which it was first written. He edited these commentaries and translated them from ancient Sinhala into Pali. His most famous work, however, is his own large treatise, the *Path of Purification*, which he regarded as the hub or centerpiece of the entire commentarial corpus, and indeed of the entire Buddhist path. The *Path of Purification* gathers the Buddha's teachings into a step-by-step training manual for purifying the mind—that is, for ridding oneself—of problematic actions, thoughts, feelings, and afflictions, in order to bring about ultimate peace, freedom, and happiness.

Our chapter occurs in the large middle section of the *Path of Purification*, concerning meditation. This section builds on the first part of the work focused on moral conduct. Moral conduct involves refraining from wrongdoing and from harmful actions. Only on a moral foundation of refraining from harming life, and from stealing, lying, and so on, can one achieve the peace of mind that makes it possible to sit on one's meditation cushion and to concentrate well enough to actually meditate.

Meditation, like morality, involves refraining and removing: one arrests and removes the distractions that clutter the mind, such as greed or attachment to the body or ego. Our specific chapter is aimed at refraining from and removing anger, hate, cruelty, envy, discontent, and passion to bring clarity, happiness, and freedom to the mind. Readers should understand that this chapter is part of a much larger program of practical techniques for developing morality, concentration, and, in the last part of the book, wisdom, that together constitute an entire therapeutic path aimed at ultimate freedom.

Buddhaghosa's advice for developing the four sublime attitudes is a classic of religious literature. His tone is gentle even when he is advising us to remonstrate sternly with our own folly and stubbornness in clinging to anger and antipathy. Readers may even note a tender humor at work in his strategies and stories urging us to learn how to change, quite literally, our minds. In his hands, a complex moral psychology comes into view, whose teachings on how emotions work invite the modern reader into new ways of relating to experience. In this respect, the ideas and mindfulness techniques in this book may have practical and therapeutic applications in the fields of mental health, clinical psychology, and the caregiving professions.

The Translation

To aid the reader, I divide the "Detailed Instructions on the Sublime Attitudes" chapter into five sections—one for each attitude and a final section on various topics—and offer commentary at certain junctures to ease the reader into what to expect. I have also added subheadings not always present as such in the text itself, but which are taken from the language used in those sections. Buddhaghosa quotes frequently from canonical sources; I provide endnotes with citations and the English translations of these texts.

To convey something of the subtle beauty of this text in English, I have taken several translational liberties. I use English instead of Pali syntax to make things accessible and lively for English readers, and I turn most of the passive constructions into active voice. Sometimes I swap a pronoun with its referent when a passage has allowed its referent to get obscured. Most audaciously, I have rendered many of the future passive participles and their impersonal subjects into imperatives with a stated or implied second person. Instead of the stodgy and detached formulation "Lovingkindness should be practiced," my translation reads "Practice lovingkindness." These ancient meditation practices are hands-on instructions to their reader on how to do them, not starchy descriptions of the sorts of things that should be done by an abstract someone.

In Pali, *dosa* means both anger and hate. To convey both meanings in English I sometimes translate the single term *dosa* as "anger and hate." At other times, I choose one or the other according to which one seems indicated by the context, but readers should keep in mind both meanings.

There are several points in the translation where I left out brief passages; these are indicated with ellipses. Most of the omitted passages elaborate technicalities on matters of advanced meditation that will be opaque to both the beginning practitioner and the reader interested primarily in the text as a moral psychology of love. In one case, the omitted passage involves a style of Pali definitional practice that relies on the sounds of Pali words to generate meaning in ways that necessarily elude English translation. For those seeking the full text in English, Bhikkhu Ñāṇamoli's superb translation of the *Path of Purification* should be the next port of call.

Buddhaghosa wrote this manual for monastics who are engaging in these practices in great earnest and in a full-time way. We see the social context of his instructions as we realize that these practices are often strategies for getting along with one's colleagues in the religious life as one lives closely with, and is often seriously annoyed by, one's fellow monks. We also come to discern the religious cosmology assumed in the text, where the ideal monastic practitioner worships the Buddha, is inspired by the scripture Buddhaghosa frequently quotes, and hopes to attain nirvana, or, failing that, to be reborn in the Brahma heavens in their next life. The text assumes the reality of rebirth (we have all lived infinite lives in the past and will continue to do so until we attain nirvana) and karma (we have inherited the fruits of our past actions, and we will experience the fruits of our present actions). Buddhaghosa makes creative use of these ideas to fashion thought experiments helpful for shifting perspective, thought, and feeling.

The sublime attitudes are mindfulness practices. Within Buddhist meditation, they are techniques for calming and unifying the mind called serenity practices (*samatha*). Serenity practices have a fourfold structure of increasingly deep immersion or concentration (the four "absorptions," or *jhānas*).[3] For each of the four deep concentrations, there is a "preliminary" entry into the topic on which one is meditating, and then "full absorption." The aim of practicing the sublime attitudes is to achieve full absorption in each attitude as it is directed to each case. That is, when I have flooded each person with lovingkindness to the point where I feel it equally toward dear ones, strangers, and enemies, I have broken down barriers between them and in this way have achieved "full absorption" in the meditation practice.

Another Word on Meditation and Cosmology

In addition to being meditation practices, the sublime attitudes are also heavenly realms. Part of the richness of this text is that it is always working on (at least) two planes at once. One level is what we have been describing—how these experiences work in everyday life (a mother loving her children) and in one's meditation practice (the discipline of expanding that love to others). The second level is cosmological: the four sublime attitudes are also heavenly or divine realms into which one will be reborn through the very practice of these meditations. In this way, meditation maps onto cosmology.[4]

When one participates in the four sublime attitudes, one is experiencing what the gods in certain heavens experience. There are many heavens in Buddhism, and the heavens are truly wonderful. However, they are not permanent: the acts of good karma that take us to them eventually run out and one is reborn into another realm, good (fortunate human or divine realms) or bad (unfortunate human, animal, and hell realms). The four sublime attitudes are called "Brahma abodes" or "Brahma ways of living" (*brahmavihāra*), because their content is what certain types of Brahma deities experience in their heavens. Brahma gods are gentle and loving and their worlds are beautiful, radiant, and spacious. We can learn of their worlds through these meditation experiences, as Buddhaghosa shows us directly at the end of his chapter.

That the four *brahmavihāras* refer both to sublime meditation experiences available in this very life *and* to heavenly realms presents a conundrum for the translator. To call them, as I do here, "sublime attitudes" might suggest a modernist set of assumptions that strips them of their cosmological significance in the tradition. To call them "Brahma abodes" or "heavenly states" might suggest that these are chiefly religious states addressing those who share Buddhist cosmological assumptions. Unfortunately, translators have to make choices. I have chosen the former, imperfect as the decision may be, because I want this translation to speak most of all to readers seeking freedom, love, and beauty in this very life. That the minds we make for ourselves here and now give us direct access to transcendent heavenly worlds is one of the most marvelous ideas in Buddhism: we create the minds we want to have in this life and so can experience heaven right here on earth.

THE SUBLIME ATTITUDES

LOVINGKINDNESS

Buddhaghosa dives right into his chapter on the sublime attitudes with practical instructions for lovingkindness. The content of this experience is friendly good will—that is, one longs for others to be happy. As we will see with all of the sublime attitudes, the attitude must be directed toward a specific someone, a living flesh-and-blood person toward whom you can get the emotion flowing. There is nothing abstract about this practice: it involves real emotions toward specific beings ("beings" is mentioned advisedly, as it is not just humans toward whom we will want to feel universal friendliness).

You'll want to start where it is easy and the emotion comes naturally. We will see that

Buddhaghosa does not think that you should start with enemies or even neutrals, because feeling lovingkindness toward them is just too hard at first. Instead, you should start by feeling lovingkindness toward yourself since it is very easy to long for your own happiness. The idea is to get kindness flowing, for a mind full of kindness can't at the same time hold hate or anger. There may also be deeper psychological truth in his insisting, against possible detractors, on starting with loving yourself. He perceives that those who hate themselves can never truly love another. It may be that much hatred, cruelty, and apathy are, at bottom, the result of self-loathing.

In any case, you cannot get far in the meditation practice simply by flooding yourself with friendly thoughts, so you learn to gradually extend them to others—first a dear one, then one for whom you have only neutral feelings (per-

*haps a mere acquaintance), then a hostile person. Of course, it is at the stage of contemplating the hostile person—someone either you dislike or who dislikes you—that things get sticky. Interestingly, in Pali, the word for anger and hatred (*dosa*) is the same, a point itself worth reflecting on. It is a deeply unpleasant experience that by its very nature harms both you and others.*[5]

Buddhists do not think that there is any context in which anger is a good or helpful thing (a view quite different from many modern people who think that anger is justified, inevitable, and can even helpfully prompt action toward a righteous cause). Buddhists take the ferocity of anger to entail a lack of control conducive to harmful action; or, if it is the simmering type of anger, it quietly corrodes one's inner peace, clear vision, and basic decency. It should be combated with its opposites, either the friendly good will of lovingkindness, or patience, the ability to endure harm from others without getting angry.

As you go deeper into this practice examining more and more closely your feelings toward particular others, it is likely that you will come upon a person toward whom—when you reflect on them—anger, resentment, or hostility flares up. Most of the lovingkindness practice is a series of techniques for removing this anger so that you can eventually break down all barriers and feel universal lovingkindness toward everyone equally.

These techniques are a kind of cognitive or affective therapy that involves transforming one's negative emotional biases into more positive orientations. They also might be seen as a kind of philosophical therapy of attending to the world more justly and lovingly, and thus more freely, as philosopher Iris Murdoch also suggests.[6] Ideally, the practitioner is engaging these practices daily, over a long period of time, to bring about a subtle psychological refashioning. The practices shift mood and perspective by undermining our usual fixed and tenacious sense of grievance, resentment, and disaffection.

And so you learn to change the way you think and feel about the person by various strategies ranging from reproaching yourself for nourishing an anger that only makes you upset to realizing that you are only gratifying your enemy by permitting your anger to make you ugly. As a good Buddhist—Buddhaghosa is addressing an in-house audience—you should, he thinks, be moved by the Buddha's own words and example. So another technique is to consider the extraordinary patience the Buddha practiced as a bodhisatta, that is, in his long run-up in previous lives to becoming the Buddha. In this technique you are to consider the extraordinary—and perhaps over-the-top—stories of his astonishing patience and lack of anger in these previous lives. Holding up the Bodhisatta as an ideal against which to measure your own petty grievances can shake you out of stubbornly nurturing your anger.

Buddhaghosa thinks that because we have been habituated to anger and hatred for so long, and because what works for some of us may not work for others, many techniques should be offered. If one technique fails or seems unrealistic, he offers another one following it. Some of these involve imaginative exercises that depend on Buddhist ideas of karma and rebirth. When I consider the workings of karma, where actions have previous conditions and will issue in future results, I realize that my enemy and I are both conditioned by our past actions and will be held to account for our present and future actions.

This can caution me about my own reactions, even while it reminds me that my enemies will experience the effects of their own actions. They will be dealt with justly without need for my angry feelings of reprisal.

The idea of rebirth too can prompt a shift in perspective: If the doctrine of rebirth is true and we have all been reborn infinitely in the past in all manner of different relationships with one another, then it is very possible that my current enemy was in a past life my mother. In that life, she tenderly nourished and cared for me. Buddhaghosa expounds on the tender acts of care we receive as infants to help shift our mood and perspective. Reflecting on my own vulnerability and how I was once the recipient of loving care—perhaps by this same person in a distant life—I realize that it can only be churlish for me to continue harboring hate toward them now.

Other techniques that may need some explanation take a different tack by deploying Buddhist ideas of "no self" to dismantle anger.[7] *Persons are real up to a point, but on closer analysis they are only a collection of constantly changing momentary events. So the person I am angry with now is not the "same" person who initially caused me distress. Like me, they are changing all the time, and like me, they are conditioned by a complex set of processes that I can disaggregate and analyze. In fact, looking for the stable, unchanging essence of this person on which to target my anger (and anger always wants a target), I find that they dissolve into these changing parts. Toward whom, toward what, am I actually angry?*

If all else fails, you should give the person a gift. Generosity to your enemy can almost magically wipe away anger on both sides.

The techniques call on us to consider why we want to hold on to these painful experiences and to think that maybe we would be happier and better off without them. And our wishing that the other be happy and friendly will likely affect them as well, bringing about a better overall state of affairs for us all.

Once you have flooded yourself, your dear ones, mere acquaintances, and enemies with lovingkindness, you can reach "full absorption" in the practice, which is indicated by your having "broken down barriers": only when you can see no difference in your feelings for any of these four have you achieved universal love.

Mettā

[1] Anussatikammaṭṭhānānantaraṃ uddiṭṭhesu pana mettā karuṇā muditā upekkhāti imesu catūsu brahmavihāresu mettaṃ bhāvetukāmena tāva ādikammikena yogāvacarena upacchinnapalibodhena gahitakammaṭṭhānena bhattakiccaṃ katvā bhattasammadaṃ paṭivinodetvā vivitte padese supaññatte āsane sukhanisinnena ādito tāva dose ādīnavo khantiyañca ānisaṃso paccavekkhitabbo.[8]

Kasmā? Imāya hi bhāvanāya doso pahātabbo, khanti adhigantabbā. Na ca sakkā kiñci adiṭṭhādīnavaṃ pahātuṃ, aviditānisaṃsaṃ vā adhigantuṃ. Tasmā duṭṭho kho, āvuso, dosena

Lovingkindness

[1] The four sublime attitudes—lovingkindness, compassion, sympathetic joy, and equanimity—are mentioned immediately following the meditation on the recollections. To start with, the beginning meditator who wants to practice lovingkindness should finish their duties and only then take up the meditation on this topic. After having a meal and dispelling any post-meal sleepiness, get seated comfortably on a well-prepared seat in a secluded place. First, contemplate the dangers of anger and hatred and the benefits of patience.

Why do this? This practice banishes anger and generates patience. And you cannot abandon dangers of which you are not aware or attain benefits of which you are ignorant. Therefore,

abhibhūto pariyādiṇṇacitto pāṇampi han-
atītiādīnaṃ vasena dose ādīnavo daṭṭhabbo.

Khantī paramaṃ tapo titikkhā, nibbānaṃ
paramaṃ vadanti buddhā.
Khantibalaṃ balānīkaṃ, tamahaṃ brūmi
brāhmaṇaṃ.
Khantā bhiyyo na vijjatītiādīnaṃ vasena khan-
tiyaṃ ānisaṃso veditabbo.

Athevaṃ diṭṭhādīnavato dosato cittaṃ vivecanatthāya, viditānisaṃsāya ca khantiyā saṃyojanatthāya mettābhāvanā ārabhitabbā.

[2] Ārabhantena ca āditova puggalabhedo jānitabbo imesu puggalesu mettā paṭhamaṃ na[11]

teachings such as "Friends, an angry person overcome and obsessed with hatred harms living beings" reveal the dangers of anger and the benefit of patience.

> The buddhas say that patience is the highest
> endurance.
> And that nirvana is supreme.
> I call anyone whose real strength is the
> power of patience a brahmin.[9]
> There is nothing greater than patience.[10]

Therefore, for the sake of removing hate from the mind—its danger now seen—and connecting it to patience—its benefit now known—take up the practice of lovingkindness.

[2] Now, at the very beginning, one starting out should recognize that there are different

bhāvetabbā, imesu neva bhāvetabbā ti. Ayañhi mettā appiyapuggale, atippiyasahāyake, majjhatte, verīpuggaleti imesu catūsu paṭhamaṃ na bhāvetabbā. Liṅgavisabhāge odhiso na bhāvetabbā. Kālakate na bhāvetabbāva.

Kiṃkāraṇā appiyādīsu paṭhamaṃ na bhāvetabbā? Appiyaṃ hi piyaṭṭhāne ṭhapento kilamati. Atippiyasahāyakaṃ majjhattaṭṭhāne ṭhapento kilamati, appamattakepi cassa dukkhe uppanne ārodanākārappatto viya hoti. Majjhattaṃ garuṭṭhāne ca piyaṭṭhāne ca ṭhapento kilamati. Verimanussarato kodho uppajjati, tasmā appiyādīsu paṭhamaṃ na bhāvetabbā.

classes of persons and that at first lovingkindness should be cultivated toward certain people and not toward others. At the beginning, lovingkindness should not be practiced toward these four: someone one dislikes, a dear friend, a person toward whom one feels neutral, and a hostile person. And it should not be practiced toward someone of the opposite sex or someone who has died.

Why should lovingkindness meditation not be practiced at first toward these kinds of people, the disliked person and the others? It is exhausting to put someone one dislikes in the position of someone dear. Placing a dear friend in the place of a mere acquaintance is also exhausting and if they incur even a trifling sorrow, one can be moved to tears. To put a mere acquaintance in the place of a teacher or a dear friend is also

Liṅgavisabhāge pana tameva ārabbha odhiso bhāventassa rāgo uppajjati. Aññataro kira amaccaputto kulūpakattheraṃ pucchi bhante, kassa mettā bhāvetabbā ti? Thero piyapuggale ti āha. Tassa attano bhariyā piyā hoti. So tassā mettaṃ bhāvento sabbarattiṃ bhittiyuddhamakāsi. Tasmā liṅgavisabhāge odhiso na bhāvetabbā.

Kālakate pana bhāvento neva appanaṃ, na upacāraṃ pāpuṇāti. Aññataro kira daharabhikkhu ācariyaṃ ārabbha mettaṃ ārabhi. Tassa mettā nappavattati. So mahātherassa santikaṃ gantvā

exhausting. And anger flares up when one thinks about a hostile person. So at first do not practice this meditation toward these people.

And passion is aroused when practicing this meditation toward a person of the opposite sex. It is said that there was once a monk associated with a certain household who was asked by a friend's son, "Sir, toward whom should lovingkindness be practiced?" The monk replied, "Toward a person who is dear." The man's own wife was dear to him. Practicing lovingkindness toward her, he spent the night beating his head against the wall. This is why it should not be practiced toward a person of the opposite sex.

And one practicing specifically for someone deceased achieves neither preliminary nor full meditative absorption. It seems that a certain young monk undertook lovingkindness directed

bhante, paguṇāva me mettājhānasamāpatti, na ca naṃ samāpajjituṃ sakkomi, kiṃ nu kho kāraṇanti āha. Thero nimittaṃ, āvuso, gavesāhīti āha. So gavesanto ācariyassa matabhāvaṃ ñatvā aññaṃ ārabbha mettāyanto samāpattiṃ appesi. Tasmā kālakate na bhāvetabbāva.

[3] Sabbapaṭhamaṃ pana ahaṃ sukhito homi niddukkho ti vā, avero abyāpajjo anīgho sukhī attānaṃ pariharāmīti vā evaṃ punappunaṃ attaniyeva bhāvetabbā.

Evaṃ sante yaṃ vibhaṅge vuttaṃ

toward his teacher. But his lovingkindness did not advance. So he approached an eminent monk and reported, "Sir, I am very well-versed in practicing deep concentration on lovingkindness, but I am not able to enter into it. Why is this?" The monk replied, "Seek out the mental object of the meditation, friend." Seeking him out, he realized that his teacher had died, and so he generated lovingkindness toward someone else and achieved it. This shows that it cannot be practiced toward someone who has died.

[3] So develop it first aimed specifically toward yourself, again and again, in this way: "May I be happy and free of suffering!" or "Let me be friendly, without ill will, untroubled, and happy!"

But, one might think, surely this contradicts what is said in the texts. The *Book of Analysis* says:

Kathañca bhikkhu mettāsahagatena cetasā ekaṃ disaṃ pharitvā viharati? Seyyathāpi nāma ekaṃ puggalaṃ piyaṃ manāpaṃ disvā mettāyeyya, evameva sabbe satte mettāya pharatīti.

Yañca paṭisambhidāyaṃ

Katamehi pañcahākārehi anodhisopharaṇā mettā cetovimutti bhāvetabbā, sabbe sattā averā hontu abyāpajjā anīghā sukhī attānaṃ pariharantu. Sabbe pāṇā... sabbe bhūtā... sabbe puggalā... sabbe attabhāvapariyāpannā averā abyāpajjā anīghā sukhī attānaṃ pariharantū ti ādi

Vuttaṃ. Yañca mettasutte

> And how does a monk live flooding one direction with a mind full of lovingkindness? Imagine how one would feel lovingkindness upon seeing a dear and likable person. Just like that one floods all beings with lovingkindness.[12]

And the *Treatise on Analytic Knowledge* says:

> What are the five ways that freedom of the loving mind is to be practiced universally?[13] First, may all *beings* go about friendly, without ill will, untroubled, and happy! Second, may all *living creatures*; third, all *who exist*; fourth, all *people*; and five, all *individuals* be friendly, without ill will, untroubled, and happy![14]

And the "Teaching on Lovingkindness" says:

Sukhinova khemino hontu,
Sabbasattā bhavantu sukhitattātiādi.

Vuttaṃ, taṃ virujjhati.

Na hi tattha attani bhāvanā vuttāti ce. Tañca na virujjhati. Kasmā? Tañhi appanāvasena vuttaṃ. Idaṃ sakkhibhāvavasena. Sacepi hi vassasataṃ vassasahassaṃ vā ahaṃ sukhito homītiādinā nayena attani mettaṃ bhāveti, nevassa appanā uppajjati. Ahaṃ sukhito homīti bhāvayato pana yathā ahaṃ sukhakāmo dukkhapaṭikkūlo jīvitukāmo amaritukāmo ca, evaṃ aññepi sattāti attānaṃ sakkhiṃ katvā aññasattesu hitasukhakāmatā uppajjati.

May all beings be happy and peaceful!
May they be at ease![15]

Nowhere is it said that this meditation is to be done toward oneself.

But in fact, this does not contradict the texts. Why not? These statements concern full absorption. But here we are concerned with just directly experiencing lovingkindness. True, even if one were to say "May I be happy" for a hundred or a thousand years with this method of practicing lovingkindness toward oneself, full absorption would never arise. But by practicing "May I be happy," one generates longing for the well-being and happiness of other beings by first directly experiencing it for oneself. For just as I wish for happiness and to avoid suffering, and I wish to live and not to die, so too do other beings.

Bhagavatāpi—

Sabbā disā anuparigamma cetasā,
Nevajjhagā piyataramattanā kvaci;
Evaṃ piyo puthu attā paresaṃ,
Tasmā na hiṃse paramattakāmoti.
vadatā ayaṃ nayo dassito.

[4] Tasmā sakkhibhāvatthaṃ paṭhamaṃ attānaṃ mettāya pharitvā tadanantaraṃ sukhappavattanatthaṃ yvāyaṃ piyo manāpo garu bhāvanīyo ācariyo vā ācariyamatto vā upajjhāyo vā upajjhāyamatto vā tassa dānapiyavacanādīni piyamanāpattakāraṇāni sīlasutādīni garubhāvanīyattakāraṇāni ca anussaritvā esa sappuriso sukhī hotu niddukkho tiādinā nayena mettā bhāvetabbā.

This interpretation is confirmed by the Buddha's statements such as this:

> Casting around with the mind in every
> direction,
> no one finds anyone more dear than oneself.
> Each holds their own self most dear.
> And so, loving oneself, one does not harm
> others.[16]

[4] Now, having first flooded yourself with lovingkindness in order to experience it directly, and so that you may proceed easily and continuously, recollect someone dear and likable, or a teacher, someone respected, a religious leader or one of similar status, or a mentor or someone like a mentor. And in the case of the dear and likable person, recall such things as their kind

Evarūpe ca puggale kāmaṃ appanā sampajjati, iminā pana bhikkhunā tāvatakeneva tuṭṭhiṃ anāpajjitvā sīmāsambhedaṃ kattukāmena tadanantaraṃ atippiyasahāyake, atippiyasahāyakato majjhatte, majjhattato verīpuggale mettā bhāvetabbā. Bhāventena ca ekekasmiṃ koṭṭhāse muduṃ kammaniyaṃ cittaṃ katvā tadanantare tadanantare upasaṃharitabbaṃ.

words and generosity and your own considerate actions toward them. In the case of one respected and honored, recall such things as their virtue and learning and your own deferential actions toward them. And in this way, practice lovingkindness: "May this good person be happy and free of suffering!"

Full absorption easily arises when directed toward such a person. But the monastic practitioner not satisfied with only this and who also wants to break down barriers should immediately turn to practicing lovingkindness toward the very dear friend, and after the very dear friend, the mere acquaintance, and after the mere acquaintance, the hostile person. Practicing toward persons in each category one after the other, open and soften your heart toward each before taking up the next.

Yassa pana verīpuggalo vā natthi, mahāpurisajātikattā vā anatthaṃ karontepi pare verīsaññāva nuppajjati, tena majjhatte me mettacittaṃ kammaniyaṃ jātaṃ, idāni naṃ verimhi upasaṃharāmīti byāpārova na kātabbo. Yassa pana atthi, taṃ sandhāya vuttaṃ majjhattato verīpuggale mettā bhāvetabbāti.

[5] Sace panassa verimhi cittamupasaṃharato tena katāparādhānussaraṇena paṭighamuppajjati, athānena purimapuggalesu yattha katthaci punappunaṃ mettaṃ samāpajjitvā vuṭṭhahitvā

But it may be that you do not know any hostile people, either because you are a truly great person or because you do not perceive hostility in others even when they have done you harm. In this case, you may disregard this step: "Now that the loving mind has grown supple toward the mere acquaintance, let me turn to the hostile person." For it is for those who do have one that it is instructed that "after the mere acquaintance, lovingkindness should be practiced toward the hostile person."

Techniques for Dispelling Anger and Hate

[5] But if anger arises when turning the mind to an enemy because you keep remembering the wrongs they have done, then repeatedly go back to lovingkindness toward any of the earlier

punappunaṃ taṃ puggalaṃ mettāyantena paṭighaṃ vinodetabbaṃ.

Sace evampi vāyamato na nibbāti, atha

Kakacūpamaovāda-ādīnaṃ anusārato;
Paṭighassa pahānāya, ghaṭitabbaṃ
punappunaṃ.

Tañca kho iminā ākārena attānaṃ ovadanteneva are kujjhanapurisa, nanu vuttaṃ bhagavatā. Ubhatodaṇḍakena cepi, bhikkhave, kakacena corā ocarakā aṅgamaṅgāni okanteyyuṃ, tatrāpi yo mano padoseyya. Na me so tena sāsanakaro ti ca

Tasseva tena pāpiyo, yo kuddhaṃ
paṭikujjhati;

persons, and then, emerging while feeling lovingkindness again and again, dispel anger toward that person.

But if going all out in this way doesn't cool it down, then consider:

> In order to eliminate anger, one should
> make repeated effort
> by recalling such teachings as the simile of
> the saw.

That is, reproach yourself this way: "Hey you, angry person! Didn't the Buddha say 'Monks, even if thieves were to savagely saw off your limbs with a two-handled saw, to respond with an angry mind would not be following my teaching.'" What is more:

> It is worse to lash back with anger than to
> be angry first.

Kuddhamappaṭikujjhanto, saṅgāmaṃ jeti dujjayaṃ.

Ubhinnamatthaṃ carati, attano ca parassa ca;
Paraṃ saṅkupitaṃ ñatvā, yo sato upasammatīti ca.

Sattime, bhikkhave, dhammā sapattakantā sapattakaraṇā kodhanaṃ āgacchanti itthiṃ vā purisaṃ vā. Katame satta? Idha, bhikkhave, sapatto sapattassa evaṃ icchati aho vatāyaṃ dubbaṇṇo assāti. Taṃ kissahetu? Na, bhikkhave, sapatto sapattassa vaṇṇavatāya nandati. Kodhanāyaṃ, bhikkhave, purisapuggalo kodhābhibhūto kodhapareto kiñcāpi so hoti sunhāto suvilitto kappitakesamassu

> Not responding to anger with anger, one
> wins the hardest battle of all.
>
> One acts for the sake of both oneself and
> the other
> when, seeing that the other is angry, one is
> mindful and stays calm.[17]

And also:

> Monks, when a woman or a man gets angry, there are seven things that please and gratify their enemies. What are the seven things? Monks, an enemy wants their enemy to be ugly. Why is this? Monks, an enemy does not delight in the beauty of their enemy. And an angry person overpowered by anger and oppressed with anger is ugly in being overpowered by anger even if freshly bathed,

odātavatthavasano, atha kho so dubbaṇṇova hoti kodhābhibhūto. Ayaṃ, bhikkhave, paṭhamo dhammo sapattakanto sapattakaraṇo kodhanaṃ āgacchati itthiṃ vā purisaṃ vā.

Puna caparaṃ, bhikkhave, sapatto sapattassa evaṃ icchati ahovatāyaṃ dukkhaṃ sayeyyāti ... pe ... na pacurattho assāti ... pe ... na bhogavā assāti ... pe ... na yasavā assāti ... pe ... na mittavā assāti ... pe ... na kāyassa bhedā paraṃ maraṇā sugatiṃ saggaṃ lokaṃ upapajjeyyāti. Taṃ kissa hetu? Na, bhikkhave, sapatto sapattassa sugatigamanena nandati. Kodhanāyaṃ, bhikkhave, purisapuggalo kodhābhibhūto kodhapareto kāyena duccaritaṃ carati, vācāya manasā duccaritaṃ carati. So kāyena vācāya manasā duccaritaṃ caritvā kāyassa bhedā paraṃ maraṇā apāyaṃ duggatiṃ vinipātaṃ nirayaṃ upapajjati kodhābhibhūtoti

perfumed, with hair well styled, and wearing clean clothes. This is the first thing that pleases and gratifies an enemy when a woman or a man gets angry.

Furthermore, monks, an enemy wants their enemy to sleep badly, to be unsuccessful, to fail, to be infamous, to become friendless, to not make it to heaven or another good place after death. Why is this? Monks, an enemy does not delight in the happiness and well-being of their enemy. An angry person overpowered by anger and oppressed with anger behaves badly physically, verbally, and mentally. Behaving badly physically, verbally, and mentally, a person overpowered by anger goes to hell, to a lower realm, and to a bad fate when the body breaks down and they die.[18]

Ca,

Seyyathāpi, bhikkhave, chavālātaṃ ubhatopadittaṃ majjhe gūthagataṃ neva gāme kaṭṭhatthaṃ pharati, na araññe kaṭṭhatthaṃ pharati. Tathūpamāhaṃ, bhikkhave, imaṃ puggalaṃ vadāmīti.

Ca so dāni tvaṃ evaṃ kujjhanto na ceva bhagavato sāsanakaro bhavissasi, paṭikujjhanto ca kuddhapurisatopi pāpiyo hutvā na dujjayaṃ saṅgāmaṃ jessasi, sapattakaraṇe ca dhamme attāva attano karissasi, chavālātūpamo ca bhavissasīti.

[6] Tassevaṃ ghaṭayato vāyamato sace taṃ paṭighaṃ vūpasammati, iccetaṃ kusalaṃ. No ce vūpasammati, atha yo yo dhammo tassa puggalassa vūpasanto hoti parisuddho, anussariyamāno

And:

> Monks, I tell you that the angry person is much like a log from a pyre burnt on both ends and coated with excrement in the middle—useful as lumber neither in the village nor in the forest.[19]

And so, reproach yourself: "Remaining angry in this way, you are not following the Buddha's teaching. It is worse to lash out with anger than to be angry first and you are not winning the hardest battle. You are doing to yourself things that only please your enemy. Moreover, you will become like the pyre log!"

[6] It is good if the anger subsides when one goes all out and strives in this way. But if it still does not subside, then recalling a composed or pure quality of the person can bring one peace.

pasādaṃ āvahati, taṃ taṃ anussaritvā āghāto paṭivinetabbo.

Ekaccassa hi kāyasamācārova upasanto hoti. Upasantabhāvo cassa bahuṃ vattapaṭipattiṃ karontassa sabbajanena ñāyati. Vacīsamācāramanosamācārā pana avūpasantā honti. Tassa te acintetvā kāyasamācāravūpasamoyeva anussaritabbo.

Ekaccassa vacīsamācārova upasanto hoti. Upasantabhāvo cassa sabbajanena ñāyati. So hi pakatiyā ca paṭisanthārakusalo hoti sakhilo sukhasambhāso sammodako uttānamukho pubbabhāsī madhurena sarena dhammaṃ osāreti, parimaṇḍalehi padabyañjanehi dhammakathaṃ katheti. Kāyasamācāramanosamācārā pana avūpasantā honti, tassa te acintetvā vacīsamācāravūpasamoyeva anussaritabbo.

The irritation should subside as one recalls this or that quality.

Now, some people are composed only in their physical conduct. Everyone recognizes their composure by their fulfilling many duties and responsibilities, even if they are not composed in their verbal and mental conduct. Without thinking of these, recall only the composure of their physical conduct.

Others are composed only in their verbal conduct. Everyone recognizes their composure by their eloquence, because they are kind, friendly, welcoming, easy to talk to, and the first to speak up. They teach sweetly and speak articulately when giving instruction, even if they are not composed in their physical and mental conduct. Without thinking of these, recall only the composure of their verbal conduct.

Ekaccassa manosamācārova upasanto hoti, upasantabhāvo cassa cetiyavandanādīsu sabbajanassa pākaṭo hoti. Yo hi avūpasantacitto hoti, so cetiyaṃ vā bodhiṃ vā there vā vandamāno na sakkaccaṃ vandati, dhammassavanamaṇḍape vikkhittacitto vā pacalāyanto vā nisīdati. Upasantacitto pana okappetvā vandati, ohitasoto aṭṭhiṃkatvā kāyena vā vācāya vā cittappasādaṃ karonto dhammaṃ suṇāti. Iti ekaccassa manosamācārova upasanto hoti, kāyavacīsamācārā avūpasantā honti, tassa te acintetvā manosamācāravūpasamoyeva anussaritabbo.

Ekaccassa pana imesu tīsu dhammesu ekopi avūpasanto hoti, tasmiṃ puggale kiñcāpi esa idāni manussaloke carati, atha kho katipāhassa

Still others are composed only in their mental conduct. Everyone is well aware of their composure in honoring shrines and so on. For if one's mind is not composed, one does not pay proper respect when honoring a shrine, the Bodhi Tree, or monks, or is distracted or dozes off when sitting in the pavilion listening to the Teaching. But one with a composed mind gives credence to something and honors it, listening attentively, and staying focused. Enacting peace of mind with body and words, they listen to the Teaching. The mental conduct of this person is composed even if their physical and verbal conduct is not. Without thinking of these, recall only the composure of their mental conduct.

Yet others are composed in none of these three respects. One should extend compassion toward such people, realizing "Even though this

accayena aṭṭhamahānirayasoḷasaussadanirayaparipūrako bhavissatīti kāruññaṃ upaṭṭhapetabbaṃ. Kāruññampi hi paṭicca āghāto vūpasammati.

Ekaccassa tayopime dhammā vūpasantā honti, tassa yaṃ yaṃ icchati, taṃ taṃ anussaritabbaṃ. Tādise hi puggale na dukkarā hoti mettābhāvanāti.

Imassa ca atthassa āvibhāvatthaṃ pañcime, āvuso, āghātapaṭivinayā. Yattha bhikkhuno uppanno āghāto sabbaso paṭivinodetabbo ti idaṃ pañcakanipāte āghātapaṭivinayasuttaṃ vitthāretabbaṃ.

[7] Sace panassa evampi vāyamato āghāto uppajjatiyeva, athānena evaṃ attā ovaditabbo

Attano visaye dukkhaṃ, kataṃ te yadi verinā;

one is moving around in the human realm now, it won't be long now before they will pass away and enter the eight great hells or the sixteen auxiliary hells." For resentment is also calmed through compassion.

Finally, some people are composed in all three respects. Recall whichever of them you prefer, for practicing lovingkindness toward such a person is not difficult.

For the sake of making the meaning clear, the "Dispelling Resentment" Teaching in the *Book of the Fives* should be given in detail. It starts with "Friend, there are five ways of removing resentment whereby any resentment that occurs in a monk can be completely removed."[20]

[7] But if the resentment still occurs despite your efforts, reproach yourself in this way:

> Okay, let's grant that the hater has caused suffering in their sphere of influence.

Kiṃ tassāvisaye dukkhaṃ, sacitte
kattumicchasi.

Bahūpakāraṃ hitvāna, ñātivaggaṃ
rudammukhaṃ;
Mahānatthakaraṃ kodhaṃ, sapattaṃ na
jahāsi kiṃ.

Yāni rakkhasi sīlāni, tesaṃ mūlanikantanaṃ;
Kodhaṃ nāmupaḷālesi, ko tayā sadiso jaḷo.

Kataṃ anariyaṃ kammaṃ, parena iti kujjhasi;
Kiṃ nu tvaṃ tādisaṃyeva, yo sayaṃ
kattumicchasi.

Dosetukāmo yadi taṃ, amanāpaṃ paro kari;
Dosuppādena tasseva, kiṃ pūresi
manorathaṃ.

But your mind is not part of their domain.
Why let them cause suffering there?

Your family was so helpful to you, but you
tearfully relinquished their embrace.
Anger never helps you at all. So, why don't
you relinquish it?

You nurture the anger that eradicates your
precious virtue.
Who else is that stupid?

Someone else does something reprehensible,
and *you* get angry?
Does that mean you want to act just like
them?

Seeking to rile you up, someone else offends
you.
Doesn't getting angry just satisfy their aim?

Dukkhaṃ tassa ca nāma tvaṃ kuddho kāhasi
vā na vā;
Attānaṃ pana idāneva, kodhadukkhena
bādhasi.

Kodhaṃ vā ahitaṃ maggaṃ, ārūḷhā yadi
verino;
Kasmā tuvampi kujjhanto,
tesaṃyevānusikkhasi.

Yaṃ dosaṃ tava nissāya, sattunā appiyaṃ
kataṃ;
Tameva dosaṃ chindassu, kimaṭṭhāne
vihaññasi.

Khaṇikattā ca dhammānaṃ, yehi khandhehi
te kataṃ;
Amanāpaṃ niruddhā te, kassa dānīdha
kujjhasi.

Maybe you caused their suffering; maybe
not.
Either way, right now your anger is making
you suffer.

If hostile people set out on an angry and
unhelpful path
why on earth would you also get angry and
follow their lead?

If your enemy does something disagreeable
in response to your anger,
then let that be the end of it. Why pile on
more pain?

All of the causes of the problem were momentary. Now they have stopped.
So what exactly are you angry with now?

Dukkhaṃ karoti yo yassa, taṃ vinā kassa so
kare;
Sayampi dukkhahetu tvam iti kiṃ tassa
kujjhasīti.

[8] Sace panassa evaṃ attānaṃ ovadatopi paṭighaṃ neva vūpasammati, athānena attano ca parassa ca kammassakatā paccavekkhitabbā. Tattha attano tāva evaṃ paccavekkhitabbā ambho tvaṃ tassa kuddho kiṃ karissasi? Nanu taveva cetaṃ dosanidānaṃ kammaṃ anatthāya saṃvattissati? Kammassako hi tvaṃ kammadāyādo kammayoni kammabandhu kammapaṭisaraṇo, yaṃ kammaṃ karissasi, tassa dāyādo bhavissasi, idañca te kammaṃ neva sammāsambodhiṃ, na paccekabodhiṃ, na sāvakabhūmiṃ, na brahmattasakkattacakkavattipadesarājādisampattīnaṃ aññataraṃ sampattiṃ sādhetuṃ samatthaṃ, atha kho sāsanato cāvetvā vighāsādādibhāvassa ceva

Whoever created the harm is no longer present, but you are creating new harm now.
So you alone are the cause of suffering!
Why be angry at them?

[8] But if the anger is *still* not calmed despite reproaching yourself in this way, then reflect on the fact that you are responsible for your actions, just as others are responsible for theirs. Now, first reflect on this with respect to yourself, like this: "Hey you! What is the point of getting angry with them? Surely any action this anger causes will only lead to misfortune for you. 'For you are responsible for your actions, you experience the consequences of your actions, and you are the source of your actions; you are bound to your actions and actions are your refuge. You will experience the consequences of any action you perform.'[21] And *this*

nerayikādidukkhavisesānañ ca te saṃvattanikamca te saṃvattanikamidaṃ kammaṃ. So tvaṃ idaṃ karonto ubhohi hatthehi vītaccite vā aṅgāre, gūthaṃ vā gahetvā paraṃ paharitukāmo puriso viya attānameva paṭhamaṃ dahasi ceva duggandhañca karosīti.

Evaṃ attano kammassakataṃ paccavekkhitvā parassapi evaṃ paccavekkhitabbā esopi tava kujjhitvā kiṃ karissati? Nanu etassevetaṃ anatthāya saṃvattissati? Kammassako hi ayamāyasmā kammadāyādo ... pe ... yaṃ kammaṃ karissati, tassa dāyādo bhavissati. Idañcassa kammaṃ neva

action cannot succeed in bringing you to the perfect awakening of a buddha, to the awakening of a solitary buddha, or even to the level of a disciple. Nor will it bless you with the status of a Brahma god, a Sakka god, a universal emperor, or even that of a minor king. Quite the opposite! This kind of action makes you fall away from the true doctrine and you will wind up living on scraps and suffering the various miseries of the hell realms. You are like those who grab a glowing ember or excrement with both hands wanting to hit someone and only burn and foul themselves!"

Having reflected on your responsibility for your own actions, reflect on the fact that the other person is also responsible for theirs, like this: "Having been angry with you, what is the point of their staying angry? Surely, this will lead them to a bad place. For this respected

sammāsambodhiṃ, na paccekabodhiṃ, na sāvakabhūmiṃ, na brahmattasakkattacakkavattipadesarājādisampattīnaṃ aññataraṃ sampattiṃ sādhetuṃ samatthaṃ, atha kho sāsanato cāvetvā vighāsādādibhāvassa ceva nerayikādidukkhavisesānañcassa saṃvattanikamidaṃ kammaṃ. Svāyaṃ idaṃ karonto paṭivāte ṭhatvā paraṃ rajena okiritukāmo puriso viya attānaṃyeva okirati. Vuttañhetaṃ bhagavatā—

Yo appaduṭṭhassa narassa dussati, suddhassa
  posassa anaṅgaṇassa;

monk is responsible for their actions, experiences the results of their actions, and so on: they will experience the consequences of whatever they do. And this kind of action cannot succeed in bringing them to the perfect awakening of a buddha, to the awakening of a solitary buddha, or even to the level of a disciple. Nor can it bless them with the status of a Brahma god, a Sakka god, a universal emperor, or even with that of a minor king. Quite the opposite! This action makes them fall away from the true doctrine and they wind up living on scraps and suffering the various miseries of the hell realms. They are like those who throw dust at someone against the wind and ends up just flinging it on themselves." For the Buddha said this:

> Like fine dust flung against the wind, evil
> rebounds to the fool

Tameva bālaṃ pacceti pāpaṃ, sukhumo rajo paṭivātaṃva khitto ti.

Sace panassa evaṃ kammassakatampi paccavekkhato neva vūpasammati, athānena satthu pubbacariyaguṇā anussaritabbā.

[9] Tatrāyaṃ paccavekkhaṇānayo ambho pabbajita, nanu te satthā pubbeva sambodhā anabhisambuddho bodhisattopi samāno cattāri asaṅkhyeyyāni kappasatasahassañca pāramiyo pūrayamāno tattha tattha vadhakesupi paccatthikesu cittaṃ nappadūsesi.

Seyyathidaṃ, sīlavajātake tāva attano deviyā paduṭṭhena pāpaamaccena ānītassa paṭirañño tiyojanasataṃ rajjaṃ gaṇhantassa nisedhanatthāya uṭṭhitānaṃ amaccānaṃ āvudhampi chupituṃ na adāsi. Puna saddhiṃ amaccasahassena āmakasusāne galappamāṇaṃ bhūmiṃ khaṇitvā

who is hostile to someone who is pure,
faultless, and free of hostility.[22]

But if even reflecting in this way on the responsibility for our actions does not bring composure, then you should recall the virtues of the Teacher's former conduct.

[9] Here is how to do this: "Hey you, monk! Your Teacher was once an unawakened bodhisatta fulfilling the perfections for four incalculable ages and a hundred thousand eons, and he never once entertained an angry thought even when his adversaries were trying to kill him.[23]

"For example, the tale 'The Virtuous' tells of how once the Bodhisatta's kingdom, three hundred leagues in size, was seized by an enemy king who had been brought in by an evil minister. The minister had been turned hostile by the Bodhisatta's own queen. Though his men rose

nikhaññamāno cittappadosamattampi akatvā kuṇapakhādanatthaṃ āgatānaṃ siṅgālānaṃ paṃsuviyūhanaṃ nissāya purisakāraṃ katvā paṭiladdhajīvito yakkhānubhāvena attano sirigabbhaṃ oruyha sirisayane sayitaṃ paccatthikaṃ disvā kopaṃ akatvāva aññamaññaṃ sapathaṃ katvā taṃ mittaṭṭhāne ṭhapayitvā āha

Āsīsetheva puriso, na nibbindeyya paṇḍito;
Passāmi vohamattānaṃ, yathā icchiṃ tathā
ahū ti.

up to defend the kingdom, he did not permit them even to touch a weapon. Moreover, when the earth was dug and he was buried up to his neck in a charnel ground together with a thousand of his men, he still did not allow himself so much as an angry thought. Nor did he become angry when the jackals came to eat their corpses. In fact, they loosened the dirt, and he added his human strength to theirs and saved all their lives. Through the supernatural powers of a helpful spirit, he was able to appear suddenly in his own royal bedchamber and see his enemy luxuriating on his royal bed. But he made a pact with his enemy and turned him into a friend. And then he declared:

> Let a man have hope, and the wise not
> give up.
> I see myself just as I wish to be.

Khantivādījātake dummedhena kāsiraññā kiṃvādī tvaṃ samaṇā ti puṭṭho khantivādī nāmāhanti vutte sakaṇṭakāhi kasāhi tāḷetvā hatthapādesu chijjamānesu kopamattampi nākāsi.

[10] Anacchariyañcetaṃ, yaṃ mahallako pabbajjūpagato evaṃ kareyya. Cūḷadhammapālajātake pana uttānaseyyakopi samāno

Candanarasānulittā, bāhā chijjanti
  dhammapālassa;
Dāyādassa pathabyā, pāṇā me deva
  rujjhantīti.

"And in the 'Teacher of Patience' story, when asked by that idiot king of Benares, 'What doctrine do you teach, renunciant?' he replied, 'I just teach patience.' And when the king had him whipped with sharp lashes and his hands and feet cut off, he still he did not feel even a twinge of anger.

[10] "Perhaps this is not so astounding in the case of an older person, but even as a young novice he did likewise. In the tale 'Little Dhammapala,' he was a tiny infant lying on his back. His mother wailed when his hands and feet, like four bamboo sprouts, were cut off by his father, King Mahapatapa:

> Dhammapala's arms, rubbed with sandal
> oil, are chopped off!
> He was the heir to the kingdom. Your majesty, my life is destroyed!

Evaṃ vippalapamānāya mātuyā pitarā mahāpatāpena nāma raññā vaṃsakaḷīresu viya catūsu hatthapādesu chedāpitesu tāvatāpi santuṭṭhiṃ anāpajjitvā sīsamassa chindathāti āṇatte ayaṃ dāni te cittapariggaṇhanakālo, idāni ambho dhammapāla, sīsacchedāṇāpake pitari, sīsacchedake purise, paridevamānāya mātari, attani cāti imesu catūsu samacitto hohīti daḷhaṃ samādānamadhiṭṭhāya paduṭṭhākāramattampi nākāsi.

Idañcāpi anacchariyameva, yaṃ manussabhūto evamakāsi. Tiracchānabhūtopi pana chaddanto nāma vāraṇo hutvā visappitena sallena nābhiyaṃ viddhopi tāva anatthakārimhi luddake cittaṃ nappadūsesi. Yathāha

"But the king was not satisfied with just that and ordered his head chopped off too! Still, the Bodhisatta had no trace of ire since he had firmly resolved thus: 'Now, this is the time to remain in complete control of your mind. Look here, Dhammapala: maintain the same attitude toward all four of them—the father who ordered the decapitation, the man who did it, the mother who lamented, and yourself.'

"Perhaps even that is not so astounding because it was done by a human. But even as an animal, the Bodhisatta did likewise. When he was born as the elephant Chaddanta, he did not corrupt his mind with hostility toward the hunter who inflicted grave injury by stabbing him in the belly with a poison-dipped arrow. For it is said:

Samappito puthusallena nāgo,
Aduṭṭhacitto luddakaṃ ajjhabhāsi;
Kimatthayaṃ kissa vā samma hetu,
Mamaṃ vadhī kassa vāyaṃ payogo ti.

Evaṃ vatvā ca kāsirañño mahesiyā tava dantānamatthāya pesitomhi bhadanteti vutte tassā manorathaṃ pūrento chabbaṇṇarasminiccharaṇasamujjalitacārusobhe attano dante chetvā adāsi.

[11] Mahākapi hutvā attanāyeva pabbatapapātato uddharitena purisena

Bhakkho ayaṃ manussānaṃ, yathevaññe
vane migā;

The elephant pierced by a large arrow
kept his mind free of anger and asked the
hunter:
'Friend, what is the point of this? For what
reason did you kill me?
What purpose does it serve?'

And when told, 'Good sir, I was dispatched by the king of Benares to get your tusks for the queen,' to fulfill her wish, he himself cut off his brilliant and magnificent tusks shining and flashing with beams of light in six colors and handed them over to him.

[11] "And as the Great Monkey, he once rescued a man fallen into a mountain cleft. The man plotted:

This one is human food, like the other
beasts in the forest.

Yaṃnūnimaṃ vadhitvāna, chāto khādeyya
vānaraṃ.

Āhitova gamissāmi, maṃsamādāya
sambalaṃ;
Kantāraṃ nittharissāmi, pātheyyaṃ me
bhavissatīti.

Evaṃ cintetvā silaṃ ukkhipitvā matthake sampadālite assupuṇṇehi nettehi taṃ purisaṃ udikkhamāno

Mā ayyosi me bhadante, tvaṃ nāmetādisaṃ
kari;
Tvaṃ khosi nāma dīghāvu, aññaṃ
vāretumarahasīti.

And so why should a hungry man not kill
this monkey and eat him?

Stocked up, I will travel taking the meat as
provisions,
and cross the wilderness with food for the
road.

So thinking, he grabbed a stone and dashed open the monkey's head. Eyes filled with tears, the monkey looked at the man and uttered these words:

Do not do this to me, good sir! For what
you have done will
deter others from doing as I have done for a
very long time.

Vatvā tasmiṃ purise cittaṃ appadūsetvā attano ca dukkhaṃ acintetvā tameva purisaṃ khemantabhūmiṃ sampāpesi.

Bhūridatto nāma nāgarājā hutvā uposathaṅgāni adhiṭṭhāya vammikamuddhani sayamāno kapputṭhānaggisadisena osadhena sakalasarīre siñciyamānopi peḷāya pakkhipitvā sakalajambudīpe kīḷāpiyamānopi tasmiṃ brāhmaṇe manopadosamattampi na akāsi. Yathāha

Peḷāya pakkhipantepi, maddantepi ca pāṇinā;
Alampāne na kuppāmi, sīlakhaṇḍabhayā
mamā ti.

Without a trace of hostility toward this man and not thinking of his pain, he helped him reach safety.

"And so too when he was Bhuridatta, king of the serpents. Vowing to observe the penances, he was once lying on top of an anthill when a brahmin seized him, sprinkled his entire body with medicinal herbs like those that emerged at the great conflagration at the beginning of an eon, and put him in a basket. Even when the brahmin treated him as a plaything throughout all of India, he did not allow even a trace of hostility into his mind. As he put it:

> Trapped in a basket and man-handled,
> out of alarm for my moral practice, I did
> not get angry at Brahmin Alampana.

[12] Campeyyopi nāgarājā hutvā ahituṇḍikena viheṭhiyamāno manopadosamattampi nuppādesi. Yathāha

Tadāpi maṃ dhammacāriṃ,
upavutthauposathaṃ;
Ahituṇḍiko gahetvāna, rājadvāramhi kīḷati.

Yaṃ so vaṇṇaṃ cintayati, nīlaṃ pītaṃ va
lohitaṃ;
Tassa cittānuvattanto, homi cintitasannibho.

Thalaṃ kareyyaṃ udakaṃ, udakampi thalaṃ
kare;
Yadihaṃ tassa kuppeyyaṃ, khaṇena chārikaṃ
kare.

[12] "And as another serpent king, Campeyya, he also did not generate a trace of hostility when harassed by a snake trainer. As he told the story:

As I was living virtuously and keeping the observances,
a snake trainer seized me and teased me at the gate of the kingdom.

I became whatever he thought of, following his thoughts,
turning whatever color he conceived—blue, yellow, red.

I would turn dry land to water, and then make water into dry land.
Had I gotten angry at him, I could have turned him to ash in a second.

Yadi cittavasī hessaṃ, parihāyissāmi sīlato;
Sīlena parihīnassa, uttamattho na sijjhatīti.

Saṅkhapālanāgarājā hutvā tikhiṇāhi sattīhi aṭṭhasu ṭhānesu ovijjhitvā pahāramukhehi sakaṇṭakā latāyo pavesetvā nāsāya daḷhaṃ rajjuṃ pakkhipitvā soḷasahi bhojaputtehi kājenādāya vayhamāno dharaṇītale ghaṃsiyamānasarīro mahantaṃ dukkhaṃ paccanubhonto kujjhitvā olokitamatteneva sabbe bhojaputte bhasmaṃ kātuṃ samatthopi samāno cakkhuṃ ummīletvā paduṭṭhākāramattampi na akāsi.Yathāha

Cātuddasiṃ pañcadasiñcaḷāra,
Uposathaṃ niccamupāvasāmi;

But were I to do so, I would fall from moral
practice,
and one fallen from virtue does not reach
the highest goal.

"And when he was the serpent king Sankhapala, the sixteen sons of the village headman pierced his body in eight places with sharp spears, stuck a thorny creeper into each open wound, and threaded a sturdy cord through his nose. They dragged him along the ground with a pole, smashing his body and causing him extreme agony. If he had become angry, he would have been able to turn each of those village boys to ash with just a glance. But he opened his eyes without even a trace of anger. As he tells it:

Alara, I always kept the observances
on the fourteenth and fifteenth days of the
month.

Athāgamuṃ soḷasa bhojaputtā,
Rajjuṃ gahetvāna daḷhañca pāsaṃ.

Bhetvāna nāsaṃ atikassa rajjuṃ,
Nayiṃsu maṃ samparigayha luddā;

Etādisaṃ dukkhamahaṃ titikkhaṃ,
Uposathaṃ appaṭikopayanto ti.

Na kevalañca etāneva, aññānipi mātuposakajātakādīsu anekāni acchariyāni akāsi.

Tassa te idāni sabbaññutaṃ pattaṃ sadevaloke kenaci appaṭisamakhantiguṇaṃ taṃ bhagavantaṃ satthāraṃ apadisato paṭighacittaṃ nāma uppādetuṃ ativiya ayuttaṃ appatirūpanti.

Sixteen sons of the village headman came at
that time
holding a cord as a strong noose.

They pierced my nose and drew the cord
through;
savagely, they took me and dragged me all
around.

I endured such agony
without a hint of anger disrupting my
observances.

He performed such wonders not only in these cases, but in others also, such as in the story 'Supporting One's Mother.'[24]

"Having borne witness to your teacher, the Buddha, who has attained omniscience and whose quality of patience is unequaled by anyone even in the heavens, it is extremely

[13] Sace panassa evaṃ satthu pubbacaritaguṇaṃ paccavekkhatopi dīgharattaṃ kilesānaṃ dāsabyaṃ upagatassa neva taṃ paṭighaṃ vūpasammati, athānena anamataggiyāni paccavekkhitabbāni. Tatra hi vuttaṃ—

> Na so, bhikkhave, satto sulabharūpo, yo na mātābhūtapubbo, yo na pitābhūtapubbo, yo na bhātā, yo na bhaginī, yo na putto, yo na dhītābhūtapubbā ti.

Tasmā tasmiṃ puggale evaṃ cittaṃ uppādetabbaṃ ayaṃ kira me atīte mātā hutvā dasamāse kucchiyā pariharitvā muttakarīsakheḷasiṅghāṇikādīni haricandanaṃ viya ajigucchamānā apanetvā ure naccāpentī aṅgena pariharamānā posesi, pitā

unbecoming and inappropriate to become angry now."

[13] But if reflecting on the virtues of the Teacher's former conduct does not dispel the anger—given that you are long used to being a slave of your pathologies—then reflect on the endless cycle of rebirths. Regarding this, it is said:

> Monks, it is not easy to find anyone who has not previously been your mother, your father, your brother, your sister, your son, or your daughter.[25]

Therefore, here is how you should think about this person: "In the past this one may have been my mother; and she would have carried me in her womb for ten lunar months. She cleaned up my urine, feces, spit, snot, and so on without

hutvā ajapathasaṅkupathādīni gantvā vāṇijjaṃ payojayamāno mayhamatthāya jīvitampi pariccajitvā ubhatobyūḷhe saṅgāme pavisitvā nāvāya mahāsamuddaṃ pakkhanditvā aññāni ca dukkarāni karitvā puttake posessāmīti tehi tehi upāyehi dhanaṃ saṃharitvā maṃ posesi. Bhātā, bhaginī, putto, dhītā ca hutvāpi idañcidañcupakāraṃ akāsīti tatra me nappatirūpaṃ manaṃ padūsetunti.

Sace pana evampi cittaṃ nibbāpetuṃ na sakkotiyeva, athānena evaṃ mettānisaṃsā paccavekkhitabbā ambho pabbajita, nanu vuttaṃ bhagavatā mettāya kho, bhikkhave, cetovimuttiyā āsevitāya

disgust as if they were golden-colored sandalwood. Dangling me on her lap and carrying me around on her body, she nourished me. As my father, he went along goat paths and roads full of perils to earn a livelihood, perhaps even giving his own life for my sake by marching to battle in double array, setting out on the high seas in a vessel, and doing other difficult things to earn money by this or that means, thinking, *I will provide for my young child*. He nourished me. Or, as my brother, sister, son, or daughter, this person provided this or that care. It is unbecoming for me to corrupt my mind with hostility toward them now."

But if even this thought is unable to extinguish your anger, then reflect on the benefits of lovingkindness like this: "Hey you, renunciant! Didn't the Buddha say: 'Monks, eleven benefits

bhāvitāya bahulīkatāya yānīkatāya vatthukatāya anuṭṭhitāya paricitāya susamāraddhāya ekādasānisaṃsā pāṭikaṅkhā. Katame ekādasa? Sukhaṃ supati, sukhaṃ paṭibujjhati, na pāpakaṃ supinaṃ passati, manussānaṃ piyo hoti, amanussānaṃ piyo hoti, devatā rakkhanti, nāssa aggi vā visaṃ vā satthaṃ vā kamati, tuvaṭaṃ cittaṃ samādhiyati, mukhavaṇṇo pasīdati, asammūḷho kālaṅkaroti, uttarimappaṭivijjhanto brahmalokūpago hotīti. Sace tvaṃ idaṃ cittaṃ na nibbāpessasi, imehi ānisaṃsehi paribāhiro bhavissasīti.

[14] Evampi nibbāpetuṃ asakkontena pana dhātuvinibbhogo kātabbo. Kathaṃ? Ambho pabbajita, tvaṃ etassa kujjhamāno kassa kujjhasi? Kiṃ kesānaṃ kujjhasi, udāhu lomānaṃ, nakhānaṃ... pe ... muttassa kujjhasi? Atha vā pana

can be anticipated when freedom of the loving mind is practiced, cultivated, repeated, familiarized, mastered, established, consolidated, and fully engaged. What are the eleven? One sleeps comfortably, wakes up with ease, is free of nightmares, is beloved by humans, and is beloved by nonhumans. The gods protect them, neither fire, poison, nor weapon can touch them, their mind can concentrate easily, their complexion becomes bright, they die unconfused, and if they don't reach the highest spiritual aim, they will at least go to the Brahma heaven.'[26] If you don't extinguish your anger, you will be a stranger to these benefits."

[14] But if you are unable to extinguish it even by this method, then try the technique of disaggregating a person into their elements. How? "Hey renouncer! You are angry with this person, but with what, exactly, are you angry? The

kesādīsu pathavīdhātuyā kujjhasi, āpodhātuyā, tejodhātuyā, vāyodhātuyā kujjhasi? Ye vā pañcakkhandhe dvādasāyatanāni aṭṭhārasa dhātuyo upādāya ayamāyasmā itthannāmoti vuccati, tesu kiṃ rūpakkhandhassa kujjhasi, udāhu vedanā saññā saṅkhāraviññāṇakkhandhassa kujjhasi? Kiṃ vā cakkhāyatanassa kujjhasi, kiṃ rūpāyatanassa kujjhasi ... pe ... kiṃ manāyatanassa kujjhasi, kiṃ dhammāyatanassa kujjhasi? Kiṃ vā cakkhudhātuyā kujjhasi, kiṃ rūpadhātuyā, kiṃ cakkhuviññāṇadhātuyā... pe ... kiṃ manodhātuyā, kiṃ dhammadhātuyā, kiṃ manoviññāṇadhātuyā ti?

hairs on their head? Their body hairs? Their fingernails? Their urine? Their other body parts?[27] If it is the hair on their head, is it the earth element with which you are angry? Or are you angry at the water element, fire element, or wind element? This fellow monk is called 'So and so,' but he is actually conditioned by the five clusters, the twelve sensory bases, and the eighteen elements.[28] Among these, is it the cluster of their bodily experience with which you are angry? Or are you angry with the clusters of phenomena constituting their feelings, perceptions, habitual patterns, and consciousness? Or perhaps you are angry with the sensory bases that constitute their visual processes, or their objects? And so on with the other senses including the mind sense and its phenomenal objects—is *this* the object of your anger? Or is it with the elements of the eye, the elements of its visual objects, or of

Evañhi dhātuvinibbhogaṃ karoto āragge sāsapassa viya ākāse cittakammassa viya ca kodhassa patiṭṭhānaṭṭhānaṃ na hoti.

Dhātuvinibbhogaṃ pana kātuṃ asakkontena dānasaṃvibhāgo kātabbo. Attano santakaṃ parassa dātabbaṃ, parassa santakaṃ attanā gahetabbaṃ. Sace pana paro bhinnājīvo hoti aparibhogārahaparikkhāro, attano santakameva dātabbaṃ. Tassevaṃ karoto ekanteneva tasmiṃ puggale āghāto vūpasammati.

actual visual awareness that you are angry? And so on with the other senses—are you actually angry with the elements of mind, its phenomenal objects, or mental awareness?"

Anyone who performs this disaggregation into elements finds that there is no place or foundation for their anger; it is like trying to land a falling mustard seed on the tip of a needle or mounting a painting in the air.

But someone unable to perform the disaggregation into elements should give a gift. Give something of your own to the other, or receive something from the other. But if the other person has acquired their possessions improperly or unjustly, you should give something of your own. This will completely eliminate all resentment toward the person; even anger that has been dogging the other person from past lives vanishes in an instant.

Itarassa ca atītajātito paṭṭhāya anubandhopi kodho taṅkhaṇaññeva vūpasammati, cittalapabbatavihāre tikkhattuṃ vuṭṭhāpitasenāsanena piṇḍapātikattherena ayaṃ, bhante, aṭṭhakahāpaṇagghanako patto mama mātarā upāsikāya dinno dhammiyalābho, mahāupāsikāya puññalābhaṃ karothāti vatvā dinnaṃ pattaṃ laddhamahātherassa viya. Evaṃ mahānubhāvametaṃ dānaṃ nāma. Vuttampi cetaṃ

Adantadamanaṃ dānaṃ, dānaṃ
sabbatthasādhakaṃ;
Dānena piyavācāya, unnamanti namanti cā ti.

[15] Tassevaṃ verīpuggale vūpasantapaṭighassa yathā piyātippiyasahāyakamajjhattesu, evaṃ

This happened at a monastery on Mount Cittala when a monk subsisting only on alms was made to move his lodgings three times by a senior monk. He gave the senior monk an almsbowl, saying, "Sir, this bowl worth eight silver coins was given to me by my mother, a laywoman, and acquired properly. Please let the good laywoman obtain merit." A gift has great efficacy in this way. It is said:

> Giving tames the untamed; giving is every-
> where efficacious;
> with generosity and kind words, people
> incline upward and reach higher.

Breaking Down Barriers

[15] Once you have dispelled the anger toward the hostile person, you can turn the mind with

tasmimpi mettāvasena cittaṃ pavattati. Athānena punappunaṃ mettāyantena attani piyapuggale majjhatte verīpuggaleti catūsu janesu samacittataṃ sampādentena sīmāsambhedo kātabbo.

Tassidaṃ lakkhaṇaṃ, sace imasmiṃ puggale piyamajjhattaverīhi saddhiṃ attacatutthe ekasmiṃ padese nisinne corā āgantvā bhante, ekaṃ bhikkhuṃ amhākaṃ dethā ti vatvā kiṃ kāraṇā ti vutte taṃ māretvā galalohitaṃ gahetvā balikaraṇatthāyā ti vadeyyuṃ, tatra ceso bhikkhu asukaṃ vā asukaṃ vā gaṇhantū ti cinteyya, akatova hoti sīmāsambhedo. Sacepi maṃ gaṇhantu, mā ime tayo tipi cinteyya, akatova hoti sīmāsambhedo. Kasmā? Yassa yassa hi gahaṇamicchati, tassa tassa ahitesī hoti, itaresaṃyeva hitesī hoti.

lovingkindness toward them just as one would to the dear person, the very dear friend, and the mere acquaintance. Break down barriers by repeatedly cultivating friendliness toward yourself, toward one dear to you, toward the mere acquaintance, and toward the enemy, striving to feel the same friendliness toward all of them.

Here is what is distinctive about breaking down barriers in this way: suppose you were sitting in the company of three people—one dear to you, a mere acquaintance, and an enemy—and robbers came up and demanded, "Hand over one of these monks!" When asked, "What for?" they reply, "So that we can kill him and take blood from his throat to offer as a sacrifice." Anyone who would think "Let them take this one or that one" has not broken down barriers. Even to say, "Take me, not the other three," is

Yadā pana catunnaṃ janānamantare ekampi corānaṃ dātabbaṃ na passati, attani ca tesu ca tīsu janesu samameva cittaṃ pavatteti, kato hoti sīmāsambhedo. Tenāhu porāṇā

Attani hitamajjhatte, ahite ca catubbidhe;
Yadā passati nānattaṃ, hitacittova pāṇinaṃ.
Na nikāmalābhī mettāya, kusalīti pavuccati;

to not break down barriers. Why not? To prefer that they seize anyone—no matter whom—is to not wish well for that person and to wish well for the others.

It is only when you concentrate your mind equally on yourself and the other three and still cannot see a single person among the four to give to the robbers that you have broken down barriers. For the ancients say:

> One may have an attitude of benevolence
> toward living beings,
> but if one still sees a difference among the
> four—oneself, one's benefactor, the neutral, and the adversary—
> then one is not considered skillful in
> lovingkindness.

Yadā catasso sīmāyo, sambhinnā honti
bhikkhuno
Samaṃ pharati mettāya, sabbalokaṃ
sadevakaṃ;
Mahāviseso purimena, yassa sīmā na ñāyatīti.

Evaṃ sīmāsambhedasamakālameva ca iminā bhikkhunā nimittañca upacārañca laddhaṃ hoti. Sīmāsambhede pana kate tameva nimittaṃ āsevanto bhāvento bahulīkaronto appakasireneva pathavīkasiṇe vuttanayeneva appanaṃ pāpuṇāti.

▪ ▪ ▪

The monk who has broken down the four
barriers
floods the whole world and even the gods
with lovingkindness.
The greatest achievement is to know no
barriers at all.

In this way, the monk achieves both the mental image of meditation and the preliminary absorption only when these barriers are broken. When one has broken those barriers, one attains full absorption while practicing, cultivating, and developing this image, as was described in the earth image meditation device.[29]

■ ■ ■

Finer Points

At this point, Buddhaghosa, in classic commentarial style, shifts to offering more precise definitions of some of the passages that have gone before, fine tuning what is meant by key terms and what exactly all this feels like. The detailed attention to these ideas has a meditative purpose as one slows down and asks what it actually means to have one's mind full of lovingkindness and to flood others with it. How does one do so systematically? Can I really flood all beings in each direction with friendliness and goodwill? By taking us through each aspect of the practice and examining more closely these modes of friendliness toward each category of beings, and in each direction, we linger on the concrete specificity of universal love, and attempt to achieve full absorption in each case. This love is never abstract even as it extends further and further to reach more and more beings in every direction.

The reader will, I hope, be struck by the freedom and spaciousness this way of living affords. The aim is "freedom of the loving mind," where one moves through the world without the usual barriers we throw up against others. The ease and happiness of a universally friendly outlook on the world are to be celebrated, along with a list of practical benefits kindness brings, including better sleep, easier dreams, and the reciprocated kindness of others.

[16] So hi paṭhamajjhānādīnaṃ aññataravasena mettāsahagatena cetasā ekaṃ disaṃ pharitvā viharati. Tathā dutiyaṃ, tathā tatiyaṃ, tathā catutthaṃ. Iti uddhamadho tiriyaṃ sabbadhi sabbattatāya sabbāvantaṃ lokaṃ mettāsahagatena cetasā vipulena mahaggatena appamāṇena averena abyāpajjena pharitvā viharati. Paṭhamajjhānādivasena appanāppattacittasseva hi ayaṃ vikubbanā sampajjati.

Ettha ca mettāsahagatenāti mettāya samannāgatena. Cetasāti cittena. Ekaṃ disanti ekamekissā disāya paṭhamapariggahitaṃ sattaṃ upādāya ekadisāpariyāpannasattapharaṇavasena vuttaṃ. Pharitvāti phusitvā ārammaṇaṃ katvā. Viharatīti brahmavihārādhiṭṭhitaṃ iriyāpathavihāraṃ

[16] It is by means of one or another of these absorptions, starting with the first one, that one comes to live *flooding one direction with a mind full of lovingkindness.*[30] And so too for the second, third, and fourth directions: with a mind full of lovingkindness, one lives friendly and without ill will, expansive, enlarged, and immeasurable everywhere, equally, toward the entire world above, below, and horizontally. Only for one whose mind has achieved full absorption by means of the meditation states beginning with the first one does this extraordinary transformation occur.

To be *full of lovingkindness* is to keep up lovingkindness. And by *mind* is meant thoughts. To adopt the attitude in *one direction* is to direct it to the beings that are contained within a single direction. *To flood* is to feel something intensely and to make it one's object of meditation. *To*

pavatteti. Tathā dutiyanti yathā puratthimādīsu disāsu yaṃkiñci ekaṃ disaṃ pharitvā viharati, tatheva tadanantaraṃ dutiyaṃ tatiyaṃ catutthañcāti attho. Iti uddhanti eteneva nayena uparimaṃ disanti vuttaṃ hoti. Adho tiriyanti adhodisampi tiriyaṃdisampi evameva. Tattha ca adhoti heṭṭhā. Tiriyanti anudisāsu. Evaṃ sabbadisāsu assamaṇḍale assamiva mettāsahagataṃ cittaṃ sāretipi paccāsāretipīti.

Ettāvatā ekaṃ disaṃ pariggahetvā odhiso mettāpharaṇaṃ dassitaṃ.

[17] Sabbadhītiādi pana anodhiso dassanatthaṃ vuttaṃ. Tattha sabbadhīti sabbattha. Sabbattatāyāti sabbesu hīnamajjhimukkaṭṭhamittasapattamajjhattādippabhedesu attatāya. Ayaṃ parasattoti vibhāgaṃ akatvā attasamatāyāti vuttaṃ hoti. Atha

live is to keep going, to be committed to living and behaving in this divine way. *And so too for the second* indicates, say, the eastern direction after one has flooded the first direction, and then one should flood all of the other directions. And *above* indicates the direction overhead, and *below* and *horizontally* just mean in these directions as well, where *below* means underneath and *horizontally* means sideways. You should send out thoughts full of lovingkindness forward and backward in every direction, like a horse in its training ring.

So far, flooding with lovingkindness is shown with respect to each direction separately.

[17] But in order to show that this practice is to be universal, the text says *everywhere*, and so on. Here, *everywhere* means in all places. *Equally* means that all beings whether of lower, equal, or higher status, whether friendly, hostile, or

vā sabbattatāyāti sabbena cittabhāgena īsakampi bahi avikkhipamānoti vuttaṃ hoti. Sabbāvantanti sabbasattavantaṃ, sabbasattayuttanti attho. Lokanti sattalokaṃ. Vipulenātievamādipariyāyadassanato panettha puna mettāsahagatenāti vuttaṃ. Yasmā vā ettha odhiso pharaṇe viya puna tathāsaddo itisaddo vā na vutto, tasmā puna mettāsahagatena cetasāti vuttaṃ. Nigamanavasena[31] vā etaṃ vuttaṃ. Vipulenāti ettha ca pharaṇavasena vipulatā daṭṭhabbā. Bhūmivasena pana etaṃ mahaggataṃ paguṇavasena ca appamāṇasattārammaṇavasena ca appamāṇaṃ, byāpādapaccatthikappahānena averaṃ, domanassappahānato abyāpajjaṃ, niddukkhanti vuttaṃ hoti.

neutral, are considered to be just like oneself; and *equality with oneself* is described as not distinguishing between them and oneself, by saying, "this is a different being." Alternatively, *equally* means that no part of one's mind is even a tiny bit distracted by external things. *Entire* means encompassing and applied to all beings, and *world* means the world of creatures. And *full of lovingkindness* is repeated in the passage in order to show additional ways of teaching, starting with the word *expansive*. Alternatively, *mind full of lovingkindness* is repeated because the word *likewise* was not said here as it was in the earlier mention of flooding with specifications; or else it is repeated as a summary. The word *expansive* indicates the capaciousness of this flooding. *Enlarged* is said with respect to the whole earth, and *immeasurable* means both mental mastery and having infinite beings as its

Ayaṃ mettāsahagatena cetasātiādinā nayena vuttāya vikubbanāya attho.

Yathā cāyaṃ appanāppattacittasseva vikubbanā sampajjati, tathā yampi paṭisambhidāyaṃ pañcahākārehi anodhisopharaṇā mettācetovimutti, sattahākārehi odhisopharaṇā mettā cetovimutti, dasahākārehi disāpharaṇā mettā cetovimuttīti vuttaṃ, tampi appanāppattacittasseva sampajjatīti veditabbaṃ.

Tattha ca sabbe sattā averā abyāpajjā anīghā sukhī attānaṃ pariharantu, sabbe pāṇā, sabbe

object. One becomes *friendly* by relinquishing its opposite—malice; and *free of ill will* by relinquishing unhappiness. This is why those who cultivate this attitude lack any suffering.

This is the meaning of the extraordinary transformation mentioned in the beginning starting with "a mind full of lovingkindness."

Now, there is this passage in the *Treatise on Analytical Knowledge* that explains the phrase *in one whose mind has achieved full absorption this extraordinary transformation occurs*: "Freedom of the loving mind floods universally in five ways; freedom of the loving mind floods with specifications in seven ways; freedom of the loving mind floods the directions in ten ways." This explains what occurs in the mind that has achieved full absorption.

Specifically, *freedom of the loving mind floods universally in five ways* should be understood as

bhūtā, sabbe puggalā, sabbe attabhāvapariyāpannā averā... pe ... pariharantūti imehi pañcahākārehi anodhisopharaṇā mettā cetovimutti veditabbā.

Sabbā itthiyo averā... pe ... attānaṃ pariharantu, sabbe purisā, sabbe ariyā, sabbe anariyā, sabbe devā, sabbe manussā, sabbe vinipātikā averā... pe ... pariharantūti imehi sattahākārehi odhisopharaṇā mettā cetovimutti veditabbā.

[18] Sabbe puratthimāya disāya sattā averā... pe ... attānaṃ pariharantu. Sabbe pacchimāya disāya, sabbe uttarāya disāya, sabbe dakkhiṇāya disāya, sabbe puratthimāya anudisāya, sabbe pacchimāya anudisāya, sabbe uttarāya anudisāya, sabbe dakkhiṇāya anudisāya, sabbe heṭṭhimāya disāya, sabbe uparimāya disāya sattā averā... pe ... pariharantu.

thinking, "May all *beings* be friendly, without ill will, untroubled, and happy! And may all *living creatures*, all who *exist*, all *people*, and all *individuals* be friendly, free of ill will, untroubled, and happy!"

Freedom of the loving mind that floods with specifications in seven ways should be understood as thinking, "Let each of these seven in turn—all women, all men, all noble ones, all ordinary people, all gods, all humans, all hell beings—be friendly, free of ill will, untroubled, and happy!"

[18] And *freedom of the loving mind floods the directions in ten ways* should be understood as thinking, "Let all beings in the eastern direction be friendly, free of ill will, untroubled, and happy! And then let them all—everyone in the western direction, everyone in the northern direction, everyone in the southern direction,

Sabbe puratthimāya disāya pāṇā, bhūtā, puggalā, attabhāvapariyāpannā, averā... pe ... pariharantu. Sabbā puratthimāya disāya itthiyo, sabbe purisā, ariyā, anariyā, devā, manussā, vinipātikā averā... pe ... pariharantu. Sabbā pacchimāya disāya, uttarāya, dakkhiṇāya, puratthimāya anudisāya, pacchimāya, uttarāya, dakkhiṇāya anudisāya, heṭṭhimāya disāya, uparimāya disāya itthiyo ... pe ... vinipātikā averā abyāpajjā anīghā sukhī attānaṃ pariharantūti imehi dasahākārehi disāpharaṇā mettā cetovimutti veditabbā.

everyone in the intermediate eastern direction, everyone in the intermediate western direction, everyone in the intermediate northern direction, everyone in the intermediate southern direction, everyone below, and everyone above—be friendly, free of ill will, untroubled, and happy! And then may all *beings* in the eastern direction go about friendly, free of ill will, untroubled, and happy! And then all *living creatures*, all who *exist*, all *people*, and all *individuals* in the eastern direction, and so on each in turn with each of the other directions. And then all women in the eastern direction, and so on. And then all men, noble ones, ordinary people, gods, humans, hell beings in each of the other directions in turn—west, north, south, northwest, northeast, southwest, southeast, below and above—may they all go about friendly, free

Tattha sabbeti anavasesapariyādānametaṃ.

■ ■ ■

Ettha ca sabbe sattā averā hontūti ayamekā appanā. Abyāpajjā hontūti ayamekā appanā. Abyāpajjāti byāpādarahitā. Anīghā hontūti ayamekā appanā. Anīghāti niddukkhā. Sukhī attānaṃ pariharantūti ayamekā appanā. Tasmā imesupi padesu yaṃ yaṃ pākaṭaṃ hoti, tassa tassa vasena mettā pharitabbā. Iti pañcasu ākāresu catunnaṃ appanānaṃ vasena anodhisopharaṇe vīsati appanā honti.

■ ■ ■

of ill will, untroubled, and happy!" This is what freedom of the loving mind flooding the directions in ten ways means.

The word "all" means exhaustively, without exceptions.

■ ■ ■

Note that here, the attitude, "May all beings be friendly" is one instance of full absorption. The attitude, "May they be free of ill will" is another instance of full absorption. To be *free of ill will* is to lack malice. The attitude, "May they be untroubled" is another instance of full absorption, and to be *untroubled* is to be free of suffering. The attitude, "May they be happy" is another instance of full absorption. Therefore, you should make lovingkindness flood each of these cases. And so there are twenty instances

[19] Iti etāsu appanāsu yassa kassaci vasena mettaṃ cetovimuttiṃ bhāvetvā ayaṃ yogāvacaro sukhaṃ supatītiādinā nayena vutte ekādasānisaṃse paṭilabhati.

Tattha sukhaṃ supatīti yathā sesā janā samparivattamānā kākacchamānā dukkhaṃ supanti, evaṃ asupitvā sukhaṃ supati. Niddaṃ okkantopi samāpattiṃ samāpanno viya hoti.

Sukhaṃ paṭibujjhatīti yathā aññe nitthunantā vijambhantā samparivattantā dukkhaṃ

of full absorption when flooding universally—these four concentrations multiplied by the five ways.

■ ■ ■

Some Practical Benefits

[19] The meditator who has practiced freedom of the loving mind with any of these kinds of full absorption receives eleven benefits, such as sleeping comfortably.

One *sleeps comfortably* means that they sleep well, unlike other people, who toss and turn, snore, and sleep fitfully. Falling asleep is like slipping into a stage of meditation.

They *wake up with ease* means that they wake up untroubled and comfortable, expanding like

paṭibujjhanti, evaṃ appaṭibujjhitvā vikasamānamiva padumaṃ sukhaṃ nibbikāraṃ paṭibujjhati.

Na pāpakaṃ supinaṃ passatīti supinaṃ passantopi bhaddakameva supinaṃ passati, cetiyaṃ vandanto viya pūjaṃ karonto viya dhammaṃ suṇanto viya ca hoti. Yathā pana aññe attānaṃ corehi samparivāritaṃ viya vāḷehi upaddutaṃ viya papāte patantaṃ viya ca passanti, evaṃ pāpakaṃ supinaṃ na passati.

Manussānaṃ piyo hotīti ure āmuttamuttāhāro viya sīse piḷandhamālā viya ca manussānaṃ piyo hoti manāpo. Amanussānaṃ piyo hotīti yatheva manussānaṃ, evaṃ amanussānampi piyo hoti visākhatthero viya. So kira pāṭaliputte kuṭumbiyo ahosi. So tattheva vasamāno assosi tambapaṇṇidīpo kira cetiyamālālaṅkato kāsāvapajjoto icchiticchitaṭṭhāneyeva ettha sakkā nisīdituṃ vā nipajjituṃ vā utusappāyaṃ senāsanasappāyaṃ

a lotus blossoming. They do not wake up painfully like others, who grumble, yawn, and roll over.

They are *free of nightmares* means that their dreams are only good since they dream of things like worshiping a shrine, making an offering, and discussing the Teaching. They are spared the nightmares that others have of being surrounded by robbers, being menaced by ferocious animals, or falling off a cliff.

They are *beloved by humans* means that they are beloved and attractive to people as though they were wearing a pearl necklace over the heart or a jeweled garland over the head.

They are *beloved by nonhumans* means that just as they are beloved by humans, they are also beloved by nonhumans, as in the case of the elder monk Visakha. The story has it that he was a householder in Pataliputta. While he was

puggalasappāyaṃ dhammassavanasappāyanti sabbamettha sulabhanti.

So attano bhogakkhandhaṃ puttadārassa niyyādetvā dussante baddhena ekakahāpaṇeneva gharā nikkhamitvā samuddatīre nāvaṃ udikkhamāno ekamāsaṃ vasi. So vohārakusalatāya imasmiṃ ṭhāne bhaṇḍaṃ kiṇitvā asukasmiṃ vikkiṇanto dhammikāya vaṇijjāya tenevantaramāsena sahassaṃ abhisaṃhari. Anupubbena mahāvihāraṃ āgantvā pabbajjaṃ yāci. So pabbājanatthāya sīmaṃ nīto taṃ sahassatthavikaṃ ovaṭṭikantarena bhūmiyaṃ pātesi. Kimetan ti ca vutte kahāpaṇasahassaṃ, bhante ti vatvā upāsaka, pabbajitakālato

living there, he heard reports that "The island of Sri Lanka is encircled throughout with religious shrines and is bright with the yellow robes of monks. One can sit down or sleep wherever one likes, and it is easy to get everything one needs. The climate is favorable, the lodgings are accommodating, people are helpful, and hearing the Teaching there is beneficial."

So he handed over his pile of wealth to his wife and children, and set out from his household with only a single coin sewn into the hem of his garment. He stayed at the seashore for a month looking for a ship, and while there, owing to his skill in trade, he bought various goods and sold them. By trading lawfully with just that small investment, he made a profit of a thousand coins. Eventually he made his way to the Great Monastery and asked for ordination as a monk. As he was being taken to the grounds of

paṭṭhāya na sakkā vicāretuṃ, idānevetaṃ vicārehīti vutte visākhassa pabbajjaṭṭhānamāgatā mā rittahatthā gamiṃsū ti muñcitvā sīmāmāḷake vippakiritvā pabbajitvā upasampanno.

So pañcavasso hutvā dvemātikā paguṇā katvā pavāretvā attano sappāyaṃ kammaṭṭhānaṃ gahetvā ekekasmiṃ vihāre cattāro māse katvā samappavattavāsaṃ vasamāno cari. Evaṃ caramāno

the monastery for ordination, his purse with the thousand coins fell out of his waistband onto the ground. They asked him, "What is that?" And when he replied that it was a thousand coins, he was told, "Layman, once you have renounced the world it will not be possible to distribute this, so you should do so now." And so he announced, "May no one who comes to the place of my ordination leave empty-handed!" And he gave it all away, strewing the coins throughout the enclosure of the monastic grounds. He was then ordained.

Five years passed, and he learned two scriptures by heart. He celebrated the end of the monastic rainy-season retreat and took up a meditation topic that would be beneficial for him. He set out to wander, stopping and living for four months at each monastery along the way. This is what people said about his wandering:

Vanantare ṭhito thero, visākho gajjamānako;
Attano guṇamesanto, imamatthaṃ abhāsatha.
Yāvatā upasampanno, yāvatā idha āgato;
Etthantare khalitaṃ natthi, aho lābhā te
mārisā ti.

[20] So cittalapabbatavihāraṃ gacchanto dvedhā pathaṃ patvā ayaṃ nu kho maggo udāhu ayan ti cintayanto aṭṭhāsi. Athassa pabbate adhivatthā devatā hatthaṃ pasāretvā esa maggo ti vatvā dasseti. So cittalapabbatavihāraṃ gantvā tattha cattāro māse vasitvā paccūse gamissāmīti cintetvā nipajji.

Caṅkamasīse maṇilarukkhe adhivatthā devatā sopānaphalake nisīditvā parodi. Thero ko eso ti āha. Ahaṃ, bhante, maṇiliyāti. Kissa rodasīti?

The monk Visakha stood in the middle of
the forest roaring,
as he examined his merits. He said to
himself:
"Since your ordination until you came here,
and all times in between,
you have never so much as stumbled—this
is truly a blessing for you!"

[20] Heading then to Mount Cittala Monastery, he came to two roads and stood there wondering which one to take. A deity who lived in the mountain stuck out his hand and showed him the way, "This is the road." He reached the monastery at Mount Cittala and stayed there for four months. One night before falling asleep he resolved to leave the next morning.

But then a deity living in a *manila* tree on the terrace sat down on a step and wept. "Who is that?" "It is I, the *manila* tree spirit." "Why are

Tumhākaṃ gamanaṃ paṭiccāti. Mayi idha vasante tumhākaṃ ko guṇoti? Tumhesu, bhante, idha vasantesu amanussā aññamaññaṃ mettaṃ paṭilabhanti, te dāni tumhesu gatesu kalahaṃ karissanti, duṭṭhullampi kathayissantīti.

Thero sace mayi idha vasante tumhākaṃ phāsuvihāro hoti, sundaranti vatvā aññepi cattāro māse tattheva vasitvā puna tatheva gamanacittaṃ uppādesi. Devatāpi puna tatheva parodi. Etenevupāyena thero tattheva vasitvā tattheva parinibbāyīti evaṃ mettāvihārī bhikkhu amanussānaṃ piyo hoti.

Devatā rakkhantīti puttamiva mātāpitaro devatā rakkhanti.

Nāssa aggi vā visaṃ vā satthaṃ vā kamatīti mettāvihārissa kāye uttarāya upāsikāya viya aggi

you crying?" "Because you are leaving." "But what benefit does my staying here give you?" "Sir, while you are staying here the nonhuman beings have lovingkindness toward one another, but when you go they will resume their quarreling and say vulgar things."

The monk replied: "If my staying here makes your life comfortable, it is a good thing," and he lived there another four months. But then he thought again of leaving, and again the deity wept. So he stayed on there because of this, and it was there that he died, having attained nirvana. This is the sense in which one living in lovingkindness may be said to be *beloved by nonhumans*.

The gods protect them means that the deities watch over them like parents their child.

Neither fire, poison, nor weapon can touch them means that neither fire, poison, nor

vā, saṃyuttabhāṇakacūḷasivattherasseva visaṃ vā, saṃkiccasāmaṇerasseva satthaṃ vā na kamati, na pavisati. Nāssa kāyaṃ vikopetīti vuttaṃ hoti. Dhenuvatthumpi cettha kathayanti. Ekā kira dhenu vacchakassa khīradhāraṃ muñcamānā aṭṭhāsi. Eko luddako taṃ vijjhissāmīti hatthena samparivattetvā dīghadaṇḍasattiṃ muñci. Sā tassā sarīraṃ āhacca tālapaṇṇaṃ viya pavaṭṭamānā gatā, neva upacārabalena, na appanābalena, kevalaṃ vacchake balavapiyacittatāya. Evaṃ mahānubhāvā mettāti.

Tuvaṭaṃ cittaṃ samādhiyatīti mettāvihārino khippameva cittaṃ samādhiyati, natthi tassa dandhāyitattaṃ.

weapons affect or penetrate the body, much as the laywoman Uttara was safe from fire, the elder monk Culasiva who recited the *Connected Discourses* was safe from poison, and Samkicca the novice was safe from weapons. They remained unharmed. There is also a story of a cow that is relevant in this context. Once a cow was feeding her calf from her udders when a hunter wanted to shoot her. He pulled back and hurled a long spear at her. But when it reached her body, it fell off as if it were a palm leaf. This was not due to the power of her preliminary or full absorption, but owing only to the strength of her love for her calf. Such is the great power of lovingkindness.

Their mind can concentrate easily means that one practicing lovingkindness can quickly concentrate the mind, without hesitation.

Mukhavaṇṇo vippasīdatīti bandhanā pavuttaṃ tālapakkaṃ viya cassa vippasannavaṇṇaṃ mukhaṃ hoti.

Asammūḷho kālaṅkarotīti mettāvihārino sammohamaraṇaṃ nāma natthi, asammūḷhova niddaṃ okkamanto viya kālaṃ karoti.

Uttarimappaṭivijjhantoti mettāsamāpattito uttariṃ arahattaṃ adhigantuṃ asakkonto ito cavitvā suttappabuddho viya brahmalokamupapajjatīti.

Ayaṃ mettābhāvanāyaṃ vitthārakathā.

Their complexion becomes bright means that their face has a clear complexion like a palm nut freed from its husk.

They die unconfused means that there is no bewilderment at the time of death for one practicing lovingkindness. When the time comes it will be like falling asleep peacefully.

If they don't reach the highest spiritual aim means that if they are accomplished in lovingkindness but are still unable to achieve the highest aim of nirvana, then when they move on from here they will be reborn in the Brahma heaven, as though waking up from sleep.

This concludes the detailed explanation of the practice of lovingkindness.

COMPASSION

We turn now to compassion. Since the instructions on lovingkindness were so detailed and lay the foundation for the other sublime attitudes, Buddhaghosa moves much more quickly through them, offering chiefly a sense of their content and their objects.

Recall that the content of compassion is wanting that someone suffering will be relieved of it. As with lovingkindness, one works gradually to feel compassion universally toward all beings. But to start, one begins with where it is easiest, and again with a concrete and specific person. Buddhaghosa thinks that even the most hard-hearted among us will be moved when we see a truly wretched person with hands and feet cut off and begging on the street, so we should start here to get the feeling flowing. But failing to find such a person (and we should hope such sights never occur!), we still need an actual being to focus on as the object of our compassion.

Here he takes a perhaps surprising turn: start with a guilty criminal being led to his death. Buddhaghosa thinks that reflecting on this person, who may seem to be happy as he eats the delicacies of his last meal, will be an easy object of compassion. No one will think he is actually happy as he faces his executioner; anyone considering the horror of his impending death will react with dismay. Unlike many Western conceptions of compassion, there is no sense that compassion should be directed only toward innocents, those who do not "deserve" their suffering. The question of whether the suffering is deserved never even comes up. Instead, by starting with a guilty criminal about to die as an easy object at the beginning, Buddhaghosa centers our understanding of compassion on its content—the longing that suffering be removed. To be truly universal, compassion cannot be concerned with our judgments about whether or not the person deserves their suffering—what is pertinent is the suffering, and criminals and evildoers are in a great deal of pain. Compassion is the desire that suffering everywhere end. It is as simple, or rather, as difficult, as this.

As we come to practice it, we can come to notice more and more varieties of suffering and their more subtle forms. Buddhaghosa will note later in the text that the sublime attitudes are four kinds of "attention" to beings. Here one attends to the pain that is so frequent in life, and seeks to address it. Opening one's heart to those suffering by longing for their pain to end is its own distinctive variety of freedom and breaking down barriers.

Karuṇā

[21] Karuṇaṃ bhāvetukāmena pana nikkaruṇatāya ādīnavaṃ karuṇāya ca ānisaṃsaṃ paccavekkhitvā karuṇābhāvanā ārabhitabbā. Tañca pana ārabhantena paṭhamaṃ piyapuggalādīsu na ārabhitabbā. Piyo hi piyaṭṭhāneyeva tiṭṭhati. Atippiyasahāyako atippiyasahāyakaṭṭhāneyeva. Majjhatto majjhattaṭṭhāneyeva. Appiyo appiyaṭṭhāneyeva. Verī veriṭṭhāneyeva tiṭṭhati. Liṅgavisabhāgakālakatā akhettameva.

Kathañca bhikkhu karuṇāsahagatena cetasā ekaṃ disaṃ pharitvā viharati? Seyyathāpi nāma ekaṃ puggalaṃ duggataṃ durūpetaṃ disvā

[21] If you want to develop compassion, you should first reflect on the dangers of not having compassion and on the benefits of having compassion. But you should not focus on those dear to you when starting on compassion. This is because you will continue to hold such a person dear to you, and to maintain that friendship. Similarly, a mere acquaintance will continue to be a mere acquaintance; you will continue to dislike someone you already dislike; and your enemies will remain your enemies. Moreover, you should not start with members of the opposite sex or those who have passed away as the objects of this meditation.

The *Book of Analysis* says: "How does a monk live flooding one direction with a mind full of compassion? Imagine the compassion

karuṇāyeyya, evameva sabbasatte karuṇāya pharatīti vibhaṅge pana vuttattā sabbapaṭhamaṃ tāva kiñcideva karuṇāyitabbarūpaṃ paramakicchappattaṃ duggataṃ durūpetaṃ kapaṇapurisaṃ chinnahatthapādaṃ[32] kapālaṃ purato ṭhapetvā anāthasālāya nisinnaṃ hatthapādehi paggharantakimigaṇaṃ aṭṭassaraṃ karontaṃ disvā kiccham vatāyaṃ satto āpanno, appeva nāma imamhā dukkhā mucceyyā ti karuṇā pavattetabbā.

Taṃ alabhantena sukhitopi pāpakārī puggalo vajjhena upametvā karuṇāyitabbo. Kathaṃ? Seyyathāpi saha bhaṇḍena gahitacoraṃ vadhetha nanti rañño āṇāya rājapurisā bandhitvā catukke catukke pahārasatāni dentā āghātanaṃ nenti. Tassa manussā khādanīyampi bhojanīyampi

you would feel upon seeing a miserable and unfortunate person, and use that feeling to flood all beings with compassion."[33] Accordingly, you should first arouse compassion by observing someone whose body is truly pitiable, such as someone who has fallen into extreme agony, miserable, unfortunate, begging, hands and feet cut off, sitting in a shelter with a begging bowl set in front of them, moaning and with maggots pouring out of their arms and legs. When you see such a person, you should think, "This being has fallen to a terrible state. If only they could be free from this misery!"

But if you cannot find such a person, arouse compassion toward an evildoer, even if he seems happy, by comparing him to a man about to be executed. How should you do this? Imagine a robber caught with stolen goods and condemned to death by the king. The executioners

mālāgandhavilepanatambulānipi denti. Kiñcāpi so tāni khādanto ceva paribhuñjanto ca sukhito bhogasamappito viya gacchati, atha kho taṃ neva koci sukhito ayaṃ mahābhogo ti maññati, aññadatthu ayaṃ varāko idāni marissati, yaṃ yadeva hi ayaṃ padaṃ nikkhipati, tena tena santike maraṇassa hotīti taṃ jano karuṇāyati.

[22] Evameva karuṇākammaṭṭhānikena bhikkhunā sukhitopi puggalo evaṃ karuṇāyitabbo ayaṃ varāko kiñcāpi idāni sukhito susajjito bhoge paribhuñjati, atha kho tīsu dvāresu ekenāpi katassa kalyāṇakammassa abhāvā idāni apāyesu anappakaṃ dukkhaṃ domanassaṃ paṭisaṃvedissatīti.

tie him up, flog him with a hundred blows at each crossroads, and lead him off to be executed. People give him both substantial and fine food, garlands, fragrances, ointments, and betel nuts. Even though he eats and enjoys these and goes along as if he were happy and well-off, no one actually thinks that this guy is happy and well-off. Quite the contrary, people feel compassion for him, thinking, "This poor wretch is about to die. Every footfall brings him closer to death."

[22] In a similar way, a monk working on compassion as a meditation topic should feel compassion for a person who may only seem happy, realizing "However much this poor wretch is now happy and cheerfully enjoying fine things, they will later experience considerable pain and distress in states of misery because they are not performing virtuous actions using their body, speech, or mind right now."

Evaṃ taṃ puggalaṃ karuṇāyitvā tato paraṃ eteneva upāyena piyapuggale, tato majjhatte, tato verimhīti anukkamena karuṇā pavattetabbā. Sace panassa pubbe vuttanayeneva verimhi paṭighaṃ uppajjati, taṃ mettāya vuttanayeneva vūpasametabbaṃ.

Yopi cettha katakusalo hoti, tampi ñātirogabhogabyasanādīnaṃ aññatarena byasanena samannāgataṃ disvā vā sutvā vā tesaṃ abhāvepi vaṭṭadukkhaṃ anatikkantattā dukkhitova ayanti evaṃ sabbathāpi karuṇāyitvā vuttanayeneva attani piyapuggale majjhatte verimhīti catūsu janesu sīmāsambhedaṃ katvā taṃ nimittaṃ āsevantena bhāventena bahulīkarontena mettāya vuttanayeneva tikacatukkajjhānavasena appanā vaḍḍhetabbā.

Once you develop compassion for this person in this way you can then arouse it successively toward others by the same method. Do so first toward someone dear to you, then toward a mere acquaintance, and finally toward an enemy. But if anger arises toward the enemy as described earlier, then extinguish it with lovingkindness by the method already explained.

And in the case of someone who has done good things, you may come to see or hear of them facing some calamity, such as the loss of wealth or an illness in their family. But even if they are not suffering from misfortune such as this, you can come to know that they are in fact actually suffering because they have not transcended the round of suffering that is life in this world. This realization enables you to feel compassion for everyone. Through this process,

Aṅguttaraṭṭhakathāyaṃ pana paṭhamaṃ veripuggalo karuṇāyitabbo, tasmiṃ cittaṃ muduṃ katvā duggato, tato piyapuggalo, tato attāti ayaṃ kamo vutto, so duggataṃ durūpeta nti pāḷiyā na sameti, tasmā vuttanayenevettha bhāvanamārabhitvā sīmāsambhedaṃ katvā appanā vaḍḍhetabbā. Tato paraṃ pañcahākārehi anodhisopharaṇā sattahākārehi odhisopharaṇā dasahākārehi disāpharaṇā ti ayaṃ vikubbanā, sukhaṃ supatī tiādayo ānisaṃsā ca mettāyaṃ vuttanayeneva veditabbāti.

break down barriers among the four kinds of people—yourself, those dear to you, your mere acquaintances, and your enemies. Meditating on these images frequently and practicing this compassion meditation as was explained in the context of the cultivation of lovingkindness, you can develop full absorption by way of the third or fourth levels of deep concentration.

However, it says in the commentary on the *Numerical Discourses* that you should first develop compassion toward a hostile person. Having softened one's mind toward them, then you turn to miserable person, one dear to you, and then to yourself, in that order. But this advice is inconsistent with the mention of "miserable and unfortunate" in the canonical text. Therefore, you should undertake the meditation by the method described here, break down barriers,

Ayaṃ karuṇābhāvanāya vitthārakathā.

and develop full absorption. And after that, do this in the different modalities—flooding universally in terms of the five ways, flooding with specifications in the seven ways, and flooding directionally in the ten ways. The benefits of this should be understood exactly as described in the case of lovingkindness, such as getting a good night's sleep.

This concludes the detailed explanation of the practice of compassion.

SYMPATHETIC JOY

The content of sympathetic joy is the happy sharing in others' good fortune and success. It is your genuine delight when good things happen to others, even to your enemies. Sympathetic joy is the removal of envy and discontent, both of which can be ubiquitous and often largely unrecognized features of our lives.

Western moral sense theorists also note that we often sympathize with happy others.[34] *We can readily shift from a sour mood when arriving at a joyful party or hearing a friend's good news. Parents enjoy unalloyed happiness at their children's success. What would life be like if we expanded these feelings, and shared the pleasure of all beings? Buddhaghosa recommends starting with the fun-loving pal whose easy cheerfulness is infectious. Once the feeling flows, we can extend it to others, with each new embrace of joy breaking down the walls of our own narrow self-regard, envy, and discontent.*

Muditā

[23] Muditābhāvanaṃ ārabhantenāpi na paṭhamaṃ piyapuggalādīsu ārabhitabbā. Na hi piyo piyabhāvamatteneva muditāya padaṭṭhānaṃ hoti, pageva majjhattaverino. Liṅgavisabhāgakālakatā akhettameva.

Atippiyasahāyako pana siyā padaṭṭhānaṃ, yo aṭṭhakathāyaṃ soṇḍasahāyoti vutto. So hi muditamuditova hoti, paṭhamaṃ hasitvā pacchā katheti, tasmā so vā paṭhamaṃ muditāya pharitabbo. Piyapuggalaṃ vā sukhitaṃ sajjitaṃ modamānaṃ disvā vā sutvā vā modati vatāyaṃ satto, aho sādhu aho suṭṭhūti muditā uppādetabbā. Imameva hi atthavasaṃ paṭicca vibhaṅge vuttaṃ kathañca bhikkhu muditāsahagatena cetasā ekaṃ disaṃ pharitvā

SYMPATHETIC JOY

[23] When you begin to cultivate sympathetic joy, don't start with those who are dear to you. Such a person cannot be the immediate cause of sympathetic joy simply because you already love them, and the same is true, *mutatis mutandis*, of your casual acquaintances and enemies. Nor are those of the opposite sex or who have passed away good objects for beginning this practice.

But a *very close* buddy—one who is always cheerful, laughing first and speaking second, the kind of person the commentaries call one's *fun-loving pal*—can be the immediate cause of sympathetic joy.[35] So flood this person with sympathetic joy first. When you see such a person happy, rejoicing, and all decked out, you should generate sympathetic joy, thinking, "This person is joyful! This is really great! This is excellent!"

viharati? Seyyathāpi nāma ekaṃ puggalaṃ piyaṃ manāpaṃ disvā mudito assa, evameva sabbasatte muditāya pharatīti.

Sacepissa so soṇḍasahāyo vā piyapuggalo vā atīte sukhito ahosi, sampati pana duggato durūpeto, atītameva cassa sukhitabhāvaṃ anussaritvā esa atīte evaṃ mahābhogo mahāparivāro niccappamudito ahosīti tamevassa muditākāraṃ gahetvā muditā uppādetabbā anāgate vā pana puna taṃ sampattiṃ labhitvā hatthikkhandhaassapiṭṭhisuvaṇṇasivikādīhi vicarissatīti anāgatampissa muditākāraṃ gahetvā muditā uppādetabbā.

Evaṃ piyapuggale muditaṃ uppādetvā atha majjhatte tato verimhīti anukkamena muditā

Speaking to this very point, the *Book of Analysis* says: "How does a monk live flooding one direction with a mind full of sympathetic joy? Imagine seeing a dear and beloved person and feeling happy for them; in exactly the same way, flood all beings with sympathetic joy."[36]

But if that fun-loving pal or dear friend was once happy but has now become miserable and unfortunate, then recall only their past happiness, getting hold of an aspect of their previous happiness—"in the past they were delighted, prosperous, and enjoyed a large following"—and generate sympathetic joy for them under that description. Or try imagining their future happiness—"in the future they will again be successful and will travel on the backs of elephants and horses or in a golden palanquin"—and generate sympathetic joy that way.

Extend your sympathetic joy in stages, first generating it toward those you hold dear, then

pavattetabbā. Appanā vaḍḍhetabbā. Sace panassa pubbe vuttanayeneva verimhi paṭighaṃ uppajjati, taṃ mettāyaṃ vuttanayeneva vūpasametvā imesu ca tīsu attani cā ti catūsu janesu samacittatāya sīmāsambhedaṃ katvā taṃ nimittaṃ āsevantena bhāventena bahulīkarontena mettāyaṃ vuttanayeneva tikacatukkajjhānavaseneva appanā vaḍḍhetabbā. Tato paraṃ pañcahākārehi anodhisopharaṇā sattahākārehi odhisopharaṇā dasahākārehi disāpharaṇā ti ayaṃ vikubbanā, sukhaṃ supatīti ādayo ānisaṃsā ca mettāyaṃ vuttanayeneva veditabbāti.

Ayaṃ muditābhāvanāya vitthārakathā.

toward mere acquaintances, then toward your enemies. This is how to generate the full absorption. But if anger toward the enemy occurs as previously described, then extinguish it by means of the method described for lovingkindness. Having broken down barriers in order to cultivate an impartial mind toward the four classes of people—yourself, your dear friends, your mere acquaintances, and your enemies—meditate earnestly and frequently. And, just as in the case of lovingkindness, develop full absorption by way of the third or fourth deep concentration. And after that, do this in the different modalities—flooding universally in terms of the five ways, flooding with specification in the seven ways, and flooding directionally in the ten ways. The benefits of this are the same as those of lovingkindness—you will sleep well, and so on.

This concludes the detailed explanation of the practice of sympathetic joy.

EQUANIMITY

Perhaps the most sublime of the sublime attitudes is equanimity. It is to be built on the foundation of the other three—only when one has flooded all beings equally with lovingkindness, compassion, and sympathetic joy should one step back from these warm feelings and aim for a less reactive and more peaceful attention to beings. Since the first three attitudes involve sizing up the experiences of other beings with strong feelings about them, they involve judgments. Such judgments of "resentment and approval" are, Buddhaghosa says, "too close." In contrast, equanimity involves stepping back and cultivating a feeling of impartiality, equality, and neutrality toward others. It stays unruffled through the ups and downs of beings' experience. And it reminds us of the Buddhist aspirations to achieve, perhaps above all, the freedom that comes from a truly peaceful mind.

Upekkhā

[24] Upekkhābhāvanaṃ bhāvetukāmena pana mettādīsu paṭiladdhatikacatukkajjhānena paguṇatatiyajjhānā vuṭṭhāya sukhitā hontū ti ādivasena sattakelāyanamanasikārayuttattā, paṭighānunayasamīpacārittā, somanassayogena oḷārikattā ca purimāsu ādīnavaṃ, santabhāvattā upekkhāya ānisaṃsañca disvā yvāssa pakatimajjhatto puggalo, taṃ ajjhupekkhitvā upekkhā uppādetabbā. Tato piyapuggalādīsu.

[24] A monk seeking to practice the meditation on equanimity should have attained the third or the fourth level of deep concentration in the meditations on lovingkindness, compassion, and sympathetic joy.[37] Once you have mastered the third level of deep concentration, you will come to see that these other three attitudes are in fact perilous, because they involve attending to and cherishing beings, as when one says "May they be happy!" Moreover, resentment and approval are too close, and their connection with mental pleasure is too substantial for them to be entirely safe. You should see that the benefit of equanimity is tranquility. You should generate equanimity by viewing with impartiality a person toward whom you have a neutral attitude,

Vuttañhetaṃ kathañca bhikkhu upekkhāsahagatena cetasā ekaṃ disaṃ pharitvā viharati? Seyyathāpi nāma ekaṃ puggalaṃ neva manāpaṃ na amanāpaṃ disvā upekkhako assa, evameva sabbe satte upekkhāya pharatīti. Tasmā vuttanayena majjhattapuggale upekkhaṃ uppādetvā atha piyapuggale, tato soṇḍasahāyake, tato verimhīti evaṃ imesu ca tīsu attani cā ti sabbattha majjhattavasena sīmāsambhedaṃ katvā taṃ nimittaṃ āsevitabbaṃ bhāvetabbaṃ bahulīkātabbaṃ. Tassevaṃ karoto pathavīkasiṇe vuttanayeneva catutthajjhānaṃ uppajjati.

Kiṃ panetaṃ pathavīkasiṇādīsu uppannatatiyajjhānassāpi uppajjatīti? Nuppajjati. Kasmā? Ārammaṇavisabhāgatāya. Mettādīsu uppannatatiyajjhānasseva pana uppajjati, ārammaṇasabhāgatāyāti. Tato paraṃ pana vikubbanā

and then extend that attitude to those who are dear and then to your enemies.

This has been said: "How does one live flooding one direction with a mind full of equanimity?"[38] Imagine being nonreactive upon seeing a mere acquaintance, and then flood this equanimity toward all beings in this way. And so, generate equanimity toward such a person in the method stated, then direct it toward someone dear to you, to the fun-loving pal, and to an enemy, breaking down barriers by adopting a neutral attitude toward yourself, toward your dear ones, and to your enemies. Pursue, practice, and develop this mental image.

As one does so, the fourth *jhāna* arises in the way described with the earth meditation device.

But can one who has reached the third level of deep concentration through *other* practices like the earth meditation device cultivate such

ca ānisaṃsapaṭilābho ca mettāyaṃ vuttanayeneva veditabboti.

Ayaṃ upekkhābhāvanāya vitthārakathā.

equanimity and impartiality? No, this is impossible. Why is this? Because of the difference in meditation object. It arises only for one who has reached the third level of deep concentration on lovingkindness, and so on, because of it being a related topic. You should understand the extraordinary transformation and the attainment of the benefits of this practice just as you understand them in the context of lovingkindness.

This concludes the detailed explanation of the practice of equanimity.

VARIOUS TOPICS

We turn last to "Various Topics," a section in which Buddhaghosa gives further details on each of the four sublime attitudes—what they feel like, what conditions them, how they manifest, how they work, and so on. And we reflect further on how these are "immeasurables," ever-expanding practices in both scope and in habit.

Much Buddhist psychology involves noticing and then managing mental states and their opposites. For example, Buddhaghosa sees each sublime attitude as having a "near" enemy and a "distant" enemy. The enemies of the attitudes stop us from experiencing them and so need to be identified as such and relinquished. Near enemies are emotions that are close to the sublime attitudes in content and so might be easily mistaken for them, while the distant enemies are their hostile adversaries.

The near enemy of lovingkindness, for example, is passion, the desire-driven love or affection that we often have toward others based on our own wants instead of a genuine longing for the other's well-being. It should not be mistaken for lovingkindness, which is entirely about the other's well-being and happiness. Lovingkindness's far enemy, ill will, is easier to spot, but as we have seen at length, quite hard to drive out.

Notice too a subtle point concerning compassion: its near enemy is sorrow. When we attend closely to the pain of the world we can easily succumb to grief. This sorrow should not be confused with compassion, which is not the debilitating pain and fatigue of sharing others' suffering. It is rather the longing for their pain to end, and the work of removing it. It is not itself a negative or painful state.

This final section gives additional particulars about meditation (though I have omitted one very technical passage). Beginning and experienced meditators can track how these levels of concentration work to develop access to the sublime realms of greater and greater serenity, spaciousness, and freedom. Recall that these realms are both sublime experiences possible here and now, and the Brahma heavens that these practices lead to after death. Readers will be fascinated with the psychology of this mapping of phenomenology, meditation states, and the heavenly worlds.

We see, for example, that lovingkindness is linked to, and culminates in, the experience of beauty and the beautiful realm. The logic here is that lovingkindness seeks out what is lovable, and perhaps what is most naturally lovable is beauty. In a different way, a compassionate mind is attentive to the sharp stabs and blows of material pain—thus, it launches quite readily to the realm of pure and infinite space free of materiality. A sympathetic mind is attentive to and aware of others' consciousness and feelings—it picks out the workings of consciousness itself and so it has natural affinities to the realm of infinite consciousness. Finally, the stepping back from resentment and approval that is equanimity culminates in the insight of the emptiness of all things—nothing has inherent essence, whether good, bad, or any of the other limited labels we reductively attach to the world.

The "Detailed Instructions for the Sublime Attitudes" chapter ends with Buddhaghosa grafting the four sublime attitudes onto the ten perfections of a bodhisatta. Bodhisattas, also called "Great Beings," are buddhas-in-training in their long, multi-lifetime preparations to achieve a buddha's awakening. They are said to develop ten perfections or excellences over these vast previous lives. In the Theravada tradition, these perfections are generosity, morality, renunciation, wisdom, effort, patience, truthfulness, unshakable determination, lovingkindness, and equanimity. Someone practicing the four sublime attitudes is also developing and creating the conditions for these "beautiful states" to emerge over time. With practice, they can yield ultimate freedom, happiness, and peace.

Pakiṇṇakakathā

[25] Brahmuttamena kathite, brahmavihāre ime iti viditvā; bhiyyo etesu ayaṃ, pakiṇṇakakathāpi viññeyyā.

Etāsu hi mettākaruṇāmuditāupekkhāsu atthato tāva mejjatīti mettā, siniyhatīti attho. Mitte vā bhavā, mittassa vā esā pavattītipi mettā.

Paradukkhe sati sādhūnaṃ hadayakampanaṃ karotīti karuṇā. Kiṇāti vā paradukkhaṃ hiṃsati vināsetīti karuṇā. Kiriyati vā dukkhitesu pharaṇavasena pasāriyatīti karuṇā.

Definitions and Characteristics

[25] Once you have grasped these sublime attitudes as described by the supreme Brahma, you should turn to various related topics that also must be understood.

First, consider the meanings of *lovingkindness*, *compassion*, *sympathetic joy*, and *equanimity*. The sense of *lovingkindness* comes from *becoming tender*—that is, softening. *Lovingkindness* can also mean *friendliness* and the state of being a friend.

Compassion makes the hearts of good people tremble when others suffer. Compassion also combats, destroys, and terminates others' suffering. And compassion is bestowed—that is, extended—to those who are suffering by flooding them with it.

Modanti tāya taṃsamaṅgino, sayaṃ vā modati, modanamattameva vā tanti muditā.

Averā hontū tiādibyāpārappahānena majjhatta-bhāvūpagamanena ca upekkhatīti upekkhā.

Lakkhaṇādito panettha hitākārappavattilak-khaṇā mettā, hitūpasaṃhārarasā, āghātavinayap-accupaṭṭhānā, sattānaṃ manāpabhāvadassana-padaṭṭhānā. Byāpādūpasamo etissā sampatti, sinehasambhavo vipatti.

Dukkhāpanayanākārappavattilakkhaṇā karuṇā, paradukkhāsahanarasā, avihiṃsāpaccupaṭṭhānā, dukkhābhibhūtānaṃ anāthabhāvadassana-padaṭṭhānā. Vihiṃsūpasamo tassā sampatti, so-kasambhavo vipatti.

Sympathetic joy refers to the joy one feels because of the joy of others. It is enjoyment itself as well as simply rejoicing.

Equanimity is looking on beings' comings and goings with neutrality by letting go of worries like "May they be friendly."

They each also have defining characteristics, and other features. *Lovingkindness* is characterized as advancing different kinds of well-being; its function is to bring about well-being; it manifests as the removal of resentment; and its immediate cause is seeing the lovableness of beings. It succeeds when it stops ill will and it fails when it produces partiality.

Compassion is characterized as advancing ways of removing suffering; its function is to make one incapable of tolerating others' suffering; it manifests as not being cruel; and its immediate cause is seeing the helplessness of those

Pamodanalakkhaṇā muditā, anissāyanarasā, arativighātapaccupaṭṭhānā, sattānaṃ sampattidassanapadaṭṭhānā. Arativūpasamo tassā sampatti, pahāsasambhavo vipatti.

Sattesu majjhattākārappavattilakkhaṇā upekkhā, sattesu samabhāvadassanarasā, paṭighānunayavūpasamapaccupaṭṭhānā kammassakā sattā, te kassa ruciyā sukhitā vā bhavissanti, dukkhato vā muccissanti, pattasampattito vā na parihāyissantīti evaṃ pavattakammassakatādassanapadaṭṭhānā. Paṭighānunayavūpasamo tassā sampatti, gehasitāya aññāṇupekkhāya sambhavo vipatti.

overcome with pain. It succeeds when it stops cruelty, and it fails when it produces grief.

Sympathetic joy is characterized as delight; its function is to lack envy; it manifests as getting rid of discontent; and its immediate cause is seeing other beings' success. It succeeds when it stops discontent, and it fails when it produces amusement.

Equanimity is characterized as advancing modes of impartiality toward beings; its function is to see equality in beings; it manifests as the subsiding of resentment and approval; and its immediate cause is observing that beings are responsible for their continuing actions, as one considers: *Beings are responsible for their actions. Whose choice is it but theirs to be happy, to get rid of suffering, or to not fall away from success already achieved?* It succeeds when it stops resentment and approval, and it fails when,

[26] Catunnampi panetesaṃ brahmavihārānaṃ vipassanāsukhañceva bhavasampatti ca sādhāraṇappayojanaṃ. Byāpādādipaṭighāto āveṇikaṃ. Byāpādapaṭighātappayojanā hettha mettā. Vihiṃsāaratirāgapaṭighātappayojanā itarā. Vuttampi cetaṃ nissaraṇañhetaṃ, āvuso, byāpādassa yadidaṃ mettā cetovimutti. Nissaraṇañhetaṃ, āvuso, vihesāya yadidaṃ karuṇā cetovimutti. Nissaraṇañhetaṃ, āvuso, aratiyā yadidaṃ muditā cetovimutti. Nissaraṇañhetaṃ, āvuso, rāgassa yadidaṃ upekkhā cetovimuttīti.

due to mundane concerns, it produces apathy toward others.

Purposes

[26] The general purpose of these four sublime attitudes is success in rebirth and the happiness deriving from insight. More specifically, they ward off things like ill will. Lovingkindness has the purpose of warding off ill will, and the others have the purposes of warding off cruelty, discontent, and passion, respectively. For this is said: "Friend, freedom of the loving mind is the escape from ill will. Freedom of the compassionate mind is the escape from viciousness. Freedom of the sympathetic mind is the escape from discontent. And, friend, the freedom of the mind that is equanimity is the escape from passion."[39]

Ekekassa cettha āsannadūravasena dve dve paccatthikā. Mettābrahmavihārassa hi samīpacāro viya purisassa sapatto guṇadassanasabhāgatāya rāgo āsannapaccatthiko, so lahuṃ otāraṃ labhati, tasmā tato suṭṭhu mettā rakkhitabbā. Pabbatādigahananissito viya purisassa sapatto sabhāgavisabhāgatāya byāpādo dūrapaccatthiko, tasmā tato nibbhayena mettāyitabbaṃ. Mettāyissati ca nāma, kopañca karissatīti aṭṭhānametaṃ.

Karuṇābrahmavihārassa cakkhuviññeyyānaṃ rūpānaṃ iṭṭhānaṃ kantānaṃ manāpānaṃ manoramānaṃ lokāmisapaṭisaṃyuttānaṃ appaṭilābhaṃ vā appaṭilābhato samanupassato pubbe vā paṭiladdhapubbaṃ atītaṃ niruddhaṃ

Near and Distant Enemies

Now in each case, there are two enemies, one near and one distant. Passion is the near enemy of lovingkindness because both see their object as good. It is like a person's rival who keeps near trying to find a point of entry. Therefore, lovingkindness really needs to be protected from it. Ill will is lovingkindness's distant enemy because it has nothing in common with it, like a rival lurking in dense thickets away in the hills. Lovingkindness must be practiced without threat from it, since it is not possible to feel lovingkindness while being angry.

Mundane distress is the near enemy of compassion because both notice others suffering from misfortune. Here is a definition: "Mundane distress refers to the distress that occurs for someone dwelling on things they don't

vipariṇataṃ samanussarato uppajjati domanassaṃ, yaṃ evarūpaṃ domanassaṃ, idaṃ vuccati gehasitaṃ domanassantiādinā nayena āgataṃ gehasitaṃ domanassaṃ vipattidassanasabhāgatāya āsannapaccatthikaṃ. Sabhāgavisabhāgatāya vihiṃsā dūrapaccatthikā. Tasmā tato nibbhayena karuṇāyitabbaṃ. Karuṇañca nāma karissati, pāṇiādīhi ca viheṭhissatīti aṭṭhānametaṃ.

Muditābrahmavihārassa cakkhuviññeyyānaṃ rūpānaṃ iṭṭhānaṃ... pe ... lokāmisapaṭisaṃyuttānaṃ paṭilābhaṃ vā paṭilābhato samanupassato pubbe vā paṭiladdhapubbaṃ atītaṃ niruddhaṃ vipariṇataṃ samanussarato uppajjati somanassaṃ, yaṃ evarūpaṃ somanassaṃ, idaṃ vuccati gehasitaṃ somanassantiādinā nayena āgataṃ gehasitaṃ somanassaṃ sampattidassanasabhāgatāya āsannapaccatthikaṃ, sabhāgavisabhāgatāya arati dūrapaccatthikā. Tasmā tato nibbhayena muditā

have, things connected with worldly pleasures, appealing and pleasurable material things delightful and charming to the eye; or it occurs for someone recalling changes and reversals of fortune in the past."[40] Cruelty is compassion's distant enemy because it has nothing in common with it. Compassion must be practiced without threat from it, since it is not possible to feel compassion while being cruel to living creatures.

Mundane happiness is the near enemy of sympathetic joy because both notice others who are successful. Here is a definition: "Mundane happiness refers to the happiness that occurs for someone dwelling on things they do have, things connected with worldly pleasures, appealing and pleasurable material things delightful and charming to the eye; or it occurs for someone recalling changes and reversals of fortune in the past." Discontent is sympathetic joy's distant

bhāvetabbā. Mudito ca nāma bhavissati, pantasenāsanesu ca adhikusalesu dhammesu vā ukkaṇṭhissatīti aṭṭhānametaṃ.

Upekkhābrahmavihārassa pana cakkhunā rūpaṃ disvā uppajjati upekkhā bālassa mūḷhassa puthujjanassa anodhijinassa avipākajinassa anādīnavadassāvino assutavato puthujjanassa yā evarūpā upekkhā, rūpaṃ sā nātivattati. Tasmā sā upekkhā gehasitāti vuccatīti ādinā nayena āgatā gehasitā aññāṇupekkhā dosaguṇāvicāraṇavasena sabhāgattā āsannapaccatthikā. Sabhāgavisabhāgatāya rāgapaṭighā dūrapaccatthikā. Tasmā tato nibbhayena upekkhitabbaṃ. Upekkhissati ca nāma, rajjissati ca paṭihaññissati cāti aṭṭhānametaṃ.

enemy because it has nothing in common with it. Sympathetic joy must be practiced without threat from it, since it is not possible to be joyful while also being discontent with highly meritorious practices and quiet lodgings.

Mundane equanimity toward others is the near enemy of equanimity because neither goes looking for problems or good features. Here is a definition: "Mundane equanimity refers to how a fool, an ordinary deluded person who has not overcome their limitations or the results of their actions, a clueless regular person, sees a visual object with their eyes and fails to see any problems at all; they have equanimity in not going beyond just what they see." Passion and resentment are equanimity's distant enemies because they have nothing in common with it. Equanimity must be practiced without threat from them, since it is not possible to feel equanimity while also being passionate or resentful.

[27] Sabbesampi ca etesaṃ kattukāmatā chando ādi, nīvaraṇādivikkhambhanaṃ majjhaṃ, appanā pariyosānaṃ. Paññattidhammavasena eko vā satto aneke vā sattā ārammaṇaṃ. Upacāre vā appanāya vā pattāya ārammaṇavaḍḍhanaṃ.

Tatrāyaṃ vaḍḍhanakkamo, yathā hi kusalo kassako kasitabbaṭṭhānaṃ paricchinditvā kasati, evaṃ paṭhamameva ekamāvāsaṃ paricchinditvā tattha sattesu imasmiṃ āvāse sattā averā hontūtiādinā nayena mettā bhāvetabbā. Tattha cittaṃ muduṃ kammaniyaṃ katvā dve āvāsā paricchinditabbā.

The Beginning, Middle, and End—and How to Extend Them

[27] Moreover, each of these *begins* with eagerness, which is the desire to act; the *middle part* of each is sustained by withdrawing one's support for their obstacles; and their *last part* is full absorption. The meditation object is a single being or many beings, taking them as a mental object of focus consisting of a concept. And when one has attained preliminary or full absorption, then one should extend it to further meditation objects.

Here is the sequence for extending them. Practice lovingkindness by the method described at the beginning of this discussion, thinking, "May beings be friendly." One starts with beings in this residence, limiting it at first to a single place. A good farmer plows having first demarcated

Tato anukkamena tayo, cattāro, pañca, cha, satta, aṭṭha, nava, dasa, ekā racchā, upaḍḍhagāmo, gāmo, janapado, rajjaṃ, ekā disāti evaṃ yāva ekaṃ cakkavāḷaṃ, tato vā pana bhiyyo tattha tattha sattesu mettā bhāvetabbā. Tathā karuṇādayoti ayamettha ārammaṇavaḍḍhanakkamo.

Yathā pana kasiṇānaṃ nissando āruppā, samādhinissando nevasaññānāsaññāyatanaṃ, vipassanānissando phalasamāpatti, samathavipas-

one area that needs plowing. After making one's heart soft and pliable toward one place, focus on two residences. And gradually from there, three, four, five, six, seven, eight, nine, ten, then a main road, half the village, the whole village, the countryside, the kingdom, and then a single direction, all the way up to one world system, and from there, practice lovingkindness toward more and more beings in each place. Likewise with compassion and the rest. This is how to extend them to further objects.

Outcomes in the Sublime and Heavenly Realms

Now, the outcome of the meditation devices is the achievement of the formless states; the outcome of calm concentration is the achievement

sanānissando nirodhasamāpatti, evaṃ purimabrahmavihārattayanissando ettha upekkhābrahmavihāro. Yathā hi thambhe anussāpetvā tulāsaṅghāṭaṃ anāropetvā na sakkā ākāse kūṭagopānasiyo ṭhapetuṃ, evaṃ purimesu tatiyajjhānaṃ vinā na sakkā catutthaṃ bhāvetunti.

[28] Ettha siyā, kasmā panetā mettākaruṇāmuditāupekkhā brahmavihārāti vuccanti? Kasmā ca catassova? Ko ca etāsaṃ kamo, abhidhamme ca kasmā appamaññāti vuttāti?

of the realm of neither perception nor non-perception; the outcome of insight practice is the attainment of the effect; and the outcome of both serenity and insight meditation is the attainment of cessation. Similarly, the sublime abiding of equanimity is the outcome of the first three sublime attitudes. A crossbeam cannot be mounted without first having secured it to the ceiling joists, since it is not possible to attach the beams of a roof to the open air. So too it is not possible to practice the fourth level of deep concentration without the first three.

Additional Nuances

[28] Now here it might be asked, "Why are lovingkindness, compassion, sympathetic joy, and equanimity called 'sublime attitudes'? Why are there only four? What is their sequence? And

Vuccate, seṭṭhaṭṭhena tāva niddosabhāvena cettha brahmavihāratā veditabbā. Sattesu sammāpaṭipattibhāvena hi seṭṭhā ete vihārā. Yathā ca brahmāno niddosacittā viharanti, evaṃ etehi sampayuttā yogino brahmasamā hutvā viharantīti seṭṭhaṭṭhena niddosabhāvena ca brahmavihārāti vuccanti.

Kasmā ca catassovātiādi pañhassa pana idaṃ vissajjanaṃ.

Visuddhimaggādivasā catasso,
Hitādiākāravasā panāsaṃ
Kamo pavattanti ca appamāṇe,
Tā gocare yena tadappamaññā.

why are they called 'immeasurables' in the Abhidhamma?"[41]

Here are the answers to these questions: "These attitudes are sublime in the sense of 'supreme' and in the sense of 'lacking harmful thoughts.' They are *supreme* modes of living because they entail right conduct toward beings. And since the minds of the Brahma gods lack harmful thoughts, practitioners connected with the sublime attitudes live as the equals of Brahma.[42] And so the sublime attitudes are considered supreme and lacking harmful thoughts."

Here are the answers to the other questions—"Why are there only four," and so on.

> They are *four* with respect to their paths to purification;
> and there is a *sequence* in terms of their modalities,

Etāsu hi yasmā mettā byāpādabahulassa, karuṇā vihesābahulassa, muditā aratibahulassa, upekkhā rāgabahulassa visuddhimaggo. Yasmā ca hitūpasaṃhāraahitāpanayanasampattimodanaanābhogavasena catubbidhoyeva sattesu manasikāro.

Yasmā ca yathā mātā daharagilānayobbanappattasakiccapasutesu catūsu puttesu daharassa abhivuḍḍhikāmā hoti, gilānassa gelaññāpan-

starting with wishing for well-being.
And they are *immeasurables* because they
progress with a measureless scope.

"They are *paths to purification* because lovingkindness purifies those full of ill will, compassion purifies those full of cruelty, sympathetic joy, those full of discontent, and equanimity, those full of passion. And they are *four* because they are four kinds of attention to beings—focusing on their well-being, removing their hurts, rejoicing at their successes, and dispassion."

The Mother with Four Sons

One who lives by these immeasurables toward all beings should practice lovingkindness and the rest like a mother with four sons—namely, a

ayanakāmā, yobbanappattassa yobbanasampattiyā ciraṭṭhitikāmā, sakakiccapasutassa kismiñci pariyāye abyāvaṭā hoti, tathā appamaññāvihārikenāpi sabbasattesu mettādivasena bhavitabbaṃ. Tasmā ito visuddhimaggādivasā catassova appamaññā.

[29] Yasmā catassopetā bhāvetukāmena paṭhamaṃ hitākārappavattivasena sattesu paṭipajjitabbaṃ, hitākārappavattilakkhaṇā ca mettā. Tato evaṃ patthitahitānaṃ sattānaṃ dukkhābhibhavaṃ disvā vā sutvā vā sambhāvetvā vā dukkhāpanayanākārappavattivasena, duk-

little boy, a sick child, a youth, and a grown-up son engaged in his own affairs. She wants her little one to flourish, her sick child to be free of illness, and her young son to enjoy the beauty of youth for a long time. And she is unruffled about the doings of her grown-up son engaged in his own affairs. This is what is meant by their being the paths to purification, their being only four, and their being immeasurables.

Sequencing

[29] This is the sequence in which they should be cultivated. For someone wishing to practice all four, lovingkindness toward beings should be practiced first because it advances modes of their well-being. This is because the very characteristic of lovingkindness is advancing modes

khāpanayanākārappavattilakkhaṇā ca karuṇā. Athevaṃ patthitahitānaṃ patthitadukkhāpagamānañca nesaṃ sampattiṃ disvā sampattipamodanavasena, pamodanalakkhaṇā ca muditā. Tato paraṃ pana kattabbābhāvato ajjhupekkhakattasaṅkhātena majjhattākārena paṭipajjitabbaṃ, majjhattākārappavattilakkhaṇā ca upekkhā. Tasmā ito hitādiākāravasā panāsaṃ paṭhamaṃ mettā vuttā, atha karuṇā muditā upekkhāti ayaṃ kamo veditabbo.

of well-being. But then one may see, hear, or consider that those beings whose well-being one sought are now overcome with suffering. So compassion—which is characterized by advancing ways of removing suffering—should be practiced by finding ways of removing their suffering. And then, seeing the success of those whose well-being and relief from suffering one sought, one should practice sympathetic joy by rejoicing in their success, since it is characterized by delight. After that, one should practice equanimity with an impartial disposition, like that of an onlooker, since there is nothing to be done. Equanimity is characterized by modes of advancing impartiality. Therefore, since their respective aims are well-being, and so on, loving-kindness is taught first, and then compassion, sympathetic joy, and equanimity.

Yasmā pana sabbāpetā appamāṇe gocare pavattanti. Appamāṇā hi sattā etāsaṃ gocarabhūtā. Ekasattassāpi ca ettake padese mettādayo bhāvetabbāti evaṃ pamāṇaṃ agahetvā sakalapharaṇavaseneva pavattāti. Tena vuttaṃ

Visuddhimaggādivasā catasso,
Hitādiākāravasā panāsaṃ;
Kamo pavattanti ca appamāṇe,
Tā gocare yena tadappamaññāti.

▪ ▪ ▪

Taken together, these attitudes are measureless in scope. Their range encompasses unlimited beings. Moreover, one can practice lovingkindness and the rest toward even a single being in one place without reaching a limit, to say nothing of continuing by flooding it everywhere. And so it is said:

> They are four with respect to their paths to purification;
> and there is a sequence in terms of their modalities, starting with wishing for well-being.
> And they are immeasurables because they progress with a measureless scope.

▪ ▪ ▪

[30] etāsaṃ subhaparamādivasena aññamaññaṃ asadiso ānubhāvaviseso veditabbo. Haliddavasanasuttasmiṃ hi etā subhaparamādibhāvena visesetvā vuttā. Yathāha subhaparamāhaṃ, bhikkhave, mettaṃ cetovimuttiṃ vadāmi. Ākāsānañcāyatanaparamāhaṃ, bhikkhave, karuṇaṃ cetovimuttiṃ vadāmi. Viññāṇañcāyatanaparamāhaṃ, bhikkhave, muditaṃ cetovimuttiṃ vadāmi. Ākiñcaññāyatanaparamāhaṃ, bhikkhave, upekkhaṃ cetovimuttiṃ vadāmīti.

Culminating in the Heavenly Realms

[30] A distinction in their efficacy should be understood because they are different from one another with respect to their highest culmination, such as in the beautiful sphere. These are mentioned in the "Teaching in Hallidavasana," which defines the highest culmination in the beautiful sphere, and the others.[43] There it is said, "Monks, I say that the mental freedom that is lovingkindness has its highest culmination in the beautiful sphere. I say that the mental freedom that is compassion has its highest culmination in the sphere of awareness of infinite space. I say that the mental freedom that is sympathetic joy is the sphere of awareness of infinite consciousness. I say that the mental freedom that is equanimity is the sphere of awareness of emptiness."

Kasmā panetā evaṃ vuttāti? Tassa tassa upanissayattā. Mettāvihārissa hi sattā appaṭikkūlā honti. Athassa appaṭikkūlaparicayā appaṭikkūlesu parisuddhavaṇṇesu nīlādīsu cittaṃ upasaṃharato appakasireneva tattha cittaṃ pakkhandati. Iti mettā subhavimokkhassa upanissayo hoti, na tato paraṃ, tasmā subhaparamāti vuttā.

Karuṇāvihārissa pana daṇḍābhighātādirūpanimittaṃ pattadukkhaṃ samanupassantassa karuṇāya pavattisambhavato rūpe ādīnavo parivídito hoti. Athassa parividitarūpādīnavattā pathavīkasiṇādīsu aññataraṃ ugghāṭetvā rūpanissaraṇe ākāse cittaṃ upasaṃharato appakasireneva tattha cittaṃ pakkhandati. Iti karuṇā ākāsānañcāyatanassa upanissayo hoti, na tato paraṃ, tasmā ākāsānañcāyatanaparamāti vuttā.

Why is this said? Because each one is the support for one of these. For someone living with lovingkindness, beings are lovely. And because of the mind's familiarity with what is lovely, when focusing on pure and lovely colors like blue, and so forth, the mind leaps easily to only what is beautiful there. Lovingkindness is the support for the freedom that is beauty, and so it is said to culminate in the beautiful sphere, but not higher.

For someone living with compassion, the danger in material experience is well known from birth through life. They see with compassion the suffering that occurs, taking it as a mental image associated with material experience such as being beaten with sticks. Because they fully grasp the danger in material experience, when they release the mind from the meditation device of the earth disk, and so on, and shift it to focus on the open space that is the escape from

Muditāvihārissa pana tena tena pāmojjakāraṇena uppannapāmojjasattānaṃ viññāṇaṃ samanupassantassa muditāya pavattisambhavato viññāṇaggahaṇaparicitaṃ cittaṃ hoti. Athassa anukkamādhigataṃ ākāsānañcāyatanaṃ atikkamma ākāsanimittagocare viññāṇe cittaṃ upasaṃharato appakasireneva tattha cittaṃ pakkhandatīti muditā viññāṇañcāyatanassa upanissayo hoti, na tato paraṃ, tasmā viññāṇañcāyatanaparamāti vuttā.

material experience, the mind leaps easily into it. Compassion is the support for the sphere of awareness of infinite space, and so is said to culminate in the sphere of awareness of infinite space, but not higher.

For someone living with sympathetic joy, the mind is familiar with apprehending consciousness from birth through life. They see with sympathetic joy the consciousness of beings given over to joy through the many causes of joy. They go beyond the sphere of awareness of infinite space acquired in the sequence. Shifting the mind to focus on the consciousness that has as its range the image of open space, the mind leaps easily into it. Sympathetic joy is the support for the sphere of awareness of infinite consciousness, and so is said to culminate in the sphere of awareness of infinite consciousness, but not higher.

Upekkhāvihārissa pana sattā sukhitā vā hontu dukkhato vā vimuccantu, sampattasukhato vā mā vimuccantūti ābhogābhāvato sukhadukkhādi-paramatthagāhavimukhabhāvato avijjamānag-gahaṇadakkhaṃ[44] cittaṃ hoti. Athassa para-matthagāhato vimukhabhāvaparicitacittassa paramatthato avijjamānaggahaṇadukkhacittassa ca anukkamādhigataṃ viññāṇañcāyatanaṃ sama-tikkamma sabhāvato avijjamāne paramatthabhū-tassa viññāṇassa abhāve cittaṃ upasaṃharato appakasireneva tattha cittaṃ pakkhandati. Iti up-ekkhā ākiñcaññāyatanassa upanissayo hoti, na tato paraṃ, tasmā ākiñcaññāyatanaparamāti vuttāti.

For someone living with equanimity, the mind has become able to take in what does not exist due to turning away from clutching at happiness and suffering and so on as ultimately significant. This occurs from one's lack of involvement in such concerns as, "May beings be happy, may they be released from suffering, may the happiness they have acquired not leave them," and so forth. Because of their mind's familiarity with turning away from clutching at ultimate significance, and because the mind is able to take in what does not exist in the ultimate sense, the mind goes completely beyond the sphere of awareness of infinite consciousness acquired in the sequence. Shifting the mind to focus on the lack of consciousness for a being in the ultimate sense—in that no inherent natures exist—the mind leaps easily to it. Equanimity is the support for the sphere of awareness that

[31] Evaṃ subhaparamādivasena etāsaṃ ānubhāvaṃ viditvā puna sabbāpetā dānādīnaṃ sabbakalyāṇadhammānaṃ paripūrikāti veditabbā. Sattesu hi hitajjhāsayatāya sattānaṃ dukkhāsahanatāya, pattasampattivisesānaṃ ciraṭṭhitikāmatāya, sabbasattesu ca pakkhapātābhāvena samappavattacittā mahāsattā.

Imassa dātabbaṃ, imassa na dātabbanti vibhāgaṃ akatvā sabbasattānaṃ sukhanidānaṃ dānaṃ denti. Tesaṃ upaghātaṃ parivajjayantā

is emptiness, and so is said to culminate in the sphere of awareness that is emptiness, but not higher.

The Perfections of Great Beings

[31] Once you have discovered the efficacy of each one in the ways in which it culminates in the beautiful and the rest, you should also understand how each of them perfects each of the beautiful states, such as generosity. Great Beings are those whose minds stay balanced through seeking beings' well-being, by not tolerating their suffering, by wishing that their special successes continue, and by not being partisan.

They *give gifts* that bring happiness to all beings, without making distinctions like "One should give to this one, but not to that one."

sīlaṃ samādiyanti. Sīlaparipūraṇatthaṃ nekkhammaṃ bhajanti. Sattānaṃ hitāhitesu asammohatthāya paññaṃ pariyodapenti. Sattānaṃ hitasukhatthāya niccaṃ vīriyamārabhanti. Uttamavīriyavasena vīrabhāvaṃ pattāpi ca sattānaṃ nānappakārakaṃ aparādhaṃ khamanti. Idaṃ vo dassāma karissāmā ti kataṃ paṭiññaṃ na visaṃvādenti. Tesaṃ hitasukhāya avicalādhiṭṭhānā honti. Tesu avicalāya mettāya pubbakārino honti. Upekkhāya paccupakāraṃ nāsīsantīti.

Evaṃ pāramiyo pūretvā yāva dasabalacatuvesārajjachaasādhāraṇañāṇaaṭṭhārasabuddhadhammappabhede sabbepi kalyāṇadhamme

They practice *morality* by completely recoiling from causing them harm. The engage in *renunciation* for the sake of perfecting morality. They purify their *wisdom* for the sake of not being confused about what is beneficial or not for beings. They constantly arouse *effort* for the sake of the well-being and happiness of beings. When they have become heroic by means of the highest effort, they become *patient* with beings' many failures. They *do not deceive* when they promise to do something, such as "We shall give this or do that." They remain *unshakably fixed* on beings' well-being and happiness, and because of their unshakable *lovingkindness* toward them, they help before being asked. Because of their *equanimity*, they do not look for any reward.

Having fulfilled the perfections, they perfect all of these beautiful states, including the ten powers, the four confidences, the six uncommon

paripūrentīti evaṃ dānādisabbakalyāṇadhammaparipūrikā etāva hontīti.

Iti sādhujanapāmojjatthāya kate
visuddhimagge
Samādhibhāvanādhikāre
Brahmavihāraniddeso nāma
Navamo paricchedo.

knowledges, and the eighteen qualities of a buddha. In this way, they completely engage all the beautiful states starting with generosity.

"Detailed Instructions for the
Sublime Attitudes"
is the name of the ninth chapter,
in the section on cultivating concentration,
of the *Path of Purification*—
a book composed to make good
people happy.

ACKNOWLEDGMENTS

Three readers of an early draft of this book are owed special thanks—Jay Garfield, Steve Jenkins, and Steve Heim. Each took patient and thoughtful care in reading and marking up the manuscript, pushing me on my choices, and helping me spot and remove infelicities. I am so grateful.

I cannot think of this text without acknowledging Charlie Hallisey, with whom I have spent many happy hours reading and discussing Buddhaghosa. I am grateful too for my many students over the years with whom I have read this chapter in the brilliant translation of Bhikkhu Ñāṇamoli, and from whom I have learned so much about how to talk and think about love.

I am also eternally grateful to my two sons, Soren and Zack, who have made it possible for me to learn what Buddhaghosa means about the varieties and nuances of immeasurable mother love.

Thanks to Amherst College for the spring sabbatical in 2025 that gave me the time to translate and write. Finally, thank you to Rob Tempio, Chloe Coy, Jennifer Harris, and the rest of the staff at Princeton University Press for including this book in the series and their work bringing it into being.

NOTES

1 For a philosphical and moral critique of the way Americans do anger, see Flanagan 2021.

2 For a translation of a canonical account of these four forms of attention, see Heim 2025, 180–193.

3 Readers seeking to understand how these meditation practices work should consult Shaila Catherine's *The Jhānas: A Practical Guide to Deep Meditative States* (Catherine 2024); for an excellent introduction to mindfulness, see Sarah Shaw, *Mindfulness: Where It Comes from and What It Means* (Shaw 2024).

4 In addition to being the best introductory textbook on Buddhism, *The Foundations of Buddhism* by Rupert Gethin helpfully charts mind and cosmos in Buddhist thought (Gethin 1998, see especially chapter 5).

5 The twentieth-century Christian thinker Thomas Merton agrees: "Hatred is the sign and the expression of loneliness, of unworthiness, of insufficiency. Hate in any form is self-destructive, and even when it triumphs physically it triumphs in its own spiritual ruin." Hell is hatred: "Hell is where no one has anything in common with anybody else except the fact that they all hate one another and cannot get away from one another and from themselves" (*New Seeds of Contemplation*, Merton 1961, 72–73). As Buddhaghosa sees too, hate is something one needs to actively get rid of.

6 Iris Murdoch, *The Sovereignty of Good* (Murdoch 1970). She too sees the profound connections between attention, love, and freedom, and the struggle they require to achieve.

7 Buddhists think that clinging to self is a key source of anger and hate. For Buddhist no-self teachings, see *How to Lose Yourself: An Ancient Guide to Letting Go* (Garfield et al. 2025).

8 Base edition used: C = Chaṭṭha Saṅgāyana Tipiṭika 4.1 (1995). Also consulted: W = Warren (1950); and RD = Rhys Davids (1989–1996).

9 Brahmin in this context refers to an admired holy person. These verses are from the *Dhammapada*, 184 and 399 (translated by Acharya Buddharakkhita at https://www.accesstoinsight.org/tipitaka/kn/dhp/dhp.intro.budd.html).

10 *Saṃyutta Nikāya* i.222, translated by Bodhi (2000, 322).

11 na] RD, W; C omits.

12 *Vibhaṅga* 272, translated by P. A. Thiṭṭila (1969, 357).

13 There are different ways to translate *mettā cetovimutti.* One way is "the freedom of the mind by means of lovingkindness," where *mettā* is in the instrumental case. *Mettā* can also be nominative here, in apposition to *cetovimutti:* "the freedom of the mind that is lovingkindness," and I follow this reading here, but more felicitously, I translate it as

"freedom of the loving mind." This is similar to Sharon Salzberg's "the liberation of the heart, which is love" (Salzberg 2004, 1). The key idea is that the sublime attitudes are practices of freedom, freeing the mind (and heart) from ill will and other constrictions that confine it.

14 *Paṭisambhidā* ii.130, translated by Ñāṇamoli (1982, 317).

15 The Metta Sutta in the *Sutta Nipāta*, translated by Bodhi (2017, 179–180).

16 *Saṃyutta Nikāya* i.75, translated by Bodhi (2000, 171).

17 *Saṃyutta Nikāya* i.162, translated by Bodhi (2000, 256).

18 *Aṅguttara Nikāya* iv.94–96, translated by Bodhi (2012, 1066–1067).

19 *Saṃyutta Nikāya* iii.93, translated by Bodhi (2000, 920).

20 *Aṅguttara Nikāya* iii.186–190, translated by Bodhi (2012, 774–777).

21 *Aṅguttara Nikāya* iii.186, translated by Bodhi (2012, 774).

22 *Dhammapada*, verse 125 (translated by Acharya Buddharakkhita at https://www.accesstoinsight.org/tipitaka/kn/dhp/dhp.intro.budd.html).

23 Our Buddha was a bodhisatta—that is, a buddha-in-training—for a vast number of lifetimes, preparing him for his final birth and discovery of awakening as Siddhattha Gotama. In these lifetimes, he is said to be perfecting ten virtues, one of which is the patience or forbearance described in these stories. (These ten virtues will be listed in the final paragraph of the "Detailed Instructions for the Sublime Attitudes" chapter. Stories about these past lifetimes are called *jatakas*, several of which Buddhaghosa relates briefly in the pages that follow.

24 This story tells of an elephant who cared for his blind mother. By an act of treachery by someone he had helped, he was captured and brought to the king. But the elephant refused to eat out of worry

for his mother, and the king was so impressed with this that he restored him to his mother (Mātuposika Jātaka).

25 *Saṃyutta Nikāya* ii.189–190, translated by Bodhi (2000, 659).

26 *Aṅguttara Nikāya* v.342, translated by Bodhi (2012, 1573).

27 I add this line to indicate the ellipses in the text where the other body parts are abbreviated.

28 The clusters, sensory bases, elements and the other technical terms in this paragraph are categories of the phenomena that make up human life. The term for clusters, *khandha*, often translated as "aggregates," refers to a classification of the phenomena of human life into bodily experience, feeling, perception, habitual patterns, and consciousness.

29 The earth meditation device (*kasiṇa*) is a meditation practice given much earlier in the *Path of Purification*, at the beginning of its section on concentration. It is a useful practice for calming and focusing the mind, and functions as a kind of prototype or

model for the practice of the rest of the serenity meditations in the book.

30 In the next few pages, italicized words and phrases are being picked up from an earlier passage in the text to receive additional exegesis. This is the commentary on the verse given on page 23. In the next paragraph, phrases from this paragraph are glossed.

31 nigamanavasena] W; nigamavasena RD, C.

32 chinnahatthapādaṃ] W; chinnāhāraṃ C, RD.

33 *Vibhaṅga* 273, translated by P. A. Thiṭṭila (1969, 359).

34 Adam Smith (*The Theory of Moral Sentiments*, 1759) and David Hume (*Treatise of Human Nature*, 1739–1740) argue that sympathy with others' emotions quite broadly, and perhaps especially with their positive emotions, is fundamental to morality and social cohesion.

35 I understand the difference between the person "dear to you" and the "very close buddy" here to be that the latter is simply a fun and easy pal to

hang out with. The dear person is often a mentor or friend whom you love, but is not necessarily the merry chum whose contagious sense of joy spreads.

36 *Vibhaṅga* 274, translated by P. A. Thiṭṭila (1969, 360).

37 The third or fourth levels of deep concentration (*jhāna*) refers to two different *jhāna* schemas that Buddhaghosa has in mind. The usual schema has four *jhānas*, and in this schema, the other three sublime attitudes can only reach the third *jhāna* (since the fourth *jhāna* involves equanimity, which precludes their presence). In a lesser-known schema there are five *jhānas*, and in this schema, one can practice the first three sublime attitudes up through the fourth *jhāna*.

38 *Vibhaṅga* 275, translated by P. A. Thiṭṭila (1969, 357).

39 *Dīgha Nikāya* iii.248, translated by Walshe (1995, 248).

40 The definitions here and in the next two paragraphs are found in *Majjhima Nikāya* iii. 218–219, translated by Ñāṇamoli and Bodhi (2001, 1067–1069).

41 The Abhidhamma is one branch of Buddhist canonical scripture. It analyzes moral phenomenology in great detail. Buddhaghosa has been working closely with Abhidhamma treatises, such as the *Book of Analysis (Vibhaṅga)*, throughout.

42 This definition expands on the term for the sublime attitudes—the *brahmavihāras*—which are ways of living that are those of the Brahma gods, the deities that reside in a calm, gentle, and blissful heaven.

43 *Saṃyutta Nikāya* v.119–121, translated by Bodhi (2000, 1607–1611).

44 Following Ñāṇamoli in taking *avijjamānaggahaṇadukkhaṃ* to be *avijjamānaggahaṇadakkhaṃ*.

BIBLIOGRAPHY

Editions

Chaṭṭha Saṅgāyana Tipiṭika 4.1. 1995. Igatpuri: Vipassana Research Institute.

Rhys Davids, C.A.F., ed. 1989–1996. *Visuddhimagga*. Khlong Luang: Input Dhammakaya Foundation. (Originally published in 1920–1921, London: Pali Text Society.)

Warren, H. C., ed. (with revisions by D. Kosambi). 1950. *Visuddhimagga of Buddhaghosācariya*. Delhi: Motilal Banarsidass, 1950.

Translations

Bodhi, Bhikkhu, trans. 2000. *The Connected Discourses of the Buddha (Saṃyutta Nikāya)*. Somerville, MA: Wisdom Publications.

BIBLIOGRAPHY

Bodhi, Bhikkhu, trans. 2012. *The Numerical Discourses of the Buddha (Aṅguttara Nikāya).* Somerville, MA: Wisdom Publications.

Bodhi, Bhikkhu, trans. 2017. *The Sutta Nipāta.* Somerville, MA: Wisdom Publications.

Garfield, Jay, Maria Heim, and Robert Sharf, trans. 2025. *How to Lose Yourself: An Ancient Guide to Letting Go.* Princeton, NJ: Princeton University Press.

Heim, Maria, trans. 2025. *How to Feel: An Ancient Guide to Minding Our Emotions.* Princeton, NJ: Princeton University Press.

Ñāṇamoli, Bhikkhu, trans. 1982. *The Path of Discrimination (Paṭisambhidāmagga).* London: Pali Text Society.

Ñāṇamoli, Bhikkhu, trans. 1991. *The Path of Purification (Visuddhimagga).* Onalaska, WA: BPS Pariyatti Editions.

Ñāṇamoli, Bhikkhu, and Bhikkhu Bodhi, trans. 2001. *The Middle Length Discourses of the Buddha (Majjhima Nikāya).* Somerville, MA: Wisdom Publications.

Thiṭṭila, Paṭhamakyaw Ashin, trans. 1969. *The Book of Analysis (Vibhaṅga)*. London: Pali Text Society.

Walshe, Maurice, trans. 1995. *The Long Discourses of the Buddha (Dīgha Nikāya)*. Somerville, MA: Wisdom Publications.

Other Works

Catherine, Shaila. 2024. *The Jhānas: A Practical Guide to Deep Meditative States*. New York: Wisdom Publications.

Flanagan, Owen. 2021. *How to Do Things with Emotions: The Morality of Anger and Shame across Cultures*. Princeton, NJ: Princeton University Press.

Gethin, Rupert. 1998. *The Foundations of Buddhism*. Oxford: Oxford University Press.

Heim, Maria. 2017. "Buddhaghosa on the Phenomenology of Love and Compassion." In *The Oxford Handbook of Indian Philosophy*, ed. Jonardon Ganeri, 171–189. New York: Oxford University Press.

hooks, bell. 1994. *Outlaw Culture: Resisting Representations.* New York: Routledge.

Hume, David. 1888. *Treatise of Human Nature*, ed. L. A. Selby-Bigge. Oxford: Clarendon Press. (Originally published in 1739–1740.)

Merton, Thomas. 1961. *New Seeds of Contemplation.* Trappist, KY: Abbey of Gethsemeni.

Murdoch, Iris. 1970. *The Sovereignty of Good.* London: Routledge and Kegan Paul.

Salzberg, Sharon. 2004. *Lovingkindness: The Revolutionary Art of Happiness*. Boulder, CO: Shambala.

Shaw, Sarah. 2020. *Mindfulness: Where It Comes from and What It Means*. Boulder, CO: Shambala.

Smith, Adam. 2009. *The Theory of Moral Sentiments.* New York: Penguin Books. (Originally published in 1759.)